Instructor's Manual

to accompany

EIGHTH EDITION

Life-Span Development

JOHN W. SANTROCK

Prepared by

K. Laurie Dickson

Cynthia Jenkins

Instructor's Manual

to accompany

Life-Span Development

Eighth Edition

John W. Santrock
University of Texas at Dallas

Prepared by
K. Laurie Dickson
Northern Arizona University

Cynthia Jenkins
University of Texas at Dallas

Boston   Burr Ridge, IL   Dubuque, IA   Madison, WI   New York   San Francisco   St. Louis
Bangkok   Bogotá   Caracas   Lisbon   London   Madrid
Mexico City   Milan   New Delhi   Seoul   Singapore   Sydney   Taipei   Toronto

McGraw-Hill Higher Education

*A Division of The **McGraw-Hill** Companies*

Instructor's Manual to accompany
LIFE-SPAN DEVELOPMENT: EIGHTH EDITION
JOHN W. SANTROCK

Published by McGraw-Hill Higher Education, an imprint of The McGraw-Hill Companies, Inc., 1221 Avenue of the Americas, New York, NY 10020. Copyright © The McGraw-Hill Companies, Inc., 2002, 1999. All rights reserved.

This book is printed on acid-free paper.

3 4 5 6 7 8 9 0 BKM BKM 0 3 2

ISBN 0-07-241436-7

www.mhhe.com

Contents

To the Professor   vi
Ideas for Planning and Teaching Your Course   xi
    Organizing Your Course   xi
    Assessment of Student Performance   xii
    Creating Your Syllabus   xiii
    Connecting with Students   xiv
    Teaching Tips   xv
Answering Essay and Critical Thinking Questions   xxi
Ethics, Human Subjects, and Informed Consent   xxii
About Our Supplements   xxiv
Overhead Transparencies   xxvii
Film and Video Sources   xxxi
Useful Web Sites   xxxiii

Chapter 1: Introduction

Total Teaching Package Outline 1 Chapter Outline 2 Learning Objectives 5 Key Terms 6 Key People 6 Lecture Suggestions 6 Classroom Activities 9 Personal Applications 12 Research Project Ideas 14 Film and Video List 15 Web Site Suggestions 15 Handouts 16

Chapter 2: The Science of Life-Span Development

Total Teaching Package Outline 24 Chapter Outline 26 Learning Objectives 33 Key Terms 34 Key People 34 Lecture Suggestions 34 Classroom Activities 37 Personal Applications 40 Research Project Ideas 41 Film and Video List 42 Web Site Suggestions 43 Handouts 44

Chapter 3: Biological Beginnings

Total Teaching Package Outline 54 Chapter Outline 55 Learning Objectives 60 Key Terms 60 Key People 61 Lecture Suggestions 61 Classroom Activities 63 Personal Applications 67 Research Project Ideas 69 Film and Video List 70 Web Site Suggestions 71 Handouts 72

Chapter 4: Prenatal Development and Birth

Total Teaching Package Outline 80 Chapter Outline 82 Learning Objectives 86 Key Terms 86 Key People 87 Lecture Suggestions 87 Classroom Activities 89 Personal Applications 92 Research Project Ideas 93 Film and Video List 94 Web Site Suggestions 96 Handouts 97

Chapter 5: Physical Development in Infancy

Total Teaching Package Outline 107 Chapter Outline 108 Learning Objectives 113 Key Terms 114 Key People 114 Lecture Suggestions 114 Classroom Activities 116 Personal Applications 119 Research Project Ideas 120 Film and Video List 121 Web Site Suggestions 122 Handouts 124

Chapter 6: Cognitive Development in Infancy

Total Teaching Package Outline 132 Chapter Outline 133 Learning Objectives 137 Key Terms 137 Key People 137 Lecture Suggestions 138 Classroom Activities 140 Personal Applications 143 Research Project Ideas 144 Film and Video List 145 Web Site Suggestions 146 Handouts 147

Chapter 7: Socioemotional Development in Infancy

Total Teaching Package Outline 155 Chapter Outline 156 Learning Objectives 161 Key Terms 161 Key People 161 Lecture Suggestions 162 Classroom Activities 164 Personal Applications 167 Research Project Ideas 168 Film and Video List 169 Web Site Suggestions 171 Handouts 172

Chapter 8: Physical and Cognitive Development in Early Childhood
Total Teaching Package Outline **179** Chapter Outline **181** Learning Objectives **186** Key Terms **187** Key People **187** Lecture Suggestions **187** Classroom Activities **190** Personal Applications **194** Research Project Ideas **195** Film and Video List **197** Web Site Suggestions **198** Handouts **200**

Chapter 9: Socioemotional Development in Early Childhood
Total Teaching Package Outline **209** Chapter Outline **211** Learning Objectives **219** Key Terms **219** Key People **220** Lecture Suggestions **220** Classroom Activities **224** Personal Applications **228** Research Project Ideas **229** Film and Video List **230** Web Site Suggestions **232** Handouts **234**

Chapter 10: Physical and Cognitive Development in Middle and Late Childhood
Total Teaching Package Outline **244** Chapter Outline **246** Learning Objectives **253** Key Terms **253** Key People **254** Lecture Suggestions **254** Classroom Activities **257** Personal Applications **261** Research Project Ideas **263** Film and Video List **265** Web Site Suggestions **266** Handouts **267**

Chapter 11: Socioemotional Development in Middle and Late Childhood
Total Teaching Package Outline **277** Chapter Outline **279** Learning Objectives **286** Key Terms **286** Key People **287** Lecture Suggestions **287** Classroom Activities **291** Personal Applications **294** Research Project Ideas **296** Film and Video List **297** Web Site Suggestions **298** Handouts **299**

Chapter 12: Physical and Cognitive Development in Adolescence
Total Teaching Package Outline **311** Chapter Outline **313** Learning Objectives **320** Key Terms **320** Key People **320** Lecture Suggestions **321** Classroom Activities **324** Personal Applications **329** Research Project Ideas **330** Film and Video List **331** Web Site Suggestions **332** Handouts **334**

Chapter 13: Socioemotional Development in Adolescence
Total Teaching Package Outline **343** Chapter Outline **345** Learning Objectives **349** Key Terms **350** Key People **350** Lecture Suggestions **350** Classroom Activities **353** Personal Applications **356** Research Project Ideas **358** Film and Video List **359** Web Site Suggestions **360** Handouts **361**

Chapter 14: Physical and Cognitive Development in Early Adulthood
Total Teaching Package Outline **369** Chapter Outline **370** Learning Objectives **377** Key Terms **377** Key People **377** Lecture Suggestions **378** Classroom Activities **381** Personal Applications **384** Research Project Ideas **385** Film and Video List **386** Web Site Suggestions **387** Handouts **388**

Chapter 15: Socioemotional Development in Early Adulthood
Total Teaching Package Outline **402** Chapter Outline **404** Learning Objectives **410** Key Terms **411** Key People **411** Lecture Suggestions **411** Classroom Activities **415** Personal Applications **418** Research Project Ideas **419** Film and Video List **421** Web Site Suggestions **422** Handouts **423**

Chapter 16: Physical and Cognitive Development in Middle Adulthood
Total Teaching Package Outline **435** Chapter Outline **436** Learning Objectives **441** Key Terms **441** Key People **441** Lecture Suggestions **441** Classroom Activities **444** Personal Applications **447** Research Project Ideas **447** Film and Video List **449** Web Site Suggestions **449** Handouts **450**

Chapter 17: Socioemotional Development in Middle Adulthood
Total Teaching Package Outline **460** Chapter Outline **461** Learning Objectives **464** Key Terms **465** Key People **465** Lecture Suggestions **465** Classroom Activities **468** Personal Applications **470** Research Project Ideas **471** Film and Video List **473** Web Site Suggestions **473** Handouts **474**

Chapter 18: Physical Development in Late Adulthood
Total Teaching Package Outline **483** Chapter Outline **485** Learning Objectives **489** Key Terms **489** Key People **490** Lecture Suggestions **490** Classroom Activities **493** Personal Applications **496** Research Project Ideas **497** Film and Video List **498** Web Site Suggestions **499** Handouts **501**

Chapter 19: Cognitive Development in Late Adulthood
Total Teaching Package Outline **509** Chapter Outline **510** Learning Objectives **515** Key Terms **516** Key People **516** Lecture Suggestions **516** Classroom Activities **523** Personal Applications **524** Research Project Ideas **526** Film and Video List **527** Web Site Suggestions **528** Handouts **530**

Chapter 20: Socioemotional Development in Late Adulthood
Total Teaching Package Outline **541** Chapter Outline **542** Learning Objectives **546** Key Terms **546** Key People **546** Lecture Suggestions **546** Classroom Activities **551** Personal Applications **553** Research Project Ideas **554** Film and Video List **555** Web Site Suggestions **556** Handouts **557**

Chapter 21: Death and Grieving
Total Teaching Package Outline **566** Chapter Outline **567** Learning Objectives **571** Key Terms **572** Key People **572** Lecture Suggestions **572** Classroom Activities **575** Personal Applications **578** Research Project Ideas **579** Film and Video List **580** Web Site Suggestions **3581** Handouts **583**

Appendix A: Cognitive Maps 590

To the Professor

Teaching offers a thrill that nothing else can match. To come before a group of people eager and interested in what you have to share with them is a unique and very rewarding experience. It is also one which is renewed time and time again with the beginning of each semester. It provides us with the chance to continually experience the promise of fresh minds, and the ability to reinvigorate our lessons. Wherever we begin our teaching journey, how we engage our students and the strategies we use to connect with them evolves over the years. The ability to learn from ourselves, our colleagues, and our students and in turn incorporate the freshness and insight we have gained into our continuing goal to educate carries us through. We are able to repeatedly find enthusiasm in our work and generate excitement about our effort. Thus is the nature of teaching. Or so it *should* be. With the right materials and resources at our disposal, it can be.

Welcome to the Instructor's Manual for John Santrock's *Life-Span Development*, eighth edition. Combined with the new and improved edition of the text, this manual offers a wealth of ideas, tips, and sources to pave the way for you to experience teaching the way you most certainly want to: with confidence, knowledge, variety, and engaging strategies to inspire and enlighten your students. Whether you are new to teaching, new to teaching this course, or have many years of experience behind you, this supplement has much to offer.

To begin with, you will find in this letter a full description of each feature contained in this Instructor's Manual along with its potential applications. This complete overview will enable you to see all of the resources available to you for teaching life-span development. You will also find a section dedicated to helping you plan and teach your course. Ideas for Planning and Teaching Your Course offers suggestions for approaching and organizing the class, along with a guide to preparing a syllabus, and time-tested tips on various aspects of teaching. Thus, if you are new to the teaching field, you will find specific information to guide you as you develop a class for the first time. For those of you who are seasoned instructors, the many suggestions may help you restructure aspects of previous classes and generate some new ideas and a fresh approach.

Also, because students sometimes have difficulty in the following areas, we have included sections on Answering Essay and Critical Thinking Questions and Ethics, Human Subjects, and Informed Consent. Both of these can be duplicated and distributed to students. Finally, as further aids to your teaching, you will find descriptions of all of the supplements available in the Santrock, *Life-Span Development* package, a complete listing of the Overhead Transparencies available, source information for obtaining the films and videos mentioned throughout the manual, and addresses for many general web sites that offer useful information for a variety of topics.

The second part of this Instructor's Manual includes a chapter corresponding to each chapter in the textbook. Each of these will include all of the vital information you will need to feel knowledgeable and secure in working from Santrock's *Life-Span Development*, such as an extensive chapter outline, learning objectives keyed to both the Test Bank and Study Guide, and key terms and people. A new feature presented in this manual is the Total Teaching Package Outline: a complete outline of each textbook chapter, with specific topics paired with the recommended ideas, activities, projects, and media sources. Subsequent to this are the specific teaching ideas to incorporate into your class for a variety of student experiences: lecture suggestions, classroom activities, personal applications, and research projects, as well as film, video, and web sources. Again, if you are new to teaching altogether, you will have at your disposal more ideas than you can possibly use in a semester, and from this begin to discover your teaching style. If you are simply new to teaching life-span development, you probably have several techniques you are comfortable with, and can thus use this manual to find topic-specific ideas and activities to fit within your usual format. And for those of you who already have experience teaching in this field, the manual will most certainly offer some fresh perspectives on what can be incorporated into your usual routine.

Total Teaching Package Outline

New to this edition is the Total Teaching Package Outline (affectionately called TTPOs). This unique feature highlights the integrative nature of this Instructor's Manual. It is our hope that the TTPOs will facilitate your teaching by providing you with relevant resources and pertinent support materials for each lecture outline. For all major headings and many subheadings in each chapter, we have noted relevant learning objectives, lecture suggestions, classroom activities, personal applications, research projects, films/videos, web sites, transparencies, and image bank files. This integrative feature should provide you with a variety of teaching materials and suggestions to enhance student enjoyment and learning.

In addition, Appendix A provides a complete set of cognitive maps that can be used as student handouts or as transparencies to introduce and/or review each chapter. A complete list of available Overhead Transparencies, many of which also appear in the Image Bank found at the Online Learning Center, is provided on page xxvii. Below we have provided a key to the reference codes we use throughout the Instructor's Manual in the TTPOs.

Reference	Resource	Reference	Resource
LO	Learning Objective	F/V	Film and Video
LS	Lecture Suggestion	WS	Web Site
CA	Classroom Activity	OHT	Overhead Transparency
PA	Personal Application	IB	Image Bank
RP	Research Project		

Chapter Outline

At the beginning of each chapter, we have provided an outline of the chapter content that demonstrates the organization of topics by heading levels. We have expanded these chapter outlines extensively for this edition. These expanded outlines provide a clear synopsis of each chapter, with key terms from the text in boldface. The outlines allow for a quick overview of the content and the chapter organization. Thus, they can facilitate your lecture development and can also serve as an introduction to each chapter for students prior to delving into your lecture or classroom activity.

Learning Objectives

Learning objectives are provided to help focus students' attention on the key points in each chapter and can facilitate students' preparation for exams. The learning objectives can be used individually by students or you can use them as an in-class activity. You can copy the learning objectives and distribute them to students for use as a study aid for exam preparation. That is, students can use the learning objectives to help them focus their attention on the key points in each chapter. Or, you can use them as a tool to organize your lectures. Another option is to use them as a review mechanism prior to exams. These objectives are also provided in the Student Study Guide and Test Bank. New for this edition, all questions in the Test Bank and the multiple-choice questions in the Study Guide are keyed to a particular learning objective. This feature facilitates an integrative approach to teaching life-span development.

Key Terms

For each chapter, we have listed, alphabetically, important key terms that students should be familiar with after reading the chapter. The key terms are highlighted in each textbook chapter and in the chapter outline in the Instructor's Manual. The list of key terms can be used as a review mechanism prior to exams. Consider having students define or give an example of each key concept in order to review the chapter material prior to an exam.

Key People

For each chapter, we have also listed, alphabetically, important people that students should be familiar with after reading the chapter. Although not all names mentioned in the chapters are included in the list, we have attempted to provide a comprehensive list of significant contributors. This list could also be used as a review mechanism for exam preparation.

Lecture Suggestions

Lecture suggestions for each chapter will assist in your lecture development. Some suggestions expand on topics mentioned in the textbook, while others introduce new, complementary ideas. In this edition, we have extensively revised, updated, and expanded the information provided to facilitate lecture development. When appropriate, we have suggested references that will aid the development of your lectures. We made a special effort to focus on developmental themes and to make connections across chapters. The lecture suggestions vary from a focus on research findings and methodological issues to more application-oriented suggestions. Some of these suggestions will serve as complete lectures. Others are not meant to be complete lectures, but will, however, serve as an impetus for lecture creation. You will want to incorporate your own course objectives and individual style into the provided suggestions.

Classroom Activities

We have suggested several classroom activities for each chapter. Some of these activities directly relate to suggested lectures, others illustrate material in *Life-Span Development*, and still others relate to material not contained in either the text or suggested lectures. Many of the activities listed vary from chapter to chapter, ranging from demonstrations, structured interactions between you and your students, small group discussions, field trips, panel discussions, and debates. The intent of these is to provide diverse ways to involve students in classroom activity. Some of them require considerable preparation by you or your students, whereas others require very little preparation by either. New for this edition, we have included logistical information for each activity. We have highlighted what materials, if any, will be needed for the activity. For example, many of the activities have an accompanying ready-to-use handout. When appropriate, we have provided ready-to-use handouts. These handouts were designed for immediate use, thus they can be duplicated for students or made into transparencies. We have also noted the recommended group size for each activity. For example, some of the activities involve small group (2 – 4 students) work prior to having a full class discussion. The approximate time required for each suggestion is noted as well. Please keep in mind that these times are mere approximations and will vary depending on classroom dynamics. Also, noted under the Logistics heading, are the sources, if any, used in the classroom activity.

Given the importance placed on critical thinking, in each chapter we have included critical thinking multiple-choice questions that can be used as a classroom activity. A unique feature of this multiple-choice format is that students must identify the best answer, explain why it is the best answer, and explain why the other answers are not as good. We have developed various kinds of problems for students to solve as they read and study the text. For example, many questions ask students to analyze material in terms of the "nature of development" as presented in chapter 1. Students may be asked which of several aspects of development are illustrated by material in the text, or they may be asked to identify which of several developmental themes receives greatest emphasis in particular topics. A second type of question requires students to integrate material within chapters. For example, an exercise for chapter 10 asks students to identify which of five statements about physical development or children's health provides the basis for the most compelling criticism of the Chinese sports schools sketched in the provided vignette. A third type of question requires students to interpret the figures or tables in the text. Finally, a fourth type of question requires students to learn how to recognize assumptions and distinguish them from inferences and observations. This last type of exercise probably represents what is most widely viewed as critical thinking, but we believe critical thinking also involves using and analyzing information that students study. Importantly, the common task across all of the questions is asking students to give reasons for the answers they choose.

We have found that students need and want discussion while working on these questions. Although you will discover points of your own to discuss, we have suggested lines of discussion that may help students with the exercises. We have also written sample answer keys for each question that are presented as handouts.

An additional activity for each chapter involves discussing the critical thinking essay questions. Several objectives can be met with these questions. First, these questions further facilitate students' understanding of concepts in the chapter. Second, this type of essay question affords the students an opportunity to apply the concepts to their own lives, which will facilitate their retention of the material. Third, the essay format also will give students practice expressing themselves in written form.

Personal Applications

New to this edition, we have included a unique feature. The personal application suggestions afford students an opportunity to apply the concepts they are learning to their own lives. Students often recall information better if they understand how it relates to them personally. Life-span development courses offer a perfect opportunity for students to live what they are learning. For each of the suggestions, we have provided instructions for students. These instructions guide their work and are typically presented as a series of questions. The personal application suggestions can be used as journal writing entries throughout the semester. Or, they can be used periodically to illustrate particular issues raised in the textbook. For example, one of the personal application suggestions in chapter 10 involves students reflecting back to their childhood physical activities. They are encouraged to think about the activities they engaged in and the pressures they may have felt to excel in certain areas. Then, as a class, students can share their experiences while relating them to concepts from the textbook.

Research Project Ideas

Consistent with Santrock's emphasis on the relationship between research and student learning, we have designed two out-of-class research projects for each chapter. These research projects typically involve some form of data collection and a brief report. These projects usually entail relatively simple types of systematic observation that students can do in everyday settings such as playgrounds, stores, schools, or malls. Occasionally they call for interviews, use of questionnaires, or experiment-life manipulations. The instructions for each project and any necessary data collection sheets are provided as ready-to-use handouts at the end of each chapter. Specific suggestions for incorporating these projects into classroom presentation and/or discussions appear at the end of each project description.

An important concern is that student projects conform to ethical guidelines for research. Given that data collection is involved, a majority of the projects will require Institutional approval and written consent. To facilitate students' awareness of research ethics, see the section on Ethics, Human Subjects, and Informed Consent on page xxii of this Instructor's Manual.

Film and Video List

We have updated the film and video lists for each chapter in an attempt to provide a useful collection that can be used to supplement your teaching. As you can imagine, the film and video offerings available for teaching life-span development are considerable. We have provided a brief content description of each video or film to facilitate your selection. These selections are generally readily available and easy to obtain from well-known sources. Given the time required to obtain video resources, we recommend that you order your films and videos well in advance of the start of the semester. To aid you in obtaining your selections, we have provided below on page xxi the names, addresses, URLs for web sites, and telephone numbers of all distributors mentioned in this manual. Most distributors maintain a web site, however, because Internet addresses often change, you might encounter a dead link. In this event, a new search will usually take you to the proper site.

Web Site Suggestions

An exciting feature of this Instructor's Manual is a list of relevant web sites for each chapter. Descriptive titles and Internet addresses have been noted for each web site suggestion. These addresses are just a starting point, as they each have multiple links that can provide you with useful information. You may want to incorporate Internet technology into your course by encouraging students to use these web sites to gather information. (If you choose to assign the Study Guide to your students, you will also find a new section there on interesting Internet projects.) For web sites that are specific to only one or two individual chapters, we have provided the URLs under Web Site Suggestions for each chapter and referenced those within the Total Teaching Package Outlines. Comprehensive developmental psychology web sites that are common to all chapters are provided on page xxxiii. At the time of publication, all sites were current and active, however, please be advised that you may occasionally encounter a dead link.

Handouts

As mentioned above, many of the classroom activities and research project ideas have an accompanying ready-to-use handout. These handouts were designed for immediate use, thus they can be duplicated for students or made into transparencies.

It is our hope that with such a tool as this Instructor's Manual to assist you in class planning and execution, you will be free to spend your time focusing on the more pleasing aspects of teaching: interacting with students, driving their motivation, and observing their progress in understanding and appreciating the field of life-span development. Teaching is an adventure; an experience like no other that continually takes us down new and different paths. Through your own knowledge, dedication, and creativity, you can employ this manual to accompany you and enhance the journey ahead.

K. Laurie Dickson

Cynthia Jenkins

Ideas for Planning and Teaching Your Course

Teaching is a profession that affords us a great deal of creativity. Even if you don't consider yourself a creative person in the traditional sense, you are still in a position to develop something that can have a profound impact on many people. A college course is not a static thing; it is a fluid, flexible entity that emerges from the interaction of students, professor, and format. You can't possibly predict semester-to-semester what the nature of each of your classes will be, and that's part of the excitement of teaching. We can continually have new and unique experiences as our students change, and as we alter the approach we take to teaching them. All this even when the information stays the same. This is why even seasoned instructors can maintain an elevated level of enthusiasm for what they do; they never have to do the same thing twice, and will thus never experience the same class twice! Learning by doing is the essence of teaching, as we experiment with our methods and discover the results from our students. Did they enjoy the course? Were they motivated to participate? What worked for them? What didn't? Did they *learn*? How wonderful that we get the chance to collect such data every few months and go back to the drawing board to once again try to develop, or *create*, our ideal class experience.

If you have an established teaching career, you probably are closer to this ideal than you were when you began, but chances are you are still looking to further enhance your class, instill more motivation, and bring about greater understanding in your students. For those of you who are new to teaching, the task you are about to undertake, although thrilling in its potential, looks daunting for sure. The implications of being solely responsible for students' exposure to and exploration of the material under your tutelage loom very large. An exciting journey to embark on, but one in which most feel a need for direction and guidance as to how to take their first steps.

This section will provide you with just that direction. For those with very little or no experience putting together an entire college course, you will find very explicit guidelines and strategies for doing even the most basic course planning. For those who are familiar with such tasks, they may offer you new insights as to how to approach developing your class, something many of us appreciate after years of doing the same thing. Beyond the basics of course planning lies further creative approaches. A collection of time-tested teaching tips is presented. Whether you are able to employ them now, or tuck them away for later application, a variety of proven techniques is a wonderful thing to have on hand. So, like the colors on an artist's palette, the following suggestions and ideas will provide you with an array of creative potential. Use some of them, use all of them; intermingle them, or create your own; they are the seeds from which successful courses can grow.

Organizing Your Course

Begin with the end in sight. In order to avoid teaching disjointed facts to fill the time, it is important to create course objectives. Decide what it is that you want students to take away from the course. This may be an overall understanding of the subject, knowledge of key ideas, the ability to think critically, and/or a desire to learn. From this starting point, the course will take shape.

On the first day of class, clearly communicate the course objectives and your strategies for achieving them. Do not merely post them in the syllabus and expect the students to catch the vision. Be sure to elaborate on your goals and elicit feedback as to their goals for the course. It is important to get them excited about the course and provide a framework of meaning for their assignments. If your students do not understand the course objectives and your anticipated strategies, they are merely floating around rather than taking an active role in the learning process.

Time is sometimes a concern when developing a course such as this. If you do not feel you will be able to cover the book in its entirety, begin by deciding which topics and stages of development you think are most important for students to learn in order to gain a substantial knowledge and understanding of life-span development. This may be in relation to material both within chapters and entire chapters themselves. *Life-Span Development* is one of the most complete texts on the subject matter. Its extensive coverage of the field of developmental psychology is one of its primary strengths. Sometimes the reality of class time dictates that not all aspects of all topics can be covered in the course. It can be frustrating and difficult to omit material, but in some cases it is necessary in order to enable students to experience the more basic concepts and information at a comfortable pace that enables them to absorb it more fully. In situations where you are really pressed for time, you may be forced to choose only a subset of major topics, forgoing either entire stages of development or areas of development.

In addition to what you determine is most important for your students to gain from the course, you may also base such decisions on what topics *you* like the best. Teaching those areas that excite you will most certainly excite your students, as instructor enthusiasm is contagious. In any of the above cases, build your course around the chosen group of topics. Organize them in such a way as to connect them to the context of life-span development as much as possible. Have a back-up plan with additional topics and the order in which you'll approach them should you have time for additional course content. You may, however, choose to provide a more in-depth exploration of a fewer number of topics during the allotted time, rather than a superficial look at everything.

Again, you have the freedom to determine the experience your students will have with the material. If you are new to teaching this course, reflect back on the manner in which your life-span course was taught.
- Was it effective?
- Did you feel the information was presented in the best way possible?
- What approach do you think will enable you to teach the material to your best ability?
- If you have been teaching this course for a while, is it time for a change?
- Have your students been responding to the information as you would like?

Assess the possibility of approaching the course differently to maybe discover new inspiration for both you and your students.

Assessment of Student Performance

To determine the testing schedule for your class, you need to spend some time thinking about your entire grading scheme. Some departments may have a pre-determined grading policy which all instructors must follow. This may be as rigid as specifying all aspects of grading (in which case the work has been done for you), or as loose as assigning certain percentages of the course grade and what work must contribute to each. Some departments leave the entire format up to you. Working within your particular boundaries, you should begin by answering the following questions.
- Is attendance something you want to include in the student's grade?
- Will there be regularly graded homework assignments?
- Will you encourage involvement in class discussions by giving a grade for participation?
- Do you want students to do any large research projects? If so, how many?
- Will you offer extra credit?
- Will there be tests and quizzes? How often? How many?

To help you answer these questions, consider the following.
- What is your course load?
- Will you have time to prepare for and grade all of the required work?
- Will you have a teaching assistant to help you?

Remember that it's important to give students timely feedback on their work. Then decide what you want your students to get out of the class.
- Is reading the material and coming to class for lecture enough?
- Is it important to you that they regularly work with the material through questions and critical thinking exercises?

- Would you rather focus on this during class time and allow them outside time to read their text?
- Do you want them to have practical experiences related to the field of life-span development such as live behavior observations or reading research articles from professional journals?

What is your philosophy on testing?
- Do you believe in giving quizzes to help students prepare for the larger exams?
- Do you feel a midterm and final is sufficient, or do you wish to evaluate them several times throughout the semester?
- Do you believe the final should be cumulative?

Once you have answered these questions, you can develop your grading structure. Prioritize students' efforts to determine how much you will weigh everything with regard to the final grade. It is also important to carefully think about your schedule of exams and assignment due dates. Do this with you and your students in mind. Consider your ability to grade related homework assignments and return them to students with enough time for them to use the assignments to study for the exam. Be aware of the drop date for which students can still receive a "W" —what grades will they have the opportunity to receive prior to this time in order for them to make an informed decision regarding whether they will remain in the class? Keep in mind their ability to work on reading assignments, homework questions, large projects, and prepare for exams. While planning your course, sit with the calendar and identify the midterm mark, finals week, and possibly the quarter points of the semester. Pencil in possible exam dates and assignment due dates to get a feel for your prep time and grading load. Try to create a schedule in which the most demanding times are evenly distributed across the semester, and there is a balance between when students must spend time on outside work and preparing for exams.

If you are new to teaching, all of the possibilities at your disposal can seem overwhelming at first. Recognize that you will hone your grading format over the years as you discover the balance of assignments, projects, tests, and quizzes that works best for you. Try not to implement everything all at once. You may be excited and anxious to have your students experience lots of things through the use of homework items, outside reading, research papers, and involvement in outside projects. This can be overwhelming for them too, so remember that while your goal is to teach them through a variety of mediums, they need to have time to focus on and absorb what it is they're working on. Too many responsibilities will lead to frustration and poor performance. Consider any departmental requirements, then begin by choosing the modes of evaluation you think will best bring about learning. Imagine what activities students will be most motivated to engage in, and how you think they can best demonstrate their understanding of the material. As you gain teaching experience, you will recognize an appropriate assignment load and the ways in which students best respond to information. Each semester provides you with the opportunity to adjust and augment your methods for achieving an effective course format.

Creating Your Syllabus

Content
Unless your department has a standard syllabus, you have creative freedom in preparing yours. The syllabus is generally considered a contract between you and your students; they are responsible for knowing and following assignments, schedules, and policies contained within it, as you are responsible for upholding the parameters you set down. Your syllabus should thus include all the information that is vital for your students to know to function successfully in class. Never assume your students will automatically know your policies, how you grade, or any aspect of what you expect from them. The best tactic is to create a very complete, very explicit description of the course and its requirements, including the following:
- Course name, number, and credit hours
- Time and place the course meets

- Your name, title, and position at the university
- Your office hours, phone number, and location
- Titles and edition number of required and optional texts, and citations of additional reading material
- Brief description of course and course objectives (may be taken from college catalog)
- Class format (what will be done during class time, question/answer format, submitting papers, etc.)
- List and description of assignments and projects
- Description of grading standards and point values for assignments and projects
- Description of quiz/exam format and point values for quizzes/exams
- Description of how course grade is determined
- Outline of class schedule, including all due dates, exam dates, holidays, and drop dates

Your policies on
- Attendance
- Tardiness
- Format of work turned in (typed, double-spaced, etc.)
- Late work
- Make-up exams
- Cheating and plagiarism
- Use of Internet sources for assignments and projects
- Cell phones and pagers
- Food and drink

Style

Keep in mind that the syllabus conveys the first impression that students will have of your class. It can be a source of dread and discouragement, or of excitement and motivation. To attract your students right from the start, develop an interesting and visually stimulating syllabus. Experiment with various font styles and sizes. Vary the look of each section of information. Add clip art to draw their attention to particularly important pieces of information (test dates, for example). For the most imaginative among you, present the information within the context of a certain theme. A syllabus titled *Days of Our Lives, One Life to Live,* or *Survivor* can capture their attention and inspire them to positively anticipate the semester to come. It can also make your work with the syllabus more fun. Let your theme guide you in how you design the presentation of the information. Preface information on required readings as "Scripts," for example. Title the section delineating grading policies "Compensation." Lead into the course description with "The Plot." It's your vision – follow it! As long as you include the necessary information, the syllabus can be a graphic representation of your approach to the course and the experience you want students to have in your class.

Connecting with Students

It can only benefit students to get to know and feel comfortable with their professors. While some students are quite outgoing and make this happen for themselves, others are much more intimidated by the thought of speaking with a college instructor. On the first day of class, make it a point to go over where your office is located and when they can find you there. Have students circle your phone number and sincerely encourage them to call and come by whenever they would like. If possible, plan to arrive early and remain after class, and let them know you will be available at those times for brief questions or discussions. You may even require a face-to-face meeting with each student at least once during the semester. This can have several benefits. First of all, it will give you the chance to interact with everyone, and discuss issues pertaining to their performance in class. For students who are having difficulty, you can help them discover what the problem might be, and direct them to resources that will get them back on track. For enthusiastic students, it's an opportunity to discuss what they've found interesting and liked about the course thus far, and possibly to give them supplemental sources of information. For some of the shy students, a required meeting often "breaks the ice," and rids them of the feeling of intimidation about meeting with faculty. In all cases, it enables you and your students to get to know each other better, something that will enhance learning, participation, and enjoyment of the class.

Another means of connecting with students is to share personal stories. Everyone has their own comfort level in this regard; however, when an instructor provides examples of phenomena through personal stories and experiences (and humor always helps!), students come to appreciate both the instructor and the material a little more. Having an instructor with funny and interesting tales to tell will also encourage greater attendance.

Teaching Tips

Teaching is a "live and learn" experience. Sometimes we have what we think are great ideas that fall completely flat when implemented in the classroom, and other times we do something that develops into a wonderful means of accomplishing our teaching goals. If you are new to teaching at the college level, you may need some good, time-tested ideas to help you approach the task before you. For those of us who are experienced instructors, new ideas are always welcome, often serving to reinvigorate our methods and motivate our enthusiasm. We have compiled a collection of tips to help you achieve your teaching goals. Some of these tips are suggestions for specific situations, whereas other tips are pedagogical ideas for you to ponder. Whether useful for immediate application, or as an inspiration for your own new ideas, they should serve to enhance your teaching of life-span development.

Student Motivation

One barrier for instructors is the perception that students are unmotivated. Motivation directly affects learning, and learning is driven by interest. While your purpose is not necessarily to entertain students, it should be your goal to engage their interest in the material. Students are motivated by both intrinsic and extrinsic factors. Without minimizing their concern with the extrinsic motivation of grades, you should strive to increase their intrinsic motivation to learn. One way to accomplish this is to emphasize the relevance of the material to their lives. Utilizing the students' questions generated at the beginning of the term (see Research Project 1: Answering Questions about Development in chapter 1), design lectures, discussions, and activities to incorporate their interests as much as possible. In order to avoid monotony, vary the teaching techniques you employ. For example, you can occasionally invite a guest speaker, incorporate class discussions and activities, and show relevant videos. A primary way to motivate students is to demonstrate enthusiasm for the material and their learning.

Pop Quizzes

Sometimes it is difficult to get students to read the textbook and ask questions. This is not surprising, as most students tend to procrastinate and either save it all until right before the exam, or not read it at all. It can be especially frustrating when they hardly ask any questions in class, even regarding difficult lecture material. Their test grades may even show that it was certainly not because they understood everything! To get them over their shyness, intimidation, or laziness (whatever the case may be), consider implementing the following policy: every day at the beginning of class they are to ask 5 questions. Require that the questions come from 5 different people, and that they can be about the reading material or previous lecture material. If there are not at least 5 questions posed at the beginning of class, administer a pop quiz covering relevant material (reading assignments or previous lectures). Given that you do not know at the beginning of the semester how many quizzes there will be, design it so that the points are theirs to *lose*. They all began the semester with 150 "Question Points" and should they have a pop quiz, any item they miss costs them 5 points. It works! You may find that not a single class period goes by without numerous students asking questions—and they never have to take a quiz.

Lecture Topic?

Although it is a good idea to plan your class periods ahead of time—either focusing on a few difficult concepts or demonstrating a particular phenomenon, there are days when nothing particular stands out to address. On these occasions consider using your students' questions to inspire the lecture and class discussion. As suggested in the Pop Quizzes tip, require 5 questions to be posed at the beginning of each class period (see "Pop Quizzes"). Every once in a while write each one on the board as it is asked, not answering any of them until all questions have been collected. Then, once you see them on the board, plan your presentation—addressing each of them in the best order and context with regard to the rest of them. Often this leads to related lecture tangents and class discussions of the material in ways unique to the particular group of students, as they stem from their own particular interests, curiosities, and confusions. It's interesting and enjoyable for the instructor as well, as there is no prep time involved and you know the students are truly learning something.

Lecture: More Is Not Necessarily Better!

When presenting a lecture, more information is not necessarily better. One of the most common mistakes instructors make is attempting to cover too much material in any one class period. Students are often frantically writing down information rather than listening and processing the material. Or, they give up their note-taking in frustration. You can prevent this from happening by reflecting on the purpose of the lecture and trying to limit the number of key points. There is no set number of key points; this varies as a function of class period duration, as well as the difficulty of the material. The old saying, "Tell them what you are going to say, say it, and tell them what you said" applies to lecture development. Thus, present your lecture outline to introduce the topic, provide supporting evidence and examples for each of your key points, and then, in conclusion, restate the main points using the original lecture outline. An additional strategy involves incorporating class discussions into your lecture. This ensures that the students will actively process the information and that you will not attempt to cover too many key points.

Self-Disclosure in the Classroom

Does the teaching of values have a place in our classrooms? Research has found that students find lectures more interesting if their professors occasionally reveal their personal beliefs about the topic at hand (Minnich, 1994). The distinction between stating your beliefs and indoctrinating students is an important one. There are several issues to keep in mind. In order to have a balanced presentation, it is important to articulate multiple perspectives. Clearly delineate your beliefs from scientific research. To demonstrate the process of critical thinking, be sure to explain how you developed your beliefs. In addition, elicit students' perspectives and encourage them to articulate the evolution of their beliefs.

- Source: Minnich, E. K. (1994). *What is at stake? Risking the pleasures of politics.* Annual SVHE Fellows Lecture, Emory University.

Peer Teaching

Regardless of the class content, course objectives, and students' abilities, peer teaching and learning have been found to be effective (Johnson & Johnson, 1975; Johnson, Maruyama, Johnson, Nelson, & Skon, 1981). Several strategies have been proposed by McKeachie (1994) that will facilitate your use of cooperative learning in the classroom. Prior to implementing these techniques, it is imperative to reveal to the students the value of cooperative learning. The benefits are motivational and cognitive. The increased stimulation and break from lecture can motivate students to be more actively engaged in the material. The cognitive benefits are primarily for students to elaborate on the material in their own words, which increases comprehension and retention. Each time you incorporate peer learning, clearly explain the assignment and the expected procedures. You may want to give students some class time to work together on the assignment. This stresses the importance you place on this type of learning. Monitor the group work by circulating throughout the classroom to answer questions. Other examples of cooperative learning can involve student-led discussions and peer tutoring.

- Sources: Johnson, D.W., & Johnson, R.T. (1975). *Learning together and alone: Cooperation, competition and individualization.* Englewood Cliffs, NJ: Prentice-Hall. Johnson, D.W., Maruyama, G., Johnson, R., Nelson, D., & Skon, L. (1981). The effects of cooperative, competitive, and individualistic goal structures on achievement: A meta-analysis. *Psychological Bulletin, 89,* 47-62. McKeachie, W. J. (1994). *Teaching tips: Strategies, research, and theory for college and university teachers* (9th ed.). Lexington, MA: Heath and Company.

Class Size

While class size is rarely under your control, you will undoubtedly teach large classes at some point in your career. The lecture format is typically the most effective method of instruction in larger classes. Although large classes are generally not considered to be conducive for discussion, you can set the stage at the beginning of the term by encouraging questions from your students and you can facilitate discussion by asking questions of the students. After posing a question to the class, allow ample time for them to reflect on the question and write out their answer. This may increase their comfort level which, in turn, may increase the likelihood that they respond orally. Be sure to either write the student's question or comment on the board or restate it so that everyone in the auditorium understands. Another way to encourage active participation is to divide the students into small groups. After each group has had time to discuss the issue, a representative from some of the groups can present their ideas to the class. It may be challenging to teach a large class, though you can improve your experience by being creative and willing to try innovative techniques.

Small Group Discussions

Consider incorporating small group discussions throughout the course. There are several benefits for the student. First, small groups facilitate the development of rapport between students which increases both their comfort level and their active participation. Second, the practice students get from interacting in small groups improves their ability to articulate their thoughts and opinions. Third, when in small groups, students are directly exposed to diverse opinions and ideas which can broaden their minds and stimulate self reflection regarding their own beliefs. Small group activities are beneficial for both small and large classes. Throughout this manual, we have developed numerous suggestions for small group activities.

Study Aids

Studying for exams is a daunting task for most students, and at least once a semester you will undoubtedly be faced with the question, "Is this going to be on the test?" In order to help students feel more in control of what to expect on the exams, create explicit study aids and include them in the syllabus. You can preface them with the statement: "This is a list of *concepts* to be understood, not just terms to be defined. You are responsible for knowing them to the extent they are presented in the text and discussed in lecture, along with examples and related study findings." You can provide a list of the concepts, terms, people, studies, and so on for each unit. Having the study aid that you personally made up, they are more confident that they know what material will be represented on the exams. It also gives them a hard copy on which they can write, cross-off items, and note the progress of their preparation. You can also advise them to use it as a guide for their notes as well, enabling them to make sure that they have focused on the important topics.

Exam Questions

We are sure you will hear students over the years say things like "I'm much better at multiple-choice questions!" or "I'm terrible at multiple-choice questions, but I do well on essay exams!" Given these differences consider including several different types of questions on your exams, such as multiple-choice, true-false, fill-in-the-blank, matching, short answer, and essay questions. The main factors to consider are the objectives you have developed for your course, the learning styles of the students, the length of the class period, and the time you have available for grading.

For an introductory course, your primary objective may be for the students to learn the basic concepts, thus multiple-choice, matching, fill-in-the-blank, and/or true-false questions may suffice. If the primary objective is integration, application, and analysis of information, consider short answer and/or essay questions. Some students are frustrated by multiple-choice questions, yet succeed when completing essay exams. In addition, consider having more than one type of question on your exams so that students have an opportunity to demonstrate their acquired knowledge in various formats. Reflect upon the length of time your students will need to complete the exam. A proposed guideline is to allow at least one minute per multiple-choice, true-false, fill-in-the-blank, and matching question. The length of time required for short answer and essay questions varies considerably due to the nature of the question. If your objectives dictate both multiple-choice and essay questions, you may want to devote two class periods to the exam (i.e., multiple-choice questions one class period and essay questions the next class period). For obvious reasons, the grading of essay questions requires more of your time, therefore, plan accordingly.

Writing Skills

An important skill students must develop or improve during college is the ability to write well. Consider assigning several brief papers, a longer, more in-depth paper, or a combination of both, depending on the number of students in your class and the course difficulty level. There are two main objectives for most writing assignments. First, they provide an opportunity for students to learn about a specific topic, to apply their emerging critical thinking skills, and to gain experience integrating information. Second, writing assignments afford students an opportunity to practice their writing skills and to organize their thoughts coherently. There are numerous types of writing assignments, including literature reviews, annotated bibliographies, case studies, research reports, and critical thinking papers. As an example, critical thinking papers require students to apply concepts from the textbook and/or lectures to real-world issues. Throughout this manual we have provided several suggested research report topics and other in-class writing assignments. If you choose to assign an in-depth research paper, you may want to consider having students turn in a rough draft so that you can provide written feedback about the content, as well as the writing. It is important to stress that writing skills will improve as a result of the process of multiple drafts. While this is a time-consuming endeavor, we have been pleasantly surprised and encouraged by the magnitude of improvement in students' writing.

Extra Credit

Depending on your pedagogical ideas, you may want to consider giving your students an opportunity to earn extra credit. You may recognize that despite some students' best efforts, occasionally things can go wrong—a misunderstanding of what to expect on the first exam, an illness or personal situation presenting itself too late to enable the student to qualify to take a make-up exam, or the demand of several difficult courses bearing down at once, with the sacrifice coming in the form of a less than desirable grade on an exam or assignment. The problem that can arise, however, is that oftentimes students would either be lazy, not learn much, and do poorly for the first two-thirds of the course then load up on extra credit to salvage their grade, or, they would immediately pursue all extra credit opportunities and, due to the extra load, perform only moderately on that and their required work. Neither of these scenarios is appealing, and may cause you to question even offering the extra credit. One solution is to implement a unique format for using extra credit. Set a policy that there will be no opportunity for extra credit until *after* midterm, and students must have at least a C average to be eligible to take advantage of it. This way, students have the opportunity to focus on the required material for the first half of the course—there is no distraction of additional work. If they have performed sufficiently on the required material (C average), but wish to improve on their grade, they are then presented with the extra credit options. For students who have a D or are failing at midterm, they can no longer rely on extra credit to carry them through. Inform these students that they should reconsider remaining in the course as there is ample time for them to drop the course and still receive a "W." If this is not an option for them, they still have an opportunity to pass the class if they apply themselves to the remaining required work.

Academic Dishonesty

Academic dishonesty can take many forms. This ranges from blatant forms of cheating, such as a student copying exam answers, to more subtle means, such as a student plagiarizing a journal article while writing a research report. Prevention should be your primary goal. McKeachie (1994) has suggested several ways to prevent cheating. First, reduce the pressure on students by providing multiple opportunities for evaluation. This lessens the emphasis on any one project, exam, or activity. Second, clearly define and provide examples of academic dishonesty, so that students fully understand concepts such as plagiarism. When assigning research projects, require students to submit copies of the research articles they are citing as they are less likely to copy the ideas directly if they think you might find out. Third, structure the classroom environment during exams, such as assigning alternate seats, so that the opportunity for cheating is reduced. Another way to reduce the opportunity for cheating is to create alternate versions of the examination so that adjacent students receive different versions of the test.

Despite your best preventive efforts, you will most likely encounter cheating. If academic dishonesty does occur, consult your university guidelines. In the classroom, if you suspect a student is copying from a classmate, make a general announcement regarding the importance of not allowing their eyes to wander. If this is ineffective, approach the student you suspect of cheating and politely suggest that he/she change seats. Further discussion about this behavior should occur in your office; if at all possible, have a colleague present for this discussion. Regarding plagiarism, invite the student into your office and go through the various sections that appear to be plagiarized. Discuss the American Psychological Association rules for citing resources and the use of quotations in writing. In many cases, students do not realize that they are plagiarizing, thus you can use this opportunity to educate them. If the pattern of academic dishonesty persists, you may have to take further action such as documenting the incidences with your university's upper administration.

- Sources: American Psychological Association (1994). *Publication manual of the American Psychological Association* (4th ed.). Washington, DC: Author. McKeachie, W. J. (1994). *Teaching tips: Strategies, research, and theory for college and university teachers* (9th ed.). Lexington, MA: Heath and Company.

Problem Student

The troublemaker . . . there is one in every class. The question is how to handle a so-called "problem student." There are several types of students that may require extra patience on your part, such as "angry and aggressive," "attention seekers," "dominators," "silent," "inattentive," "unprepared," "flatterer," and "con man (or woman)." The angry and aggressive student is often verbally and nonverbally hostile to you, his/her peers, and the educational process in general. One way to handle this problem is to ignore his or her hostility, which will prevent public confrontation and the problem may go away on its own. Another strategy is to become better acquainted with the student, which may reduce his or her hostility towards you and may reassure the student that you are concerned about him or her as a person, as well as his/her education. Another difficult student to deal with is the con man or woman who is full of excuses and always demands special treatment. One preventative technique is to have students sign a contract at the beginning of the term that clearly outlines the requirements for the course, deadlines, and policies for make-up work. Regardless of whether you implement a contract system, it is important that you clearly delineate the requirements, deadlines, and policies for make-up work at the beginning of the course and consistently enforce them. McKeachie (1994) discusses a range of problem students and methods for interacting with them.

- Source: McKeachie, W. J. (1994). *Teaching tips: Strategies, research, and theory for college and university teachers* (9 ed.). Lexington, MA: Heath and Company.

Course Critique

Although most universities administer their own evaluations at the end of each semester, consider creating your own. Rather than a multiple-choice or Likert-type scale to get students' feedback on the class, assign an open-ended critique that they turn in to you. You can make it a required assignment to demonstrate its importance to you—we value their feedback and use it to improve our subsequent classes. Encourage them to be open, honest, and constructively critical, as well as positive about what they liked. It is important to assure them that their grade is based on the time, effort, and thought that goes into their critique, and not whether they discuss positive or negative things. They may need some structure to guide them, so you can make a list of the things you want them to address, such as the text, the class format, the assignments, lecture style, projects, and so on. We both have received a great deal of wonderful, useful comments over the years; some that have encouraged us to continue certain practices, some that have enlightened us to difficulties we did not anticipate, and some that have inspired new and effective teaching techniques and assignment ideas. Students also enjoy the fact that their input matters.

Congratulations!

You've made it to the end of the course! Now is a good time to reflect on your teaching and how the course went. Throughout the term you have probably noticed that certain lectures and assignments worked better than others. While it seems that you will never forget those awkward moments when things didn't flow well, it is important to document necessary changes for future reference. First, note your teaching strengths and areas that need improvement. Second, develop strategies for improvement while this information is still fresh in your mind. Third, if your institution implements formal student evaluations, try to incorporate reasonable student suggestions. The key to being an effective instructor is to continually strive to improve your teaching ability.

Answering Essay and Critical Thinking Questions

The following is a statement you may wish to duplicate and distribute to students to help them think about and plan answers to essay and critical thinking questions:

Santrock argues that children must learn to think critically. For Santrock, critical thinking is "grasping the deeper meaning of problems, keeping an open mind about different approaches and perspectives, and thinking reflectively rather than accepting statements and carrying out procedures without significant understanding and evaluation."

Learning to think critically requires activity rather than passivity on the part of students. To improve your critical thinking skills (e.g., developing problem-solving strategies, seeing things from multiple points of view, expanding your knowledge base, and becoming motivated to use newly acquired critical thinking skills in daily life), you must actively: (a) read, listen, and observe carefully, (b) identify or formulate questions, (c) organize your thoughts on an issue or topic, (d) note similarities and differences, (e) make deductions by reasoning from the general to the specific, and (f) distinguish between logically valid and invalid inferences.

In answering the essay and critical thinking questions you should demonstrate each of these aspects of critical thinking and satisfy the following criteria regarding content, organization, and writing skills. *Appropriate content* includes a sentence that restates the question, and a sentence or paragraph that answers all parts of the question. Additional aspects of content include major points and supporting evidence that are accurate and related to the answer. Provide credit for information from others that you include in your response. Finally, end your response by restating the answer to the question and summarizing major points. *Appropriate organization* requires that your answer to the question appear near the beginning of your response. Major points and supporting evidence should be arranged in an order that is logical and coherent. The answer should be summarily restated at the end of your response. *Appropriate writing skills* require that you use complete sentences, correct punctuation, and other mechanics of good writing.

- Source: Santrock, *Instructor's Manual to accompany Child Development*, ninth edition, 2001. Reproduced with permission from The McGraw-Hill Companies.

Ethics, Human Subjects, and Informed Consent

The following section is duplicated in the Student Study Guide. It presents information about the ethics involved in doing research with human subjects. It also provides information about what is involved in both a Human Subjects Review Committee Application and in an informed consent form.

It has been our experience that many students today are concerned with issues involving the risks to and the rights of potential subjects in psychological and other research. Many of them have had experience as subjects participating in our research projects. It is in their best interests and ours to provide them with information so that they can understand the issues involved.

Ethical Practices in Research with Human Subjects[1]

There are four issues of major importance in conducting research with human subjects:

1. Informed consent is required from the subject prior to any psychological testing. In doing research with children, written consent of the parents is required. Informed consent means that the purpose of the research and the procedures involved have been explained to the parents and that they understand what is involved and agree to allow their child to participate in the study. The procedures should then be explained to the child at the child's level of understanding, the child's cooperation should be enlisted, and an attempt should be made to maintain the child's interest during his or her participation in the project. Parents must be informed that both they and their child have the right to withdraw from participating at any time for any reason.

2. A Human Subjects Review Committee, by that or some similar name, exists at all institutions that do research with human subjects to evaluate the research projects and to safeguard the rights and the safety of potential subjects. Determinations of such review committees are usually based, in part, upon the possible use of deception and any potential risk to subjects. The concept of informed consent assumes that the real purpose of the experiment has been revealed to subjects and that the subjects are competent to decide whether or not to participate. This condition is violated when the experiment requires deception of the subject. None of the projects in this supplement package requires deception of the subjects. The second problem is possible risk to subjects. None of the projects presented here involves risk to the subjects. However, they do not provide positive benefits to the subjects either; they are neutral.

3. The requirement for informed consent is violated when coercion is used on the subjects because, when coercion is used, subjects are not free to refuse to participate. This freedom to refuse must be guaranteed to the subjects. When working with children as subjects, it is necessary to make the study as playful and gamelike as possible to enlist the interest of children. However, their rights to refuse to participate and to not be coerced must also be respected and protected.

4. Privacy and confidentiality must be guaranteed. It is important to inform the parents that, in any report of the information gained, their child will not be identified by name but only by averages or identifiers that cannot be traced to the individual child. The child's privacy will be protected. This requires that, when you present data in class, you report the data only by age and sex of the child, never by name.

---

[1]Carroll, M.A., Schneider, H.G., & Wesley, G.R. (1985). *Ethics in the practice of psychology.* Englewood Cliffs, NJ: Prentice-Hall.

- Source: Santrock, *Instructor's Manual to accompany Child Development*, ninth edition, 2001. Reproduced with permission from The McGraw-Hill Companies.

Human Subjects Information

Your school should have forms available to use for the submission of research studies to the Human Subjects Review Committee on your campus. The kind of information generally required on these forms includes:

1. A description of the purpose of the research and a detailed description of the procedure used, including potential hazards and benefits to the subjects.

2. A copy of the informed consent form that subjects will sign, along with a description of the way in which their consent will be elicited.

3. A description of any possible harm—physical, emotional, or psychological—that might come from participation in the project.

4. A description of the subjects to be seen, including number, age, and other characteristics.

It is also possible that your school allows, as many do, for entire supplements such as this one to be submitted for consideration so that all the research exercises can be considered at once. This is a great convenience. Ask whether your school has such a policy.

Informed Consent Form

The informed consent form that parents sign should include several kinds of information:

1. A description of the procedures and the purpose of the study.

2. A statement of the rights of the subject to refuse to participate and to withdraw from participation at any time.

3. A statement guaranteeing the privacy and confidentiality of the results of the study. This usually involves a statement saying that results will not be reported by name and that any identifying information will be omitted from the report.

4. A description of any possible risks or discomforts that the subject might experience.

5. A description of any possible benefits to be expected for the subject. In the exercises presented in this supplement, the benefits tend to simply be the enjoyment of playing some of the games.

It is very likely that your school has such a form already prepared for use by faculty researchers. You can use the same form.

About Our Supplements

The supplements listed here accompany *Life-Span Development*, eighth edition. This comprehensive and fully integrated package includes offerings written specifically for instructors and students of life-span development, as well as a variety of generic supplements that are also applicable. Please contact your local McGraw-Hill representative for details concerning policies, pricing, and availability as some restrictions may apply.

For the Instructor

Printed Test Bank
by Angela Sadowski, Chaffey College
This comprehensive Test Bank has once again been extensively revised to include over 2,400 multiple-choice and short answer/brief essay questions for the text's 21 chapters. Each multiple-choice item is classified as factual, conceptual, or applied, as defined by Benjamin Bloom's taxonomy of educational objectives. Learning objectives have been added to this edition and are similarly included in both the Instructor's Manual and Study Guide. Test items are keyed to the learning objectives so that instructors can pinpoint areas in which students may have difficulty.

Computerized Test Bank (Mac/IBM) CD-ROM
The computerized test bank contains all of the questions in the print test bank and is available in both Macintosh and Windows platforms. This CD-ROM provides a fully-functioning editing feature that enables instructors to integrate their own questions, scramble items, and modify questions.

Overhead Transparencies
The overhead transparency package provides full-color acetates for use in the classroom. Many of the images in this package are taken directly from the eighth edition of *Life-Span Development*, and they include key illustrations, tables, and charts that highlight key concepts in the course. New to this edition are a number of conceptual transparencies that illustrate key concepts in ways different from those in the text. A complete list can be found below, following this section of the Instructor's Manual.

Instructor's Resource CD-ROM
This tool offers instructors the opportunity to customize McGraw-Hill materials to create their lecture presentations. Resources offered for instructors include complete material from the Instructor's Manual, PowerPoint presentation slides, computerized test bank, and the Image Database for life-span development. The chapter-by-chapter PowerPoint lectures were completely redone for this edition by one of the Instructor's Manual coauthors, Cynthia Jenkins. You will find great cohesiveness between the comprehensive lectures and the presentation of material in the text and in this manual, particularly in the use of the cognitive maps as an organizing feature.

The McGraw-Hill Developmental Psychology Image Bank
This set of 200 full-color images was developed using the best selection of our human development art and tables and is available online for both instructors and students at the text's Online Learning Center.

Online Learning Center
The extensive web site, designed specifically to accompany Santrock, *Life-Span Development*, eighth edition, offers an array of resources for both instructors and students. For instructors, the web site includes a full set of PowerPoint presentations, and hotlinks for the text's topical web links that appear in the margins and for the Taking it to the Net exercises that appear at the end of each chapter. These resources and more can be found by logging on to the web site at http:// www.mhhe.com/santrockld8.

The AIDS Booklet
by Frank D. Cox
This brief but comprehensive text has been recently revised to provide the most up-to-date information about acquired immune deficiency syndrome (AIDS).

The Critical Thinker
by Richard Mayer and Fiona Goodchild, University of California, Santa Barbara
The authors use excerpts from introductory psychology textbooks to show students how to think critically about psychology.

Annual Editions—Developmental Psychology
Published by Dushkin/McGraw-Hill, this is a collection of articles on topics related to the latest research and thinking in human development. These editions are updated annually and contain helpful features including a topic guide, an annotated table of contents, unit overviews, and a topical index. An Instructor's Guide containing testing material is also available.

Sources: Notable Selections in Human Development
This volume presents a collection of more than 40 articles, book excerpts, and research studies that have shaped the study of human development and our contemporary understanding of it. The selections are organized topically around major areas of study within human development. Each selection is preceded by a headnote that establishes the relevance of the article or study and provides biographical information of the author.

Taking Sides
This debate-style reader is designed to introduce students to controversial viewpoints on the field's most crucial issues. Each issue is carefully framed for the student, and the pro and con essays represent the arguments of leading scholars and commentators in their fields. An Instructor's Guide containing testing material is also available.

For the Student

Study Guide
by Anita Rosenfield, DeVry Institute of Technology
The revised Study Guide has benefited from the author's experience in teaching courses in Student Success Strategies as well as student feedback on what makes an effective study guide. The Study Guide provides a complete introduction for students on how best to use each of the various study aids plus invaluable strategies on setting goals, benefiting from class, reading for learning, taking tests, and memory techniques in the section "Being an Excellent Student." For each chapter, features include learning objectives from the Instructor's Manual and Test Bank and a chapter outline. A self-test section contains multiple-choice questions keyed to the learning objectives, matching sets on key people found in the text, comprehensive essays with suggested answers, and new word scramblers on key terms found in the text. In addition, new to this edition of the Study Guide are personal application projects and Internet exercises that complement the revised student research projects and allow for effective student learning.

Making the Grade CD-ROM

This user-friendly CD-ROM gives students an opportunity to test their comprehension of the course material. Written specifically to accompany Santrock, *Life-Span Development*, eighth edition, this CD-ROM provides 15–25 multiple-choice questions for each chapter to help students further test their understanding of key concepts. Feedback is provided for each answer. In addition, the CD-ROM provides a Learning Assessment questionnaire to help students discover which type of learner they are, of the three types covered in the program.

Online Learning Center

The extensive web site, designed specifically to accompany Santrock, *Life-Span Development*, eighth edition, offers an array of resources for both instructors and students. For students, the web site includes interactive quizzing and exercises, as well as hotlinks for the text's topical web links that appear in the margins and for the Taking it to the Net exercises that appear at the end of each chapter. These resources and more can be found by logging on to the web site at http:// www.mhhe.com/santrockld8.

Guide to Life-Span Development for Future Educators and Guide to Life-Span Development for Future Nurses

These course supplements help students apply the concepts of human development to education and nursing careers. They contain information, exercises, and sample tests designed to help students prepare for certification and understand human development from a professional perspective.

Resources for Improving Human Development

This informative booklet provides descriptions and contact information for organizations and agencies that can provide helpful information, advice, and support related to particular problems or issues in life-span development. Recommended books and journals are also described and included. The booklet is organized in chronological order of the periods of the life span.

Overhead Transparencies

Following is a complete list of overhead transparencies available with Santrock, *Life-Span Development*, eighth edition. You will find references to each image within the Total Teaching Package Outlines for each chapter where they are most relevant.

No. Title
1   Two Contrasting Perspectives on Developmental Change
2   The Aging of America
3   Human Life Expectancy
4   Maximum Recorded Life Spans for Different Species
5   Characteristics of the Life-Span Perspective
6   Influences on Developmental Change
7   Conceptions of Age
8   Critical Thinking about Life-Span Development
9   Increases in Ethnic Minority Populations
10 Critical Thinking about Children's Development
11 Piaget's Four Stages of Cognitive Development
12 Classical Conditioning Procedure
13 Little Albert's Generalized Fear
14 Possible Explanations for Correlational Data
15 Principles of Experimental Strategy
16 Influences on Context: An Ecological Approach
17 Experiments
18 Design for an Experiment
19 Two Most Common Ways to Obtain Data
20 Classical Conditioning
21 Operant, or Instrumental Conditioning
22 Biological, Cognitive, and Socioemotional Processes in Development
23 Human Reproductive Systems
24 Heredity Composition of the Zygote
25 Determination of Sex
26 Phenotypes and Genotypes
27 Dominant Inheritance of a Birth Defect
28 Recessive Inheritance of a Birth Defect
29 Sex-Linked Inheritance of a Birth Defect
30 Some Conditions and Characteristics Showing Genetic Influence
31 Early Development of a Human Embryo
32 Proportion of American Mothers with Late or No Prenatal Care
33 Piaget's Stages of Cognitive Development
34 A Model of Cognition
35 Possible Explanations of Correlational Data
36 Principles of the Experimental Strategy
37 Fertility Problems and Solutions
38 The Placenta and the Umbilical Cord
39 Drug Use during Pregnancy
40 Percentage of Low-Birthweight Infants
41 Changes in Body Form and Proportion
42 The Brain's Four Lobes
43 The Neuron
44 The Development of Fine Motor Skills in Infancy

45 How Infants Scan the Human Face
46 How Brown-Eyed Parents Can Have a Blue-Eyed Child
47 Developmental Changes in Height and Weight from Birth to 18 Months
48 Embryological Development of the Nervous System
49 Piaget's Description of Sensorimotor Thought
50 Developmental Course of Facial Expressions of Emotion
51 Infant Mortality Rates in Industrialized Countries
52 Growth in Height and Weight during Infancy
53 Primary, Secondary, and Tertiary Circular Reactions
54 Piaget's Conservation Task
55 Classification: An Important Ability
56 Characteristics of Concrete Operational Thought
57 Growth of Mental Abilities
58 The Four Stages of Cognitive Development
59 Average Correlations
60 Preoperational Thought's Characteristics
61 Primary Child-Care Arrangements Used by Employed Mothers
62 Child Poverty Rates in 18 Industrialized Countries
63 Piaget's Mountain Task
64 Average Height and Weight of Girls and Boys 2–6 Years
65 Three Mountain Task Perspective
66 Growth Curves
67 Development of Gross Motor Skills in Early Childhood
68 Development of Fine Motor Skills in Early Childhood
69 Piaget's Substages of Sensorimotor Development
70 Array of Objects
71 Conservation
72 Classification
73 Time Frames of Memory
74 Cubes Used to Study Mental Rotation Abilities
75 Balance Scale Used by Siegler
76 Normal Curve and the Stanford-Binet IQ Scores
77 Approaches to Children's Learning, Cognitive Development, and Intelligence
78 Approaches to Children's Learning, Cognitive Development, and Intelligence (continued)
79 The Snowflake Model of Creativity
80 Developmental Information-Processing Model of Reading
81 Chess and Thomas's Basic Clusters of Temperament
82 Proportion of Youngsters Living in Single-Parent Households
83 Changes in Height and Weight in Middle and Late Childhood
84 Children Under 18 Living with One Parent
85 Peer Aggression
86 Identification and Social Learning Views of Gender Development
87 Identification and Social Learning Theories of Gender
88 A Comparison of Cognitive Development and Gender Schema Theories
89 Gender-Role Classification
90 Damon's Description
91 Profile of Poor Children
92 Four Main Ways to Improve Self-Esteem
93 Characteristics of Formal Operational Thought
94 Dunphy's Progression of Peer Group Relations in Adolescence
95 Models of Pubertal Change and Behavior

96   Adolescent Sexual Intercourse
97   Understanding AIDS
98   Adolescents' Self-Understanding
99   Behavioral Indicators of Self-Esteem
100 Marcia's Four Stages of Identity
101 Freshman Life Goals
102 Rest's Components of Moral Development
103 Classification of Parenting Styles
104 Models of Parent-Adolescent Relationships
105 The Development of Communication Skills
106 Reading and Television Habits of High School Students from Working-Class Families
107 Usual Sequence of Physiological Changes in Adolescence
108 Primary Sex Characteristics: Sex Origins
109 Secondary Sex Characteristics
110 A Sharp Increase in Marijuana Use
111 Parents Involvement and High School Students' Grades
112 School Dropout Rates among Youth Ages 16–24
113 Growth in High School Graduation
114 Continuity and Discontinuity in Development
115 Critical Thinking about Adolescent Development
116 Model of Information Processing
117 Bandura's Model of the Reciprocal Influences of Behavior
118 Possible Explanations of Correlational Data
119 Principles of the Experimental Strategy
120 Hormone Levels by Sex and Pubertal Stage
121 Major Endocrine Glands Involved in Pubertal Change
122 Models of Pubertal Change and Behavior
123 Steps Involved in Processing Information to Solve an Algebra Problem
124 Approaches to Adolescent Learning
125 Old and New Models of Parent-Adolescent Relationships
126 Mean Scores for Peer Conformity on Different Types of Behavior
127 The Functions of Friendship
128 Living in Distressed Neighborhoods
129 Weekly After-School Activities of Eighth-Graders
130 Four Stages of Ethnic Minority Identity Development
131 Five Stages of White Ethnic Identity Development
132 Gender-Role Classification
133 Teenagers Who Have Had Sexual Intercourse
134 Contraceptive Use by Adolescent Females
135 Trends in the Teenage Birth Rate
136 Agreements/Disagreements: American and Indian Hindu Brahman Children about Right and Wrong
137 Rest's Components of Moral Development
138 Fowler's Stage Theory of Religious Development
139 How Employment Change Will Vary
140 Unemployment Rates of Youth: 1988
141 Eight-, Tenth-, and Twelfth-Graders Who Have Been Drunk
142 Rate of Suicide Rate Is Rising
143 Selye's General Adaptation Syndrome
144 Levels of Sex Hormones
145 Height at Different Ages
146 Important Sex Differences

147 Average Menarcheal Age of Adolescent Girls
148 The Age of Menarche Has Declined
149 IQ Scores Fluctuate Very Little
150 Some Consequences of Attaining Adult Status
151 The Divorce Rate
152 Employment of Mothers with School-Aged Children
153 Similarities and Differences
154 Percentage of U.S. Population
155 Self-Esteem Is Affected Differently
156 Between 1950 and 1970, US College Enrollments
157 More US High School Students Are Working
158 Percentage of Boys versus Girls in Common Adolescents' Jobs
159 Scales Used to Measure "Cynicism toward Work" & "Tolerance of Unethical Business Practices"
160 Percentages of 18- to 21-Year-Olds in Various Roles
161 Eight Stages of Development
162 Identity Status Categories
163 Susceptibility to Peer Pressure
164 Age Differences in Intimacy
165 First Marriages
166 An Overview of Adolescent Pregnancy
167 SAT Scores
168 Over Time Changes in Scores of SATs
169 Percentages of American High School Seniors Who Have Ever Used Drugs
170 Drug Use Trends
171 Drug Use among Younger Adolescents
172 Monthly and Daily Use of Various Drugs
173 Aggravated Assault and Murder Trends
174 Suicide
175 Cognitive Stages of Adulthood
176 The Life Contour of Work in Adulthood
177 Sternberg's Triangle of Love
178 Single-Parent Families with Children Under 18 Years of Age
179 Death Rates
180 Proportion of Women Aged 20-44 Who Have Not Yet Given Birth
181 Four Paths to Developing Generativity
182 Adult Development Stages Proposed by Levinson, Gould, and Vaillant
183 Some Typical Life Events and Weighted Values
184 Differences in the Life Expectancies of Females and Males
185 Perceptual Decline in Old Age and Late Old Age
186 The Six Leading Causes of Death in Americans 65 and Older
187 Fluid and Crystallized Intellectual Development across the Life Span
188 Cross-Sectional and Longitudinal Comparisons of Reasoning Ability
189 Social Breakdown
190 Life Expectancy at Birth
191 Number of Men per 100 Women by Age
192 Percentages of Older Adults Who Needed Help with Daily Activities
193 Cognitive-Appraisal Model of Coping
194 Sources of Income for Older Americans
195 Living Arrangements of Noninstitutionalized Persons 65 and Older
196 Suicide Rates in the US
197 Kubler-Ross' Stages of Dying

Film and Video Sources

The film and video offerings available for teaching life-span development are countless and variable in quality. For each chapter contained in this manual, we have provided a dozen or so selections that we have found to be worth consideration for use in the classroom. These selections are generally readily available and easy to obtain from well-known sources. We recommend that you order your films and videos well in advance of the start of the semester.

To aid you in obtaining your selections, we have provided below the names, addresses, URLs for web sites, and telephone numbers of all distributors mentioned in this manual. Most distributors maintain a web site, however, because Internet addresses often change, you might encounter a dead link. In this event, a new search will usually take you to the proper site.

Film and Video Distributor List

Ambrose Video Publishing, Inc.
28 W. 44th Street, Suite 2100
New York, NY 10036-6600
(212)768-7373
http://www.ambrosevideo.com

Annenberg/CPB Project
The Corporation for Public Broadcasting
901 E Street NW
Washington, DC 20004-2037
http://www.learner.org

Cambridge Documentary Films, Inc.
P.O. Box 390385
Cambridge, MA 02139-0004
(617)484-3993
http://www1.shore.net/~cdf/films1.html

Carousel Film and Video
260 Fifth Avenue
New York, NY 10001
(212)683-1660
carousel@pipeline.com

Cinema Guild
130 Madison Avenue, 2nd floor
New York, NY 10016-7038
(212)685-6242
http://www.cinemaguild.com

Davidson Films
668 Marsh Street
San Luis Obispo, CA 93401
(805)594-0532
http://www.davidsonfilms.com

Direct Cinema Ltd.
c/o Transit Media Library
P.O. Box 315
779 Susquehanna Avenue
Franklin Lakes, NJ 07417
(310)636-8200
http://www.directcinemalimited.com

Education Development Center, Inc.
Distribution Center
55 Chapel Street
Newton, MA 02458-1060
(617)969-7100
http://www.edc.org

Fanlight Productions
4196 Washington Street, Suite 2
Boston, MA 02131
(800)937-4113
http://www.fanlight.com

Films for the Humanities & Sciences
P.O. Box 2053
Princeton, NJ 08543-2053
(800)257-5126
http://www.films.com

Filmakers Library
124 East 40th Street
New York, NY 10016
(212)808-4980
http://www.filmakers.com

The Glendon Association
5383 Hollister Avenua
Suite 230
Santa Barbara, CA 93111
(800)663-5281
http://www.glendon.org

Indiana University
Instructional Support Services
Franklin Hall
Bloomington, IN 47405-1223
(812)855-8065
http://www.indiana.edu/~mediares/catalog.htm

Insight Media, Inc.
2162 Broadway
New York, NY 10024-0621
(800)233-9910
http://www.insight-media.com

Magna Systems, Inc.
P.O. Box 576
Itasca, NY 60143-0576
(708)382-6477

Media Education Foundation
26 Center Street
Northampton, MA 01060
(800)897-0089
http://www.mediaed.org

Morton Publishing Company
(800)348-3777
http://www.morton-pub.com

National Film Board of Canada
1251 Avenue of the Americas, 16th floor
New York, NY 10020-1173
(800)542-2164
http://www.nfb.ca

New Yorker Films
16 West 61st Street
New York, NY 10023
(212)247-6110
http://www.newyorkerfilms.com

PBS Video
1320 Braddock Place
Alexandria, VA 22314
(800)344-3337
http://www.pbs.org

Pennsylvania State University
Audio-Visual Services
Special Services Building
1127 Fox Hill Road
University Park, PA 16803-1824
(800)826-0132
http://www.medianet.libraries.psu.edu

Syracuse University Film Rental Center
1455 East Colving Street
Syracuse, NY 13210

Terra Nova Films, Inc.
9848 South Winchester Avenue
Chicago, IL 60643
(800)779-8491
http://www.terranova.org

Time-Life Film & Video
100 Eisenhower Drive
Paramus, NJ 07652
http://www.time-life.com

University of Illinois
Visual Aids Service
1325 South Oak Street
Champaign, IL 61820

University of Minnesota Film & Video
University of Minnesota
1313 Fifth Street S.E., Suite 108
Minneapolis, MN 55414-1524
In-state: (800)542-0013
Out-of-state: (800)847-8251

Women Make Movies, Inc.
462 Broadway, Suite 500WI
New York, NY 10013
(212)925-0606
http://www.wmm.com

Useful Web Sites

Probably the most valuable web site you will investigate for this course is the one developed specifically for the eighth edition of Santrock, *Life-Span Development*. As noted above, you can access the online learning center at http://www.mhhe.santrockld8 At the site, you will find resources for both instructors and students.

In addition, there are many useful web sites that provide information valuable to many or all of the chapters. The URLs for those sites are listed below. Because most of these are for established organizations, they should remain current over the life of this edition of the Instructor's Manual. However, please be advised that you may occasionally encounter an inactive link. For web sites that are more specific to only one or two individual chapters, we have provided the URLs under Web Site Suggestions for each chapter and referenced those within the Total Teaching Package Outlines.

American Psychological Association
http://www.psy.utexas.edu/psy/div7/div7.html

American Psychological Association Division 7: Developmental Psychology
http://www.apa.org/about/division/div7.html

American Psychological Society
http://www.adec.org/

Faculty Connection: Teaching Technologies
http://www.facultyconnection.org/

Films for the Humanities and the Sciences
http://www.films.com/

The Gerontological Society of America
http://www.geron.org/

McGraw-Hill for Psychology
http://www.mhhe.com/catalogs/hss/psychology/

McGraw-Hill/Dushkin: Publisher of Annual Editions and Taking Sides
http://www.dushkin.com/online/contentsmain.mhtml

Monitor on Psychology: Publication of the American Psychological Association
http://www.apa.org/monitor/

National Institute on Aging
http://www.nih.gov/nia/

Online Psychology Web
http://www.onlinepsych.com/index.html/

Other Lists of Psychological Resources on the Net
http://psych.hanover.edu/Krantz/lists.html

Psychological Resources on the Net
http://psych.hanover.edu/Krantz/lists.html

A Psychologist's Internet Guide
http://www.paonline.com/pwallin/pwallin/framespsysearch.htm

PsycSCAN: Developmental Psychology
http://www.apa.org/psycinfo/products/scan-dev.html

Psyc Site: Science of Psychology Resources
http://stange.simplenet.com/psycsite/

Society for Research in Child Development
http://www.srcd.org/

University of Chicago Press: Journal Division
http://www.journals.uchicago.edu/pub-alpha.html

Chapter 1: Introduction

Total Teaching Package Outline

Lecture Outline	Resource References
Introduction	PowerPoint Presentation: See www.mhhe.com Cognitive Maps: See Appendix A
The Life-Span Perspective • Why Study Life-Span Development?	LO1 CA1: Ice Breaker PA1: Who Are You? PA2: What Do You Want to Know? RP1: Answering Questions about Development
• The Historical Perspective	LO2
-Child Development	OHT1 & IB: Contrasting Views on Development LS1: Historical Views of Childhood F/V: Child Development
-Life-Span Development	OHT2 & IB: The Aging of America OHT3 & IB: Human Life Expectancy OHT4 & IB: Maximum Recorded Life Spans
-The Twentieth Century	
• Characteristics of the Life-Span Perspective	LO3 OHT5 & IB: Characteristics of the Life-Span Pers.
-Development is Lifelong -Development is Multidimensional -Development is Multidirectional -Development is Plastic -Development is Contextual	 LO4 OHT6: Influences on Developmental Change PA3: Event of a Lifetime
-Development is Multidisciplinary -Development Involves Growth, Maintenance, and Regulation	
• Some Contemporary Concerns -Health and Well-Being	LO5 LS2: Interesting Statistics Regarding Dev. Psych RP2: Monitoring Contemporary Concerns
-Parenting and Education -Sociocultural Contexts	 F/V: Culture, Time, and Place F/V: Childhood: Great Expectations
-Social Policy	WS: American Family Policy Institute WS: Children's Action Alliance WS: Children's Defense Fund WS: The Future of Children

The Nature of Development
• Biological, Cognitive, Socioemotional
  Processes
	LO6
	OHT22 & IB: Biological, Cognitive, and
	                Socioemotional Processes
	LS3: The Concept of Development and Interaction

• Periods of Development
    -Prenatal Period
    -Infancy
    -Early Childhood
    -Middle and Late Childhood
    -Adolescence
    -Early Adulthood
    -Middle Adulthood
    -Late Adulthood
	LO7
	CA2: Developmental Myths Quiz
	F/V: Development and Diversity

• Age and Happiness	

• Conceptions of Age
    -Chronological Age
    -Biological Age
    -Psychological Age
    -Social Age
	LO8
	OHT7 & IB: Conceptions of Age
	F/V: Development and Diversity

• Developmental Issues
    -Nature and Nurture
    -Continuity and Discontinuity
    -Stability and Change
    -Evaluating Developmental Issues
	LO9
	F/V: Nature/Nurture
	OHT114: Continuity and Discontinuity

Careers in Life-Span Development	LO10 IB: Jobs and Careers in Life-Span Development LS4: Guest Speaker Idea WS: Chronicle of Higher Education Job List
Review	OHT8: Critical Thinking about Life-Span CA3: Critical Thinking Multiple-Choice CA4: Critical Thinking Essays

Chapter Outline

THE LIFE-SPAN PERSPECTIVE
  Why Study Life-Span Development?
  • **Development** is the pattern of movement or change that begins at conception and continues through the human life span.
  • Individuals can gain insight into their own childhood and better anticipate potential changes they may experience in adulthood.
  • Life-span development is an important college course, as it links many areas of psychology.

The Historical Perspective

Child Development

- Historically, three philosophical views have been proposed to explain the nature of children and how they should be reared.
  - The concept of **original sin** from the Middle Ages viewed children as being bad, born into the world as evil beings. Childrearing focused on salvation.
  - The 17th century English philosopher Locke's concept of **tabula rasa** stated that children were not innately bad, rather children were blank slates. Children acquired their characteristics through experience. Parenting focused on shaping children to be good citizens.
  - In the 18th century, the French philosopher Jean-Jacques Rousseau proposed the **innate goodness** view that children were born inherently good. Children should be allowed to develop with little monitoring or supervision.

Life-Span Development

- The traditional approach emphasizes extreme change from birth to adolescence, little or no change in adulthood, and decline in old age.
  - The life-span approach emphasizes that developmental change occurs during adulthood as well as childhood.

The Twentieth Century

- Life expectancy has changed considerably in the last century. Improvements in sanitation, nutrition, and medical knowledge led to this increase of 30 years.

Characteristics of the Life-Span Perspective

- Baltes states that the **life-span perspective** has seven basic characteristics.

Development is Life-Long

- Individuals continue to develop and change from conception to death. No one age dominates development.

Development is Multidimensional

- Development consists of biological, cognitive, and socioemotional components.

Development is Multidirectional

- Some components of a dimension increase in growth, others decrease.

Development is Plastic

- Plasticity involves the degree to which characteristics change or remain stable.

Development is Contextual

- Individuals respond to and act upon contexts, including one's biological makeup, physical environment, cognitive processes, and social, historical, and cultural contexts. Within the contextual view, the following three sources influence development:
  - Normative age-graded influences are biological and environmental influences that are similar for individuals in a particular age group.
  - Normative history-graded influences are common to people of a particular generation because of the historical circumstances they experience.
  - Nonnormative life events are unusual occurrences that have a major impact on an individual's life. The occurrence, pattern, and sequence of these events are not applicable to many individuals.

Development is Studied by a Number of Disciplines

- Psychologists, sociologists, anthropologists, neuroscientists, and medical researchers all study human development.

Development Involves Growth, Maintenance, and Regulation

- The mastery of life often involves conflicts and competition among three goals of human development: growth, maintenance, and regulation.

Some Contemporary Concerns
    Health and Well-Being
    - An individual's behavior and psychological states influence health and well-being.
    Parenting and Education
    - In today's society, family functioning and education are influenced by various issues (e.g., day care, maltreatment, homelessness, ethnicity and social class, and bilingualism).
    Sociocultural Contexts
    - A **context** is the setting in which development occurs. This setting is influenced by historical, economic, social, and cultural factors.
    - **Culture** is the behavior patterns, beliefs, and all other products of a particular group of people that are passed on from generation to generation.
    - **Cross-cultural studies** involve a comparison of a culture with one or more other cultures. The comparison provides information about the degree to which development is similar across cultures or is instead culture-specific.
    - **Ethnicity** involves cultural heritage, nationality characteristics, race, religion, and language.
    - **Gender** is the sociocultural dimension of being female or male.
    Social Policy
    - **Social Policy** is a government's course of action designed to influence its citizen's welfare.
    - **Generational inequity** is the condition in which an aging society is being unfair to its younger members (older members receiving inequitably large allocations of resources).

THE NATURE OF DEVELOPMENT
- **Development** is the pattern of movement or change that begins at conception and continues through the life span. Development involves an interplay of biological, cognitive, and socioemotional processes.

Biological, Cognitive, and Socioemotional Processes
- **Biological processes** involve changes in the individual's physical nature.
- **Cognitive processes** involve changes in the individual's thought, intelligence, and language.
- **Socioemotional processes** involve changes in the individual's relationships with other people, changes in emotions, and changes in personality.

Periods of Development
- The life span is commonly divided into the following periods of development:
    - Prenatal period is the time from conception to birth.
    - Infancy is the developmental period extending from birth to 18 or 24 months.
    - Early childhood (preschool years) extends from the end of infancy to about 5 or 6 years.
    - Middle and late childhood (elementary school years) extends from about 6 to 11 years.
    - Adolescence is the developmental period of transition from childhood to early adulthood, entered at approximately 10 to 12 years of age and ending at 18 to 22 years of age.
    - Early adulthood begins in the late teens or early twenties and lasts through the thirties.
    - Middle adulthood begins at approximately 35 to 40 years of age and extends to the sixties.
    - Late adulthood is the developmental period beginning in the sixties or seventies and lasting until death.

Age and Happiness
- When individuals report how happy they are and how satisfied they are with their lives, no particular age group says they are happier or more satisfied than any other age group.

Conceptions of Age
- A full consideration of age requires consideration of four dimensions:
    - **Chronological Age** is the number of years that have elapsed since a person's birth.
    - **Biological Age** is a person's age in terms of biological health.
    - **Psychological Age** is an individual's adaptive capacitates compared to those of other individuals of the same chronological age.
    - **Social Age** refers to social roles and expectations related to a person's age.

Developmental Issues
Nature and Nurture
- The nature-nurture controversy involves the debate about whether development is primarily influenced by nature or nurture. Nature refers to an organism's biological inheritance, nurture to its environmental experiences.
Continuity and Discontinuity
- This issue focuses on the extent to which development involves gradual, cumulative change (continuity) or distinct stages (discontinuity).
Stability and Change
- This issue involves the degree to which we become older renditions of our early experience or we develop into someone different from who we were at an early point in development.

Evaluating the Developmental Issues
- The way in which researchers and policy makers approach development is influenced by their stance on several issues (nature and nurture, continuity and discontinuity, stability and change). Most developmentalists do not take extreme positions on these issues, though debates still ensue.

CAREERS IN LIFE-SPAN DEVELOPMENT
- Rewarding careers can be built around life-span developmental psychology. A variety of career options are offered in education, helping, and health professions.

Learning Objectives

1. Explain the importance of studying life-span development.
2. Describe the history of interest in children and adolescents and indicate how contemporary concerns have arisen from previous views.
3. Describe the seven basic characteristics of the life-span perspective.
4. List and describe the three interacting systems of contextualism.
5. Describe the role that experts in developmental psychology have regarding health and well-being, parenting and education, sociocultural contexts, and social policy.
6. Define and distinguish between biological processes, cognitive processes, and socioemotional processes.
7. Understand the major developmental periods from conception to death.
8. Define and distinguish between chronological age, biological age, psychological age, and social age.
9. Understand the three major developmental issues (nature and nurture, continuity and discontinuity, stability and change).
10. Identify several options that are available to individuals who are interested in careers in life-span development.

Key Terms

biological age
biological processes
chronological age
cognitive processes
context
continuity-discontinuity issue
cross-cultural studies
culture
development
ethnicity
gender

generational inequity
innate goodness view
life-span perspective
nature-nurture issue
original sin view
psychological age
social age
social policy
socioemotional processes
stability-change issue
tabula rasa view

Key People

Philippe Aries
Paul Baltes
Marian Wright Edelman
Jerome Kagan

John Locke
Bernice Neugarten
Jean-Jacques Rousseau

Lecture Suggestions

Lecture Suggestion 1: Historical Views of Childhood The purpose of this lecture is to supplement the textbook material regarding changing perceptions of children. Somerville's book, *The Rise and Fall of Childhood*, is easy reading and provides an interesting historical view of children. The purpose of this book is to show ways children have been important to adults throughout history and reasons for the changes in their status. It is an examination of adult attitudes toward children and childhood and how these attitudes have changed over history. The actual plight of children in the past and currently is explored in order to examine the relationship between attitudes and reality with respect to children. Specific issues that are discussed include major trends in childrearing attitudes and practices from ancient Greece to Puritan times, practice of infanticide, views concerning education, control over children, and the changing family structure and function over the history of Western Civilization.

The first chapter asks, "What would others notice about our treatment of our children, and which of our attitudes would strike them as curious?" In these questions, "others" refers to our ancestors or future historians. Have your students generate their own answers to these questions. We've noted a few of Somerville's ideas.

- Most would notice that our attitudes are contradictory. We claim to care about children, yet 25 percent of children in the U.S. live in poverty. Child abuse is believed to have increased in last few decades. One could assume that the increase is due to an increase in reporting, however, most violent crimes have increased (e.g., between 1960 and 1980, the U.S. murder rate doubled, assault tripled, robbery and rape quadrupled), so many experts assume that child abuse has increased too.

- We read a lot about children; the all-time best-selling book in American history (excluding the Bible) is Dr. Benjamin Spock's *Baby and Child Care* (it has sold over 30 million copies in its first 30 years). Despite our many concerns for children, the amount of interaction between parents and children has been declining for at least 20 years. Smaller families are more common, so one might assume that parents could spend more time with children, though this is not the case.

- Are there any potential problems with parents seeking expert advice? Spock admits expert advice often undermines parents' self-confidence for parenting. Many parents don't use the advice they seek anyway. One study found that child-rearing books affect primarily what parents say they are doing and have little relation to what they can be observed doing under pressure of circumstances.

- Ann Landers (advice columnist) found that 70 percent of the readers answering one of her polls reported that they would not have children if they could do it over again. Why? (Expensive, fear of responsibility, general disenchantment with children).

- According to Somerville, the modern crisis with regard to children is that Americans are having an identity crisis in that there is confusion about which values to transmit to our children. He thinks Americans lack direction and cultural cohesion. The commitment to children and families is deteriorating. He states that we need to re-establish the significance of the family and commitment to children and transmit the value of service to others to our children.

We've noted several interesting issues that are raised in the book and can be used to stimulate discussion. Some of these issues may spark significant emotion in students. Be sure to discuss the importance of discussing ideas that are either consistent or inconsistent with one's personal opinions as part of one's educational experience. Stress the importance of discussing ideas and not attacking individuals for their ideas. Encourage them to keep an open mind to ideas that they may initially disagree with. It is important to understand varying points of view.
- The book discusses the significance of maternal nursing in the history of childhood, specifically the consequences of nursing or not and how these choices reflect the views about and treatment of babies and children. The consequences include health reasons and mortality rates, bonding and mother-child relationships, and babies being neglected by wet nurses. Historically, nursing has been seen as inconvenient and unfashionable and the lack of nursing reflected parents' indifference to children and a lack of caring or responsibility.
  - What are the consequences of breast-feeding today? How do current views reflect attitudes towards children?

- The book describes the high and low points in the history of childhood. The high point was the extreme sentimentalism and romanticism about children in literature. Children were seen as good and innocent but corrupted by society with time. The low point was the suffering of children in industrial factories. These points are connected because they occurred simultaneously during the industrial revolution and reflected the common plight that people's actual behavior and ideals are often not consistent. Somerville thinks that some of the apparent contradiction may actually reflect SES differences.
  - Have students provide examples for how these high and low points continue today. (High points: representation of TV, movies, literature, religion as pure and innocent; idealization by parents of the perfect baby; advertising. Low points: child labor, especially farm and migrant workers, increasing abuse; latchkey and other deserted children.)

- The historical pros and cons of infanticide are discussed. (Pros: economic survival of family, deformities are eliminated, evidence of premarital sex is eliminated, population control, the practice of sacrifices in religion, only wanted babies survive. Cons: abortion risk for mother's health, religion, morality, disrespect for human life, children as disposable, people want to adopt.)
  - Have students generate the pros and cons of infanticide.

- Child socialization (including childrearing and education) occurs within a culture and is directed at shaping children into adults with behavior, attitudes, and values appropriate to the culture. The book discusses Spartan harsh physical training and psychological toughening for both boys and girls. The boys learned war-related skills so that they could be soldiers in a military machine. Girls were toughened up so they would bear strong children and be able to give them up to the state for service. In Athens, boys (citizen class) spent the first 7 years with the mother and were neglected by the father. Boys were educated to be thinking citizens. Girls stayed at home and received no education, except domestic skills. As adults, men were leaders and women were restricted to house and domestic activities.

- Have students compare and contrast any two cultural groups (historic or current) in terms of the socialization of gender, with a specific focus on how socialization of boys versus girls is connected to adult gender roles in that culture.
- Source: Somerville, C. J. (1982). *The rise and fall of childhood.* Beverly Hills, CA: Sage.

Lecture Suggestion 2: Interesting Statistics Regarding Developmental Psychology In order to introduce the importance of life-span developmental research and understanding, you can provide interesting statistics regarding child abuse, teenage pregnancy, elder abuse, and public policy in your state, as well as national statistics. We've provided some summary national statistics, as well as state statistics for Arizona, from The Children's Defense Fund (2000) as an example.

Summary National Statistics:

- Health Insurance: While Vermont ranks 1st in the nation with only 6.4 percent of children without health coverage, Arizona and Texas rank last with 25.9 percent and 25.3 percent (respectively) of children without health coverage.
- Babies Born to Mothers Who Received Early Prenatal Care: While New Hampshire ranks 1st with 89.6 percent of babies born to mothers receiving early prenatal care, New Mexico and the DC rank last with only 70.2 percent and 66.6 percent (respectively) of babies born to mothers receiving early prenatal care.
- Low Birthweight (LBW): While Oregon ranks 1st with 5 percent of babies born at LBW, Louisiana and DC rank last with 10 percent and 13 percent (respectively) of babies born at LBW.
- Infant Mortality: While New Hampshire ranks 1st with an infant death rate of 4.3 per 1,000 live births, the DC ranks last with an infant death rate of 13.2 per 1,000 live births.
- Immunizations: While Vermont ranks 1st with 90 percent of 2-year-olds fully immunized, Oregon and Idaho rank last with 72 percent and 69 percent (respectively) of 2-year-olds fully immunized.
- Children in Poverty: While New Hampshire ranks 1st with 7.5 percent of children in poverty, West Virginia and the DC rank last with 29.9 percent and 35.6 percent (respectively) of children in poverty.
- Child Support Collected: While Vermont ranks 1st with 43.9 percent of child support collected, Tennessee and the DC rank last with only 11 percent and 9.7 percent (respectively) collected.
- Spending for Education per Public School Student: While New Jersey ranks 1st with $9,361 spent per public school student, Mississippi and Utah rank last with $3,951 and $3,604 (respectively) spent per student.

National Rankings for Arizona - With 1 being the best and 51 being the worst:

- Arizona ranks 51st in the percentage of children without health insurance. 1996-1998
- Arizona ranks 49th in the percentage of babies born to mothers who had early prenatal care. 1997
- Arizona ranks 24th in infant mortality. 1997
- Arizona ranks 16th in the percentage of low birthweight births. 1997
- Arizona ranks 48th in child immunizations for 2-year-olds. 1999
- Arizona ranks 39th in the percentage of children in poverty. 1996
- Arizona ranks 40th in its lowest fair market rent as a percentage of the minimum wage. 2000
- Arizona ranks 47th in its child support enforcement. 1997
- Arizona ranks 48th in per pupil expenditures in the public schools. 1995-1996
- Sources: Children's Defense Fund (2000). *The state of America's children.* Children's Defense Fund Publications. http://www.childrensdefense.org/

Lecture Suggestion 3: The Concept of Development and Interaction One of the ways in which life-span developmental psychology is distinct from other areas in psychology is its focus on a special kind of behavioral and psychological change. Developmental change is said to be different from other types of change such as learning and maturation. In order to introduce this topic and stimulate discussion regarding this issue, have students generate ideas about what development involves. Use these ideas to demonstrate the difference between development, learning, change, and maturation.

Give a lecture that explores the nature of developmental change, its causes, and what distinguishes it from other types of change. Although there are different views about what characterizes developmental change, consider these four features: Developmental change (a) is orderly; (b) is relatively long lasting; (c) produces something that is new or qualitatively different from what was present earlier; and (d) results in superior functioning. Elaborate and exemplify each of these points with brief descriptions of material that you will cover in the course. Motor development is an excellent vehicle, as are Piaget's theory and material on language development.

After characterizing development, discuss some causes of development. Consider these possibilities: (a) heredity; (b) biological maturation; (c) psychological change; and (d) environmental forces. Then address the question of whether any one of these causes is more important than any other. In this context, begin a treatment of the concept of interaction as a way to understand development. Useful examples include phenylketonuria, language development, Vygotsky's theory of the zone of proximal development, the concept of critical period, gene interactions—in fact, virtually any developmental topic.

Lecture Suggestion 4: Guest Speaker Idea Invite a panel of individuals that have careers that directly or indirectly relate to life-span developmental psychology. Individuals that you might consider inviting to participate on the panel would include a research developmental psychologist, a child clinical psychologist, a clinical psychologist, a child advocate, a child-care worker, and a lawyer that specializes in child custody, child abuse, or elder issues. The focus of the panel would be to illustrate that there are multiple ways to be involved with developmental issues. Not only would the students learn how they could create a career in developmental psychology, but they could also learn what steps need to be taken to attain those careers. A condensed, yet related, option would be to invite an individual who specializes in developmental psychology and have that person discuss his/her career and career development.

Classroom Activities

Classroom Activity 1: Ice Breaker The purpose of this activity is to break the ice and to introduce various concepts that will be presented throughout the course. During the first class meeting, have the students draw a picture of a memory from childhood. This picture can be of anything related to their own childhood, for example, getting ice cream with Dad at the beach, or hitting baby brother over the head with a stuffed animal. Solicit volunteers to show and describe their pictures and attempt to relate those topics to theories and/or concepts that will be covered during the term. If you have a pad camera it is fun to display drawings from volunteers or have a couple students draw their picture on the board.
Logistics:
- Materials: One piece of paper per student, enough crayons so each student has one.
- Group size: Individual, then full class.
- Approximate time: 5 minutes for individual drawings, then 10 to 15 minutes for full class discussion.

Classroom Activity 2: Developmental Myths Quiz The two primary objectives of this activity are to introduce ideas and concepts that you will address during the course and to illustrate the relationship between research and everyday life. Often students get frustrated in college courses because they fail to see a connection between research and their lives. In order to achieve these objectives, first, present ten developmental myths commonly espoused by parents, teachers, and others, that are presented as **Handout 1** at the end of this chapter. Have the students express their ideas about each belief. You might have the students get into groups of three or four to discuss their answers. Second, as a class lead a discussion of relevant research evidence that contradicts these long-held beliefs. This will foster more discussion and help the students get acquainted with each other and with developmental psychology. Below we have provided sample instructions to the students, quick notes, and relevant resources to aid your discussion. The first four myths were adapted from Segal's (1989) paper.

Logistics:

- Materials: Handout 1 (Development Quiz).
- Group size: Small groups (2-4) to discuss the myths, and then full class for a larger discussion.
- Approximate time: 15 to 20 minutes for small groups, then 30 to 40 minutes for full class discussion.
- Source: Segal, J. (1989). 10 myths about child development. *Parents*, July issue, 81-84, 87.

Development Quiz

Instructions for Students: You already have many beliefs about development. You might have picked up these opinions from parents, friends, relatives, and/or Oprah. These sources may or may not be accurate. Historically, parents relied on these anecdotal sources because they did not have access to developmental research findings. Today, scientific data are more readily available. So, parents now are able to formulate their own educated ideas regarding human development. For each statement on the handout, indicate whether you agree or disagree with the statement and write down your ideas regarding the statement.

1. My baby started walking and talking earlier than other babies. I know he will be a smart adolescent.
   - Infant behavior (timing of walking and language) in general is not predictive of later intelligence. Some infant developmental tests (Bayley) are helpful to assess developmental delays or advancement. If delays are noted, enrichment may be necessary. Basically, infant "intelligence" tests measure different types of behaviors (sensorimotor and social abilities) compared to adult intelligence tests (spatial and verbal). Habituation and dishabituation procedures have been found more predictive of later intelligence (less attention in habituation phase and more attention in dishabituation phase). See chapter 6 for a discussion and predictability of infant intelligence testing.

2. I pick up my baby as soon as she starts to cry, but my mother-in-law thinks I'm going to spoil her.
   - Crying is one way infants communicate their needs. In early months, crying is not an attempt to manipulate caregivers; thus, quick responses will not spoil the infant. Ainsworth's attachment research has found that more sensitive, responsive caregiving is related to more secure attachments, more independence, more exploration of environment, and less crying. See chapter 7 for a discussion of the effects of sensitive parenting on the development of attachment relationships.

3. I want to have only one child, but my wife thinks that only children have problems relating to other children.
   - Papalia and Old's research on only children found that only children are achievement oriented, bright, successful, popular individuals with good personalities. They are less likely to join organizations and have fewer friends. Yet, if they do join a group, the only child is more likely to be the leader of the group. See chapter 9 for a discussion of only children.

4. I think that in order to raise a well disciplined child I will have to use physical discipline.
   - Children disciplined with physical means are more likely to be angry, aggressive, fear the "abuser," model violence, and learn how not to get caught. See chapter 7 or Segal (1987) for a discussion of physical punishment.

5. My son just turned 13 and I'm worried about how our relationship is going to change because adolescence is always a difficult time for parents and children.
   - For the majority of adolescents, this period is not particularly difficult, yet the stereotype of adolescence persists. Approximately 20 percent of adolescents have serious, prolonged conflict with a parent. Moderate conflict is often due to cognitive changes (idealism, logical reasoning), biological changes (puberty), and social changes (autonomy, identity development). Conflict between parents and adolescents can be viewed as positive, as the adolescent transitions to independence and explores his/her own ideas and identities. See chapter 13 for a discussion of parent-child relationships during adolescence.

6. I'm looking for a wife and my grandmother keeps telling me that opposites attract.
   - Individuals that are similar with respect to attitudes, behavior, intelligence, education, and attractiveness are more likely to be attracted to each other. See chapter 15 for a discussion of mate selection.

7. My husband is about to turn 40 and I know he is going to go through a mid-life crisis because all men have a mid-life crisis.
   - Most individuals do not experience a classic mid life crisis. Many individuals in middle adulthood reflect upon their choices and re-evaluate their lives. See chapter 17 for a discussion of mid-life crises.

8. I've just moved out of my parents' house. I wonder if their marriage will suffer now that I am gone.
   - Marital satisfaction tends to increase after children leave home, as the couple can spend more time and energy on their marital relationship. Most parents do not experience the "empty nest syndrome" when their children leave home. See chapter 17 for a discussion of these issues.

9. I know my grandparents don't have sex anymore because old people are not interested in sex.
   - The most common reason for not having sex in later adulthood is the lack of a capable partner. See chapter 18 for a discussion of sexuality in late adulthood.

10. My great aunt has been diagnosed with terminal cancer and she acts as if nothing is wrong. This must be very unusual for a person in her situation.
    - Kubler-Ross' theory of death and dying specifies five stages: denial-isolation, anger, bargaining, depression, and acceptance. See chapter 21 for a discussion of stages of dying.

Classroom Activity 3: Critical Thinking Multiple-Choice Questions and Suggested Answers Discuss the answers to the critical thinking multiple-choice questions (**Handout 2**). The purpose of this activity is to facilitate student understanding of various concepts in chapter 1. For each question on this handout, students are asked to indicate which is the best answer and to explain why the alternate answers are incorrect. You may want to assign Handout 2 as homework or as a small group activity. The suggested answers are presented in **Handout 3**.

For the first two questions for chapter 1, you may want to review the concepts students need to understand in order to answer the questions. You will find that students are often uncertain of the distinction between continuity/discontinuity and stability/change, for example, and are apt to confuse descriptions of each. The third question requires abstract application and a thorough understanding of the characteristics of the life-span perspective.

You may want to discuss the critical thinking exercises on three different occasions: when you assign them, while students are doing them, and after students have completed them. Chances are students will not be familiar with these exercises and will need support from you as they get used to doing them. When you first assign critical thinking exercises, make sure that students understand that they are to identify both the best answer and the answers that are not as good. Also, they must give their reasons for both types of decision. If you wish, emphasize that their reasoning behind the decisions is really the most important part of the exercises. Present the first thinking exercise in class and discuss it with the class. Verify that they know what it means to argue for and against answers. You may want to give tips about how to do that. In particular, stress that you are not interested in opinions or feelings, but that you want logical arguments that apply concepts or evidence to the problem posed in the exercise. You may also duplicate and distribute to students the section on Answering Essay and Critical Thinking Questions found in the front of this Instructor's Manual.

Consider devoting class time to having students work together. Have them form groups of three or four, and encourage them to share their ideas and argue their points of view. The objective is for each group to reach a consensus on the answers. Circulate among the groups to listen to their discussions, and possibly deal with difficulties they are having with the assignment. When students finish the assignment, discuss the answers as an entire class or discuss any potential concerns they may have. Have people present their arguments for and against the alternatives. You should find that over the course of the term this becomes a spontaneous activity among your students. In addition, it may afford you clues about material that students would especially like to discuss.

- These suggestions will not be repeated in subsequent chapters, but they are applicable to each. When appropriate, we will suggest specific points you may want to explore with students before, during, or after they have completed the critical thinking questions.

Logistics:
- Materials: Handout 2 (the critical thinking multiple-choice questions) and Handout 3 (answers).
- Group size: Small groups (2-4) to discuss the questions, then a full class discussion.
- Approximate time: Small groups (15 to 20 minutes), full class discussion of any questions (5 minutes).

Classroom Activity 4: Critical Thinking Essay Questions and Suggestions for Helping Students Answer the Essays Discuss the answers to the critical thinking essay questions. The purpose of **Handout 4** is threefold. First, answering the essay questions further facilitates students' understanding of concepts in chapter 1. Second, this type of essay question affords the students an opportunity to apply the concepts to their own lives, which will facilitate their retention of the material. Third, the essay format also will give students practice expressing themselves in written form. Ideas to help students answer the critical thinking essay questions are provided as **Handout 5**.

Logistics:
- Materials: Handout 4 (essay questions) and Handout 5 (helpful suggestions for the answers).
- Group size: Individual, then full class.
- Approximate time: Individual (60 minutes), full class discussion of any questions (30 minutes).

Personal Applications

Personal Application 1: Who are You? The purpose of this exercise is to get students thinking about, and interested in, human development by focusing on themselves and their experiences. When we think about human development, we often do so in terms of a person's life story, such as those of Ted Kaczynski and Alice Walker presented at the beginning of the chapter. When we read the summary of someone's experiences, it creates an image of who they are, and the road they traveled to get there. Our interest in human behavior is generated by the history each one of us has, and the role it has played in creating the individual we are.

- Instructions for Students: Write your own profile in the style of those presented in the text, and begin your journey into the realm of life-span development with a description of your own life's journey. How would *you* be written up to this point in your life? What is your background, and what have you experienced that would tell the story of who you've become?

- Use in the Classroom: This can also be a classroom activity if students are willing to share. Ask for volunteers to present some events/aspects of their life that they feel have had a significant impact on who they are. As students share their stories, ask for reasons *why* they believe certain aspects of their life have influenced who they are. Also, ask them if they experienced any major events/experiences that they *don't* think impacted the person they've become. To what do they attribute their strengths? Their weaknesses? For additional impact and interest, share your own life story and the influences on your development.

Personal Application 2: What Do You Want to Know? The purpose of this exercise is to get students to focus on what they want to get out of the class, as well as expose them to the variety of topics addressed in the course. One of the unique aspects of taking a course in life-span development is that everyone can relate to it! The required material focuses on aspects of everyone's life, whether they have experienced it themselves, or have a relationship with an older person who has. Certainly there are new concepts, theories, and research findings to learn, but at their core are the fundamental developmental milestones that make up our life's journey, and the results of those experiences.
- Instructions for Students: Make a list of what you want to learn from this course. Do you want practical information for parenting purposes? Do you have aspects of your own life that you're curious about? What behaviors have you observed in people around you, of all ages, that you'd like to understand better?
- Use in the Classroom: Help students understand some of the practical applications of this course. Illustrate how, although it involves a great many theories and new concepts, the information they will learn has real-life implications, and can provide insight on many of the behaviors and issues that they encounter on a daily basis. Specifically acknowledge students who are taking the course simply to fill a degree requirement. Challenge them to find something that interests them with regard to life-span development. Keep careful note of your students' responses. This will guide you in planning your course, enabling you to spend additional time focusing on what your students are particularly motivated to learn about.
- Another option is to have students share their interests in class, at which time you can respond with some introductory "teasers" (a brief anecdote about an area of study, or a particularly amazing research finding) about their particular areas of interest. This will assure them that their interests will be addressed at some point during the course, and whet their appetite for all the material to come

Personal Application 3: Event of a Lifetime This exercise demonstrates the impact of nonnormative life events on an individual's development. During this period of introducing students to the study of life-span development, it is important for them to recognize the numerous influences on an individual's behavior. From this perspective they learn what influences are common to everyone, and how certain people experience different circumstances which contribute to their development as well. Not only is it important to consider the particular experiences in one's life, but how one *responds* to those experiences as well. This is necessary for a more complete understanding of life-span development, and nonnormative events can contribute significantly.
- Instructions for Students: Write about any nonnormative life events you, or someone close to you, have experienced. What happened? How did you (or your friend) react? What visible effect has it had on your behavior since it occurred? Why do you think it has affected your development in this way? Can you imagine what your personality and life might be like had you not had this particular experience? If you are considering someone else as the focus of this answer, ask if they would be willing to share these thoughts with you, promising them anonymity for their responses.
- Use in the Classroom: The best way for students to understand a particular concept is for them to have a very explicit, concrete example to refer to and contemplate. See if you can draw upon personal experience, or that of someone you have known (even family members of a past generation), and present a vivid example of a nonnormative life event and it's resulting effect.

Research Project Ideas

Research Project 1: Answering Questions about Development The goal of this research project is to have students conduct research on a topic they find interesting in developmental psychology (**Handout 6**). On the first day of class, have your students write down one or two questions they would like to have answered by the end of this course. Presumably, they are interested in at least one aspect of development about which they have specific questions they would like to have answered (e.g., Does bilingualism influence cognitive development?). This will involve going to the library and finding at least ten relevant journal articles. Over the course of the semester, have the students investigate the topic and write a brief report that incorporates the following questions:

- What is the question you are investigating?
- Why is this question interesting to you?
- How did you go about determining the answer to your question?
- Describe the information you located to address your question.
- What questions has this new information stimulated?
- Use in the Classroom: Two options exist for incorporating this assignment. First, you can have students present the question they researched and the results of their investigation. If possible, organize these presentations so that students present their questions when you are discussing the chapter that is most relevant to their topic. A second option for incorporating this research project is to ask each student to answer the question they researched as part of their final exam. This will mean that each student will be answering a different question on the final exam.

Research Project 2: Monitoring Contemporary Concerns in the Media Chapter 1 highlights life-span developmental topics, such as health and well-being, parenting and education, sociocultural contexts, and social policy, which are issues that receive frequent media attention. Have students monitor a newspaper, radio news program, or television news program for a week and keep a record of stories that reflect each of these concerns (**Handout 7**). When they are done, they should tally the number of stories that reflect each concern. Then students should write a brief report in which they answer the following questions:

- What was the most frequently expressed concern?
- Were the concerns you encountered in each category focused on one particular kind of story? Or, were there a number of different kinds of news items that reflected a variety of concerns within each category? Explain your answer.
- Did the stories reflect a life-span perspective? Or, did they reflect some other way of viewing the contemporary concerns? Explain your answer.
- Can you find information in *Life-Span Development* that is related to each story and that helps you to understand it better? Explain your answer.
- What information do you wish you had in order to understand the story better?
- Use in the Classroom: Discuss students' answers to these questions. Find out what the dominant concerns are, what kinds of stories express these concerns, and whether the stories are examples of the life-span perspective. Be on the lookout for how well students appear to understand text material in terms of the answers they provide, and use their answers as opportunities to affirm their understanding or to amend it. In order to introduce the importance of rigorous, systematic inquiry for understanding life-span development, contrast media presentations with textbook presentations. Have students compare and contrast topics they have found in the media with similar material in the textbook, and see what they identify as important differences in the respective treatments.

Film and Video List

The following films and videos supplement the content of chapter 1. Contact information for film distributors can be found at the front of this Instructor's Manual under Film and Video Sources.

Child Development (Insight Media, 30 minutes). This is a historical overview of contributions from Locke to modern theorists. It stresses the idea of interaction and deals with research methods of the field.

Childhood: Great Expectations (Ambrose Video, 60 minutes). This seven-part video series explores development from a cross-cultural perspective. This episode introduces such concepts as the nature/nurture debate by exploring three childbirths in different cultures.

Culture, Time, and Place (Insight Media, 30 minutes). This video shows how language, school, and relationships bring about acculturation concerning attitudes, values, and beliefs.

Development and Diversity (Insight Media, 30 minutes). This video explores historical and cultural definitions of childhood and probes the prolongations of infancy and childhood. In addition, there is an emphasis on children in different cultures.

Nature/Nurture (Indiana University, 52 minutes). Acquired and inherited characteristics, results of twin studies, and environmental influences on behavior are illustrated in this video.

Web Site Suggestions

The URLs for general sites, common to all chapters, can be found at the front of this Instructor's manual under Useful Web Sites. At the time of publication, all sites were current and active, however, please be advised that you may occasionally encounter a dead link.

American Family Policy Institute
http://www.familypolicy.com/goalsreport96.html

Children's Action Alliance
http://www.azchildren.org/caa/welcome.asp

Children's Defense Fund
http://www.childrensdefense.org/release000926-info.htm

Chronicle of Higher Education Job Listings
http://chronicle.merit.edu/.ads/.ads-by-group/.faculty/.sscience/.psychology/.links.html

The Future of Children
http://www.futureofchildren.org/

Development Quiz

For each statement on the handout, indicate whether you agree or disagree and why.

- My baby started walking and talking earlier than other babies. I know he will be a smart adolescent.

- I pick up my baby as soon as she starts to cry, but my mother-in-law thinks I'm going to spoil her.

- I want to have only one child, but my wife thinks that only children have problems relating to other children.

- I think that in order to raise a well disciplined child I will have to use physical discipline. ("Spare the rod, and spoil the child.")

- My son just turned 13 and I'm worried about how our relationship is going to change because adolescence is always a difficult time for parents and children.

- I'm looking for a wife and my grandmother keeps telling me that opposites attract.

- My husband is about to turn 40 and I know he is going to go through a mid-life crisis because all men have a mid-life crisis.

- I've just moved out of my parents' house. I wonder if their marriage will suffer now that I am gone.

- I know my grandparents don't have sex anymore because old people are not interested in sex.

- My great aunt has been diagnosed with terminal cancer and she acts as if nothing is wrong. This must be very unusual for a person in her situation.

Critical Thinking Multiple-Choice Questions

1. Chapter 1 begins with sketches of the lives of Ted Kaczynski and Alice Walker. Which of the following ideas about the nature of humans or human development best applies to these portraits? Circle the letter of the best answer and explain why it is the best answer and why each other answer is not as good.

   a. original sin
   b. tabula rasa
   c. innate goodness
   d. storm and stress
   e. nonnormative life events

2. In chapter 1, Santrock describes some contemporary concerns in the study of development, including health and well-being, parenting and education, and sociocultural contexts. Which concept below relates best to these contemporary concerns? Circle the letter of the best answer and explain why it is the best answer and why each other answer is not as good.

   a. cognitive processes
   b. nurture
   c. genetics
   d. discontinuity
   e. change

3. Near the end of chapter 1, Roger Rosenblatt wrote, "One's children's children's children. Look back to us as we look to you; we are related by our imaginations. If we are able to touch, it is because we have imagined each other's existence, our dreams running back and forth along a cable from age to age." Which of the following characteristics of life-span development best relates to this quotation? Circle the letter of the best answer and explain why it is the best answer and why each other answer is not as good.

   a. life long
   b. multidimensional
   c. plastic
   d. contextual
   e. studied by a number of disciplines

Suggested Answers for Critical Thinking Multiple-Choice Questions

1. Chapter 1 begins with sketches of the lives of Ted Kaczynski and Alice Walker. Which of the following ideas about the nature of humans or human development best applies to these portraits? Circle the letter of the best answer and explain why it is the best answer and why each other answer is not as good.

   a.   Original sin is not the best answer. These individuals seem to express opposite basic natures, and they represent different reactions to social interactions. Kaczynski avoided social interaction, whereas Walker overcame and learned from negative social interactions.

   b.   Tabula rasa is not the best answer. If it were, the lives of both people should more clearly and exactly mirror the conditions of their upbringing. Alice Walker, in particular, appears to have developed well beyond what might have been predicted from the circumstances of her childhood, while Ted Kaczynski committed acts of violence despite his higher education.

   c.   Innate goodness is not the best answer. As was the case in "a" above, Kaczynski and Walker seem to have opposite natures and represent different reactions to life events.

   d.   Storm and stress is not the best answer because this theme does not apply to Kaczynski. By all accounts, his adolescence was quite privileged, while Walker's was stressful.

   e.   Nonnormative life events seems to be the best answer, though the match is not direct. Walker experienced a nonnormative life event that probably influenced who she became as an adult. Recall that her brother accidentally shot her in the eye, which left her blind in one eye. Kaczynski traces his difficulties to growing up as a genius in a kid's body and not fitting in as a child. Of the alternatives, only the nonnormative life events concept seems able to explain the diversity of life-span development suggested by the lives of these people.

2. In chapter 1, Santrock describes some contemporary concerns in the study of development, including health and well-being, parenting and education, and sociocultural contexts. Which concept below relates best to these contemporary concerns? Circle the letter for the best answer and explain why it is the best answer and why each other answer is not as good.

   a.   Cognitive processes is not the best answer. If so, the issues Santrock raised would have concerned how changes in thought, intelligence, or language influence the behavior of a child or the quality of a child's adaptation to the environment. But the contemporary concerns—changes in the family, educational reform, and sociocultural issues—are aspects of the child's environment and how they potentially influence child development.

   b.   Nurture is the best answer. As indicated in "a," the focus of the contemporary concerns is children's environments and how they affect children. These are explicitly listed in the text as examples of the nurture side of the nature-nurture controversy.

   c.   Genetics is not the best answer. Genetics refers to one's biological makeup based on heredity. This would entail a focus on heredity and, perhaps, genetic engineering as a means of enhancing child development outcomes. Instead, the focus is on improving children's environments to enhance developmental outcomes.

   d.   Discontinuity is not the best answer. If this were the concern, much would be said about the importance of describing child development as a series of stages or about developing the notion of childhood as a distinct stage from adulthood. This is not the sense of the contemporary concerns at all.

   e.   Change is not the best answer. If it were, the issue would be that patterns of behavior expressed arly in a child's life are not especially predictive of later developmental outcomes. Again, the emphasis is on environmental conditions that promote optimal developmental outcomes.

3. Near the end of chapter 1, Roger Rosenblatt wrote "One's children's children's children. Look back to us as we look to you; we are related by our imaginations. If we are able to touch, it is because we have imagined each other's existence, our dreams running back and forth along a cable from age to age." Which of the following characteristics of life-span development best relates to this quote? Circle the letter of the best answer and explain why it is the best answer and why each other answer is not as good.

   a. Lifelong is not the best answer because it highlights that no age period dominates development. This quote does not focus on age-related phenomena.

   b. Multidimensional is not the best answer. This concept refers to the fact that development consists of cognitive, socioemotional, and biological aspects. This quote makes no reference to domains of development.

   c. Plastic is not the best answer because it refers to the flexible nature of development, which is not applicable to the quote.

   d. Contextual seems to be the best answer. The idea that development is contextual best captures the sense in which each person acts on and reacts to social and historical conditions. This quote reflects the idea that each generation is influenced by the development of previous generations. The development of individuals is embedded in their own family history as well as the historical context.

   e. Studied by a number of disciplines is not the best answer because the quote does not mention the study of development.

Critical Thinking Essay Questions

Your answers to this kind of question demonstrate an ability to comprehend and apply ideas discussed in this chapter.

1. Describe each of the three historical views about the nature of the child (i.e., tabula rasa, original sin, and innate goodness views). Also explain how one's belief in each view affects what life-span developmentalists do and study.

2. Explain the seven basic characteristics of the life-span perspective in your own terms.

3. Explain contextualism by expressing the meaning of normative age-graded influences, normative history-graded influences, and nonnormative life events in your own terms. Provide an example of each concept from your own life and times.

4. Your textbook provides current and comprehensive coverage of four contemporary concerns in life-span development: health and well-being, parenting and education, sociocultural contexts, and social policy. In your own words, explain the nature and importance of each of these four contemporary concerns. Also, for each concern, provide one example from your own life and times that illustrates how it relates to you personally.

5. What do you believe is the most important social policy issue involving human development today? How would you persuade the government to improve citizen's lives related to this particular issue?

6. Explain the meaning of biological, cognitive, and socioemotional processes. Also give an example of each from a source other than chapter 1.

7. Think about your life during the past 24 hours in terms of the life-span perspective. Demonstrate your understanding of periods of development by indicating one example of how you have, or could have, interacted with individuals from each of the following seven developmental periods: infancy, early childhood, middle and late childhood, adolescence, early adulthood, middle adulthood, and late adulthood.

8. Explain the meaning of (a) nature and nurture, (b) continuity and discontinuity, and (c) stability and change. Also, explain why current life-span developmentalists do not adopt extreme positions on the three issues.

9. Imagine a career in life-span development. Given your abilities and interests, consider what you would like to do, with which age group you would like to work, and what factors might or could encourage or discourage you from pursuing this career.

Ideas to Help You Answer Critical Thinking Essay Questions

1. Often it is easiest to describe things through the use of examples. Thus, after you familiarize yourself with the text's description of the three historical views, incorporate your own personal descriptions of each into your answer. Two suggested areas to consider: 1) discipline, and 2) the issue of the potential effects of violent television and movies on children's behavior.

2. Consider examples from your own life for each of the seven characteristics of the life-span perspective. For example, for the characteristic that development is multidimensional you may reflect on the ways in which you've changed physically (growing larger, increased hair growth during puberty), cognitively (changing music preferences from simple children's tunes to an appreciation for adult music with deeper, more substantial meaning), and socioemotionally (your shift in desire to spend time only with same-sex peers to a focus on interacting with the opposite sex).

3. Begin by identifying your own examples of each concept. After you have become comfortable with them through relating them to your own life, incorporate them into an explanation of contextualism.

4. Keep in mind that the *nature* of something refers to what it is—the characteristics which define it. The *importance* of something refers to the impact that it has in the context in which is occurs or functions. As you think and write about each of the four contemporary concerns in life-span development and consider them in terms of your own life, combine your consideration of their nature and importance on the particular *influence* they have on growing and developing human beings.

5. Use this essay as an opportunity to learn about yourself. As you consider your views about social policy, first assess the scope of your awareness of the issues, the viewpoints, who supports them, and the reasoning behind them. When you determine your position, you may gain some valuable insight into your values and what's meaningful to you. This, in turn, might lead you to discover a greater interest and enthusiasm in your exploration of life-span development.

6. To help you gain a comfortable recognition and understanding of the terms biological, cognitive, and socioemotional, think: *physical, mental, personal*. Characteristics of what each is concerned with can be easily associated with each of these more familiar terms. Use the former, however, to begin exploring your text. Not only will you find a multitude of examples of each, you will gain a greater understanding of the field that you will be studying in the upcoming semester.

7. To begin thinking about the many periods of development, familiarize yourself with the characteristics of each stage by re-reading this section of the book. This will enable you to reflect with a new perspective on the individuals who've passed through your life in the past few days.

8. After you identify the nature of the issues of nature and nurture, continuity and discontinuity, and stability and change, think about an *extreme* position for each. Work through the process of disproving such drastic viewpoints with reasoning and examples, and present your explanation as to why such extremes are not supported by life-span developmentalists.

9. In addition to the stated questions, consider these (based on your experience with chapter 1):
   -What issues explored by developmentalists appeal to you and interest you the most?
   -What theories do you find useful and meaningful in understanding aspects of life-span development?
   -What concepts presented motivate you to think about aspects of development at various stages of life?

Answering Questions about Development

The goal of this research project is to conduct research on a topic you find interesting in developmental psychology. On the first day of class, your instructor asked you to write down one or two questions you would like to have answered by the end of this course (e.g., Does bilingualism influence cognitive development?). Over the course of the semester, investigate the topic and write a brief report that incorporates the following questions. This will involve going to the library and finding at least ten relevant journal articles.

Questions:

• What is the question you are investigating?

• Why is this question interesting to you?

• How did you go about determining the answer to your question?

• Describe the information you located to address your question.

• What questions has this new information stimulated?

Monitoring Contemporary Concerns in the Media

Chapter 1 highlights life-span developmental topics, such as health and well-being, parenting and education, sociocultural contexts, and social policy, which are issues that receive frequent media attention. Monitor a newspaper, radio news program, or television news program for a week and keep a record of stories that reflect each of these concerns. Search the paper for news items or listen to news broadcasts, and make a record of stories that reflect these concerns. When you are done, tally the number of stories that reflect each concern. Then write a brief report in which you answer the following questions.

Questions:

- What was the most frequently expressed concern?

- Were the concerns you encountered in each category focused on one particular kind of story? Or, were there a number of different kinds of news items that reflected a variety of concerns within each category? Explain your answer.

- Did the stories reflect a life-span perspective? Or, did they reflect some other way of viewing the contemporary concerns? Explain your answer.

- Can you find information in *Life-Span Development* that is related to each story and that helps you to understand it better? Explain your answer.

- What information do you wish you had in order to understand the story better?

Chapter 2: The Science of Life-Span Development

Total Teaching Package Outline

Lecture Outline	Resource References
The Science of Life-Span Development	PowerPoint Presentation: See www.mhhe.com Cognitive Maps: See Appendix A
Theories of Development	LO1 CA1: Theoretical Perspectives
• Psychoanalytic Theories	LO2
-Freud's Theory	IB: Freudian Stages
-Erikson's Theory	IB: Erikson's Eight Life-Span Stages OHT161: Eight Stages of Development PA1: Erik Erikson and You F/V: Erik Erikson: A Life's Work
-Evaluating the Psychoanalytic Theories	F/V: Theories of Personality F/V: Personality
• Cognitive Theories	LO3 OHT34 & IB: A Model of Cognition
-Piaget's Cognitive Developmental Theory	OHT11 & IB: Piaget's Four Stages
-Vygotsky's Sociocultural Theory	
-The Information-Processing Approach	OHT116 & IB: Model of Information Processing
-Evaluating the Cognitive Theories	LS1: The Concept of Stage in Life-Span Dev. PA2: But What Can You Do with It? F/V: Cognitive Development F/V: Cognitive Development F/V: Learning in Context
• Behavioral and Social Cognitive Theories -Behaviorism	LO4 OHT12: Classical Conditioning Procedure OHT20: Classical Conditioning OHT21: Operant, or Instrumental Conditioning LS2: Applications of Learning Concepts PA3: Do I Look Like a Pigeon?

-Social Cognitive Theory
   -Evaluating the Behavioral and Social
      Cognitive Theories
	LO5
	OHT117 & IB: Bandura's Model
	F/V: Learning
	F/V: Classical and Operant Conditioning

• Ethological Theory -Evaluating Ethological Theory	LO6
• Ecological Theory -Evaluating Ecological Theory	LO7 OHT 16: An Ecological Approach F/V: The Ecology of Development

• An Eclectic Theoretical Orientation	LO8
	IB: Time Line for Major Developmental Theories
	IB: A Comparison of Theories in Life-Span Dev.
	CA2: Critical Analysis of Theories Using
	        Developmental Themes
	CA3: Psychological Theories and Methods
	        and Everyday Information

Research Methods • Observation	LO9 IB: Connection of Research Methods to Theories OHT19: Two Most Common Ways to Obtain Data LS3: Examination of Research Methodology CA4: Design an Experiment CA5: Theoretical Perspectives Influence Observations F/V: Research Methods for the Social Sciences RP1: Parent-Child Interaction
• Interviews and Questionnaires	
• Case Studies	
• Standardized Tests	
• Life-History Records	
• Physiological Research and Research with Animals	F/V: The Family of Chimps
• Correlational Research	LO10 IB: Possible Explanations for Correlational Data OHT14 & IB: Explanations for Correlational Data LS4: Understanding Correlational Research
• Experimental Research	LO11 OHT15 & IB: Principles of Experimental Strategy OHT 17: Experiments OHT 18: Design for an Experiment CA6: Sampling Errors F/V: Decisions Through Data Parts 1 & 2

• Time Span of Research
    -Cross-Sectional Approach
    -Longitudinal Approach
    -Sequential Approach
    -Cohort Effects
	LO12

Research Journals	LO13
	RP2: Journal Article Critique
	WS: American Psychological Association (APA)
	WS: American Psychological Society
	WS: CEC Division Journals
	WS: PsycSCAN: Developmental Psych
	WS: University of Chicago Press Journals
Research Challenges • Ethics • Gender • Ethnicity and Culture	LO14 WS: Office for Human Research Protections LS3: Sexism, Ageism, and Heterosexist Bias in Psychological Research
Review	CA7: Critical Thinking Multiple-Choice CA8: Critical Thinking Essays F/V: Research Methods for the Social Sciences

Chapter Outline

THEORIES OF DEVELOPMENT
- Researchers draw on theories and develop hypotheses as they study development.
- A **theory** is an interrelated, coherent set of ideas that helps to explain and to make predictions.
- **Hypotheses** are specific predictions that can be tested to determine their accuracy.

Psychoanalytic Theories
  Freud's Theory
- Sigmund Freud developed **psychoanalytic theory** in Austria in the late 1800s and early 1900s. His theory was based on the study of mentally ill patients and describes development as primarily unconscious.
- Behavior is merely a surface characteristic and, to truly understand development, symbolic meanings of behavior and the deep inner workings of the mind must be analyzed.
- Freud believed that personality has three structures:
    - The id consists of instincts, which are an individual's reservoir of psychic energy. This unconscious component has no contact with reality.
    - The ego deals with the demands of reality and uses reasoning to make decisions. Neither the id nor the ego has any morality.
    - The superego is the moral component of personality. The ego must balance the demands of the id and the conscience of the superego.
- Freud stated that all individuals proceed through five psychosexual stages and that at each stage individuals experience pleasure in one part of the body more than in others (erogenous zones).
- Adult personality is determined by the way individuals resolve conflicts between these erogenous zones and the demands of reality. Fixation occurs when the individual remains locked in an earlier developmental stage because needs are either under- or overgratified.
- The five psychosexual stages follow:
    - During the oral stage (0 to18 months), the infant's pleasure centers around the mouth.
    - During the anal stage ($1 \frac{1}{2}$ to 3 years), the child's greatest pleasures involves the anus, or the eliminative functions associated with it.

- The phallic stage (3 to 6 years) involves self-manipulation of the genitals in order to provide pleasure and reduce tension.
    - The Oedipus complex is the young child's intense desire to replace the same-sex parent and enjoy the affections of the opposite-sex parent. At 5 or 6 years, children anticipate that the same-sex parent may punish them for these desires. Thus, they identify with and strive to be like the same-sex parent.
- During the latency period (6 years to puberty), children repress all interest in sexuality and develop social and intellectual skills.
- The genital stage (from puberty on) involves sexual reawakening. Sexual pleasure comes from outside the family.

Erikson's Theory
- Erik **Erikson's theory** modified Freud's psychoanalytic theory by replacing sexual motivations with social motivations as the primary motivation for behavior.
- Erikson's theory consists of eight psychosocial stages that extend through the life span. Each stage consists of a unique developmental task that confronts individuals with a crisis that must be faced.
- The eight psychosocial stages follow:
    - Trust vs. Mistrust (1st year): A sense of trust requires a feeling of physical comfort and a minimal amount of fear and apprehension about the future.
    - Initiative vs. Shame and Doubt: (1 to 3 years): After gaining trust in their caregivers, the challenges of a widening social world appear. Guilt may result if the child is irresponsible and is made to feel too anxious.
    - Industry vs. Inferiority (elementary school years): Children's initiative helps them focus their energy on mastering knowledge and intellectual skills.
    - Industry vs. Identity Confusion (adolescence): Individuals are faced with finding out who they are, what they are about, and where they are going in life.
    - Intimacy vs. Isolation (early adulthood): Individuals face the task of forming intimate relationships with others.
    - Generativity vs. Stagnation (middle adulthood): Generativity results from assisting the younger generation in developing and leading useful lives.
    - Integrity vs. Despair (late adulthood): This stage involves reflecting on the past and either piecing together a positive review or concluding that one's life has been wasted.

Evaluating the Psychoanalytic Theories
Contributions of psychoanalytic theory:
- Early experiences and family relationships play an important part in development.
- Personality can be better understood if it is examined developmentally.
- Unconscious aspects of the mind need to be considered.
- Changes take place in adulthood as well as childhood (Erikson).
Criticisms of psychoanalytic theory:
- The main concepts of psychoanalytic theories have been difficult to test scientifically.
- Much of the data used to support psychoanalytic theories come from individual reconstruction of the past, often the distant past, and are of unknown accuracy.
- The sexual underpinnings of development are given too much importance (Freud).
- The unconscious mind is given too much credit for influencing development.
- Psychoanalytic theories present an image of humans that is too negative (Freud).
- Psychoanalytic theories are culture- and gender-biased.

Cognitive Theories
  Piaget's Cognitive Developmental Theory
  - Jean **Piaget's theory** of cognitive development states that children actively construct their understanding of the world and go through four stages of cognitive development. Each of the four stages is age-related and consists of qualitatively different ways of thinking.
  - Two processes, organization and adaptation, underlie this cognitive construction of the world.
    - Organization involves the rearrangement of schemes based on experience.
    - Adaptation involves the changing of cognitive schemes to further understanding through assimilation and accommodation.
      - **Assimilation**: Incorporation of new information into existing knowledge.
      - **Accommodation**: Creation of new knowledge or modification of existing knowledge.
  - Piaget's four major stages of cognitive development follow:
    - Sensorimotor (0 to 2 years): Infants construct an understanding of the world by coordinating sensory experiences with physical, motor actions.
    - Preoperational (2 to 7 years): Children begin to represent the world with words, images, and drawings. Children still lack the ability to perform operations (internalized mental actions).
    - Concrete Operational (7 to 11 years): Children perform operations, and logical reasoning replaces intuitive thought. Reasoning is limited to specific or concrete examples.
    - Formal Operational (11 to 15 through adulthood): Individuals move beyond concrete experiences and think in abstract and more logical terms.

  Vygotsky's Sociocultural Cognitive Theory
  - **Vygotsky's theory** emphasizes development analysis, the role of language, and social relations.
  - The following three tenets form the basis for Vygotsky's theory:
    - To understand cognitive skills, they need to be developmentally analyzed and interpreted.
    - Cognitive skills are mediated by words, language, and forms of discourse, which serve as psychological tools for facilitating and transforming mental activity.
    - Cognitive skills originate in social relations and are embedded in a sociocultural backdrop.

  The Information-Processing Approach
  - The **information-processing approach** emphasizes that individuals manipulate information, monitor it, and strategize about it. This approach describes the development of thinking and memory as a continuous process.
  - A computer analogy is used to explain the relation between cognition and the brain. The physical brain is described as the computer's hardware, cognition as its software.

  Evaluating the Cognitive Theories
  Contributions of cognitive theories:
  - The cognitive theories present a positive view of development, emphasizing individuals' conscious thinking.
  - The cognitive theories (Piaget's and Vygotsky's) emphasize the individual's active construction of understanding.
  - Piaget's and Vygotsky's theories underscore the importance of examining developmental changes in children's thinking.
  - The information-processing approach offers detailed descriptions of cognitive processes.

Criticisms of cognitive theories:
- There is skepticism about the pureness of Piaget's stages.
- The cognitive theories do not attend to individual variations in cognitive development.
- The information-processing approach does not provide an adequate description of developmental changes in cognition.
- Psychoanalytic theorists argue that the cognitive theories do not give enough credit to unconscious thought.

Behavioral and Social Cognitive Theories

Behaviorism
- Behaviorists propose that scientists should only study observable behaviors.
- Ivan Pavlov's classical conditioning occurs when a neutral stimulus acquires the ability to produce a response originally produced by another stimulus.
- John Watson applied classical conditioning to a boy named Little Albert.
- Skinner's operant conditioning involves changing the probability of the behavior's occurrence. Rewards increase the likelihood of reoccurrence. Punishment reduces the likelihood of the behavior.

Social Cognitive Theory
- **Social cognitive theory** emphasizes the reciprocal relationship between behavior, environment, and cognition as the key factors in development. Imitation and modeling are the main concepts in this theory.
- Albert Bandura and Walter Mischel are the leading proponents of this theory.

Evaluating the Behavioral and Social Cognitive Theories
Contributions of behavioral and social cognitive theories:
- An emphasis on the importance of scientific research.
- Focus on the environmental determinants of behavior.
- Underscoring the importance of observational learning (Bandura).
- An emphasis on person and cognitive factors (social cognitive theory).

Criticisms of behavioral and social cognitive theories:
- Too little emphasis on cognition (Pavlov, Skinner).
- Too much emphasis on environmental determinants.
- Inadequate attention to developmental changes.
- Too mechanical and inadequate consideration of the spontaneity and creativity of humans.

Ethological Theory
- **Ethology** stresses that behavior is strongly influenced by biology, is tied to evolution, and is characterized by critical or sensitive periods.
- By studying greylag geese, Konrad Lorenz observed the process of imprinting (innate learning within a limited critical period of time that involves attachment to the first moving object seen).
- A critical period is a fixed time period very early in development during which certain behaviors optimally emerge.
- Attachment theory focuses on mother-infant interactions from an ethological perspective.

Evaluating Ethological Theory
Contributions of ethological theory:
- Increased focus on the biological and evolutionary basis for development.
- Use of careful observations in naturalistic settings.
- Emphasis on sensitive period of development.

Criticisms of ethological theory:
- The critical and sensitive period concepts may be too rigid.
- Too strong an emphasis on biological foundations.
- Inadequate attention to cognition.
- The theory has been better at generating research with animals than with humans.

Ecological Theory
- **Ecological theory** is Urie Bronfenbrenner's view of development. It consists of five interacting environmental systems ranging from direct interactions with social agents to cultural influences.
- Bronfenbrenner's five interacting systems follow:
  - The microsystem is the setting in which the individual lives, including direct interactions with the person's family, peers, school, and neighborhood.
  - The mesosystem involves relations between microsystems or connections between contexts. Relations of family experiences to school experiences, school experiences to church experiences, and family experiences to peer experiences would be included in this system.
  - The exosystem is involved when experiences in another social setting—in which the individual does not have an active role—influence what the individual experiences in an immediate context.
  - The chronosystem involves the patterning of environmental events and transitions over the life course, as well as sociohistorical circumstances.

Evaluating Ecological Theory
Contributions of ecological theory:
- A systematic examination of macro and micro dimensions of environmental systems.
- Attention to connections between environmental settings (mesosystem).
- Consideration of sociohistorical influences on development (chronosystem).
Criticisms of ecological theory:
- Even with added discussion of biological influences in recent years, there is still too little attention to biological foundations of development.
- Inadequate attention to cognitive processes.

An Eclectic Theoretical Orientation
- An **eclectic theoretical orientation** does not follow any one theoretical approach, but rather selects and uses from each theory whatever is considered the best in it.

RESEARCH METHODS
Observation
- Scientific observation is highly systematic: it requires knowing what to look for, conducting observations in an unbiased manner, accurately recording and categorizing what you see, and communicating your observations.
- Observations occur in either laboratories or naturalistic settings.
  - A **laboratory** is a controlled setting from which many of the complex factors of the real world have been removed.
  - In **naturalistic observations**, behavior is observed outside of a laboratory in the real world.

Interviews and Questionnaires
- One way to gather information quickly is through interviews or by using **questionnaires** (surveys) to find out about experiences, beliefs, and feelings.

- Good interviews and surveys involve concrete, specific, and unambiguous questions and a means for checking the authenticity of the responses.
  - One limitation of interviews and questionnaires is that people often give socially described answers rather than honest answers.

Case Studies
- A **case study** is an in-depth look at an individual to examine unique aspects of a person's life that cannot be duplicated.
- Generalizability can be a problem, as the subject has a unique genetic makeup and experiences.

Standardized Tests
- **Standardized tests** are commercially prepared tests that assess performance in different domains, where test scores can be compared across individuals.

Life-History Records
- **Life-history records** are records of information about a lifetime chronology of events and activities. They often involve a combination of data records on education, work, and family.

Physiological Research and Research with Animals
- Measurement of the biological basis of behavior and technological advances have produced remarkable insights about development.
- Animal studies permit researchers to control their subjects' genetic background, diet, and experiences; thus "controlling for noise" that arises in human research.

Correlational Research
- The goal of **correlational research** is to describe the strength of the relation between two or more events or characteristics. It is useful because the stronger the two events are correlated, the more effectively we can predict one from the other.
- Correlation does not equal causation.

Experimental Research
- **Experimental research** allows researchers to determine the causes of behavior by carefully regulated procedures in which one or more of the factors believed to influence the behavior being studied are manipulated and all other factors are held constant. If the behavior changes when a factor is manipulated, we say the manipulated factor causes the behavior to change.
- "Cause" is the manipulated factor being studied. "Effect" is the behavior that changes due to the manipulation.
  - The **independent variable** is the manipulated, influential, experimental factor.
  - The **dependent variable** is the factor that is measured in an experiment. It can change as the independent variable is manipulated.
  - An experimental group is a group whose experience is manipulated.
  - A control group is a group that is treated in every way like the experimental group except for the manipulated factor.
  - **Random assignment** involves assigning participants to experimental and control groups by chance in order to reduce the likelihood that the experimenter's result will be due to any preexisting differences between the groups.

Time Span of Research
Developmentalists study the relation of age to other variables using three research strategies:

Cross-Sectional Approach
- Individuals of different ages are compared at one time in the **cross-sectional approach**.
  - This time-efficient approach does not require time for the individuals to age.
  - This approach provides no information about how individuals change or about the stability of their characteristics.

Longitudinal Approach
- The same individuals are studied over a period of time in the **longitudinal approach.**
  - This approach provides information regarding stability and change in development and the importance of early experience for later development.
  - This approach is expensive and time-consuming.
  - There is potential for subjects to drop out due to sickness, loss of interest, or moving away.
  - The subjects that remain in the study could bias the results, as they may be dissimilar from the ones that dropped out.

Sequential Approach
- The **sequential approach** is a combination of the cross-sectional and longitudinal approaches.
  - Individuals of different ages (cross-sectional) are tested over a period of time (longitudinal).
  - Oftentimes, a new group of subjects are added throughout the study for assessment of changes that may have occurred in the original group (dropping out, retesting differences).
  - This approach is complex, expensive, and time-consuming, yet it is an important strategy because cohort effects can be assessed.

Cohort Effects
- **Cohort effects** are important because they can affect the dependent measures in a study ostensibly concerned about age.
- Cross-sectional studies can show how different cohorts respond but they can confuse age changes and cohort effects.
- Longitudinal studies are effective in studying age changes but only within one cohort.
- With sequential studies, both age changes in one cohort can be examined and compared to age changes in another cohort.

RESEARCH JOURNALS
- A journal publishes scholarly and academic information. Most journal articles are reports of original research.
- Most research journal articles follow this format:
  - Abstract: brief summary of article.
  - Introduction: introduces the problem or issue that is being studied and provides a concise review of relevant research, theoretical ties, and the hypotheses.
  - Methods: clear description of the subjects evaluated in the study, the measures used, and the procedures.
  - Results: reports the analysis of the data collected.
  - Discussion: describes the author's conclusions, inferences, and interpretation of what was found relative to the hypotheses. Limitations of the study and future are discussed.
  - References: bibliographic information for each source cited in the article.

RESEARCH CHALLENGES

Ethics

- Researchers recognize ethical concerns that must be met when conducting research.
- Ethical guidelines proposed by the American Psychological Association (APA) follow:
  - Researchers must protect participants from mental and physical harm.
  - All participants must give their informed consent (if under 7 years, parents provide consent). Informed consent involves understanding what participation entails and potential risks.
  - Participants can withdraw at any time during the study.

Gender

- Historically, research has often been biased against females. Every effort should be made to make research equitable for both males and females.

Ethnicity and Culture

- Historically, ethnic minority individuals have been ignored in research or viewed as variations from the norm. Researchers need to include more ethnic minority individuals in developmental research.
- Ethnic gloss is using an ethnic label, such as African American, in a superficial way that makes an ethnic group look more homogeneous than it really is.

Learning Objectives

1. Define and distinguish between theory, hypotheses, and the scientific method.
2. Compare and contrast Freud's psychoanalytic theory with Erikson's psychoanalytic theory.
3. Describe Piaget's theory of cognitive development and explain how it differs from Vygotsky's sociocultural cognitive theory and the information-processing approach.
4. Understand the basic principles underlying the behavioral theories.
5. Understand how social cognitive theory has been modified in recent years.
6. Describe the basic concepts from ethological theories.
7. Consider how Bronfenbrenner's ecological theory is similar to and different from social cognitive theory.
8. Describe what is meant by an eclectic theoretical orientation.
9. Describe the different research measures used by developmental psychologists.
10. Compare and contrast the correlational and experimental strategies for collecting information scientifically.
11. Define independent variable, dependent variable, and random assignment, and explain why causal conclusions cannot be made from correlational studies.
12. Describe cross-sectional, longitudinal, and sequential approaches to research, then define cohort effects and their role in each type of study.
13. Grasp the basics of understanding professional journal articles.
14. Understand the standard ethics of developmental research.

Key Terms

accommodation

assimilation

case study

cohort effects

correlational research

cross-sectional approach

dependent variable

eclectic theoretical orientation

ecological theory

ethology

experimental research

Erikson's theory

hypotheses

independent variable

information-processing approach

laboratory

life-history records

longitudinal approach

naturalistic observation

Piaget's theory

psychoanalytic theory

questionnaire

random assignment

sequential approach

social cognitive theory

standardized tests

theory

Vygotsky's theory

Key People

Albert Bandura

Urie Bronfenbrenner

Erik Erikson

Sigmund Freud

Karen Horney

Konrad Lorenz

Walter Mischel

Ivan Pavlov

Jean Piaget

Robert Siegler

B. F. Skinner

Lev Vygotsky

Lecture Suggestions

Lecture Suggestion 1: The Concept of Stage in Life-Span Developmental Psychology The concept of stage has long been useful in life-span developmental psychology. It appears in the earliest developmental theories and continues to be used in modern theories. However, the concept is frequently misunderstood and misused, and also is often the subject of controversy and debate. For example, Piaget's theory has been criticized on the grounds that cognitive development at all levels proceeds more continuously than his theory suggests. Give a lecture that begins with an overview of the historical uses of the concept of stage. A starting point might be Hall's idea that the stages of development represent various stages of evolution. This can be followed by a brief description of the stages identified by Gesell. These treatments will establish clearly the strongest meanings of the concept and probably also provide clear criticisms of the concept. Next, distinguish various uses of the concept. These might include (a) description, or a handy way to summarize developmental events typical of given points in the life span; (b) metaphor, which chiefly involves applying analogies (which may be misleading) to periods of life ("adolescence is the spring of life"); and (c) genuine theoretical statements, which indicate that there are definite periods of development characterized by the emergence of qualitatively different types of thinking or behaving.

Flavell (1971) states that four criteria are essential to the concept of a developmental stage. Briefly, they are (a) qualitative change, (b) movement from one stage to the next involves simultaneous changes in multiple aspects of the child's behavior, (c) the transition between stages is rapid once it begins to occur, and (d) the changes (e.g., behavioral and physical changes) that indicate the next stage form a coherent pattern. Finally, give examples of contemporary uses of the stage concept (e.g., Kohlberg's stages of moral reasoning). You may want to draw on various theories of social cognition that extensively use the concept. Other possibilities include stages of motor development, emotional development, or newer theories of cognitive development. If time permits, you may wish to examine the extent to which a particular theory meets or violates Flavell's criteria or exemplifies one of the three ways in which the stage concept is used.

- Sources: Flavell, J. H. (1971). Stage-related properties of cognitive development. *Cognitive Psychology, 2,* 241-453. Ross, D. (1972). *Stanley Hall: The psychologist as prophet.* Chicago: University of Chicago Press. Thelen, E., & Adolph, K. E. (1992). Arnold L. Gesell: The paradox of nature and nurture. *Developmental Psychology, 28,* 368-380.

Lecture Suggestion 2: Applications of Learning Concepts Although classical learning theories have not figured large in developmental accounts of age-related behavioral change, they have contributed greatly to techniques for managing and teaching children and to the scientific study of children's behavior. The concepts of classical and operant conditioning continue to be valuable to teachers and parents, and are enjoying a renaissance in educational practice throughout the country.

Lecture on the fundamental concepts of classical and operant conditioning. Spice your treatment liberally with sample applications of the concepts to child management or teaching. Point out how various features of behavioral control are operating even as you speak (the students are sitting in chairs, oriented to the front of the room, writing down what you have presented on overheads—all examples of stimulus control). Students often erroneously define negative reinforcement as punishment. Negative reinforcement occurs when an unpleasant event is removed following a desired behavior, thereby increasing the probability of the behavior occurring again. Differentiate these terms. All reinforcements (positive and negative) increase the likelihood of the behavior reoccurring. All punishments (positive and negative) decrease the likelihood of the behavior reoccurring. Positive refers to the addition of something (giving candy or slapping). Negative refers to the removal of something (removing the child's toy or the uncomfortable shoes). Note that positive and negative are not referred to in the traditional sense. This lecture is most effective if you use multiple examples and if you encourage students to create their own examples.

Lecture Suggestion 3: Examination of Research Methodology These controversial statistics come from a 270-page book, *The Day America Told the Truth—What People Really Believe About Everything That Really Matters (1991),* written by James Patterson, chairman of the J. Walter Thompson, and Peter Kim, director of Research Services and Consumer Behavior for the national advertising firm.

- 13 percent of Americans believe in all 10 of the Biblical Commandments
- 90 percent lie regularly
- 30 percent of married Americans have had an affair
- 20 percent have lost their virginity by age 13
- 14 percent carry a handgun or have one in their car
- 20 percent of women have been date raped
- 7 percent would kill a stranger for $10 million

The data was gathered using what the authors call the "cathartic method" of polling. At 50 regionally representative locations across the country, 2,000 people each answered 1,800 questions. The respondents were assured anonymity and completed their questionnaires in privacy. These findings were augmented by another survey of 3,700 Americans who filled out shorter forms. The book concluded that, "Americans are making up their own rules and laws." There is absolutely no moral consensus in the country—as there was in the 1950s and 1960s. Religion plays almost no role in shaping most lives. While the statistics are approximately 10 years old, interesting discussion topics could be conducted regarding this lecture idea.

- Consider asking students to anonymously respond to these statements one class period prior to discussing them. Compute the percentages and compare your class statistics to the national ones presented here.

- Discuss possible reasons for similarities and differences that arise.
- What other statements would the students like to know about? Have dyads generate statements to assess cohort differences.
- Probe the students to consider possible methodological issues. After briefly describing the polling methods, ask students for their critical analysis of the methods used. What information is not provided (age of respondents, SES, ethnicity)? Would the statistics differ for various groups? If so, how?
  - Potential methodological problems: questionnaire length (1,800), format (true-false, Likert).
  - Why is this method called the "catharsis method"? Feels good to reveal their true thoughts (Freud).
- Source: Patterson, J., & Kim, P. (1991). *The Day America Told the Truth— What People Really Believe About Everything That Really Matters*. New York, NY: Prentice-Hall.

Lecture Suggestion 4: Understanding Correlational Research Give a lecture on correlational research as students often misunderstand the important concepts. It is beneficial to provide numerous examples.

- Correlation does not equate to causation. For example, exercise is associated with less severe depression. However, it would be a mistake to conclude that exercise causes less severe depression (severely depressed people may not have the energy to exercise). It could be that some third variable affects the other two variables (interacting with others during exercise may affect depression, not exercise per se).
- Define correlation coefficient (a statistic that provides numerical description of the extent of the relatedness of two variables and the direction of the relationship).
- Values of this coefficient may range from −1.0 to +1.0. Thus, each correlation coefficient indicates the direction of the relationship and the strength of the relationship.
- Direction of the relationship:
  - A positive relationship is indicated by a correlation value that falls between 0 and 1.0.
    - A positive relationship means that as one variable increases, the other variable increases (the more a student studies, the higher his grades).
  - A negative relationship is indicated by a correlation that is between 0 and −1.0.
    - A negative relationship means that as one variable decreases, the other variable decreases (the more television a student watches, the lower his grades).
- Strength of the relationship:
  - Zero indicates no relationship between the two variables; they do not vary together.
  - The closer the number is to 0, regardless of the direction of the relationship (positive or negative), the weaker the relationship between the two variables.
  - The closer the number is to 1.0, regardless of the direction of the relationship (positive or negative), the stronger the relationship between the two variables.

Lecture Suggestion 5: Sexism, Ageism, and Heterosexist Bias in Psychological Research While progress has been made regarding sexism in psychological research, little progress has been made regarding ageism and heterosexist bias. An interesting question to raise and discuss is whether sexism, ageism, and heterosexism influence psychological research. First, define sexism, ageism, and heterosexism. Second, discuss how one's beliefs, whether conscious or unconscious, can influence the scientific method (e.g., the research questions that are asked, the interpretation of data, and the subject populations). In addition, the language that is used to describe phenomena often reflects sexism, ageism, and heterosexist bias. Schaie's (1993) article focuses on potential problems in the use of ageist language, and provides recommendations for reducing ageism in psychological research and practice. Herek et al.'s (1991) discussion of heterosexist bias in scientific research raises several important points that mirror the questions that could be asked for ageism and sexism. The following questions were pulled from that discussion:

- Formulating the Research Question: Does the research question ignore or deny the existence of homosexual individuals? Does the research question devalue or stigmatize homosexual individuals? Does the research question reflect cultural stereotypes of homosexuals?
- Sampling: Is the sample representative? Is the sample appropriate for the research question?
- Research Design and Procedures: Is sexual orientation the variable of interest? Is sexual orientation assessed appropriately? Are comparison groups appropriate to the research design? Do questionnaire items or interview protocols assume heterosexuality? Do the researchers' personal attitudes influence participants' responses? Does the experimental manipulation presume that participants are heterosexual?
- Protection of Participants: Is information obtained about sexual orientation and behavior truly confidential? Does the research procedure reinforce prejudice or stereotypes among heterosexual respondents? Does the recruitment procedure intrude inappropriately on potential participants' privacy?
- Interpreting and Reporting Results: Is an observed difference assumed to reflect a problem or pathology of homosexual participants? Does the language reflect heterosexist bias? Has the researcher attempted to anticipate distortions or misinterpretations of findings by the lay public and in the popular media?
- Sources: Herek, G.M., Kimmel, D.C., Amaro, H., & Melton, G.B. (1991). Avoiding heterosexist bias in psychological research. *American Psychologist, 46*, 957-963. Schaie, K. W. (1993). Ageist language in psychological research. *American Psychologist, 48*, 49-51.

Classroom Activities

Classroom Activity 1: Theoretical Perspectives This project introduces various theoretical perspectives, and also allows students to realize how much of the material they already know. What students offer will depend on how many psychology courses they have had prior to this course and their retention after reading the chapter. As an instructor, you will learn which theoretical perspectives need the most class coverage, what misconceptions the students have, and what strengths they have coming into the course. On the blackboard, list each of the following perspectives (you may use fewer, or modify labels, to fit how you cover the course material), leaving room below each to add comments. Then one by one have students contribute terms, ideas, and "great psychologists" associated with each. By the end of the exercise, they will be able to see some similarities and dissimilarities for each group.

Here is an example of this exercise from one class:
- PSYCHOANALYTIC: Freud, Adler, id, ego, superego, sex, early childhood, psychosexual stages, "mom's fault," Erikson, unconscious, defense mechanisms, dreams, Jung, Oedipal complex, birth order, sibling rivalry, inferiority, libido.
- BEHAVIORAL/SOCIAL LEARNING: Skinner, Pavlov, reinforcement, punishment, imitation, Bandura, classical conditioning, operant conditioning, modeling, delay of gratification, Watson, token economy, systematic desensitization, behavioral modification, mazes, mechanistic.
- BIOLOGICAL/ETHOLOGICAL: Lorenz, split-brain, neurotransmitter, dopamine, genetics, heredity vs. environment, central nervous system, instinct, critical periods, pregnancy, genes, genetic counseling, DNA, autonomic nervous system, stress.
- COGNITIVE: Piaget, Ellis, memory, information-processing, Binet, Terman, intelligence tests, accommodation, assimilation, language, development, moral development, Kohlberg.
- ECOLOGICAL: environment, culture, ethnicity, Bronfenbrenner.

Logistics:
- Group size: Full class discussion.
- Approximate time: 45 minutes for full class discussion.
- Source: Irwin, D. B., & Simons, J. A. (1984). *Theoretical perspectives class activity*. Ankeny, IA: Des Moines Area Community College.

Classroom Activity 2: Critical Analysis of Theories Using Developmental Themes We are never quite sure that students have grasped the basic components of developmental theories or that they know how the theories are the same and how they differ. To check their understanding and their ability to discriminate, list several theories and theorists down one side of a piece of paper and the distinguishing characteristics of the theories across the top of the paper. Characteristics that could be used to discriminate between the theories include whether development is deterministic (yes or no), biology versus environment, stability versus change, whether there are critical periods for different aspects of development (yes or no), whether culture plays a role in development (cultural universal or cultural relativism), and the role of the participant in development (active or passive). The students' task is to indicate where each theorist or theory stands on each of the characteristics and to provide an explanation for their answer. Emphasize that their reasoning behind their decisions is the primary focus. Students find the activity difficult; however, answers to essay questions about the theories show that they seem to learn a lot from the exercise.

Logistics:
- Group size: Small groups (2 -4), and then full class discussion.
- Approximate time: 30 minutes for small groups, then 30 minutes for full class discussion.

Classroom Activity 3: Psychological Theories and Methods and Everyday Information The purpose of this activity is for students to see the relationship between psychological theories and methods and everyday reading material and information. One week before you want to use this in class, have students find two or three articles on human development from parenting or other popular magazines. They should bring the magazine issue or copies of the specific articles to class. Have the students get into small groups to discuss their answers to the following questions: Who is the audience for the articles (e.g., parents, teachers, adolescents)? What is the topic of the article? What are some examples of information provided? Does the article emphasize heredity (nature) or environment (nurture)? What theoretical perspective does the author seem to use (e.g., psychoanalytic, behavioral, humanistic, biological, cognitive, ecological)? Does the article rely on scientific findings, expert opinion, or case example? Do the conclusions of the articles seem valid?

For the following questions, consider all of the magazine articles that your group has collected. Which theoretical perspectives seem to be most popular with these magazines? What topics are getting the most coverage in the magazines? Are most articles well-done and useful?

Logistics:
- Materials: Students must gather popular magazine articles.
- Group size: Individual, small group, and full class discussion.
- Approximate time: Individual (1 hour), small group (15 minutes), and full class discussion (30 minutes).
- Source: Simons, J. A. (1990). *Evaluating psychological value of magazine articles*. Central Iowa Psychological Services.

Classroom Activity 4: Design an Experiment The purpose of this activity is to take students step by step through the basic processes of designing a research experiment. Given the numerous new concepts (such as independent and dependent variables, random selection, etc.), the most effective way for students to understand what they are and how they are used is to see them implemented.

Choose a very basic study, such as, "Does watching violent television increase aggressive behavior in children?" Begin by identifying the independent variables (What will your "violent" show be? Might you have a passive, non-violent show too? Will there be a control group who watches nothing?) and dependent variables (How are you going to measure "aggression"? Determining both this and what constitutes a "violent" program should prompt an explanation of operationalizing.) Determine the age of subjects you wish to study (have students determine this and explain *why* they think that it is a valid/useful age group to focus on). Go through the process of how and where you might obtain subjects, how you will assign them to the various groups. Develop a procedure for carrying out the experiment

—where they will watch the show, what they will do following the viewing so that you may observe behavior to assess aggressiveness (playground, room with toys, problem solving activity). Consider whether the study needs to be blind or double blind; the importance and logistics of both. Then create some results and discuss possible interpretations, making sure to include consideration of any confounds or methodological limitations. To go even further, demonstrate how a write-up of this study would conform to the standard professional journal format.

Logistics:
- Group size: Small groups (2 -4), and then full class discussion.
- Approximate time: 30 minutes for small groups, then 15 minutes for full class discussion.

Classroom Activity 5: Theoretical Perspectives Influence Observations Divide the class into small discussion groups to consider the following questions: How does one's theoretical view of development affect the kinds of behaviors one notices? What behaviors would be observed by Freud, Piaget, an information-processing theorist, Skinner, Bandura, an ethological theorist, and Bronfenbrenner when watching two children interact on a playground? Option 1: Have each group discuss each theory. Option 2: Have each group address one theory. Ask each group to nominate someone to write down the results of the discussion. The summary of each group's comments can be the basis for a general class discussion regarding the similarities and differences among the major theories of life-span development.

Logistics:
- Group size: Small groups (2-4), and then full class for a larger discussion.
- Approximate time:
  - Option 1: 30 minutes for small groups, then 30 to 40 minutes for full class discussion.
  - Option 2: 5 minutes for small groups, then 30 to 40 minutes for full class discussion.
- Source: King, M. B., & Clark, D. E. (1990). *Instructor's manual to accompany children*. Dubuque, IA: Brown.

Classroom Activity 6: Sampling Errors The goal of this activity is for students to better understand sample populations and the potential confounds that result from sampling error. First, define sampling error or sampling bias. Sampling error is caused by having a nonrepresentative sample, or generalizing the probable behavior of a population from a nonrepresentative sample. Second, present the situations in **Handout 1** to your students and ask them to uncover any possible sampling biases and potential confounds.

Logistics:
- Materials: Handout 1 (Sampling Bias Activity).
- Group size: Full class discussion.
- Approximate time: 15 minutes for full class discussion.
- Source: Simons, J. A., Irwin, D. B., & Drinnin, B. A. (1987). *Instructor's manual to accompany psychology, the search for understanding*. St. Paul, MN: West.

Classroom Activity 7: Critical Thinking Multiple-Choice Questions and Suggested Answers Discuss the answers to the critical thinking multiple-choice questions (**Handout 2**). The purpose of this activity is to facilitate student understanding of various concepts in chapter 2. For each question on this handout, students are asked to indicate which is the best answer and to explain why the alternate answers are incorrect. You may want to assign Handout 2 as homework or as a small group activity. The answers are presented in **Handout 3**.

Discuss the critical thinking questions. For question 1, find out if students know who the "observers" are in the quote. They probably will not know, in which case you will want to explain that they were people who introspected about their mental processes in early perception and cognition experiments.

For question 2, students will appreciate a careful review of the differences between correlational and experimental research; they are apt to see Chi's research as experimental if left to their own devices. They will have little difficulty with the other concepts, but note that Chi's measures do not fit neatly with any of those offered, which may entail some discussion of how to interpret Santrock's catalogue of measures.

For question 3, discuss with your class the notion that assumptions are not always directly expressed, but may be very important motivations in researchers' work. That is, assumptions suggest how to solve problems and lead to choices of methods, techniques, or strategies to solve them. Remember that an inference is a conclusion that is drawn because it is a logical extension of a statement or a fact.
Logistics:
- Materials: Handout 2 (the critical thinking multiple-choice questions) and Handout 3 (answers)
- Group size: Small groups to discuss the questions, then a full class discussion.
- Approximate time: Small groups (15 to 20 minutes), full class discussion of any questions (15 minutes).

Classroom Activity 8: Critical Thinking Essay Questions and Suggestions for Helping Students Answer the Essays Discuss the answers to the critical thinking essay questions (**Handout 4**). The purpose of this activity is threefold. First, answering these questions facilitates students' understanding of concepts in chapter 2. Second, this type of essay question affords the students an opportunity to apply the concepts to their own lives, which will facilitate their retention of the material. Third, the essay format also will give students practice expressing themselves in written form. Ideas to help students answer the critical thinking essay questions are provided as **Handout 5**.
Logistics:
- Materials: Handout 4 (essay questions) and Handout 5 (helpful suggestions for the answers).
- Group size: Individual, then full class.
- Approximate time: Individual (60 minutes), full class discussion of any questions (30 minutes).

Personal Applications

Personal Application 1: Erik Erikson and You The purpose of this exercise is for students to consider their own lives and the lives of their friends and family in terms of Erikson's psychosocial stages of development. Erikson viewed behavior as the manifestation of an individual's progressive responses to social "dilemmas" that present themselves throughout the life span. The direction that people take in dealing with the dilemma at each stage provides the perspective from which they will approach subsequent stages. Examining one's current behavior can indicate which stage of Erikson's theory an individual is experiencing, as well as provide some insight into how he/she may have responded to previous stages.
- Instructions for Students: What stage of Erikson's psychosocial theory are you currently in? Your friends? Your parents? Provide evidence to support your reasoning.
- Use in the Classroom: Demonstrate how to think through behavior with regards to Erikson's theory by using yourself as an example. Discuss the current stage of your life, behaviors that reflect your response to the dilemma, as well as memories from past stages and relevant behavioral manifestation.

Personal Application 2: But What Can You *Do* with It? The purpose of this exercise is for students to critically think about the possible applications of several theories. The information-processing approach is very practical in nature, and the text talks about how psychologists actually use it. In their efforts to understand and explain behavior, theories should serve a greater purpose—that of providing a tool that is useful and meaningful for real-life application to human behavior.
- Instructions for students: Familiarize yourself with the theories of Freud, Erikson, and Piaget. Consider practical applications for each.
- Use in the Classroom: To help students see the potential usefulness of each of the theories, begin by having them identify particular behaviors to approach from a practical standpoint. Once they have thought about the area of application, prompt them to identify ways in which these behaviors may be approached, enhanced, used, etc. Lead them through the process of using the tenets and assumptions of the theories to answer questions about, and provide solutions to, issues in human development.

Personal Application 3: Do I Look Like a Pigeon? The purpose of this exercise is to get students to understand the process of operant conditioning by employing it themselves. The processes identified by learning theorists are constantly occurring in our everyday lives. We don't realize how much of our behavior is followed by some kind of reinforcement. The impact of many of these consequences usually affects us only at a subconscious level, but if we are tuned in to their occurrence, the results are very clear. Bandura acknowledged that we are cognitive beings, and that not only do we have the ability to self-reward and self-punish, but we do so regularly.

- Instructions for Students: Design an operant conditioning experiment to shape someone's behavior (yours, your roommate's, your boyfriend's). Identify either a bad habit that you'd like to break or a good new one that you'd like to establish. Write up what you did, identifying your desired or undesired behavior, your reinforcement, the schedule of reinforcement implemented, and the results. Plan on two to three weeks to carry this out.

- Use in the Classroom: Have students brainstorm the behavior(s) they'd like to tackle prior to starting the experiment. Provide your own example of something you'd like to change about yourself or your spouse, and how you might go about accomplishing it. Once they've established their plan of action, tell them you will compare results of all experiments in class at the end of the time period allotted.

Research Project Ideas

Research Project 1: Parent-Child Interaction In this project, your students will observe a parent-child interaction and interpret it according to psychoanalytic, behavioral, and cognitive theoretical approaches. They should go to a local supermarket and watch a mother or father shop with a 2- to 4-year-old child. They should describe the interactions that they observe, including demands on the part of the child, verbal exchanges between parent and child, and ways in which the parent responds to the demands of the child. Then have them answer the questions on **Handout 6**.

- On what would a psychoanalytic theorist focus in this example? How would the sequence of observed events be explained?
- How would a behavioral psychologist analyze the situation? What reinforcers or punishers characterized the interaction? Did specific things occur that would make a behavior more likely to occur in the future? Less likely to occur?
- On what would a cognitive theorist focus in this situation? Why?
- What is the child learning in this situation? What does the child already know?
- Use in the Classroom: Have several students present their observations to the class. Are there commonalities to the observations, or is each unique? How would the various theories interpret aspects of the interactions? Do some of the interpretations seem more comprehensive than others? Do some of the interpretations seem more reasonable than others?

Research Project 2: Journal Article Critique Part of conducting psychological research is reviewing and understanding published research studies. In this research project (**Handout 7**), students will choose one of the topics that will be covered in this course (e.g., play, gender roles, moral development, effects of television) and find a research report in a journal (e.g., *Adolescence, Child Development, Developmental Psychology, Family Therapy, Journal of Marriage and the Family*) on the chosen topic. They should read the article and write a report about the article. Request that they enclose a copy of the research article with their report. In addition to including the main points of the study, they should give their personal reactions to the research findings and address the questions in the handout.

- Can you use the title of the study to identify the independent and dependent variables? (Many titles are in this format: "The effects of IV on the DV.")
- What did you learn from the introduction section? What is the historical background of the research topic? Which earlier research findings are most relevant to this study? What theoretical explanations are emphasized in this section? What is the hypothesis of the present study?

- What did you learn from the methods section? Who were the subjects? What procedures (e.g., apparatus, directions, assessment tools) were used?
- What did you learn from the results section? What kinds of statistical procedures were used? What did you learn from charts, frequency tables, and bar graphs? What results did the authors say were statistically significant?
- What did you learn from the discussion section? How did the authors interpret their results? Did they provide alternative explanations? Did they talk about the limitations of the research study? What future research studies were suggested?
- What kinds of ideas did this article make you think about? Can you design a similar study on this topic?

- Use in the Classroom: Possible modifications of the project are: (1) assign specific articles to students; (2) have students choose articles all on one topic; (3) have students choose articles from only one journal; (4) have students read two different articles on the same topic; (5) have students read research articles that address a current social issue— e.g., abortion, teenage pregnancy, racial prejudice—and decide what the research findings would suggest for social policy; (6) have students compare journal reading to textbook reading and magazine reading. Which sections were difficult to understand? Which sections of their articles were comprehended? How did the article compare to their expectations? Were their articles based on basic or applied research? What did the students see as the value of their articles?

Film and Video List

The following films and videos supplement the content of chapter 2. Contact information for film distributors can be found at the front of this Instructor's Manual under Film and Video Sources.

Classical and Operant Conditioning (Films for the Humanities and Sciences, 56 minutes). This program explains the nature of Behaviorism and its applications in therapy, education, and child-rearing. It features archival footage of laboratory work with dogs and rats as well as examples from everyday life.

Cognitive Development (Films for the Humanities and Sciences, 58 minutes). This program examines Piaget's theory in light of modern research. The program suggests that children are more cognitively capable at an earlier age than Piaget proposed.

Cognitive Development (Insight Media, 30 minutes). This video focuses on Piaget's theory of cognitive development and criticisms of that theory. In addition, it looks at the development of thought, reasoning, memory, and language.

The Ecology of Development (Insight Media, 30 minutes). This video profiles children of twelve families in five countries to illustrate the influence of family, peers, school, culture, and history on development. In addition, terms from Bronfenbrenner's ecological theory are defined.

Erik Erikson: A Life's Work (Insight Media, 38 minutes). This program uses biography and interviews to introduce Erikson's theory.

The Family of Chimps (Filmakers Library, 55 minutes). This video focuses on a study by ethologist Frans de Waal at the Arnhem Zoo in Holland and explores issues of comparative psychology and the ethics of animal research.

Learning (Insight Media, 30 minutes). This video presents information about classical and operant conditioning with a special focus on helping hyperactive children using operant conditioning.

Learning in Context: Probing the Theories of Piaget and Vygotsky (Films for the Humanities and Sciences, 31 minutes). This program examines three sets of experiments using gender-biased task instructions, cooperation between asymmetrical pairs of peers, and tasks involving students trained by adults and peers. The results emphasize the importance of self-perception on competence and the influence of different teaching approaches on learning.

Personality (Insight Media, 30 minutes). This program looks at social learning, psychoanalytic, humanistic, and behavioral approaches to personality. It also deals with the five factor theory and the use of twin studies to deal with genetic issues.

Research Methods for the Social Sciences (Insight Media, no time given). This video covers types of experimental designs and describes with basic features of experiments, clinical, correlational, and field methods. It also lays out the seven steps of the scientific method, interpretation of data, and ethical issues.

Statistics: Decisions through Data, Part 1 (Insight Media, 3 volumes, 60 minutes each). Basic descriptive statistics, their calculation, and various graphing methods are presented. Graphics and animation are used to integrate real examples.

Statistics: Decisions through Data, Part 2 (Insight Media, 2 volumes, 60 minutes each). Experimental design is presented with a discussion of causation and sampling. It also deals with confidence intervals and statistical significance.

Theories of Personality (Insight Media, 20 minutes). This video uses discussions with clinicians and research psychologists to cover psychoanalytic, humanistic, social learning, cognitive, and trait approaches. It also addresses the stability of personality over time.

Web Site Suggestions

The URLs for general sites, common to all chapters, can be found at the front of this Instructor's manual under Useful Web Sites. At the time of publication, all sites were current and active, however, please be advised that you may occasionally encounter a dead link.

American Psychological Association (APA)
http://www.apa.org/

American Psychological Society (APS)
http://www.adec.org/

CEC Division Journals
http://www.cec.sped.org/bk/17.htm

Office for Human Research Protections (Ethics for human and animal research)
http://ohrp.osophs.dhhs.gov/

PsycSCAN: Developmental Psychology: Journal Descriptions, Pricing, and Subscription Information
http://www.apa.org/journals/psd.html

University of Chicago Press Journals
http://www.journals.uchicago.edu/pub-alpha.html

Sampling Bias Activity

Identify possible sampling biases in the following statements:

1. Teenage males at a drive-in movie, a local tavern, the beach, and the baseball park were surveyed about their driving records and habits. The results led researchers to some interesting conclusions about male adolescent driving abilities and habits.

2. Parents at a PTA meeting were interviewed about the quality of the public school system.

3. A telephone survey assessed a community's attitudes toward ADC (Aid for Dependent Children) recipients.

4. On December 28, children were asked about their impressions of Santa Claus.

5. The elderly population of Palm Springs was sampled on the advantages and disadvantages of being old.

6. The effectiveness of a new and innovative science teaching program in the elementary schools of Ankeny, Iowa was judged by comparing their scientific knowledge on a standardized test with their peers in Brooklyn, New York.

7. Ten different churches' Sunday school classes were asked about their impressions of God, in order to understand how children from 3 to 12 years of age develop a concept of God and religion.

Critical Thinking Multiple-Choice Questions

1. Chapter 2 presents several different schools of thought about the appropriate subject matter and methods of life-span developmental psychology. The author of the following quote was most likely a proponent of which of the perspectives below: "I never wanted to use human subjects. I hated to serve as a subject. I didn't like the stuffy, artificial instructions given to subjects. I was uncomfortable and acted unnaturally. With animals I was at home. I felt that, in studying them, I was keeping close to biology with my feet on the ground. More and more the thought presented itself: Can't I find out by watching their behavior everything the other students are finding out by using observers?" Circle the letter of the best answer and explain why it is the best answer and why each other answer is not as good.

   a. cognitive
   b. behavioral
   c. life-span
   d. psychoanalytic
   e. ecological

2. Read the following description of a study that compared memory performances of children and adults:

   Do adults remember more than children because they know more about what they are trying to remember? Would children remember more than adults if they knew more than adults did about a topic? These were questions Michelene Chi tried to answer by comparing the memory performances of children and adults with differing levels of knowledge about the information they tried to remember.

   Chi asked children from grades three through eight who were experienced chess players to study either ten numbers or the positions of chess pieces in a chess game for ten seconds. The children then tried to remember all the numbers or the chess positions, after which they studied the items again for ten seconds. The look-recall cycle continued until the children remembered all the items. Memory performance was measured in two ways: The total number of items remembered on the first trial, and the number of trials that were needed to remember all the items. Chi compared the children's performances on both tasks to the performances of adults who were novice chess players. The results suggested that knowledge of to-be-remembered material is important to memory. The child chess experts remembered more chess positions and needed fewer trials to achieve perfect recall than did the adult novices. On the other hand, the adults—who presumably knew more about numbers than the children—outperformed the children in both ways when remembering the numbers.

   • Source: Chi, M. T. H. (1978). Knowledge structures and memory development. In R. S. Siegler (Ed.), *Children's thinking: What develops?* Hillsdale, NJ: Erlbaum.

   Which of the following types of studies best describes Chi's research? Circle the letter of the best answer and explain why it is the best answer and why each other answer is not as good.

   a. cross-sectional, experimental study using interviews
   b. longitudinal, correlational study using standardized tests
   c. cross-sectional, correlational study using observations
   d. longitudinal, experimental study using questionnaires
   e. cross-sectional, experimental study using multiple measures

3. Read the passage about Jess and his teachers that follows:
    Jess and His Teachers

    Jess is an eighth-grader at a junior high school in California. At 14 years old, he already weighs 185 pounds. He is the school's best athlete, but he used to get some of his biggest thrills out of fighting. Jess knocked out several fellow students with bottles and chairs and once hit the principal with a stick, for which he received a 40-day suspension from school. Jess's teachers unanimously agreed that he was an impossible case. No one was able to control him. But one week, his teachers began to notice a complete turnabout in Jess's behavior. His math teacher was one of the first to notice the strange but improved behavior. Jess looked at her one day and said, "When you are nice, you help me learn a lot." The teacher was shocked. Not knowing what to say, she finally smiled. Jess continued, "I feel really good when you praise me." Jess continued a consistent pattern of such statements to his teachers and even came to class early or sometimes stayed late just to chat with them. What was responsible for Jess's turnabout? Some teachers said he attended a mysterious class every day that might provide some clues to his behavior change. In that "mysterious" class, a teacher was training students in behavior modification, which emphasizes that behavior is determined by its consequences. Those consequences weaken some behaviors and strengthen others.

    In an experiment, Paul Graubard and Henry Rosenberg (1974) selected seven of the most incorrigible students at a junior high school—Jess was one of them—and had a teacher give them instruction and practice in behavior modification in one 43-minute class period each day. In their daily training session, the students were taught a number of rewards to use to shape a teacher's behavior. Rewards included eye contact, smiling, sitting up straight, and being attentive. The students also practiced ways to praise the teacher, saying such things as, "I like working in this class where there is a good teacher." And they worked on ways to discourage certain teacher behaviors by saying such things as, "I just have a rough time working well when you get mad at me." Jess had the hardest time learning how to smile. He was shown a videotape of his behavior and observed that he actually leered at people when he was told to smile. Although it was somewhat hilarious, Jess practiced in front of a camera until he eventually developed a charming smile.

    During the five weeks in which the students implemented their behavior-change tactics, observations indicated that teacher-student interchanges were becoming much more positive. Informal observations and comments after the program ended suggested that positive student-teacher interchanges were continuing. But what happened in the long run? In the case of this experiment, we do not know, but in many cases such behavior modification interventions do not result in long-lasting changes once the consequences for behavior are removed (Masters & others, 1988).

    *   Source: Graubard, P., & Rosenberg, H. (1974). *Classrooms that work: Prescriptions for change.* New York: E.P. Dutton.

Which of the following statements is most likely to have been the researchers' (Graubard and Rosenberg) assumption about difficult students, rather than an inference or an observation? Circle the letter of the best answer, and explain why it is the best answer and why each other answer is not as good.

a. The difficult students' behavior was not caused by disturbed personalities or mental abnormalities.
b. The normal reactions of teachers reinforced the disruptive or harmful behavior of difficult students.
c. Students exerted control over their teachers' behavior.
d. Students changed the way that they interacted with their teachers.
e. The improved interaction between students and teachers continued for a short time after the students finished their behavior modification class.

Suggested Answers for Critical Thinking Multiple-Choice Questions

1. Chapter 2 presents several different schools of thought about the appropriate subject matter and methods of life-span developmental psychology. The author of the presented quote was most likely a proponent of which of the following perspectives:

   a. Cognitive is not the best answer. The main reasons are that the speaker (a) is mainly interested in animals, whereas cognitivists typically (though not exclusively) are interested in people, and (b) prefers to focus on observing behavior. Cognitivists are interested in making inferences about the mind and studying conscious mental activity.

   b. Behavioral is the best answer. The first reason is the speaker's interest in the objective study of behavior, and the second is the interest in studying animals rather than people. This seems to parallel the development of Skinner's behaviorism—though the speaker is actually John Watson.

   c. Life-span is not the best answer. The main reasons are that the researcher (a) is mainly interested in animals, and (b) says nothing that relates clearly to the seven characteristics of the life-span perspective. For example, the focus of observation is on the "here and now" without reference to the context in which development is embedded; the researcher is delighted to be grounded in biology, to the exclusion of other disciplines.

   d. Psychoanalytic is not the best answer. Psychoanalysts are interested in people and the inner workings of their thoughts. They also do not typically rely on formal observation as a technique for finding things out, preferring instead various forms of clinical interviews or clinical devices for revealing the nature of personality and personality function.

   e. Ecological is not the best answer. Bronfenbrenner's ecological theory is based on an analysis of systems of human behavior, not the observation of individuals—especially not of animals.

2. Which of the following types of studies best describes Chi's research? Circle the letter of the best answer and explain why it is the best answer and why each other answer is not as good.

   a. A cross-sectional, experimental study using interviews is not the best answer. Chi's study is cross-sectional because it compares children to adults. However, the researchers did not manipulate the independent variables (age, chess expertise), but rather selected subjects who had these characteristics. Finally, the researchers did not interview children about their performance, but rather asked them to remember as many items as they could.

   b. A longitudinal, correlational study using standardized tests is not the best answer. As indicated in "a," Chi used a cross-sectional design not a longitudinal one. Correlational strategy does best describe the research strategy because Chi attempted to show an association (more knowledge is associated with better memory, regardless of age). However, Chi did not use standardized tests to measure performance; this was measured with a recall task designed for the study.

   c. A cross-sectional, correlational study using observations is the best answer. See "a" for cross-sectional and "b" for correlational study. Although the claim that Chi used observations is not exactly correct, this term better fits the kind of research she conducted than the possibilities mentioned in the other answers. One can say that she observed how well children remembered the items by counting the number that they were able to name when asked to remember them.

   d. A longitudinal, experimental study using questionnaires is not the best answer. See "b" for longitudinal and "a" for experimental study. Chi did not measure performance in terms of respondents' written responses to questions they had read.

   e. A cross-sectional, experimental study using multiple measures is not the best answer. See "a" for cross-sectional and experimental. Identifying the measures as multiple measures is not correct because the term implies the use of several different types of measures—for example, combining interviews and questionnaires, or observations, interviews, and standardized tests.

3. Which of the following statements is most likely to have been the researchers' (Graubard and Rosenberg) assumption about difficult students, rather than an inference or an observation? Circle the letter of the best answer, and explain why it is the best answer and why each other answer is not as good.

    a. The answer <u>the difficult students' behavior was not caused by disturbed personalities or mental abnormalities</u> is the best because it is indeed an assumption. This appears to be a key belief of the researchers who worked with students like Jess. If they had not believed this, they would not have focused on specific behaviors that students could change, which, in turn, might change the way teachers treated them. The statement is not made explicitly in the passage, nor does it seem to be a conclusion of the research, nor is it an observation.

    b. The answer <u>the normal reactions of teachers reinforced the disruptive or harmful behavior of difficult students</u> is not the best answer because it is an inference based on the following reasoning: The article demonstrated that a change in the students' behavior produced a change in the teachers' behavior and that, in fact, the changes reinforced each other. The suggestion is that in "normal" day-to-day interactions, the specific pattern of behaviors that people engage in reinforce and maintain each other. For example, the students report things like, "I have a rough time working well when you get mad at me." In order change behavior, one has to intervene in this self-maintaining pattern.

    c. The answer <u>students exerted control over their teachers' behavior</u> is not the best answer because it is an inference or a conclusion that one might derive from the research. The teachers' behavior changed when the students changed their own behavior. Since no other factors appear to have generated this change, the inference is that what the students did actually caused the change (controlled it).

    d. <u>Students changed the way that they interacted with their teachers</u> is not the best answer because it is an observation. This is a "fact"—something deliberately done and directly observable. A teacher/trainer taught students to smile, make pleasant comments, and so on. Students' teachers in other classes then noticed these changed behaviors.

    e. <u>The improved interaction between students and teachers continued for a short time after the students finished their behavior modification class</u> is not the best answer as it is an observation. Teachers reported informally after the study that they continued to see pleasant interactions between the so-called problem students and their teachers.

Critical Thinking Essay Questions

Your answers to this kind of question demonstrate an ability to comprehend and apply ideas discussed in this chapter.

1. What is science? How does a scientific understanding of life-span development differ from an understanding produced by everyday experiences with people of various ages?

2. Compare and contrast the psychoanalytic theories of Freud and Erikson. Also explain whether Erikson changed psychoanalytic theory in a fundamental way.

3. Explain the Piagetian concepts of organization, adaptation, assimilation, and accommodation. Also indicate how these concepts help explain cognitive change during the development of a child.

4. Compare and contrast the Piagetian and information-processing approaches to cognitive development. Which approach appears to be more "developmental"? Defend your answer using the characteristics of life span development outlined in chapter 1.

5. Think about your life during the past 24 hours from the perspective of behavioral and social cognitive theories. Provide at least two examples of how (a) rewards, (b) punishments, and (c) observational learning have influenced your behavior during this time frame.

6. Explain and evaluate ethological theory by indicating its strengths, limitations, and aspects of development that are not explained by this approach to life span development.

7. Define and distinguish the five systems in Bronfenbrenner's ecological theory. Provide at least two examples of each system by citing aspects from your own personal life.

8. Explain the meaning of an eclectic theoretical orientation to life span development. Evaluate the pros and cons of such an approach before you explain which approach is most agreeable to you personally.

9. Discuss what factors influence a researchers selection of a method (e.g., controlled observation in a laboratory, naturalistic observation, interviews and questionnaires, case studies, standardized tests, cross-cultural studies, physiological research, research with animals, or multimeasure, multisource, and multicontext approach) for scientifically collecting data about life-span development.

10. Compare and contrast correlational and experimental strategies for research in life span development. What do you gain and lose by using a correlational rather than experimental strategy in research?

11. What are the strengths and weaknesses of the cross-sectional and longitudinal approaches to research? In what ways do cross-sectional and longitudinal designs differ from experimental strategies? What kinds of conclusions can you draw from each?

12. Explain how research on development can be sexist. Also, discuss ways to reduce sexism in lifespan developmental research.

13. What precautions must be taken to safeguard the rights and welfare of a child who might be a psychological subject? In your answer, relate each precaution to a specific ethical concern. In addition, discuss at least two examples of other types of subjects who pose similar ethical difficulties for researchers.

Ideas to Help You Answer Critical Thinking Essay Questions

1. Think about how you view and interpret behavior of people around you on a daily basis. Recall some judgements and conclusions you've drawn about how and why individuals, of any age, acted as they did. Now review your book's description of science as it relates to life span development. What does it do when attempting to understand and explain behavior that you don't? What do you do in attempting the same thing that is not a part of the scientific process?

2. Start by separately listing characteristics of each theory in a column. Then, match up the concepts that appear in both columns to delineate the similarities. After you have completed the similarities, note the characteristics that appear in only one of the columns to delineate the differences.

3. The Piagetian concepts of organization, adaptation, assimilation, and accomodation are fundamentally understood through the use of examples of cognitive change during childhood. The essence of the concepts themselves is inexorably linked to the processes of development. Thus you may find that beginning with a description of an early cognitive change will clarify your understanding of each concept and enable you to provide a more complete and accurate explanation.

4. Begin by reviewing the main themes of development outlined in chapter 1, and create a graph of the two approaches with regard to each theme. You will then be able to literally visualize the areas in which they converge and differ, and depending on what you find, you can more easily draw your conclusion about their "developmentalness."

5. Our own lives are rich with demonstrations of the processes of behavioral and social cognitive theories. When you identify your own personal experiences with them, it will ensure that you will both understand and remember the basic tenets of these approaches to behavior. Keep in mind when thinking about the last 24 hours of your life that your example doesn't necessarily have to include your actual *experiencing* of the learning process, but rather much behavior reflects the *manifestation* or results of that process. Also, always check with your instructor that your personal examples are correct. Cognitive theories and processes can be tricky and, if your example isn't quite right, it can really mislead you.

6. Review the main themes of development outlined in chapter 1. Create a chart of the themes and note where ethological theory falls with regard to each. This will provide you with the basis for identifying it's strengths and weaknesses, which in turn, will provide you with the answer for what may be missing from this approach.

7. Examples of concepts and phenomena are not separate and distinct entities from the concepts themselves. Sometimes in order to understand something, we must incorporate the example as part of the explanation—it gives us the ability to not only recognize the nature of the concept itself, but to identify it's importance and contextual impact. Use your examples to guide you in your definitions and delineation of Bronfenbrenner's systems for a more comprehensive coverage of the theory.

8. Begin by re-reading and familiarizing yourself with all of the various theories. Pull them apart piece by piece and decide what aspects *you* think are useful in addressing and explaining human development. What concepts are not effective or are not applicable scientifically? After you have spent time viewing the theories from this perspective, you will then be able to understand both the origin and implementation of eclectic theoretical orientations. You will also have done the leg work to enable you to identify which approach you prefer.

9. For each research method, consider what it is you might be studying were you to employ it. What information would you expect to gain by using each particular method? From here, take the next step and identify the specific factors that would serve to influence your selection of a certain research method.

10. Begin by re-reading and making certain you understand correlational and experimental strategies. Then design your own (very basic) studies using each method. Compare and contrast what you are able to learn from each study based on the method you chose to approach it with.

11. Choose a behavior you would like to study developmentally. Approach it both longitudinally and using a cross-sectional design. Where would you have challenges with each? What would you gain from each approach? How might you decide which one to ultimately use? Answers to these questions will enlighten you on the strengths, weaknesses, and useful contexts of each design.

12. Create a sexist research study. In what ways could someone claim that it is sexist? Why would this be problematic? Now, alter your design to study the same behavior, but eliminate the problematic factors. Was this difficult? What general recommendations can you make that might apply to numerous studies in life-span development?

13. As you read through each ethical concern for life-span developmentalists, consider it's relevance to subjects of all ages. Do they relate and apply to all potential age groups that are studied or are they only relevant to individuals of a particular age? Are there ethical concerns that are only valid for certain ages, but wouldn't be an issue with others? Which concerns cover all age groups, thus indicating a greater issue of general unethical methodology? By familiarizing yourself with these aspects of research design, you will gain a greater understanding of issues life-span developmentalists must consider when studying human behavior.

Parent-Child Interaction

In this project, you will observe a parent-child interaction and interpret it according to psychoanalytic, behavioral, and cognitive theoretical approaches. Go to a local supermarket and watch a mother or father shop with a 2- to 4-year-old child. Describe the interactions you observe, including demands on the part of the child, verbal exchanges between parent and child, and ways in which the parent responds to the demands of the child. Then answer the questions that follow, referring to your observations.

Child: Age _____ Sex _____
Parent: Age _____ Sex _____

Description:

Questions:
- On what would a psychoanalytic theorist focus in this example? How would the sequence of observed events be explained?

- How would a behavioral psychologist analyze the situation? What reinforcers or punishers characterized the interaction? Did specific things occur that would make a behavior more likely to occur in the future? Less likely to occur?

- On what would a cognitive theorist focus in this situation? Why?

- What is the child learning in this situation? What does the child already know?

Handout 7 (RP 2)

Journal Article Critique

Part of conducting psychological research is reviewing and understanding published research studies. In this research project, you will choose one of the topics that will be covered in this course (e.g., play, gender roles, moral development, effects of television) and find a research report in a journal (e.g., *Adolescence, Child Development, Developmental Psychology, Family Therapy, Journal of Marriage and the Family*) on the chosen topic. Read the article and write a report about the article. Enclose a copy of the research article with your report. In addition to including the main points of the study, give your personal reactions to the research findings.

Questions:

- Can you use the title of the study to identify the independent and dependent variables? (Many titles are in this format: "The effects of IV on the DV.")

- What did you learn from the introduction section? What is the historical background of the research topic? Which earlier research findings are given as most relevant to this study? What theoretical explanations are emphasized in this section? What is the hypothesis of the present study?

- What did you learn from the methods section? Who were the subjects? What procedures (e.g., apparatus, directions, assessment tools) were used?

- What did you learn from the results section? What kinds of statistical procedures were used? What did you learn from charts, frequency tables, and bar graphs? What results did the authors say were statistically significant?

- What did you learn from the discussion section? How did the authors interpret their results? Did they provide alternative explanations? Did they talk about the limitations of the present research study? What future research studies were suggested?

- What kinds of ideas did this article make you think about? Can you design a similar study on this topic?

Chapter 3: Biological Beginnings

Total Teaching Package Outline

Lecture Outline	Resource References
Biological Beginnings	PowerPoint Presentation: See www.mhhe.com Cognitive Maps: See Appendix A

The Evolutionary Perspective
• Natural Selection and Adaptive Behavior
 	
• Evolutionary Psychology
    -Evolution and Life-Span Development
    -Evaluating Evolutionary Biology
	LO1

Genetic Foundations • What Are Genes?	LO2 IB: Cells, Chromosomes, Genes, and DNA
• Mitosis and Meiosis	LO3 IB: Mitosis and Meiosis

• Genetic Principles
 	
    -Dominant-Recessive Genes
	LO4
	OHT25-30: Genetic Principles
	OHT46 & IB: Eye Color
	CA1: Principles of Genetic Transmission
	RP1: Heritability of Height
	F/V: Boy or Girl? When Doctors Choose a
	      Child's Sex
	F/V: How Babies Get Made
	F/V: Keltie's Beard: A Woman's Story
	F/V: Reproduction: Designer Babies
	WS: Gender: Biology vs. Environment?

• Behavior Genetics	LO5 LS1: Three Laws of Behavior Genetics WS: Behavior Genetics Association WS: National Society for Genetic Counselors

• Molecular Genetics
• Chromosome and Gene-Linked Abnormalities
    -Chromosome Abnormalities
 	
    -Gene-Linked Abnormalities
	LO6
	IB: Some Chromosome Abnormalities
	LS2: Guest Speaker and Prenatal Counseling
	CA2: Ethical Dilemmas Regarding Genetic
	      Counseling
	IB: Some Gene-Linked Abnormalities
	CA3: Pros and Cons of Genetic Testing for
	      Huntington's Disease
	RP2: Genetic Counseling Available to You
	F/V: Down's Syndrome
	F/V: Yours to Keep
	F/V: Little People
	WS: Down's Syndrome

Reproduction Challenges and Choices	LO7
• Prenatal Diagnostic Tests	LO8 IB: Amniocentesis and Chorionic Villi Sampling WS: Prenatal Diagnostic Techniques
• Infertility	IB: Fertility Problems, Causes, and Treatments OHT37 & IB: Fertility Problems and Solutions WS: A Weekly Digest of Fertility WS: Infertility
• Adoption	LO9 WS: Holt International Children's Services: Specializes in Adoptions
Heredity-Environment Interaction	PA1: All in the Family F/V: Biological Growth: Nature's Child
• Intelligence	LO10 CA4: Debate on Heritability of Intelligence
• Heredity-Environment Correlations	LO11 LO12 PA2: I Am What I Am
• Shared and Nonshared Environmental Experiences	LO13 PA3: The Same But Different
• Conclusions about Heredity-Environment Interaction	LO14 LS: 3 Interaction Concepts PA4: But Everybody's Doing It!
Review	CA5: Critical Thinking Multiple-Choice CA6: Critical Thinking Essays

Chapter Outline

THE EVOLUTIONARY PERSPECTIVE
    Natural Selection and Adaptive Behavior
- Natural selection is the evolutionary process proposed by Charles Darwin that favors individuals of a species that are best adapted to survive and reproduce.
- Adaptive behavior is behavior that promotes an organism's survival in the natural habitat.

    Evolutionary Psychology
- **Evolutionary psychology** emphasizes the importance of adaptation, reproduction, and "survival of the fittest" in explaining behavior.
- The evolutionary process of natural selection favors behaviors that increase an organism's reproductive success and it's ability to pass it's genes to the next generation.

Evolution and Life-Span Development
- According to Paul Baltes, the benefits of evolutionary selection decrease with age mainly because of a decline in reproductive fitness.
- Baltes also stresses that a life-span shift in the allocation of resources takes place away from growth and toward maintenance and regulation of loss.
- While evolutionary selection benefits decrease with age, cultural needs increase.

Evaluating Evolutionary Biology
- Albert Bandura, the social cognitive theorist, acknowledges evolution's important role in human adaptation and change. Yet, he rejects "one-sided evolutionism," in which social behavior is the product of evolved biology. He argues for a bidirectional view that enables organisms to alter and construct new environmental conditions.
- Learnability and plasticity allow humans to adapt to diverse contexts. Human behavior is not biologically fixed. Biology allows for a broad range of cultural possibilities.

GENETIC FOUNDATIONS
- The principles of genetics explain the mechanism for transmitting characteristics from one generation to the next. Each individual has a genetic code that we inherited from our parents within every cell in our bodies.

What Are Genes?
- The nucleus of each human cell contains 46 chromosomes.
- **Chromosomes** are threadlike structures that come in 23 pairs, one member of each pair coming from each parent. Chromosomes contain the genetic substance deoxyribonucleic acid (DNA).
- **DNA** is a complex molecule that contains genetic information. The double helix shape looks like a spiral staircase.
- **Genes** are short segments composed of DNA. Genes act as a blueprint for cells to reproduce themselves and manufacture proteins that maintain life.

Mitosis and Meiosis
- Mitosis and meiosis are biological processes that are important to understanding how genes function.
- **Mitosis** is the process by which each chromosome in the cell's nucleus duplicates itself.
- **Meiosis** is the process by which cells divide into gametes (testes/sperm in males, ovaries/eggs in females) which have half the genetic material of the parent cell.
  - In mitosis, the focus is on cell growth and repair, while meiosis involves sexual reproduction.
  - In mitosis, the number of chromosomes present remains the same (the chromosomes copy themselves), while in meiosis, the chromosomes are halved.
  - In mitosis, two daughter cells are formed, while in meiosis four daughter cells are formed.
- Human reproduction begins when a female gamete (ovum) is fertilized by a male gamete (sperm) to create a single cell called a **zygote**.

Genetic Principles
- Dominant-recessive genes principle: if one gene of a pair is dominant and one is recessive, the dominant gene exerts its effect, overriding the potential influence of the recessive gene. A recessive gene exerts its influence only if the two genes of a pair are both recessive.
- Sex of offspring is determined by 2 of the 46 chromosomes. Females ordinarily have two X chromosomes, and males have an X and a Y.
- Polygenetic inheritance is the genetic principle that many genes can interact to produce a particular characteristic.

- A **genotype** is the person's genetic heritage, the actual genetic material.
- A **phenotype** is the way an individual's genotype is expressed in observed and measurable characteristics.
- The **reaction range** is the range of possible phenotypes for each genotype, suggesting the importance of an environment's restrictiveness or enrichment. Humans have a range of potential that is genetically determined and environmental influences determine where within the range the individual's characteristic will develop.
- **Canalization** describes the narrow path, or developmental course, that certain characteristics take. Apparently, preventative forces help protect, or buffer, a person from environmental extremes.

Behavior Genetics
- Behavior genetics is the study of the degree and nature of behavior hereditary basis. Behavior is assumed to be jointly determined by the interaction of heredity and environment.
- Twin studies and adoption studies are used to examine the influences of heredity and environment.
  - **Twin studies** compare the behavioral similarity of identical twins to fraternal twins.
    - Identical twins (monozygotic twins) develop from a single fertilized egg that splits into two genetically identical replicas, each of which becomes a person.
    - Fraternal twins (dizygotic twins) develop from separate eggs and separate sperm, making them no more similar than ordinary siblings.
    - Comparing fraternal and identical twins, behavioral geneticists capitalize on the basic knowledge that identical twins are more similar genetically than are fraternal twins.
    - Potential concerns regarding twin studies include the notion that identical twins may be treated more similarly than fraternal twins and have more similar environments. If so, observed similarities may be due to environmental influences rather than genetics.
  - In **adoption studies**, researchers assess whether adopted children are more like their adoptive parents (environment), or more like their biological parents (genetics) with respect to behavior and psychological characteristics.
    - Another form of adoption studies compares adoptive and biological siblings.

Molecular Genetics
- The field of molecular genetics seeks to discover the precise locations of genes that determine an individual's susceptibility to various diseases and other aspects of health and well-being.
- Genome refers to the complete set of instructions for making an organism (DNA). It contains the master blueprint for all cellular structures and activities for the life span of the organism.
- The Human Genome Project which began in the 1970s is mapping out the human genome.

Chromosome and Gene-Linked Abnormalities
  Chromosome Abnormalities
  - Chromosome abnormalities occur when chromosomes do not divide evenly.
  - Down Syndrome
    - **Down syndrome** is a chromosomally transmitted form of mental retardation, caused by the presence of an extra chromosome (approximately 1 out of 700 live births). An individual with Down syndrome typically has a round face, a flattened skull, an extra fold of skin over the eyelids, a protruding tongue, short limbs, and retardation of motor and mental abilities.
    - Maternal age may contribute to this syndrome.

Sex-Linked Chromosomal Abnormalities
- Sex-linked chromosome abnormalities occur when there is a deviation from the typical XX or XY combination of sex chromosomes. Sex-linked chromosomal disorders include:
  - **Klinefelter syndrome** is a genetic disorder in which males have an extra X chromosome, making them XXY instead of XY (approximately 1 in 800 live births). Males with this disorder have undeveloped testes and enlarged breasts.
  - **Fragile X syndrome** is a genetic disorder that results from abnormality in the X chromosome (becomes constricted and breaks). Mental deficiency is the primary outcome.
  - **Turner syndrome** is a chromosome disorder in which females are missing an X chromosome, making them XO instead of XX. These females (one in 3,000 live births) are short in stature, mentally retarded, and sexually underdeveloped, and have webbed necks.
  - The **XYY syndrome** is a disorder in which the male has an extra Y chromosome. Despite assumptions, XYY males are no more likely to commit crimes than are XY males.

Gene-Linked Abnormalities
- More than 7,000 genetic disorders are caused by harmful genes, though most are rare.
  - **Phenylketonuria** (PKU) is an easily detected genetic disorder in which the individual cannot properly metabolize an amino acid. If left untreated, mental retardation and hyperactivity result.
  - **Sickle-cell anemia**, which occurs in 1 of 400 African Americans, is a genetic disorder affecting the red blood cells and results in early death.

REPRODUCTION CHALLENGES AND CHOICES
Prenatal Diagnostic Tests
- Scientists have developed the following tests to determine whether a fetus is developing normally:
  - Amniocentesis is a prenatal medical procedure in which a sample of amniotic fluid is withdrawn by syringe and tested to discover if the fetus is suffering from any chromosomal or metabolic disorders. Amniocentesis can be performed between 12 and 16 weeks post conception.
  - Ultrasound sonography is a prenatal medical procedure in which high-frequency sound waves are directed into the pregnant woman's abdomen. The echo from the sounds is transformed into a visual representation of the fetus's inner structures.
  - Chronic villi sampling is a prenatal medical procedure in which a small sample of the placenta is removed at some point between the 8th and 11th weeks of pregnancy. This technique provides information about the presence of birth defects.
  - The maternal blood test (alpha-fetoprotein or AFP) is a prenatal diagnostic technique typically performed between 14 and 20 weeks post conception that is used to assess blood alphaprotein levels, which are associated with neural-tube defects.

Infertility
- Approximately 10 to 15 percent of couples in the U.S. experience infertility which is the inability to conceive after 12 months of regular intercourse without contraception.
- Causes of female infertility include lack of ovulation, abnormal ova, blocked fallopian tubes, or implantation difficulties.
- Causes of male infertility include too few sperm, poor sperm mobility, or blocked passageways.

- Infertility treatments include:
  - In vitro fertilization (IVF): Egg and sperm combined in laboratory dish and transferred to woman's uterus (less than 20 percent success rate).
  - Gamete intrafallopian transfer (GIFT): Eggs and sperm directly inserted into woman's fallopian tubes (approximately 30 percent success rate).
  - Intrauterine insemination (IUI): Frozen sperm directly inserted into the uterus (10 percent success rate).
  - Zygote intrafallopian transfer (ZIFT): Two-step procedure involving eggs being fertilized in laboratory then transferred into a fallopian tube (approximately 25 percent success rate).
  - Intracytoplasmic sperm injection (ICIS): Single sperm injected into an egg, then the zygote is returned to the uterus (approximately 25 percent success rate).
- Multiple births have increased due to infertility treatments.

Adoption
- Another alternative to infertility problems involves adoption which is the social and legal process by which a parent-child relationship is established between persons unrelated at birth.
- Adopted children and adolescents have more problems than their nonadopted counterparts.
- When adoption occurs very early in development the outcomes for the child are improved.

HEREDITY-ENVIRONMENT INTERACTION
- Development is the result of the interaction of heredity and environment. Intelligence is discussed to highlight this interaction.

Intelligence
- Using data from twin studies, Arthur Jensen concluded that intelligence is primarily inherited, thus environment and culture play a minimal role in intelligence.
- Criticism of Jensen's work focused on his definition of intelligence (standardized IQ test scores) and the homogeneity of environments among his participants (influence would not be apparent when environments are similar).
- Current research estimates that heredity's influence on intelligence is in the 50 percent range.

Heredity-Environment Correlations
- The concept of heredity-environment correlations is that individuals' genes influence the types of environments to which they are exposed.
- Scarr proposes three ways that heredity and environment are correlated:
  - **Passive genotype-environment correlations** occur when biological parents, who are genetically related to the child, provide a rearing environment for the child.
  - **Evocative genotype-environment correlations** occur because a child's genotype elicits certain types of physical and social environments.
  - **Active (niche-picking) genotype-environment correlations** occur when children and adolescents seek out environments they find compatible and stimulating.
- Scarr proposes that the relative importance of these genotype-environment correlations changes as children develop from infancy to adolescence.

Shared and Nonshared Environmental Experiences
- Robert Plomin found that common rearing, or shared environments, accounts for little of the variation in children's personality or interests.
- **Shared environmental experiences** are children's common experiences, such as their parents' personalities and intelligence, the family's social class, and the neighborhood in which they live.

- **Nonshared environmental experiences** are a child's unique experiences, within the family and outside the family, that are not shared with another sibling. Experiences occurring within the family can be part of the "nonshared environment."

Conclusions about Heredity-Environment Interaction
- Both genes and environment are necessary for a person to exist. They interact extensively to determine behavior and development.
- Complexity captures this relationship. Many complex behaviors have some genetic loading that gives people a propensity for a particular development trajectory.

Learning Objectives

1. Discuss natural selection and the evolutionary perspective of human development.
2. Understand the relationship between chromosomes, DNA, genes, and human reproduction cells.
3. Distinguish between mitosis and meiosis.
4. Discuss the genetic principles of dominant-recessive genes, sex-linked genes, polygenic inheritance, genotype and phenotype, reaction range, and canalization.
5. Discuss the goals of twin studies and adoption studies in behavior genetics, being sure to mention the difference between the two types of twins.
6. Discuss the disorders associated with abnormalities in genes and chromosomes.
7. Describe the method and purpose for tests such as amniocentesis, ultrasound sonography, chorionic villi sampling, and the maternal blood test.
8. Describe the five most common techniques for helping infertile couples.
9. Present the common explanations for why outcomes for adopted children may be problematic.
10. Discuss the controversy surrounding research on the heritability of intelligence.
11. Explain Sandra Scarr's views that genotypes drive experience and outline criticisms of Scarr's views.
12. Define and distinguish between passive, evocative, and active genotype-environment interactions.
13. Distinguish shared environmental experiences from nonshared environmental experiences.
14. Present some conclusions about the research on heredity-environment interaction.

Key Terms

active (niche-picking) genotype-
   environment correlations
adoption study
canalization
chromosomes
DNA
Down syndrome
evocative genotype-environment
   correlations
evolutionary psychology
Fragile X syndrome
genes
genotype
Klinefelter syndrome
meiosis

mitosis
nonshared environmental
   experiences
passive genotype-environment
   correlations
phenotype
phenylketonuria
reaction range
sickle-cell anemia
shared environmental
   experiences
Turner syndrome
twin study
XYY syndrome
zygote

Key People

Paul Baltes

Albert Bandura

Thomas Bouchard

David Buss

Charles Darwin

Theodore Dobzhansky

Gilbert Gottlieb

Stephen Jay Gould

Judith Harris

Richard Hernstein and Charles Murray

Arthur Jensen

Robert Plomin

Craig Ramey

Sandra Scarr

Lecture Suggestion

Lecture Suggestion 1: Three Laws of Behavior Genetics The purpose of this lecture is to extend the discussion of behavior genetics relative to the nature-nurture debate. The traditional nature-nurture debate focused on whether genes influenced complex behavioral outcomes. The answer is yes. The current nature-nurture debate focuses on how to proceed from partitioning sources of variance to specifying concrete developmental processes. Turkheimer (2000) has synthesized three laws of behavior genetics:

- First Law: All human behavioral traits are heritable.
- Second Law: The effect of being raised in the same family is smaller than the effect of genes.
- Third Law: A substantial portion of the variation in complex human behavioral traits is not accounted for by the effects of genes or families.

If the first two laws are taken literally, the nature side of the great nature-nurture debate won. That is, genes matter and families or environment do not. However, this is a massive oversimplification. The claim that genes are involved in all traits does not preclude environmental influences. Individual genes and their environments (including other genes) interact to influence developmental processes. Interactivity is the primary component of this process. Subsequent environments are influenced by prior states, and these interactions influence developmental trajectories of the organism which affect future expression of genes. There are no direct cause and effect relationships in developmental processes. Rather any individual gene or environmental event influences development only by interacting with other genes and environments.

Heritability per se has few implications for scientific understanding of development. It is important to keep in mind the following point. Heritability does not have one certain consequence. Correlations among biologically related family members are not prima facie evidence of sociocultural causal mechanisms. Just because a child of a depressed mother becomes depressed does not demonstrate that being raised by depressed mothers is itself depressing. That child might have become depressed regardless of the environment, due to the influence of the mother's genes.

Related to the second and third law, Plomin and Daniels (1987) asked the question: Why are children in the same family so different from one another? They proposed that children in the same family are different because nonshared environmental events are more potent causes of developmental outcomes than shared environmental factors. In other words, children's environments, their peers, and the aspects of parenting their siblings do not share help explain differences between siblings. The part of the family environment that siblings do not share appears to matter more than the part of the family environment that siblings do share. Plomin and Daniels also state that the salient environment is almost impossible to research because it is a combination of unsystematic, idiosyncratic, or serendipitous events.

Genetic material is a more systematic source of variability in development than environment. Yet this statement is based on methodological issues rather than substantive issues. Genetic experiments (identical and fraternal twins) statistically assess this component better than social scientists ability to assess unsystematic and idiosyncratic events within environments. Turkheimer states that twin studies are a methodological shortcut, but they do not demonstrate that genes are more important than environments. Turkheimer further states that human developmental social science is difficult to conduct for two major reasons: 1) human behavior develops out of complex, interactive nonlinear processes, and 2) experimental control is impossible to implement in human developmental processes because of ethical constraints.

- Sources: Plomin, R., & Daniels, D. (1987). Why are children in the same family so different from one another? *Behavioral and Brain Sciences, 10,* 1-60. Turkheimer, E. (2000). Three laws of behavior genetics and what they mean. *Current Directions in Psychological Science, 9,* 160-164.

Lecture Suggestion 2: Guest Speaker Idea and Prenatal Counseling Students often find the role of a genetics counselor difficult to understand. They confuse abortion counseling with genetic counseling. Invite a genetic counselor to come and discuss what he or she does to assist couples who want testing. You might ask the counselor to discuss the most common reasons why couples come for testing (see below) and methods of testing. If you are not able to have a guest speaker attend your class, give a lecture on these ideas.

Genetic counseling involves using potential parents' medical and genetic histories and tests to help couples estimate their chances of having a healthy baby and to discuss the best course of action in view of risks and family goals. Individuals likely to seek prenatal counseling include:

- Couples who have a child with a serious defect (Down syndrome, spina bifida, limb malformation, etc.)
- Couples with a family history of genetic diseases or mental retardation.
- Couples who are blood relatives (1st or 2nd cousins).
- Any woman over 35 years.
- Women who have taken potentially harmful substances early in pregnancy or are habitual drug users.
- Women who have had a serious infection early in pregnancy (HIV, rubella, etc.)
- Members of high-risk ethnic groups (e.g., African Americans, Ashkenazi Jews, Italians, Greeks)
- Women who have had an X-ray early in pregnancy.
- Sources: Feinbloom, R. I., and Forman, B.Y. (1987*). Pregnancy, birth and the early months: A complete guide.* Reading, MA: Addison-Wesley.

Lecture Suggestion 3: Interaction Concepts The concept of interaction takes some time to master. There are numerous examples of interaction among the topics taught in a life-span development course. One of the clearest examples comes from the principles of gene expression.

- Dominant and recessive genes are examples of interaction involving heredity. The effect of a recessive gene depends on the presence or absence of its corresponding dominant gene.
- The genotype/phenotype contrast further illustrates the fact that heredity does not always find direct expression in the outward appearance of organisms. Statements based on the results of genotypes are probabilistic. That is, if you possess a particular set of genes you are more likely to develop a particular characteristic than a person without those genes is. Genes are not deterministic, since environmental influences may lessen the impact of those genes on the behavioral outcome (Scarr & McCartney, 1983). Fogel (1983, p. 37) states that, "the genotype determines the opportunities by which the environment may have an influence on the phenotype." A particular genetic predisposition may never result in the phenotype because the "needed" environment was not present. Some genetic disorders (PKU, diabetes, etc.) can be eliminated in the phenotype through environmental intervention (surgery, drug treatments, diet, etc.). Point out there are other ways that a phenotype may not directly express its genotype, which can lead to a discussion of canalization and range of reaction.
- Canalization and range of reaction indicate that heredity/environment interactions come in different types. Heredity and environment both may play a role in determining individual differences in the expression of traits. Unique combinations of heredity and environment lead to both similarity and differences in people's behavior.

- Reaction range highlights the relationship between heredity and environment.
  - Each person has a unique genetic makeup, thus we respond differently to the same environment.
    - Two individuals with similar genetic intellectual potentials may result in very different IQ scores due to their environment. The individual raised in a highly enriched environment would have a higher IQ than an individual in a less stimulating environment.
  - Different genetic-environmental combinations can produce individuals that look the same.
    - An individual with less genetic intellectual potential raised in an enriched environment may have the same intelligence score as an individual with more genetic potential raised in a less stimulating environment.
- Canalization is the tendency of heredity to restrict the development of some characteristics to just one or a few outcomes.
  - Strongly canalized behaviors (infant perceptual, motor development) follow a genetically set growth plan. Only strong environmental forces can change the developmental path.
  - Behaviors that are less strongly canalized (personality, intelligence) vary much more with changes in the environment.
  - The concept of canalization has been expanded to include the notion that environments can limit development. Harmful environments early in life may impede the influence of later experiences to change the characteristic (prenatal exposure to alcohol may make it difficult for enriched environments to enhance cognitive development).
- Sources: Fogel, A. (1983). *Infancy*. St. Paul, MN: West Publishing. Scarr, S., and McCartney, K. (1983). How people make their own environments: A theory of genotype-environments effects, *Child Development, 21*, 391-402.

Classroom Activities

Classroom Activity 1: Principles of Genetic Transmission The purpose of this activity is to help students understand the principles of genetic transmission. Ask students to bring in as complete a description as possible of the hair type (straight or curly) of their siblings, parents, grandparents, and, if possible, great grandparents. Some students will be unable to get the information, so it might be a good idea to break them into groups and have them use the data of the student with the most complete history. Using Mendel's principles of genetic transmission, have students draw genetic models that explain how they and their siblings got their hair type. Encourage the students to include their parents and grandparents in their models.
- The allele for curly hair is dominant (represent it as C) and the allele for straight hair is recessive (c). Children who inherit either a homozygous pair (CC) of dominant alleles or a heterozygous pair (Cc) will have curly hair (though the Cc individuals could pass on a straight hair gene to their children, thus they are called carriers). Children who inherit a homozygous recessive pair (cc) will have straight hair.
- If the father is homozygous for straight hair (cc) and the mother is heterozygous for curly hair (Cc), 50 percent of the children will be heterozygous for curly hair and 50 percent will be homozygous for straight hair.

Logistics:
- Group size: Individual or small group (2-4).
- Approximate time: 10 minutes.

Classroom Activity 2: Ethical Dilemmas Regarding Genetic Counseling In order for students to appreciate the value of the information they are learning, it is sometimes useful to present them with situations faced by people every day in which knowledge of life-span development can be useful, but at the same time, controversial. This activity also affords students an opportunity to review concepts from the chapters (recessive-dominant, genetic testing, etc.) In the November 1994 issue of *Science News*, four ethical dilemmas were presented and readers were asked to write in and indicate how they would respond to each situation. We will present two of the dilemmas and suggest issues for students to consider as **Handout 1**.

The first scenario deals with dwarfism and is quoted from *Science News*.

A husband and his pregnant wife seek genetic counseling. Each carries one flawed copy of the gene responsible for achondroplasia; therefore, they are both dwarfs. Recently, a California research team described the mutation in a gene on chromosome 4 that causes achondroplasia. The counselor explains that genetic testing can determine whether the fetus has inherited the mutated gene. In the discussion, the couple informs the counselor that they will abort any fetus that carries two mutant genes. That's not surprising, since children born with two such genes rarely survive beyond infancy. This couple has had a child in this circumstance who died when 2 months old.

This time around, they say, they want a baby who is heterozygous for the achondroplasia trait. This child inherits a flawed gene from one parent and a healthy gene from the other parent. That genetic combination means the child will be a dwarf—just like the parents. At the same time, the parents say, they will abort any fetus that does not inherit one copy of the mutant gene. Should the counseling center perform the test, knowing that the couple plans to abort a healthy fetus?

Some of the things to consider include the fact that achondroplasia is a serious disorder. The bones can be abnormal in structure, sometimes requiring the use of a wheelchair. Yet, many dwarfs live long, healthy lives and don't regard their condition as a disability. In addition, some couples with this condition worry about problems involved in raising a normal-sized child.

- Have students determine what the ethical dilemma is for the scenario (perform the test or not?).
- What would they do if they were the genetic counselor?
- Have students present arguments for both sides of the issue.
- Remind students that genetic counselors should present options to clients and not make decisions.

The second scenario deals with paternity and is quoted from *Science News*.

A husband and wife have a child who suffers from cystic fibrosis (CF), an incurable, fatal hereditary disease that results in frequent infections and difficulty breathing. The couple wants to determine their risk of having another child with this disorder. Because CF is a recessive disorder, a child usually must inherit the CF gene from both parents to get the disease. A child with just one CF gene is a carrier: Such a person doesn't have the disorder but can pass the trait on to the next generation. The DNA test revealed that the mother of the child carried the CF trait. However, her husband did not. The DNA tests showed that he was not the biological father of the child.

The fact significantly decreased the couple's chance of having another child with CF. But the test has put the counselor in a difficult situation. Should the counselor tell the couple about the nonpaternity findings? Should the mother be told privately? If so, is the center colluding with the mother to withhold information from the husband?

In addition, this case brings up issues concerning the biological father of the child. This man has not contracted with the genetics center for the test, yet the counselor now knows that this man is probably a carrier of the mutant gene for CF. Should the genetic counselor call this man and tell him about his risk?

- Have students determine what the ethical dilemmas are for the scenario (reveal paternity to wife?, reveal paternity to husband?, reveal carrier status to biological father?).
- What would they do if they were the genetic counselor?
- Have students present arguments for both sides of the issue.

In the December 1994 issue of *Science News*, the author presents the results of people's responses to these dilemmas. Compare the opinions of your class with those of the people who responded to the article.

Scenario 1:
- Of the adults who answered, 84 percent said the center should perform the test for this couple.
- The students were split more evenly, 59 percent said they would okay the test, 41 percent would veto the test.

Scenario 2:
- Of the adults, 35 percent believed the counselor should explain the low risk of having another child with CF without revealing the paternity issue (some said to reveal paternity if the couple wanted more details).
- Of the adults, 35 percent believed the counselor should tell the couple about the paternity data (some thought to tell the mother separately first).
- Of the adults, 30 percent thought the counselor should relay the paternity findings to the mother only.
- Of the students, 9 percent would reveal only the CF risk.
- Of the students, 56 percent would tell the couple about the paternity (most would tell the mother first).
- Of the students, 35 percent would tell only the mother the paternity results.
- 71 percent of the students and 52 percent of the adults wanted the biological father to know he was a CF carrier.
- Most genetic clinics now tell prospective clients that paternity can be determined through DNA testing and ask them how they want the situation handled if it arises.

Logistics:
- Materials: Handout 1 (ethical dilemmas).
- Group size: Small groups (2-4) and full class.
- Approximate time: Small groups (20 minutes) and full class (10 -15 minutes per dilemma).

- Sources: Fackelmann, K. (1994). Beyond the genome: The ethics of DNA testing. *Science News, 146,* 298-299. Fackelmann, K. (1994). DNA dilemmas: Readers and "experts" weigh in on biomedical ethics. *Science News, 146,* 408-410.

Classroom Activity 3: Pros and Cons of Genetic Testing for Huntington's Disease A genetic diagnostic test has been developed for the 100,000 Americans with a history of Huntington's disease in their families. The test identifies which individuals have inherited the defective gene. These individuals will usually begin to show symptoms between ages 35 and 45. The symptoms include progressive dementia and loss of body control, irritability and depression, and symptoms that mimic "drunkenness" such as slurred speech, slowed thought processes, impaired memory, and diminished problem-solving ability. These individuals also exhibit uncontrolled movements. Students should discuss the disadvantages and advantages of conducting these simple blood tests, and if they would have the test and why.

Disadvantages:
- Some people may be unable to cope with the knowledge that they will inevitably suffer from an incurable disease. Some individuals diagnosed with symptoms of the disease attempt suicide (25 percent).
- Some families may break up and some people may not be able to concentrate on their jobs.
- Sibling relationships may change as one is "liberated" from the disease and another is "doomed."
- Fetal testing will cause some families to make decisions about abortions that they are uncomfortable making, or they will have to live with the belief that their children are "doomed."

Advantages:
- Some people will be relieved to know that they will not get Huntington's disease, lifting a lifetime burden from their shoulders.
- Some people who are informed that they will get the disease may prefer the knowledge and plan their lives accordingly, just as many cancer patients would rather know their fates.
- The 50 percent of family members who will not get the disease can have children without wondering whether they are passing on a serious genetic condition. The rest can be more certain about their decisions not to have children.
- This genetic screening test represents a first step in prevention and successful treatment of Huntington's disease. Somewhere down the line, potential victims may be treated with medicines or genetic surgery.

Logistics:
- Group size: Full class discussion.
- Approximate time: 15 minutes.

Classroom Activity 4: Debate on Heritability of Intelligence The purpose of this activity is to foster thinking about the contribution of life-span developmental research for setting public policy. Divide the class into two groups to debate the issue of heritability of intelligence and its effect on public policy. Should data about parents' (or grandparents') intelligence be used to determine what kinds of schooling to give to children? One group should provide evidence consistent with a strong genetic position on intelligence. The other group should argue a strong environmental position on intelligence. Students should think about how this issue would be further complicated by information about whether heritability of intelligence is high or low. Each side of the debate should generate evidence from the text that supports their side. The groups can select a couple of spokespersons, and let the debate begin. Bringing in a colleague to judge the debate can keep you from having to take sides and may motivate the students to prepare better arguments.

Logistics:
- Group size: Divide class in half, and then full class for a debate.
- Approximate time: 25 minutes for evidence/argument development and 25 minutes for debate.

Classroom Activity 5: Critical Thinking Multiple-Choice Questions and Suggested Answers Discuss the answers to the critical thinking multiple-choice questions presented as **Handout 2**. For question 1, be sure the class understands the genetic principles. They need not fully understand the ramifications of the dominant-recessive genes principle, but it will help to work toward that understanding. Students often do not comprehend the other concepts well either, and you may want to work through them carefully. Their performance on this exercise should be a good indication of their learning of the concepts.

The purpose of question 2 is to review the material presented in chapter 1 by applying it. The idea is that these developmental issues are not easily mastered, but that doing so is important because they define the nature of developmental psychology.

The point of question 3 is to make students aware of an important assumption in the hereditarian argument about causes of intellectual differences. This exercise will help students confront Jensen's claim about the nature of intelligence by locating potential weaknesses in his argument, which otherwise appears quite strong. The answers to these multiple-choice critical thinking questions are presented as **Handout 3.**

Logistics:
- Materials: Handout 2 (the critical thinking multiple-choice questions) and Handout 3 (answers).
- Group size: Small groups (2-4) to discuss the questions, then a full class discussion.
- Approximate time: Small groups (15 to 20 minutes), full class discussion of any questions (15 minutes).

Classroom Activity 6: Critical Thinking Essay Questions and Suggestions for Helping Students Answer the Essays Discuss the answers to the critical thinking essay questions (**Handout 4**). The purpose of this activity is threefold. First, answering these questions facilitates students' understanding of concepts in chapter 3. Second, this type of essay question affords the students an opportunity to apply the concepts to their own lives, which will facilitate their retention of the material. Third, the essay format also will give students practice expressing themselves in written form. Ideas to help students answer the critical thinking essay questions are provided as **Handout 5**.

Logistics:
- Materials: Handout 4 (essay questions) and Handout 5 (helpful suggestions for the answers).
- Group size: Individual, then full class.
- Approximate time: Individual (60 minutes), full class discussion of any questions (30 minutes).

Personal Applications

Personal Application 1: All in the Family The purpose of this exercise is for students to recognize the varied influence of heredity and environment within a family. The power of genetics is phenomenal, and though each cell only contains 23 pairs of chromosomes, the possible manifestations of this hereditary material is nearly limitless. Sayings such as, "Blood is thicker than water," indicate that we feel very close to our family members because we share inherited traits. However, we can't ignore the fact that we grow up in the same environment. To what extent does that contribute to our similarity to our siblings? Or does it? The challenge of identifying the relative influences of nature and nurture is tremendous.
- Instructions for Students: Describe the major traits you share with each of your siblings. What major traits are very different for you and your siblings? Which ones do you believe are biologically based, and which ones do you think are the result of your environment? How do you explain the differences, given you have the same parents and grew up in the same family? If you are an only child, compare and contrast your traits with those of each of your parents.
- Use in the Classroom: Have students contribute examples of both similar and dissimilar traits shared with siblings. Make a list on the board of all traits and discuss which ones appear to be more "nature" based and which ones seem to be more a function of "nurture." Are there discrepancies among what students believe or is there a common perception of inherited and non-inherited traits? Challenge students to provide evidence, counterarguments, reasoning, or research methods that might serve to determine the answer.

Personal Application 2: I Am What I Am The purpose of this exercise is for students to understand the correlation between heredity and environment from Sandra Scarr's perspective of the three major influences on development. Genetic and situational contributions to an individual's make-up are inexorably linked, and the combination of influences impacts individuals in three distinct ways. The way in which we are raised not only impacts us because of the experience itself, but because those very experiences are the result of the combination of genetic and environmental influences on our *parents*. And it is our own genetic make-up that influences both the environmental influences that come to us, and those that we particularly seek out. The combination of these three processes of confounded influence creates the person we become.
- Instructions for Students: Present your profile with regard to Sandra Scarr's three ways in which heredity and environment are correlated.
  - Passive: What kind of environmental experiences did you parents provide for you because of who they were?
  - Evocative: What environmental experiences did you have due to your genetic make-up?
  - Active: What environmental experiences did you seek out due to aspects of your genetic make-up?

- Use in the Classroom: Plan to help your students get in the frame of mind for thinking through these concepts. Provide examples from your own life—including specifics about parents and their characteristics, and particular inherited traits that obviously served to influence life experiences. This may be a difficult one to grasp, so you may have students work through it in class. If certain students feel they have good examples, have them share in order to provide as many concrete examples as possible, then have students proceed to write their full responses.
- Source: Scarr, S. (1993). Biological and cultural diversity: The legacy of Darwin for development. *Child Development, 64*, 1333-1353.

Personal Application 3: The Same But Different The purpose of this exercise is to enable students to realize that a combination of factors contributes to one's environmental experiences. We automatically assume that because we live in the same house and have the same parents, we share the same environment with our siblings. But very few siblings would admit that they share similar life experiences. The older siblings will swear that the younger ones always get their way, and that their parents aren't nearly as hard on their younger brother or sister as they were on them. The younger ones believe the older siblings get to do everything, and they are treated like babies with all their restrictions. Then there are the middle children! Developmental psychologists know that it is very different to be an older brother than to have an older brother, and that despite living under the same roof, siblings' environments are not, in fact, the same.
- Instructions for Students: Consider how your environment growing up was different from those of your siblings, given you were raised in the same household.
- Use in the Classroom: This can be a fun way to get students talking and sharing childhood (and even current) stories. Feel free to share some of your own, and encourage students to compare their experiences with those of their siblings. How many felt they had an overall easier time of it than their siblings? A harder time? Were their parents' reactions to them stricter, harsher, more unfair? Conclude by emphasizing the varying circumstantial influences experienced by people functioning in very close proximity, and how that contributes to differences in behavior.

Personal Application 4: But *Everybody's* Doing It! The purpose of this exercise is to get students to consider the various individual influences on the person they've become. Judith Harris presented a shocking and controversial theory stating that parents have very little to no influence on the development of their children. She believes that genes and one's peer group are what determine the path our lives will take. This contrasts directly with numerous existing notions about human development, and the irreplaceable role that parents play. However, much data exists illustrating the profound influence of peers over parents, particularly during the adolescent years.
- Instructions for Students: Discuss the evidence from your life that supports or refutes Judith Harris' provocative contention that what parents do does not make a difference in their children's and adolescents' behavior —that genes and peers are the primary influence.
- Use in the Classroom: Given the controversial nature of this theory, it makes a great topic for class discussion! If you can read Harris' book prior to class, come prepared with some specific quotes from the book to prompt discussion and debate. Make sure that students back up their arguments for or against with specific reasoning and examples. You could also plan a more formal debate on the topic, giving students a week or two to prepare and research the material.
- Source: Harris, J.R. (1998). *The nurture assumption: Why children turn out the way they do: Parents matter less than you think and peers matter more.* New York: Free Press.

Research Project Ideas

Research Project 1: Heritability of Height The purpose of this project is to demonstrate the concept of heritability by using height as an example (**Handout 6**). Have students do a kinship study of two families (one of the families can be their own) to collect the necessary data. Students should record the height of all family members over 18 years of age and separate them by sex. Next, they should calculate the mean and range of heights of both sexes for both families and compare them. This exercise is intended to give them experience both with a kinship study design and with the concept of heritability for a variable with a clear operational definition. Once data collection is done they should answer the questions that follow.

- Which family in your sample is on average taller (for both males and females)?
- Of the taller family, how many females are taller than the females in the shorter family? How many of the males are taller than the males in the shorter family?
- From your data, does it appear that height is an inherited trait?
- What is the advantage of examining the heritability of a variable like height rather than a variable such as temperament or intelligence?
- Use in the Classroom: Have students examine family differences for the following factors:
  - Evidence for the heritability of height: The expectation is that the closer the relative is genetically, the more similar the characteristic measured will be—identical twins, fraternal twins and siblings, parents, (blood) uncles and aunts, cousins, etc.
  - Ideas about environmental differences that might play a role in height: The data from those in the older generations may be difficult to interpret because 60 or more years ago different health and nutrition standards may have influenced growth (cohort effects).
  - Reasons for separating the data according to sex: The data must be segregated by sex because humans are sexually dimorphic in height. Males are characteristically larger than females.
  - Advantages of using height as a measure rather than intelligence or temperament: Height is a good measure to use because it has an easy, noncontroversial, operational definition. Intelligence and temperament are harder to define in exact terms and are therefore more controversial.

Research Project 2: Genetic Counseling Available to You Chapter 3 introduces the concept of genetic counseling and how genetic counseling can help expectant couples learn about the possibility that their infants will suffer from genetically-based problems. While the focus in the text is on the process of counseling, it does not say much about how this service is delivered from community to community.

For this project, have students find out and report if genetic counseling services are made available in your community (**Handout 7**). They will want to discuss where one can go for these services in your community, as well as how people can find out about genetic counseling services. Form groups of up to four individuals, and divide the following tasks between individuals or pairs. Students should contact hospitals to learn whether they disseminate information about genetic counseling, and, if they do, students should obtain the pamphlets or handouts that they provide. If there are other services or organizations for expectant couples (e.g., Planned Parenthood, or divisions of social service agencies), they should find out what they offer. If the students can identify individuals in the community who provide such information, they should contact them to see if they will allow the students to interview them about their services. In addition, they can go to the public library and look up books or other reference materials about genetic counseling.

Once they have determined what information is publicly available, have them write a report that summarizes:

- How current is the information?
- What source of information is most easily and cheaply available?
- What attitude does the material seem to take toward genetic counseling?
- Are couples able to make their own decisions about their infants' chances of suffering a genetic defect with the information they obtain from genetics counselors in your community?

- What options or alternatives are available in your community?
- Are any alternatives discouraged by the genetic counselors?
- Are the services uniformly available to all community members?
- Are there significant controversies about their use?
- What political/ethical/legal issues did you discover?

- Use in the Classroom: Have the groups report their findings to the class. Use a format comfortable to you; an interesting one would be to have teams present their findings as panels. In any case, have the rest of the class carefully attend to the presentations by taking notes in a systematic way. One way to do this would be to have them prepare a data sheet with categories on which they can pool the groups' answers to the questions posed above. When all individuals or panels have reported their findings, hold a general discussion of the things people have found out. Are their reports consistent? Why or why not? How well do their efforts correspond to the material in the text? What implications do their findings have for people seeking genetic counseling in your area?

Film and Video List

The following films and videos supplement the content of chapter 3. Contact information for film distributors can be found at the front of this Instructor's Manual under Film and Video Sources.

Biological Growth: Nature's Child (Insight Media, 60 minutes). This video explores the nature/nurture controversy with a focus on genetic influences on intelligence, personality, temperament, sex differences, and mental illness. It also deals with environmental influences on prenatal development.

Boy or Girl? When Doctors Choose a Child's Sex (Films for the Humanities and Sciences, 14 minutes). *ABC News* correspondent Dr. Nancy Snyderman investigates the once-accepted belief that surgical sex assignment determines gender. Arguments are made for the notion that gender comes from the brain, not the body, and no operation can alter that basic fact.

Down's Syndrome (Films for the Humanities and Sciences, 28 minutes). This is a Phil Donahue program that is devoted to presenting medical and psychological break-throughs in the treatment of Down's syndrome.

How Babies Get Made (BBC-TV, 58 minutes). This video examines the processes by which embryos develop from single cells into complex organisms and the efforts of scientists to discover the cellular and genetic mechanisms that account for both normal and abnormal embryological development.

Keltie's Beard: A Woman's Story (Filmakers Library, 9 minutes). This touching film illustrates genetic variations and personal reactions to a unique woman who comes from a family in which the women have heavy facial hair. Keltie takes the atypical course of not removing this hair.

Little People (Filmakers Library, 58 minutes). This video focuses on a genetic condition that influences one's entire life by highlighting discrimination and difficulties of access for dwarfs.

Reproduction: Designer Babies (Films for the Humanities and Sciences, 20 minutes). This program examines some of the issues raised by the potential uses and misuses of genetic technology. Topics include DNA, implications of genetic manipulation, prenatal screening techniques, genetic abnormalities, artificial insemination, and embryo transplants.

Yours to Keep (Direct Cinema Limited, 75 minutes). This is a movie focuses on an individual with Down's syndrome who is "just like other people, but lower."

Web Site Suggestions

The URLs for general sites, common to all chapters, can be found at the front of this Instructor's manual under Useful Web Sites. At the time of publication, all sites were current and active, however, please be advised that you may occasionally encounter a dead link.

Behavior Genetics Association Home Page
http://www.bga.org/

Down Syndrome
http://dir.yahoo.com/Health/Diseases_and_Conditions/Down_Syndrome/

Fertility Weekly: A Weekly Digest of Fertility and Human Reproduction
http://www.newsfile.com/homepage/060297fn.htm

Holt International Children's Services: Specializes in Adoptions
http://www.holtintl.org/

Infertility
http://dir.yahoo.com/Health/Reproductive_Health/Infertility/

National Society for Genetic Counselors
http://www.nsgc.org/

Prenatal Development and Prenatal Diagnostic Techniques
http://www.amnionet.com/

Sex Reassignments – Gender: Biology vs. Environment?
http://www.indiana.edu/~lggender/john-joan.html

Handout 1 (CA 2)

Ethical Dilemmas Regarding Genetic Counseling

In order to appreciate the value of the information you are learning, it is sometimes useful to examine situations faced by people every day in which knowledge of life-span development can be useful, but at the same time, controversial. In the November 1994 issue of *Science News*, four ethical dilemmas were presented and readers were asked to write in and indicate how they would respond to each situation. Two of the dilemmas are presented below. Answer the questions that follow the dilemma.

The first scenario deals with dwarfism and is quoted from *Science News*.

A husband and his pregnant wife seek genetic counseling. Each carries one flawed copy of the gene responsible for achondroplasia; therefore, they are both dwarfs. Recently, a California research team described the mutation in a gene on chromosome 4 that causes achondroplasia. The counselor explains that genetic testing can determine whether the fetus has inherited the mutated gene. In the discussion, the couple informs the counselor that they will abort any fetus that carries two mutant genes. That's not surprising, since children born with two such genes rarely survive beyond infancy. This couple has had a child in this circumstance who died when 2 months old.

This time around, they way, they want a baby who is heterozygous for the achondroplasia trait. This child inherits a flawed gene from one parent and a healthy gene from the other parent. That genetic combination means the child will be a dwarf—just like the parents. At the same time, the parents say, they will abort any fetus that does not inherit one copy of the mutant gene. Should the counseling center perform the test, knowing that the couple plan to abort a healthy fetus?

Some of the things to consider include the fact that achondroplasia is a serious disorder. The bones can be abnormal in structure, sometimes requiring the use of a wheelchair. Yet, many dwarfs live long, healthy lives and don't regard their condition as a disability. In addition, some couples with this condition worry about problems involving in raising a normal-sized child.

- What is the ethical dilemma for the scenario?
- What would you do if you were the genetic counselor?
- Present arguments for both sides of the issue.

The second scenario deals with paternity and is quoted from *Science News*.

A husband and wife have a child who suffers from cystic fibrosis (CF), an incurable, fatal hereditary disease that results in frequent infections and difficulty breathing. The couple wants to determine their risk of having another child with this disorder. Because CF is a recessive disorder, a child usually must inherit the CF gene from both parents to get the disease. A child with just one CF gene is a carrier: Such a person doesn't have the disorder but can pass the trait on to the next generation. The DNA test revealed that the mother of the child carried the CF trait. However, her husband did not. The DNA tests showed that he was not the biological father of the child.

The fact significantly decreased the couple's chance of having another child with CF. But the test has put the counselor in a difficult situation. Should the counselor tell the couple about the nonpaternity findings? Should the mother be told privately? If so, is the center colluding with the mother to withhold information from the husband?

This case brings up issues concerning the biological father of the child. This man has not contracted with the genetics center for the test, yet the counselor now knows that this man is probably a carrier of the mutant gene for CF. Should the genetic counselor call him and tell him about his risk?

- What are the ethical dilemmas for the scenario?
- What would you do if you were the genetic counselor?
- Present arguments for both sides of the issue.
- Sources: Fackelmann, K. (1994). Beyond the genome: The ethics of DNA testing. *Science News, 146,* 298-299. Fackelmann, K. (1994). DNA dilemmas: Readers and "experts" weigh in on biomedical ethics. *Science News, 146,* 408-410.

72

Critical Thinking Multiple-Choice Questions

1. Many developmentalists believe that an important inherited determinant of personality is temperament. Look ahead to chapter 7 (Socioemotional Development in Infancy) to find out how researchers have attempted to identify basic dimensions of temperament and to describe the extent of their stability in individuals' lives. Which genetic principle is best illustrated by this work? Circle the letter of the best answer and explain why it is the best answer and why each other answer is not as good.

   a. dominant-recessive genes principle
   b. polygenic inheritance
   c. genotype/phenotype differences
   d. reaction range
   e. canalization

2. Review The Nature of Development box in chapter 1, which describes several important issues in developmental psychology. Which of these issues receives the greatest emphasis in chapter 3? Circle the letter of the best answer and explain why it is the best answer and why each other answer is not as good.

   a. biological, cognitive, and social processes in development
   b. continuity versus discontinuity
   c. nature versus nurture
   d. stability versus change
   e. periods of development

3. A recurrent and often bitter controversy in the study of intelligence is the issue of how heredity and environment contribute to intelligence. Arthur Jensen, a leading figure in the debate, has contributed both data and argument to the "nature" view. Which of the following statements represents an important assumption, rather than an inference or an observation, of Jensen's argument? Circle the letter of the best answer and explain why it is the best answer and why each other answer is not as good.

   a. Identical twins have identical genetic endowments.
   b. Identical twins should have IQs that are more similar than the IQs of ordinary siblings.
   c. The correlation between IQs of twins reared together is .89.
   d. Differences between the correlations of IQs for twins reared together versus those of twins reared apart indicate that environment has only a weak effect on intelligence.
   e. The environments of twins reared together versus those of twins reared apart are very different.

Suggested Answers for Critical Thinking Multiple-Choice Questions

1. Many developmentalists believe that an important inherited determinant of personality is temperament. Look ahead to chapter 7 to find out how researchers have attempted to identify basic dimensions of temperament and to describe the extent of their stability in individuals' lives. Which genetic principle is best illustrated by this work? Circle the letter of the best answer and explain why it is the best answer and why each other answer is not as good.

   a. The <u>dominant-recessive genes principle</u> is not the best answer. This principle refers to a single gene pairing in which one gene determines a quality of the trait governed by the gene. There is a distinctive pattern of probabilities for the expression of each variation of the trait. In any case, temperament is not thought to be controlled by a single gene pair, nor is there a known pattern of probabilities for any given dimension of temperament. The text presents no information on how specific genes influence temperament.

   b. <u>Polygenic inheritance</u> is not the best answer. The important point, as above, is that no information specific to this point appears in the text with regard to temperament. The textbook does indicate, however, that traits such as intelligence are probably based on polygenic inheritance.

   c. <u>Genotype/phenotype differences</u> is not the best answer. The problem is that no systematic comparisons are presented to indicate the relationship for temperament between genotypes and phenotypes.

   d. <u>Reaction range</u> is the best answer. The text points out that the heritability of temperament seems to decline with age. Traits such as introversion and extroversion seem to be change, within limits. This most clearly corresponds to what is meant by the concept of range of reaction. Different environments seem to produce different expressions of the genetic basis for temperament.

   e. <u>Canalization</u> is not the best answer. Canalization refers to traits that show little environmentally caused variability in their expression. Such traits should have uniform heritability during the individual's life span, but the dimensions of temperament do not.

2. Review The Nature of Development box in chapter 1, which describes several important issues in developmental psychology. Which of these issues receives the greatest emphasis in chapter 3? Circle the letter of the best answer and explain why it is the best answer and why each other answer is not as good.

   a. <u>Biological, cognitive, and social processes in development</u> is not the best answer. These processes are simply not uniformly discussed in the chapter. The focus of the chapter is on one aspect of biological processes: genetic determination.

   b. <u>Continuity versus discontinuity</u> is not the best answer. The course of development—either prenatally or postnatally—is not described.

   c. <u>Nature versus nurture</u> is the best answer. This is a continuing theme of the chapter, throughout which the point is made that environments interact with genotypes in the course of development. For example, natural selection determines which genotypes survive. In the discussion of genetic principles, it is clear that genetic expression is a function, in varying degrees, of environmental influence. Research on intelligence is driven by the question of how much of the variation in each individual is determined by heredity and how much by environment.

   d. <u>Stability versus change</u> is not the best answer. There is material on this issue in the discussion of intelligence, but the issue is not as pervasive as the nature-nurture issue.

   e. <u>Periods of development</u> is not the best answer. These simply receive no treatment in this chapter. The discussion of the biological bases of development is not organized around separate developmental periods.

3. A recurrent and often bitter controversy in the study of intelligence is the issue of how heredity and environment contribute to intelligence. Arthur Jensen, a leading figure in the debate, has contributed both data and argument to the "nature" view. Which of the following statements represents an important assumption, rather than an inference or an observation, of Jensen's argument? Circle the letter of the best answer and explain why it is the best answer and why each other answer is not as good.

    a. Identical twins have identical genetic endowments is an observation. It is a factual statement about the nature of identical twins' heredity.

    b. Identical twins should have IQs that are more similar than the IQs of ordinary siblings is an inference. It is a hypothesis about the correlations based on the belief that heredity makes an important and direct contribution to individual differences in intellectual ability.

    c. The correlation between IQs of twins reared together is .89 is an observation taken directly from research on the correlations of IQs in twins reared together.

    d. Differences between the correlations of IQs for twins reared together versus those of twins reared apart indicate that environment has only a weak effect on intelligence is an inference. It interprets the finding that these two types of correlation do not differ very much.

    e. The environments of twins reared together versus those of twins reared apart are very different is the assumption. According to the text, Jensen and others have not verified this belief about the environments of twins reared together and twins reared apart, but rather take it for granted that these environments differ. In fact, this belief is a point that critics of Jensen's work have challenged.

Critical Thinking Essay Questions

Your answers to these questions demonstrate an ability to comprehend and apply ideas discussed in this chapter.

1. Explain the concepts of natural selection and evolutionary psychology.

2. Explain the relationship between genes, chromosomes, and DNA. Also indicate how these entities function in reproduction.

3. In your own words, what is a genotype and a phenotype? Also explain how these concepts relate to the concepts of dominant and recessive genes.

4. Compare and contrast the concepts of reaction range and canalization.

5. Describe the methods used by behavior geneticists to study heredity's influence on behavior.

6. Indicate and explain at least three examples of abnormalities in genes and chromosomes.

7. Assume that you have received a number of tests to assess fetal abnormalities. Identify and explain each procedure and what you would learn from it.

8. What is infertility? What causes infertility? Explain what an infertile couple can do to have a baby.

9. Indicate how you would explain to a friend that heredity and environment interact in various ways to produce developments. Also provide an example of each of the three types of interaction and shared and nonshared environmental influences that you would use to help your friend understand this concept.

Ideas to Help You Answer Critical Thinking Essay Questions

1. These concepts are inherently connected to specific examples of the phenomena of this aspect of development. Read the examples presented in the text, then come up with your own example(s). Use this to launch your explanation of natural selection and evolutionary psychology and their tenets.

2. A visual representation will be helpful when approaching this essay. Create a careful drawing of genes, chromosomes, and DNA, as there is a building block structure. Establishing their physical relationship to one another will provide a clearer context in which to explain their roles in reproduction.

3. The best way to describe something in your own words is to either teach someone else about it or pretend to teach it to someone else. When you imagine approaching an audience who knows nothing about the subject matter, it causes you to explain things in a number of different ways, anticipate questions regarding the topic, and provide explicit examples to demonstrate the concepts. Do this as you write about genotypes, phenotypes, dominant and recessive genes.

4. Create a grid to more clearly illustrate the relationship between the concepts of reaction range and canalization.

5. Begin by describing the bigger issue of trying to assess the relative influences of biology and the environment on behavior. This will provide the context to better explain and understand the methods used to study the specific contributions of heredity.

6. For a more complete learning experience, combine your efforts on this question and the next. Create a grid delineating genetic and chromosomal abnormalities on one axis. On the other, list the tests used to assess fetal abnormalities. In the resulting intersecting squares, describe the characteristics and causes of the abnormalities, and the procedures and results of the testing methods relating to them.

7. Look at the suggestion for question 6 above for help on this question.

8. Pretend you are providing counseling to couples having difficulty conceiving a child. Your job is to inform them about the nature of infertility, what may contribute to it, and their options to overcome it.

9. Begin with either a brief story about your life and description of the person you've become, or have your friend provide one. Make a list of what you believe are genetic-based trait, and a list of traits you've acquired from experience. This will demonstrate the difficulty in knowing for certain the contributions of nature and nurture in an individual's development, and will provide a preface for your presentation of examples for each of the three types of interaction and shared and nonshared environmental influences.

Handout 6 (RP 1)

Heritability of Height

The purpose of this project is to demonstrate the concept of heritability by using height. You will do a kinship study of two families (one of the families can be your own) to collect the necessary data. Record the height of all family members over 18 years of age and separate them by sex. Calculate the mean and range of heights of both sexes for both families and compare them. This exercise is intended to give you experience both with a kinship study design and with the concept of heritability for a variable with a clear operational definition. Use the following data sheet to record heights. Then answer the questions below.

Person/Sex	Family 1	Family 2		Data	Family 1	Family 2
Self	____	____		Average female	____	____
Mother	____	____		Average male	____	____
Father	____	____		Tallest female	____	____
Grandmother 1	____	____		Tallest male	____	____
Grandmother 2	____	____		Shortest female	____	____
Grandfather 1	____	____		Shortest male	____	____
Grandfather 2	____	____				
Sibling	____	____				
Sibling	____	____				
Sibling	____	____				
Aunt	____	____				
Aunt	____	____				
Aunt	____	____				
Uncle	____	____				
Uncle	____	____				
Uncle	____	____				
Cousin	____	____				
Cousin	____	____				
Cousin	____	____				
Cousin	____	____				
Other	____	____				
Other	____	____				
Other	____	____				

Questions:

- Which family in your sample is on average taller (for both males and females)?
- Of the taller family, how many females are taller than the females in the shorter family? How many of the males are taller than the males in the shorter family?
- From your data, does it appear that height is an inherited trait?
- What is the advantage of examining the heritability of a variable like height rather than a variable such as temperament or intelligence?

Genetic Counseling Available to You

Chapter 3 introduces the concept of genetic counseling and how genetic counseling can help expectant couples learn about the possibility that their infants will suffer from genetically-based problems. While the focus in the text is on the process of counseling, it does not say much about how this service is delivered from community to community.

For this project, you will find out and report if genetic counseling services are made available in your community. You will want to discuss where one can go for these services in your community, as well as how people can find out about genetic counseling services. Form groups of up to four individuals, and divide the following tasks between individuals or pairs. Contact hospitals to learn whether they disseminate information about genetic counseling, and, if they do, obtain the pamphlets or handouts that they provide. If there are other services or organizations for expectant couples (e.g., Planned Parenthood, or divisions of social service agencies), find out what they offer. If you can identify individuals in the community who provide such information, contact them to see if they will allow you to interview them about their services. Go to the public library and look up books or other reference materials about genetic counseling.

Once you have determined what information is publically available, write a report that summarizes the information that you obtained. In addition, address the following questions/statements:

Once you have determined what information is publicly available, write a report that summarizes:
- How current is the information?
- What source of information is most easily and cheaply available?
- What attitude does the material seem to take toward genetic counseling?
- Are couples able to make their own decisions about their infants' chances of suffering a genetic defect with the information they obtain from genetics counselors in your community?
- What options or alternatives are available in your community?
- Are any alternatives discouraged by the genetic counselors?
- Are the services uniformly available to all community members?
- Are there significant controversies about their use?
- What political/ethical/legal issues did you discover?

Chapter 4: Prenatal Development and Birth

Total Teaching Package Outline

Lecture Outline	Resource References
Prenatal Development and Birth	PowerPoint Presentation: See www.mhhe.com Cognitive Maps: See Appendix A

Prenatal Development
• The Course of Prenatal Development
 	
    -The Germinal Period
    -The Embryonic Period
    -The Fetal Period
	LO1
	OHT 23, 24, 31, OHT 38 & IB, OHT 48 & IB:
	     Prenatal Development
	LS1: Technology and Images of Prenatal Dev.
	F/V: Developmental Phases Before and After Birth
	F/V: Invasion of the Embryo
	F/V: Prenatal Development
	F/V: Pregnancy and Birth
	F/V: Psychological Development Before Birth
	F/V: Reproduction: Fetal Development
	WS: The Visible Embryo
	
	LO2
	LO3

• Cultural Beliefs about Pregnancy	LO4 CA1: Reproductive Double Standards for Men and Women PA1: In a Family Way
Teratology and Hazards to Prenatal Development • Exploring Teratology	 WS: Teratology Society LS2: Principles of Teratogenic Effects

• Prescription and Nonprescription Drugs
 	
• Psychoactive Drugs
	LO5
	OHT39 & IB: Drug Use during Pregnancy
	LS3: Dangers of Drug Use during Pregnancy
	CA2: Court's Treatment of Substance
	     Abusing Pregnant Women
	F/V: Pregnancy and Substance Abuse
	
	LS4: Birth Defects Are Too Often Blamed on
	     Alcohol

- Alcohol
 	
   -Nicotine
 	
   -Illegal Drugs
	CA3: Fetal Alcohol Syndrome Quiz
	F/V: David with Fetal Alcohol Syndrome
	F/V: Fetal Alcohol Syndrome and Other Drug
	     Use During Pregnancy
	F/V: Fetal Alcohol Syndrome: Life Sentence
	RP1: Why Do Some Pregnant Women Drink,
	     Smoke, or Use Drugs?
	
	F/V: Unborn Addicts

• Environmental Hazards	LO6
• Other Maternal Factors -Infectious Diseases -Nutrition -Emotional States and Stress -Maternal Age	F/V: AIDS Babies WS: Caffeine in Pregnancy
• Paternal Factors	LO7
• Prenatal Care	OHT32: Mothers with Late or No Prenatal Care
• Positive Prenatal Development	
Birth • Exploring the Birth Process	PA2: Oh, the Pain!
-Stages of Birth	LO8
-The Fetus/Newborn Transition	LO9
-Childbirth Strategies	LO10 F/V: Birth without Violence F/V: Contemporary Childbirth F/V: A Human Life Emerges F/V: The Process of Birth WS: Childbirth
• Preterm Infants and Age-Weight Considerations -Preterm and Low-Birthweight Infants -Long-Term Outcomes for Low-Birthweight Infants	LO11 OHT40 & IB: Percentage of LBW Infants WS: Evidence-Based Ethics and the Care of Premature Infants
• Measures of Neonatal Health and Responsiveness	LO12 F/V: Brazelton Neonatal Behavioral Assessment Scale: An Introduction WS: Apgar Scoring
The Postpartum Period • What Is the Postpartum Period? • Physical Adjustments • Emotional and Psychological Adjustments • Bonding	LO13 RP2: Fatherhood F/V: The Newborn: Development and Discovery WS: Postpartum Depression CA4: Reasons to Have Children or Not F/V: The Newborn: Development and Discovery

Review	PA3: The Pitter Patter of Little Feet
	CA5: Critical Thinking Multiple-Choice
	CA6: Critical Thinking Essays
	F/V: The Mind: Development

Chapter Outline

PRENATAL DEVELOPMENT

The Course of Prenatal Development

- Prenatal development is divided into three periods:

  The Germinal Period

  - The **germinal period** takes place in the first 2 weeks after conception. It includes the creation of the zygote, continued cell division, and the attachment of the zygote to the uterine wall.
    - The **blastocyst** is the inner layer of cells that develop into the embryo.
    - The **trophoblast** is the outer layer of cells that develops and provides nutrition and support for the embryo.
    - Implantation, attachment of the zygote to the uterine wall, occurs 10 days after conception.

  The Embryonic Period

  - The **embryonic period** occurs from 2 to 8 weeks after conception.
  - The rate of cell differentiation intensifies, support systems for the cells form, and organs appear.
    - Endoderm, inner layer of cells, develops into the digestive and respiratory systems.
    - Ectoderm, outermost layer of cells, becomes the nervous system, sensory system, and skin.
    - Mesoderm, middle layer of cells, becomes the circulatory system, bones, muscles, excretory system, and reproductive system.
  - Life-support systems for the embryo mature and develop rapidly:
    - The **placenta** is a life-support system that consists of a disk-shaped group of tissues in which small blood vessels from the mother and the offspring intertwine but do not join.
    - The **umbilical cord** is a life-support system, containing two arteries and one vein, that connects the baby to the placenta.
    - The **amnion** is a bag that contains clear fluid in which the developing embryo floats.
    - **Organogenesis** is the process of organ formation that takes place during the first 2 months of prenatal development.

  The Fetal Period

  - The **fetal period** begins 2 months after conception and lasts for 7 months, on average.
  - Growth and development continue their dramatic course and organ systems mature to the point at which life can be sustained outside of the womb.

Cultural Beliefs about Pregnancy

- Specific actions in pregnancy are often determined by cultural beliefs (whether pregnancy is viewed as a medical condition or a natural occurrence).
- Certain behaviors (prenatal care) are expected if pregnancy is viewed as a medical condition.

Teratology and Hazards to Prenatal Development
Exploring Teratology
- A **teratogen** is any agent that causes a birth defect.
- Teratology is the field of study that investigates the causes of birth defects.
- Sensitivity to teratogens begins about 3 weeks after conception. The probability of a structural defect is greatest early in the embryonic period, during organogenesis.
- Exposure during the fetal period usually is more likely to stunt growth or cause problems in the way organs function.

Prescription and Nonprescription Drugs
- In the 1960s, thalidomide was taken by some women in order to reduce morning sickness and caused limb malformation in some of the developing fetuses.
- Prescription drugs, such as antibiotics, some antidepressants, estrogen, and Accutane (acne medicine) have teratogenic effects.
- Nonprescription drugs, such as diet pills, aspirin, and caffeine have potential teratogenic effects.

Psychoactive Drugs
- Psychoactive drugs are drugs that act on the nervous system to alter states of consciousness, modify perceptions, and change moods.

Alcohol
- **Fetal alcohol syndrome** (FAS) is a cluster of abnormalities that appears in the offspring of mothers who drink alcohol heavily during pregnancy. The abnormalities include facial deformities, and defective limbs and heart. Most of these children are below average in intelligence, and some are mentally retarded.
- When pregnant women drink moderately (1-2 drinks a day) negative effects on their offspring have been found.

Nicotine
- Cigarette smoking by pregnant women can adversely influence prenatal development. There is a higher incidence of preterm births and lower birthweights, and a higher chance of fetal and neonatal deaths.

Cocaine
- The most consistent finding is that cocaine exposure during prenatal development is associated with reduced birthweight, length, and head circumference. Information-processing deficits have been found as well.
- Caution is necessary when interpreting these findings as poverty, malnutrition, etc. may contribute to the negative effects found.

Marijuana
- Marijuana use during pregnancy has been associated with increased tremors and startles in newborns and poor verbal and memory development at 4 years of age.

Heroin
- Young infants exposed prenatally to heroin are addicted and show withdrawal symptoms at birth. Behavioral problems and attention deficits continue to be present.

Environmental Hazards
- Potential environmental hazards include radiation, environmental pollutants, toxic wastes, prolonged exposure to heat in saunas and hot tubs, and low-level electromagnetic radiation from computer monitors.

Other Maternal Factors
Infectious Diseases
- Maternal diseases and infections can produce defects by crossing the placental barrier or they can cause damage during the birth process.
  - Rubella (German measles), syphilis, genital herpes, and human immunodeficiency virus (HIV) can all affect the developing organism.

Nutrition
- A developing fetus depends completely on its mother for nutrition, which comes from the mother's blood. The total number of calories and appropriate levels of protein, vitamins, and minerals are important factors.
  - The lack of folic acid is linked to neural tube defects in the offspring (spina bifida).

Emotional States and Stress
- Maternal anxiety and stress are linked with less than optimal prenatal and birth outcomes (premature delivery).

Maternal Age
- Two age periods may lead to problems for the offspring's development: adolescence (higher incidence of premature infants and infant mortality) and mothers of age 30 or older (infertility and increased risk for Down syndrome).

Paternal Factors
- Men's exposure to lead, radiation, certain pesticides, and petrochemicals can cause abnormalities in sperm that lead to miscarriage or diseases. Father's smoking during the mother's pregnancy can cause newborns to be lighter at birth and increase the risk of childhood cancers.

Prenatal Care
- Prenatal care varies extensively, but usually involves medical-care services with a defined schedule of visits. Screening for treatable conditions, education about pregnancy, labor and delivery, and newborn care are included.

Positive Prenatal Development
- Most pregnancies proceed without negative outcomes. It is important for prospective mothers and pregnant women to avoid the vulnerabilities that teratogens produce.

BIRTH
Exploring the Birth Process
Stages of Birth
- The birth process occurs in three stages:
  - The first stage lasts about 12 to 24 hours for a woman having her first child. The cervix dilates to about 4 centimeters due to uterine contractions.
  - The second stage, which lasts approximately $1\frac{1}{2}$ hours, begins when a baby's head moves through the cervix and ends with the baby's complete emergence.
  - The third stage, which lasts a few minutes, is called afterbirth at which time the placenta, umbilical cord, and other membranes are detached and expelled.

The Fetus/Newborn Transition
- Anoxia is the condition in which the fetus/newborn has an insufficient supply of oxygen due to the placenta and umbilical cord being compressed during uterine contractions. Anoxia can cause brain damage.
- Hormones, adrenaline and noradrenalin, are secreted to protect the fetus against stress.

Childbirth Strategies
- Childbirth Setting and Attendants
  - Most births in the U.S. take place in hospitals with physicians in attendance. Many women have the baby's father or a birth coach in the room during delivery.
  - In many countries, the birth is attended by a **doula**, a caregiver who provides continuous physical, emotional, and educational support for the woman before, during, and after childbirth.

Methods of Delivery
- Three basic kinds of drugs are used for labor:
  - Analgesics (tranquilizers, barbiturates, and narcotics) relieve pain.
  - Anesthesia is used in late first-stage labor and during expulsion of the baby to block sensation in an area of the body or to block consciousness.
    - An epidural block is regional anesthesia that numbs the body from the waist down.
    - Oxytocics are synthetic hormones that are used to stimulate contractions.
  - The current trend is for women to use some medication during delivery, but to keep it to a minimum and to broadly educate the pregnant woman regarding labor medication.
  - **Natural childbirth** was developed in 1914 by an English obstetrician, Grantley Dick-Read. It attempts to reduce the mother's pain by decreasing her fear through education about childbirth and by teaching her to use breathing methods and relaxation techniques during delivery.
  - Ferdinand Lamaze developed **prepared childbirth**. This strategy is similar to natural childbirth but includes a special breathing technique to control pushing in the final stages of labor.
- In a cesarean delivery, the baby is removed from the mother's uterus through an incision made in her abdomen. A cesarean section is often performed if the baby is in a **breech position**, which causes the baby's buttocks to be the first part to emerge from the vagina.

Preterm Infants and Age-Weight Considerations
Preterm and Low-Birthweight Infants
- Full-term infants have grown in the womb for 38 to 42 weeks between conception and delivery.
- Preterm and low-birthweight infants are considered high-risk.
  - A **preterm infant** is one who is born prior to 38 weeks after conception.
  - A **low-birthweight infant** is born after a regular gestation period of 38 to 42 weeks but weighs less than $5\frac{1}{2}$ pounds. The number of low-birthweight babies has increased in the last two decades (adolescents having babies, drug use, and poor nutrition).
Long-Term Outcomes for Low-Birthweight Infants
- Although most low-birthweight infants are normal and healthy, as a group they have more health and developmental problems than normal-birthweight infants do.
- The number and severity of these problems increases as birthweight decreases (brain damage, cerebral palsy, lung or liver disease, learning disability, attention deficit disorder, asthma).

Measures of Neonatal Health and Responsiveness
- The **Apgar Scale** is a method widely used to assess the health of newborns at 1 and 5 minutes after birth. The Apgar Scale evaluates infants' heart rate, respiratory effort, muscle tone, body color, and reflex irritability.
- More thorough assessments can be made with the **Brazelton Neonatal Behavioral Assessment Scale**, performed within 24-36 hours after birth to evaluate the newborn's neurological development, reflexes, and reactions to people.

THE POSTPARTUM PERIOD
What Is the Postpartum Period?
- The **postpartum period** is the period after childbirth or delivery. It is a time when the woman's body adjusts, both physically and psychologically, to the process of childbearing. It lasts for about 6 weeks or until the body has completed its adjustment and has returned to a prepregnant state.

Physical Adjustments
- Fatigue is common and can undermine the new mother's sense of well-being and confidence in her ability to cope with a new baby and a new family life.
- Involution is the process by which the uterus returns to its prepregnant state (5-6 weeks).

Emotional and Psychological Adjustments
- Common maternal emotional fluctuations may be due to a number of factors: hormonal changes, fatigue, inexperience or lack of confidence with newborns, or extensive caregiving demands.
- The following signs may indicate a need for professional counseling for postpartum adaptation: excessive worrying, depression, extreme changes in appetite, crying spells, and insomnia.
- Paternal reactions may include jealousy regarding the woman's attention to the baby.

Bonding
- **Bonding** is the occurrence of close contact, especially physical, between parents and newborn in the period shortly after birth.
- Some physicians consider this time critical for the development of emotional attachment. However, research findings do not support this claim.

Learning Objectives

1. Describe the germinal, embryonic, and fetal periods of prenatal development
2. Define placenta and umbilical cord, and describe how they prevent the transmission of harmful substances from mother to infant.
3. Define organogenesis and explain its importance.
4. Understand how cultural beliefs affect the experience of pregnancy.
5. Describe the effects that drugs can have on the unborn child.
6. Discuss maternal diseases and conditions that influence prenatal development such as rubella, syphilis, herpes, and HIV/AIDS.
7. Explain how maternal and paternal characteristics affect prenatal development.
8. Describe the three stages of birth.
9. State what researchers know and do not know about the effects of drugs administered during childbirth.
10. Contrast the different childbirth strategies, noting the pros and cons of each.
11. Define and distinguish between preterm infants and low-birthweight infants.
12. Describe the two most widely used measures of neonatal health and responsiveness.
13. Describe the physical, emotional, and psychological adjustments women have to make after pregnancy.

Key Terms

amnion
Apgar scale
blastocyst
bonding
Brazelton Neonatal Behavior
   Assessment Scale
breech position
doula
embryonic period
fetal alcohol syndrome
fetal period

germinal period
low-birthweight infants
natural childbirth
organogenesis
placenta
postpartum period
prepared childbirth
preterm infant
teratogen
trophoblast
umbilical cord

Key People

T. Berry Brazelton
Grantley Dick-Read
Christine Dunkel-Scheltter

Ferinand Lamaze
Ann Streissguth

Lecture Suggestions

Lecture Suggestion 1: Technology and Images of Prenatal Development A compelling way to bring home the value of observation as a research technique and, at the same time, stress the importance of prenatal development as a pivotal period in human development is to present and discuss images of prenatal development. Amazing images of prenatal development are available at The Visible Embryo web site (http://www.visembryo.com). The spiral represents the 23 stages occurring in the first trimester of pregnancy and every two weeks of the second and third trimesters. Use the spiral to navigate through the 40 weeks of pregnancy and preview the unique changes in each stage of human development. Images are provided for the first trimester with in-depth descriptions for all 40 weeks of pregnancy.

Lecture Suggestion 2: Principles of Teratogenic Effects The concept of an interaction was introduced in chapter 3 and can be further elaborated with a lecture about the principles that govern the effects of teratogens on the developing embryo. These effects vary depending upon the genotype of the mother and the baby, as well as the amount and timing of exposure to the teratogen. Some of the principles of teratogenic effect are:

- The effects of a teratogen vary with the developmental stage of the embryo.
  - Systems or organs in the process of development (organogenesis) are generally affected more than are completed organs and systems. Since the various organ systems begin and end their prenatal development at different times, their sensitivity to agents varies over time.
  - The most vulnerable time for the brain is from 15 to 25 days post conception, for the eye from 24 to 40 days post conception, and the heart from 20 to 40 days post conception. Figure 4.5 in your textbook further illustrates this point.
- Individual teratogens influence specific developing tissue, which leads to particular patterns of developmental deviations.
  - German measles affect mainly the heart, eyes, and brain. Thalidomide, the anti-nausea drug from the 1960s, results in malformation of the limbs.
- Both maternal and fetal genotypes can affect the developing organism's response to teratogenic agents and may play an important role in the appearance of abnormalities in offspring.
  - Not all pregnant women who used Thalidomide or had German measles during early pregnancy produced infants with abnormalities.
- The physiological or pathological status of the mother will influence the action of a teratogen.
  - Not only will nutritional deficiencies themselves directly affect prenatal development, they may intensify the adverse effects on the fetus of certain drugs ingested by the mother. Other maternal factors such as obesity, high blood pressure, and liver dysfunction may increase the impact of damage by teratogens.
- The level of teratogenic agent that will produce malformations in the offspring may show only mild detrimental effects on the mother, or none at all.
  - Radiation from x-rays, drugs (alcohol, thalidomide, etc.), and dietary deficiencies may have no impact on the mother, but cause gross deviations in the infant.

As you present each principle, relate it to the concept of interaction as well as other relevant developmental concepts. For example, the first principle is an example of an interaction in which developmental level mediates the influence of a specific experience. This idea is related to the concepts of critical/sensitive period, fixation, and developmental readiness. The third principle provides a complicated example of heredity/environment interaction, and an example of dyadic interaction (physiological level).

- Sources: Hogge, A. (1990). Teratology. In I.R. Merkatz & J. E. Thompson (Eds.), *New perspectives on prenatal care*. New York: Elsevier. Moore, K., & Persaud, T. (1993). *The developing human: Clinically oriented embryology* (5th). Philadelphia: Saunders.

Lecture Suggestion 3: Dangers of Drug Use during Pregnancy Information about the teratogenic effects of "everyday drug use" is very important to students as present or future parents. You may wish to underscore this with a lecture that explores this issue in greater depth than is possible in the text. Place special emphasis on the potential dangers of even normal everyday drug use, in particular the use of caffeine (coffee), nicotine (cigarettes), and alcohol. Some important points to address include:

- These teratogens have graded effects, which make it risky to talk about "safe" levels of exposure. For example, having just one serving of alcohol a day increases risks for developmental disorders. Fetal alcohol syndrome can have mild, moderate, or severe effects on the developing fetus.
- Effects of drug exposure may be direct or indirect. Alcohol use may lead to organic abnormalities; nicotine use may lead to temperamental difficulties in babies, which can reduce the quality of their interactions with their caregivers.
- Risks can be vitiated by discontinuing use of the drug. It is not reasonable to continue using a drug on the grounds that harm has already been done and cannot be reversed.
- Risks may be dependent on the timing of prenatal exposure (see Lecture Suggestion 1: Technology and Images of Prenatal Development).
- The drug use habits of both parents can affect the fetus, either directly or indirectly.
  - Second-hand smoke has been found to adversely affect fetuses. Maternal exposure to environmental tobacco smoke for 1 hour or more per day is associated with spontaneous abortion (Windham et al., 1992).
  - The quality of care and support a husband can provide to his pregnant wife could influence the outcome of the pregnancy.
- Caffeine exposure is common in pregnancy. The consumption of greater than 300 mg/d of caffeine during pregnancy is potentially harmful. This is equivalent to three (8 oz) cups of coffee or 7.5 cups of tea/cola. The results indicated that women who consumed caffeine in moderation (less than 300 mg/day) did not have a significant risk for pregnancy loss, intrauterine growth retardation, or microcephaly. (http://www.mostgene.org/gd/gdvol11d.htm)
- An important addition to your lecture could be a treatment of how mothers (and fathers) can deal with drug use habits that may endanger their unborn baby. Classroom Activity 2: The Court's Treatment of Substance Abusing Pregnant Women addresses issues related to drug use during pregnancy and the social ramifications for the mother, father, and child.
- Sources: Mills, J., et al. (1993). Moderate caffeine use and the risk of spontaneous abortion and intrauterine growth retardation. *Journal of the American Medical Association, 269*, 593-597. Eskenazi, B. (1993).Caffeine during pregnancy: Grounds for concern? 2973-4. Windham, G.C., Swan, S.H., & Fenster, L. (1992). Parental cigarette smoking and the risk of spontaneous abortion. *American Journal of Epidemiology, 135*, 1394-1403.

Lecture Suggestion 4: Birth Defects are Too Often Blamed on Alcohol Students are aware that pregnant women should not drink alcohol during pregnancy because alcohol exposure has been linked to birth defects such as small heads, small eye openings, smooth upper lips, and intelligence deficits. Fetal alcohol syndrome (FAS) is one of the most common causes of birth defects (1 in 500 - 1000 births). Diagnosis of FAS depends on the presence of facial abnormalities, short stature, and low IQ. Children who do not meet all three criteria are often diagnosed with fetal alcohol effects (FAE), considered a mild form of fetal alcohol syndrome, on the assumption that their birth defects arose from exposure to alcohol prenatally.

Researchers at the University of Arizona Health Sciences Center in Tucson reanalyzed 437 cases involving Arizona children (19 percent diagnosed with FAS, the rest with some FAE). Using facial abnormalities as the criteria, they found that 56 percent could be diagnosed FAS, and 13 percent of children diagnosed with FAS suffered from misdiagnosed genetic problems (Down syndrome, neurofibromatosis). The researchers classified 41percent as having some prenatal alcohol exposure, but they could not claim that alcohol had caused the birth defects. Dr. H. Eugene Hoyme urges doctors and geneticists to eliminate the diagnosis of fetal alcohol effects. He states that the risk of stigmatizing children and missing other serious diagnoses is too great if doctors too easily point to alcohol.

- You may want to use Classroom Activity 3: Fetal Alcohol Syndrome Quiz before beginning this lecture. This activity assesses students' knowledge of the prevalence of FAS.
- Source: Seachrist, L. (1995). Birth defects too often blamed on alcohol. *Science News, 148*.

Classroom Activities

Classroom Activity 1: Reproductive Double Standards for Men and Women Pro-choice legislator Pruitt introduced some legislative bills restricting male reproductive rights to illustrate how abortion restrictions amount to unequal treatment of women and men in reproductive matters. She said, "If women's rights and bodies are going to be violated, then men's should be too." Her proposed bills would require that:
- Men who failed to keep up with child support payments be sterilized.
- A husband must get his wife's permission before undergoing a vasectomy.
- Husbands must be counseled about having a vasectomy as if their wives are considering tubal ligation.

Ask the students the following questions:
- Do you think Pruitt has made her point? Why or why not?
- Do you approve of any of her proposals that she herself labels "absolutely outrageous"?

Logistics:
- Group size: Full class discussion.
- Approximate time: Full class (10 – 15 minutes).
- Source: Powell, M. (1990). Bills take aim at double standard. *Insight, 49*.

Classroom Activity 2: The Court's Treatment of Substance Abusing Pregnant Women In August 1989, 23-year-old Jennifer Johnson was found guilty of delivering a controlled substance to a minor; the minor was her baby who was born a cocaine addict. She could have received a 30-year sentence, but she was sentenced to a year house arrest in a drug rehabilitation center and 14 years of probation. In your discussion, inform students of typical effects of cocaine in personality and physical aspects of offspring (babies whose mothers used cocaine during pregnancy had significantly lower cardiac output, lower stroke volume, and higher mean arterial blood pressure with a higher heart rate). Divide students into groups and have them discuss the following questions (**Handout 1**):

- Do you think that mothers who use drugs during pregnancy should face criminal prosecution?
- Might this policy keep some pregnant women from getting prenatal care?
- How far should the prosecution go?
- What alternative solutions can you suggest?
- Is fetal abuse equivalent to child abuse?
- Should fathers who use drugs during their partner's pregnancy face criminal prosecution?
  - Maternal exposure to environmental tobacco smoke for 1 hour or more per day is associated with spontaneous abortion (Windham et al., 1992) and paternal smoking is related to mental retardation in offspring (Roeleveld, et al., 1992).
- How responsible is a drug-using male in infertility and newborn health problem situations? Do you think a wife should be able to sue her husband for infertility problems caused by cocaine?
  - Cocaine usage lowers sperm count, increases abnormally shaped sperm, and decreases sperm mobility. Infertility problems may last more than 2 years after a man quits using cocaine.
- Research, for example, suggests that mothers who smoke tobacco during pregnancy and up to the time their children are 5 years old increase the risk of their offspring getting asthma. Should smoking mothers also be prosecuted?

Logistics:
- Materials: Handout 1 (The Court's Treatment of Substance Abusing Pregnant Women Activity).
- Group size: Small groups.
- Approximate time: Small groups (30 minutes).
- Sources: Roeleveld, N, Vingerhoets, E., Zielhuis, G.A., & Gabreels, F. (1992). Mental retardation associated with parental smoking and alcohol consumption before, during, and after pregnancy. *Preventive Medicine, 21*, 110-119. Van Bel, F., Van de Bor, M., Stijnen, T., Baan, J., & Ruy, J. (1990). Decreased cardiac output in infants of mothers who abused cocaine. *Pediatrics, 85*, 30-32. Van Pelt, D. (1990). Smokers' offspring more prone to asthma. *Insight, 47*. Van Pelt, D. (1990). Sperm abnormalities among cocaine users. *Insight, 50*. Windham, G.C., Swan, S.H., & Fenster, L. (1992). Parental cigarette smoking and the risk of spontaneous abortion. *American Journal of Epidemiology, 135*, 1394-1403.

Classroom Activity 3: Fetal Alcohol Syndrome Quiz The purpose of this activity is to increase students' understanding of fetal alcohol syndrome (FAS). Have students get into groups of two or three and answer the Fetal Alcohol Syndrome Quiz presented as **Handout 2**. After they have discussed the questions and indicated the answer they believe to be correct, discuss the correct answers as a class. The answers below are also included as **Handout 3**, in case you want the students to have a copy on which to take notes. This activity should clear up some misconceptions students have about this syndrome. Ask students to generate ideas about how this information can be disseminated to the public so that the incidences of FAS can be reduced.

<u>Answers to the Fetal Alcohol Syndrome Quiz</u>
1. (E) Some argue that this is a conservative estimate.
2. (C) Characteristic abnormalities include facial deformities, mental retardation, and heart abnormalities.
3. (D) FAS is the primary threat to children's mental health, much greater than either Down syndrome or spina bifida.
4. (C) The risk for African Americans is 6.7 times that of European Americans. Native Americans are 33 times more likely to suffer from FAS than European Americans.
5. (B) Risk may be minimal during the first 2 weeks, however during the rest of the first trimester the organs are developing and tremendous damage can be caused by exposure to alcohol.
6. (A) Alcohol can be ingested in the breast milk.
7. (A) Scandinavian, Boston, and Atlanta studies all indicate that some correction may occur. Size and healthiness improve, at least, but there is no evidence that intelligence is improved.
8. (B) Barbiturates and opiates affect the nervous system; alcohol can affect any cell.

Logistics:
- Materials: Handout 2 (Fetal Alcohol Syndrome Quiz) and Handout 3 (answers).
- Group size: Small group discussion and full class discussion.
- Approximate time: Small groups (10 minutes) and full class (10 – 15 minutes).
- Sources: Simons, J. A. (1989). *Quiz on Fetal Alcohol Syndrome*. Des Moines, IA: Central Iowa Psychological Services. Dorfman, A. (August 28th, 1989). Alcohol's youngest victims. *Time, 60.*

Classroom Activity 4: Reasons to Have Children or Not Have Children Students often take for granted that they will have children, without considering why they will have them. Ask class members to list reasons why couples have children (i.e., What value do children serve?). Compare their suggestions to those offered by Hoffman and Hoffman (1973) below. Discuss the advantages and the disadvantages of having children and of choosing to remain childless.

Reasons to Have Children or Not Have Children:
- adult social status and identity
- expansion of the self, tie to a larger entity, sense of immortality
- morality, religion, good of the group, altruism, normality
- primary group ties, affiliation
- stimulation, novelty, fun
- creativity, accomplishment, competence
- power, effectiveness, influence
- social comparison, competition
- economic utility

Logistics:
- Group size: Full class discussion.
- Approximate time: Full class (10 – 15 minutes).
- Source: Hoffman, L. W., & Hoffman, M. L. (1973). The value of children to parents. In J. T. Fawcett (Ed.), *Psychological perspectives on population* (pp.19-76). New York: Basic Books.

Classroom Activity 5: Critical Thinking Multiple-Choice Questions and Answers Discuss the answers to the critical thinking multiple-choice questions that are presented as **Handout 4**. The answers are described in **Handout 5.** Question 1 continues the theme of applying the issues from The Nature of Development box in chapter 1. Review these as necessary; again, you may want to work with a few examples from topics in chapter 4.

Question 2 stresses the limitations of research involving teratogens. Some of the issues presented were not addressed in the textbook, however, these are important issues to consider. This question requires students to think about how the research is conducted and the conclusions that can be drawn from the various methodologies employed.

Question 3 continues to provide practice in identifying inferences, assumptions, and observations. A good discussion prior to this exercise would involve asking students whether they are beginning to develop their own criteria or procedures for discriminating these different sorts of propositions. They may find the material for this question difficult because it is largely descriptive; in fact, three of the alternatives in this question are observations. You may want to alert your students that the pattern of two inferences, two observations, and one assumption established in previous exercises of this type changes in this exercise.

Logistics:
- Materials: Handout 4 (the critical thinking multiple-choice questions) and Handout 5 (answers)
- Group size: Small groups (2-4) to discuss the questions, then a full class discussion.
- Approximate time: Small groups (15 to 20 minutes), then 5 minutes for full class discussion.

Classroom Activity 6: Critical Thinking Essay Questions and Suggestions for Helping Students Answer the Essays Discuss students' answers to the critical thinking essay questions presented in **Handout 6**. The purpose of this exercise is threefold. First, answering the essay questions further facilitates students' understanding of concepts in chapter 4. Second, this type of essay question affords the students an opportunity to apply the concepts to their own lives, which will facilitate their retention of the material. Third, the essay format also gives students practice expressing themselves in written form. Ideas to help students answer the critical thinking essay questions are provided as **Handout 7**.
Logistics:
- Materials: Handout 6 (essay questions) and Handout 7 (helpful suggestions for the answers).
- Group size: Individual, then full class.
- Approximate time: Individual (60 minutes), full class discussion of any questions (30 minutes).

Personal Applications

Personal Application 1: In a Family Way The purpose of this exercise is to demonstrate the significance of pregnancy from a cultural standpoint. Each culture takes it's own particular view of the major stages of life: birth, childhood, puberty, parenthood, work, old age, and death. It's interesting and important to be aware of the different cross-cultural perspectives, especially in our multi-cultural society.
- Instructions for Students: Describe your cultural views of pregnancy. How are pregnant women viewed and treated by society? What beliefs are held about the biological processes occurring with regard to her body? What is the perception of the developing fetus? What preparations are made for the upcoming labor, delivery, and birth? How is impending parenthood anticipated?
- Use in the Classroom: If you are fortunate and have an ethnically diverse group of students, make a grid on the board comparing and contrasting beliefs for each of the above categories. If you have a homogeneous class, put students in groups and assign them particular cultures to research with regard to the various aspects of pregnancy and childbirth. Each group will then present their findings to the class.

Personal Application 2: Oh, the Pain! The purpose of this exercise is for students to recognize the various ways the human body carries out and experiences the same biological processes. Mammals giving birth is one of nature's most fundamental experiences. It involves a series of physiological stages that all members of the same species are programmed to go through. However, rarely are they experienced in the same way and to the same degree by different mothers. As we have been studying the influences of both biology and environmental factors on human behavior, it is important to recognize the varying contributions of both to such a fundamental life process.
- Instructions for Students: Ask your mother if she can recall her experience giving birth to you and your siblings. If you are a parent, recall the experience of the birth of your child/children. What's different about each situation? What's similar? What might account for the differences? What factors might contribute to the variety of birthing experiences women have?
- Use in the Classroom: Comparing labor and delivery stories can be a very interesting and informative thing. If you feel comfortable, share your own stories of the birth of your children, and bring in contrasting stories from friends and family. Have students share their stories, and follow these up with a discussion of what might contribute to each mother's particular experiences. Have students then try to conclude which of those factors result from nature and which may be due to environmental circumstances. Were there any aspects of labor and delivery that the mother may have been able to change somehow? Were there any mothers who had drastically different birthing experiences with their different children? Why might this have been?

Personal Application 3: The Pitter Patter of Little Feet The purpose of this exercise is to prompt students to think about all that is involved in preparing to become parents. It's not just becoming a parent that is demanding and has numerous implications; planning, conceiving, and sustaining a healthy pregnancy also require a great deal of preparation as well—from both the mother and the father! The more we understand about each person's role in this delicate process, the more we can ensure a successful outcome.

- Instructions for Students: If you are not yet a parent, think and write about the following.
  - Women: Your physical condition prior to becoming pregnant—how will you take care of and prepare your body for conception? Address nutrition, physical shape, drugs, alcohol, smoking, and other environmental stressors. What might be your health care plans? (Physician, mid-wife, etc.) What kind of labor and delivery experience do you want? (Hospital, home delivery) Who will you want with you during this time? What post-partum situation do you anticipate? How might you prepare yourself to be an exceptional mother?
  - Males: Your physical condition prior to conception—nutrition, physical shape, drugs, alcohol, smoking, and other environmental stressors. How do you plan to support the mother during pregnancy? Labor and delivery? Post-partum? Were you surprised to read of the important role fathers play in this extensive process? How might you prepare yourself to be an exceptional father?
- Use in the Classroom: Put together several different profiles of couples wanting to conceive or already experiencing pregnancy. You could include married, unwed, women with absent partners, working women, uneducated women (and partners varying along those lines as well), financial variations, social support systems, etc. Present the profiles to students to read, then have a class discussion on the implications of the various circumstances surrounding each pregnancy and impending birth. Emphasize the dangers of poor choices, the risks of particular behaviors, and the benefits of planning, preparation, and healthy living.

Research Project Ideas

Research Project 1: Why do Some Pregnant Women Drink, Smoke, or Use Drugs? The dangers of drinking alcohol, smoking, and other drug use on fetal development are now well known and widely publicized. Despite this fact, many women continue to use these substances while they are pregnant. This research activity attempts to find out why (**Handout 8**).

Have students ask a number of female friends who smoke or drink to talk to them about whether they will do these things when they are pregnant. Then have them ask their friends whether they know that smoking and drinking endanger prenatal development and about what they know in detail. Have them talk about the dangers, and then ask again whether their friends will drink and smoke. You may want to suggest that they prepare an interview schedule of questions to ask. Be sure to instruct the students to avoid judgmental statements and to interview the women individually so their answers will be confidential.

- Discuss the findings in class. Do different people give different reasons? Or are there common reasons among many? Discuss whether the women suggested ways that the message about the dangers of drinking and smoking for prenatal development can be made more convincing to prospective parents.
- Source: Salkind, N. (1990). *Child development*. Fort Worth: Holt, Rinehart, & Winston.

Research Project 2: Fatherhood How actively are fathers participating in the births of their children these days? Have the students find out by carrying out an interview project (**Handout 9**). They should identify two first-time, expectant fathers and two fathers of children under the age of 2, and then interview these men using the following sets of questions:

Expectant fathers:
- What are your feelings about becoming a father?
- How have you been involved in your partner's pregnancy?
- What part will you play in your child's birth? What part would you like to play?
- What do you think being a "good father" means?
- How will having a child change your life?

Fathers:
- What part did you play in the birth(s) of your child (children)? What were your feelings about this experience?
- What are the three biggest challenges you face as a father?
- What do you think a "good father" is?
- How has having a child changed your life?
- What advice would you give a new father?

Instruct students to write a brief report indicating what they were trying to find out. They need to describe their sample and how they interviewed the fathers and soon-to-be fathers, and then summarize similarities and differences between the two pairs of men. Finally, they should relate what they learned to material on fathers' participation in childbirth from the text.
- Have students form groups of three or four to discuss and compare their findings. Have each group report to the class to identify any trends and generalizations that seem warranted by their findings.
- Source: Salkind, N. (1990). *Child development*. Fort Worth: Holt, Rinehart, & Winston.

Film and Video List

The following films and videos supplement the content of chapter 4. Contact information for film distributors can be found at the front of this Instructor's Manual under Film and Video Sources.

AIDS Babies (Cinema Guild, 58 minutes). This documentary examines the plight of babies born with AIDS. It is filmed in various countries around the world, and compares the reaction of different governments to the AIDS crisis and speculates on future consequences of a generation of AIDS babies.

Birth without Violence (New Yorker Films, 21 minutes). Dr. Frederick Leboyer shows his method of quiet childbirth during this video.

Brazelton Neonatal Behavioral Assessment Scale: An Introduction (EDC Distribution Center, 20 minutes). In this video, Brazelton introduces his Neonatal Behavioral Assessment Scale and conducts an assessment on a 2-day-old normal infant.

Contemporary Childbirth (Films for the Humanities and Sciences, 19 minutes). This video portrays the various ways of giving birth.

David with Fetal Alcohol Syndrome (Films for the Humanities and Sciences, 45 minutes). David Vandenbrink seems like a normal 21-year-old man, however David suffers from FAS. This program provides a personal look at what it is like to live with the effects of FAS.

Developmental Phases Before and After Birth (Films for the Humanities and Sciences, 30 minutes). This program examines the development of the fetus and child during the first year. It concludes that no matter the culture, development and growth is identical for children throughout the world.

Fetal Alcohol Syndrome and Other Drug Use During Pregnancy (Films for the Humanities and Sciences, 19 minutes). This program profiles an 8-year-old boy born with FAS, and also examines babies born to cocaine-addicted mothers.

Fetal Alcohol Syndrome: Life Sentence (Films for the Humanities and Sciences, 24 minutes). This video deals with injury that can result from prenatal exposure to alcohol.

A Human Life Emerges (Films for the Humanities and Science, 35 minutes). This program presents a close-up view of reproduction, beginning with the fertilization of the egg, through gestation and cell divisions, into the birth of a fully formed individual. It uses computer animation and technical narration to explain gestation and the birth process for the advanced learner.

Invasion of the Embryo (Films for the Humanities and Sciences, 24 minutes). This program follows the life of a couple expecting a baby. Using 3-D animation, one can follow the changes the body goes through during the nine months of pregnancy.

The Mind: Development (PBS, 60 minutes). This video examines the development of the human brain from a single cell to that of a 6-year-old child.

The Newborn: Development and Discovery (Magna Systems, Inc., 29 minutes). This video focuses on the newborn. Topics include the newborn's physical appearance and behavior states, bonding, high risk newborns, assessment scales, physiological functioning, and breast- versus bottle-feeding.

Pregnancy and Birth: Caring and Preparing for the Life Within (Magna Systems, Inc., 26 minutes). This video highlights fertilization, pregnancy, maternal prenatal care, prenatal tests and interventions, fetal abuse, childbirth choices, labor, and birth.

Pregnancy and Substance Abuse (Films for the Humanities and Sciences, 28 minutes). This program follows several couples through pregnancy and prenatal care.

Prenatal Development: A Life in the Making (Magna Systems, Inc., 26 minutes). This video shows the stages of prenatal development and discusses critical periods and factors that influence development.

The Process of Birth (Films for the Humanities and Sciences, 23 minutes). This program shows how different cultures and individuals within the same culture respond to birthing issues. Aspects of birth including stress, who should aid in the process, and bonding are discussed.

Psychological Development Before Birth (Films for the Humanities and Sciences, 22 minutes). This program shows how it is possible to determine the well-being of the fetus and how it begins to react to sound. It also discusses differences in how women of different cultures prepare themselves for pregnancy and birth.

Reproduction: Fetal Development (Films for the Humanities and Sciences, 23 minutes). The first part of this program examines the components and processes of human reproduction. MRI scans and endoscopic imaging provide an outstanding look at elements of conception and cell division. The second part of this program focuses on the stages of fetal development.

Unborn Addicts (Films for the Humanities & Sciences, 50 minutes). This program presents case studies of two pregnant women who are drug addicts who have entered a treatment program.

Web Site Suggestions

The URLs for general sites, common to all chapters, can be found at the front of this Instructor's manual under Useful Web Sites. At the time of publication, all sites were current and active, however, please be advised that you may occasionally encounter a dead link.

Apgar Scoring
http://www.childbirth.org/articles/apgar.html

Caffeine in Pregnancy: Is There an Increased Risk for Miscarriage?
http://www.mostgene.org/gd/gdvol11d.htm

Childbirth
http://www.childbirth.org/

Evidence-Based Ethics and the Care of Premature Infants
http://www.futureofchildren.org/LBW/13LBWTYS.htm

Post-partum Depression
http://www.psycom.net/depression.central.post-partum.html

Teratology Society: Birth Defects Research | Education | Prevention
http://www.teratology.org/

The Visible Embryo
http://www.visembryo.com/baby/hp.html

The Court's Treatment of Substance Abusing Pregnant Women Activity

1. Do you think that mothers who use drugs during pregnancy should face criminal prosecution?

2. Might this policy keep some pregnant women from getting prenatal care and having a hospital delivery?

3. How far should the prosecution go?

4. What alternative solutions can you suggest?

5. Is fetal abuse equivalent to child abuse?

6. Should fathers who use drugs during their partner's pregnancy face criminal prosecution? (Maternal exposure to environmental tobacco smoke for 1 hour or more per day is associated with spontaneous abortion (Windham et al., 1992) and paternal smoking is related to mental retardation in offspring (Roeleveld, et al., 1992).)

7. How responsible is a drug-using male in infertility and newborn health problem situations? Do you think a wife should be able to sue her husband for infertility problems caused by use of cocaine? (Cocaine usage lowers sperm count, increases abnormally shaped sperm, and decreases sperm mobility. Infertility problems may last more than 2 years after a man quits using cocaine.)

8. Research, for example, suggests that mothers who smoke tobacco during pregnancy and up to the time their children are 5 years old increase the risk of their offspring getting asthma. Should smoking mothers also be prosecuted?

Fetal Alcohol Syndrome (FAS) Quiz

1. About _____ American babies are born each year with alcohol-related defects.
    A. 5,000   D. 40,000
    B. 15,000   E. 50,000
    C. 25,000

2. Of babies affected by alcohol, _____ are affected enough to be diagnosed with fetal alcohol syndrome.
    A. 2,000   D. 18,000
    B. 6,500   E. 25,000
    C. 12,500

3. FAS is responsible for _____ percent of all cases of mental retardation in this country.
    A. 5   D. 20
    B. 10   E. 35
    C. 15

4. Which group has the highest risk for having a child with FAS?
    A.   African Americans
    B.   European Americans
    C.   Native Americans
    D.   There are no differences in FAS rates among ethnic groups.

5. Drinking during the first trimester does not lead to FAS.
    A.   True
    B.   False

6. Motor development can be impaired for breast-feeding babies whose mothers drink alcohol.
    A.   True
    B.   False

7. Some injuries to the fetus resulting from alcohol exposure may be corrected in the womb if a mother gives up alcohol before her third trimester.
    A.   True
    B.   False

8. Barbiturates, opiates, and alcohol have similar effects on developing fetuses.
    A.   True
    B.   False

Handout 3 (CA 3)

Answers to the Fetal Alcohol Syndrome (FAS) Quiz Activity

1. E is the correct answer. Some argue that this is a conservative estimate.

2. C is the correct answer. Characteristic abnormalities include facial deformities, mental retardation, and heart abnormalities.

3. D is the correct answer. FAS is the primary threat to children's mental health, much greater than either Down syndrome or spina bifida.

4. C is the correct answer. The risk for African Americans is 6.7 times that of European Americans. Native Americans are 33 times more likely to suffer from FAS than European Americans.

5. B is the correct answer. Risk may be minimal during the first 2 weeks, however during the rest of the first trimester the organs are developing and tremendous damage can be caused by exposure to alcohol.

6. A is the correct answer. Alcohol can be ingested in the breast milk.

7. A is the correct answer. Scandinavian, Boston, and Atlanta studies all indicate that some correction may occur. Size and healthiness improve, at least but there is no evidence that intelligence is improved.

8. B is the correct answer. Barbiturates and opiates affect the nervous system; alcohol can affect any cell.

Critical Thinking Multiple-Choice Questions

1. Chapter 4 illustrates a number of the issues discussed in The Nature of Development box presented in chapter 1. Which of the following topics taken from chapter 4 correctly illustrates the chapter 1 topic paired with it? Circle the letter of the best answer and explain why it is the best answer and why each other answer is not as good.

    a. germinal, embryonic, and fetal periods: stability
    b. embryonic development: maturation
    c. teratology: biological determinants and influences
    d. miscarriage/abortion: discontinuity
    e. what to expect when you are expecting: cognitive processes

2. Teratology is the field that investigates the causes of birth defects. Research has found that certain agents influence the development of birth defects. Which of the following is NOT a concern regarding the research methodology involved in teratology? Circle the letter of the best answer and explain why it is the best answer and why each other answer is not as good.

    a. exposure to many teratogens
    b. long term effects
    c. animal research
    d. correlational research
    e. potential effects

3. During the past two decades, parents, researchers, and physicians have reacted against the so-called standard childbirth, once very widely practiced in American hospitals. Most have begun to favor a variety of prepared or natural forms of childbirth. Which of the following statements represents a basic assumption of standard childbirth practice that critics have rejected? Circle the letter of the best answer and explain why it is the best answer and why each other answer is not as good.

    a. Important individuals were excluded from the birth process.
    b. The mother was separated from her infant in the first minutes and hours after birth.
    c. Giving birth was like a disease.
    d. Babies were slapped or spanked.
    e. Babies were scared with bright lights.

Suggested Answers for Critical Thinking Multiple-Choice Questions

1. Chapter 4 illustrates a number of the issues discussed in The Nature of Development box presented in chapter 1. Which of the following topics taken from chapter 4 correctly illustrates the chapter 1 topic paired with it? Circle the letter of the best answer and explain why it is the best answer and why each other answer is not as good.

   a. <u>Germinal, embryonic, and fetal periods</u> do not illustrate the concept of <u>stability</u>. Prenatal development involves rapid and radical change, not stability. These phases better illustrate periods of development.

   b. <u>Embryonic development</u> illustrates the concept of <u>maturation</u>. Embryonic development illustrates clear, orderly sequence of changes that most likely are dictated by a genetic blueprint.

   c. <u>Teratology</u> does not illustrate the concept of <u>biological determinants and influences</u>. Teratogens do influence biological development, but they are environmental influences.

   d. <u>Miscarriage/abortion</u> do not illustrate the concept of <u>discontinuity</u>. The concept of discontinuity is that development produces qualitatively new and different features, often in what appears to be a progression of stages. These events represent an end to development.

   e. <u>What to expect when you are expecting</u> does not illustrate the concept of <u>cognitive processes</u>. Cultural beliefs live in the minds of people, but their practical influence on the developing fetus is social—shaping the parental practices that dictate the fetus's environment and their relationships with the unborn child.

2. Teratology is the field that investigates the causes of birth defects. Research has found that certain agents influence the development of birth defects. Which of the following is NOT a concern regarding the research methodology involved in teratology? Circle the letter of the best answer and explain why it is the best answer and why each other answer is not as good.

   a. <u>Exposure to many teratogens</u> is not the best answer. Given that every fetus is exposed to teratogens it is difficult to determine which one influenced the birth defect, thus exposure to many teratogens is a methodological issue.

   b. <u>Long term effects</u> is not the best answer. Given that some of the effects of teratogens are not evident until later in development (about half are evident at birth), long-term effects are a methodological concern.

   c. <u>Animal research</u> is not the best answer. Much of teratology is conducted on animals and there are questions as to the generalizability to human prenatal development of the animal research findings.

   d. <u>Correlational research</u> is not the best answer. Given that experiments involving exposure to teratogens cannot ethically be conducted on humans, cause and effect statements should not be made.

   e. <u>Potential effects</u> is the best answer. Given the correlational nature of teratogen studies, one avoids methodological issues if potential effects are discussed rather than stating cause and effect relationships.

3. During the past two decades, parents, researchers, and physicians have reacted against the so-called standard childbirth, once very widely practiced in American hospitals. Most have begun to favor a variety of prepared or natural forms of childbirth. Which of the following statements represents a basic assumption of standard childbirth practice that critics have rejected? Circle the letter of the best answer and explain why it is the best answer and why each other answer is not as good.

    a. <u>Important individuals were excluded from the birth process</u> is an observation. It is a straightforward statement about who was allowed to be present at a birth.

    b. <u>The mother was separated from her infant in the first minutes and hours after birth</u> is an observation.

    c. <u>Giving birth was like a disease</u> is the assumption. The statement does not describe any specific practice, but rather expresses the guiding analogy that directed medical procedures for assisting a birth.

    d. <u>Babies were slapped or spanked</u> is an observation. It is a practice that Lamaze vehemently rejected.

    e. <u>Babies were scared with bright lights</u> is an inference. It states the presumed (but not directly known) effect of bright lights on newborn infants.

Critical Thinking Essay Questions

Your answers to this kind of question demonstrate an ability to comprehend and apply ideas discussed in this chapter.

1. Describe development during the germinal, embryological, and fetal periods. Also, explain what factors might contribute to complications at specific times during gestation.

2. What is organogenesis, and why is this concept important to the process of development?

3. Discuss medical, ethical, psychological, and personal issues pertinent to the decision to have an abortion.

4. Define *teratogen* and give at least two examples of teratogens and their specific effects.

5. Compare and contrast the risks to expectant mothers who are either teenagers, twenty-something, or thirty-something.

6. Describe the stages of birth, and also explain three birth complications.

7. Imagine that you are about to give birth. What questions about cesarean sections and the use of drugs during delivery would be important to you? What reasons would lead you to accept or reject a cesarean section and drugs such as tranquilizers, sedatives, and analgesics during delivery?

8. Imagine that you are an expectant parent. What would you do and learn in a parent education class on pregnancy, prenatal development, and childbirth strategies?

9. Why and how have fathers become more involved in childbirth? Discuss the pros and cons of this involvement.

10. How do preterm and low-birthweight infants differ?

11. What would you learn about your newborn from the Apgar and Brazelton Neonatal Behavioral Assessment Scales?

12. Explain why some claim that the postpartum period should be termed the fourth trimester.

Ideas to Help You Answer Critical Thinking Essay Questions

1. Create a timeline for the prenatal stages of development. Note developmental milestones along with periods associated with particular concerns about complications.

2. In describing the nature of organogenesis, you will automatically address why it is important to the process of development.

3. Few people can address this issue from an objective standpoint, yet that is your challenge here. Make a chart and include each of the four issues listed as pertinent to the consideration of an abortion. Referring to the text, list the relevant information in each category to compile a substantial presentation of information upon which to base such a decision. As you discuss what you have considered for each category, weigh the significance of your information based on its scientific merit, objectiveness, and meaningfulness with regard to the contribution towards a sound conclusion.

4. Do this in your own words. Read the text's description, then proceed to expand on it, including a presentation and discussion about examples and their particular effects.

5. Create a chart with all the possible risks, both physiologically and environmentally based, for the varying age groups of pregnant women. Color code each maternal age group, then indicate the particular groups associated with each risk. This will provide a concrete illustration of maternal age and the associated risks of pregnancy shared by, and different for, each group.

6. Imagine you are teaching a childbirth class and your job is to inform expectant parents of the stages of birth and to explain the three particular birth complications. Anticipate their particular questions and concerns to create a more complete presentation of the information.

7. Begin by re-reading the relevant sections of the text, imagining that either you are pregnant or your wife is about to give birth. As you bring this personal perspective to your consideration of the information, you should easily begin to develop questions as you would if you were actually facing these circumstances yourself.

8. If you are an expectant parent, you will approach pregnancy, prenatal development, and childbirth in very practical terms. You are less interested in the information for the information itself, but rather you want to be able to apply it. This is a primary reason for the existence of childbirth classes—to inform parents on what they can do to successfully experience each of these stages, based on the scientific information.

9. Begin by thinking about your own father's involvement. Ask your mother, or your father, about the extent of his role during your mother's pregnancy, labor and delivery, and childrearing. Compare what you find out to what you now know about the new and changing role of fathers.

10. Preterm infants always experience low-birthweight, but the opposite is not true. Explain why that is, and what leads to each.

11. Present this information as if you were a pediatrician explaining these assessments to new parents. Remember, they most likely have no working knowledge of developmental psychology.

12. Begin by describing the "first" three trimesters to establish the context for explaining the views about the post-partum period. Then discuss whether or not it should be considered the fourth trimester.

Why do Some Pregnant Women Drink, Smoke, or Use Drugs?

The dangers of drinking alcohol, smoking, and other drug use on fetal development are now well known and widely publicized. Despite this fact, many women continue to use these substances while they are pregnant. This research activity attempts to find out why.

Ask a number of female friends who smoke or drink to talk to you about whether they will do these things when they are pregnant. Then ask them whether they know that smoking and drinking endanger prenatal development and about what they know in detail. Talk about the dangers, and then ask again whether your friends will drink and smoke. You may want to prepare an interview schedule of questions to ask before meeting with your friends. You will want to come up with a list of about ten questions to ask. Be sure to avoid judgmental statements/questions. You will want to interview the women individually so their answers will be confidential.

Fatherhood

How actively are fathers participating in the births of their children these days? Find out by carrying out an interview project. Identify two first-time, expectant fathers and two fathers of children under the age of 2, and interview these men using the following sets of questions:

Expectant fathers:

- What are your feelings about becoming a father?
- How have you been involved in your partner's pregnancy?
- What part will you play in your child's birth? What part would you like to play?
- What do you think being a "good father" means?
- How will having a child change your life?

Fathers:

- What part did you play in the birth(s) of your child (children)? What were your feelings about this experience?
- What are the three biggest challenges you face as a father?
- What do you think a "good father" is?
- How has having a child changed your life?
- What advice would you give a new father?

Write a brief report indicating what you were trying to find out, describe your sample and how you interviewed the fathers and soon-to-be fathers, and then summarize similarities and differences between the two pairs of men. Relate what you learn to material on fathers' participation in childbirth from the text.

Chapter 5: Physical Development in Infancy

Total Teaching Package Outline

Lecture Outline	Resource References
Physical Development in Infancy	PowerPoint Presentation: See www.mhhe.com
	Cognitive Maps: See Appendix A
Physical Growth and Development in Infancy	F/V: Infancy: Landmarks of Development
	F/V: Physical Development: The First Five Years
• Cephalocaudal and Proximodistal Sequences	LO1
	OHT41 &IB: Changes in Body Proportions
• Height and Weight	LO2
	OHT47 & IB: Height and Weight (0 - to 18 m .)
	OHT52: Height and Weight during Infancy
• The Brain	OHT42 & IB: The Brain's Four Lobes
	OHT43 & IB: The Neuron
-The Brain's Development	F/V: The Brain
	F/V: The Brain-Mind Connection
	F/V: The Brain: An Inside Look
-The Brain's Hemispheres	F/V: The Development of the Human Brain
	F/V: The Brain and How it Works
-Early Experience and the Brain	F/V: Brain Dev.: The Importance of Head Start
	F/V: Pediatric Neuroscience: Rage of Innocents
	RP1: Infant Brain Development and Childcare Settings
• Infant States	LO3
	IB: Sleep across the Human Life Span
	PA1: Remember When
	F/V: How Relationships Are Formed
-REM Sleep	
-Shared Sleeping	
-SIDS	LO4
	LS1: The SIDS Controversy
	F/V: Sudden Infant Death Syndrome: An Update
	F/V: Sudden Infant Death Syndrome
	WS: American SIDS Institute
	WS: National SIDS Resource Center
	WS: Center for Disease Control: Growth Charts
• Nutrition	LO5
-Nutritional Needs and Eating Behavior	
-Breast-Versus-Bottle Feeding	F/V: Mothers, Fathers, and Babies
	WS: Breastfeeding
-Malnutrition in Infancy	LS2: The Effects of Malnutrition
	WS: Malnutrition
• Toilet Training	LO6

Motor Development • Reflexes	LO7 CA1: Assessing Infant Reflexes F/V: Evolution, Environment, and Growth F/V: Infancy: Landmarks of Development

• Gross and Fine Motor Skills
  -Gross Motor Skills
  -Fine Motor Skills
	LO8
	IB: Milestones in Gross Motor Development
	OHT44 & IB: Fine Motor Skills in Infancy

• Developmental Biodynamics	LO9 LS3: Current Views of Infant Motor Development RP2: Replication of Thelen's Work on Infant Motor Development
Sensory and Perceptual Development	PA2: If I Could Read Your Mind
• What Are Sensation and Perception?	LO10 F/V: Mystery of the Senses

• Visual Perception
 	
  -Visual Acuity and Color
  -Visual Preferences
  -Depth Perception
  -Visual Expectations
	LO11
	OHT45 & IB: How Infants Scan the Human Face

• Other Senses
  -Hearing
  -Touch and Pain
 	
  -Smell
  -Taste
	LO12
	
	CA2: To Circumcise or Not to Circumcise
	WS: Ritual Female Genital Mutilation in Africa

• Intermodal Perception	LO13
• Perceptual-Motor Coupling and Unification	
Review	CA3: Assessing Infant Abilities CA4: Critical Thinking Multiple-Choice CA5: Critical Thinking Essays WS: Zero to Three: Infants, Toddlers, and Families

Chapter Outline

PHYSICAL GROWTH AND DEVELOPMENT IN INFANCY
Cephalocaudal and Proximodistal Sequences
- The **cephal0caudal pattern** is the sequence in which the greatest growth occurs at the top with physical growth in size, weight, and feature differentiation gradually working its way down from top to bottom (i.e., head, neck, shoulders, middle trunk, etc.).
- The **proximodistal pattern** is the sequence in which growth starts at the center of the body and moves toward the extremities (control over arms, hands, fingers).

Height and Weight
- The average North American newborn is 20 inches long and weighs 7.5 pounds.
- Infants grow about one inch per month in the first year and nearly triple their weight by 12 months.
- By 2 years, the average infant's height is 32 to 35 inches and weight is 26 to 32 pounds.

The Brain
- A **neuron** is a nerve cell that handles information processing at the cellular level.

The Brain's Development
- Dendritic spreading (connections between neurons) is substantial in the first 2 years.
- Myelination, the process of encasing axons with fat cells, begins prenatally and continues throughout childhood and into adolescence.
- The newest brain imaging techniques cannot be used with babies, as PET scans pose radiation risks and infants wiggle too much for MRIs.
- Researcher Charles Nelson uses 128 electrodes on babies' scalps to measure brain waves.
  - Newborns can distinguish their mother's voices from another woman's voice.

The Brain's Hemispheres
- The cerebral cortex (the highest level of the brain) is divided into two halves, or hemispheres.
- **Lateralization** is the specialization of functions in the two hemispheres of the cerebral cortex.
  - Greater electrical brain activity occurs in the newborn's left hemisphere when listening to speech.
- Complex functions (reading, creating art, performing music) involve both hemispheres.

Early Experience and the Brain
- Animal research in the 1960s revealed that animals raised in enriched environments had more sophisticated brains than animals reared in standard or isolated conditions.
- Neural connections are formed early in life. Before birth, genes direct neurons to locations. The brain produces trillions more connections than are necessary.
- Connections that are not used are eliminated (pruning). After birth, stimulation from the environment helps the brain's connections take shape.

Infant States
- Infant states, or states of consciousness, and levels of awareness have been classified:
  - No REM (rapid eye movement) sleep: reoccurring sleep stage during which vivid dreams occur. Eyes are closed and still, virtually no motor activity.
  - Active sleep without REM: sleep in which the eyes are closed and still, some motor activity.
  - **REM (rapid eye movement) sleep**: sleep, eyes are closed, rapid eye movement can be detected, motor activity may or may not be present.
  - Indeterminate sleep: all transitional states that cannot fit the above codes.
  - Drowsy: opening and closing eyes (dull, glazed appearance), minimal motor activity.
  - Inactive alert: relatively inactive, eyes wide open (bright and shiny).
  - Active awake: eyes are open and there is motor activity.
  - Crying: eyes can be open or closed, motor activity, and agitated vocalizations are present.
- Newborns usually sleep 16 to 17 hours a day. By 4 months, many American infants approach adultlike sleeping patterns.

REM Sleep
- Adults spend 20 percent of their night in REM sleep, newborns spend about 50 percent (40 percent by 3 months).
- The large amount of REM sleep may provide added stimulation and promote brain development.

Shared Sleeping
- Newborns' sleeping arrangements vary by culture.
    - In the U.S., most infants sleep in a crib in a separate room.
    - Possible benefits of shared sleeping (sleeping in the same bed with a baby) include: promotion of breast-feeding, quick response to cries, and detection of pauses in breathing.
    - The American Academy of Pediatrics (AAP) Task Force on Infant Position and SIDS recommends against shared sleeping as it may lead to sudden infant death syndrome.

SIDS
- **Sudden infant death syndrome (SIDS)** is a condition that occurs when infants stop breathing, usually during the night, and suddenly die without apparent cause.
- Researchers have found that SIDS decreases when infants sleep on their backs (due to the inability to swallow effectively in the prone sleeping position).
- SIDS is the highest cause of infant death in the U.S. (13%) with risk highest at 4 to 16 weeks of age.
- Researchers have found the following risk factors:
    - Low-birthweight; twins and triplets; infants with a sibling who died of SIDS; infants with sleep apnea (temporary cessation of breathing in which the airway is completely blocked, usually 10 seconds or longer); African American or Eskimo infants; lower SES; and infants exposed to secondhand cigarette smoke.

Nutrition

Nutritional Needs and Eating Behavior
- Nutritionists recommend as a guideline that infants consume 50 calories per day for each pound that they weigh (more than twice an adult's requirement per pound).
- For growing infants, high-calorie, high-energy foods are part of a balanced diet.

Breast-Versus Bottle-Feeding
- There is growing consensus that breast-feeding is better for the baby's health than bottle-feeding.
- Some of the benefits of breast-feeding include:
    - Appropriate weight gain; fewer allergies; prevention of diarrhea, respiratory infections, bacterial and urinary tract infections, and otitis media; bone density; reduced childhood cancer and reduced incidence of breast cancer in mothers and their female offspring; lower incidence of SIDS; neurological and cognitive development; and visual acuity.
- The AAP strongly endorses breast-feeding throughout the first year of life.
- No psychological differences have been found for breast-fed and bottle-fed infants.

Malnutrition in Infancy
- **Marasmus** is a wasting away of body tissues in the infant's first year, caused by severe protein-calorie deficiency.
- **Kwashiorkor** is a condition caused by a deficiency in protein in which the child's face, legs, and abdomen swell with water. This condition usually occurs between 1 and 3 years of age.
- These conditions are often caused by early weaning from breast-feeding.
- Severe, lengthy malnutrition is detrimental to physical, cognitive, and social development.

Toilet Training
- North American culture emphasizes that toilet training is a physical and motor skill that is expected by 3 years of age.
- Toilet training should be accompanied by warm, relaxed, supportive parents.

MOTOR DEVELOPMENT

Reflexes

- Reflexes are genetic survival mechanisms which serve as a foundation for later motor development.
- These built-in reactions to stimuli are adaptive, automatic, and beyond the newborn's control.
    - The **sucking reflex** occurs when newborns automatically suck an object placed in their mouth. This reflex enables newborns to get nourishment before they have associated a nipple with food.
    - The **rooting reflex** occurs when the infant's cheek is stroked or the side of the mouth is touched. In response, the infant turns its head toward the side that was touched in an apparent effort to find something to suck.
        - The sucking and rooting reflexes are present at birth and later disappear around 3 or 4 months when they are replaced by voluntary eating.
    - The **Moro reflex** is a neonatal startle response that occurs in response to a sudden, intense noise, or movement. When startled, the newborn arches its back, throws back its head, and flings out its arms and legs. The newborn rapidly closes its arms and legs to the center of its body.
    - The **grasping reflex** occurs when something touches the infant's palms. The infant responds by grasping tightly.

Gross and Fine Motor Skills

Gross Motor Skills

- **Gross motor skills** involve large muscle activities, such as moving one's arms and walking.
- The accomplishment of these milestones can vary by as much as 2 to 4 months, however, the sequence of accomplishments remains fairly stable.
    - By the first month, infants can lift their head from a prone position.
    - At about 3 months, infants can hold their chest up and use their arms for support.
    - At 3 to 4 months, infants can roll over.
    - At 4 to 5 months, infants can support some weight on their legs.
    - By 6 months, infants can sit without support.
    - By 7 to 8 months, infants can crawl and stand without support.
    - At 8 months, infants can pull themselves up to a standing position.
    - At 10 to 11 months, they can walk using furniture for support.
    - By 12 to 13 months, they can walk without assistance.

Fine Motor Skills

- **Fine motor skills** involve movements that are more finely tuned than gross motor skills and a number of milestones are achieved in infancy (grasping, wrist movements, thumb-finger coordination, etc.).
- Contrary to past assumptions, early reaching for an object is not visually guided.
    - Clifton et al. found that proprioceptive (muscle, tendon, joint sense) cues, not sight of the reaching limb, guide early reaching for 4-month-old infants.

Developmental Biodynamics

- **Developmental biodynamics** seeks to explain how motor behaviors are assembled for perceiving and acting. Perception and action are coupled when new skills are learned.
- This new view of motor development emphasizes the importance of exploration and selection in finding solutions to new task demands.
    - Infants need to assemble adaptive patterns by modifying their current movement patterns. The task and the challenge of the context drive change, not prescribed genetic instructions.

SENSORY AND PERCEPTUAL DEVELOPMENT

What Are Sensation and Perception?

- **Sensation** occurs when information interacts with sensory receptors (eyes, ears, tongue, nostrils, skin).
- **Perception** is the interpretation of what is sensed.

Visual Perception

Visual Acuity and Color

- William James was wrong—the newborn's visual world is not a blooming, buzzing confusion.
- Newborn's vision is estimated to be 20/400 to 20/800 (10 to 30 times lower than adult vision).
- By 6 months, vision is 20/100 or better, and by 12 months, vision approximates adult vision.
- Newborns can distinguish green and red, and by 2 months, they can perceive blue.

Visual Preferences

- Robert Fantz's pioneering study of visual perception found that infants look at different things for different lengths of time.
  - Infants, as young as 2 days old, prefer to look at patterns, such as faces, printed matter, or a bull's-eye longer than colored discs.
- These findings led to the inference that pattern perception has an innate basis or at least is acquired after only minimal environmental experience.

Depth Perception

- Gibson and Walk demonstrated through the use of the visual cliff that infants as young as 6 months have depth perception.
- Is depth perception innate?
  - 2- to 4-month-old infants' heart rate changes when they are placed directly on the deep side of the visual cliff instead of the shallow side.
  - It is clear that young infants can perceive the difference between the shallow and deep side of the visual cliff.

Visual Expectations

- Haith's research demonstrated that infants develop expectations about future events in their world by the time they are 3 months old.
- Spelke's research also demonstrated that 4-month-old infants can recognize where a moving object is when it has left their visual field and can infer where it should be when it comes into their sight again.

Other Senses

Hearing

- DeCasper and Spence's research showed that fetuses can hear several weeks before birth.
- Two important conclusions from DeCasper and Spence's research are that:
  - Ingenious scientists can assess the development of fetuses.
  - Infants' brains have the ability to learn even before birth.
- Immediately after birth, newborns can hear (their sensory threshold is higher than adults).
- Very young infants can discriminate between subtle phonetic differences (*ba* and *pa*), their mother's voice, and their mother's native language.
  - Between 6 and 12 months infants lose the ability to discriminate between phonetic sounds that they have not heard.

Touch and Pain

Touch

- Newborns respond to touch.

Pain
- It was once thought that newborns are indifferent to pain.
- However, research on male circumcision demonstrates that newborns are sensitive to pain. Newborn males show a higher level of cortisol (an indicator of stress) after circumcision than prior to the surgery.

Smell
- Newborns can differentiate odors.
- Using facial expressions as an indicator, researchers infer that newborns prefer vanilla and strawberry smells, but do not like rotten egg or fish smells.
- By 6 days (but not by 2 days), breast-fed babies prefer the smell of their mother's breast pad, indicating that this preference requires several days of experience to recognize the odor.

Taste
- Taste sensitivity is present at birth.
- When saccharin was added to amniotic fluid, fetal swallowing increased.
- By 2 hours old, babies make different facial expressions when they taste sweet, sour, and bitter solutions.

Intermodal Perception
- **Intermodal perception** is the ability to relate and integrate information about two or more sensory modalities.
  - Infants as young as 3 months of age can connect visual and auditory stimuli.
    - Infants looked more at their mother when they also heard her voice and longer at their father when they heard his voice.

Perceptual-Motor Coupling and Unification
- It was once believed that perceptual and motor development are isolated from each other.
- Increasingly, it is believed that perceptual-motor development is coupled and unified.
  - Babies are continually coordinating their movements with concurrent perceptual information to learn how to maintain balance, reach for objects, and locomote across various surfaces.

Learning Objectives

1. Distinguish between cephalocaudal and proximodistal growth patterns.
2. Describe the physical changes during the first 2 years, including those in height and weight, and changes in brain organization and structure.
3. Describe each of the eight categories of infant states, then define REM sleep and explain its purpose.
4. Describe sudden infant death syndrome (SIDS), and list its risk factors.
5. Discuss the array of nutritional needs for the infant, including the pros and cons of breast- versus bottle-feeding and findings about infant malnutrition.
6. Summarize the arguments surrounding the question of when to toilet train.
7. Describe the various infant reflexes and explain their importance.
8. Explain how the development of gross motor skills and fine motor skills follows the principles of cephalocaudal and proximodistal sequences.
9. State how developmental biodynamics explains how motor behaviors are assembled for perceiving and acting.
10. Differentiate between sensation and perception.
11. Describe the infant's visual abilities, including visual acuity, color vision, visual preferences, depth perception, and visual expectations.
12. Describe the infant's senses in addition to vision, explaining how we know that infants can hear before birth and identifying odors and tastes that newborns can discriminate.
13. Define intermodal perception and the notion of perceptual-motor coupling and unification.

Key Terms

cephalocaudal pattern
developmental biodynamics
fine motor skills
grasping reflex
gross motor skills
intermodal perception
kwashiorkor
lateralization
marasmus

Moro reflex
neuron
perception
proximodistal pattern
REM (rapid eye movement) sleep
rooting reflex
sensation
sucking reflex
sudden infant death syndrome (SIDS)

Key People

T. Berry Brazelton
Rachel Clifton
Robert Fantz
Eleanor Gibson and James Gibson
Marshall Haith
William James

Ernesto Pollitt
Charles Nelson
Mark Rosenzweig
Elizabeth Spelke
Esther Thelen
Richard Walk

Lecture Suggestions

Lecture Suggestion 1: The Sudden Infant Death Syndrome Controversy Students are usually very interested in sudden infant death syndrome (SIDS).
SIDS IS:

- a major cause of death in infants from 1 to 12 months (most between 2 to 4 months).
- characterized by a seemingly healthy victim.
- currently, unpredictable and unpreventable.
- a death that occurs quickly, with no signs of suffering, and is usually associated with sleep.
- a syndrome the first symptom of which is death.
- determined only after an autopsy, death scene examination, and a case history review.
- a diagnosis established by exclusion.
- a syndrome where the cause or causes are still unknown.
- Most researchers now believe that babies who die of SIDS are born with one or more conditions that make them vulnerable to both internal and external stresses that occur in the normal life of an infant.
- There is a 60-to- 40percent male-to-female ratio.
- Medical researchers have identified some typical pathological characteristics of SIDS deaths (several subtle tissue changes common in SIDS autopsies).
  - An increased number of star-shaped cells in the brainstem, referred to as brainstem gliosis, as a "non-specific response to injury" (Goyco & Beckerman, 1990).
  - The occurrence of tiny red or purple spots (minute hemorrhages) on the surface of the heart, lungs, and thymus. These spots have been identified in approximately 80 percent of SIDS cases (Krous, 1988).

SIDS IS NOT:
- caused by vomiting and choking, or minor illnesses such as colds or infections.
- caused by the diphtheria, pertussis, tetanus (DPT) vaccines, or other immunizations.
- contagious.
- child abuse.
- the cause of every unexpected infant death.

CAN SIDS BE PREVENTED?

No product can stop SIDS from happening. However, research has identified factors commonly associated with SIDS, such as passive smoke exposure, stomach sleeping, and soft bedding. Risk factors can play an important part in the chain of events culminating in a SIDS death. In some cases, the elimination of a risk factor can alter the outcome, influencing the baby's ability to survive. Since 1992, when the Back To Sleep advisory was first announced, the rate of SIDS has dropped 38%—the equivalent of sparing the lives of 2,000 infants a year in the U.S.
- Sources: Goyco, P.G., & Beckerman, R.C. (1990). Sudden infant death syndrome. *Current Problems in Pediatrics 20*, 297-346. Krous, H.F. (1988). Pathological considerations of sudden infant death syndrome. *Pediatrician, 15*, 231-239.
- http://www.circsol.com/SIDS/SIDSFACT.HTM, http://www.sids.org/researchproj.htm,

Lecture Suggestion 2: The Effects of Malnutrition The purpose of this lecture is to expand upon Santrock's introduction of the effects of malnutrition. The prevalence of malnutrition is overwhelming. Nearly 195 million children under the age of 5 are undernourished. Malnutrition affects physical and cognitive development, and the environment in which malnutrition occurs also influences the outcome.

Brown and Pollitt's article, *Malnutrition, Poverty, and Intellectual Development*, overviews several interesting studies related to this complex relationship. Recent research has stimulated a conceptual shift in understanding the relationship between malnutrition and cognitive impairments. Traditionally, the "main-effect" model guided our understanding. This model states that malnutrition during the first 2 years of life caused severe, permanent brain damage which in turn resulted in cognitive impairment. This linear model is too simplistic: brain growth retardation is not always permanent. Rather, brain growth is "put on hold temporarily" when malnourished. If diet is improved, brain growth can rebound, especially if an appropriate environment is involved. In addition, other factors such as physical growth, quality of the environment, and intellectual stimulation impact the effects of malnutrition on cognitive development. Thus, an "interactional model" more accurately describes the complicated relationship between malnutrition and cognitive development. Malnutrition has a bi-directional relationship with illness, which can cause delays in motor development and physical growth, which in turn leads to lowered expectations of the child from others; these lowered expectations can impede cognitive development. In parallel, delayed motor development and physical growth and lethargy from illness can reduce exploration of the environment, which impacts cognitive development. If you add poverty to the equation, the effects can be exacerbated given the quality of the environment in which the child can explore and the lack of educational and medical resources.
- Source: Brown, J.L., & Pollitt, E. (1996). Malnutrition, poverty and intellectual development. *Scientific American*, 38-43.

Lecture Suggestion 3: Current Views of Infant Motor Development The purpose of this lecture is to expose students to the current view of infant motor development. Esther Thelen's developmental biodynamic perspective is introduced in the chapter, while this lecture extension describes one of her research studies (1984; 1987; 1994). This perspective contrasts sharply with the traditional view of motor development, which views motor development as a maturationally determined stagelike progression. In contrast, Thelen views motor development and walking, in particular, to be the result of "self-organization." That is, systems exhibit complex patterns over time without a genetic blueprint. Movement develops from the interaction of constraints in the organism and the environment. Thus, it is the dynamic interaction of developing neuromuscular pathways and the changing environmental demands that determine when an infant will first walk independently. This new view of motor development emphasizes the importance of exploration and selection in finding solutions to new task demands. Infants need to assemble adaptive patterns by modifying their current movement patterns. The task and the challenge of the context drive change, not prescribed genetic instructions.

The so-called "disappearing reflex" intrigued Thelen. Newborn infants, when held upright with their feet on a support surface, perform alternating steplike motions and appear to be walking. This phenomenon is referred to as the "stepping reflex." The intriguing aspect of this is that this ability "disappears" a few months later and does not reappear until approximately 12 months of age. Experts assumed that the reflex "disappears" because of some genetic maturationally determined switch in the brain. This explanation made sense because they assumed that motor development was single-causal. However, Thelen and her colleagues (1984) observed infants kicking their legs and noted that they were actually engaged in the same movement as the stepping reflex. Thus, the kicking movement was actually the "stepping reflex" in a supine position. Interestingly, when they positioned the kicking infant in an upright position, the infant ceased the motion, yet when they laid the same infant down, the infant resumed the kicking/stepping movement. They questioned how the maturing brain could inhibit this reflex in one position and not in a different position.

During the same time period that the "stepping reflex" is not evident in the upright position (after it disappears), Thelen noted that infants are experiencing rapid weight gain. The infants were getting heavier, but not necessarily any stronger. She then speculated that it was the interaction of the heavier legs and the biomechanically demanding posture of being upright that suppressed the "stepping reflex." Thelen and her colleagues ingeniously tested their hypothesis (Thelen, Fisher, & Ridley-Johnson, 1984). They experimentally manipulated the weight of the infants' legs by submerging the infants in waist deep water. The infants, without the added weight because their legs were submerged in water, could "walk." The point to stress is that motor development is not single-causal, but rather a multicausal developmental phenomenon.

- Research Project 2: Replication of Thelen's Work on Infant Motor Development complements this lecture suggestion.
- Sources: Thelen, E. (1994). Motor development: A new synthesis. *American Psychologist, 50,* 79-95. Thelen, E., Fisher, D. M., & Ridley-Johnson, R. (1984). The relationship between physical growth and a newborn reflex. *Infant Behavior and Development, 7,* 479-493. Thelen, E., Kelso, J. S., & Fogel, A. (1987). Self-organizing systems and infant motor development. *Developmental Review, 7,* 39-65.

Classroom Activities

Classroom Activity 1: Assessing Infant Reflexes The purpose of this classroom activity is twofold. First, students will gain experience assessing infant reflexes. Second, students will further develop their understanding of infant reflexes. The goal is to assess two infants, one aged 1 to 4 months and the other infant aged 6 to 12 months. Invite two parents and their infants to class. Oftentimes, one of your students has an infant in his or her family or knows someone who does; most often a phone call is all it takes to get the parent to bring the baby to the class. **Handout 1** describes seven infant reflexes and the conditions that elicit each of the reflexes. For each infant, have the parent perform the stimulation necessary to elicit the reflexive behavior. Students can note on the handout which of the reflexes are present (P) or absent (A) for each infant. After performing the demonstration with each infant, they should answer the provided questions.

- How many of the reflexive behaviors were exhibited by the younger infants and by the older infants?
- Which reflexes dropped out early?
- What responses seem to replace each of the reflexive behaviors in the older infants?
- What might be the adaptive value of each reflex in the infant's repertoire?

- Use in the Classroom: Discuss the observation techniques and possible problems with the methods used. Have students discuss any discrepancies and the reasons for why reflexes drop out.

Logistics:
- Materials: Handout 1 (Assessing Infant Reflexes).
- Group size: Full class.
- Approximate time: 10 minutes for the reflex assessment, and 15 minutes for a full class discussion.

Classroom Activity 2: To Circumcise or Not to Circumcise—That Is the Cutting Question This activity affords students an opportunity to debate the controversy of infant circumcision. Oftentimes, students have preformed ideas regarding circumcision, or neglect to consider the implications of circumcision. Students usually assume that circumcisions are only performed on male infants. In small groups, have students identify the advantages and disadvantages of male circumcision and the advantages and disadvantages of female circumcision. Also, the groups should determine whether they are in favor of male and female circumcision. Frequently, students in the United States are appalled by the practices of female circumcision in Africa, yet they fail to reflect on the practice of male circumcision in the United States. Then as a class, you can tally the groups' ideas, positions, and the mitigating circumstances for whether they would encourage the circumcision of male and female infants. Do the students' decisions differ based upon gender, age, religion, or parenting status? The following ideas will help you get started:
- Current national rates for male circumcision: Australia 15%(1), Canada 20%(2), the United States 60%(3). In the U.S., over 1.25 million infants annually (3,300 per day, 1 child every 26 seconds).

Advantages of male circumcision:
- Parents can make sure that after-surgery care is properly done to avoid infection.
- Parents can request safe local anesthesia for the baby during the procedure.
- Circumcised males have easier hygiene to practice.
- Circumcised men are less likely to contract cancer of the penis.

Disadvantages of male circumcision:
- Surgery has a little risk, as do all surgeries; after-surgery care is important for avoiding infection.
- Physical trauma occurs because most circumcisions are performed without anesthesia.
- There is no evidence that a circumcised male is less likely to acquire or transmit venereal disease.
- Cancer of the penis is quite rare.

Two interesting films related to female genital mutilation:
- "Warrior Marks" by Alice Walker: This is a documentary film that follows Alice Walker and Pratibha Parmar through a journey in Africa and England, where they seek to educate people about the harmful, sometimes deadly aftereffects of female genital mutilation.
- "Rites," a documentary film by the American Anthropological Association (AAA), also outlines the harmful effects of female genital mutilation.

For additional information, visit the interesting web site that highlights the ritual female genital mutilation in Africa (http://hamp.hampshire.edu/~mnbF94/whatis.FGM.html). The following information was taken from that web site.
- Female genital mutilation has often been referred to as female circumcision and compared to male circumcision. However, such comparison is often misleading. Both practices include the removal of well- functioning parts of the genitalia and are quite unnecessary. Both rituals also serve to perpetuate customs which seek to regulate and keep control over the body and sexuality of the individual. However, female genital mutilation is far more drastic and damaging than male circumcision. A more appropriate analogy would be between clitoridectomy and penisdectomy where the entire penis is removed.
- The term female genital mutilation covers three main varieties of genital mutilation:
  - "Sunna" circumcision: Consists of the removal of the prepuce and/or the tip of the clitoris. Sunna in Arabic means "tradition."
  - Clitoridectomy (also referred to as excision): Consists of the removal of the entire clitoris (both prepuce and glans), and the removal of the adjacent labia.

- Infibulation: This most extreme form consists of the removal of the clitoris, the adjacent labia (majora and minora), and the joining of the scraped sides of the vulva across the vagina, where they are secured with thorns or sewn with catgut or thread. A small opening is kept to allow passage of urine and menstrual blood. An infibulated woman must be cut open to allow intercourse on the wedding night and is closed again afterwards to secure fidelity to the husband.

Logistics:
- Group size: Small group, then full class.
- Approximate time: Small group (15 minutes) and full class discussion (30 minutes).
- Sources: (1) Average of state and territory circumcision rates NOCIRC of Australia. (2) Average of provincial circumcision rates compiled from Health & Welfare Canada and Statistics Canada. (3) Average of regional circumcision rates compiled by National Center for Health Statistics. Denniston, G. C. (1992). Unnecessary circumcision. *The female patient*, 17. Romberg, R. (1985). *Circumcision: The painful dilemma*. South Hadley, MA: Bergin & Garvey Publishers. Squires, S. (June 1990). Medinews. *Ladies' Home Journal*, 94.

Classroom Activity 3: Assessing Infant Abilities The purpose of this activity is to expose students to an infant and allow them to observe an assessment of an infant's abilities. Invite a parent and his/her infant to class. Oftentimes, one of your students has an infant in his or her family or knows someone who does; most often a phone call is all it takes to get the parent to bring the baby to the class. It is important to demonstrate various infant assessment instruments or scales to the students before the infant is brought into the class. Consider covering the Apgar, the Brazelton Neonatal Assessment Scale, and the Denver Developmental Screening Test. If your Psychology Department, Educational Psychology Department or library does not have a copy of the screening devices, a local pediatrician may be convinced to part with a copy of what they use and to offer some quick instruction on how to use it. Another option is to invite a local pediatrician to come to the class and give the screening.

The students' task will be to determine the age of the infant as well as the baby's developmental scores. It is best if each student gets a copy of the screening devices ahead of time. During the class period, run the infant through some of the components of each of the screening devices. It would probably be best if you conducted the behavioral tests, but only at the direction of the students. The infant will experience less stress if you minimize the number of individuals manipulating him/her. The infant, if awake, will tolerate between 10 and 20 minutes of manipulation before deciding that he/she is too young to be in college. After the infant leaves or refuses to play anymore, have students try to determine what the baby's scores would be on the various measures and to give their best guess as to the specific age of the infant. Ask the parent to reveal the infant's actual age and, if known, the baby's latest developmental scores. If the infant is unresponsive during the class period, allow the students to ask the parent questions regarding the infant (e.g., can he/she differentiate the infant's cries).

Logistics:
- Materials: One or more of the following assessment instruments (Apgar, Brazelton Neonatal Assessment Scale, and Denver Developmental Screening Test). Copies of the screening devices for students.
- Group size: Full class.
- Approximate time: 20 minutes to review assessment devices, 10-20 minutes for the assessment, and 30 minutes for a full class discussion.

Classroom Activity 4: Critical Thinking Multiple-Choice Questions and Suggested Answers Discuss the answers to the critical thinking multiple-choice questions on **Handout 2**. Suggested answers are provided as **Handout 3**. The point of question 1 is to get students to pay attention to figures and tables provided in the text. Students often do not understand this material very well; you probably will want to discuss with them how to interpret tables and figures. For example, you may want to discuss with students how inferences can be drawn from the tables and figures beyond what is indicated in text or captions.

The point of question 2 is to have students attend to the difference between sensation and perception, and to examine the sorts of inferences researchers make about infant perceptual capacities based on infant behavior. Both of these issues are good topics for discussion prior to having students do this exercise. The distinction between sensation and perception is not clear to people working in the field, and some researchers do not feel it is productive to make the separation. Nevertheless, an interesting way to apply the distinction is to discuss whether infants' discrimination between stimuli or their reaction to stimulating events represents some sort of innate, reflexive response or whether it is based on active interpretation. You can guide students' solutions to this question by having them try to decide which of the results for each of the senses described in the text most convincingly indicates active perceptual processes.

Question 3 continues to provide practice with the distinctions between inferences, observations, and assumptions.

Logistics:

- Materials: Handout 2 (the critical thinking multiple-choice questions) and Handout 3 (answers).
- Group size: Small groups to discuss the questions, then a full class discussion.
- Approximate time: Small groups (15 to 20 minutes), full class discussion of any question (15 minutes).

Classroom Activity 5: Critical Thinking Essay Questions and Suggestions for Helping Students Answer the Essays Discuss students' answers to the critical thinking essay questions presented as **Handout 4**. The purpose is threefold. First, answering these questions further facilitates students' understanding of concepts in chapter 5. Second, this type of essay question affords the students an opportunity to apply the concepts to their own lives, which will facilitate their retention of the material. Third, the essay format also will give students practice expressing themselves in written form. Ideas to help students answer the critical thinking essay questions are provided as **Handout 5**.

Logistics:

- Materials: Handout 4 (essay questions) and Handout 5 (helpful suggestions for the answers).
- Group size: Individual, then full class.
- Approximate time: Individual (60 minutes), full class discussion of any questions (30 minutes).

Personal Applications

Personal Application 1: Remember When The purpose of this exercise is for students to connect with the material on infant development through stories about themselves. Since we have no active memories dating back to our first couple of years, it is not possible to recall experiences related to reflex-based functioning, milestones such as rolling over and searching for a hidden object, and parental responses. The dramatic nature of development during these early stages is difficult to grasp when simply read in a book. A more real-life connection can demonstrate that these phenomena do occur and make quite an impact to those experiencing them through parenthood.

- Instructions for Students: Ask your parents to spend some time talking with you about when you were a baby. Maybe they can get out the pictures and your baby book! Ask them what they remember about the early days after birth. Did your mother breast feed or not? Why? What were the views during that time about doing so? What are their memories of your sleep habits, eating habits, motor development, crying, stimulus response, potty training? In what ways do they remember you changing the most? Enjoy this walk down memory lane with your parents and either read your text prior to your conversation or soon afterwards to link your own story with the specific developmental issues covered.
- Use in the Classroom: Have students share their stories in class. Compare and contrast what they experienced and discuss how much is likely to indicate individual differences and how much is a function of their parents' memories!

Personal Application 2: If I Could Read Your Mind The purpose of this exercise is to get students thinking more in-depth about infant sensory experiences and the research methods used to study them. Until quite recently, babies have been believed to experience the world in very limited ways. This was most likely because people relied only on what they could see babies do overtly. Some amazing developments have been made with regard to assessing the early experiences of infants, and we now know that even in utero, babies are capable of sensing and encoding sensory information.

- Instructions for Students: Read through your text and familiarize yourself with infants' sensory functioning and the studies psychologists have done to learn more about this amazing area. Choose a behavior you would like to explore with an infant, and write up how you would go about studying it. Use a journal article format to write up your proposal, beginning with the behavior of interest, why it's of interest, and your methodology. Base your results section on what you expect you might find, and conclude with any questions you may have that would lead to additional scientific investigation.

Research Project Ideas

Research Project 1: Infant Brain Development and Child-Care Settings The purpose of this activity is to have students review research studies regarding infant brain development and to apply the research findings to the development of an infant child-care setting. The first step involves the literature review. Either have students gather research articles or you can have a few selected articles for the students to use. Nash's (1997) article, Fertile Minds, in *Time* magazine is very interesting and relevant. In small groups, the students should then generate a list of perceptual abilities that develop over the first year of life. Second, the students should develop a child-care program for infants that would facilitate infants' brain development. The child-care program should be based on suggestions from current research findings that would enhance infants' development. For example, they should determine what toys would be appropriate for infants of different ages and they should decide how they would decorate the setting. Consider using Gunzenhauser's (1988) edited book as a resource for this activity. It is important to point out that more stimulation is not always better. See **Handout 6**.

- Have students complete the following tasks: First, using research articles and your textbook, identify how the brain develops during the first year of life. Explain how experiences influence brain development. Second, develop a child-care program for infants that would facilitate infant brain/perceptual development. The child-care program should be based on suggestions from current research that would enhance infants' development. For example, you will want to consider what toys would be appropriate for infants of different ages and decide how you would decorate the setting.
- Sources: Gunzenhauser, N. (1988). *Infant stimulation: For whom, what kind, when, and how much? Pediatric Round Table No. 13.* Johnson & Johnson Baby Products. Nash, J.M. (Feb. 3, 1997). Fertile minds. *Time*, 49-56.

Research Project 2: Replication of Thelen's Work on Infant Motor Development This research project idea will help students understand the complex nature of the development of infant motor skills, especially the development of walking, and give them practice replicating a research study. Lecture Suggestion 3 regarding Thelen's perspective on infant motor development will provide relevant background knowledge. This project will require approval by the school's human subjects review board and the parent's informed consent.

First, have students read the Thelen, Fisher, and Ridley-Johnson (1984) article. They should also write a summary of the introduction section and specify the hypotheses. Second, have students in groups of two to four people replicate the procedure in this study. Given that two separate manipulations were conducted in the Thelen et al. study, have half of the students manipulate the leg mass by adding small weights to the infant's legs. The other half of the class can manipulate the effects of leg mass by submerging the infant's legs in water. Third, students should write up their results and relate their results to the hypotheses. If the results are not consistent with Thelen et al.'s, have the students explain why they think the results were inconsistent. Finally, students should present their findings to the class. See **Handout 7**.

- Summarize the introduction section of the Thelen et al. (1984) article.
- Identify the hypotheses of the study.
- Describe the study's procedures and explain if your procedures differ from Thelen et al.'s procedures.
- Summarize the results of your study.
- Discuss how your results compare to Thelen et al.'s results. Discuss any discrepancies.
- Use in the Classroom: Discuss whether the students had to modify the procedures. Did they obtain the same findings? If not, why?
- Source: Thelen, E., Fisher, D. M., & Ridley-Johnson, R. (1984). The relationship between physical growth and a newborn reflex. *Infant Behavior and Development, 7*, 479-493.

Film and Video List

The following films and videos supplement the content of chapter 5. Contact information for film distributors can be found at the front of this Instructor's Manual under Film and Video Sources.

The Brain (Insight Media, 50 minutes). This animated BBC production explores the brain and covers physiology, levels of function, and brain structure.

The Brain: An Inside Look (Films for the Humanities and Sciences, 20 minutes). This program provides an introduction to the brain. Techniques for studying brain development and functioning including computerized tomography (CT), magnetic resonance imaging (MRI), and advanced surgical techniques are discussed.

The Brain-Mind Connection (Insight Media, 30 minutes). This program explores how the brain interacts with thought, behavior, culture, and environment; shows the resilience and plasticity of the brain; and discusses structure and function, lateralization, and effects of enriched environments.

The Development of the Human Brain (Films for the Humanities and Sciences, 40 minutes). This program follows the physiological development of the human brain from conception to the moment of birth.

Evolution, Environment, and Growth (Insight Media, 30 minutes). The relation between central nervous system development and motor development from infancy to childhood is examined. The interaction between motor development and social development is explored as well.

How Relationships Are Formed (Films for the Humanities and Sciences, 24 minutes). This program shows that as the infant's need for sleep decreases, his need for relationships increases. The baby seeks attention and the mother-child relationship grows.

Infancy: Landmarks of Development (Magna Systems, 22 minutes). There are four focuses of this video: physical and motor development; principles of development; factors that influence development; and regulation of basic processes.

Inside Information: The Brain and How It Works (Films for the Humanities and Sciences, 58 minutes). This program examines research on the brain's processes: how individual parts of the brain work, how the brain uses pattern recognition rather than logic to interpret reality, experiments with computer analogs have been successful and unsuccessful.

Mothers, Fathers, and Babies (Films for the Humanities and Sciences, 26 minutes). This program observes the role of breast-feeding in different cultures and its effect on the role of the father. Fathers in industrialized countries have a positive opportunity to assume an active part in infant care since babies are often weaned at two and three months.

Mystery of the Senses (Insight Media, 5 volumes, total 300 minutes). This series covers the five senses, dealing with neural pathways, visual images, dreams, taste mechanism, touch and infant growth, development of perfume scents, and use of sound.

Pediatric Brain Development: The Importance of Head Start (Films for the Humanities and Sciences, 17 minutes). *ABC News* anchor Diane Sawyer reports on the neurological connections that form in a child's brain during pregnancy and early childhood and the long-term effects of sensory stimulation and deprivation.

Pediatric Neuroscience: Rage of Innocents (Films for the Humanities and Sciences, 47 minutes). Emotional neglect of children during the early years can have long-term biochemical consequences. In this documentary, anthropologists from Cornell and Emory Universities report on research findings regarding the subtle biochemical link between parental attentiveness and the proper development of the child's brain regions that control stress responses.

Physical Development: The First Five Years (Films for the Humanities and Sciences, 19 minutes). This program shows children at each stage of physical development between birth and age five. Commentary is provided by a pediatrician and child development specialist.

Sudden Infant Death Syndrome: An Update (Films for the Humanities and Sciences, 17 minutes). This program explores what is known about SIDS and describes practices that may reduce risk factors. Doctors discuss the mystery of this silent killer.

Sudden Infant Death Syndrome (Films for the Humanities and Sciences, 49 minutes). Parents discuss losing infants to SIDS, and doctors and researchers discuss trying to understand and defeat the syndrome. Recent research findings are discussed.

Web Site Suggestions

The URLs for general sites, common to all chapters, can be found at the front of this Instructor's Manual under Useful Web Sites. At the time of publication, all sites were current and active, however, please be advised that you may occasionally encounter a dead link.

American SIDS Institute
http://www.sids.org/

Breastfeeding
http://dir.yahoo.com/Society_and_Culture/Cultures_and_Groups/Women/Mothering/Breastfeeding

Center for Disease Control
New Pediatric Growth Charts Provide Tool To Ward Off Future Weight Problems
http://www.cdc.gov/nchs/releases/00news/growchrt.htm

Malnutrition: Determinants, extent and effects
http://www.odc.com/anthro/tutorial/tunit18.html

National Sudden Infant Death Syndrome Resource Center
http://www.circsol.com/SIDS/

Ritual Female Genital Mutilation in Africa
http://hamp.hampshire.edu/~mnbF94/whatis.FGM.html

Zero to Three: National Center for Infants, Toddlers, and Families
http://www.zerotothree.org/

Assessing Infant Reflexes

The purpose of this exercise is twofold. First, you will gain experience assessing infant abilities. Second, you will further develop your understanding of infant reflexes. The goal is to assess two infants, one aged 1 to 4 months and the other infant aged 6 to 12 months. For each infant, perform the stimulation necessary to elicit the reflexive behavior. Note which of the reflexes are present (P) or absent (A) for each infant. After performing the demonstration with each infant, you should answer the questions that follow.

Reflex	Stimulation and reflex	Infant 1 Sex __ Age __	Infant 2 Sex __ Age __
Placing	Backs of infant's feet are drawn against a flat surface's edge: Baby withdraws foot	P/A	P/A
Walking	Hold baby under arms with bare feet touching flat surface: Baby makes steplike motions that appear like coordinated walking	P/A	P/A
Darwinian (grasping)	Stroke palm of infant's hand: Baby makes strong fist; if both fists are closed around a stick, the infant could be raised to standing position	P/A	P/A
Tonic neck	Baby is laid down on back: Infant turns head to one side and extends arms and legs on preferred side and flexes opposite limbs	P/A	P/A
Moro (startle)	Make a sudden, loud noise near infant: Infant extends legs, arms, and fingers, arches back, and draws back head	P/A	P/A
Babinski	Stroke sole of baby's foot: Infant's toes fan out and foot twists in	P/A	P/A
Rooting	Stroke baby's cheek with one's finger: Baby's head turns, mouth opens, and sucking movements begin	P/A	P/A

Questions:
- How many of the reflexive behaviors were exhibited by the younger infant? By the older infant?
- Which reflexes dropped out early?
- What responses seem to replace each of the reflexive behaviors in the older infant?
- What might be the adaptive value of each reflex in the infant's repertoire?

Critical Thinking Multiple-Choice Questions

1. Chapter 5 contains a number of tables and figures that illustrate various topics. Five of them are listed below. Each of the figures is paired with an interpretation of the information it presents. Which interpretation is most accurate? Circle the letter of the best answer and explain why it is the best answer and why each other answer is not as good.

   a. Figure 5.3: The number of brain cells increases dramatically during the first 2 years of life.
   b. Figure 5.7: Reflexes that disappear involve gross motor behavior.
   c. Figure 5.8: Most infants can walk by themselves before they are 1 year old.
   d. Figure 5.11: There is no evidence that 2-month-old infants can discriminate between colors.
   e. Figure 5.13: Four-month-old infants can differentiate between expected and unexpected events.

2. In this chapter, Santrock distinguishes between the concepts of sensation and perception, and then takes the reader on a tour of the sensory and perceptual capacities of human infants. For which sense do we appear to know the most about the perceptual capabilities of infants? Circle the letter of the best answer and explain why it is the best answer and why each other answer is not as good.

   a. vision
   b. hearing
   c. smell
   d. taste
   e. touch

3. Robert Fantz's pioneering study of visual perception found that infants look at different things for different lengths of time. Which of the following statements represents an important assumption, rather than an inference or an observation? Circle the letter of the best answer and explain why it is the best answer and why each other answer is not as good.
   a. Infants, as young as 2 days old, prefer to look at patterns, such as faces, printed matter, or bull's-eyes longer than colored discs.
   b. Infants, as young as 2 days old, look longer at patterns, such as faces, printed matter, or bull's-eyes than colored discs.
   c. Pattern perception has an innate basis.
   d. Fantz's "looking chamber" advanced the ability of researchers to investigate infant vision perception.
   e. Two-month-old infants prefer to look at patterns, such as faces, printed matter, or bull's-eyes longer than colored discs.

Suggested Answers for Critical Thinking Multiple-Choice Questions

1. Chapter 5 contains a number of tables and figures that illustrate various topics. Five of them are listed below. Each of the figures is paired with an interpretation of the information it presents. Which interpretation is most accurate? Circle the letter of the best answer and explain why it is the best answer and why each other answer is not as good.

   a. The interpretation of <u>Figure 5.3</u> is not accurate. It illustrates the increasing richness of connections between neurons, not an increase in the number of neurons. Dendrites connect neurons, they are not separate nerve cells.

   b. The interpretation of <u>Figure 5.7</u> is not accurate. The grasping reflex involves fine, not gross, motor skills.

   c. The interpretation of <u>Figure 5.8</u> is not accurate. The figure shows a time range during which infants begin to walk unaided. This time frame extends well past 1 year of age.

   d. The interpretation of <u>Figure 5.11</u> is not accurate. Although the differences are small, 2-month-old infants appear to fixate on red, yellow, and white discs for different amounts of time. This suggests that they can discriminate between these colors.

   e. The interpretation of <u>Figure 5.13</u> is accurate. Spelke's research on infant perception found that 4-month-old infants look longer at unexpected actions than at expected actions, which indicates the infant's ability to differentiate

2. In this chapter, Santrock distinguishes between the concepts of sensation and perception, and then takes the reader on a tour of the sensory and perceptual capacities of human infants. For which sense do we appear to know the most about the perceptual capabilities of infants? Circle the letter of the best answer and explain why it is the best answer and why each other answer is not as good.

   a. <u>Vision</u> is the best answer. We know of several kinds of visual discriminations that infants can make (e.g., striped versus gray fields, stages of face perception, depth perception, and coordination of vision and touch). These all seem to require different kinds of interpretations of visual stimuli and involve a greater variety of interpretations compared with the other senses.

   b. <u>Hearing</u> is not the best answer. Facts are presented about auditory discrimination, the coordination of hearing and vision, and hearing sensitivity. The first two are arguably aspects of perception, but the last seems more an example of sensation (registering the occurrence of a stimulus). So "vision" is a better answer.

   c. <u>Smell</u> is not the best answer. We know about a small number of smell discriminations that infants can make (perceptions). We have fewer examples of olfactory perceptions than visual perceptions.

   d. <u>Taste</u> is not the best answer. Again, we mainly know about various discriminations that are possible. Some of these discriminations, however, appear to be based on responses newborns make to very specific taste stimuli, which may indicate that "true" perception is not involved.

   e. <u>Touch</u> is not the best answer. Much of the information about touch comes from studies of reflexes; hence, it is unclear whether perception is involved. Nothing is indicated about touch discriminations, and the only perceptual phenomenon noted is the coordination of touch and vision.

3. Robert Fantz's pioneering study of visual perception found that infants look at different things for different lengths of time. Which of the following statements represents an important inference, rather than an assumption or an observation? Circle the letter of the best answer and explain why it is the best answer and why each other answer is not as good.

    a. <u>Infants, as young as 2 days old, prefer to look at patterns</u>, such as faces, printed matter, or bull's-eyes longer than colored discs is not the best answer as it is an assumption. Researchers assume that a preference is displayed when an infant looks longer at one stimuli compared to other stimuli.

    b. <u>Infants, as young as 2 days old, look longer at patterns</u>, such as faces, printed matter, or bull's-eyes than colored discs is not the best answer as it is an observation. Fantz found that infants did look longer at patterns compared to colored discs.

    c. <u>Pattern perception has an innate basis</u> is the best answer as it represents an inference. Given that it is not possible to determine if pattern perception is innate, researchers infer that it is innately based or at least is acquired after only minimal environmental experience given that pattern perception has been observed in infants only 2 days old.

    d. <u>Fantz's "looking chamber" advanced the ability of researchers to investigate infant vision perception</u> is not the best answer as it reflects an observation. Fantz's pioneering work has stimulated significant research and understanding of infant visual perception.

    e. <u>Two-month-old infants prefer to look at patterns</u>, such as faces, printed matter, or bull's-eyes longer than colored discs is not the best answer as it is an assumption. Same as the answer for "a."

Handout 4 (CA 5)

Critical Thinking Essay Questions

Your answers to this kind of question demonstrate an ability to comprehend and apply ideas discussed in this chapter.

1. Provide examples of cephalocaudal and proximodistal patterns of development.

2. Sketch brain development during infancy, and speculate about how brain development relates to behavioral and psychological development during this period of life.

3. Describe the various states of infant consciousness. Also explain their relationship to sleep and waking.

4. Discuss the pros and cons of breast- versus bottle-feeding.

5. How would you explain the importance of reflexes, and their development, to a friend?

6. Describe the general patterns in the development of infant motor capabilities during the first year.

7. Compare and contrast the development of gross and fine motor skills during infancy.

8. Describe the new perspective on motor development called developmental biodynamics. Explain how it differs from the traditional view of motor development.

9. Define and distinguish *sensation*, *perception*, and *intermodal perception*. Also explain why they make interesting problems for study by developmentalists and what practical problems their study might solve.

10. Explain how it is possible for researchers to study infants' early competencies.

11. Apparently, infants can imitate facial expression nearly at birth, but have 20-200 to 20-400 vision at birth. Provide a rationale for understanding this apparent inconsistency.

12. Explain what we know about the ability of infants to hear.

13. Do infants feel pain? In answering, also indicate evidence that challenges the traditional practice of not administering anesthetics to infants having operations.

14. Describe the relationship between perception and motor development. Give an example.

Ideas to Help You Answer Critical Thinking Essay Questions

1. Present your examples in a directional format, following the flow of each pattern of development.

2. Approach these areas as a hierarchy—begin with brain development and map out behavioral development and then psychological development.

3. Think of the states of infant consciousness as baby "moods"—the way in which they are experiencing and respond to their world at any particular time. This applies to both sleep states and waking states.

4. Imagine that your job is to objectively inform mothers-to-be about their feeding options, keeping in mind that their concern is for what's in the best interest of their baby.

5. Begin by defining what a reflex is, then explicitly describe several infant reflexes. Tell the purpose of each then conclude with the overall importance of reflexes early in development.

6. Create a time line and mark the general onset of particular motor capabilities. Draw your conclusions about the overall patterns that emerge.

7. Make a list of gross motor skills and fine motor skills in the order in which they develop to provide an illustration of what you're comparing. You can derive similarities and differences from this.

8. Begin with a description of the traditional view of motor development and it's weaknesses Lead into a description of developmental biodynamics and how it addresses the shortcomings of the former.

9. Describe what an individual experiences with regard to sensation, perception, and intermodal perception. This will provide a basis for explaining why they are pertinent to study, and the possible practical applications resulting from doing so.

10. Address this issue through descriptions of several infant research methodologies. Describe a study or two and the findings they've yielded. What factors contribute to our confidence in those results? What makes these studies (and their findings) different from those done years ago? Are infants getting smarter, or are the research methods getting better? Comment.

11. Take another look at the pictures in your text demonstrating infants' visual abilities. Also review what the text says about the extent to which infants imitate, and the kinds of expressions they copy.

12. During your explanation, keep in mind the fact that infants can't tell us what they can and cannot perceive. Also address how we know what we do about their auditory experiences.

13. Begin with a discussion of the historical view of infants and pain. How was it viewed, and thus responded to? Why has thinking changed, and in what ways is it different? What practical implications have resulted from the change?

14. First define perception and explain what constitutes motor development—this will lay the foundation for a discussion about their relationship. The best explanations come out of approaching your audience as being completely naïve about the subject matter.

Handout 6 (RP 1)

Infant Brain Development and Child-Care Settings

The purpose of this activity is to review research studies regarding infant brain development and to apply the research findings to the development of an infant child-care setting.

- Using research articles and your textbook, identify how the brain develops during the first year of life. Explain how experiences influence brain development.

- Develop a child-care program for infants that would facilitate infant brain/perceptual development. The child-care program should be based on suggestions from current research findings that would enhance infants' development. For example, you will want to consider what toys would be appropriate for infants of different ages and decide how you would decorate the setting. It is important to point out that more stimulation is not always better.

- Sources: Gunzenhauser, N. (1988). *Infant stimulation: For whom, what kind, when, and how much? Pediatric Round Table No. 13*. Johnson & Johnson Baby Products. Nash, J.M. (Feb. 3, 1997). Fertile minds. *Time*, 49-56.

Replication of Thelen's Work on Infant Motor Development

The purpose of this research project idea is to help you better understand the complex nature of the development of infant motor skills, especially the development of walking, and to give you practice replicating a research study. In order to proceed, you will need to clear this project through the human subjects review board at your school and get a signed Informed Consent form from the baby's parents. You will first write a summary of the Thelen, Fisher, and Ridley-Johnson (1984) article. Then you should attempt to replicate the procedure in this study. Half of the class will manipulate the infant's leg mass by adding small weights to the infant's legs. The other half of the class will manipulate the effects of leg mass by submerging the infant's legs in water. You will then write up your results and relate the results to the proposed hypotheses. If the results are not consistent with Thelen et al.'s, you should explain why you think the results were inconsistent.

* Summarize the introduction section of the Thelen et al. (1984) article.
* Identify the hypotheses of the study.
* Describe the study's procedures and explain if your procedures differ from Thelen et al.'s procedures.
* Summarize the results of your study.
* Discuss how your results compare to Thelen et al.'s results. Discuss any discrepancies.

* Source: Thelen, E., Fisher, D. M., & Ridley-Johnson, R. (1984). The relationship between physical growth and a newborn reflex. *Infant Behavior and Development, 7*, 479-493.

Chapter 6: Cognitive Development in Infancy

Total Teaching Package Outline

Lecture Outline	Resource References
Cognitive Development in Infancy	PowerPoint Presentation: See www.mhhe.com Cognitive Maps: See Appendix A
Piaget's Theory of Infant Development	LO1 OHT11 & IB: Piaget's Four Stages PA1: Something Old, Something New F/V: Scales of Infant Psychological Development WS: Jean Piaget-Intellectual Development
• The Stage of Sensorimotor Development	LO2 OHT49 & IB: Sensorimotor Thought OHT 53 & IB: Circular Reactions
• Substages	OHT 69 & IB: Substages of Sensorimotor Dev.
• Object Permanence	RP1: Object Permanence
• Evaluating Piaget's Sensorimotor Stage 　　　-Perceptual Development 　　　-Conceptual Development	LO3 F/V: The Infant Mind
Learning and Remembering	WS: Breakthrough: Infant Learning F/V: Discovering the Outside World F/V: Mastering Early Skills F/V: Young Minds: Is Zero-to-Three Destiny
• Conditioning	LO4
• Habituation and Dishabituation	LO5 PA2: Oh, That Again?!
• Imitation	LO6
• Memory	LS1: Why Can't We Remember Events from 　　　Our Early Childhood?
Individual Differences in Intelligence	LO7 LS2: To Test or Not to Test F/V: Individual Differences and Developmental 　　　Milestones
Language Development	WS: Understanding Language Dev. and Hearing
• Defining Language	LO8 F/V: Language and Thinking F/V: Symbolic Formation and the Acquisition 　　　of Language

• How Language Develops	LO9 CA1: Testing Language Development F/V: Developing Language F/V: Language Development F/V: Symbolic Formation and the Acquisition of Language WS: Babies Don't Forget What They Hear WS: The Language Explosion: Newsweek

• Biological Influences
   -Biological Evolution
 	
   -Biological Prewiring
	LO10
	LS3: Infant Speech Perception: Use It or Lose It?
	
	CA2: Do Animals Have the Ability to
	     Communicate?

• Behavioral and Environmental Influences	LO11 CA3: Observation of Parent-Infant Interaction RP2: Caregiver-Infant Language

Review	LS4: Is It Possible to Accelerate Infant
	     Cognitive Development?
	CA4: Supporting Arguments for Three Views
	     of Language Development
	CA5: Critical Thinking Multiple-Choice
	CA6: Critical Thinking Essays
	F/V: Infancy: Cognition and Language
	F/V: Language and Thinking
	F/V: The Mind: Development

Chapter Outline

PIAGET'S THEORY OF INFANT DEVELOPMENT
- Piaget believed that children pass through four stages of thought from infancy to adolescence.
- Passage through the stages results from biological pressures to adapt to the environment (assimilation and accommodation) and organize structures of thinking.
- **Schemes**, cognitive structures that help individuals organize and understand their experiences, change with age.
- The stages of thought are qualitatively different from one another. The way individuals think at one stage is different from thinking at other stages.

The Stage of Sensorimotor Development
- The first stage of thought for Piaget is the sensorimotor stage which lasts from birth to about 2 years of age. Mental development is characterized by progression in infant's ability to organize and coordinate sensations with physical movements and actions.
- Sensorimotor stage is divided into six substages in which schemes change in organization.
Substages
- The **simple reflexes** (0-1 month) substage involves coordinating sensation and action through reflexive behaviors (rooting and sucking). Babies develop the ability to produce behaviors that resemble reflexes in the absence of obvious reflexive stimuli which is evidence that the infant is initiating action and is actively structuring experiences in the first month.

- The **first habits and primary circular reactions** (1-4 months) substage involves infants' reflexes evolving into adaptive schemes that are more refined and coordinated.
  - A habit is a scheme based on simple reflex that is separate from its eliciting stimuli.
  - A **primary circular reaction** is a scheme based on the infant's attempt to reproduce an interesting or pleasurable event that initially occurred by chance.
- The **secondary circular reactions** (4-8 months) substage involves the infant becoming more object-oriented or focused on the world, moving beyond preoccupation with the self in sensorimotor interactions.
- The **coordination of secondary circular reactions** (8-12 months) substage includes several significant changes that involve the coordination of schemes and intentionality.
- In the **tertiary circular reactions, novelty, and curiosity** (12-18 months) substage, the infant becomes intrigued by the variety of properties that objects possess and by the many things they can make happen to objects.
- In the **internalization of schemes** (18-24 months) substage, the infant's mental functioning shifts from a purely sensorimotor plane to a symbolic plane, and the infant develops the ability to use primitive symbols.

Object Permanence
- **Object permanence** involves understanding that objects and events continue to exist, even when they cannot directly be seen, heard, or touched.

Evaluating Piaget's Sensorimotor Stage
- Infant development is viewed in terms of coordinating sensory input with motor actions.
- In the last three decades, many research studies in the areas of perceptual development and conceptual development have suggested that Piaget's theory needs to be revised.
  Perceptual Development
  - In perceptual development, researchers have found that a stable and differentiated perceptual world is formed earlier than Piaget envisioned.
    - Spelke found that 4-month-old infants have intermodal perception (the ability to coordinate information from two or more sensory modalities).
    - Baillargeon found that 4-month-olds demonstrate object permanence.
  Conceptual Development
  - Researchers have found that memory and other forms of symbolic activity occur at least by the second half of the first year of life, much earlier than Piaget believed.

LEARNING AND REMEMBERING
  Conditioning
  - Classical and operant conditioning occur in infancy.
  - Operant conditioning techniques (behavior is more likely reoccur if followed by a reward) have been useful for researchers to determine what infants perceive.
    - Infants will suck faster on a nipple when the sucking behavior is followed by a visual display, music, or a human voice.

  Habituation and Dishabituation
  - **Habituation** is the repeated presentation of the same stimulus that causes reduced attention to the stimulus.
  - **Dishabituation** is an infant's renewed interest in a stimulus.
    - Newborns are capable of habituation, but it becomes more acute over the first three months.
    - Habituation allows researchers to determine what infants perceive, the extent to which they see, hear, smile, taste, and experience touch.
    - Habituation also allows researchers to determine if infants recognize previously seen stimuli.

Imitation
- Meltzoff assessed infants' imitative abilities which he believes are biologically based because infants can imitate facial expressions as neonates.
- Other researchers say that babies are merely engaging in automatic responses to a stimulus, not imitating the facial expressions.
- **Deferred imitation** occurs after a time delay of hours or days.
  - Meltzoff found that 9-month-olds could imitate actions they had seen the day before.

Memory
- **Memory** involves the retention of information over time.
  - Research found that 2-month-olds can retain information about perceptual-motor actions.
  - However, critics argue that research fails to distinguish between retention of a perceptual-motor variety that is involved in conditioning tasks. Many experts argue that what many of us think of as memory does not occur until the second half of life.
- Infantile amnesia is the inability to remember anything from the first three years of life.
  - One explanation of this is the lack of maturation of the brain, especially the frontal lobes, which occurs during infancy.

INDIVIDUAL DIFFERENCES IN INTELLIGENCE
- It is important to know whether an infant is developing at a slow, a normal, or an advanced pace.
- The current version of Gesell's developmental test provides a **developmental quotient (DQ)**, which is an overall developmental score that combines subscores in motor, language, adaptive, and personal-social domains.
- The **Bayley Scales of Infant Development** are widely used in the assessment of infant development. The current version has three components: a mental scale, a motor scale, and an infant behavior profile.
  - The mental score includes assessment of the following:
    - auditory and visual attention to stimuli, manipulation (combining objects or shaking a rattle), examiner interaction (babbling and imitation), relation with toys (banging spoons together), memory involved in object permanence (finding a hidden toy), goal-directed behavior that involves persistence (putting pegs in a board), and ability to follow directions and knowledge of objects' names (understanding the concept of "one").
- Global infant intelligence measures are not good predictors of childhood intelligence because the developmental scales are considerably less verbal than later tests.
  - However, specific aspects of infant intelligence, such as information-processing tasks involving attention, are better predicators of childhood intelligence, especially in a specific area.

LANGUAGE DEVELOPMENT
Defining Language
- **Language** is a form of communication, whether spoken, written, or signed, that is based on a system of symbols.
- All languages have some common characteristics (infinite generativity and organizational rules).
  - **Infinite generativity** is the ability to produce an endless number of meaningful sentences using a finite set of words and rules.

How Language Develops
- Milestones in infant language include:
  - babbling (3-6 months).
  - first words understood (6-9 months).
  - growth of receptive vocabulary (reaches 300 or more words by age 2).
    - **Receptive vocabulary** refers to the words an individual understands.
  - first instructions understood (9-12 months).
  - first word spoken (10-15 months). Infants' first words are usually holophrases.
    - The **holophrase hypothesis** states that a single word can be used to imply a complete sentence.
  - growth of spoken vocabulary (reaches 200-275 words by age 2).
  - By 18 to 24 months of age, infants often speak in two-word utterances (usually telegraphic).
    - **Telegraphic speech** is the use of short and precise words to communicate.

Biological Influences
- The strongest evidence for the biological basis of language is that children all over the world reach language milestones at about the same time developmentally and in about the same order despite the vast variation of language input.

Biological Evolution
- In evolution, language clearly gave humans an enormous edge over other animals and increased their chance of survival.

Biological Prewiring
- Linguist Chomsky proposed the concept of **language acquisition device (LAD)** which is a biological endowment that enables the child to detect certain language categories, such as phonology, syntax, and semantics.
- Support for the LAD involves the uniformity of language milestones across languages and cultures, biological substrates for language, and deaf children's ability to create language.

Behavioral and Environmental Influences
- Behaviorists argue that language reinforcement and imitation are factors in language acquisition.
  - Critics argue that there is no evidence to document that reinforcement is responsible for language's rule systems and that this view fails to explain the extensive orderliness of language.
- Environmental influences do influence the acquisition of competent language skills.
- Adults teach language to children through various means:
  - **Infant-directed speech** is often used by parents and other adults when they talk to babies, it has higher than normal pitch and involves the use of simple words and sentences.
  - Recasting involves rephrasing something the child has said in a different way, perhaps by turning it into a question.
  - Echoing involves repeating what the child says, especially if it is an incomplete phrase or sentence.
  - Expanding is stating, in a linguistically sophisticated form, what a child has said.
  - Labeling is identifying the names of objects.
- Parents should talk extensively with an infant, especially about what the baby is attending to (live talk, not mechanical talk).

Learning Objectives

1. Grasp the four stages in Piaget's theory of cognitive development, and the role the concepts of assimilation, accommodation, and schemes play in the individual's adaptation.
2. Describe Piaget's sensorimotor stage of development, including the six substages and object permanence.
3. Discuss the contributions of Piaget's theory to the perceptual and conceptual development of infants, and then discuss how more modern researchers might modify his views.
4. Explain how research with infants has demonstrated the role of conditioning in early cognitive abilities.
5. Describe the concepts of habituation and dishabituation.
6. Understand the infant's memory capabilities and how that relates to imitation.
7. Discuss the history of intelligence testing, the tests that are used to test infant intelligence, and the relationship between infant cognitive abilities and cognitive functioning in childhood and adolescence.
8. Describe what language is and how it relates to the concept of infinite generativity.
9. Explain the developmental milestones in language development including receptive vocabulary, the holophrase hypothesis, and telegraphic speech.
10. Describe how biological development influences the development of language and cite evidence to support Chomsky's view of language development.
11. Describe the behavioral view of language development and be able to indicate how environmental factors influence the development of language.

Key Terms

Bayley Scales of Infant
   Development
coordination of secondary
   circular reactions
deferred imitation
developmental quotient (DQ)
dishabituation
first habits and primary
   circular reactions
habituation
holophrase hypothesis
infant-directed speech
infinite generativity

internalization of schemes
language
language acquisition device (LAD)
memory
object permanence
primary circular reaction
receptive vocabulary
scheme
secondary circular reaction
simple reflexes
telegraphic speech
tertiary circular reactions,
    novelty, and curiosity

Key People

Renee Baillargeon
Nancy Bayley
Roger Brown
Noam Chomsky
Arnold Gesell
Eleanor Gibson

Betty Hart and Todd Risley
Jean Mandler
Andrew Meltzoff
Jean Piaget
Carolyn Rovee-Collier
Elizabeth Spelke

Lecture Suggestions

Lecture Suggestion 1: Why Can't We Remember Events from Our Early Childhood? The purpose of this lecture is to delve into the issue of childhood amnesia. The following questions should be addressed: What is the earliest age at which people can remember specific events? Why can't people remember events from early childhood? What are some problems with retrospective research on early childhood memories?

Infantile or childhood amnesia refers to the inability to remember events from infancy and early childhood. Freud first described this phenomenon based largely on anecdotal evidence. Early research asked people to report their earliest memories. Most could only remember a scarcity of events from before the age of 8, with the average age being $3\frac{1}{2}$ years for the earliest memory. The scarcity of early memories could not be explained by the idea that greater forgetting is due to the increased time since the event. Childhood amnesia does not expand with increasing age and has been found as early as age 18 and as late as age 70. Memories of childhood events are conspicuous in their absence. People typically are unable to remember events that occurred before the age of 3 (Eacott & Crawley, 1998). There appears to be a qualitative difference between early and later memories as childhood memories are often fragmentary, and lacking in social and temporal context and narrative structure ("I remember sitting by the window").

In order to explain the phenomenon of childhood amnesia, a theory would have to explain adults' failure to recall their earliest childhood memory and the gradual increase in memories from the age of 3. Given the age range of 2 to 8 years for recall of one's earliest memories, individual differences would have to be explained as well. Nelson states that children need conventionalized narrative structures in order to build and interpret their personal past. Organized memories last longer and are easier to recall than unorganized memories. Thus, early memories that are unorganized due to young children's inability to structure the episodic memories are prone to forgetting. As language skills develop in early childhood, language-based narrative skills can aid in the formation of organized narrative autobiographical memories. Caregivers can aid in the development of narrative structure by asking questions such as, "What happened next?" Social interaction may be key in the initial development of these skills, and later these types of questions become internalized.

- What are some of the problems with asking people to recall their earliest memories?
    - Tough to accurately date memories.
    - Report false memories.
    - Confuse memories of events with what people have told them about the event.
    - Imagined the event.
    - Can't validate the memories.
- Have students discuss how to best study aspects related to childhood amnesia.
    - Probe for memories of notable events on specific dates e.g., sitting in basement during tornado on July 24, 1975).
    - Events that can be validated by people that were actually there.
    - Events that are not likely to have been videotaped or photographed.
- Sources: Eacott, M.J. (1999). Memory for the events of early childhood. *Current Directions in Psychological Science, 8,* 46-49. Eacott, M.J., & Crawley, R.A. (1998). The offset of childhood amnesia: Memory for events that occurred before age 3. *Journal of Experimental Psychology: General, 127,* 22-33. Nelson, K. (1992). Emergence of autobiographical memory at age 4. *Human Development, 35,* 172-177.

Lecture Suggestion 2: To Test or Not to Test, That Is the Question A problem of long-standing interest is the question of whether individual differences in infant intelligence can be measured and whether they have predictive value. A lecture on this topic is an opportunity to explore how basic values influence what researchers consider to be important questions, a chance to illustrate and elaborate on the stability/change issue, and a further vehicle to discuss how modern methodological advances have contributed both to our scientific and, potentially, applied knowledge of infants.

First, explore the reasons why it is valuable to identify individual differences in infants. In doing this you may wish to review the reasons why Binet developed the intelligence test. Point out that Binet was optimistic that if he were able to identify intellectual deficits early in the life of a child, he would be able to develop intervention techniques to enhance the child's intelligence.

Students should address the following questions:

- Do you think that it is important to know the intelligence of infants? Why or why not?
- Do intelligence tests predict later intellectual abilities?
- If intelligence testing in infancy can validly predict later intellectual abilities, do you think all infants should be tested? Why or why not?
- Discuss the potential advantages and disadvantages of knowing an infant's intellectual abilities.
- Finally, discuss the advantages and disadvantages of a system that would allow intellectual potential to be measured in a 3-month-old fetus.

Second, briefly trace the history of attempts to develop developmental scales for infants, expanding on the textbook's coverage. Note that these early tests never yielded impressive correlations with later intelligence. This acknowledgment presents an opportunity to review the meaning and uses of correlational findings. More recent work has highlighted the continuous nature of cognitive abilities. Recent fine-grained analyses of performance on Bayley scales have shown that some subscales on this test predict later language ability (Seigel, 1989). Also, McCall and Carriger (1993) have noted that the rate of habituation in very young infants correlates with later measured intelligence.

Finally, speculate about the meaning of this correlation. Does it mean that intelligence is basically a biological trait? Or, does it suggest that differences in information-processing capacity lead to differential rates of learning and remembering? Is rate of habituation a cause of intellectual development or is it related to something else?

- Sources: McCall, R. B., & Carriger, M. S. (1993). A meta-analysis of infant habituation and recognition memory performance as predictors of later IQ. *Child Development, 64,* 57-79. Seigel, L. S. (1989). *Perceptual-motor, cognitive, and language skills as predictors of cognitive abilities at school age.* Paper presented at the biennial meeting of the Society for Research in Child Development, Kansas City. Simons, J. A., Irwin, D. B., & Drinnin, B. A. (1987). *Instructor's manual to accompany psychology, the search for understanding.* St. Paul, MN: West Publishing.

Lecture Suggestion 3: Infant Speech Perception: Use It or Lose It? Create a lecture on the speech perception abilities in young infants and the contribution of biology and experience to this ability. Discuss research evidence of categorical perception (the ability to discriminate when two sounds represent two different phonemes and when they lie within the same phonemic category). Very young infants have the ability to discriminate speech contrasts that are found in languages they have not heard (Best, McRoberts, & Sithole, 1988), which suggests that categorical perception is an innate ability and universal among infants. The biological component of speech perception is complemented by the experiential component. Experience plays an important role in the development of speech perception and language. The lack of exposure to various sounds thwarts speech perception abilities. The Japanese language does not have a phonemic distinction between *r* and *l* sounds. Your students may well have noticed that native Japanese speakers have trouble pronouncing and discriminating between *r* and *l* sounds. Interestingly, Japanese infants have no trouble discriminating between these sounds (Eimas, 1975). Research suggests that infants gradually lose their ability to discriminate sound contrast that they are not exposed to (Werker & Lalonde, 1988). Consider showing the *Development* video from *The Mind* series as it demonstrates Werker's research.

- Sources: Best, C. T., McRoberts, G. W., & Sithole, N. M. (1988). Examination of perceptual reorganization for nonnative speech contrast: Zula click discrimination by English-speaking adults and infants. *Journal of Experimental Psychology: Human Perception and Performance, 14,* 345-360. Eimas, P. D. (1975). Auditory and phonetic coding of the cues for speech: Discrimination of the r-l distinction by young infants. *Perception and Psychophysics, 18,* 341- 347. Werker, J. F., & Lalonde, C. E. (1988). Cross-language speech perception: Initial capabilities and developmental change. *Developmental Psychology, 24,* 672-683.

Lecture Suggestion 4: Is It Possible to Accelerate Infant Cognitive Development? If you visit the parenting section of your local bookstore, you will come across works by numerous psychologists and other experts that proclaim that, "Yes, you can create a Super Baby." Programs and books attest to their methods to create a high-IQ, superior child. Some of the titles of such books are *Give Your Child a Superior Mind, How to Give Your Baby Encyclopedic Knowledge*, and *Awakening your Child's Natural Genius*. Present the ideas in one of these books to your class. In your lecture, delineate the issues and problems surrounding these programs. Obtain a more detailed description of the typical practices of better-baby institutes. What evidence do they describe to support their claims of success. If possible, find parents who have actually enrolled their babies in such schools or who have been inspired to employ their practices in raising their children. Next, present more formal evidence on the question of whether environment influences intellectual development in young children. Review some of the classic studies of institutionalized infants (Hunt, 1961; Thompson & Grusec, 1970); the influence of early home environments on later intelligence (Bradley & Caldwell, 1984; Campbell & Ramey, 1994; Olson, Bates, & Kaskie, 1992); and the interesting animal studies that have been conducted, such as those done with rats raised in impoverished versus enriched environments (Greenough, 1992). Speculate on the relevance of recent work that demonstrates a connection between brain development and stimulation. Consider having your students read the *Newsweek* article, Your Child's Brain (Feb. 19, 1996). Finally, discuss whether and how the techniques of the Doman Institute and its competitors seem to apply what is known about the correlates of individual differences in intellectual performance among infants and young children. You can relate this discussion to the issue discussed in the second lecture suggestion regarding the measurement of infant intelligence. A goal of this lecture is to illustrate how to think critically about the information that is provided by the Superbaby Institutes and how it relates to the scientific data.

- Sources: Bradley, R. H., & Caldwell, B. M. (1984). The relation of infants' home environments to achievement test performance in first grade: A follow-up study. *Child Development, 55*, 803-809. Campbell, F. A., & Ramey, C. T. (1994). Effects of early intervention on intellectual and academic achievement: A follow-up study of children from low-income families. *Child Development, 65*, 684-698. Greenough, W. T. (1992). Determinants of brain readiness for action: Experience shapes more than neuronal form. *Brain Dysfunction, 5*, 129-149. Hunt, J. McV. (1961). *Intelligence and experience*. New York: Ronald Press. Olson, S. L., Bates, J. E., & Kaskie, B. (1992). Caregiver-infant interaction antecedents of children's school-age cognitive ability. *Merrill-Palmer Quarterly, 38*, 309-330. Thompson, W. R., & Grusec, J. E. (1970). Studies of early experience. In P. H. Mussen (Ed.), *Carmichael's manual of child psychology* (3rd ed., Vol. 1). New York: Wiley. Your Child's Brain. (Feb. 19, 1996). *Newsweek*.

Classroom Activities

Classroom Activity 1: Testing Language Development The purpose of this activity is to have students relate their own development to the information provided in the textbook and to design a research study regarding parental reports of infant development. Santrock describes the development of language in infants in sufficient detail to allow for a comparison.

- First, have students ask their parents to indicate how old the students were when: (a) the parents could tell the difference between the cry communicating hunger and the cry communicating wet diapers, (b) they spoke their first word (indicate what the word was), (c) they first put two words together, and (d) they created their first sentence.
- Second, students should bring their data to class and compare it to that provided in the text. Once the comparison is made, have students indicate why the differences exist.
- Third, break the students into groups and ask them to design a retrospective study that would determine when each of the initial stages of language development occurred. They should also identify the problems with this type of study.

- Fourth, after sufficient time has passed, bring them back together and have them describe their studies and the difficulties they had in designing them.
- Fifth, as a large class have students design a more realistic study of the progression of language development (longitudinal, naturalistic observation).

Logistics:
- Group size: Individual, small group (2–4 students), and full class discussion.
- Approximate time: Individual (10 minutes prior to class meeting), small group (30 minutes), and full class discussion (30 minutes).
- Sources: King, M. B., & Clark, D. E. (1989). *Instructor's manual to accompany Santrock and Yussen's child development: An introduction*, 4th ed. Dubuque, IA: Wm. C. Brown Communications, Inc.

Classroom Activity 2: Do Animals Have the Ability to Communicate? This activity affords students an opportunity to discuss the utility of animal research in the study of language development. Begin this discussion by describing research studies such as Washoe (the first ape to be taught sign language) (Gardner & Gardner, 1971) and Koko the gorilla (Patterson, 1978). Below is some information about Gua, who was the first chimpanzee whom psychologists raised as if human.

In 1933, Winthrop Niles Kellogg, his wife, and their son Donald (10 months old) engaged in an experiment in which Donald was raised with a chimpanzee (Kellogg & Kellogg, 1933). Robert Yerkes, Yale's ape expert, arranged for the loan of Gua, a 7-month-old female chimpanzee. For nine months, the Kelloggs and Gua lived in a bungalow near Yale Anthropoid Experiment State in Florida. Both Donald and Gua were cuddled, fed, dressed, and tested. The Kelloggs reported in *The Ape and the Child* that Gua learned to walk upright more quickly than did Donald. Gua liked to pull at hangings, such as curtains, tablecloths, and skirts. Gua also recognized people better than Donald, by the smell of their chests and armpits, and did better recognizing by clothes than by faces. Donald, on the other hand, recognized faces. Although Donald liked perfume, Gua did not. Both reacted the same to sweet, salty, and bitter substances, except that Gua was more likely to enjoy sour things. Gua recognized herself in a mirror before Donald did, and she was also the first to become interested in picture books. However, Gua did not learn to speak human words. At the end of the study, the Kelloggs concluded that when Gua was treated as a human child she behaved like a human child in all ways that her body and brain structure allowed. Donald and his parents went on to Indiana University; Gua was returned to Yerkes, where she lived in a cage and was part of experiments.

- Have students discuss their opinions regarding the value of language learning studies with primates. What have researchers learned from animal studies about the development or cause of language? Do they have any ethical concerns? If they think that animal studies are beneficial for the understanding of language development, they should describe how they think this type of research should be conducted.
- Sources: Gardner, B. T., & Gardner, R. A. (1971). Two-way communication with an infant chimpanzee. In A. M. Schrier and F. Stollnitz (Eds.), *Behavior of nonhuman primates*. New York: Academic Press. Gerow, J. (1988). *Time retrospective: Psychology 1923-1988*. 16-17. Kellogg, W. N., & Kellogg, I. A. (1933). *The ape and the child*. New York: McGraw-Hill. Patterson, F. G. (1978). The gestures of a gorilla: Language acquisition in another pongid. *Brain and Language, 5*, 72-97.

Classroom Activity 3: Observation of Parent-Infant Interaction With this activity, students will assess the communication patterns of infants and the interactional synchrony between caregiver and infant. If possible, videotape at least two infants between the ages of 9 and 18 months interacting with their caregiver in face-to-face play for approximately 10 minutes. Have students identify the infant's vocal and nonverbal communication behaviors. Depending on the videotaped segment and the age of the infant, students should notice eye contact, cooing, pointing, babbling, crying, laughing, facial expressions, intonation patterns, etc. Next, the students should focus on what the caregiver is doing to elicit communication from the infant.

- Instructions for Students:
  - List all of the infant's behaviors that you consider to be communication.
  - List all of the caregiver's behaviors that you think are eliciting communication from the infant.
  - What sounds did the infant produce? Were all of his/her sounds part of his/her native language?
  - What babbling patterns were used? Did the infant have the same intonation patterns as his/her parents' native language?
  - Did it appear that the caregiver and the infant were having a conversation? Why or why not?
- Use in the Classroom: Discuss the students' observations and highlight the interactional dance that occurs and the many different ways that very young infants communicate with their world. Note whether the students considered all behavior to be communication or whether they discriminated between communicative and noncommunicative behavior.

Logistics:
- Materials: Two videotapes of parent-infant interaction.
- Group size: Full class discussion.
- Approximate time: Full class (25 minutes per videotape).
- Sources: King, M. B., & Clark, D. E. (1989). *Instructor's manual to accompany Santrock and Yussen's child development: An introduction*, 4th ed. Dubuque, IA: Wm. C. Brown Communications, Inc.

Classroom Activity 4: Supporting Arguments for Three Views of Language Development The purpose of this activity is to afford students an opportunity to further their understanding of the three major views of language development.
- First, have them break into small groups and assign them one of the three positions (Biological, Behavioral, and Interactionalist). As a group, they should identify the basis of language development that their theoretical perspective assumes and generate evidence that supports that view using their textbooks.
- Second, select one group from each perspective to present their theoretical position on language development to the class. You can have the groups debate their positions or merely present the arguments and evidence.
- Third, have the students that are not presenting determine which position makes the most sense to them. If they cannot come to a consensus, or if they dispute all three of the theoretical claims, have them generate a new perspective on the development of language. The new perspective can include components of the three perspectives that were provided.

Logistics:
- Group size: Small groups (2–4 students), and full class discussion.
- Approximate time: Small group (15 minutes), and full class discussion (30 minutes).

Classroom Activity 5: Critical Thinking Multiple-Choice Questions and Suggested Answers Discuss the answers to the critical thinking multiple-choice questions on **Handout 1**. Suggested answers are provided as **Handout 2**. Question 1 is a new type of exercise compared to those from previous chapters. The question requires students to integrate information from different parts of the chapter in a novel way. Students are likely to have difficulty because (a) Santrock does not always explicitly trace the implications of the new research for Piaget's claims; (b) students are not always clear about the concrete meaning of Piaget's stages of sensorimotor development, which makes it difficult for them to discover when a new finding contradicts a Piagetian claim or finding; (c) students do not always understand the inferential nature of our understanding of infant cognition; and (d) students do not expect material in textbooks to be self-contradictory. Therefore, it is important to discuss each of these problems; students usually prompt the discussion with questions of their own. For point (a), consider discussing the tentative and often controversial nature of claims about infant cognition. Explore how researchers make inferences about the qualitative and quantitative aspects of infant cognition for point (c). Finally, for point (d) discuss the notion that what we know about infant cognition is a synthesis of many separate studies and involves dealing with inconsistent and contradictory findings.

Question 2 revisits the "nature of development," this time in a less direct way than in previous chapters. You may want to review the issues presented in chapter 1 again, but this time give students an opportunity to define and illustrate these on their own. A good idea would be to ask them how each issue would be applied to the study of language development without directly referring to material in the text.

Question 3 is an extension of Classroom Activity 2 (Do Animals Have the Ability to Communicate?). Notice that the assumption in this exercise revolves around the definition of language. You may wish to discuss how definitions become assumptions, and how questioning or reformulating definitions can reshape arguments and lead to new discoveries. For example, questioning the assumption that language had to be oral produced new insights into the essential nature of language (e.g., sign language) and kept alive the hope that chimpanzees could learn a language.

Logistics:
- Materials: Handout 1 (the critical thinking multiple-choice questions) and Handout 2 (answers)
- Group size: Small groups (2-4) to discuss the questions, then a full class discussion.
- Approximate time: Small groups (15 to 20 minutes), then 15 minutes for full class discussion.

Classroom Activity 6: Critical Thinking Essay Questions and Suggestions for Helping Students Answer the Essays Discuss students' answers to the critical thinking essay questions presented as **Handout 3**. The purpose is threefold. First, answering these questions further facilitates students' understanding of concepts in chapter 6. Second, this type of essay question affords the students an opportunity to apply the concepts to their own lives, which will facilitate their retention of the material. Third, the essay format also will give students practice expressing themselves in written form. Ideas to help students answer the critical thinking essay questions are provided as **Handout 4**.

Logistics:
- Materials: Handout 3 (essay questions) and Handout 4 (helpful suggestions for the answers).
- Group size: Individual, then full class.
- Approximate time: Individual (60 minutes), then 30 minutes for full class discussion.

Personal Applications

Personal Application 1: Something Old, Something New The purpose of this exercise is to help students understand Piaget's concept of scheme—a cognitive structure that helps individuals organize and understand their experiences. Schemes play a major role in infant development where infants are experiencing everything for the first time and the world is a huge, unfamiliar place. However, even as adults we have new experiences and adapt to them through the use of what Piaget conceptualized as schemes.
- Instructions for Students: Write about something you did for the first time as an adolescent or adult. Remember how, until you first had the experience, you really had no understanding of what it would really be like. When you first encountered the new "thing" you were encoding all of the new information about it. That initial "scheme" then guided you to build your expectations, and to prepare for and understand the experience better the next time you had it. Certainly, your initial scheme was altered somewhat by the second experience, and all subsequent experiences both evolved out of, and contributed to, your mental scheme for this particular event.
- Use in the Classroom: Share some common adult first-time experiences and talk students through both assimilation and accomodation using something they can relate to. Good examples are flying on an airplane, roller blading (as related to ice skating), eating at a very ethnic restaurant (Japanese and sitting on the floor; Morroccan and eating with your fingers), bungee jumping.

Personal Application 2: Oh, That Again?! The purpose of this exercise is to get students to think about the phenomenon of habituation in terms of their own experiences. Habituation is fundamental to many studies of infant perceptual and cognitive functioning. It is, of course, employed purposefully, but there are cases in our daily lives that demonstrate the naturally occurring effects of habituation.

- Instructions for Students: Write about something you have been habituated to. What was the stimulus? How was it repeatedly presented to you? What is the behavioral outcome? What might happen to bring about dishabituation? Would you like to be dishabituated? What are some other real-life issues related to habituation and dishabituation?

- Use in the Classroom: Probably one of the biggest and most noticeable issues regarding habituation is that of violence and children. We know that children see an astounding number of deaths on television and movies early in life (in the thousands before they reach the age of 10), and the concern is that they show no particular reaction of dismay or disgust. The notion that our violent society and repeated media exposure have habituated even young children to such acts is a hot topic of debate with regard to the effect this habituation may have. Can this account for children bringing weapons to school and settling their "differences" with others through violence and killing? Or, does it simply enable them to tune it out when they see it, and not concern themselves with it (and succumb to bad dreams)? The same argument can be made about sexual images. When clothing advertisements use partially nude models, and the covers of newsstand magazines flaunt only partially clad women, clothing trends for younger and younger children can follow suit and society may think it's perfectly acceptable. Have students discuss their views, using examples to back up their claims.

Research Project Ideas

Research Project 1: Object Permanence For this project, students should work in groups of two to four. Each group will need an infant from two of the following four age groups: 4 to 8 months, 8 to 12 months, 12 to 18 months, and 18 to 24 months. Prior to the start of the research, the project must be approved by the human subjects review board at your school and the students must get a signed informed consent form from the infants' parents. See the section at the front of this Instructor's Manual entitled Ethics, Human Subjects, and Informed Consent. Using **Handout 5**, the students should perform each of the tasks with both of the infants and record the infants' responses. The students should address the following questions as well.

- How do the younger and older infants respond in task one? Do both seem to understand that the object is under the cloth? When part of the object is exposed, does the baby exhibit surprise? Does the infant reach out for the object?

- In the second task, which infants realize the object is behind the screen? Can either baby follow the action when the object is moved to a second screen?

- How does each of the infants respond when the object is in the box? When the box no longer contains a the object, does either of the infants look behind the screen?

- How does object permanence change as infants get older? Do your observations agree with Piaget's findings about object permanence?

- Use in the Classroom: Have students present data in class from the research project, pooling the data for the four age groups of infants. Discuss how the younger and older infants responded to the three tasks. How does object permanence improve during infancy? Discuss the consistency between the students' observations and Piaget's findings.

Research Project 2: Caregiver-Infant Language In this project, students will gain a better understanding of communication techniques caregivers use when interacting with infants and they will gain experience with naturalistic observation methods. Students will examine recasting, echoing, and expanding using naturalistic observation. They should go to a local shopping mall and observe a caregiver with an infant 18 to 24 months old. The observation period should be approximately 15 minutes. Using the provided data sheet (**Handout 6**), they should record three instances of speech by the caregiver to the infant, and classify each instance as recasting, echoing, or expanding. In addition to noting the caregiver's statements, they should also note the infant's response to each statement. Finally, they should answer the provided questions.

- What types of techniques did the caregiver use with the infant you observed?
- How did the infant respond to the statement made by the caregiver?
- From your observations, do you think recasting, echoing, and expanding are effective techniques in aiding infants to learn language? Why or why not?
- What variables might have affected the quality of data you collected? Might your conclusions have been different if you had observed a different caregiver-infant pair? How?
- Use in the Classroom: Have the students present data from the research project in class. Do the observations agree with the presentation in the textbook?

Film and Video List

The following films and videos supplement the content of chapter 6. Contact information for film distributors can be found at the front of this Instructor's Manual under Film and Video Sources.

Cognitive Development (Films for the Humanities and Sciences, 58 minutes). This program examines Piaget's theory in light of modern research. The program suggests that children are more cognitively capable at an earlier age than Piaget proposed.

Developing Language (Insight Media, 24 minutes). This program charts the development of children's language from birth to age 5, and then asks the question, "What is left to learn?"

Discovering the Outside World (Films for the Humanities and Sciences, 23 minutes). This program examines infant cognitive development. As the infant grows, the child acquires many skills and much information. Curiosity leads to exploration of the world and further intellectual development depends on the willingness of adults to help satisfy the child's curiosity.

Individual Differences and Developmental Milestones (Insight Media, 30 minutes). Sensory motor development in first year is charted, with a focus on temperament, auditory and visual acuity, depth perception, phonemic perception, and bimodal perception in this video.

Infancy: Beginnings in Cognition and Language (Magna Systems, 29 minutes). This video explores infant senses and perception and the development of cognition and language during the first year of life. In addition, the role that parents play in language learning is discussed.

The Infant Mind (Insight Media, 30 minutes). This video explains and challenges Piaget's claims about sensorimotor intelligence. New research on infant memory, conceptual development, perception, number and object permanence is presented.

Language and Thinking (Insight Media, 30 minutes). Brain development and language acquisition are explored. This video features Elizabeth Bates, Jean Mandler, and Susan Curtiss' perspectives on beginning of language and grammar.

Language Development (Films for the Humanities and Sciences, 40 minutes). The emphasis of this program is language development of infants and young children. In addition, the video covers the nature-nurture debate, the Whorf-Sapir hypothesis, and non-human language abilities.

Mastering Early Skills (Insight Media, 60 minutes). This video explores the relationship between physical growth and early learning through habituation, classical and operant conditioning, and observational learning.

The Mind: Development (PBS, 60 minutes). This video examines the development of the human brain from a single cell to that of a 6-year-old child.

Scales of Infant Psychological Development (University of Illinois, up to 40 minutes each). These six films explore cognitive acquisitions during the sensorimotor period. The topics featured include object permanence, causality, object relations in space, imitation, gestures, vocalization, and development of schemas.

Symbolic Formation and the Acquisition of Language (Insight Media, 30 minutes). This video discusses how symbolic capacity relates to language development by following a child's development and profiling a deaf child's language acquisition.

Young Minds: Is Zero-to-Three Destiny (Films for the Humanities and Sciences, 12 minutes). *NewsHour* correspondent Betty Ann Boweser explores the questions of whether or not Mozart's music can have a lasting impact on the growth of a baby's brain. She talks with members on both sides of the debate.

Web Site Suggestions

The URLs for general sites, common to all chapters, can be found at the front of this Instructor's Manual under Useful Web Sites. At the time of publication, all sites were current and active, however, please be advised that you may occasionally encounter a dead link.

Babies Don't Forget What They Hear
http://www.apnet.com/inscight/09261997/grapha.htm

Breakthrough: Infant Learning
http://www.uvol.com/family/infant.html

Jean Piaget-Intellectual Development
http://www.english.sk.com.br/sk-piage.html

The Language Explosion: Newsweek (Special Issue) 1997
http://www.thriveonline.com/health/Library/CAD/abstract27104.html

Understanding Language Development and Hearing
http://www.kidsears.com/milestones/frmilestone_intro.htm

Critical Thinking Multiple-Choice Questions

1. In this chapter, Santrock presents findings about infant cognitive development from the Piagetian, learning and memory, and individual differences perspectives. The Piagetian perspective is the oldest and most influential of the three; however, both the learning and memory and individual differences perspectives have challenged basic claims of Piaget. Which of the following statements from either information-processing or individual differences research does NOT contradict one of Piaget's observations? Circle the letter of the best answer and explain why it is the best answer and why each other answer is not as good.

    a. In Rovee-Collier's study, 10-week-old infants moved a leg or an arm to rotate a mobile. They "remembered" to do so again 2 weeks later.
    b. Andrew Meltzoff watched 3-day-old babies imitate facial expressions.
    c. Carolyn Rovee-Collier found that infants as young as 2 to 6 months can remember some experiences through $1\frac{1}{2}$ to 2 years of age.
    d. Tested on the Bayley Scales, an average 6-month-old infant will search persistently for objects just out of reach.
    e. Elizabeth Spelke documented intermodal perception in 4-month-old infants.

2. Santrock's treatment of early language development uses many of the organizing concerns and questions that developmentalists employ to study other aspects of human development. Which one of the following concepts, issues, or themes receives the LEAST coverage during Santrock's discussion of early language development? Circle the letter of the best answer and explain why it is the best answer and why each other answer is not as good.

    a. Development is a product of biological, cognitive, and social processes.
    b. The nature versus nurture issue.
    c. The continuity versus discontinuity issue.
    d. The issue of qualitative versus quantitative change.
    e. Culture influences development.

3. Read the following passage, "Ape Talk—From Gua to Nim Chimpsky," that outlines the history of attempts to teach apes to talk and sketches the controversy resulting from these attempts:

    It is the early 1930s. A 7-month-old chimpanzee named Gua has been adopted by humans (Kellogg & Kellogg, 1933). Gua's adopters want to rear her alongside their 10-month-old son, Donald. Gua was treated much the way we rear human infants today—her adopters dressed her, talked with her, and played with her. Nine months after she was adopted, the project was discontinued because the parents feared that Gua was slowing down Donald's progress.

    About twenty years later, another chimpanzee was adopted by human beings (Hayes & Hayes, 1951). Viki, as the chimp was called, was only a few days old at the time. The goal was straightforward: teach Viki to speak. Eventually she was taught to say "Mama," but only with painstaking effort. Day after day, week after week, the parents sat with Viki and shaped her mouth to make the desired sounds. She ultimately learned three other words—papa, cup, and up—but she never learned the meanings of these words and her speech was not clear.

    Approximately twenty years later, another chimpanzee named Washoe was adopted when she was about 10 months old (Gardner & Gardner, 1971). Recognizing that the earlier experiments with chimps had not demonstrated that apes have language, the trainers tried to teach Washoe the American sign language, which is the sign language of the deaf. Daily routine events, such as meals and washing, household chores, play with toys, and car rides to interesting places, provided many opportunities for the use of sign language. In two years, Washoe learned 38 different signs and by the age of 5 she had a vocabulary of 160 signs. Washoe learned how to put signs together in novel ways, such as "you drink" and "you me tickle."

Yet another way to teach language to chimpanzees exists. The Premacks (Premack & Premack, 1972) constructed a set of plastic shapes that symbolized different objects and were able to teach the meanings of the shapes to a 6-year-old chimpanzee, Sarah. Sarah was able to respond correctly using such abstract symbols as "same as" or "different from." For example, she could tell you that "banana is yellow" is the same as "yellow color of banana." Sarah eventually was able to "name" objects, respond "yes," "no," "same as," and "different from," and tell you about certain events by using symbols (such as putting a banana on a tray). Did Sarah learn a generative language capable of productivity? Did the signs Washoe learned have an underlying system of language rules?

Herbert Terrace (1979) doubts that these apes have been taught language. Terrace was part of a research project designed to teach language to an ape by the name of Nim Chimpsky (named after famous linguist Noam Chomsky). Initially, Terrace was optimistic about Nim's ability to use language as human beings use it, but after further evaluation he concluded that Nim really did not have language in the sense that human beings do. Terrace says that apes do not spontaneously expand on a trainer's statements as people do; instead, the apes just imitate their trainer. Terrace also believes that apes do not understand what they are saying when they speak; rather they are responding to cues from the trainer that they are not aware of. The Gardners take exception to Terrace's conclusions (Gardner & Gardner, 1986). They point out that chimpanzees use inflections in sign language to refer to various actions, people, and places. They also cite recent evidence that the infant chimp Loulis learned over 50 signs from his adopted mother Washoe and other chimpanzees who used sign language.

The ape language controversy goes on. It does seem that chimpanzees can learn to use signs to communicate meanings, which has been the boundary for language. Whether the language of chimpanzees possesses all of the characteristics of human language, such as phonology, morphology, syntax, semantics, and pragmatics, is still being argued (Maratsos, 1983; Rumbaugh, 1988).

Which of the following statements represents an assumption shared by individuals on each side of the argument, rather than an inference or an observation? Circle the letter of the best answer and explain why it is the best answer and why each other answer is not as good.

a. Communication cannot be called language unless it has phonology, morphology, syntax, semantics, and pragmatics.
b. Washoe put signs together in ways that her trainer had not taught her.
c. Apes do not understand language; rather, they learn to imitate their trainers.
d. Sarah used a symbol that meant "same as" when she asked whether "banana is yellow" was the same as "yellow color of bananas."
e. Chimps use signs to communicate meaning.

Suggested Answers for the Critical Thinking Multiple-Choice Questions

1. In this chapter, Santrock presents findings about infant cognitive development from the Piagetian, information processing, and individual differences perspectives. The Piagetian perspective is the oldest and most influential of the three; however, both the information- processing and individual differences perspectives have challenged basic claims of Piaget. Which of the following statements from either information-processing or individual differences research does NOT contradict one of Piaget's observations? Circle the letter of the best answer and explain why it is the best answer and why each other answer is not as good.

   a. Rovee-Collier's findings contradict Piaget's observations. What Rovee-Collier described (moving the mobile) is what Piaget called a secondary circular reaction. Piaget claimed that this occurred between 4 and 8 months of age. Piaget also provided no descriptions of memory in infants as young as 10 weeks old, and his theory seems to suggest that infants that young do not have memories.

   b. Meltzoff's findings contradict Piagetian claims. Piaget did not observe imitation until 4 to 8 months, when he saw imitations of baby talk, babbling, and physical gestures. These examples involved actions the infant already was able to perform, whereas newborn infants may imitate facial expressions they have never produced on their own.

   c. This is not the correct answer. Piaget thought that memory did not form until the end of the sensorimotor stage, thus Rovee-Collier's finding that 2-year-olds could remember experiences they had up to two years later, when put in the same context, contradicts Piaget.

   d. This is the correct answer. The finding that an average 6-month-old will search persistently for an object just out of reach is consistent to Piaget's finding during the third stage of object permanence development. The infant persists in looking for the object. If the object disappears, the baby will examine the spot where it vanished.

   e. Spelke's research findings contradict Piaget's theory. According to Piaget's theory, the basis of intermodal perception, a mental scheme that integrates information from several senses, should not exist until the end of the sensorimotor period or the beginning of the preoperational period of development.

2. Santrock's treatment of early language development uses many of the organizing concerns and questions that developmentalists employ to study other aspects of human development. Which one of the following concepts, issues, or themes receives the LEAST coverage during Santrock's discussion of early language development? Circle the letter of the best answer and explain why it is the best answer and why each other answer is not as good.

   a. Development is a product of biological, cognitive, and social processes is not the best answer. The chapter discusses the biological bases of language and the behavioral and environmental views. Language itself is dependent on cognitive processes (e.g., symbolic function). One cognitive characteristic of language is that it is rule-based and generative.

   b. The nature versus nurture issue is not the best answer. The chapter explicitly talks about biological and environmental influences on language, which is one way of talking about nature-nurture issues. The chapter also touches on the classic nature view (that language acquisition is the product of a language acquisition device) and the definitive nurture view (that language is learned in the same way as any other behavior through processes of reinforcement).

   c. The continuity versus discontinuity issue is the best answer. This issue receives the least attention. For example, it is not clear whether changes described in the chapter are relatively continuous or abrupt. Likewise, nothing is said about whether individual language styles or abilities persist into later life (the stability/change issue).

    d.   <u>The issue of qualitative versus quantitative change</u> is not the best answer. Much of the material is about qualitative changes. The rule systems of phonology and syntax change as language develops. There are also quantitative changes, such as the increase in the number of words learned.

    e.   <u>Culture influences development</u> is not the best answer. Santrock described a study in which the language environments of children from middle-income professional families and families on welfare (cultures) were examined relative to the children's language development. Researchers estimated that by the age of 4, the average welfare family child would have 13 million fewer words of cumulative language experience. Despite the finding that language milestones are universal, cultural influences still impact language development.

3. After reading the passage, "Ape Talk—From Gua to Nim Chimpsky," that outlines the history of attempts to teach apes to talk and sketches the controversy resulting from these attempts, which of the following statements represents an assumption shared by individuals on each side of the argument, rather than an inference or an observation? Circle the letter of the best answer and explain why it is the best answer and why each other answer is not as good.

    a.   The statement <u>Communication cannot be called language unless it has phonology, morphology, syntax, semantics, and pragmatics</u> is the assumption shared by both sides. The criterion used to determine whether a communication system qualifies as a language is the presence of one or more rule systems that govern features of the communication system. Individuals on both sides of the debate appear to accept this as a rule for the debate, and what they argue about is whether the communications of apes possess this particular language attribute.

    b.   <u>Washoe put signs together in ways that her trainer had not taught her</u> is an observation. Researchers noted and recorded that Washoe put together new combinations of the 160 signs that she had learned.

    c.   <u>Apes do not understand language; rather, they learn to imitate their trainers</u> is an inference. It is Herbert Terrace's interpretation of ape behavior that others have called language. He noted that trainers made signs that the apes reproduced and inferred that this meant that the apes were merely imitating their trainers.

    d.   <u>Sarah used a symbol that meant "same as" when she asked whether "banana is yellow" was the same as "yellow color of bananas."</u> is an observation. It is what researchers saw Sarah do in response to the question.

    e.   <u>Chimps use signs to communicate meaning</u> is an inference. It is the conclusion many researchers have reached from attempts to teach language to apes. Terrace, however, disputes this claim.

Critical Thinking Essay Questions

Your answers to this kind of question demonstrate an ability to comprehend and apply ideas discussed in this chapter.

1. Explain Piaget's concept of scheme, and give an example of a sensorimotor scheme. Explain the processes of assimilation and accommodation (discussed in chapter 2) using that concept.

2. Compare and contrast the methods used by Piaget and learning and memory researchers to study infant cognition.

3. What is the relationship between each of the substages in Piaget's theory of the sensorimotor period? How does the infant get from one stage to the next?

4. Explain the attacks on Piaget's theory. That is, describe them, and indicate what impact they should have on our belief in Piaget's theory as an accurate description and explanation of infant cognitive development.

5. Describe what we know about infants' ability to pay attention, remember, and imitate. Then speculate about how these abilities may be related to each other.

6. How do learning and memory theorists approach development? How would you convince a friend that imitation and deferred imitation demonstrate learning and memory by infants?

7. Compare and contrast the learning and memory and individual differences approaches to infant cognitive development. Is there any overlap in uses of these perspectives?

8. If you were a parent of an infant, what would you learn about your infant from the Gesell and the Bayley Scales of Infant Development?

9. Define language, and explain the concept of infinite generativity.

10. Discuss evidence regarding the nature and nurture bases for language development.

11. Summarize the milestones in the development of language by infants.

12. Discuss how information about language development relates to information about cognitive development in infants. That is, do the two areas of study reinforce, contradict, or both reinforce and contradict each others' findings and conclusions about infant cognitive capacities?

Ideas to Help You Answer Critical Thinking Essay Questions

1. Begin by describing a particular experience that an infant might have for the first time. Tell the story of what happens in Piagetian terms (incorporating the concepts of scheme, assimilation, and accomodation), as the infant encounters the experience, and variations of it, again and again.

2. List the methods and who employed them. Note what each specifically tested, what age group they observed, what was required of the subjects, and what kinds of results they yielded. Also identify any inherent weaknesses in the methods.

3. Think about the fundamental aspects of the stage as a whole. What was Piaget's theoretical basis for identifying this particular time frame as a single "stage" of development? What differentiates the sensorimotor period from the pre-operational period? Upon answering this, you can establish your answer for the transition that the infant must make.

4. Begin with a brief summary of the distinguishing characteristics of Piaget's theory. Next, present the specifics of the attacks on his theory. Consider the validity of their claims, their motivations for finding fault with Piaget, and their alternative explanations.

5. Discuss each of these experiences separately to begin with. Bring them together as a behavioral sequence to delineate their relationship.

6. For your argument to be convincing, your friend will need a solid understanding of the phenomena and theoretical context. Approach this as an entire teaching opportunity. Provide the background of the learning and memory theorists' perspective, then proceed to discuss the role of imitation and deferred imitation, along with relevant examples.

7. As you list and relate the aspects of each approach to infant cognitive development, keep in mind their potential implications for practical application. Not only will this create a more complete comparison overall, but it will also enable you to more directly relate theory and practice.

8. This exercise will be more interesting if you can think about a real infant you know, or imagine you are a parent who wants to know anything and everything about your baby. With either of these perspectives in mind, make a list of the information provided by each assessment tool, then write a general summary. Take a step back and also mention the theoretical issues addressed by the assessment tools.

9. Use your own lifetime of experiencing language to guide you. Come up with your own personal demonstration of infinite generativity.

10. Begin by establishing the basic perspective of both the nature and nurture approach to development. Provide specific evidence for each, and discuss whether the evidence is contradictory or complimentary—or both!

11. Summarize the milestones of language development by creating a story of a child as he/she experiences the first two years of life.

12. Summarize the principles of cognitive development, then map out the principles of language development. Point out connections, parallels, contradictions, gaps, etc.

Object Permanence

For this project, in which you may work in groups of two to four, you will need an infant from two of the following four age groups: 4 to 8 months, 8 to 12 months, 12 to 18 months, and 18 to 24 months. In order to do the object permanence task with these two infants, you need to clear your project through the human subjects review board at your school and get a signed informed consent form from the infants' parents. With each infant, perform each of the following three tasks and record the infants' responses. Then write a report incorporating your answers to the accompanying questions.

	Infant Responses	
	Infant 1	Infant 2
Task Description	Sex ___ Age ___	Sex ___ Age ___

1. Show each infant an interesting object (e.g., ball or object). Then cover it with a piece of cloth. Note the response.

   Now move the cloth so that part of the object is exposed. Note the response.

2. Show the child the object again. Now move it so that it disappears behind a screen. Note the response.

   Now do the task again, but this time have the toy go behind one screen and then another screen located close by. Note the response.

3. Show the infant the object, then cover it with a small box. Move the box behind the screen. Let the object remain behind the screen, but bring the box back into view. Note the response.

Questions:
- How do the younger and older infants respond in task one? Do both seem to understand that the object is under the cloth? When part of the object is exposed, does the baby exhibit surprise? Does the infant reach out for the object?
- In the second task, which infants realize the object is behind the screen? Can either baby follow the action when the object is moved to a second screen?
- How do each of the infants respond when the object is in the box? When the box no longer contains the object, does either of the infants look behind the screen?
- How does object permanence change as infants get older? Do your observations agree with Piaget's findings about object permanence?

Caregiver-Infant Language

In this project, you will examine recasting, echoing, and expanding using naturalistic observation. Go to a local shopping mall and observe a caregiver with an infant 18 to 24 months old. Observe them for 15 minutes. Record three instances of speech by the caregiver to the infant, and classify each instance as recasting, echoing, or expanding. Note the caregiver's statements and then the infant's response to each statement. Then answer the questions that follow.

<u>Speech</u>   <u>Response of Infant</u>   Age _____ Sex _____

Statement 1

Statement 2

Statement 3

Questions:

- What types of techniques did the caregiver use with the infant you observed?

- How did the infant respond to the statement made by the caregiver?

- From your observations, do you think recasting, echoing, and expanding are effective techniques in aiding infants to learn language? Why or why not?

- What variables might have affected the quality of data you collected? Might your conclusions have been different if you had observed a different caregiver-infant pair? How?

Chapter 7: Socioemotional Development in Infancy

Total Teaching Package Outline

Lecture Outline	Resource References
Socioemotional Development in Infancy	PowerPoint Presentation: See www.mhhe.com Cognitive Maps: See Appendix A
Emotional and Personality Development • Emotional Development	OHT50 & IB: Facial Expressions of Emotion F/V: First Feelings F/V: Life's First Feelings

-Defining Emotion
      -Affect in Parent-Infant Relationships
      -Developmental Timetable of Emotions
      -Crying
 	
      -Smiling
      -Stranger Anxiety
	LO1
	LO2
	
	LO3
	PA1: Don't Be Such a Cry Baby!

•   Temperament
 	
      -Defining and Classifying Temperament
 	
      -Goodness of Fit
 	
      -Parenting and the Child's Temperament
	LO4
	
	OHT81 & IB: Basic Clusters of Temperament
	LS1: Biological Basis of Shyness and
	           Sociability
	WS: Temperament

•   Personality Development
      -Trust
      -The Developing Sense of Self and
         Independence
	LO5
	
	RP1: Development of Self in Infants
	F/V: The Development of the Self
	F/V: Infancy: Self and Social World
	WS: Comparison of Mahler and Stern's
	        Theories of the Development of the Self

Attachment • What Is Attachment? • Individual Differences	LO6 F/V: Attachment F/V: Mother Love F/V: Rock-a-Bye-Baby WS: Attachment Research @ Stony Brook WS: Bowlby: Attachment Theory

•   Caregiving Styles and Attachment
      Classification
	LO7
	LS2: The Influence of Caregiving on
	        Attachment Classification
	RP2: Attachment Behaviors

• Attachment, Temperament, and the Wider Social World	LO8 LS3: How Do Toddlers Regulate Their Emotions?

Social Contexts	F/V: Early Relationships: Habits of the Heart
	F/V: Infancy: Early Relationships
• The Family	F/V: Children of Poverty
	F/V: Developing the Sense of Family
	F/V: Early Relationships: Habits of the Heart
	F/V: Early Socialization: From Birth to Age Two
-The Transition to Parenthood	CA1: Erikson's Psychosocial Theory and Parenting
-Reciprocal Socialization	LO9
-The Family as a System	LO10
-Maternal and Paternal Infant Caregiving	LS5: Father Love
• Day Care	LO11
	CA2: Assessment of Child Care in Your Community
	CA3: Child-Care Laws in Your State?
	PA2: The Big Debate
	F/V: Early Child Care and Education
	WS: Babes in Day Care
	WS: Infant Care: How Do You Know Quality?
	WS: National Child Care Information Center
	WS: The NICHD Study of Early Child Care
Review	CA4: Baby in a Box
	CA5: Critical Thinking Multiple-Choice
	CA6: Critical Thinking Essay Questions
	PA3: Remember When…

Chapter Outline

EMOTIONAL AND PERSONALITY DEVELOPMENT
  Emotional Development
    Defining Emotion
    • **Emotion** is a feeling, or affect, that can involve physiological arousal, conscious experience, and behavioral expression.
    • Infants gradually develop the ability to inhibit, or minimize, the intensity and duration of emotional reaction which is called emotional regulation.
    Affect in Parent-Infant Relationships
    • Before infants acquire speech, parents and infants communicate through emotion.
    • Face-to-face interactions between infant and adults are bidirectional and mutually regulated.
    Developmental Timetable of Emotions
    • Izard developed a system for coding infants' facial expressions related to emotion, the **Maximally Discriminative Facial Movement Coding System (MAX)**.
    • Based on Izard's coding scheme, distress, interest, and disgust are present at birth; a social smile appears at 4 to 6 weeks; anger, surprise, and sadness emerge at 3 to 4 months; fear is displayed at 5 to 7 months; shame and shyness appear at 6 to 8 months; and contempt and guilt appear around 2 years of age.

Crying
- Crying is the infant's most important mechanism for communication.
- Babies have at least three types of cries:
  - The **basic cry** is a rhythmic pattern that usually consists of a cry, followed by a briefer silence, then a shorter inspiratory whistle that is somewhat higher in pitch than the main cry, then another brief rest before the next cry.
  - The **anger cry** is a variation of the basic cry, however, there is more excess air forced through the vocal cords.
  - The **pain cry**, which is stimulated by high-intensity stimuli, differs from the other types of cries. A sudden appearance of loud crying without preliminary moaning and a long initial cry followed by an extended period of breath holding characterize the pain cry.
- Most parents, and adults in general, can distinguish between the anger and pain cry. Parents can distinguish the cries of their own infant better than a strange baby.
- Controversy surrounds the issue of whether parents should respond to an infant's cries.
  - Most developmentalists argue that an infant cannot be spoiled in the first year, which suggests that parents should soothe a crying baby. Infants will likely develop a sense of trust and secure attachment to the caregiver due to responsive caregiving.

Smiling
- Smiling is another important communicative affective behavior.
- Two types of smiles can be distinguished in babies:
  - A **reflexive smile** does not occur in response to external stimuli. It appears during the first month, usually during irregular patterns of sleep, not when the infant is in an alert state.
  - A **social smile** occurs in response to an external stimulus, which early in development typically is in response to a face around 2 to 3 months of age.

Stranger Anxiety
- **Stranger anxiety** occurs when infants show fear and wariness of strangers.
- It usually emerges gradually around 6 months and escalates until 12 months, though not all infants show distress.
- Several factors influence whether an infant will display stranger anxiety.
  - Infants show less anxiety when in familiar settings (at home or on mom's lap), when the stranger is another child, and when the stranger is friendly and outgoing.

Temperament
Defining and Classifying Temperament
- **Temperament** is an individual's behavioral style and emotional response style.
- Chess and Thomas believe that there are three basic types of temperament:
  - An **easy child** is generally in a positive mood, quickly establishes regular routines in infancy, and adapts easily to new experiences (40 percent of children).
  - A **difficult child** tends to react negatively and cry frequently, engages in irregular daily routines, and is slow to accept new experiences (10 percent of children).
  - A **slow-to-warm-up child** has a low activity level, is somewhat negative, shows low adaptability, and displays a low intensity of mood (15 percent of children).
- Rothbart and Bates' modified framework for classifying temperament focuses more on positive affect and approach, negative affectivity, and effortful control (self-regulation).
- Temperament is perceived to be a stable characteristic of newborns, which comes to be shaped and modified with experience.
- Twin and adoption studies indicate that the heritability index for temperament is in the .50 to .60 range which suggests there is a moderate influence of heredity on temperament.

Goodness of Fit
- Goodness of fit refers to the match between a child's temperament and the environment; demands the child must cope with.

Parenting and the Child's Temperament
- Sarason and Rothbart speculate as to the implications of temperamental variations for parenting.
  - Attention to and respect for individuality: It is important to modify one's parenting to fit the child's temperament.
  - Structuring the child's environment: It is important to consider the child's reaction to different contexts based upon the child's temperament.
  - The "difficult child" and packaged parenting programs: Parents may consider seeking help when parenting a child with a difficult temperament as they may face more challenges.
- Overall, it is a good idea for parents to be sensitive to individual characteristics of the child, be flexible in responding to these characteristics, and avoid negative labeling of the child.

Personality Development

Trust
- According to Erikson, infancy is characterized by the trust-versus-mistrust stage of development.
  - Infants learn trust when they are cared for in a consistent, warm manner and these feelings influence later social interactions.

The Developing Sense of Self and Independence

The Self
- At some point in the second half of the second year, the infant develops a sense of self.
- Researchers have used a mirror technique to determine if an infant can recognize her own image.

Independence
- Mahler argues that the infant separates herself from her mother and then develops individuation in the second year of life.
- Erikson stressed that the second year of life is characterized by the stage of autonomy versus shame and doubt.

ATTACHMENT

What Is Attachment?
- **Attachment** is a close emotional bond between the infant and the caregiver.
- Freud believed that infants become attached to the person that provides oral satisfaction.
  - Harlow and Zimmerman's classic study demonstrated that feeding is not the crucial element in the attachment process: contact comfort is more important.
- Bowlby explained from an ethological perspective that the newborn is biologically equipped to elicit attachment behaviors from the caregiver.
- Four phases characterize the gradual development attachment between infant and caregiver:
  - Phase 1 (0-2 months): Infants instinctively direct their attachment to human figures. Infants indiscriminately respond to people.
  - Phase 2 (2-7 months): Attachment becomes focused on the primary caregiver.
  - Phase 3 (7-24 months): Specific attachments form and the infant is able to actively seek contact from regular caregivers.
  - Phase 4 (24 months on): A goal-directed partnership is formed. Children become aware of others' feelings, goals, and plans and take them into account in forming their actions.

Individual Differences
- Mary Ainsworth documented variation in the types of infant-caregiver attachments.
  - In secure attachments, infants use the caregiver as a secure base from which to explore the environment. Ainsworth proposed that secure attachments provide an important foundation for psychological development later in life.
- Ainsworth created the **Strange Situation** which is an observational measure of infant attachment that requires the infant to move through a series of introductions, separations, and reunions with the caregiver and an adult stranger in a prescribed order.
  - Infants with a **secure attachment** explore the room and play with the toys when their caregivers are in the room. When the caregiver leaves, the infant may protest mildly and then reestablishes positive interactions when the caregiver returns.
  - **Insecure avoidant babies** show insecurity by avoiding the mother during the strange situation. They do not engage very much with the caregiver, yet they cry when she leaves the room. Avoidant babies do not establish contact when the caregiver returns.
  - **Insecure resistant babies** may cling to the caregiver then resist her by fighting against the closeness, perhaps by kicking or pushing away. When the caregiver leaves the room, these infants often cry loudly.
  - **Disorganized babies** are disorganized and disoriented during the Strange Situation. The often appear dazed, confused, and fearful.
- Critics of the Strange Situation highlight that the isolated, controlled events of the setting might not necessarily reflect the interactions that would happen in the babies' natural environment.
- Researchers have found that early attachments seem to foreshadow later functioning and that consistency in caregiving is likely an important factor in connecting early attachment and later functioning.

Caregiving Styles and Attachment Classification
- Caregivers of secure babies are sensitive to the babies' signals and are consistently available to meet their needs.
- Caregivers of avoidant babies tend to be unavailable or rejecting.
- Caregivers of ambivalent-rejecting babies tend to be inconsistently available to their babies and usually are not very affectionate.
- Caregivers of disorganized babies are often neglectful or physically abuse their babies.

Attachment, Temperament, and the Wider Social World
- Not all research supports attachment classification predictions of later development.
  - Research found that parental divorce, not early attachment classification, was a better predictor of attachment classification at age 18.
- Some critics believe that too much emphasis has been placed on early attachment relationships.
  - Kagan stresses that infants are highly resilient and adaptive in the face of wide variations in parenting. He thinks genetics and temperament are more important to children's social competence than attachment relationships.
- Cultural variations have been found, yet the most frequent classification in every culture studied so far is the secure attachment.
  - German babies are more likely to be classified as avoidant because their parents stress independence.
  - Japanese babies are more likely to be categorized as resistant-ambivalent given the emphasis on dependence.
- Another criticism is that attachment theory ignores the diversity of socializing agents and contexts that exist in an infant's world.
- Researchers acknowledge the importance of competent, nurturant caregivers, yet some question whether a secure attachment to a single caregiver is critical.

SOCIAL CONTEXTS
The Family
The Transition to Parenthood
- Parenthood requires considerable adaptation and adjustment on the part of the parents.
- Research has found that martial relations change with the birth of a baby (some couples grow apart, others feel closer to each other, and others experience both sentiments).

Reciprocal Socialization
- **Reciprocal socialization** is socialization that is bidirectional. Children socialize parents just as parents socialize children.
- Mutual regulation and scaffolding are important aspects of reciprocal socialization.
  - **Scaffolding** is parental behavior that supports children's efforts, allowing them to be more skillful than they would be if they were to rely only on their own abilities.

The Family as a System
- As a social system, the family can be thought of as a constellation of subsystems defined in terms of generation, gender, and role.
- Belsky's model illustrates that marital relations, parenting, and infant behavior and development can have both direct and indirect effects on each other.

Maternal and Paternal Infant Caregiving
- Mothers and fathers have the ability to act sensitively and responsively with their infants.
- Maternal interactions usually center around child care activities, paternal interactions are more likely to focus on play.
  - Fathers engage in more rough-and-tumble play, whereas mothers play with their infants in a less physical and arousing manner.
- In stressful circumstances, infants show a stronger attachment to the mother.
- Lamb's study of nontraditional families found that when fathers assume the primary caregiving role, their interactions continue to resemble the patterns described above.
  - It is unclear whether these interactions are biological or a result of deeply ingrained socialization patterns.

Day Care
- Day care has become a basic need of the American family. More children are in day care now than at any point in history.
- The U.S. does not have a policy of paid leave for child care.
- The quality of day care in the U.S. is uneven.
  - One study found that day-care centers that served high-income children delivered better quality care than did centers that served middle- and low-income children.
- Children in low-quality child care tend to be less socially competent. Unfortunately, children with few resources are more likely to experience poor quality day care.
- The National Institute of Child Health and Human Development studied the long-term effects of day care for over 1,400 children in 10 locations in the U.S. Some of the results include:
  - Infants from low-income families were more likely to receive low-quality child care than were their higher-income counterparts.
  - Child care in and of itself neither adversely affected nor promoted the security of infants' attachments to their mothers.
  - Child care quality, especially sensitive and responsive attention from caregivers, was linked with fewer child problems.

Learning Objectives

1. Understand the difficulty of defining emotion and the complexity of its components.
2. Describe the use of MAX in determining a developmental timetable of emotions.
3. Discuss how crying, smiling, and stranger anxiety are important communication mechanisms for infants.
4. Explain the concept of temperament, including the types of temperament, goodness of fit, and the implications of temperamental variations for parenting.
5. Discuss early personality development, including trust and the developing sense of self and independence.
6. Define attachment, then describe the importance of the research of Harlow and Zimmerman and the theories of Erik Erikson and John Bowlby.
7. Describe the types of attachment and the Strange Situation, being sure to mention what behaviors manifest themselves for each type and what caregiving styles will predict each type.
8. Discuss criticisms of attachment theory and the Strange Situation laboratory procedure, understanding the role played by cultural differences.
9. Understand reciprocal socialization and scaffolding, and the notion of the family as a system.
10. Describe the roles of the mother and the father in the development of an infant.
11. Indicate the effects of day care on developmental processes in infancy and what constitutes high-quality day care for infants.

Key Terms

anger cry
attachment
basic cry
difficult child
disorganized babies
easy child
emotion
insecure avoidant babies
insecure resistant babies
Maximally Discriminative Facial
    Movement Coding System (MAX)

pain cry
reciprocal socialization
reflexive smile
scaffolding
secure attachment
slow-to-warm-up child
social smile
stranger anxiety
Strange Situation
temperament

Key People

Mary Ainsworth
John Bowlby
Alexander Chess and Stella Thomas
Erik Erikson
Jacob Gerwirtz
Harry Harlow and Robert Zimmerman

Carroll Izard
Jerome Kagan
Margaret Mahler
Mary Rothbart and John Baltes
John Watson

Lecture Suggestions

Lecture Suggestion 1: Biological Basis of Shyness and Sociability The purpose of this lecture is to examine the biological basis of shyness and sociability. Kagan (1998) found that about 20 percent of 4-month-olds are easily upset by novelty, whereas 40 percent thrive on novelty and new experiences. Approximately 30 percent of children in these extreme groups maintained their temperamental style as they grew older. That is, the ones that were easily upset as infants became fearful, inhibited toddlers and preschoolers. The ones that thrived on novelty developed into outgoing, uninhibited preschoolers. Kagan proposes that the arousal of the amygdala (inner brain structure that controls avoidance reactions) may be responsible for the individual differences seen in temperament styles. In some children, especially the shy, inhibited ones, minimal stimulation is necessary to excite the amygdala and its connections to the cerebral cortex. In contrast, the same level of stimulation evokes minimal excitation in the highly social, uninhibited children.

In addition, shy infants and preschoolers display greater right than left frontal brain activity. Sociable children show the opposite pattern. The left cortical hemisphere is specialized to respond to positive emotion, whereas the right hemisphere is associated with negative emotion (Calkins et al., 1996). Neural activity in the amygdala is transmitted to the frontal lobes and may influence the temperament styles. There are other physiological differences between shy and sociable children:

- The heart rates of shy children are consistently higher and speed up further in response to novel events (Snidman et al., 1995).
- Cortisol, a stress hormone, tends to be higher in shy children (Gunnar & Nelson, 1994).
- Shy children have more pupil dilation and rise in blood pressure during novel events (Kagan, 1994).
- Sources: Calkins, S.D., Fox, N.A., & Marshall, T.R. (1996). Behavioral and physiological antecedents of inhibited and uninhibited behavior. *Child Development, 67*, 523-540. Gunnar, M.R. & Nelson, C.A. (1994). Event-related potentials in year-old infants: Relations with emotionality and cortisol. *Child Development, 65*, 80-94. Kagan, J. (1994). *Galen's prophecy.* New York: Basic Books. Kagan, J. (1998). Biology and the child. In N. Eisenberg (Ed.), *Handbook of child psychology: Vol. 3, Social, emotional, and personality development* (5th ed.) pp. 177-236. New York: Wiley. Snidman, N., Kagan, J., Riordan, L., & Shannon, D.C. (1995). Cardiac function and behavioral reactivity. *Psychophysiology, 32*, 199-207.

Lecture Suggestion 2: The Influence of Caregiving on Attachment Classification The purpose of this lecture is to examine influences on individual differences in attachment security. Rosen and Burke (1999) assessed attachment relationships within the context of two-parent families with two young children. With this approach, they could examine attachment relationships with mother and father and make comparisons between the younger and older children. Given the interactive nature of families it is important to examine relationships in this context. In this study, the mean age for the younger child was 1 year, 10 months and the Strange Situation was used to assess attachment security. The older children had a mean age of 4 years, 8 months and interpersonal interactions were used to assess attachment quality. Parental caregiving scores for both children were obtained as well.

Concordance in both younger and older children's attachments to their mothers and fathers was found. Based on the caregiving scores, parents were consistent in their caregiving behavior toward their two children. Yet, the patterns of attachment to their two children were not necessarily the same. It was equally likely that there was congruence as incongruence in the attachment relationships with their children. Caregiving and attachment was associated for younger children and their mothers, but the association was only moderate for other dyad combinations. Rosen and Burke hypothesize that characteristics of children and their parents differentially influence attachment at different ages. They propose that younger children place greater demand on mothers for accommodation based on their individual behavioral styles. This difference may account for the stronger relationship between caregiving and attachment for mothers and younger children. The weaker association for the older children's attachment and caregiving may be explained by the lessened significance of caregiving in determining attachment status for children in early childhood.

Rosen and Burke conclude that temperament and children's cognitive representations of attachment interact with parental caregiving and parents' cognitive representation of attachment to determine attachment security. While parental caregiving does influence attachment security, it appears to account for only a modest portion of the individual differences in attachment relationships.

- Source: Rosen, K.S., & Burke, P.B. (1999). Multiple attachment relationships within families: Mothers and fathers and two young children. *Developmental Psychology, 35*, 436-444.

Lecture Suggestion 3: How Do Toddlers Regulate Their Emotions? The purpose of this lecture is to examine research that describes how toddlers regulate their emotions. Before you talk about the research findings, have students generate methods they have used or have seen others use to calm a distressed toddler. Did some work better than others? Were all toddlers calmed by the same techniques?

Grolnick, Bridges, and Connell (1996) studied four behaviors that toddlers typically use to regulate their negative affective responses. The modulating behaviors they examined included symbolic reassurance (repeating phrases such as "I'm a big girl" or "Mommy will be back later"), shifting attention (looking away, high involvement in toy play), self-soothing comfort (thumb-sucking, hair-stroking, seeking comfort contact from caregiver), and maintaining focus on the stressful situation (active searching for the mother). Grolnick et al. assessed these behaviors during both separation from the mother and when faced with a delay in receiving a desirable gift.

Individual differences were seen, in that some toddlers were very upset by both of the situations, whereas others were only mildly distressed. Active engagement with toys was a very effective method for coping with the distressed toddler and was used the most when an adult was present. The children who used active involvement in toy play as a regulatory event were the least distressed. The ones that maintained focus on the stressful situation continued to be the most upset. It is important to note that the researchers acknowledge that these findings do not elucidate the causal relations between coping strategy and emotional expressiveness.

- Source: Grolnick, W.S., Bridges, L.J., & Connell, J.P. (1996). Emotion regulation in two-year-olds: Strategies and emotional expression in four contexts. *Child Development, 67*, 928-941.

Lecture Suggestion 4: Father Love The purpose of this lecture is to examine the role of fathers in children's development. The research reviewed illustrates that father love is influential in children's psychological well-being and health, and in an array of psychological and behavioral problems. Historically, the cultural construction of fatherhood had two main emphases. The first emphasis was that fathers were incapable of competent childrearing (they were biologically unsuited for the job). The second emphasis was that fathers' influence was not important, or peripheral at best. These cultural views influenced the scientific community as well. Researchers virtually ignored the role of fathers in children's development in behavioral science research for the first seven decades of the 20th century. More recently, researchers have attempted to better understand the influence of father love on children's development. Rohner (1998) defines father love in terms of parental acceptance and rejection. Acceptance involves real and perceived feelings and behaviors of nurturance, affection, support, etc. Rejection involves the absence or withdrawal of these real and perceived feelings and behaviors. Rohner reviewed research that highlights the relationship between father love and offspring development.

Variations in the Influence of Father Love

- Gender role development research has found that the masculinity of fathers per se did not influence the masculinity of their sons. Lamb (1997) found that cultural sex-role standards were more influential than the masculinity of the fathers when the father-son relationships were warm. The higher the quality of the father-child relationship, not just the amount of time a father spends with his child, the more cognitively and socially competent, less gender stereotypic, more empathic, and more psychologically healthy the children were (Lamb, 1997; Veneziano & Rohner, 1998).

Father Love Is as Important as Mother Love
- Young et al. (1995) found that perceived paternal love and caring was predictive of children's life satisfaction with a national sample of 640 12- to 16-year-olds living in two-parent families.

Father Love Predicts Specific Outcomes Better than Mother Love
- Fathers may be particularly influential in the development of some psychopathology (depression, conduct disorders, aggression) and substance abuse (drug and alcohol use and abuse) (Rohner, 1998).
- Amato (1994) in a national sample found that perceived closeness of fathers contributed (above and beyond the perceived closeness of mothers) to adult children's happiness, life satisfaction, and psychological well-being.

Father Love is the Sole Predictor of Specific Outcomes
- Father-child conflict, but not mother-child conflict, was positively associated with adolescent depression (Cole & McPherson, 1993).

Father Love Moderates the Influence of Mother Love
- Forehand and Nousianen (1993) found that when mothers were high in acceptance, the acceptance of fathers made an enormous difference. Low father acceptance scores were associated with children with poorer cognitive competence. High father acceptance scores were associated with children with significantly better cognitive competence.

Differential Outcomes for Sons and Daughters Based on Paternal vs. Maternal Parenting
- Daughters' self-esteem was best predicted by mothers' general support and fathers' physical affection, whereas sons' self-esteem was best predicted by mothers' companionship and fathers' sustained contact (Barber & Thomas, 1986).
- Paternal nurturance was positively correlated with boys' IQ scores, but not girls' (Jordan et al., 1975).

- Sources: Amato, P.R. (1994). Father-child relations, mother-child relations and offspring psychological well-being in adulthood. *Journal of Marriage and the Family, 56*, 1031-1042. Barber, B. & Thomas, D. (1986). Dimensions of fathers' and mothers' supportive behavior: A case for physical affection. *Journal of Marriage and the Family, 48*, 783-794. Cole, D. & McPherson, A.E. (1993). Relation of family subsystems to adolescent depression: Implementing a new family assessment strategy. *Journal of Family Psychology, 7*, 119-133. Forehand, R. & Nousianen, S. (1993). Maternal and paternal parenting: Critical dimensions in adolescent functioning. *Journal of Family Psychology, 7*, 213-221. Jordan, B., Radin, N., & Epstein, A. (1975). Paternal behavior and intellectual functioning in preschool boys and girls. *Developmental Psychology, 11*, 407-408. Lamb, M.E. (1997). Fathers and children development: An introductory overview and guide. In M.E. Lamb (Ed.), *The role of the father in children development* (pp.1-18). New York: Wiley & Sons. Rohner, R.P. (1998). Father love and child development: History and current evidence. *Current Directions in Psychological Science, 7*, 157-161. Veneziano, R.A. & Rohner, R.P. (1998). Perceived paternal warmth, paternal involvement, and youths' psychological adjustment in a rural, biracial southern community. *Journal of Marriage and the Family, 60*, 335-343. Young, M.H. ,Miller, B.E., Norton, M.C., & Hill, J.E. (1995). The effect of parental supportive behaviors on life satisfaction of adolescent offspring. *Journal of Marriage and the Family, 57*, 813-822.

Classroom Activities

Classroom Activity 1: Erikson's Psychosocial Theory and Parenting Students should explore the relation between Erikson's psychosocial theory and parenting skills. Erikson thought a child's sense of trust was the cornerstone of all future personality development. Thus, the interactions between the caregivers and the infant are extremely important.
- Which aspects of parenting lead to this sense of trust?
- What roles do physical comfort, consistency, lack of fearful situations, and feeding play?
- What is the role of parental attentiveness?
- Should the caregiver respond immediately to the infant's cries?

- Do you think that trust is developed more easily by later-born children because their parents are more confident?
- What aspects of being the first born counterbalance the advantages of having experienced parents?

Logistics:
- Group size: Full class discussion.
- Approximate time: Full class discussion (20 minutes).
- Sources: Maier, H. (1969). *Three theories of child development*. New York: Harper & Row.

Classroom Activity 2: Assessment of Child Care in Your Community Most students accept that day care is a fact of life for many children in the United States. Even if some of the students do not envision themselves either as parents or as a parent that would utilize child care, have them explore the issues involved in choosing a child care setting. The purpose of this activity is for students to assess the quality of infant child care in their community.
- First, have students explore the options for infant child care available in your community. Students often neglect to explore the university community when it comes to child-care issues. Most institutions have either a day-care setting on campus or a voucher system for local facilities, and, at the very least, they have a list of available child-care facilities in the community.
- Second, for each potential option, the students should assess the cost and services available. Students can use Figure 7.5 in the textbook as it provides a list of characteristics of high-quality child care.
- Third, they should decide which child-care facility would be their first and second choice. With that in mind, they should determine if that facility would be feasible given the expense.
- Use in the Classroom: Have students report their findings. Is there any consensus as to the "best" child care available? Were there different choices depending on the age and gender of the child? Did your students use other criteria than the characteristics listed in the textbook to make their decisions?

Logistics:
- Group size: Individual homework and full class discussion.
- Approximate time: Individual homework (60 minutes) and full class discussion (30 minutes).

Classroom Activity 3: What are the Child Care Laws in Your State? The purpose of this activity is for students to research the child care laws in their state and compare those laws to other states. There is enormous variability in the state laws that regulate child care. Given that standards for child care are set by states, the quality of care also varies tremendously by state. You can provide the web sites listed below to help your students get started or you can have them search the internet on their own. Internet research is a valuable skill that your students should learn.
- Have students research information about the child care standards in various states. You can assign each student one or two states depending on the size of your class. You can also divide up the assignment by age (e.g., ratios of children to caregivers vary by age of the child). They should obtain information on the following issues: curriculum requirements, space and equipment, child care staff training, child to caregiver ratios and maximum group size, criminal records, health and safety requirements, discipline, parental rights.
- Use in the Classroom: Have students report their findings. Which states have the most stringent requirements? Which have the least? Discuss whether these requirements influence quality of care and cost of care?

Logistics:
- Group size: Individual homework and full class discussion.
- Approximate time: Individual homework (45 minutes) and full class discussion (30 minutes).
- Source: http://ericps.ed.uiuc.edu/nccic/statepro.html, http://www.childrensdefense.org/cc_lookatstates.htm

Classroom Activity 4: Baby in a Box This activity introduces students to Skinner's "Baby in a Box." B. F. Skinner built a "baby box," an incubator-like apparatus in which he raised his second daughter, Deborah. Henry Hope, head of Indiana University's fine arts department, also used the invention to raise his twin boys Roy and Ray. The box had a constant temperature of 88 degrees and humidity of 50 percent. There was a canvas mattress at the bottom stretched over the air filters that regulated the temperature and humidity. The "baby box" had a picture window and sound-absorbing walls. One of the main issues for Skinner was that the "baby box" facilitated mothers' care of babies; the added convenience reduced the time to care for a baby to approximately 1 hour per day. In order for students to better understand Skinner's position, either have the students read excerpts from Skinner's original work or you can read selected excerpts in class (Skinner, 1972).

None of these three children seemed to have any developmental problems or advantages from this unusual "air crib," but attempts to manufacture and sell these cribs were not successful. For a while, rumors existed that Skinner's daughter Deborah had committed suicide, but, in reality, she became a successful artist.

Given the students' interest in this topic and the controversy it generates, small groups work well for this activity. After describing Skinner's use of the "baby box," have students answer these questions:
- What would be the advantages and disadvantages of this "baby box"?
- Would you raise a baby using this? Why or why not?
- Based on the "baby box," what modifications might you propose for other baby apparatuses—high chairs, playpens, etc.?
- Do you think it is ethical to raise a child in a "baby box"?

Logistics:
- Group size: Small groups.
- Approximate time: Small groups (20 minutes).
- Sources: Gerow, J. (1988). Time retrospective: Psychology 1923-1988, p.45. Skinner, B. F. (1972). *Baby in a box. Cumulative record: A selection of papers* (3rd ed.). New York: Appleton-Century-Crofts. Skinner, B. F. (March, 1979). My experience with the baby tender. *Psychology Today*.

Classroom Activity 5: Critical Thinking Multiple-Choice Questions and Suggested Answers Discuss the answers to the critical thinking multiple-choice questions on **Handout 1**. The answers are provided in **Handout 2**. Questions 1 and 2 are different from the previous critical thinking exercises. The first one requires a more specific evaluation of the evidence presented in the textbook. In addition to deciding whether there is any evidence to support the claim, the students are asked to evaluate whether the evidence is appropriate. In order to prepare them to do this, you will probably want to review rules for interpreting the adequacy of scientific evidence. Students will need to remember, for example, what inferences are permissible from correlational and experimental research. In this discussion, you may also want to explore how the type of questions being asked is related to the type of research that is needed. Descriptive questions need observational research; questions about patterns or associations are answered with correlational research; questions about cause and effect need experimental research.

Question 2 represents the first time since chapter 2 that students are asked to apply the theoretical perspectives. You may want to discuss with them how well they remember these perspectives, and either provide a review or have them review the theories. In any case, either give students a list of the key features of each perspective, or have them develop such a list as an in-class activity.

Question 3 is a straightforward continuation of the inference, assumption, and observation problems.

Logistics:
- Materials: Handout 1 (the critical thinking multiple-choice questions) and Handout 2 (answers).
- Group size: Small groups to discuss the questions, then a full class discussion.
- Approximate time: Small groups (15 to 20 minutes), then 15 minutes for full class discussion.

Classroom Activity 6: Critical Thinking Essay Questions and Suggestions for Helping Students Answer the Essays Discuss the students' answers to the critical thinking essay questions provided in **Handout 3**. Several objectives can be met with these questions. First, answering these questions further facilitates students' understanding of concepts in chapter 7. Second, this type of essay question affords the students an opportunity to apply the concepts to their own lives, which will facilitate their retention of the material. Third, the essay format also will give students practice expressing themselves in written form. Ideas to help students answer the critical thinking essay questions are provided as **Handout 4**.

Logistics:
- Materials: Handout 3 (essay questions) and Handout 4 (helpful suggestions for the answers).
- Group size: Individual, then full class.
- Approximate time: Individual (60 minutes), then 30 minutes for full class discussion.

Personal Applications

Personal Application 1: Don't Be Such a Cry Baby! The purpose of this exercise is to get students assessing their perceptions of a common infant emotional state: crying. Crying is the most important mechanism newborns have for communicating. We also know that babies have a minimum of three different cries—all indicating a different need (although many mothers would say there are even more!). Developmental psychologists differ in their beliefs as to the importance of responding to infants' cries and the implications it has for subsequent crying. Regardless, it is something inherent about being an infant, and in being around infants for any period of time.

- Instructions for Students: Think about when you encounter crying babies in a public place. When was the last time you were in a restaurant and had your dinner interrupted by the loud cries of an infant? How about standing in line at the grocery store? The movie theater? How did you feel upon hearing the crying? Be honest! What are most people's reaction to a crying infant? Discuss this with regard to what you've learned about the significant role crying plays in development.

- Use in the Classroom: Discuss this issue in class, and focus on people's general tolerance for crying babies. If you have any parents in the class, have them discuss their views since having a child of their own. Have mothers talk about the different types of cries their babies have, and what they each communicate. End by addressing the issue of parents bringing children to various public places—theaters, restaurants, and so on knowing that crying is inevitable. Debate the appropriateness of such behavior.

Personal Application 2: The Big Debate The purpose of this exercise is to have students explore their own personal reaction to putting children in day care. There are more children in day care today than ever before in history. Our society has come to accept, and in some ways expect, women working outside the home. This has not resulted in a dramatic drop in birth rate, rather the shift has been with regard to who takes care of the children. The findings of the effects of day care are mixed, with numerous variables influencing the results. Emotions run high on this topic, as there is a lot at stake for everyone involved.

- Instructions for Students: Write about your feelings regarding placing children in day care. Were you placed in day care? What was it like? How did you feel about it? About your parents' decision to place you there? Have you done it with your children? Why? What are the benefits? Do you have any concerns about doing so? How are they responding? What is the most difficult part? Are there any other alternatives? If you don't have children, do you think you will rely on day care in order for you to be able to work? Why or why not? What information presented in the text makes you feel comfortable with the idea of children in day care? What information concerns you about it? What do you think will be the overall effect on society of new generations of children growing up in day care environments? If you find them problematic, what might the solution be to accommodate both the children's needs and the parents'?

- Use in the Classroom: This makes an excellent topic for class discussion. Get input from students who experienced day care themselves, and input from parents whose children currently attend. Share stories, concerns, ideas, alternatives, and reactions to the research findings in this area. Do students have any other ideas for pertinent study regarding the day care issue?

Personal Application 3: Remember When… The purpose of this exercise is to get students to reflect on their childhood experiences and the accompanying emotions. Society is far removed from the traditional family life of the 1950s in which the father went away to work, the mother stayed home and cared for the children, and most families were intact units that spent dinnertime and vacations together. As the diversity of our lifestyles grows, children are experiencing any number of different experiences in the formative years of development. They don't participate in the decision-making process, and they're not asked how they feel about their circumstances. Yet, children are affected by their early experiences, and often we believe the impact lasts well into our adult years.

- Instructions for Students: Write a short autobiographical description of your childhood. Talk about your family life, relationships with your parents and siblings, who took care of you—the roles of each of your parents in this regard, and anyone else who might have contributed. Do you recall how you felt about your situation growing up? Did you feel loved and nurtured or neglected and abandoned? Did you have a lot of family time, and did you enjoy it? If you had a broken home, did you feel the burden of additional responsibility? Did you feel more independent? How do you feel your childhood experiences still influence who you are today?
- Use in the Classroom: An abbreviated option for this exercise is to have a class discussion in which students share small tidbits about their childhood, and the emotions they recall from certain experiences. Compare and contrast students who had similar backgrounds—did they respond the same way to them, or were their reactions quite different? Also see if there are students who experienced very different circumstances early on, yet had very similar emotional reactions to them.

Research Project Ideas

Research Project 1: Development of Self in Infants This project examines the development of the self in infants. Prior to the start of the research, the project must be approved by the human subjects review board at your school and the students must get a signed informed consent form from the infants' parents. See the section entitled Ethics, Human Subjects, and Informed Consent at the front of this Instructor's Manual. Students will test an 8-month-old infant and an 18-month-old infant with a mirror recognition task. Each infant will be assessed with two tasks, one will test for mirror recognition of the self and the other task will assess the infant's mirror recognition of an object near the infant. The students will then answer the questions about their observations. The task descriptions, worksheet, and questions are provided on **Handout 5**.

- Task 1: Have the mother stand behind the infant and hold an attractive toy above and slightly behind the infant's head, so that the infant can see the toy in the mirror but cannot see the toy itself. Record whether the infant reaches for the reflection of the toy in the mirror or turns around and reaches for the toy itself.
- Task 2: For one minute, count the number of times the infant touches its nose while looking in the mirror. Then have the mother put a dab of rouge on the infant's nose, and turn the infant back toward the mirror. For the next minute count the number of times the infant touches its nose and the number of times it touches the reflection of its nose.

Questions for Students:
- Does the 8-month-old infant reach for the object? Does the 18-month-old reach for the object? Does either infant reach for the reflection of the toy in the mirror? If so, which infant?

- How does the 8-month-old infant react to his or her image in the mirror with the rouge on his or her nose? How does the 18-month-old infant react to the image in the mirror with the rouge on the nose? Do the infants of different ages react differently? Explain.
- Is there a difference in the development of the ability to recognize the self and the ability to recognize an object in a mirror? If so, why would this be?
- Use in the Classroom: Have students present the data from the research project. Divide the data by age and sex of the subjects and evaluate the data for age and sex differences. Do the infants solve both tasks at the same age? If so, what age? If not, which task is solved first? What would account for the age differences in behavior? What is developing? What cognitive, social, and biological factors might account for the developmental change?
  - You can expect that the younger child will probably be oriented to the mirror for both tasks. That is, he or she will attend to the spot on the nose of the reflection and the reflection of the toy behind. Both the rouge spot on the nose and the real toy are likely to be ignored or discovered accidentally. The older child is likely to be oriented to the self for the rouge and to the toy behind him or her. He or she is likely to touch the spot on his or her nose and turn around to look at the real toy. Sex differences are unlikely to emerge. Maturation of the nervous system and visual system, the appearance of mental representation and symbolic abilities, and experience with mirrors might all be factors in this development.

Research Project 2: Attachment Behaviors The purpose of this project is for students to become more familiar with attachment behaviors and to practice their naturalistic observational techniques. Students can go to either the local shopping mall or a local park and observe a caregiver with an infant 12 to 18 months old. They should observe for a period of 15 minutes. Using **Handout 6** they should describe the behaviors they see. Possible observed behaviors are: protesting a separation when a mother walks around the shopping cart to get something from the shelf, and resistance or ambivalence when the mother picks the child up after paying for the groceries. After they have collected their data, have them answer the provided questions:
- What kinds of behaviors did your caregiver-infant pairs engage in? Did the infant use the caregiver as the base for exploration? Was the infant allowed to explore?
- According to the categories secure and insecure, how did this pair seem? Were interactions generally positive or generally negative? Did the relationship seem warm and affectionate or hostile?
- Use in the Classroom: Aggregate the students' data. How many of the infants were rated as securely attached? What behaviors led to that classification? How many infants were rated as insecurely attached? What behaviors led to that classification?

Film and Video List

The following films and videos supplement the content of chapter 7. Contact information for film distributors can be found at the front of this Instructor's Manual under Film and Video Sources.

Attachment (Insight Media, 24 minutes). This video examines research on attachment including a focus on the Strange Situation procedure.

Children of Poverty (Films for the Humanities and Sciences, 26 minutes). This program profiles children stricken by poverty. It examines the effects of finding food and shelter, how to keep children from becoming victims or perpetrators of crime, and methods to nurture self-esteem in these children.

The Development of the Self (Films for the Humanities and Sciences, 23 minutes). This program focuses on the development of self in the first year of life.

Developing the Sense of Family (Films for the Humanities and Sciences, 21 minutes). This video examines the development of social relationships within the family. At 6 months, the infant has developed a sense of familiarity with his/her surroundings and recognizes the faces of family members. He or she begins to turn away from strangers.

Early Child Care and Education (Magna Systems, 36 minutes). This video explores choices in child care and early education, quality in early childhood programs, and issues in early childhood education. In addition, factors in child abuse are discussed.

Early Relationships: Habits of the Heart (Insight Media, 60 minutes). This program looks at how infants participate in early social relationships, including bonding and attachment, the Strange Situation, and individual differences.

Early Socialization: From Birth to Age Two (Films for the Humanities and Sciences, 23 minutes) This program tracks the social development of two children, Max and Ellie. Footage covers awareness, bonding, attachment to adults, parallel play, sharing with peers, and communication by vocalization, facial expression, body language, and speech.

First Feelings (Insight Media, 30 minutes). Nature/nurture issues in infant personality development are the focus of this program. Discussion of attachment and temperament by experts Kagan, Ainsworth, Sroufe, and Bridges is presented. Footage from Harlow's work is included.

Infancy: Early Relationships (Magna Systems, 19 minutes). Socioemotional development is discussed, including the development of trust, mutuality, bonding and attachment, growth failure, and quality caregivers for infants.

Infancy: Self and Social World (Magna Systems, 15 minutes). This short video examines the development of emotions, symbiosis and separation, social awareness, and cultural effects on development.

Life's First Feelings (Pennsylvania State University, 58 minutes). While this NOVA video is somewhat dated, it does an incredible job of showing the emotional capabilities in newborns and young children.

Mother Love (Carousel Films, 26 minutes). This classic program presents Harlow's experiments about rearing infant rhesus monkeys on artificial mothers made of wire mesh and terry cloth.

Rock-a-Bye-Baby (Time-Life Films, 28 minutes). The classic work of Spitz and Bowlby that demonstrated the concept of critical period and the behavior of mother-deprived institutional children is portrayed.

Web Site Suggestions

The URLs for general sites, common to all chapters, can be found at the front of this Instructor's Manual under Useful Web Sites. At the time of publication, all sites were current and active, however, please be advised that you may occasionally encounter a dead link.

Attachment: Theory and Research @ Stony Brook
http://www.psychology.sunysb.edu/ewaters/

Babes in Day Care
http://www.theatlantic.com/issues/88aug/babe.htm

Comparison of Mahler and Stern's Theories of the Development of the Self
http://www-students.biola.edu/~jay/psy-mahlervstern.html

Controversial Aspects of Bowlby's Attachment Theory
http://www.geocities.com/Athens/Acropolis/3041/controversy.html

Infant Care: How Do You Know Quality When You See It?
http://home.oit.umass.edu/~cshrc/childcare/Infant_Care.html

John Bowlby: His Life and Work on Attachment Theory
http://gamma.is.tcu.edu/~cross/histweb/bowlby.html

National Child Care Information Center
http://ericps.ed.uiuc.edu/nccic/statepro.html

The NICHD Study of Early Child Care
http://156.40.88.3/publications/pubs/early_child_care.htm

Temperament
http://www.temperament.com/

Critical Thinking Multiple-Choice Questions

1. In chapter 7, Santrock describes many claims about social development during infancy. The quality of the evidence that supports each claim is quite varied. Which of the following claims is LEAST supported? Which evidence is LEAST convincing according to scientific criteria? Circle the letter of the best answer and explain why it is the best answer and why each other answer is not as good.

    a. Caregivers of disorganized babies often neglect or physically abuse their babies.
    b. Under stress, infants show stronger attachment to their mothers than their fathers.
    c. Extensive day care during the first year of an infant's life is associated with negative outcomes later in life.
    d. The expression of emotions by infants follows a predictable developmental course.
    e. During the second year of life, an infant experiences conflict between autonomy versus shame and doubt.

2. In previous chapters, there has been little opportunity to apply the various theories of development that were outlined in chapter 2. Chapter 7, however, presents research and theorizing motivated by several of these theories. Santrock directly identifies some of these, but does not do so for all topics. Listed below are topics from chapter 7 paired with theoretical perspectives. Decide which of these pairs is accurate. Circle the letter of the best answer and explain why it is the best answer and why each other answer is not as good.

    a. reciprocal socialization: psychoanalytic theory
    b. attachment: cognitive theory
    c. temperament: ethological theory
    d. the father's role: behavioral theory
    e. day care: ecological theory

3. Attachment is a major topic in the study of infant social development. Which of the following statements best represents an assumption by researchers, rather than an inference or an observation? Circle the letter of the best answer and explain why it is the best answer and why each other answer is not as good.

    a. An infant cries when separated from its mother because it is attached to its mother.
    b. The most important relationship in an infant's life involves attachment to a primary caretaker.
    c. Stressed 12-month-old babies direct their behavior toward their mothers.
    d. Providing an infant with a comfortable, safe environment creates an attachment bond between an infant and caretaker.
    e. Some babies do not look at their mothers or try to be near them in the Strange Situation.

Handout 2 (CA 5)

Suggested Answers for Critical Thinking Multiple-Choice Questions

1. In chapter 7, Santrock describes many claims about social development during infancy. The quality of the evidence that supports each claim is quite varied. Which of the following claims is LEAST supported? Which evidence is LEAST convincing according to scientific criteria? Circle the letter of the best answer and explain why it is the best answer and why each other answer is not as good.

    a. The statement <u>caregivers of disorganized babies often neglect or physically abuse their babies</u> requires at least correlational evidence for support. Main and Solomon's research reported in the text provides it.

    b. Lamb's study reported in the text is an experimental test of the hypothesis that <u>under stress, infants show stronger attachment to their mothers than their fathers</u>. The research confirmed that tired infants exposed to a Strange Situation sought their mothers instead of their fathers.

    c. <u>Extensive day care during the first year of an infant's life is associated with negative outcomes later in life</u> is not the best answer. While the evidence is mixed, there is research that documents the association between day care early in infants' lives and later negative outcomes. The contradictions in the research seem to be satisfactorily resolved by the claim that later outcomes are a function of the quality of day care the infants attend.

    d. Izard's research represents years of observational study and the development of a meticulous system for classifying infant facial expressions. Furthermore, longitudinal work has documented that the <u>expression of emotions by infants follows a predictable developmental course</u>, as indicated in the table presented in the text.

    e. This is the best answer because no evidence is presented to support the claim that <u>during the second year of life, an infant experiences conflict between autonomy versus shame and doubt</u>. Rather, the informal observations of a clinical psychologist are described. No systematic research of any type is cited.

2. In previous chapters, there has been little opportunity to apply the various theories of development that were outlined in chapter 2. Chapter 7, however, presents research and theorizing motivated by several of these theories. Santrock directly identifies some of these, but does not do so for all topics. Listed below are topics from chapter 7 paired with theoretical perspectives. Decide which of these pairs is accurate. Circle the letter of the best answer and explain why it is the best answer and why each other answer is not as good.

    a. <u>Reciprocal socialization: psychoanalytic theory</u> is not an accurate pair. While psychoanalytic theory does stress the importance of early relationships to personality development, it does not focus on the influence of an infant's behavior on an adult caretaker's behavior. In fact, the theory seems to imply a unidirectional analysis, focusing on how adult behavior determines personality outcomes in interaction with the developmental stage of the infant. The detailed analysis of adult-infant interaction as a system of mutually regulated and synchronized behaviors, intensively studied through observational techniques, is better paired with behavioral or ethological theories.

    b. <u>Attachment: cognitive theory</u> is not an accurate pair. Cognitive theory would focus on mental processes such as schemes or information processing, or perhaps would include notions of innate abilities to discriminate attachment figures from nonattachment figures. The emphasis in research on attachment, however, is on observation of social interactions in well-defined contexts; and attachment theorists speak of interacting systems of behavior between infant and the attachment figure. While the phenomenon of attachment seems to be related to cognitive development during infancy, cognitive theory is not the source of the concept.

    c. <u>Temperament: ethological theory</u> is the most accurate pair. A major claim is that temperament has a biological basis and survival value which is the focus of ethological theory. An interest in individual differences is also a mark of the biological heritage of ethological theory.

    d. <u>The father's role: behavioral theory</u> is not an accurate pair. If behavioral theory had motivated research in this area, there would be an analysis of the rewards and punishments currently operating in families or societies to encourage or discourage fathers from taking part in child rearing. However, the focus is a more observational study of what fathers are doing. It is not clear that the material in the chapter derives from any specific theoretical perspective.

    e. <u>Day care: ecological theory</u> is not an accurate pair. As was the case with item "d," it is not clear that a specific theoretical approach has motivated research on day care. The stimulus appears to be more pragmatic and empirical—namely, the simple need to analyze and evaluate a major change in the early social life of infants that has occurred over the past three decades. Interestingly, the ecological perspective could be used to organize and discuss information in this area, but that has not been done explicitly in this chapter. Also, Belsky, who views families as subsystems of individuals, is a researcher in this area, suggesting that he has done some systems analysis of day care and its effects on children.

3. Attachment is a major topic in the study of infant social development. Which of the following statements best represents an assumption by attachment researchers, rather than an inference or an observation? Circle the letter of the best answer and explain why it is the best answer and why each other answer is not as good.

    a. The following statement is an inference: <u>an infant cries when separated from its mother because it is attached to its mother</u>. It is an explanation offered to account for the observation that infants often cry when they are separated from their mothers.

    b. <u>The most important relationship in an infant's life involves attachment to a primary caretaker</u> is the assumption. One indication is Kagan's challenge that attachment is not as important as other researchers think it is. Another is that this point is taken for granted in the text, without evidence or justification. A third is that if researchers did not believe this, so much work would probably not have been invested in studying it.

    c. The statement that <u>stressed 12-month-old babies direct their behavior toward their mothers</u> is an observation and a summary of data collected by Lamb and others in their studies of the correlates of securely and insecurely attached infants. Simply stated, infants who were classified as insecurely attached were later seen to be more likely to fuss, cry, or be angry if they were challenged with a problem or difficult task.

    d. <u>Providing an infant with a comfortable, safe environment creates an attachment bond between an infant and caretaker</u> is an inference from the conclusion of a variety of studies of the causes of attachment in humans and monkeys. Researchers have tested hypotheses about the causes of attachment in experimental and correlational studies. They have concluded from this work that comfort and safety are primary determinants of attachment.

    e. The observation that <u>some babies do not look at their mothers or try to be near them in the Strange Situation</u> is seen in both systematic and casual observations of infants. It is one way that researchers and caregivers have seen babies behave in the presence of their mothers.

Critical Thinking Essay Questions

Your answers to this kind of question demonstrate an ability to comprehend and apply ideas discussed in this chapter.

1. Explain how developmentalists have studied emotions in infants.

2. Discuss what we learn about infant cognitive and social development by studying infant smiling and crying.

3. Analyze your own temperament. Indicate whether your temperament is better explained by the Chess and Thomas or the Buss and Plomin approach. Also indicate how stable your temperament has been over the course of your development and what factors may have contributed to this stability or lack of stability.

4. Explain Erikson's concept of trust versus mistrust. Give a hypothetical situation of a parent-infant interaction that leads to the infant developing trust and an example in which the infant would develop mistrust.

5. Compare and contrast Mahler's and Erikson's explanations for the development of independence and the self during infancy.

6. Explain the main criticisms of the Strange Situation procedure.

7. Indicate and explain the individual differences in attachment, and the relationship of early attachment to later social interactions.

8. Explain reciprocal socialization. Provide at least two examples of how parents socialize their children and two examples of how children socialize their parents in your response.

9. What does it mean to think of a family as a system? Illustrate your answer using the concepts of reciprocal socialization, scaffolding, or attachment.

10. Compare and contrast fathers' and mothers' ability to care for infants, and each parent's typical caregiving practices.

11. If you were a parent who could choose whether to stay home with your children or place them in day care, what factors would you consider in making this decision?

Ideas to Help You Answer Critical Thinking Essay Questions

1. Begin by thinking about emotions. In your own words, what are they? How many are there? How easy or difficult are they to describe and explain? Have you ever felt that others don't understand your emotions? After considering the nature of emotions, explain how developmental psychologists study them, considering the tremendous challenge of this endeavor and the creativity involved in the methodology.

2. To help you put the significance of these two behaviors in perspective, consider your argument to the notion that a baby is "*just* smiling" or "*only* crying." In other words, through your discussion convey the profound developmental issues present in these behaviors.

3. Re-read the two approaches to understanding and explaining temperament. Describe and analyze yours according to each perspective. Which one does a better job of enabling you to do that? What factors does one address that the other does not?

4. Preface your explanation with a description of Erikson's basic theoretical approach to personality. What is the notion behind the concept of trust vs. mistrust? What does Erikson theorize follows this concept? Explain the stage and present your examples within this context.

5. Begin by defining independence and what is meant by the notion of self. Compare and contrast from there.

6. Briefly explain Ainsworth's approach to attachment and the reasoning behind the Strange Situation. Having established this basis, discuss the criticisms.

7. What is meant by attachment? Establish an understanding of the concept, then discuss individual differences, and how it relates to subsequent social interaction.

8. Think about your own relationships and the interactions that take place within them. Identify examples of the bidirectionality of influence. Do you exhibit behaviors or have you developed opinions similar to those close to you? Have others become more like you in their thinking and mannerisms? With these images in mind, explain the occurrence of reciprocal socialization in parents and children.

9. Describe a "scene" from your own family—current or childhood. Do you recognize aspects of a *system* present in that scene? Continue your discussion by addressing reciprocal socialization, scaffolding, and/or attachment.

10. Create a chart: "Mom vs. Dad." Make a list of the particular aspects of caregiving, and note each one's involvement, participation, effectiveness, investment, etc.

11. Address each factor presented in the text. How relevant a factor is each to you? What factors would weigh more heavily in your decision? Why?

Development of Self in Infants

This project examines the development of the self in infants. Prior to the start of the research, the project must be approved by the human subjects review board at your school and you must get a signed informed consent form from the infants' parents. You will test an 8-month-old infant and an 18-month-old infant with a mirror recognition task. Each infant will be assessed with two tasks, one will test for mirror recognition of the self and the other task will assess the infant's mirror recognition of an object near the infant. After you have completed the tasks, answer the questions about your observations. The task descriptions, worksheet, and questions are provided below.

Task 1:

Have the mother stand behind the infant and hold an attractive toy above and slightly behind the infant's head, so that the infant can see the toy in the mirror but cannot see the toy itself. Record whether the infant reaches for the reflection of the toy in the mirror or turns around and reaches for the toy itself.

Task 2:

For one minute, count the number of times the infant touches its nose while looking in the mirror. Then have the mother put a dab of rouge on the infant's nose, and turn the infant back toward the mirror. For the next minute count the number of times the infant touches its nose and the number of times it touches the reflection of its nose.

Child 1   Child 2
Sex ____ Age ____   Sex ____ Age ____

Task 1
Reaches to mirror

Reaches to toy

Task 2
Touches mirror

Touches nose

Questions:

- Does the 8-month-old infant reach for the object? Does the 18-month-old reach for the object? Does either infant reach for the reflection of the toy in the mirror? If so, which infant?

- How does the 8-month-old infant react to his or her image in the mirror with the rouge on his or her nose? How does the 18-month-old infant react to the image in the mirror with the rouge on the nose? Do the two infants react differently? Explain.

- Is there a difference in the development of the ability to recognize the self and the ability to recognize an object in a mirror? If so, why would this be?

Attachment Behaviors

The objectives of this project are for you to become more familiar with attachment behaviors and to practice your naturalistic observational techniques. Go to either the local shopping mall or a local park and observe a caregiver with an infant 12 to 18 months old. The observation period should be 15 minutes. Describe the behaviors you see occurring. Then, you should answer the provided questions.

Behaviors   Child: Age _____ Sex _____

Talking

Laughing

Tickling

Clinging

Crying

Escaping

Retrieving

Mutual gaze

Hitting

Smiling

Yelling

Generally positive interaction

Generally negative interaction

Questions:

• What kinds of behaviors did your caregiver-infant pais engage in? Did the infant use the caregiver as the base for exploration? Was the infant allowed to explore?

• According to the categories secure and insecure, how did this pair seem? Were interactions generally positive or generally negative? Did the relationship seem warm and affectionate or hostile?

Chapter 8:Physical and Cognitive Development in Early Childhood

Total Teaching Package Outline

Lecture Outline	Resource References
Physical and Cognitive Development in Early Childhood	PowerPoint Presentation: See www.mhhe.com Cognitive Maps: See Appendix A F/V: Preschoolers: Physical and Cognitive Dev. F/V: Toddlerhood: Physical and Cognitive Dev.
Physical Development in Early Childhood	F/V: How We Study Children F/V: Physical Development: The First Five Years
• Body Growth and Change	LO1
-Height and Weight	OHT64 & IB: Height and Weight (2–6 Years) OHT66 & IB: Growth Curves
-The Brain	LO2
• Motor Development	LO3 CA1: Trends in Verbal and Motor Development
-Gross Motor Skills	OHT67 & IB: Gross Motor Development PA1: Tag, You're It!
-Fine Motor Skills	OHT68 & IB: Fine Motor Development LS1: Teaching Toddlers to Draw CA2: Design a Preschool Program
-Handedness	LS2: Is Handedness Related to Life Expectancy? PA2: For Lefties Only
• Nutrition	LO4 F/V: Nutrition WS: Assessment of Nutritional Status WS: Mild-to-Moderate Malnutrition WS: State of the World's Children 1998: Nutrition.
-Energy Needs	PA3: Have It Your Way
-Eating Behavior	
• Illness and Death	LO5 CA3: What Should Parents Tell Their Ill Child?
-The United States	LS3: The State of Illness and Health in Your State
-The State of Illness and Health of the World's Children	

Cognitive Development in Early Childhood • Piaget's Preoperational Stage of Development	LO6 CA4: Illustration of Piagetian Concepts
-Symbolic Function Substage	F/V: Representation in Three to Five-Year-Olds F/V: Concepts, Memories, and Reasons OHT63 & IB: Piaget's Mountain Task OHT65 & IB: Three Mountain Task Perspective
-Intuitive Thought Substage	IB: Some Dimensions of Conservation OHT54 & IB: Piaget's Conservation Task OHT71: Conservation PA4: I'm Sure You'll Agree

• Vygotsky's Theory of Development
    -The Zone of Proximal Development
    -Scaffolding
    -Language and Thought
    -Evaluating and Comparing Vygotsky's
       and Piaget's Theories
    -Teaching Strategies Based on Vygotsky's
       Theory
	LO7
	
	F/V: Learning in Context: Probing the Theories of
	Piaget and Vygotsky

• Information Processing
    -Attention
    -Memory
 	
    -Strategies
    -The Young Child's Theory of Mind
	LO8
	F/V: The Preschooler's Mind
	OHT73: Time Frames of Memory
	RP1: Memory Span
	F/V: Memory: The Past Imperfect
	
	LO9
	PA5: Know Your Own Mind
	LS4: The Benefits of Being Wrong

Language Development	LO10 RP2: Language Errors F/V: Childhood F/V: Language Acquisition F/V: Language Development F/V: Unlocking Language
Early Childhood Education • The Child-Centered Kindergarten • The Montessori Approach • Developmentally Appropriate and Inappropriate Practices in the Education of Young Children • Does Preschool Matter? • Education for Children Who Are Disadvantaged	LO11 F/V: Early Childhood Care and Education F/V: Men in Early Childhood Education WS: Early Childhood Education Resources WS: Maria Montessori: An Historical Perspective WS: The Montessori Approach CA5: Children's Readiness to Read LO12 LS5: Does Early Intervention Have Long-Term Effects?

Chapter Outline

PHYSICAL DEVELOPMENT IN EARLY CHILDHOOD
 Body Growth and Change
  Height and Weight
  - The average child grows 2 $\frac{1}{2}$ inches in height and gains 5 to 7 pounds a year in early childhood.
  - Girls are slightly smaller and lighter than boys.
  - Body fat decreases during the preschool years.
    - The two most important contributors to height differences are ethnic origin and nutrition.
    - Congenital factors, physical problems, and emotional difficulties are the most common reasons why some children are unusually short.
  The Brain
  - Between 3 and 5 years of age, the brain grows from 75 to 90 percent of its adult size.
  - The brain's increase is due to an increase in the number and size of nerve endings within and between brain areas and myelination.
    - **Myelination** is the process by which nerve cells are covered and insulated with a fat layer.
    - Myelination increases the speed of information traveling through the nervous system.
  - Using brain scanning techniques researchers found that the amount of brain material in some areas nearly doubles within a year's time, and then there is drastic loss of tissue as the unneeded cells are purged.
  - In early childhood, the most rapid growth occurs in the frontal lobes, which are important for planning and organizing new actions and in maintaining attention to tasks.

 Motor Development
  Gross Motor Skills
  - At 3 years, children enjoy simple movements (hopping, jumping, and running back and forth) for the sheer pleasure of the activity.
  - From 4 to 5 years of age, children become more confident and organized in their motor abilities.
  Fine Motor Skills
  - Between 3 and 4 years, children's fine motor coordination improves substantially.
  - Hand, arm, and body all move together under better command of the eye by 5 years.
  Handedness
  - Left-handers have suffered unfair discrimination in the world designed for right-handers.
  - Infants display a preference for one side of their bodies (turn their heads to the right when they are lying on their stomachs) and these preferences are related to later handedness.
  - By 2 years, about 10 percent of children favor their left hand, though many preschoolers do not have a clear preference.
  - Genetic inheritance and environmental experiences influence handedness.
    - The handedness of adopted children was related to their biological parents not to the handedness of their adoptive parents.

Nutrition
  Energy Needs
- What children eat affects their skeletal growth, body shape, and susceptibility to disease.
- An average preschooler needs 1,700 calories a day.
- Individual children's energy needs are determined by **basal metabolism rate (BMR)**, which is the minimum amount of energy a person uses in a resting state.
- Differences in physical activity, basal metabolism, and efficiency of energy use help explain the differences in children's energy needs.
  Eating Behavior
- While fat is a necessary component of an infant's diet, many young American children are consuming too much fat, especially from fast foods.
  - The American Heart Association recommends that 35 percent of daily calories come from fat.
- Being overweight can be a serious problem in early childhood.
  - Except in extreme cases of obesity, overweight children are encouraged to slow their rate of weight gain in order for their height to catch up, rather than aiming for weight loss.
- Prevention of obesity is important.
  - Food should be a way to satisfy hunger and nutritional needs, not as proof of love or as a reward for good behaviors.
  - Snack foods should be low fat, simple sugars, as well as high in fiber.
  - Routine physical activity is an important daily occurrence.

Illness and Death
  The United States
- Vaccines have nearly eradicated many disabling diseases.
- Birth defects, cancer, and heart diseases are still likely to be fatal during early childhood.
- It is extremely important to keep young children on an immunization schedule.
- Car accidents, drownings, falls, and poisoning are the leading causes of death in young children.
- Parental smoking increases children's risk for many medical problems.
- Malnutrition lessens children's resistance to disease.
  The State of Illness and Health of the World's Children
- One death in three in the world is the death of a child under the age of 5.
- The leading cause of childhood death worldwide is dehydration and malnutrition due to diarrhea.
  - **Oral rehydration therapy (ORT)** involves a range of techniques designed to prevent dehydration during episodes of diarrhea by giving the child fluids by mouth.
- Education regarding adequate birth spacing, prenatal care, breast-feeding, immunization, special feeding before and after illness, and regular checkups can help improve children's health.

COGNITIVE DEVELOPMENT IN EARLY CHILDHOOD
Piaget's Preoperational Stage of Development
- The preoperational stage encompasses 2 to 7 years of age. Stable concepts are formed, mental reasoning emerges, egocentricism weakens over the period, and magical beliefs are formed.
- The term *preoperational* emphasizes that a child is not able to think in an operational way.
  - **Operations** are internalized sets of actions that allow the child to do mentally what before she did physically.

- Preoperational thought can be divided into two substages:
  Symbolic Function Substage
    - **Symbolic function substage** is the first substage of preoperational thought, occurring roughly between the ages of 2 and 4. In this substage, the young child gains the ability to mentally represent an object that is not present.
    - Two limitations of children's thinking during this substage include:
      - **Egocentrism** is the inability to distinguish between one's own perspective and someone else's perspective.
        - Piaget and Inhelder's three mountain task demonstrated that children did not have the ability to take another's perspective when viewing objects on the three mountains.
        - More recent research has found that perspective-taking does not develop uniformly in preschool children, who frequently show perspective skills on some tasks and not others.
      - **Animism** is the belief that inanimate objects have "lifelike" qualities and are capable of action.
  Intuitive Thought Substage
    - The **intuitive thought substage** occurs between approximately 4 and 7 years of age. Children begin to use primitive reasoning and want to know the answers to all sorts of questions.
    - **Centration** involves focusing or centering attention on one characteristic to the exclusion of all others.
    - Children in this substage demonstrate the lack of **conservation** which is the awareness that altering an object's or a substance's appearance does not change its basic properties.
      - Centration and children's inability to reverse actions contribute to the lack of conservation.
      - Gelman states that children are more likely to be able to conserve if they have been trained to pay attention to the relevant aspects of the task. She also states that children develop conservation earlier than Piaget thought and that attention is especially important in explaining conservation.
    - Children first start asking questions around age 3 and the rate of question asking escalates. Questioning signals the emergence of children's interest in reasoning and figuring out how things work.

Vygotsky's Theory of Development
- The basic principles of Vygotsky's theory include:
  - Children's cognitive skills should be analyzed and interpreted developmentally.
  - Cognitive skills are mediated by words, language, and forms of discourse.
  - Cognitive skills originate in social relations and are embedded in a sociocultural context.
  The Zone of Proximal Development
  - The **zone of proximal development (ZPD)** is the range of tasks too difficult for children to master alone but which can be learned with the guidance and assistance of adults or more skilled peers.
    - This concept underscores Vygotsky's emphasis on the importance of social influences on children's cognitive development.
  Scaffolding
  - **Scaffolding** means changing the level of support. Over the course of a teaching session, more skilled person (teacher or more advanced peer) adjusts the amount of guidance to fit the student's current performance level.
    - Dialogue is an important part of scaffolding in the zone of proximal development. Through interaction, children's concepts become more systemic, logical and rational.

Language and Thought
- Language allows children to have social communication, and to plan, guide, and monitor their behavior in a self-regulatory fashion.
- Language used for self-regulation is called inner speech or private speech.
  - Vygotsky thought private speech was an important tool for cognitive development, whereas Piaget thought it was egocentric and immature.
  - Researchers have found support for the positive role of private speech in children's development.

Evaluating and Comparing Vygotsky's and Piaget's Theories
- Vygotsky's theory has played an important role in evaluating contextual factors in learning.
- Some critics say Vygotsky overemphasized the role of language in thinking.
- Vygotsky's theory is considered to be a **social constructivist approach** because it emphasizes the social contexts of learning and that knowledge is mutually built and constructed.
- Piaget's theory did not emphasize the social aspect of knowledge construction.
- There is a conceptual shift from Piaget to Vygotsky that involves a shift from the individual to collaboration, social interaction, and sociocultural activity.

Teaching Strategies Based on Vygotsky's Theory
- Use the child's zone of proximal development in teaching.
- Use scaffolding.
- Use more skilled peers as teachers.
- Monitor and encourage children's use of private speech.
- Assess the child's zone of proximal development, not IQ.
- Transform the classroom with Vygotskian ideas.

Information Processing
- Two major aspects of preschool children's thoughts are attention and memory.

Attention
- Children's ability to pay attention changes significantly in the preschool years.
  - Preschoolers still have trouble attending to the relevant aspect of a problem or task.
  - By the age of 6 or 7, children can attend more efficiently to relevant aspects which may reflect a shift to cognitive control of attention, so that children act less impulsively and reflect more.

Memory

Short-Term Memory
- In **short-term memory**, individuals retain information for up to 15 to 30 seconds, assuming there is no rehearsal.
  - Memory-span tasks are used to assess short-term memory in which a short list of stimuli are presented at a rapid pace and recall is measured.
  - Memory span increases from 2 digits in 2- to 3-year-olds to about 5 digits in 7-year-olds.
- Rehearsal of information, speed, and efficiency of processing are all important.

How Accurate Are Young Children's Long-Term Memories?
- Young children can remember information if they are given appropriate cues and prompts.

Strategies
- Chen's research demonstrated that 2-year-olds can learn a strategy to help them remember.

The Young Child's Theory of Mind
- **Theory of mind** refers to individuals' thoughts about how mental processes work.
- Children's developing knowledge of the mind includes:
  - Becoming aware that the mind exists
    - By the age of 2 or 3, children refer to needs, emotions, and mental states.
  - Understanding cognitive connections to the physical world
    - Young children understand that people can see them, hear them, like them, etc.
  - Detecting accuracies/inaccuracies of the mind
    - By 4 or 5 years of age, children can understand false beliefs.
  - Understanding the mind's active role in emotion and reality
    - The shift from viewing the mind as passive to viewing it as active appears in children's knowledge that prior experiences influence current mental states, which in turn affect emotions and social inferences.

LANGUAGE DEVELOPMENT
- Young children's grasp of language's rule systems increases.
  - These rule systems include morphology (the meaningfulness of words), semantics (the meanings of phrases and sentences), and pragmatics (rules of conversation).
  - Berko's classic experiment demonstrated that young children understand morphological rules.
- Between 1 and 6 years, children learn an average of 5 to 8 words a day.

EARLY CHILDHOOD EDUCATION
The Child-Centered Kindergarten
- In the **child-centered kindergarten**, education involves the whole child and includes concern for the child's physical, cognitive, and social development.
  - Experimenting, exploring, discovering, trying out, restructuring, speaking, and listening are all words that describe excellent kindergarten programs.

The Montessori Approach
- The **Montessori approach** is a philosophy of education in which children are given considerable freedom and spontaneity in choosing activities.
- Critics claim that this approach neglects children's social development and the development of imagination. Montessori emphasizes independence and cognitive development and de-emphasizes verbal interaction between the teacher and children and peer interaction.

Developmentally Appropriate and Inappropriate Practices in the Education of Young Children
- Schools should focus on social and cognitive development.
- **Developmentally appropriate practice** is based on knowledge of the typical development of children within an age span (age appropriateness), as well as the uniqueness of the child (individual appropriateness).
- Developmentally appropriate practice contrasts with developmentally inappropriate practice, which ignores the concrete, hands-on approach to learning.
  - Direct teaching largely through abstract paper-and-pencil activities presented to large groups of young children is believed to be developmentally inappropriate.
- The National Association for the Education of Young Children has many recommendations for developmentally appropriate practice.
  - Children who attended developmentally appropriate programs displayed more appropriate classroom behavior, had better conduct records, and had better work and study habits in the first grade than children who did not attend these programs.
  - Unfortunately, only one-third to one-fifth of all early childhood programs have developmentally appropriate practices. Child-initiated activities, divergent questioning, and small-group instruction are rare.

Does Preschool Matter?

- A special concern is that education is a race and that an early academic start in preschool will help children win the race.
- Critics argue that too many preschools are academically oriented and stressful for young children.
- Children who attended highly academic programs had higher test anxiety, less creativity, and a less positive attitude toward school than those who attended low academic programs in early childhood.

Education for Children Who Are Disadvantaged

- **Project Head Start** is a compensatory education program designed to provide children from low-income families the opportunity to acquire the skills and experiences important for success in school.
- **Project Follow Through** was implemented in 1967 as an adjunct to Project Head Start. In Project Follow Through, different types of educational programs were devised to determine which programs were the most effective. In the Follow Through programs, the enriched programs were carried through the first few years of elementary school.
- Variation in early childhood education does have significant effects in a wide range of social and cognitive areas.
  - Children in effective education approaches were absent from school less often and showed more independence than children in other approaches.
  - Children in academic oriented, direct-interaction approaches did better on achievement tests and were more persistent on tasks than children in other approaches.
- The long-term effects of such interventions include:
  - lower rates of special education, dropping out of school, grade retention, and welfare use.
  - higher rates of high school graduation and employment.
- For every dollar invested in high-quality model preschool programs, taxpayers receive about $1.50 in return by the time the participants are 20 years old.
- Not all programs are created equally.
  - One estimate is that 40 percent of Head Start Programs are of questionable quality.
  - Four out of five early childhood programs do not meet quality standards.
- Early childhood programs should encourage preparation for learning, varied learning activities, trusting relationships between adults and children, and increased parental involvement.

Learning Objectives

1. Understand the changes in height and weight during the preschool years and note factors associated with individual differences in height and weight.
2. Define myelination and discuss its contribution to brain development.
3. Explain how gross motor skills and fine motor skills change during the preschool years and the role that handedness plays in motor skills and intellect.
4. Define basal metabolism rate (BMR), and explain why early exposure to fast food worries developmentalists.
5. Discuss the state of illness and health in the world's children, including the leading cause of childhood death in the world, treatment, and prevention.
6. Define Piaget's preoperational stage and be able to give examples of behaviors that differentiate children in the symbolic function and intuitive thought substages.
7. Explain Vygotsky's theory of development, including the zone of proximal development (ZPD), scaffolding, language and thought, and the educational applications of Vygotsky's theory, and compare Vygotsky's theory with that of Piaget.

8. Indicate what changes occur in attention, memory, and use of strategies in early childhood.
9. Explain the development of the young child's theory of the mind.
10. Identify observations that indicate children understand rules of morphology, semantics, and pragmatics.
11. Compare and contrast the child-centered kindergarten with the Montessori approach, and discuss developmentally appropriate and inappropriate practices in educating young children.
12. Be able to answer the question, "Does preschool matter?" by addressing developmental consequences for all children, including those who are economically disadvantaged.

Key Terms

animism
basal metabolism rate (BMR)
centration
conservation
child-centered kindergarten
developmentally appropriate practice
egocentrism
intuitive thought substage
Montessori approach
myelination

operations
oral rehydration therapy (ORT)
Project Follow Through
Project Head Start
scaffolding
short-term memory
social constructivist approach
symbolic function substage
theory of mind
zone of proximal development (ZPD)

Key People

Teresa Amabile
Jean Berko
Zhe Chen and Robert Siegler
David Elkind

Rochel Gelman
Barbel Inhelder
Maria Montessori
Jean Piaget
Lev Vygotsky

Lecture Suggestions

Lecture Suggestion 1: Teaching Toddlers to Draw Should children be taught to draw? Or should they be allowed simply to draw however they wish, letting their motor, perceptual, and cognitive skills develop and enhance their drawing skills naturally? Tackle these questions in a lecture that relates fine motor development during toddlerhood to children's drawing abilities. Consider inviting a day-care or kindergarten teacher to present information on typical experiences with drawing provided to young children, and have them comment on whether they are concerned with using training to enhance drawing abilities. You may wish to open your (or your guest's) presentation to class discussion.

- Are there reasons why we might want to teach children to draw? Can drawing skills be trained? What is the nature of individual differences in drawing skill at these ages? Are these predictive of later skill? Were great painters talented scribblers as toddlers? You may find that this information is very interesting to students. Many suspect that drawing is something each of us wish we could do better if we only had the talent. But perhaps early training could enhance our subsequent artistic skills.

Lecture Suggestion 2: Is Handedness Related to Life Expectancy? The purpose of this lecture is to examine research on life expectancy and handedness. With increasing age, left-handedness declines (15 percent of 10 year olds are left-handed compared to less than 1 percent at age 80). Cross-sectional research has found that left-handers have a shorter life expectancy than right-handers (lefties do not live as long).

- Prior to delving into the research, encourage students to critically analyze from a methodological perspective some potential problems with using cross-sectional data for this research.

Coren and Halpern (1991) summarized research in their article, "Left-handedness: A marker for decreased survival fitness." They found that left-handedness is associated with prenatal and perinatal stressors (low-birthweight, prolonged labor, and anoxia). Alcoholism, allergies, suicide, and risk of immune disorders are linked to left-handedness. The question remains as to why these differences have been found.

Are lefties inherently weaker? Harris in a rebuttal to Coren and Halpern's article argues that societal pressure and an environmental bias toward right-handers may unfairly discriminate against lefties. Lefties may experience more accidents and injuries because they are pressured to use their right hand, which is not as competent. This reliance on the unpreferred right hand may render both hands less competent. More accidents may ensue given this reliance on less proficient maneuvering in a right-hand world. Harris also notes that historically young children were forced to switch to their right hand. Thus, cohort effects may weaken the cross-sectional data presented. The greater acceptance of left-handedness today and the historic pressure to be right handed may explain the larger number of lefties in the younger generations.

The entire argument that handedness is related to life expectancy hinges on cross-sectional, rather than longitudinal data. It is possible to explain the decrease in the number of lefties among the older cohorts in that left-handers are discriminated against in a right-handed world which puts them at risk for accidents and injuries, and the cohort effect we discussed above.

- Do these arguments make sense to your students? Would these arguments explain all of the problems mentioned in the Coren and Halpern article (prenatal and perinatal stressors, allergies, immune disorders, etc.)?
- Sources: Coren, S., & Halpern, D.F. (1991). Left-handedness: A marker for decreased survival fitness. *Psychological Bulletin, 109*, 90-106. Harris, L.J. (1993). Do left-handers die sooner than right-handers? Commentary on Coren and Halpern's (1991) "Left-handedness: A marker for decreased survival fitness." *Psychological Bulletin, 114*, 203-234.

Lecture Suggestion 3: The State of Illness and Health in Your State The chapter section regarding the state of illness and health of children worldwide sparked this lecture suggestion. Oftentimes, students assume that there are not problems in their own city or state; that is, problems happen elsewhere, not in our community. Develop a lecture that focuses on demographics and issues that pertain directly to your state. Interesting demographic statistics regarding child protection (abuse, foster care, adoption, domestic violence), economics (poverty, public assistance, taxes, hunger, homelessness), maternal and child health (low birthweight, infant mortality, sexually transmitted diseases, mental health, substance abuse), juvenile justice (juvenile court, gang activity), and education (dropout rate, child care, enrollment) can be presented. It is fascinating to compare state and national statistics regarding these issues. The Children's Defense Fund's website: http://www.childrensdefense.org/states/data.html provides a wealth of statistics and information.

The Children's Defense Fund publishes an annual analysis of the status of U.S. children, *The State of America's Children*. This publication provides an overview of their work over the last quarter century and the latest information of developments affecting children and families. *The Children in the States 2000* provides state-by-state tables detailing children's status and participation in a variety of programs. Data can also be obtained from both state and federal agencies, including Office of Planning and Budget, Demographic and Economic Analysis, Department of Employment Security, Department of Human Services, Traveller's Aid Society, Planned Parenthood, Division of Services for People with Disabilities, Office of Education, and Administration of Children Youth and Families. If you are unable to obtain sufficient breadth of various demographic information, focus on one or two of the issues and examine relevant public policy in your community and/or state.

- Sources: Children's Defense Fund. (2000). *The state of America's children.* Washington, DC: Children's Defense Fund. Children's Defense Fund. (2000). *The children in the states 2000.* Washington, DC: Children's Defense Fund. http://www.childrensdefense.org/states/data.html

Lecture Suggestion 4: The Benefits of Being Wrong Generally, the holding of inaccurate beliefs is thought to be undesirable. That is, cognitive immaturity is equated with inefficiency. The goal of education is to replace erroneous beliefs with accurate ones. Yet, Bjorklund and Green (1992) have proposed that cognitive immaturity is adaptive for young children. Their cognitive system is qualitatively different from older children and it actually facilitates the attainment of important cognitive milestones such as language.

Metacognition refers to a person's knowledge of his/her own cognitions and the factors that influence thinking. Young children tend to overestimate their memory abilities and their metamemory is minimally influenced by their previous performance. They know that they have failed to remember, but they assume that they can do it the next time. Unrealistic optimism regarding their abilities and future performance is common at this age. Young children's overestimation of their abilities motivates them to keep trying to achieve tasks they have previously failed. This persistence allows for the successful completion of tasks and the development of a sense of mastery.

Bjorklund and Green also discuss the advantages of egocentrism (Piaget's concept for the inability to take the perspective on another). They speculate that interpreting events from one's own perspective may actually be advantageous. Memory research for both children and adults has found that memory recall is actually enhanced when self-reference is used to encode or retrieve information. Thus, "egocentricism" may enhance young children's retention and comprehension of information.

Language acquisition may actually be easier for young children as evidenced by the ease and proficiency in which young children acquire first and second languages. Johnson and Newport (as cited in Bjorklund & Green, 1992) speculate that slow neurological development affords children the cognitive flexibility to acquire language.

The goal of this lecture is to help students understand that young children's cognitive immaturity may allow them to learn the things they need to learn. Bjorklund and Green argue that the preschool years are not just a waiting period, but a period of adaptive cognitive limitations that facilitate cognitive development.

- Source: Bjorklund, D. F., & Green, B. L. (1992). The adaptive nature of cognitive immaturity. *American Psychologist, 47,* 46-54.

Lecture Suggestion 5: Does Early Intervention Have Long-Term Effects? The purpose of this lecture is to examine a well-conducted experiment to determine if active intervention techniques, beginning in infancy, boost IQ scores, and school performance in children from impoverished backgrounds. Campbell and Ramey (1994) studied 111 families from low SES (mothers had a mean IQ of 85) over a 8-year period. The newborns were randomly assigned to either a preschool experimental group (E) or a preschool control group (C). The treatment intervention for the infants included day care with infant programs designed to boost cognitive, perceptual-motor, language, and social skills. The intervention program for the preschoolers focused on development of language and preparing children for literacy tasks. The children in the preschool control group were provided with iron-fortified formula to eliminate early nutritional differences as a potential confound. They did not receive any special programs.

The researchers implemented a second randomization after the children reached school age. Half of the children from each group were assigned to either a school age intervention or school age control group. The school age treatment involved special attention from a resource teacher. The activities involved were designed to increase specific learning skills (reading and math). Parents were visited twice a week to discuss the learning activities and to invite the parents to school events. The children in the school age control group did not receive any treatment.

Based on the two random assignments, four groups were formed.

- Experimental-Experimental Group (EE): Children received both the preschool and school-age interventions.
- Experimental-Control Group (EC): Children received only the preschool intervention.
- Control-Experimental Group (CE): Children received only the school-age intervention.
- Control-Control Group (CC): Children received neither preschool nor school-age interventions.

Campbell and Ramey found that children in the preschool intervention group maintained significantly higher IQ scores and math and reading performance scores than the control group from age 18 months to 8 years. The researchers were interested to see if the early advantage held by the preschool intervention group was maintained following an additional four years of school. The advantage was maintained: Children in the preschool treatment had significantly higher IQ scores. The children that received the school-age intervention but not the preschool intervention did significantly worse than both groups of children that had the preschool intervention. The researchers found that the intensity and duration of the treatment intervention program significantly impacted how well a child performed across all tests. There was an overall trend when looking at measures of IQ and test performance. There was a hierarchy of benefits across the four groups (EE>EC>CE>CC). Thus, the EE group outperformed all other groups, followed by the EC, CE, and CC groups. These findings suggest that attempts to foster intellectual growth for children in impoverished environments within infancy may lead to longer lasting and more pronounced intellectual gains. Another conclusion from this study is that school age interventions may be too late to do much good.

- Source: Campbell, F., & Ramey, C. (1994). Effects of early intervention on intellectual and academic achievement: A follow-up study of children from low income families. *Child Development, 65*, 684-698.

Classroom Activities

Classroom Activity 1: Sequence and Trends in Verbal and Motor Development Fernald and Fernald (1990) have developed a class activity that is well liked by students and provides a good bridge between the chapters on infancy and the chapters on early childhood. This activity illustrates several principles of development, such as the cephalocaudal and proximodistal principles; prompts discussion of issues, such as the relative roles of maturation and experience in development; and gets students thinking about how to measure relative degrees of development. The students need to identify the order of development for a list of motor and verbal abilities.

- Give students a copy of **Handout 1** and have them complete the exercise in small groups.
- Study the list of verbal and motor accomplishments given below and list the order in which you think each accomplishment occurs:
  - The correct order is as follows:

2 months	Turns head to follow moving object
9 months	Sits alone for 1 minute; says "da-da"
1 year	Walks while holding on to something
1 year 3 months	Walks alone; says several words
1 year 6 months	Climbs stairs; says many words
2 years	Runs; uses simple word combinations
3 years	Puts on shoes
4 years	Laces shoes
5 years	Names penny, nickel, and dime
6 years	Describes the difference between a bird and a dog
7 years	Tells time to quarter hour
8 years	Tells how a baseball and an orange or an airplane and a kite are alike

- Study the order of accomplishments that you have identified. Describe any rules or patterns that you think apply to the order. Justify your conclusions with appropriate examples from the above list.
- Which of the above accomplishments do you think come about chiefly through maturation? Which involve training? Do you see any trends here? Identify them and justify your conclusions with appropriate examples.
- Use in the Classroom: After students have completed their task, you can address the following isses in a class discussion. Discuss their ideas about what the correct order should be. There is usually agreement on the items that develop first, with decreasing agreement on later items. Discuss the reasons for this pattern of agreement and disagreement. How are the cephalocaudal and proximodistal principles illustrated by the order? Which items appear to develop mainly through maturation and which develop through training? Is there an age-related pattern?

Logistics:
- Materials: Handout 1 (Motor and Verbal Abilities Activity).
- Group size: Small group discussion and full class discussion.
- Approximate time: Small groups (15 minutes) and full class discussion (20 minutes).
- Source: Fernald, P. S., & Fernald, L. D. (1990). Early motor and verbal development. In V.P. Makosky, C. C. Sileo, L. G. Whittemore, C. P. Landry, and M. L. Skutley (Eds.). *Activities handbook for the teaching of psychology*. Washington DC: American Psychological Association.

Classroom Activity 2: Design a Preschool Program The objective of this activity is for students to use information regarding gross and fine motor skill development to plan preschool program activities that would facilitate both types of motor skill development. In small groups, have students determine what activities would be appropriate for 3-year-olds. For 5-year-olds.
- For gross motor skills, the program might incorporate a game such as follow the leader, in which the leader ran, skipped, hopped, walked backwards, skipped rope, and performed similar activities for the legs. For the arms, the program could incorporate throwing a ball, bowling (with a light ball), and skipping rope.
- Fine motor activity could be promoted by work such as drawing with crayons. You could also incorporate work with puzzles, cutting and pasting, shaping clay, and playing with small blocks.

Logistics:
- Group size: Small group discussion.
- Approximate time: Small groups (15 minutes).
- Source: King, M. B., & Clark, D. E. (1989). *Instructors manual to Santrock and Yussen's child development: An introduction*, 4th ed. Dubuque, IA: Wm. C. Brown Communications, Inc.

Classroom Activity 3: What Should Parents Tell Their Seriously Ill Child? Children with serious illnesses are usually better off when families deal with their illness directly and openly. One overwhelming conclusion of a study of 117 childhood cancer survivors and their families was that they believed it was best to tell the child, in honest comprehensible terms, about the cancer early on and to provide the child with a sense of mastery over the disease. Ask students to consider the following questions.
- Do you agree with the results of this study? Are there situations in which you would not tell a child that he or she has a serious illness? How would you deal with the possibility of death? How would a child's cognitive development influence his/her understanding of the illness.

Logistics:
- Group size: Full class discussion.
- Approximate time: Full class discussion (15 minutes).
- Source: Hurley, D. (August 1987). A sound mind in an unsound body. *Psychology Today*, 34-43.

Classroom Activity 4: Illustration of Piagetian Concepts in Preschoolers This activity functions to expand students' understanding of preschoolers' cognitive abilities. Assign students the task of asking two preschoolers the following questions. They should bring back responses that include typical limitations of preoperational thinking such as egocentrism, animism, irreversibility, and artificialism.

- How did you learn to talk?
- Where does the sun go at night?
- Why is the sky blue?
- Why do dogs bark?
- Why does it rain?
- Where do babies come from?
- Who are you going to be when you grow up?
- Why do you eat breakfast in the morning instead of at night?
- Why do you have toes?
- Why are you ticklish?
- How do birds fly?
- What is your favorite toy?

Logistics:
- Group size: Individual homework and full class discussion.
- Approximate time: Individual homework (30 minutes) and full class discussion (15 minutes).
- Source: Simons, J. A., Irwin, D. B., & Drinnin, B. A. (1987). *Instructor's manual to accompany psychology, the search for understanding.* St. Paul, MN: West Publishing.

Classroom Activity 5: Children's Readiness to Read This activity focuses on children's readiness to read. Have students discuss what skills children should have before they learn to read. They should discuss which activities help young children learn these skills. Encourage them to give their opinion on the advantages and disadvantages of beginning to learn to read before attending school.
- Use the following information to aid the discussion.
    - First, young children need to know the alphabet. Children who do not know how to identify both uppercase and lowercase letters by the middle of kindergarten are likely to have trouble with first-grade reading.
    - Second, children need the ability to break up words into their component sounds. A child who cannot do this by first grade will get behind in reading skills.
    - Third, attitude is important—a love and interest in reading. Most good readers come from homes that have books and other reading material, have been read to on many occasions, and have parents who enjoy and model reading. These children also have above-average vocabularies and do well on IQ tests. Exposure to reading and the love of reading is sufficient, and experts do not recommend parental pressure or early reading training.

Logistics:
- Group size: Full class discussion.
- Approximate time: Full class discussion (15 minutes).
- Source: Bradley, L. (1988). Rhyme recognition and reading and spelling in young children. In R. Masland & M. Masland (Eds.). *Pre-school prevention of reading failures.* Parkton, MD: York Press. Ellis, N., & Large, B. (1988). The early stages of reading: A longitudinal study. *Applied Cognitive Psychology, 2,* 47-76. Jackson, N. E. (1988). Precocious reading ability: What does it mean? *Gifted Child Quarterly, 32,* 200-204. Scarborough, H. S. (1989). Prediction of reading disability from familial and individual differences. *Journal of Educational Psychology, 81,* 101-108. Walsh, D. J., Price, G. G., & Gillingham, M. G. (1988). The critical but transitory importance of letter-naming. *Reading Research Quarterly, 23,* 108-122.

Classroom Activity 6: Critical Thinking Multiple-Choice Questions and Suggested Answers Discuss the answers to the critical thinking multiple-choice questions on **Handout 2**. The answers are provided on **Handout 3**. The point of the first two questions is to get students to integrate material in chapter 8 in order to see how language and cognitive development are related to each other and how ideas about cognitive development may or may not influence caregiving and teaching practices with young children. Although questions for previous chapters have prompted students to do these types of tasks, you may still want to discuss with them what to look for in the chapter that will help them deal with the issues. For example, before assigning question 1, get them to talk about ways to assess egocentrism other than the three mountains task, and have them discuss varieties of meaning for the phrase "take another's point of view." You also may need to work with the class to distinguish different aspects of attention, such as processing multiple channels of information, maintaining attention, and avoiding distractions. Finally, discuss alternative ways to assess the other cognitive characteristics or feats mentioned in the question.

Question 2 requires students to compare and integrate information. In some respects, this is mainly a comprehension exercise and may not need as much discussion as the first question. Some students will be sensitive to the fact that there are both similarities and differences between Piaget's and Vygotsky's theories. You may want to discuss them as a means of clarifying and strengthening their understanding of both theories. Students have little difficulty with alternatives "b," "c," and "d," but there are interesting ambiguities for them to grapple with in "e." For example, the text documents quantitative changes in memory and attention, but talks about children acquiring new strategies for enhancing memory and improving attention. Those could be conceived as qualitative changes, a point that should give both you and the class pause as you seek the best answer!

Question 3 may be difficult in an unusual way, given that you are asked to distinguish inferences from observations. The inference represents implications or extensions of material presented as observations. What makes them inferences is that they are not directly stated. The observations are difficult to identify because they are not clearly identified by their source; what makes them observations is that Santrock uses them as facts in his presentation. The assumption, "a," is an assumption because it is an unexamined proposition that appears to underlie the difference between children's energy needs.

Logistics:
- Materials: Handout 2 (the critical thinking multiple-choice questions) and Handout 3 (answers)
- Group size: Small groups to discuss the questions, then a full class discussion.
- Approximate time: Small groups (15 to 20 minutes), then 15 minutes for full class discussion.

Classroom Activity 7: Critical Thinking Essay Questions and Suggestions for Helping Students Answer the Essays Discuss the students' answers to the critical thinking essay questions that are presented as **Handout 4**. Several objectives can be met with these questions. First, they facilitate students' understanding of concepts in chapter 8. Second, this type of essay question affords students an opportunity to apply the concepts to their own lives, which will facilitate their retention of the material. Third, the essay format also will give students practice expressing themselves in written form. Ideas to help students answer the critical thinking essay questions are provided as **Handout 5**.

Logistics:
- Materials: Handout 4 (essay questions) and Handout 5 (helpful suggestions for the answers).
- Group size: Individual, then full class.
- Approximate time: Individual (60 minutes), then 30 minutes for full class discussion.

Personal Applications

Personal Application 1: Tag, You're It! The purpose of this exercise is to have students recall the physical elements of their childhood. Young children are extremely active, both with regard to gross motor activities (running, jumping, climbing) and fine motor activities (coloring, cutting, manipulating blocks). These activities are both the result of, and the driving force behind, further physical development and agility—and children love them!

- Instructions for Students: Recall your favorite early childhood activities. Did you prefer gross motor oriented activities, or fine motor oriented activities? How did you spend most of your time? Do you remember any activity that you wanted to be able to participate in, but you weren't physically coordinated enough? Can you recall a time of triumph, when you accomplished a particular feat for the first time?

- Use in the Classroom: Show a video or bring in some toddlers and/or preschool age children and supply them with a variety of toys and manipulatives and possible climbing opportunities (such as a chair or step stool). Have students observe what activities children choose to engage in. Attempt to have children engage in motor activities that are too advanced and watch what happens. Discuss the in-class goings on with regard to motor development.

Personal Application 2: For Lefties Only The purpose of this exercise is to enable students who are left handed explore their experiences in a world dominated by right handedness. Left handedness has been viewed as problematic in the past; so much so that children were often forced to use their right hands, despite their difficulty in doing so. Left-handed individuals also have to function in a world that is oriented to those who are right-dominant. Given that there appears to be a dominant brain hemisphere link to handedness, that's a lot to ask!

- Instructions for Students: For those of you who are lefties, write about your experiences as such. Was your handedness met with any resistance when you were a child—by either your parents or your teachers? Did you struggle to cut with scissors for right-handed children? How did you feel (and *still* feel) writing on desks for right-handed individuals? Have you benefited in any way from your different handedness—in sports, or in a particular artistic creativity?

- Use in the Classroom: Have your left-handed students share their personal experiences with their minority handedness status with the rest of the class. Discuss the possible implications for development, and have students create ideas for studying the relationship between handedness and brain hemisphere dominance.

Personal Application 3: Have It Your Way The purpose of this exercise is for students to recognize and respond to the potential health hazards of a poor diet for young children. Fast food has become deeply ingrained in our society. Most children not only get their first taste of fast food during the toddler/preschool years, buy many eat it on a regular basis. Well, they gotta have the toy...

- Instructions for Students: Write a letter to the president of a major fast food chain. Explain, from a developmental perspective, the hazards of a poor, high-fat diet for children's development. Discuss the inappropriateness of luring children (or their parents rather) to purchase such meals with the special kid's meal and accompanying toy. Elaborate by presenting the argument that spending advertising dollars to highlight such meals and toys, along with offering popular, trendy toys contributes to the poor nutrition habits of children too young to understand the hazards.

- Use in the Classroom: Have groups of students create public service announcements geared to parents for the purpose of alerting them to the hazards of a poor, high-fat diet—particularly in young children. Include society's problematic propensity for turning to fast food for ease and convenience, and the inclusion of a toy with kids' meals.

Personal Application 4: I'm Sure You'll Agree The purpose of this exercise is for students to more fully explore the concept of *egocentrism* by recalling examples from adulthood. A predominant feature of preoperational thought is that children believe everyone thinks and experiences the world exactly like they do. This is due to the fact that they are mentally not able to consider someone else's perspective. While children between the ages of approximately 2 and 4 have actual cognitive limitations to explain this, adults often exhibit the same egocentric thinking, without the excuse!

- Instructions for Students: Familiarize yourself with Piaget's concept of egocentrism—the notion that an individual believes everyone else must think, see, hear, feel, and experience the world just as he does. Now recall experiences you have had with adults who believe the same thing. It may be someone else, or it may even be you! Many of our assumptions about those we work and live with result from egocentric tendencies. If we have particular opinions, values, or expectations, we often function as though others share those same notions. We may perceive particular situations in a way that we then expect others to do as well. It's not until we are met with disappointment or shock that we come to realize (if we even do) that just because *we* looked at something from a particular point of view, that (*oh my gosh!*) not everyone did. Start paying attention to how you initially assume other people experience the world—you may be surprised.
- Use in the Classroom: Present some examples of adult egocentricism and have students share their own. Point out that many disagreements, arguments, and hurt feelings are often the result of people simply assuming that others share their particular perspective on things. Discuss how, as adults, we are cognitively able to avoid this—with increased awareness and sensitivity to others—but that children cognitively are not capable of doing so. Also, clarify the difference between being ego*centric* and ego*tistic*.

Personal Application 5: Know Your Own Mind The purpose of this exercise is to demonstrate to students the concept of theory of mind. Developmental psychologists have studied and continue to be interested in children's recognition and understanding of the presence and functioning of their own mind. Doing so provides an important developmental milestone, and is a phenomenon that continues to evolve over time, contributing significantly to cognitive functioning.

- Instructions for Students: Assess your own cognitive functioning. Think about the classes you are taking this semester. How are you doing in each of them? Are you aware of your performance so far? Are you aware of why you have performed at the level you have? Can you explain the difference in your functioning and capabilities in your different classes? What are your strong mental areas? In which subjects are you weak? What has contributed to these strengths and weaknesses? What might you do to improve in your weaker areas? What field might you pursue to capitalize on your mental strengths?
- Use in the Classroom: Discuss student's awareness of their particular learning style. Do they know how they learn best? Can they delineate their cognitive strategies for the various aspects of information processing (identifying important information, remembering information, communicating information). Briefly introduce the various learning styles (visual, auditory, tactile, kinesthetic) and what learning environments benefit each kind the most. Provide tips on how students might work to improve their weaker areas of cognitive functioning.

Research Project Ideas

Research Project 1: Memory Span The function of this project is to provide a demonstration of memory span. The students can pair up with a classmate for this project. They will need to test four individuals: a 3-year-old, a 6-year-old, a 9-year-old, and a classmate. The task is a digit span task. They should present a list of digits to each subject at the rate of one per second, and have each subject repeat as many digits as he or she remembers. One student will present the digits and the other will record the subject's response. The worksheets for data collection and questions for them to answer are on **Handout 5**. In order to test the four children, the project will have to be approved by the human subjects review board at your school and they will need to get a signed informed consent form from the children's parents. See the section on Ethics, Human Subjects, and Informed Consent at the front of this Instructor's Manual.

- How many digits did the 3-year-old remember? Was it the same number regardless of the number of digits presented? How many did the 6-year-old, the 9-year-old, and the classmate remember? Was the number different depending on the number presented? In what way was the number different?
- Did you find age differences for memory span? What is the nature of the differences observed? Could anything besides memory span account for the differences? (Consider possible sex differences, if applicable, or differences in the child's understanding of his or her role in the task.)
- From your data, what statement could you make about the development of memory span from 3 years to adulthood? What qualifications, if any, would you need to make about your statement, based on the limitations of your data?

- Use in the Classroom: Have students present their data from the research project in class. They should discuss the developmental trend that appears in the class data. How does memory span for digits change with age? Are there any variables besides age that could account for the data? You would expect digit span to be about 2, 4 to 5, 6 to 7, and about 7 with the increasing age groups.

Research Project 2: Language Errors This class project exposes students to the kinds of errors that children make when they are acquiring language. Have each student pair up with another student in the class. One student will act as the experimenter, while the other will act as the observer. They should test two different children, one 3 to 4 years of age, the other 7 to 8 years of age. In order to test the children, the project will have to be approved by the human subjects review board at your school and they will need to get a signed informed consent form from the children's parents. See the section on Ethics, Human Subjects, and Informed Consent at the front of this Instructor's Manual.

The children will receive from the students three different tasks evaluating their understanding and use of the passive construction. Sudents should present an act-out task, an imitation task, and a production task. The task and sentence descriptions follow. **Handout 6** can be used as a data sheet to record observations. The students should answer the provided questions as well.

- **Act-out Task:** Have several objects available—a toy car and truck, a toy doll, a toy horse, cow, dog, and cat. Read the sentences below one at a time, and have the child act out the sentences with the toys.
- **Imitation Task:** Present each of the sentences below to each child, and have the child repeat the sentences back to you.
- **Production Task:** Perform the actions in each of the sentences below with the toys for the child. Ask the child to tell you what happened, starting with the first noun in the sentence. For instance, for item "e" roll the car along so that it hits the truck, and then ask the child to tell you what happened beginning with the truck.

a) The car hit the truck.
b) The dog was kicked by the cat.
c) The boy was bitten by the dog.
d) The boy hit the cat.
e) The truck was hit by the car.
f) The cow stepped on the horse.
g) The cat kicked the dog.
h) The cat was hit by the boy.
i) The dog bit the boy.
j) The horse was stepped on by the cow.

Questions:
- What did the 3- to 4-year-old child do in response to the act-out task? The imitation task? The production task? Was performance on one task better than on the others? If so, which? What sorts of errors appeared in the act-out task? What about the imitation task? The production task? Were the errors similar in the various tasks?
- What did the 7- to 8-year-old child do in response to the act-out task? The imitation task? The production task? Was performance on one task better than on the others? If so, which? What sorts of errors appeared in the act-out task? What about the imitation task? The production task? Were the errors similar in the various tasks?
- Compare the two children. What differences, if any, did you see on their performances on these three tasks? How would you account for the differences? What is the nature of language learning that seems to be occurring during this time?
- What criticisms could be leveled at the procedures you used in this demonstration? For example, do you think each task should have had different questions?

- Use in the Classroom: Have students present the data from the research project in class. What kinds of errors did the younger children make on the tasks? Were there individual differences within age groups present (that is, did some of the younger children perform all tasks well, while other children made errors with all tasks?)? How did the older children perform on these tasks? Were some tasks easier? What do these findings tell us about the development course for understanding active and passive sentences? What strategies did children use when they made errors?

Film and Video List

The following films and videos supplement the content of chapter 8. Contact information for film distributors can be found at the front of this Instructor's Manual under Film and Video Sources.

Cognitive Development: Representation in Three to Five-Year-Old Children (Films for the Humanities and Sciences, 30 minutes). Academic researchers from Cambridge University discuss the child's experiential-based understanding of causal relationships.

Concepts, Memories, and Reasons (Insight Media, 30 minutes). Cognitive changes between ages 5 and 7, including development of memory strategies, logical reasoning, and problem solving are discussed. The video also considers how these changes influence relationships to family and society.

Doing What Comes Naturally: Childhood Language Acquisition (Films for the Humanities and Sciences, 47 minutes). Experts deflate misconceptions about childhood language acquisition.

Early Child Care and Education (Magna Systems, 36 minutes). Choices in child care and early education are discussed, as are quality and other related issues. Factors in child abuse are explored.

How We Study Children (Insight Media, 24 minutes). This video illustrates methods for studying children, showing observational and experimental techniques. The pros and cons for these techniques are explored.

Language Development (Films for the Humanities and Sciences, 40 minutes). This program emphasizes the development of language in babies and young children from the first cry to the language development of a seven-year-old. In addition, the program discusses the arguments in the nature-nurture debate, as well as other theories.

Learning in Context: Probing the Theories of Piaget and Vygotsky (Films for the Humanities and Sciences, 31 minutes). This program examines three sets of experiments using gender-biased task instructions, cooperation between asymmetrical pairs of peers, and tasks involving students trained by adults and peers. The results emphasize the importance of self-perception on competence and the influence of different teaching approaches on learning.

Memory: The Past Imperfect (Insight Media, 24 minutes). Examining both short- and long-term memory, this video explores the acquisition, retention, and retrieval stages of memory. Other topics include infants' memory abilities, eyewitness testimony, and hypnosis.

Men in Early Childhood Education (Davidson Films, 24 minutes). While this film is dated, it is still valuable because it examines the role men can play as preschool educators.

Nutrition (Magna Systems, 27 minutes). Issues related to nutrition are discussed, including the food pyramid, nutrients, and optimal nutrition; as well as developmental issues during pregnancy, infancy, childhood, and adolescence.

Physical Development: The First Five Years (Films for the Humanities and Sciences, 19 minutes). This program shows children at each stage of physical development between birth and age five. Commentary is provided by a pediatrician and child development specialist.

The Preschooler's Mind (Insight Media, 30 minutes). This video recreates classic research to illustrate Piaget's theory and criticisms of it, especially from cross-cultural study and considerations of decalage. Also, it discusses Bruner's ideas about how to enhance learning and cognitive development.

Preschoolers: Physical and Cognitive Development (Magna Systems, 28 minutes). This program focuses on motor skills, perceptual development, ways of learning, and characteristics of preschool thinking and language.

Toddlerhood: Physical and Cognitive Development (Magna Systems, 26 minutes). Physical growth and motor development in toddlerhood are examined. In addition, cognitive and language development are outlined.

Unlocking Language (Films for the Humanities and Sciences, 29 minutes). Experts discuss the development and transmission of language. Topics covered include language used to express abstractions, the evolution of language, language as an innately guided behavior in unborn babies, infants and toddlers, the parts of the brain involved in language, language disorders, and isolation of the Speech 1 gene.

Web Site Suggestions

The URLs for general sites, common to all chapters, can be found at the front of this Instructor's Manual under Useful Web Sites. At the time of publication, all sites were current and active, however, please be advised that you may occasionally encounter a dead link.

Assessment of Nutritional Status
http://www.sameint.it/dietosys/dieto/englbro/bro01.htm

Idea Box: Early Childhood Education and Activity Resources
http://www.worldvillage.com/ideabox/

Maria Montessori: An Historical Perspective
http://www.montessori.org/mariawho.htm

The Montessori Approach: Interactive Materials
http://www.our-montessori.com/about_montessori.html

Relation of Mild-to-Moderate Malnutrition to Human Development
http://www.unu.edu/unupress/food2/uid04e/uid04e0b.htm

The State of Illness and Health in Your State
http://www.childrensdefense.org/states/data.html

The State of the World's Children 1998: Nutrition
http://www.unicef.org/sowc98/mainmenu.htm

Motor and Verbal Abilities Activity

1. Study the list of verbal and motor accomplishments given below and list the order in which you think each accomplishment occurs:

Order of Development	Motor and Verbal Ability
_____	Walks alone; says several words
_____	Describes the difference between a bird and a dog
_____	Turns head to follow moving object
_____	Names penny, nickel, and dime
_____	Climbs stairs; says many words
_____	Laces shoes
_____	Sits alone for 1 minute; says "da-da"
_____	Tells how a baseball and an orange or an airplane and a kite are alike
_____	Puts on shoes
_____	Tells time to quarter hour
_____	Runs; uses simple word combinations
_____	Walks while holding on to something

2. Study the order of accomplishments that you have identified. Describe any rules or patterns that you think apply to the order. Justify your conclusions with appropriate examples from the above list.

3. Which of the above accomplishments do you think come about chiefly through maturation? Which involve training? Do you see any trends here? Identify the trends and justify your conclusions with appropriate examples.

Critical Thinking Multiple-Choice Questions

1. This chapter makes many claims about diverse aspects of the cognitive functioning of preschool children. Although the picture of their cognitive skills is fairly consistently presented, some of the studies contradict one another. Which of the following statements is contradicted by information elsewhere in the chapter? Circle the letter of the best answer and explain why it is the best answer and why each other answer is not as good. Hint: Cite the specific finding (or findings) that confirms or contradicts the claim in question.

    a. As indicated by their performance on the three mountains task, young children cannot take the perspective of others.
    b. Young children find it difficult to pay attention to more than one feature, characteristic, or dimension of a task at the same time.
    c. An aspect of preoperational thought is that nonliving things have the characteristics of living things.
    d. Memory span increases rapidly between the ages of 2 and 7 years old.
    e. Around 3 years of age, children are able to talk about things that are not physically present.

2. Santrock devotes much effort in this chapter to describing the nature of cognition in early childhood and to identifying the experiences presumed to promote cognition; however, he seldom directly shows the relationship between ideas and observations. To the contrary, the job of synthesizing this information is left to the reader. According to your synthesis of information in the chapter, which of the following statements makes the most sense? Circle the letter of the best answer and explain why it is the best answer and why each other answer is not as good.

    a. Piaget's and Vygotsky's theories contradict one another.
    b. The Montessori approach is the most effective early education program.
    c. The development of language is very different from and unrelated to the development of thought.
    d. The concept of a child-centered kindergarten is clearly based on Piaget's theory of cognitive development.
    e. Both Piagetian tests and information-processing tasks reveal that the preschooler's mind is qualitative.

3. Tremendous research has examined physical development in early childhood, including research on height differences, second-hand smoke, and brain development. Which of the following statements best represents an assumption by researchers, rather than an inference or an observation? Circle the letter of the best answer and explain why it is the best answer and why each other answer is not as good.

    a. Differences in physical activity, basal metabolism, and efficiency with which children use energy help explain the varying energy needs of individual children of the same age, sex and size.
    b. The two most important contributors to height differences around the world are ethnic origins and nutrition.
    c. Exposure to tobacco smoke increases children's risk for developing a number of medical problems.
    d. Children's brains experience rapid, distinct spurts of growth.
    e. Myelination is important in the maturation of a number of children's abilities.

Suggested Answers for Critical Thinking Multiple-Choice Questions

1. This chapter makes many claims about diverse aspects of the cognitive functioning of preschool children. Although the picture of their cognitive skills is fairly consistently presented, some of the studies contradict one another. Which of the following statements is contradicted by information elsewhere in the chapter? Circle the letter of the best answer and explain why it is the best answer and why each other answer is not as good. Hint: Cite the specific finding (or findings) that confirms or contradicts the claim in question.

a. The statement that <u>as indicated by their performance on the three mountains task, young children cannot take the perspective of others</u> is contradicted by information in the text. Santrock notes that development of perspective taking is not uniform. A specific contradiction is that 2-year-olds can hide objects so that another person cannot see them, which implies that 2-year-olds have some idea of another person's perspective. Other information about the child's theory of mind suggests a more abstract understanding of perspective taking as well.

b. The finding that <u>young children find it difficult to pay attention to more than one feature, characteristic, or dimension of a task at the same time</u> is not contradicted. When Piaget observed this, he called it centration. It is consistent with Gelman's work, which showed that children can be trained to pay attention to relevant task dimensions, but do not do so on their own. It is also consistent with the difficulty young children have paying attention to television.

c. The statement that <u>an aspect of preoperational thought is that nonliving things have the characteristics of living things</u> is not contradicted, although Santrock mentions that there are alternative interpretations of the phenomenon, such as preschoolers may not be as concerned with reality as older children or they may be more fanciful and inventive. Consistent with the statement are observations of children's drawings (suns with faces). Also consistent is the implication that children like books about such characters as Winnie the Pooh because they portray toy animals that are alive.

d. Nothing contradicts the statement that <u>memory span increases rapidly between the ages of 2 and 7 years old</u>. It is consistent with the estimate that the average child learns between 5 and 8 new words a day during this period, and possibly with the ability to attend to multiple task features that emerges at about the age of 7.

e. Nothing contradicts the statement that <u>around 3 years of age, children are able to talk about things that are not physically present</u>. It is consistent with the claim that the symbolic function develops between 2 and 4 years of age. The symbolic function involves mental representation of objects not physically present, which likely underlies the capacity, in language, to talk about things that are not physically present.

2. Santrock devotes much effort in this chapter to describing the nature of cognition in early childhood and to identifying the experiences presumed to promote cognition; however, he seldom directly shows the relationship between ideas and observations. To the contrary, the job of synthesizing this information is left to the reader. According to your synthesis of information in the chapter, which of the following statements makes the most sense? Circle the letter of the best answer and explain why it is the best answer and why each other answer is not as good.

a. The statement that <u>Piaget's and Vygotsky's theories contradict one another</u> makes the most sense. Piaget and Vygotsky differ in their interpretation of the nature and meaning of egocentric speech, as well as on the primary mechanisms of cognitive development. Vygotsky sees egocentric speech as an internalized conversation that promotes cognitive development. Piaget sees egocentric speech as a sign of immature cognitive development, which interferes with more advanced and appropriate communication.

b. The sentence stating that the <u>Montessori approach is the most effective early education program</u> does not follow from information in the text. In fact, Santrock does not identify a single "best" type of early childhood education program. There are many different types, each with different strengths and weaknesses. The Montessori approach is seen as strong in fostering academic outcomes, but weak in fostering effective social outcomes.

c. The statement that <u>the development of language is very different from and unrelated to the development of thought</u> does not follow from information in the text. There are many similarities and parallels in the development of each. For example, displacement in language is similar to, and probably requires, symbolic function. Language itself appears to involve perceptual and cognitive processes. In both theories, language and thought are viewed as related, but in different ways.

d. <u>The concept of a child-centered kindergarten is clearly based on Piaget's theory of cognitive development</u> is not supported in the textbook. Piaget's theory focuses mainly on cognitive development and tries to characterize all children. In contrast, child-centered kindergartens stress individual differences and the importance of dealing with the "whole" child, which includes physical, social, emotional, and personality development.

e. The statement that <u>both Piagetian tests and information-processing tasks reveal that the preschooler's mind is qualitative</u> does not follow from information in the text. Piaget's tasks reveal qualitative changes in the sense that concrete operational children think about problems differently from preoperational children. However, information-processing tasks tend to reveal quantitative changes; for example, older children remember more from short-term memory, process information faster, and attend longer.

3. Tremendous research has examined physical development in early childhood, including research on height differences, second-hand smoke, and brain development. Which of the following statements best represents an assumption by researchers, rather than an inference or an observation? Circle the letter of the best answer and explain why it is the best answer and why each other answer is not as good.

a. The statement that <u>differences in physical activity, basal metabolism, and efficiency with which children use energy help explain the varying energy needs of individual children of the same age, sex, and size</u> is an assumption, thus it is the best answer. These reasons have been proposed to help explain this phenomenon, yet they have not been examined.

b. The statement that <u>the two most important contributors to height differences around the world are ethnic origins and nutrition</u> is an observation. Santrock states, for example, that African American children are taller than White children are in the United States.

c. <u>Exposure to tobacco smoke increases children's risk for developing a number of medical problems</u> is an observation. Research has found that exposure to tobacco smoke increases children's risk for pneumonia, bronchitis, middle ear infections, burns, and asthma.

d. The statement that <u>children's brains experience rapid, distinct spurts of growth</u> is an observation. Using repeated brain scans of the same children over a four year period, researchers found that the amount of brain material in some areas can nearly double within as little as a year, followed by drastic loss of tissue as unneeded cells are purged and the brain continues to reorganize itself.

e. The statement that <u>myelination is important in the maturation of a number of children's abilities</u> is an inference. Santrock implies that some developmentalists have reached this conclusion based on research. Myelination in the areas of the brain related to hand-eye coordination is not complete until about 4 years of age which corresponds to the development of children's motor abilities.

Critical Thinking Essay Questions

Your answers to this kind of question demonstrate an ability to comprehend and apply ideas discussed in this chapter.

1. Explain why there is so much variation in the height of children.

2. What is myelination? What is its role in development?

3. Describe the major milestones in motor development in early childhood, and explain how this information could be used by parents and teachers.

4. Explain what factors contribute to toddlers' risk of illness and death.

5. What does Piaget mean by *operations*? Also explain how preoperational thought differs from sensorimotor thought.

6. Define and give examples of the symbolic function substage and the intuitive thought substage.

7. Explain at least two examples of a Piagetian conservation task. Compare and contrast Piaget's and Gelman's analyses of children's success or failure on a conservation task.

8. What is a zone of proximal development (ZPD)? Also explain the respective activities of child and teacher as a child moves through a ZPD.

9. Compare and contrast Piaget's and Vygotsky's views about what causes the development of thought and language.

10. Describe findings about the development of attention in early childhood. Discuss whether this information confirms or contradicts aspects of Piaget's description of   cognitive   development during this time of life.

11. Describe short-term memory, and indicate how it changes in young children.

12. Outline the development of children's theory of mind. How does this information relate to Piaget's claims about children's cognitive functioning during early childhood.

13. Describe the major milestones of language development in early childhood.

14. Characterize the philosophy and activities of a child-centered kindergarten; explain whether they are developmentally appropriate.

15. Imagine that you are a parent with a prospective preschooler. Explain what you would do before attending a session with a preschool director and what kinds of questions you would ask during the meeting.

Ideas to Help You Answer Critical Thinking Essay Questions

1. To effectively illustrate the phenomenon you will be explaining, collect some easy data. Visit a pre-school classroom, or ask parents at a playground if you can measure their child's height. Graph varying heights of children of the same age, and preface your discussion with what you found.

2. Describe neural functioning without myelin before you explanation of what myelin is and it's role.

3. Approach this assignment as if you were addressing an audience of parents and teachers. Describe the major milestones and incorporate the application(s) of this information relevant to each group.

4. Imagine you are presenting this information to a group of parents-to-be, individuals highly interested in what you have to say.

5. After you explain what Piaget means by *operations*, present an example of a mental operation. This will provide a good basis for your comparison of preoperational and sensorimotor thought.

6. Begin your answer by introducing Piaget's conceptualization of the preoperational stage of cognitive development, followed by your discussion of the two substages.

7. Explain what is meant by the concept of conservation, then elaborate through your presentation of two examples of conservation tasks and behaviors that would indicate passing and failing. This will create a meaningful basis for a comparison between Piaget and Gelman.

8. Introduce Vygotsky and his theory, including the notion of zones of proximal development. Proceed to get more specific.

9. Outline each theorist's view of the development of thought and language. From these, identify the similarities and differences between them.

10. Begin by discussing what *attention* refers to with regard to cognitive functioning in children. Then, present the findings and their implications for Piaget's notions of cognitive development.

11. Describe developmentalists' overall view of memory in order to put your discussion of short-term memory development in context.

12. Explain what *theories of mind* refer to and what the significance of studying this aspect of development is. Having done this, outline it's development and relevance to Piagetian theory.

13. Imagine you are presenting a talk on language development to new parents. It is, after all, one of the most highly anticipated aspects of child development, and they'll want to know everything that's going to happen and when.

14. Imagine you are a developmental psychologist asked to make this presentation to the local school board for their consideration in planning educational opportunities and curriculum for young children.

15. When in your role as a parent, imagine the implications of putting your child in preschool—she will be away from you for the first time, this will be her first experience with "formal" learning and school, this will be the first structure placed on her valuable childhood play time. Now address the issues.

Memory Span

The function of this project is to provide a demonstration of memory span. Pair up with a classmate for this project. You will need to test four individuals: a 3-year-old, a 6-year-old, a 9-year-old, and a classmate. The task is a digit span task. Present a list of digits to each subject at the rate of one per second, and have each subject repeat as many digits as he or she remembers. One of you will present the digits and the other will record the subject's response. Use the following worksheet for data collection and answer the questions after you have completed the task. In order to test the children, the project will have to be approved by the human subjects review board at your school and you will need to get a signed informed consent form from the children's parents.

Task	Child 1	Child 2	Child 3	Adult
	Age ____	Age ____	Age ____	Age ____
	Sex ___	Sex ___	Sex ___	Sex ___
Digits	Response:	Response:	Response:	Response:
2				
74				
196				
2389				
64157				
326890				
7509621				
92503184				
849276304				

Number of correct digits out of:
one
two
three
four
five
six
seven
eight
nine

Questions:
- How many digits did the 3-year-old remember?
- Was it the same number regardless of the number of digits presented?
- How many did the 6-year-old, the 9-year-old, and the classmate remember?
- Was the number different depending on the number presented?
- In what way was the number different?
- Did you find age differences for memory span?
- What is the nature of the differences observed?
- Could anything besides memory span account for the differences?
- From your data, what statement could you make about the development of memory span from 3 years to adulthood?
- What qualifications, if any, would you need to make about your statement, based on the limitations of your data?

Handout 6 (RP 2)

Language Errors

This class project exposes you to the kinds of errors that children make when they are acquiring language. Pair up with another student in the class. One of you will act as the experimenter, while the other will act as the observer. Test two different children, one 3 to 4 years of age, the other 7 to 8 years of age. In order to test the two children, the project will have to be approved by the human subjects review board at your school and you will need to get a signed informed consent form from the children's parents.

The children will receive from you three different tasks evaluating their understanding and use of the passive construction. Present an act-out task, an imitation task, and a production task. The task and sentence descriptions follow. Use the provided data sheet to record your observations. After you have collected your data, answer the questions provided at the bottom of the page.

Act-out task: Have several objects available—a toy car and truck, a toy doll, a toy horse, cow, dog, and cat. Read the sentences below one at a time, and have the child act out the sentences with the toys.

Imitation task: Present each of the sentences below to each child, and have the child repeat the sentences back to you.

Production Task: Perform the actions in each of the sentences below with the toys. Ask the child to tell you what happened, starting with the first noun in the sentence. For instance, for item "e" roll the car along so that it hits the truck, and then ask the child to tell you what happened beginning with the truck.

a) The car hit the truck.
b) The dog was kicked by the cat.
c) The boy was bitten by the dog.
d) The boy hit the cat.
e) The truck was hit by the car.
f) The cow stepped on the horse.
g) The cat kicked the dog.
h) The cat was hit by the boy.
i) The dog bit the boy.
j) The horse was stepped on by the cow.

Questions:
- What did the 3- to 4-year-old child do in response to the act-out task? The imitation task? The production task? Was performance on one task better than on the others? If so, which? What sorts of errors appeared in the act-out task? What about the imitation task? The production task? Were the errors similar in the various tasks?

- What did the 7- to 8-year-old child do in response to the act-out task? The imitation task? The production task? Was performance on one task better than on the others? If so, which? What sorts of errors appeared in the act-out task? What about the imitation task? The production task? Were the errors similar in the various tasks?

- Compare the two children. What differences, if any, did you see on their performances on these three tasks? How would you account for the differences? What is the nature of language learning that seems to be occurring during this time?

- What criticisms could be leveled at the procedures you used in this demonstration? For example, do you think each task should have had different questions?

Handout 6 (RP 2) continued

Task	Child 1	Child 2
	Sex ____ Age ____	Sex ____ Age ____

Act-out task

Sentence a
Sentence b
Sentence c
Sentence d
Sentence e
Sentence f
Sentence g
Sentence h
Sentence i
Sentence j

Imitation task

Sentence a
Sentence b
Sentence c
Sentence d
Sentence e
Sentence f
Sentence g
Sentence h
Sentence i
Sentence j

Production task

Sentence a
Sentence b
Sentence c
Sentence d
Sentence e
Sentence f
Sentence g
Sentence h
Sentence i
Sentence j

Chapter 9: Socioemotional Development in Early Childhood

Total Teaching Package Outline

Lecture Outline	Resource References
Socioemotional Development in Early Childhood	PowerPoint Presentation: See www.mhhe.com Cognitive Maps: See Appendix A

Emotional and Personality Development
• The Self
    -Initiative vs. Guilt
 	
    -Self-Understanding
	LO1

• Emotional Development	LO2 F/V: Emotional Development of Children F/V: Preschoolers: Social and Emotional Dev. F/V: Toddlerhood: Social and Emotional Dev.
• Moral Development	LO3 OHT90: Damon's Description OHT102: Components of Moral Development PA1: Just a Little White Lie RP1: Altruism-Empathy Observations

-What Is Moral Development?
 	
    -Piaget's View of How Children's Moral
       Reasoning Develops
    -Moral Behavior
    -Moral Feelings
	F/V: Moral Development I
	F/V: Moral Development II

• Gender	LO4 OHT89 & IB: Gender-Role Classification LS1: The Study of Gender PA2: It's a Girl (Boy) Thing
-What Is Gender?	F/V: The Idea of Gender F/V: Self Identity and Sex Role Development F/V: Sex Roles
-Biological Influences	F/V: Brain Sex F/V: The Facts Behind Sex Differences
-Social Influences	IB: Psychoanalytic and Social Cognitive Views CA1: Do Parents Really Treat Boys and Girls Differently?
-Cognitive Influences	IB: Cognitive Developmental and Gender Schema F/V: Anything You Can Do, I Can Do Better WS: Achieving Gender Equity in Science

Families	F/V: The Influence of the Family
	F/V: Family Influences
	F/V: Family Life and the Active Child
• Parenting	LS2: The Problem of Studying Parenting
	PA3: The Most Important Job in the World
	WS: Scholarly Works on Parenting
-Parenting Styles	LO5
	OHT103 & IB: Classification of Parenting Styles
	F/V: Basic Parenting Skills
	WS: Do You Know Your Parenting Style?
	WS: Parenting Style and Its Correlates
-Child Abuse	LO6
	WS: Child Abuse
-Parenting: Nature and Nurture	F/V: Child in the Family
-Good Parenting Takes Time and Effort	
• Sibling Relationships and Birth Order	LO7
-Sibling Relationships	CA2: Siblings
	F/V: Brothers and Sisters: Sibling Relationships
-Birth Order	LO8
	LS3: Context-Specific Learning, Personality,
	and Birth Order
	WS: Birth Order
• The Changing Family in a Changing Society	IB: Single-Parent Families in Different Countries
	OHT82 & IB: Living in Single-Parent Households
	OHT84 & IB: Living with One Parent
	OHT178 & IB: Single-Parent Families
	CA3: Changing Family Demographics
-Working Parents	LO9
	OHT152 & IB: Employment of Mothers
	LS4: Early Parental Employment
-Effects of Divorce on Children	LO10
	PA4: I Lived It
	F/V: Children and Divorce
	F/V: For the Love of Ben: A Father's View
	WS: Children and Divorce
	F/V: Family Stress: The Child's Perspective
-Cultural, Ethnic, and Socioeconomic	LO11
Variations in Families	CA4: Family Constellations

Peer Relations, Play, and Television • Peer Relations	LO12

• Play
  -Play's Functions
  -Parten's Classic Study of Play
 	
  -Types of Play
	LO13
	
	CA5: Play Classification
	RP2: Parten's Play Styles
	F/V: Play
	F/V: Play and Imagination
	F/V: Techniques of Play Therapy

• Television
  -Television's Many Roles
 	
  -Amount of Television Watched By Children
 	
  -Effects of Television on Children's
   Aggression and Prosocial Behavior
 	
  -Television and Cognitive Development
	LO14
	CA6: Television Quiz
	CA7: Applying Concepts to Television Shows
	
	OHT106: Reading and Television Habits
	
	OHT85 & IB: Peer Aggression
	LS5: How Do Parents Teach Their Children
	      Prosocial Behavior?
	WS: Children and TV Violence
	
	WS: Mind and Media: The Effects of TV,
	      Video Games, and Computers
	CA8: Applying Concepts to Cartoons

Review	CA9: Critical Thinking Multiple-Choice CA10: Critical Thinking Essays WS: Children's Social Development: A Checklist

Chapter Outline

EMOTIONAL AND PERSONALITY DEVELOPMENT
  The Self
    Initiative Versus Guilt
    • Initiative versus guilt is the conflict in early childhood for Erikson's psychosocial theory.
    • Conscience develops during this stage and children are capable of hearing the inner voice of self-observation, self-guidance, and self-punishment.
    • Resolution of this conflict depends on how children's self-initiated activities are handled.
      • Freedom and opportunity support initiative, whereas guilt develops if children's enthusiasm for exploration and curiosity is squelched.
    Self-Understanding
    • **Self-understanding** is the child's cognitive representation of self, the substance and content of the child's self-conceptions.
    • Self-understanding begins with self-recognition around 18 months.
    • Self description usually focuses on physical characteristics, physical actions, or material possessions.

Emotional Development

Developmental Timetable of Young Children's Emotion Language and Understanding
- There is an increase in emotion language and the understanding of emotion.
  - Preschoolers are beginning to understand the causes and consequences of feelings.
  - By 4 to 5 years, children can reflect on emotions. They understand that the same event may elicit different emotions in different people.
- There is also an increase in emotion management to meet social standards.

Moral Development

What is Moral Development?
- **Moral development** involves thoughts, feelings, and behaviors.
- Moral development involves intrapersonal and interpersonal components.
  - The intrapersonal dimension involves a person's basic values and sense of self. It regulates a person's activities when she is not engaged in social interaction.
  - The interpersonal dimension involves a focus on what people should do in their interactions with other people. It regulates social interactions and arbitrates conflict.

Piaget's View of How Children's Moral Reasoning Develops
- Piaget observed and interviewed children from 4 to 12 years of age and concluded that children think in two distinctly different ways about morality depending on their maturity.
- **Heteronomous morality** is the first stage of moral development in Piaget's theory, occurring from approximately 4 to 7 years of age.
  - Justice and rules are conceived of as unchangeable properties of the world, removed from the control of people.
    - Children in this stage judge the rightness and goodness of behavior by considering the consequences of the behavior, not the intentions of the actor.
  - Another characteristic of heteronomous morality is **imminent justice** which is the belief that, if a rule is broken, punishment will be meted out immediately.
- **Autonomous morality** is the second stage of moral development in Piaget's theory, displayed by older children (about 10 years of age and older).
  - The child becomes aware that rules and laws are created by people and that, in judging an action, one should consider the actor's intentions as well as the consequences.
    - Children in this stage accept change and recognize that rules are merely convenient, socially agreed upon conventions, subject to change by consensus.
    - They also recognize that punishments are socially mediated and occur only if a relevant person witnesses the wrongdoing (even then punishment is not inevitable).
- Piaget thought the mutual give-and-take of peer relations facilitates moral development.

Moral Behavior
- Moral behavior is emphasized by behavioral and social cognitive theorists.
  - They believe there is considerable situational variability in moral behavior.
  - Self-control is an important aspect of understanding children's moral behavior.

Moral Feelings
- In psychoanalytic theory, children conform to societal standards to avoid guilt.
- Positive feelings such as empathy contribute to moral development.
  - Empathy involves reacting to another's feelings with an emotional response that is similar to other's feelings.
    - Cognition is required for empathy, such that one has the ability to discern another's inner psychological states (perspective taking).
- Hoffman and Damon emphasize that positive feelings (empathy, sympathy, admiration, and self-esteem) and negative feelings (anger, outrage, shame, and guilt) contribute to moral development. When strongly experienced, these emotions influence children to act in accord with standards of right and wrong.

Gender
  What Is Gender?
  - **Gender** refers to the social dimensions of being male or female.
  - **Gender identity** is the sense of being male or female, which most children acquire by the time they are 3 years old.
  - **Gender role** is a set of expectations that prescribe how females or males should think, act, and feel.
  Biological Influences
  - The 23rd pair of chromosomes determines our sex (XX for females, and XY for males).
  - The two main classes of sex hormones are estrogens and androgens:
    - Estrogens (estradiol) influence the development of female physical sex characteristics.
    - Androgens (testosterone) promote the development of male physical sex characteristics.
  - For the first few weeks of gestation, male and female embryos look alike. Then the XY chromosomes in the male embryo trigger the secretion of androgen, which causes the male sex organs to form.
  Social Influences
  - Males and females are treated differently shortly after birth. Parents are an important influence on gender development.
  Psychoanalytic and Social Cognitive Theories
  - The **psychoanalytic theory of gender** stems from Freud's view that the preschool child develops a sexual attraction to the opposite-sex parent. At 5 or 6 years of age, the child renounces this attraction because of anxious feelings. Subsequently, the child identifies with the same-sex parent, unconsciously adopting the same-sex parent's characteristics.
  - Most experts do not think that gender development proceeds in the manner proposed by Freud.
  - The **social cognitive theory of gender** emphasizes that children's gender development occurs through observation and imitation of gender behavior, and through the rewards and punishments children experience for gender-appropriate and inappropriate behavior.
    - Critics of this view argue that gender development is not as passively acquired as it indicates.
  Parental Influences
  - Mothers and fathers are psychologically important for children's gender development.
    - Fathers are more involved in the socializing of their sons than their daughters.
    - Fathers are also more likely to treat their sons and daughters differently.
    - Many parents encourage differential play in their sons (aggressive) and daughters (dolls).
  Peer Influences
  - Children who play in sex-appropriate activities are more likely to be rewarded by peers and children who play in cross-sex activities are more likely to be criticized.
  - There is greater pressure for boys to conform to traditional male roles than for girls to conform to traditional female roles.
  School and Teacher Influences
  - Boys and girls are not receiving an equal education:
    - Girls' learning problems are not identified as often as boys' are.
    - Boys are given more attention than girls are.
    - Girls start school testing higher in every subject, yet they have lower SAT scores upon high school graduation.
    - Boys are disproportionately represented at the top and bottom of the class.
    - Pressure to achieve is greater for males than females.

Cognitive Influences

Cognitive Developmental Theory

- In the **cognitive developmental theory of gender**, gender typing occurs after they have developed a concept of gender. Once they consistently conceive of themselves as male or female, children often organize their world on the basis of gender.
- Children use physical and behavioral cues to differentiate gender roles and to gender-type themselves early in development.

Gender Schema Theory

- A schema is a cognitive structure, a network of associations that organizes and guides an individual's perceptions.
- A gender schema organizes the world in terms of female and male.
- **Gender schema theory** states that an individual's attention and behavior are guided by an internal motivation to conform to gender based on sociocultural standards and stereotypes.
  - Gender typing occurs when individuals are ready to encode and organize information along the lines of what is considered appropriate for males and females in their society.
  - Gender constancy refers to the understanding that sex remains the same even though activities, clothing, and hairstyle might change, and may be necessary for gender typing.

FAMILIES

Parenting

Parenting Styles

- Baumrind proposed four parenting styles that are associated with different aspects of children's socioemotional development:
  - **Authoritarian parenting** is a restrictive, punitive style in which parents exhort the child to follow their directions and to respect work and effort. The authoritarian parent places firm limits and controls on the child and allows little verbal exchange.
    - Authoritarian parenting is associated with children's social incompetence.
    - Children of authoritarian parents are often unhappy, fearful, anxious about themselves with others, fail to initiate activity, and have weak communication skills.
  - **Authoritative parenting** encourages children to be independent but still places limits and controls on their actions. Extensive verbal give-and-take is allowed, and parents are warm and nurturing toward the child.
    - Authoritative parenting is associated with children's social competence.
    - Children of authoritative parents are often cheerful, self-controlled and self-reliant, achievement-oriented, cooperate with adults, and cope well with stress.
  - **Neglectful parenting** is a style in which the parent is very uninvolved in the child's life.
    - It is associated with children's social incompetence, especially a lack of self-control.
    - These children are often immature, and may be alienated from the family.
  - **Indulgent parenting** is a style of parenting in which parents are highly involved with their children but place few demands or controls on them.
    - Indulgent parenting is associated with children's social incompetence.
    - Children of indulgent parents may be impulsive, aggressive, domineering, and noncompliant.

Child Abuse

- As many as 500,000 children are physically abused each year in the U.S.
- Experts on child abuse think that child abuse is a complex phenomenon that involves the social context, the parent's coping skills, and the personality characteristics of the parents.

The Multifaceted Nature of Abuse
- Child maltreatment is the term used to refer to both child abuse and neglect.
  - Physical and sexual abuse, fostering of delinquency, lack of supervision, medical, education, and nutritional neglect, and drug and alcohol abuse are included.

Severity of Abuse
- Ninety percent of abused children suffer from temporary physical injuries. These milder injuries are likely to be experienced repeatedly in the context of daily hostile family exchanges.
- Neglected children, who suffer physical injuries, often experience extensive, long-term psychological harm.

The Cultural Context of Abuse
- The extensive violence that takes place in American culture is reflected in the occurrence of violence in the family.
- The amount of support services available to families is correlated to the amount of child abuse.
  - Family resources (relatives and friends) and formal community support systems (crisis centers) are associated with a reduction in child abuse.

Family Influences
- The interactions of all family members need to be considered in order to understand child abuse.
- Parents that abuse their child view physical punishment as a legitimate way to control a behavior.
- About one-third of parents who were abused themselves as children abuse their own children.
  - The majority of individuals who were abused as children are not locked into an intergenerational transition of abuse.

Developmental Consequences of Abuse
- Some of the consequences of abuse include poor emotion regulation, attachment problems (disorganized pattern), peer relations problems (aggression or avoidance), difficulty adapting to school, and other psychological problems (anxiety, personality problems, delinquency).

Parenting: Nature and Nurture
- Two types of research are effective in disentangling children's heredity and rearing conditions.
  - Studies have examined the effects of rearing experiences on the behavior of children who differ in temperament.
    - Parenting moderates the relationship between temperament and later adjustment.
  - Studies have compared the effects of high- and low-risk environments of children of different vulnerabilities.
    - Authoritative parenting facilitated resilience of children who displayed early developmental problems because of risk factors such as low-birthweight.
- Heredity and environment influence children's development.

Good Parenting Takes Time and Effort
- Good parenting takes a lot of time and effort.

Sibling Relationships and Birth Order
Sibling Relationships
- More than 80 percent of American children have one or more siblings.
- Given the many combinations of relationships it is hard to generalize about sibling influences.

Birth Order
- Parents typically have high expectations for firstborn children and they put more pressure on them for achievement and responsibility.
  - Firstborn children are more adult-oriented, helpful, conforming, anxious, and self-controlled than their siblings are.
  - Only children are often achievement-oriented and have desirable personalities.
- Birth order by itself is not a good predictor of behavior as age spacing, sex of siblings, heredity, temperament, parenting styles, peer influences, school influences, sociocultural factors, etc. also influence development and behavior.

The Changing Family in a Changing Society
- Variety characterizes family structures currently in the U.S.
  Working Parents
  - It is not certain that children of working parents receive less attention.
  - Maternal employment meets family needs and personal needs and may better socialize children for adult roles, especially daughters.
  - No detrimental effects of maternal employment on children's development have been found.
  Effects of Divorce on Children
  - Considerable research has examined the effects of divorce on children.
    Children's Adjustment in Divorced Families
    - Children from divorced families show poorer adjustment than their counterparts from nondivorced families.
      - Multiple divorces pose even greater risk.
    - Children from divorced families are more likely to experience academic problems, externalizing (delinquency) and internalizing (anxiety and depression) problems, to be less socially responsible, to have less competent intimate relationships, etc.
    - Experts disagree as to the effect of divorce on children.
      - The majority of children from divorce do not have these problems as most cope competently with their parents' divorce.
      - Approximately 20-25 percent of divorced children have adjustment problems compared to 10 percent of children from nondivorced families.
    Should Parents Stay Together for the Sake of Their Children?
    - If the stresses and disruptions in family relationships associated with an unhappy, conflictual marriage are reduced by divorce, then divorce may be advantageous.
    - If inept parenting and conflict accompany the diminished resources and increased risk associated with divorce, the best option is to retain the unhappy marriage.
    How Much Do Family Processes Matter in Divorced Families?
    - If the divorced parents' relationship is harmonious and they use authoritative parenting, the adjustment of children improves.
    What Factors Are Involved in the Child's Individual Risk and Vulnerability in a Divorced Family?
    - Many factors influence child outcomes:
      - Adjustment prior to divorce influences some problems that children experience.
      - Socially mature and temperamentally easy children show few problems.
      - Research regarding the effects of gender and the effects of joint custody have been inconsistent.
    What Role Does Socioeconomic Status Play in the Lives of Children of Divorced Families?
    - Custodial mothers experience the loss of about one-quarter to one-half of their predivorce income, compared to one-tenth by custodial fathers.
    - Increased workloads, job instability, and residential moves to less desirable neighborhoods and schools accompany income loss.

216

Cultural, Ethnic, and Socioeconomic Variations in Families
- Despite wide cultural variation, the most common pattern is a warm and controlling style.
- Minority families in the U.S. tend to have large and extended families, which may function as a buffer against discrimination and stress.
- Single parenting is more common among African Americans and Latinos.
- Higher SES families place more emphasis on education.

PEER RELATIONS, PLAY, AND TELEVISION
Peer Relations
- Peers are children of about the same age or maturity level.
- Peer groups provide information and allow comparisons to be made.
- Good peer relations may be necessary for normal social development.
    - Withdrawn children who are rejected by peers and/or victimized and feeling lonely are at risk for depression.
    - Children who are aggressive with their peers are at risk for developing a number of problems (delinquency and dropping out of school).

Play
- Play is a pleasurable activity that is engaged in for its own sake.
  #### Play's Functions
    - Play increases affiliation with peers, releases tension, advances cognitive development, increases exploration, and provides a safe haven to explore and learn.
    - Play therapy allows the child to work off frustrations. Through play therapy, the therapists can analyze the child's conflicts and ways of coping.
        - Children may feel less threatened and be more likely to express their true feelings in the context of play.
  #### Parten's Classic Study of Play
- Parten developed the following classification of play based on observations of children in free play. It emphasizes the role of play in the child's social world.
    - **Unoccupied play** occurs when the child is not engaging in play, as it is commonly understood. The child may stand in one spot, look around the room, or perform random movements that do not seem to have a goal.
    - **Solitary play** occurs when the child plays alone and independently of others.
    - **Onlooker play** occurs when the child watches other children play.
    - **Parallel play** occurs when the child plays separately from others, but with toys like those the others are using or in a manner that mimics their play.
    - **Associative play** occurs when play involves social interaction with little or no organization.
    - **Cooperative play** involves social interaction in a group with a sense of group identity and organized activity.
  #### Types of Play
- Bergin's view of play emphasizes both the cognitive and the social aspects of play.
  #### Sensorimotor and Practice Play
    - **Sensorimotor play** is behavior engaged in by infants to derive pleasure from exercising their existing sensorimotor schemas.
        - At 9 months, infants begin to select novel objects for exploration and play.
        - At 12 months, infants enjoy making things work and exploring cause and effect.
        - By 24 months, children understand the social meaning of objects.
    - **Practice play** involves the repetition of behavior when new skills are being learned or when physical or mental mastery and coordination of skills are required for games or sports.

217

- Sensorimotor play, which often involves practice play, is primarily confined to infancy, whereas practice play can be engaged in throughout life.

Pretense/Symbolic Play
- **Pretense/symbolic play** occurs when the child transforms the physical environment into a symbol.
  - Between 9 and 30 months, children increase their use of objects in symbolic play.
  - Make-believe play gradually declines after 5 years.
  - Pretending may help children develop imagination.

Social Play
- **Social play** is play that involves social interaction with peers.
  - Social play, including rough-and-tumble play with peers, increases dramatically during the preschool years.

Constructive Play
- **Constructive play** combines sensorimotor play and practice of repetitive activities with symbolic representation of ideas. Constructive play occurs when children engage in self-regulated creation or construction of a product or a problem solution.
  - Constructive play is the most common type of play in the preschool years.
  - It can help foster academic skill learning, thinking skills, and problem solving.

Games
- **Games** are activities engaged in for pleasure. They include rules and often competition with one or more individuals.
  - Preschoolers can play games that involve simple rules of reciprocity and turn taking.
  - The meaningfulness of challenge emerges in elementary school.

Television
- Television has had a tremendous influence on children as they spend more time in front of the TV than they do with their parents.

Television's Many Roles
- TV can have both negative influences (turning children into passive learners and presenting them with aggressive models) and positive influences (presenting motivating educational programs and providing models of prosocial behavior) on children's development.

Amount of Television Watched by Children
- Children are averaging 11 to 28 hours of TV per week, which is more than for any other activity except sleep.
- Children in the U.S. watch considerable more TV than children in other countries.

Effects of Television on Children's Aggression and Prosocial Behavior
- The amount of TV viewed at age 8 was related to the seriousness of adult criminal acts.
- Long-term exposure to TV violence was related to aggression in adolescence.
  - These findings are correlational.
- One experiment found that exposure to TV violence caused an increase in aggression.
  - TV violence is not the only cause of children's aggression, but it can induce aggression.
  - Children need to be taught critical thinking skills to counter the effects of TV violence.
- Prosocial behavior on TV is associated with increased positive behavior in children.

Television and Cognitive Development
- Children's greater attention to TV and their less complete and more distorted understanding of what they view suggest that they may miss some of the positive aspects and be more vulnerable to its negative aspects.
- TV viewing is negatively related to children's creativity and verbal skills.

Learning Objectives

1. Discuss young children's self-understanding, incorporating Erikson's view of the initiative versus guilt stage.
2. Explain how children attempt to make sense of their own and other people's emotional reactions and feelings.
3. Understand the Piagetian, social cognitive, and Freudian theories of moral development.
4. Describe the biological, social, and cognitive factors that influence gender development.
5. Understand the four major parenting styles and how parenting styles are affected by developmental changes in the child, as well as by culture, social class, and ethnicity.
6. Describe the multifaceted nature of child abuse, including contextual aspects, risk factors, and consequences of abuse.
7. Describe the complexity of sibling relationships.
8. Summarize the research that has examined birth order effects and the criticism that birth-order has been overdramatized and overemphasized.
9. Consider how families are changing in a changing society, including concerns of working mothers or both parents working.
10. Discuss the many factors involved in divorce such as the effects of divorce on children, whether parents should stay together for the sake of their children, the influence of family processes, factors involved in children's risk and vulnerability, and socioeconomic factors.
11. Outline the cultural, ethnic, and socioeconomic variations in families.
12. Indicate the role that peers play in early development and be able to differentiate peer interaction and parent-child interaction.
13. Describe the functions of play and the types of play.
14. Describe the effects of television viewing on development, including both positive and negative behavior.

Key Terms

associative play
authoritarian parenting
authoritative parenting
autonomous morality
cognitive developmental theory
    of gender
constructive play
cooperative play
games
gender
gender role
gender identity
gender schema theory
heteronomous morality

imminent justice
indulgent parenting
moral development
neglectful parenting
onlooker play
parallel play
practice play
pretense/symbolic play
psychoanalytic theory of gender
self-understanding
sensorimotor play
social cognitive theory of gender
social play
solitary play
unoccupied play

Key People

Diana Baumrind

Daniel Berlyne

William Damon

Erik Erikson

Anna Freud

Sigmund Freud

Lois Hoffman

Martin Hoffman

Lawrence Kohlberg

Mildred Parten

Jean Piaget

Lev Vygotsky

John Watson

Lecture Suggestions

Lecture Suggestion 1: The Study of Gender: Individual Differences and Social Context Approaches
This lecture highlights how gender research has changed as research philosophies have become more sophisticated. Students find the discussion of gender behavior interesting, especially as the social context approach is usually new to them. Traditionally, gender research emerged out of the individual differences approach. The individual differences approach attempts to explain wide variation among individuals by classifying individuals by some antecedent variable (such as age, sex, or an aspect of the environment). The goal is to determine how much of the variance among individuals in their performance on a given task can be accounted for by the antecedent variable.

- Issues have been raised regarding this approach. For example, very few attributes differ consistently when comparing the average values for the two sexes and, when consistent differences are found, the within-group variance is considerable relative to the between-group differences.

While there are some replicable sex differences of moderate magnitude (math and spatial abilities, aggression), most research has found null findings when making comparisons of male and female individuals. Maccoby (1990) suggests that the null findings are an artifact of the individual differences approach. That is, there really are differences between males and females when you examine behavior in a social context. Given that social behavior is never a function of the individual alone, the social context must be considered when examining social behavior. Individuals interact differently with different partners. When behavior is summed across all categories of social partners important differences may be obscured or missed altogether.

We have provided a couple of research examples from Maccoby's article to illustrate the importance of considering the social context when examining gender. Jacklin and Maccoby (1978) observed the social behavior of preschoolers on a time-sampling basis. Positive and negative behaviors (sharing, hugging, grabbing a toy, etc.) were recorded when the children were interacting with a previously unacquainted child. Same-sex dyads and opposite dyads were examined.

- Using an individual differences approach (the sex of the partner was not taken into account), there were no overall sex differences in the amount of social behavior.
- However, when the sex composition of the dyad was examined (social context approach), there were several important findings.
  - Same-sex dyads had a much higher level of social behavior than did opposite-sex dyads.
  - Girls' passive behavior was greatly influenced by the sex of the partner. Girl-girl dyads rarely displayed passive behavior, however, when girls interacted with a boy, passive behavior was prominent (boys tended to monopolize the toys).
  - The conclusion is that social behavior is situationally specific and is influenced by the sex composition of the dyad.

Greeno's (as cited in Maccoby, 1990) research provides another example that the sex composition of the group influences social behavior. Four-child groups of kindergartners played in a large playroom with attractive toys. The groups were all-boy, all-girl, or two boys and two girls. A female adult sat at one end of the room and, halfway through the session, she moved to the other side of the room. Greeno assessed whether the sex composition of the groups influences proximity to the teacher.

- Girls in the all-girl groups actually stayed farther away from the adult than did the boys in the all-boy groups. The girls moved away from the adult when she changed her position. The boys did not change their location.
- However, when two boys were present, the girls maintained close proximity to the teacher. The girls moved with the adult when she changed her location.
- Greeno concluded that proximity seeking was not a general trait of the girls, rather it was a function of the sex composition of the group.

- Source: Jacklin, C.N., & Maccoby, E.E. (1978). Social behavior at 33 months in same-sex and mixed-sex dyads. *Child Development, 49,* 557-569. Maccoby, E. E. (1990). Gender and relationships: A developmental account. *American Psychologist, 44,* 127-133.

Lecture Suggestion 2: The Problem of Studying Parenting The purpose of this lecture is to stimulate discussion regarding methodological concerns in parenting research. After lecturing on parenting styles and the child outcomes of the various parenting styles, encourage your students to critically evaluate the generalizations that have been made based on this research. This is a good time to encourage skepticism of research techniques and careful attention to one's own experience.

Understanding how variations in parenting influence child development is a complicated task. Students are rightly skeptical of generalizations in this area when they point out that mothers and fathers may parent differently from one day to the next, may differ between themselves, may respond differently depending of the social context (staying out past the curfew for a special occasion versus having a car), and may treat individual children in different ways. Furthermore, research on parenting is almost entirely observational and correlational, which renders interpretation of associations difficult and tentative. Students readily offer their reservations about such research and often generate alternative ways of conducting research to verify what parents say that they do. In addition, contemporary family configurations have changed considerably from those on whom much parenting research is based, so it is unclear how well much of the classic work applies to modern parenting.

- Sears, Maccoby, and Levin's (1957) classic study was based entirely on interviews of mothers about their child-rearing techniques.
- Baumrind's (1971) studies used in-home observations and a longitudinal design.
- Maccoby and Martin's (1983) article is useful for examples of methodological and conceptual strengths.

- Sources: Baumrind, D. (1971). Current patterns of parental authority. *Developmental Psychology Monograph, 4,* 1-103. Maccoby, E. E., & Martin, J. A. (1983). Socialization in the context of the family: Parent-child interaction. In E. M. Hetherington (Ed.), *Handbook of child psychology: Vol. 4. Socialization, personality, and social development.* New York: Wiley. Sears, R. R., Maccoby, E., & Levin, H. (1957). *Patterns of child rearing.* Evanston, IL: Row, Peterson.

Lecture Suggestion 3: Context-Specific Learning, Personality, and Birth Order Students are typically quite fascinated by (and opinionated about!) the effects of birth order on personality. Most large, well-controlled studies of birth order yield no significant effects, or only small effects that are not well replicated. A general conclusion is that birth order has no important effects on adult personality. Yet, many people, including psychologists, still believe that birth order is a major influence on personality development. Harris (2000) argues that the lack of consensus is somewhat puzzling. She explains the phenomenon by looking at the way behavior is affected by context.

Detterman (1993) concludes after reviewing 90 years of research that transfer between two situations occurs only if the situations are highly similar (and even then, it is rare). Failure to transfer learning may be adaptive as it gives the individual time to figure out if the behavior should be transferred or if a different behavior would be better. The more similar the contexts are, the higher the correlation between the behaviors in the two contexts. Harris notes several research studies that support this conclusion.

221

- Children who are obnoxious around their parents are not necessarily obnoxious around their peers (Dishion et al. 1994).
- Just because a child is dominated by an older sibling does not translate into that child being dominated by his/ her peers (Abramovitch et al., 1986).
- Children that are timid around adults are not usually timid around peers (vice versa) (Rubin et al., 1997).

Genetic influences account for a substantial amount of the variation on many personality and behavior variables. Harris proposes that "the genetic component of personality influences behavior in every social context, but that the acquired, or environmental, component is firmly linked to the context in which it was acquired." (p. 175).

- Saudino (1997) found that some children are timid in all contexts due to an innate tendency to be timid, whereas other children are timid in certain contexts because of their experiences in those contexts.
- Children learn separately how to act in each of their social contexts. Behaviors are only displayed across contexts if the behaviors are useful in that context. Often, behaviors that are displayed in the home are counterproductive outside of the home. Harris speculates that age differences in the home make birth order important in the home, but age differences are not relevant outside of the home because most people associate with age-mates.
- Ernst and Angst (1983) assessed the personalities of over 7,000 young adults using self-report of personality. No significant differences in any aspect of personality were found between first- and second-born individuals from two-child families.
  - In larger families, one significant difference was found. Last-borns were slightly lower in masculinity than older siblings.
- When parents judge the personalities of their children, they tend to describe firstborns as serious and responsible, and their later-borns as cheerful and independent.
  - To explain the discrepancy between self-report and family judgements, Ernst and Angst hypothesized that the behaviors of the "family judgment" personality may be parent-specific, in that the firstborns act in a serious and responsible manner when they are around their parents.
- Freese et al. (1999) also found no significant difference between firstborns and later borns on conservatism, support of authority, or punitiveness.
- Blake (as cited in Harris, 2000) found that education attainment was unrelated to birth order in small and medium-sized families. In large families, the two youngest children were the most likely to graduate from high school and attend college.

Harris speculates that many people still think that there are birth order effects based on subjective impressions. People incorrectly assume that people behave the same in other social contexts as they do in the family context. Research indicates that patterns of behavior developed in the family setting are not carried to other contexts. Birth order does not explain or account for variation in adult personality.

- Classroom Activity 2 (Siblings) complements this lecture.
- Sources: Abramovitch, R., Corter, C., Pepler, D.J., & Stanhope, L. (1986). Sibling and peer interaction: A final follow-up and a comparison. *Child Development, 57,* 217-229. Detterman, D.K. (1993). The case for the prosecution: Transfer as an epiphenomen. In D.K. Detterman & R.J. Sternberg (Eds.), *Transfer on trial: Intelligence, cognition, and instruction* (pp. 1-24). Norwood, NJ: Ablex. Dishion, T.J., Duncan, T.E., Eddy, J.M., Fagot, B.I., & Fetrow, R. (1994). The world of parents and peers: Coercive exchanges and children's social adaptation. *Social Development, 3,* 255-268. Harris, J.R., (2000). Context-specific learning, personality, and birth order. *Current Directions in Psychological Science, 9,* 174-177. Rubin, E.C., & Angst, J. (1983). *Birth order: Its influence on personality.* Berlin, Germany: Springer-Verlag. Freese, J., Powell, B., & Steelman, L.C. (1999). Rebel without a cause or effect: Birth order and social attitudes. *American Sociological Review, 64,* 207-231. Saudino, K.J. (1997). Moving beyond the heritability question: New directions in behavioral genetic studies of personality. *Current Directions in Psychological Science, 6,* 86-90.

Lecture Suggestion 4: Early Parental Employment, What Are the Effects? The purpose of this lecture is to go beyond the research that Santrock reviewed in the textbook regarding the effects of parental employment. Controversy surrounds the effects of early maternal employment on later development. Research has found that child-care quality and sensitive caregiving mediate the effects of maternal employment on attachment relationships.

Harvey (1999) conducted a longitudinal study involving 12,600 parents, and their children who were between 3 and 12 years of age when assessments were conducted. Family income, parents' education level, mothers' IQ and age, child race, and birth order were statistically controlled in the analyses as they were associated with parental employment and child outcomes. Overall, Harvey found no evidence of substantial negative effects of early parental employment on children's later development.

- Early parental employment status and the timing and continuity of employment were not consistently associated with children's development.
- Parental job satisfaction was not related with the effects of parental employment.
- Several small effects of early maternal employment were found.
  - Mothers who worked more hours during the child's first three years had children with slightly lower cognitive development through age 9 and slightly lower academic achievement scores before age 7.
  - Both of these effects were small and were not maintained past the ages indicated.
- Children's behavior problems, compliance, and self-esteem were not significantly affected by mothers' employment hours.
- Fathers' working more hours was not associated with children's development.
- Interesting differences were found for low-income families and single mothers.
  - A positive relationship was found for single mothers who were employed during the first three years of the child's life, and slightly higher cognitive scores.
  - Children who had fathers in low-income African-American families that worked more hours were linked with improved cognitive development. This was the opposite for children in high-income families.
- What could explain the association between cognitive scores and employment hours for low-income families?
  - Harvey speculates that the increased income could explain this relationship in low-income and single-parent families.
- Source: Harvey, E. (1999). Short-term and long-term effects of early parental employment on children of the National Longitudinal Survey of Youth. *Developmental Psychology, 35*, 445-459.

Lecture Suggestion 5: How Do Parents Teach Their Children Prosocial Behavior? The purpose of this lecture is to review research that examines how parents support the development of prosocial behavior in their young children. Before you review Grusec's (1991) research, have your students come up with ways that parents encourage prosocial behavior in their preschool-age children. Do parents use direct teaching, modeling, and reinforcement for prosocial behaviors? Should parents punish their children if they neglect to use prosocial behavior, such as sharing?

Mothers of 4- and 7-year-olds were trained to observe and record the socialization of prosocial behavior. Each incidence of prosocial behavior that occurred in their home over a one-month period was recorded. The prosocial behavior was noted along with the precipitating circumstances, and the responses that the behavior elicited from the people involved. Some of the findings include:

- Mothers used social reinforcement the most. Verbal and physical approach occurred when children helped, empathized, or displayed concern for others.
- One-third of children's prosocial acts received no response at all.
  - Do your students think that this is appropriate?

- From a learning theory perspective, this is appropriate, as it demonstrates a variable ratio reinforcement schedule. The child would not know when the reinforcement will occur, but the child would expect that reinforcement would eventually come. Thus, the child would keep acting prosocially. This reinforcement schedule tends to produce a high response rate with frequent, consistent action. Behavior that is reinforced with a variable ratio schedule is the most resistant to extinction.
- Parents almost never offered material rewards for children's spontaneous prosocial behavior.
  - Do your students think this is appropriate?
  - Grusec interpreted this as indication of the mother's sensitivity to the undermining effects of this type of reward.
- Mothers used induction most often when the children did not respond prosocially.
  - Induction is a technique that tends to motivate concern for others. This technique models appropriate behavior and encourages future prosocial action.
- Punishment was more likely when a child acted antisocially, than when he failed to act prosocially.
  - Do your students think that this is appropriate?
  - Grusec speculates that mothers were more annoyed with disobedience than lapses in concern for others.
- Parents rarely attributed good behavior to the character of the child.
  - This is interesting as laboratory research has found that these attributions actually increase morally relevant behavior.

Surprisingly, Grusec did not find a strong relationship between prosocial behavior and its reinforcement. She interpreted this finding by speculating as to many other mechanisms that encourage prosocial action. She proposed modeling, assignment of responsibility, or discussion of feelings and needs of others as possible mechanisms that explain the development of prosocial behavior.

- Source: Grusec, J.E. (1991). Socializing concern for others in the home. *Developmental Psychology, 27,* 338-342.

Classroom Activities

Classroom Activity 1: Do Parents Really Treat Boys and Girls Differently? This activity highlights the differential treatment of boys and girls by parents. This exercise works well as a full class discussion as most students are quite eager to discuss this topic. Have students discuss how parents reward and punish boys and girls differently and thereby contribute to gender differences in behaviors, beliefs, and so forth. Encourage them to provide specific examples.

- Parents, especially mothers, act consistently toward boys and girls, but the subtle differences contribute to gender-typed behavior. For example, parents are more favorably responsive to girls talking about emotions and feelings than they are toward boys. In fact, they may give negative responses to boys who act or talk about being sad. Parents are also more negative toward sons who act dependent than to daughters who act dependent. Parents are more likely to punish sons for misbehavior. They also allow sons to be more independent and expect less compliance.

Logistics:
- Group size: Full class discussion.
- Approximate time: Full class discussion (45 minutes).
- Sources: Fuchs, D., & Thelen, M. H. (1988). Children's expected interpersonal consequences of communicating their affective state and reported likelihood of expression. *Child Development 59,* 1314-1322. Russell, G., & Russell, A. (1987). Mother-child and father-child relationships in middle childhood. *Child Development, 58,* 1573-1585.

224

Classroom Activity 2: Siblings This activity is informative and entertaining for students to examine their beliefs about siblings. Using **Handout 1**, have your students answer the questions about siblings, family size, and only children.

- What is your sibling IQ? Answers: 1. c; 2. b; 3. a; 4. b; 5. c; 6. a; 7. b; 8. f; 9. c; 10. a

Logistics:
- Materials: Handout 1 (sibling quiz)
- Group size: Small group and full class discussion.
- Approximate time: Small group (5 minutes), full class (15 minutes).
- Sources: Simons, J. A. (1988). A Sibling Quiz: Classroom Activity. Ankeny, IA: Des Moines Area Community College.

Classroom Activity 3: Changing Family Demographics This activity highlights the myths that many people hold regarding how family constellations have changed over the last century. Most people believe that previous generations had numerous extended families and today we have isolated nuclear families. Actually, at the beginning of the twentieth century, shorter lifespans meant that the majority of families were one-generation families while, today, three- to five-generation families are more typical. Today's family statistics include:

- 75 percent of people over 65 are grandparents.
- 75 percent of them see their grandchildren every week or every other week; 50 percent see them almost daily.
- Middle-aged women are often caretakers of young adult children, grandchildren, and aging relatives.
- In the typical family, daughters and daughters-in-law hold families together. The women call parents (and parents-in-law), remember and plan for special occasions, and visit sick relatives.
- Use in the Classroom: After presenting the demographics, ask students the following questions: How does this information differ from our stereotypes of modern families? How have longer lifespans changed the responsibilities of family members? Why have most of these responsibilities fallen to women? What are the advantages and disadvantages of longer lifespans? What adaptations in society would better fit today's longer lives?

Logistics:
- Group size: Full class discussion.
- Approximate time: Full class (15 minutes).
- Sources: Schlossberg, N. K. (1984). Exploring the adult years. In A. M. Rogers & C. J. Scheirer (Eds.), *The G. Stanley Hall lecture series, Vol. 4.* Washington, DC: American Psychological Association.

Classroom Activity 4: Family Constellations This activity compares family members. For **Handout 2**, students are asked to examine their own family constellation. You need to stress that their impressions about parents and siblings are more influential than what the actual situation really is (See Lecture Suggestion 3: Context-Specific Learning, Personality, and Birth Order). Also, state that their family makeup and atmosphere did not force them to become the people they are today, but these factors did help to shape their decisions and personality.

Logistics:
- Materials: Handout 2 (Family constellations).
- Group size: Individual and full class discussion.
- Approximate time: Individual (15 minutes) and full class discussion (15 minutes).
- Source: Eckstein, D., Baruth, L., & Mahrer, D. (1982). *Life style: What it is and how to do it.* Dubuque, IA: Kendall/Hunt.

Classroom Activity 5: Play Classifications This chapter, with its discussion of play, is particularly fun and lends itself to good classroom discussion and debate. One way to enhance the discussion and to ensure involvement is to have students do some observing before they come to class.

- Instructions for Students: Have each student collect play observations on five children. The children can be any age and can be observed in a variety of settings such as in a home, park, or schoolyard. The observations collected should include the following:
  - The age of the child (approximations are OK if the exact age cannot be determined), the child's sex, how many other children are in the vicinity when the observation is made, whether or not there are toys present, and, if there are, what kind they are, and where the observations took place. The children can be observed wherever children play (e.g., at schools, churches, malls, in their homes, in their yards, and on playgrounds).
  - Using the descriptions of play that have been identified by different theorists, the students should break up into groups and classify the examples they observed. Consider using Parten's classification scheme, although it is a bit outdated, because the breaks between categories are clean. However, any classification scheme works as long as everybody agrees on it from the start.
- Use in the Classroom: After the observations are classified, have each group present a summary of its findings. Have students keep track of the frequency of different kinds of play for different ages and different genders. The place where the children were observed may influence the type of play as well, and so could be an interesting part of the discussion. The discussion should center on how well the data fit the predictions made by Parten or whatever classification scheme was chosen. Which theory did the best at predicting the results that were obtained?

Logistics:
- Group size: Small group and full class discussion.
- Approximate time: Small group (20 minutes), full class (15 minutes).

Classroom Activity 6: Television Quiz This seven-item quiz (**Handout 3**) about television can be used as an introductory activity for a lecture on television.
- The correct answers are as follows: 1. a; 2. c; 3. a; 4. a & c; 5. d; 6. a; 7. b

Logistics:
- Materials: Handout 3 (TV quiz).
- Group size: Small group and full class discussion.
- Approximate time: Small group (5 minutes), full class (5 minutes).
- Source: Mohler, M. (1987, April). Test your TV I.Q. *Ladies' Home Journal*, 60.

Classroom Activity 7: Applying Concepts to Television Shows This activity affords students an opportunity to relate the concepts that they are learning in this course to the "real world." This activity can also serve as a review of concepts from the textbook.
- Instructions for Students: Have students select a television series that focuses on children and/or parent-child relationships. The series can either be a comedy or a drama. The task for this activity is for the students to identify key issues from the chapter and/or the course materials that are presented in the TV show, such as sibling relationships and parenting styles.
- Use in the Classroom: Encourage students to discuss their ideas regarding the accuracy of the show and the implications of the content of the show for child-parent relationships, indicating whether the implications are negative or positive.

Logistics:
- Group size: Individual work at home and full class discussion.
- Approximate time: Individual (45 minutes), full class (50 minutes).

Classroom Activity 8: Applying Concepts to Cartoons This activity is an in-class version of Classroom Activity 6, thus it also affords students an opportunity to relate the concepts that they are learning in this course to the "real world." Bring in a videotape of a Saturday-morning cartoon.

- Instructions for Students: The students should be divided into small groups.
  - One-fourth of the groups should count the number of violent actions in the videotape.
  - One-fourth of the groups should count the number of sex-role stereotyped behaviors.
  - Another fourth of the groups should count the number of high energy, fast-paced activities, not necessarily violent.
  - The final fourth of the groups should count the number of prosocial actions.
- Use in the Classroom: Prior to viewing the videotape, the small groups should convene to discuss their task. They should operationalize the concepts (violent acts, prosocial actions, etc.) and decide how they will collect their data.

    After the class has viewed the cartoon, let the groups reconvene to organize their data. Did they agree on the number of behaviors that they were assigned to code? Did they have high inter-rater reliability? Why or why not? If not, what should they have done differently.

    Then, have each of the groups present their data and discuss the overall message and effect of the cartoon on young children. What kinds of models are being presented? What kind of world is shown? What kinds of perceptual and cognitive strategies do watching a cartoon require? How might a child who sees many of these cartoons be different in school from a child who does not watch much television?

Logistics:
- Materials: Videotape of a Saturday-morning cartoon.
- Group size: Small group and full class discussion.
- Approximate time: Initial small group meetings (20 minutes), watching of video as class (30 minutes), second small group meetings (20 minutes), and then full class discussion (45 minutes).
- Source: Modified from King, M. B., & Clark, D. E. (1990). *Instructor's manual to accompany children.* Dubuque, IA: Wm. C. Brown Communications, Inc.

Classroom Activity 9: Critical Thinking Multiple-Choice Questions and Suggested Answers The critical thinking multiple-choice questions on **Handout 4** are similar to the ones in previous chapters. Have students discuss their answers. The suggested answers are presented as **Handout 5**. Question 1 requires students to explore the documented benefits of authoritative parenting, and thus to review the scientific base for endorsement of this parenting style. Question 2 requires students to review the characteristics of the major theoretical perspective of life-span development in order to decide whether they apply to specific topics covered in chapter 9. The third question again requires students to recognize the explicit statement of an assumption and understand that it is different from a claim of fact or an interpretation of facts. It is worth noting that the assumption in this case is fundamental to virtually the entire developmental perspective, and students will probably identify it easily.

Logistics:
- Materials: Handout 4 (the critical thinking multiple-choice questions) and Handout 5 (answers).
- Group size: Small groups to discuss the questions, then a full class discussion.
- Approximate time: Small groups (15 to 20 minutes), then 30 minutes for full class discussion.

Classroom Activity 10: Critical Thinking Essay Questions and Suggestions for Helping Students Answer the Essays Discuss students' answers to the critical thinking essay questions provided in **Handout 6**. Several objectives can be met with these questions. First, students' understanding of concepts in chapter 9 will be facilitated. Second, this type of essay question affords the students an opportunity to apply the concepts to their own lives, which will increase their retention of the material. Third, the essay format also will give students practice expressing themselves in written form. Ideas to help students answer the critical thinking essay questions are provided as **Handout 7**.

Logistics:
- Materials: Handout 6 (essay questions) and Handout 7 (helpful suggestions for the answers).
- Group size: Individual, then full class.
- Approximate time: Individual (60 minutes), then 30 minutes for full class discussion.

Personal Applications

Personal Application 1: Just a Little White Lie The purpose of this exercise is for students to explore the social cognitive view of moral development. Developmental psychologists have studied children's moral behavior in a number of different situations. They have discovered that morality is often situationally based, as in a study of thousands of children where the totally honest child was virtually nonexistent, as were children who cheated in every situation possible. As adults we exhibit the same patterns of morality, defining the acceptability of our behavior by the circumstances surrounding it.
- Instructions for Students: Explore your morality. Consider lying, cheating, stealing, and any other behavior you choose. Are those behaviors wrong in *all* cases? Discuss. (Hint: When was the last time you fibbed? Have you even taken "extra" office supplies home from work?)
- Use in the Classroom: Discuss this concept of situational morality. Ask students whether they consider themselves to be honest people. After (hopefully) most of them raise their hands, ask how many have ever told a "little white lie"—telling a friend they have to stay late at work or the libraryso that they don't have to go on that blind date they arranged. Discuss tax returns (are we all completely honest, or do we fear an audit due to those little "oversights" in reporting), stealing (what happens when the grocery checker gives you more change then you were due, but you don't discover it until you're in the parking lot), cheating in school, and larger moral issues such as premarital sex. What makes something a "larger" moral issue—or are all "wrongs" equal?

Personal Application 2: It's A Girl (Boy) Thing The purpose of the exercise is to get students thinking about their own gender schemas. These cognitive networks of associations that guide our perceptions about gender begin taking shape early in childhood. We begin accumulating information as to what is "girl-like" and "boy-like." We are continually adding information to our schema to enable us to understand and form expectations about males and females. Because this is viewed as being influenced by many societal factors, what was once traditionally considered "male" and "female" is changing. Society has experienced the feminist movement, and the "sensitive male" movement, and perceptions of gender-appropriate behavior continue to evolve with the more visible presence and acceptance of homosexuality. With more women than ever being career-oriented and fathers becoming more active caregivers, gender roles and our schemas for them are not what they used to be.
- Instructions for Students: Write about your gender schema. What do you consider "female" and "male." Include notions of physical appearance and functioning, societal roles, and relationship participation. Have your current views of gender functioning changed from when you were growing up? If so, what contributed to the change? Do you have a problem with the way society currently views either gender? Explain.
- Use in the Classroom: Ask students for characteristics of "males" and "females" and write them in two columns on the board. After everyone has exhausted their list, assess the accumulation of items in each list. Are there contradictory characteristics within each list? Are there more contradictory items for one gender than another? If so, why might this be? How many characteristics do both sexes share? Are there any outdated characteristics? Why? What might be the result of society's changing gender schemas? Do students feel in any way confused as to what their gender role should encompass? Why?

Personal Application 4: The Most Important Job in the World The purpose of this experience is to help students think about parenting styles with regard to their own upbringing. The family is the primary socializing environment during childhood. Significant findings have illuminated a connection between parenting styles and behavioral outcomes later in life.

- Instructions for Students: Review Diana Baumrind's four parenting styles. Describe the style your parents exhibited, and try to recall your reactions to them growing up. How do you feel their approach continues to influence your behavior today, or does it? If you yourself are a parent, what style do you employ?
- Use in the Classroom: Is there a prevalent style of parenting exhibited by parents today? What might the effects be of the explosion of day care on parents and how they approach their children? Or might it be the other way around—that the parenting style adopted by parents contributes to their decision to place children in day care? Use explicit examples from children's behavior to demonstrate evidence of particular parenting styles. What effect might there be on society with the prevalence of a particular style of parenting? In what ways might expectant parents become educated on the most appropriate method for parenting? Why is this important?

Personal Application 4: I Lived It The purpose of this exercise is to enable students to explore their own experience with divorce. The data suggests that children of divorced parents show more problematic behavioral and adjustment outcomes than children of intact families. However, many of these children appear to be fine, thus the discrepancy between the two groups is not dramatic. Psychologists acknowledge the numerous factors that contribute to children's response to divorce, including both external (family) and internal (temperament) characteristics.

- Instructions for Students: If you have experienced the divorce of your parents, share the experience. What was family life like prior to their separation? Did you welcome the divorce, or was it painful? Were your parents amicable in their parting or did you witness a great deal of negativity? What were the arrangements for spending time with your parents after the divorce? How did you deal with your new lifestyle? Can you identify what factors contributed to your particular adjustment to the situation, or what hindered your being able to accept it? What were your coping mechanisms? Elaborate as much as you feel comfortable.
- Use in the Classroom: This can be a difficult subject matter for students to talk about, but some may be willing to share their stories. In either case, discuss the various factors that come into play in divorce situations, and how different temperament styles might react to such circumstances. Talk about parenting styles before and after the divorce, family size, and the differential effects on children based on birth order. Consider children in day care and those with stay-at-home moms, and the impact of divorce on the superego and subsequent morality.

Research Project Ideas

Research Project 1: Altruism-Empathy Observations For this project, students will observe two children playing on a playground for 20 minutes each and note any evidence of altruism or empathy. One child should be about 2 years of age, the other about 5. The students should make observations and record any behavior relevant to altruism or empathy (remind them that they may see both operations in the same situation). They can record their observations on **Handout 8**. In addition, they should write a report regarding the following questions.

- How did you define altruism and empathy?
- How many instances of empathy did you observe in the 2-year-old? In the 5-year-old?
- How many instances of altruism did you observe in the 2-year-old? In the 5-year-old?
- What seems to be the developmental progression in empathy and altruism from 2 to 5 years of age? How would you account for this? Could your data be explained on the basis of individual differences rather than on the basis of developmental changes? Why or why not?

- Use in the Classroom: Have students present their data in class. Organize the students to analyze the data for age differences and individual differences. Is there any evidence for the presence of altruism or empathy in the 2-year-olds? Is there any evidence for the presence of altruism or empathy in the 5-year-olds? Which has a stronger effect, age, or individual differences? Is there the same amount of variability in responses in the two age groups?
  - Probably both developmental and individual differences will emerge. Overall, older children will probably show more altruism and empathy than younger children will. The altruistic behavior shown by the younger children is more likely to be ineffective or egocentric. There will probably be more variability in the younger group, because some 2-year-olds may not be at a cognitive level where they perceive the distress of another. The 5-year-old children will probably show more appropriate altruistic behavior than the younger children will.

Research Project 2: Parten's Play Styles This project is an observational study of children's play. Have students pick a partner from the class and go to a neighborhood playground. One student should act as the observer, the other as the recorder. They should observe two children, one about 3 years old, the other about 5 years old, for 10 minutes each. They should determine for each child the amount of time spent in each of Parten's categories of play. Then, have them compare the differences as a function of age. **Handout 9** can be used for recording the observations. After completing the observations, they should answer the questions that follow in the form of a report.
- For the 3-year-old child, in what category was the largest amount of time spent? What category of play was the least frequent?
- For the 5-year-old child, in what category was the largest amount of time spent? What category of play was the least frequent?
- What were the differences between the children in the kinds of play in which they engaged? To what do you attribute this difference? Use information about cognitive, physical, and social development to answer this question. Are there variables besides age that could account for the differences you observed?
- How do your findings compare with those of Parten and Barnes?
- Use in the Classroom: Pool the students' results and discuss their findings. What play patterns were observed for 3-year-olds? For 5-year-olds? How might observations be affected by the play setting? Would they expect to see differences if they observed at a child's home (e.g., television and toys more accessible, maybe no friends over, maybe having built-in playmates in the form of siblings)?

Film and Video List

The following films and videos supplement the content of chapter 9. Contact information for film distributors can be found at the front of this Instructor's Manual under Film and Video Sources.

Anything You Can Do, I Can Do Better: Why the Sexes Excel Differently (Films for the Humanities and Sciences, 51 minutes). In this program, researchers debate whether differences in brain architecture lead to a division of talents between the sexes. Children are observed in classrooms, while at play, and at home.

Basic Parenting Skills (Films for the Humanities and Sciences, 50 minutes). This video focuses on parenting frustrations. Discipline techniques are illustrated with examples. Ideas for building healthy parent/child relationships are presented.

Brain Sex (Insight Media, 3 volumes, 150 minutes total). This video examines sex differences in men and women; including material on fetal hormones and later behavior, brain differences, and evolution.

Brothers and Sisters: Sibling Relationships (Films for the Humanities and Sciences, 55 minutes). This documentary explores the emotional dynamics of the sibling bond. Topics include siblicide in nature, competition, characteristic birth order differences, and environmental influence.

Child in the Family (Magna Systems, 37 minutes). This video explores functions of the family; diversity in family structures and parenting roles; stress and change within the family; teen parenting; cultural influences; and parenting styles and effective parenting.

Children of Divorce (Films for the Humanities and Sciences, 28 minutes). This program examines the effects of divorce on children. It discusses research findings that children have difficulty recovering from the effects of their parents' divorce.

Emotional Development of Children (Films for the Humanities and Sciences, 18 minutes). This program examines birth order and its effect on personality.

Family Influences (Insight Media, 30 minutes). This program defines parenting styles and their influence on children. It also deals with family background influences, birth order controversies, nontraditional families, and the effects of divorce.

Family Life and the Active Child (Insight Media, 30 minutes). This video examines the family as a context for development, looking at structure and dynamics. A comparison is made between a Russian and an American family.

Family Stress: The Child's Perspective (Insight Media, 30 minutes). The social and economic forces that influence family life during a divorce are examined in this video.

For the Love of Ben: A Father's View (The Cinema Guild, 27 minutes). This video presents a sensitive examination of a child's emotions following separation from his father by divorce.

The Idea of Gender (Insight Media, 60 minutes). James Sheehan lectures on the evolution of gender over the past 200 years.

The Influence of the Family (Insight Media, 60 minutes). This program explores complex family interactions, focusing on family structures, the circumplex model, discipline, birth order, and age span.

Moral Development I: Concepts and Theory (Magna Systems, 29 minutes). This video explains the concept of morality through the use of examples. Three major theories of moral development are presented.

Moral Development II: Learning to be Moral (Magna Systems, 29 minutes). This video describes the emergence of moral behavior from early infancy through adolescence and the roles that different facets of the environment play.

Play (Magna Systems, 29 minutes). This video discusses the importance of play in the lives of children from infancy to childhood.

Play and Imagination (Insight Media, 30 minutes). This video traces the development of play from infancy to adolescence to show how play enhances cognitive and socioemotional skills.

Preschoolers: Social and Emotional Development (Magna Systems, 29 minutes). This video outlines emotional and social development in early childhood, including fears and stress; prosocial behavior and aggression; developing conscience; and socialization.

Self Identity and Sex Role Development (Magna Systems, 33 minutes). The focus of this program is on the development of self and gender identity throughout childhood.

Sex Roles: Charting the Complexity of Development (Insight Media, 60 minutes). This program looks at myths about, and cultural aspects of, sex roles; covers psychoanalytic cognitive and social learning accounts; and deals with nature/nurture issues, stereotyping, achievement, peer interactions, and prospects for the future.

Sugar and Spice: The Facts Behind Sex Differences (Films for the Humanities and Sciences, 51 minutes). This program argues that hormones in the womb "hardwire" the brain with a sex-aligned signature even before birth. This causes a male or female orientation or a mixture of both.

Techniques of Play Therapy: A Clinical Demonstration (Insight Media, 40 minutes). This video illustrates the use of play therapy to engage, assess, and communicate with children.

Toddlerhood: Social and Emotional Development (Magna Systems, 29 minutes). This video explores aspects of emotional development, including autonomy, shame and doubt, socialization through meeting biological needs, handling emotions, and social interaction.

Web Site Suggestions

The URLs for general sites, common to all chapters, can be found at the front of this Instructor's Manual under Useful Web Sites. At the time of publication, all sites were current and active, however, please be advised that you may occasionally encounter a dead link.

Achieving Gender Equity in Science Classrooms
**http://www.brown.edu/Administration/Dean_of_the_College/homepginfo/equity/Equity_handbook.
html**

American Academy of Child and Adolescent Psychiatry Children and Divorce
http://www.aacap.org/web/aacap/publications/factsfam/divorce.htm

American Academy of Child and Adolescent Psychiatry: Children and TV Violence
http://www.aacap.org/web/aacap/publications/factsfam/violence.htm

Birth Order
http://www.ag.ohio-state.edu/~ohioline/hyg-fact/5000/5279.html

Child Abuse
http://www.jimhopper.com/abstats/#caut

Do You Know Your Parenting Style?
http://childrentoday.com/resources/articles/parent.htm

Mind And Media; The Effects of Television, Video Games, and Computers
http://www.opengroup.com/open/fabooks/067/0674576209.shtml

Parenting Style and Its Correlates
http://ericeece.org/pubs/digests/1999/darlin99.html

Scholarly Works on Parenting
http://parenthood.library.wisc.edu/Topics.html

Young Children's Social Development: A Checklist
http://www.ed.gov/databases/ERIC_Digests/ed356100.html

What Is Your Sibling IQ? Activity

1. About what percentage of children have no siblings?
   a. 25   b. 15   c. 10   d. 5   e. 1

2. What percentage of young and middle-aged adults have at least one living sibling?
   a. 95   b. 88   c. 72   d. 63   e. 51

3. The majority of adult siblings contact each other several times a year.
   a. True   b. False

4. Generally, siblings grow farther apart during adolescence than they were during the school-aged years.
   a. True   b. False

5. Which pair is most likely to experience intense sibling rivalry?
   a. Sister-Sister   b. Sister-Brother   c. Brother-Brother

6. "Intense sibling loyalties" are more likely to develop when siblings suffer parental losses, and yet get to grow up together in emotionally trying conditions.
   a. True   b. False

7. Which parenting response tends to decrease sibling-sibling aggression?
   a. Physical punishment   b. Laissez-faire

8. The _____ child in the family was more often the favorite of the mother and the _____ child was least often a parental favorite.
   a. oldest / youngest   b. oldest / middle   c. middle / oldest
   d. middle / youngest   e. youngest / oldest   f. youngest / middle

9. Aggression between two siblings is more common when their ages are
   a. more than five years apart.   b. three or four years apart.   c. less than three years apart.

10. Physically active individuals are more likely to have
    a. an older brother.   b. a younger brother.   c. an older sister.
    d. a younger sister.   e. no siblings.

Family Constellation Activity

1. List your parents (and other primary caretakers, e.g., stepparents, grandparents). For each person, answer the following questions:

   Current age?
   Occupation?
   Description?
   Favorite child? Why?
   Ambitions and goals for children?
   Relationships to children?
   Sibling most like this person? Why?
   Relationship with other adult(s)?
   Attitude toward life?
   Birth order in their childhood family?

2. Write the name and age of each sibling (including self) according to birth order. Include stepsiblings and other persons that acted as family members. Briefly describe each person on your list, then answer the following questions:

   Which one was most different from you? How?
   Which one was most like you? How?
   Who fought and argued?
   Who played together?
   Who took care of whom?
   Did any have to deal with prolonged illness or handicaps?

3. For each of the following adjectives, decide which sibling it best describes and least describes: intelligent, hard-working, conforming, rebellious, pleaser, critical, considerate, selfish, humorous, materialistic, spoiled, punished, spontaneous, attractive, strongest, idealistic, sensitive, obstinate, helping.

4. What are the subfamilies (i.e., siblings separated by 5 or more years) in your family?

5. What were the most important family values?

6. What saying could be your family motto?

7. What are your early recollections? Describe these memories and your feelings about these memories. What themes do these memories represent?

8. What kinds of patterns are revealed by these data? What factors have been most significant to you? How does your childhood influence your life now?

Television Quiz Activity

1. Daytime shows for children have more commercials than evening shows for adults.
   a. True   b. False

2. A child has spent 11,000 hours in school by the beginning of high school. How many hours has the child spent watching television?
   a. 2,000 hours   b. 10,000 hours   c. 15,000 hours

3. Is there a relationship between violence on TV and aggression in children?
   a. Yes   b. No

4. What are the two most commonly advertised products during children's programs?
   a. Toys   b. Diapers   c. Food/snacks
   d. Toothpaste   e. Soda pop

5. On Saturday, what percentage of network TV programs for children are cartoons?
   a. 25   b. 50   c. 75   d. 95

6. During children's TV programs, cartoon characters and program hosts are not permitted to talk about any commercials.
   a. True   b. False

7. There are government regulations for all advertising that children might see.
   a. True   b. False

Critical Thinking Multiple-Choice Questions

1. Child psychologists advocate authoritative parenting because this parenting style is associated with so many valued developmental outcomes. But because this parenting style is so popular and well supported, it is easy to overgeneralize its benefits and to conclude that all desirable developmental outcomes are related to it. Which of the following outcomes associated with early childhood is LEAST likely to result from authoritative parenting? Circle the letter of the best answer and explain why it is the best answer and why each other answer is not as good.

    a. competence at cooperative play
    b. relatively positive adjustment to a divorce
    c. development of a pervasive sense of guilt, especially after misbehavior
    d. development of higher levels of moral reasoning
    e. development of perspective taking

2. When he discusses gender issues in chapter 9, Santrock clearly indicates how a variety of theoretical perspectives attempt to understand developmental gender phenomena. However, his treatment of other topics in the chapter is not so explicitly linked to theoretical perspectives. For this question, your task is to decide which of the following topics is a reasonable match with the perspective paired with it. Circle the letter of the best answer and explain why it is the best answer and why each other answer is not as good.

    a. effects of divorce on children: psychoanalytic theory
    b. Parten's play categories: cognitive theory
    c. effects of television viewing: social cognitive theory
    d. self-understanding: behavioral theory
    e. working-parent solutions: ethological theory

3. The study of gender role development is fraught with assumptions. For example, one popular belief has been that males are biologically superior to females. Which of the following statements constitutes an assumption in Santrock's treatment of gender, rather than an inference or an observation? Circle the letter of the best answer and explain why it is the best answer and why each other answer is not as good.

    a. In the first few weeks of gestation, male and female embryos look alike.
    b. The development of gender roles results from an intersection of biological and environmental factors.
    c. Peers cause boys to be masculine and girls to be feminine.
    d. Parents' differential treatment of boys and girls causes boys and girls to acquire different gender roles.
    e. When not required to do otherwise, preschool boys and girls play with children of their own sex.

Handout 5 (CA 9)

Suggested Answers for Critical Thinking Multiple-Choice Questions

1. Child psychologists advocate authoritative parenting because this parenting style is associated with so many valued developmental outcomes. But because this parenting style is so popular and well supported, it is easy to overgeneralize its benefits and to conclude that all desirable developmental outcomes are related to it. Which of the following outcomes associated with early childhood is LEAST likely to result from authoritative parenting? Circle the letter of the best answer and explain why it is the best answer and why each other answer is not as good.

   a. <u>Competence at cooperative play</u> is a likely result of authoritative parenting. Baumrind found that children of authoritative parents tend to be socially competent, which is a requirement for participation in cooperative play.

   b. One of the factors associated with a <u>relatively positive adjustment to a divorce</u> is having authoritative parents. Hertherington et al. (1998) found that when divorced parents' relationship with each other is harmonious and when they use authoritative parenting, the adjustment of children improves.

   c. <u>Development of a pervasive sense of guilt, especially after misbehavior</u> is not a likely result of authoritative parenting. Erikson's theory suggests that children who suffer a pervasive sense of guilt rather than initiative have authoritarian parents. Baumrind's work seems to confirm this in the sense that children of authoritarian parents are less creative, have lower self-esteem, and get along with peers less well.

   d. The <u>development of higher levels of moral reasoning</u> is a likely outcome. Authoritative parents control their children, but they rely heavily on rules to do so and on communicating to children the reasons for the rules. They also permit children to challenge the reasoning behind rules. This sort of activity, according to Piaget, may promote the development of moral reasoning. In any case, it probably promotes the development of perspective taking, which is a component of more advanced moral reasoning (the ability to infer intentions.)

   e. The <u>development of perspective taking</u> is another likely outcome. Authoritative parenting is more likely than other types to foster perspective taking because it involves greater communication. Children come to know how their parents think about things and therefore that their parents have different perspectives from theirs. A less direct indication of this is the social competence of these children. This facility requires some ability to understand the perspectives of others.

2. When he discusses gender issues in chapter 9, Santrock clearly indicates how a variety of theoretical perspectives attempt to understand developmental gender phenomena. However, his treatment of other topics in the chapter is not so explicitly linked to theoretical perspectives. For this question, your task is to decide which of the following topics is a reasonable match with the perspective paired with it. Circle the letter of the best answer and explain why it is the best answer and why each other answer is not as good.

   a. <u>Effects of divorce on children: psychoanalytic theory</u> is not a match. If this were so, Santrock's treatment should include details about early family socialization practices and how these relate, via the first three stages of Freud's or Erikson's theory, to personality development. Instead, he details how the effects of divorce are influenced by the parenting styles and parental conflict, and how SES factors influence children's adaptation to divorce. This is more characteristic of an ecological approach.

    b. <u>Parten's play categories: cognitive theory</u> is not a match. Parten's categorization of play is a scheme based entirely on observations of play itself, making no reference to the inferred cognitive significance or correlates of the play. As such, this would better match ethological theory.

    c. <u>Effects of television viewing: social cognitive theory</u> is a match! The key is the emphasis on the idea that television shows provide models of attitudes and behavior from which children may learn stereotypes, acquire responses, and become more disposed to act in certain ways. There is also an emphasis on possible cognitive mediation of TV effects, another aspect of the social cognitive theory.

    d. <u>Self-understanding: behavioral theory</u> is not a match. This is immediately discounted by the reference to "a child's cognitive representation of the self;" and there is no indication about how these representations might influence a child's response to behavior modeled by others, or how they influence or mediate any other aspect or determinant of a child's behavior. Thus, neither radical nor cognitive variants of behavioral theory provide a match.

    e. <u>Working-parent solutions: ethological theory</u> is not a match. The attempt to understand the basis of parents' feelings of guilt about working is cognitive or psychodynamic in its orientation. Missing is any attempt to understand how this behavior represents or expresses a biological adaptation.

3. The study of gender role development is fraught with assumptions. For example, one popular belief has been that males are biologically superior to females. Which of the following statements constitutes an assumption in Santrock's treatment of gender, rather than an inference or an observation? Circle the letter of the best answer and explain why it is the best answer and why each other answer is not as good.

    a. The statement that <u>in the first few weeks of gestation, male and female embryos look alike</u> is an observation. Male sex organs start to differ from female sex organs when XY chromosomes in the male embryo trigger the secretion of androgens.

    b. The statement that <u>the development of gender roles results from an intersection of biological and environmental factors</u> is the assumption. It is a basic belief held by virtually all developmental psychologists about all features of development. In fact, Santrock directly reminds us of this principle as he introduces the topic of gender role development. He does not present it as a hypothesis to be tested, but rather a dictum to be obeyed as we attempt to understand the determinants of gender role development.

    c. The statement that <u>peers cause boys to be masculine and girls to be feminine</u> is an inference. Santrock describes research that has found that children are rewarded for engaging in sex-appropriate behavior and that children tend to criticize children for engaging in cross-sex activities. However, it is incorrect to claim a causal relationship as this research is correlational.

    d. The statement that <u>parents' differential treatment of boys and girls causes boys and girls to acquire different gender roles</u> is an inference. Parents have been observed to treat their sons and daughters differently. But to claim that this differential treatment is a cause of later differential gender role development is an extrapolation of this finding, a hypothesis about the possible effect of the parents' behavior on their sons and daughters.

    e. The statement that <u>when not required to do otherwise, preschool boys and girls play with children of their own sex</u> is an observation. Researchers and teachers see children playing in same-sex groups when children choose with whom they will play.

Critical Thinking Essay Questions

Your answers to this kind of question demonstrate an ability to comprehend and apply ideas discussed in this chapter.

1. Explain what Erikson means by saying that early childhood is dominated by feelings of initiative versus guilt.

2. Describe the development of self-understanding during early childhood, and relate what we know about it to what we know about cognitive development during this life period.

3. Identify and discuss the components of moral development. Discuss how current theorists conceptualize moral development.

4. Summarize what we know about biological, social, and cognitive influences on gender development. Clarify whether these influences are independent of each other, or whether they interact with each other. Give examples that support your conclusion.

5. Compare and contrast any two theories of gender development. Indicate whether these theories contradict each other, or whether an eclectic use of them would enhance our understanding of gender development.

6. Explain the four types of parenting styles, and describe the personalities of children who experience each type of parenting.

7. Analyze cultural, ethnic, and social class variations in families in terms of parenting styles.

8. Summarize what we know about birth order effects in children, and explain why some researchers think this information has been overdramatized.

9. Discuss the pros and cons of a mother's working outside of the home on a child's social development.

10. A friend of yours is going through a divorce and she has asked you to help her cope with her two preschool age sons. Write a letter to your friend and explain the current research on the effects of divorce and ways to facilitate her children's adaptation.

11. What are peer relations? Explain whether they are necessary for adequate social development.

12. Explain how play fulfills both developmental and educational goals and functions.

13. Compare and contrast Parten's classifications of play to the more recent classification systems.

14. Summarize what we know about the dangers and benefits of television. Then state and support a statement about whether television viewing by young children should/should not be regulated.

Ideas to Help You Answer Critical Thinking Essay Questions

1. Begin by reviewing the basics of Erikson's theory, and what *initiative versus guilt* refers to. Proceed to discuss how this concept is a defining aspect (according to Erikson) of early childhood.

2. Preface this discussion with an adult perspective of self-understanding. To what extent do you understand yourself, your thoughts, and cognitive processes? After exploring this, describe the development of self-understanding in childhood and how this is relevant to cognitive development.

3. Think back to when you were a child. What do you remember about how you thought about right and wrong? Do you remember specifically being taught these things, or did you just infer things from life around you? Now explore how developmental psychologists conceptualize moral development, and the components they identify as relevant to studying morality.

4. First discuss the importance of gender identity. When does it begin? Now address biological, social, and cognitive influences on gender development, their mutual influence, and supporting examples.

5. Provide some general background information on gender identity formation, and reasons for its significance as something to be studied by developmental psychologists. Now compare and contrast two theories of this development.

6. Preface your discussion of the four types of parenting styles with a presentation of the enormity of the responsibility of raising children. After acknowledging the scope of this job, explain the parenting styles, who delineated them, and the personalities of the children who experience each.

7. Create a chart to visually separate cultural, ethnic, and social class as they vary in terms of parenting styles. Discuss the distinctions.

8. What does *birth order* refer to? Why is it something explored by developmental psychologists? Summarize the known effects and explain the notion that this information has been overdramatized.

9. Before analyzing the pros and cons of this issue, present the particular issues of social development that are considered significant by developmental psychologists.

10. Describe a general divorce scenario involving children—whatever comes to mind. Now summarize each of the two models of divorce and compare and contrast their features. Review your text to assist you in assessing their respective degree of accuracy.

11. Don't simply define *peer relations*—paint a picture. Draw from your own childhood friendships and school days. What do peer relations involve for children? What behaviors do they elicit? What functions do they serve? Now explain their necessity for social development.

12. How do developmentalists define *play*? Further your discussion by explaining the role it plays in development and education.

13. Create a chart that defines play and all its elements according to each different classification system. Discuss the comparison.

14. Make a chart on the pros and cons of television. Develop a mature, well-stated case to present to your legislator regarding the regulation of children's television viewing.

Altruism-Empathy Observations

For this project, you will observe two children playing on a playground for 20 minutes each and note any evidence of altruism or empathy. One child should be about 2 years of age, the other about 5. Make observations and record any behavior relevant to altruism or empathy (you may see both operations in the same situation). Record your observations below. Then, write a brief report based on the provided questions.

<u>Child 1</u>   Sex ___ Age ___

<u>Child 2</u>   Sex ___ Age ___

Questions:

- How did you define altruism and empathy?

- How many instances of empathy did you observe in the 2-year-old? In the 5-year-old?

- How many instances of altruism did you observe in the 2-year-old? In the 5-year-old?

- What seems to be the developmental progression in empathy and altruism from 2 to 5 years of age? How would you account for this? Could your data be explained on the basis of individual differences rather than on the basis of developmental changes? Why or why not?

Parten's Play Styles

This project is an observational study of children's play. Pick a partner from the class and go to a neighborhood playground. One of you will act as the observer, the other as the recorder. Observe two children, one about 3 years old, the other about 5 years old, for 10 minutes each. Enter the amount of time each child spent in each type of play for the 10-minute observation period. Then calculate the percentage of time spent in each category for the time period. Determine for each child the amount of time spent in each of Parten's categories of play. Then, compare the differences as a function of age. Write a brief report using the provided questions as a foundation.

DATA SHEET

Category	Child 1 Sex ___ Age ___	Child 2 Sex ___ Age ___
Unoccupied play		
Solitary play		
Onlooker play		
Parallel play		
Associative play		
Cooperative play		

Questions:
- For the 3-year-old child, in what category was the largest amount of time spent? What category of play was the least frequent?

- For the 5-year-old child, in what category was the largest amount of time spent? What category of play was the least frequent?

- What were the differences between the children in the kinds of play in which they engaged? To what do you attribute this difference? Use information about cognitive, physical, and social development to answer this question. Are there variables besides age that could account for the differences you observed?

- How do your findings compare with those of Parten and Barnes?

Chapter 10: Physical and Cognitive Development in Middle and Late Childhood

Total Teaching Package Outline

Lecture Outline	Resource References
Physical and Cognitive Development in Middle and Late Childhood	PowerPoint Presentation: See www.mhhe.com Cognitive Maps: See Appendix A
Physical Development	LO1 F/V: Middle Childhood: Physical Growth and Dev.
• Body Growth and Proportion	OHT83 & IB: Height and Weight in Childhood
• Motor Development	

• Exercise and Sports
  -Exercise
  -Sports
	LO2
	RP1: Current Exercise Levels
	PA1: That's My Kid!

• Health, Illness, and Disease
 	
  -Accidents and Injuries
 	
  -Obesity
 	
  -Cancer
	LO3
	F/V: Stress, Health, and Coping
	
	LS1: The Long-Term Consequences of Obesity
	CA1: Weight Control for a Young Child
	
	IB: Types of Cancer in Children

• Children with Disabilities
  -Who Are Children with Disabilities?
 	
  -Learning Disabilities
 	
  -Attention Deficit Hyperactivity Disorder
 	
  -Educational Issues
	LO4
	IB: The Diversity of Children Who Have a Disability
	
	LS2: ADHD—An Intolerance for Playfulness
	LS3: Identifying Children with ADHD
	F/V: All About ADD (Parts 1 and 2)
	F/V: Medication for ADD
	F/V: Out of Control: Hyperactive Children
	WS: ADHD, Dyslexia, Learning Disabilities
	
	LO5

Cognitive Development
 	
• Piaget's Theory
 	
  -Piaget and Education
 	
  -Evaluating Piaget's Theory
	CA2: Time to Tell Time?
	F/V: Middle Childhood: Cognitive Growth and Dev.
	LO6
	OHT11 & IB, OHT55, OHT56 & IB, OHT57: Piaget
	RP2: Assessment of a Preoperational and a Concrete
	    Operational Thinker
	F/V: The Elementary Mind
	CA3: Is Psychology Just Common Sense?

• Information Processing	LO7
	OHT80: Information-Processing Model of Reading
-Memory	CA4: Training Children to Use Memory Strategies
	PA2: Remember the Time…
-Critical Thinking	
-Metacognition	
• Intelligence and Creativity	LO8
-What Is Intelligence?	LO9
	OHT77 & IB: Learning, Cognitive Dev & Intelligence
	OHT76: Stanford-Binet IQ Scores
	F/V: Intelligence
-Controversies and Issues in Intelligence	LO10
	OHT149: IQ Scores Fluctuate Very Little
-Extremes of Intelligence	LO11
	LO12
	CA5: Use of IQ Scores for Special Ed. Placement
	CA6: Child Prodigies
	PA3: Smart Move
	F/V: The Gifted Child
	WS: Gifted Children
	WS: Gifted and Learning Disabled
-Creativity	LO13
	OHT79: The Snowflake Model of Creativity
	PA4: Exploring Your Creativity
	WS: Creativity Home Page
• Language Development	
-Vocabulary and Grammar	
-Reading	LO14
	LS4: Environmental Influences on Literacy
	WS: Learning to Read and Whole-Language Ideology
	WS: Whole Language versus Phonics
-Bilingualism	LO15
	WS: Child Bilingualism
Review	CA7: Critical Thinking Multiple-Choice
	CA8: Critical Thinking Essays

Chapter Outline

PHYSICAL DEVELOPMENT
  Body Growth and Proportion
  - Slow, consistent growth characterizes middle and late childhood.
    - Children grow an average of 2 to 3 inches a year.
    - Children gain about 5 to 7 pounds a year.
  - Weight gain is mainly due to increases in skeletal and muscular systems.
  - Strength typically doubles due to an increase in muscle mass and strength.

  Motor Development
  - Smoother and more coordinated movements characterize this period.
  - Children at this age should be engaged in active, rather than passive activities.
  - Increased myelination of the central nervous system is reflected in fine motor skill improvements.

  Exercise and Sports
    Exercise
    - Only 22 percent of children in grades 4 through 12 are physically active for 30 minutes everyday due to time being devoted to television, computers, and video games.
    - Only 34 percent of children attend daily PE classes, and 23 percent don't have PE at all.
    - Some suggestions to help children to get more exercise include:
      - Offer more physical activity programs at schools.
      - Have children plan community and school activities that interest them.
      - Encourage families to focus more on physical activity.
    Sports
    - Participation in sports can have both positive and negative consequences.
      - Positive consequences include exercise, opportunities to learn how to compete, self-esteem, peer relations, and friendships.
      - Negative consequences include the pressure to achieve and win, physical injuries, a distraction from academic work, and unrealistic expectations for success as an athlete.
    - Some critics question the appropriateness of highly competitive, win-oriented sports teams due to undue stress from a win-at-all-costs philosophy.

  Health, Illness, and Disease
  - Disease and death are less prevalent in this period than at other ages in childhood and adolescence.
    Accidents and Injuries
    - Car accidents are the most common cause of serious injury and death.
    - The most effective prevention strategy is to educate the child about hazards of risk-taking and improper use of equipment.
    Obesity
    - Approximately 20 percent of children are overweight and10 percent are obese.
    - White girls are more likely than boys or African American girls to be obese in childhood. In adolescence, African American girls are more likely to be obese.
    - Approximately 25 percent of obese 6-year-olds will be obese as adults, whereas 75 percent of obese 12-year-olds will be obese as adults.
      Consequences of Obesity in Children
      - Obesity is a risk factor for many medical and psychological problems (pulmonary problems, hip problems, high blood pressure, elevated blood cholesterol, low self-esteem, depression, and exclusion from peer groups).

246

Treatment of Obesity
- There is no research support for the use of surgical procedures in obese children.
- Treatments that involve a combination of diet (moderate reduction in calories), exercise, and behavior modification have been successful.

Cancer
- Cancer is the second leading cause of death 5-14 year-old children.
- Child cancers are mainly those of the white blood cells (leukemia), brain, bone, lymph system, muscles, kidney, and nervous system.

Children with Disabilities
Who Are Children with Disabilities?
- Approximately 10 percent of all children in the U.S. receive special education. Slightly more than half have a learning disability.
- The term "children with disabilities" is preferred (emphasis is on the child not the disability).

Learning Disabilities
- Children with a **learning disability** 1) are of normal intelligence or above, 2) have difficulties in at least one academic area and usually several, and 3) have a difficulty that is not attributable to any other diagnosed problem or disorder.
- About three times as many boys as girls are classified with a learning disability.
  - The gender difference is explained by the greater biological vulnerability of boys, as well as referral bias.
- **Dyslexia** is a category that is reserved for individuals who have a severe impairment in their ability to read and spell.
  - Phonological awareness training in kindergarten has had positive effects on literacy.
  - Most children with reading difficulties are not diagnosed until the third grade or later.
  - Later interventions are not as successful unless the intervention is intensive.

Attention Deficit Hyperactivity Disorder
- **Attention deficit hyperactivity disorder** (ADHD) is a disability in which children consistently show one or more of the following characteristics over a period of time: 1) inattention, 2) hyperactivity, and 3) impulsivity.
  - Based on these characteristics, children can be diagnosed as ADHD with either predominately inattention, predominately hyperactivity/impulsivity, or both inattention and hyperactivity/impulsivity.
  - The number of children diagnosed with ADHD doubled in the 1990s and the disorder occurs as much as 4 to 9 times more in boys than girls.
    - The increase may be due to increased awareness of the disorder or to inadequate professional evaluations.
  - Definitive causes are not known, though a number of causes have been proposed (low levels of certain neurotransmitters, prenatal and postnatal abnormalities, heredity, and environmental toxins).

Educational Issues
- Prior to 1975 when Public Law 94-142 was implemented, most children with a disability were either refused enrollment or inadequately served in schools.
- **Public Law 94-142** is the Education for All Handicapped Children Act. It requires that all students with disabilities be given a free, appropriate public education and be provided the funding to help implement this education.
- In 1983, Public Law 94-142 was renamed the **Individuals with Disabilities Education Act (IDEA)**. The IDEA spells out broad mandates for services to all children with disabilities. These include evaluation and eligibility determination, appropriate education and the individualized education plan (IEP), and the least restrictive environment (LRE).

- The IDEA requires that students with disabilities have an **individualized education plan (IEP)**, a written statement that spells out a program specifically tailored for the student with a disability.
- In general, the IEP should be 1) related to the child's learning capacity, 2) specially constructed to meet the child's individual needs and not merely a copy of what is offered to other children, and 3) designed to provide educational benefits.
- Under the IDEA, children with a disability must be educated in the **least restrictive environment (LRE)**. This means a setting that is as similar as possible to the one in which children who do not have a disability are educated.
- The concept of mainstreaming has been replaced with the term **inclusion**, which means educating a child with special education needs full-time in the general school program.
- **Mainstreaming** currently refers to educating a student with special education needs partially in a special education classroom and partially in a regular classroom.
- There is controversy as to which is the best approach to educate children with special needs, some claim that separate programs may be more effective and appropriate.

COGNITIVE DEVELOPMENT

Piaget's Theory

- Concrete operational thought involves operations (mental actions that allow children to do mentally what they had done physically before) and reversible thought.
- Children in this stage can conserve. The ability to reverse mental actions on real-concrete objects and the ability to focus on more than one dimension of an object facilitate conservation.
- Children can also classify or divide things into different sets or subsets and consider their interrelationships.
- Seriation and transitivity demonstrate that children can reason about relations between classes.
    - **Seriation** is the concrete operation that involves ordering stimuli along a quantitative dimension (such as length).
    - **Transitivity** involves the ability to logically combine relations to understand certain conclusions.

Piaget and Education

- Some of Piaget's ideas that have been applied to teaching include:
    - Take a constructivist approach.
    - Facilitate rather than direct learning.
    - Consider the child's knowledge and level of thinking.
    - Use ongoing assessment.
    - Promote the student's intellectual health.
    - Turn the classroom into a setting of exploration and discovery.

Evaluating Piaget's Theory

Contributions of Piaget's Theory

- Piaget's contributions include the concepts of assimilation, accomodation, object permanence, egocentricism, and conservation.
- Piaget's careful observations were inventive and genius.

Criticisms of Piaget's Theory

- Recent theoretical revisions highlight more cognitive competencies in infants and young children and more cognitive shortcomings of adolescents and adults.
- Piaget thought stages were unitary structures of thought (synchrony was assumed).
    - Critics agree that children's cognitive development is not as stagelike as Piaget thought. For example, some concrete operational concepts do not appear at the same time.
- Piaget assumed that training was superficial and ineffective unless the child was at a maturational transition point between stages.
    - Research has found that children can be trained to reason at a higher cognitive stage.

- Culture and education exert stronger influence on children's development than Piaget thought.
- **Neo-Piagetians** modified Piaget's theory by emphasizing how children process information through attention, memory, and strategy use.

Information Processing
  Memory
- **Long-term memory** is a relatively permanent and unlimited type of memory.
    - Long-term memory increases with age during middle and late childhood and depends on the learning activities individuals engage in when learning and remembering information.
- **Control processes** are cognitive processes that do not occur automatically but require work and effort. They are under the learner's conscious control and can be used to improve memory.
- Many characteristics (age, motivation, health) determine the effectiveness of memory.
  Critical Thinking
- **Critical thinking** involves grasping the deeper meaning of ideas, keeping an open mind about different approaches and perspectives, and deciding for oneself what to believe or do.
- Experts think that students need to analyze, infer, connect, synthesize, criticize, create, evaluative, think, and rethink in order to achieve deeper understanding.
  Metacognition
- **Metacognition** is cognition about cognition or knowing about knowing.
- Kuhn distinguishes between first-order cognitive skills that enable children to know about the world, and second-order cognitive skills (meta-knowing skills) that entail knowing about one's own (and others') knowing.
    - By 5 to 6 years, children know that unfamiliar items are harder to learn, short lists are easier than long lists, recognition is earlier than recall, and forgetting is more likely over time.
    - Children gain a more realistic evaluation of their memory skills in middle childhood.

Intelligence and Creativity
  What Is Intelligence?
- **Intelligence** is verbal ability, problem-solving skills, and the ability to adapt to and learn from everyday experiences.
- **Individual differences** (the stable, consistent ways in which people are different from each other) are examined by using intelligence tests.
  The Binet Tests
- Binet devised a method to identify children who were unable to learn in school.
- **Mental age (MA)** is an individual's level of mental development relative to others.
- **Intelligence quotient (IQ)** is a person's mental age divided by chronological age (CA), multiplied by 100.
    - If mental age is the same as chronological age, then the person's IQ is 100.
- By administering intelligence tests to a large number of people of different ages from different backgrounds, researchers have found that the scores represent a normal distribution.
    - A normal distribution is symmetrical, with a majority of the scores falling in the middle of the possible range of scores and few scores appearing toward the extremes of the range.
- The current Stanford-Binet intelligence test assesses four content areas (verbal reasoning, quantitative reasoning, abstract/visual reasoning, and short-term memory), yet a composite score is still obtained to reflect overall intelligence.

The Wechsler Scales
- The Wechsler scales provide an overall IQ score, a verbal IQ score, and a performance IQ score.
- Patterns of strengths and weaknesses in different areas of the student's intelligence can be examined.

Types of Intelligence
- Sternberg's **triarchic theory of intelligence** states that intelligence comes in three forms:
  - Analytical intelligence involves the ability to analyze, evaluate, compare, and contrast.
  - Creative intelligence consists of the ability to create, design, invent, originate, and imagine.
  - Practical intelligence focuses on the ability to use, apply, implement, and put into practice.
- Children can have a combination of levels in these three areas and their pattern of intelligence influences how well they adapt and perform in traditional academic schools.

Gardner's Eight Frames of Mind
- Gardner thinks that there are eight types of intelligence:
  - Verbal skills: the ability to think in words and to use language to express meaning.
  - Mathematical skills: the ability to carry out mathematical operations.
  - Spatial skills: the ability to think in three-dimensional ways.
  - Bodily-kinesthetic skills: the ability to manipulate objects and be physically skilled.
  - Musical skills: possessing a sensitivity to pitch, melody, rhythm, and tone.
  - Interpersonal skills: the ability to understand and effectively interact with others.
  - Intrapersonal skills: the ability to understand one's self and effectively direct one's life.
  - Naturalist skills: the ability to observe patterns in nature and understand natural and human-made systems.

Evaluating the Multiple Intelligence Approaches
- These approaches have stimulated teachers to think more broadly about what makes up children's competencies, motivated educators to instruct students in multiple domains, and encouraged teachers to assess students in innovative ways.
- Some critics say that classifying musical skills as intelligence is inappropriate.
- Other critics say that research to support these approaches is lacking.

Controversies and Issues in Intelligence
Ethnicity and Culture
- In the U.S., children from African American and Latino families score below children from White families on standardized tests.
- It is important to note that there is wide variation in scores for all groups of people (15-25 percent of all African American children score higher than half of all White children).
  - The gap between the scores has narrowed as African Americans have experienced improved social, economic, and educational opportunities, which highlights that these differences are environmentally influenced.
- Many intelligence tests are biased against rural children, children from low-income families, minority children, and children who do not speak English proficiently.
- **Culture fair tests** are tests of intelligence that attempt to be free of cultural bias.
  - Two types have been devised.
    - One type includes items that are familiar to children from all SES and ethnic backgrounds.
    - The second type removes all verbal questions.
- Some people question whether it is even possible to create a culture-free test of intelligence, as intelligence itself is culturally determined.

The Use and Misuse of Intelligence Tests
- These psychological tools can be used successfully and they can be abused.
- Several concerns about IQ testing have been raised:
  - Stereotypes can be made about students based on IQ testing.
  - IQ tests should always be considered a measure of current performance and not a measure of fixed potential.
  - Problems occur when IQ scores are used as the main characteristics of competence.
  - Caution should be used when interpreting the meaningfulness of an overall IQ score.

Extremes of Intelligence
- Intelligence tests can assess incidences of mental retardation and intellectual giftedness.

Mental Retardation
- **Mental retardation** is a condition of limited mental ability in which an individual has a low IQ, usually below 70 on a traditional intelligence test, and has difficulty adapting to everyday life.
- Mental retardation can have an organic cause or it can be social and cultural in origin.
  - **Organic retardation** is mental retardation caused by a genetic disorder or by brain damage; organic refers to the tissues or organs of the body, so there is some physical damage in organic retardation.
  - **Cultural-familial retardation** is a mental deficit in which no evidence of organic brain damage can be found; individuals' IQs range from 50 to 70.

Giftedness

What Is **Giftedness**?
- People who are gifted have above-average intelligence (an IQ of 120 or higher) and/or superior talent for something.
  - Schools typically select children who have intellectual superiority and academic aptitude, whereas talented children in other areas (music, arts) are often overlooked.
- Recent research has found that gifted people tend to be more mature, have fewer emotional problems, and grow up in a positive family climate.

Characteristics of Gifted Children
- Winner described three criteria for gifted children:
  - Gifted children learn quickly and easily. They may have an innate ability in a particular domain or domains.
  - They learn in a qualitatively different way and they need minimal help or scaffolding from adults.
  - Gifted children are driven to understand the domain in which they have high ability. They display intense, obsessive interest and ability to focus.

Creativity
- **Creativity** is the ability to think about something in novel and unusual ways and to come up with unique solutions to problems.
- Guilford distinguishes between convergent and divergent thinking.
  - **Convergent thinking** produces one correct answer and is characteristic of the kind of thinking required on conventional intelligence tests.
  - **Divergent thinking** produces many different answers to the same question and is more characteristic of creativity.
- While most creative children are quite intelligent, the opposite is not true.

- Suggestions for increasing creativity:
  - Have children engage in brainstorming.
    - **Brainstorming** is a technique in which children are encouraged to come up with creative ideas in a group, play off each other's ideas and say practically whatever comes to mind.
  - Provide children with environments that stimulate creativity.
  - Don't overcontrol.
  - Encourage internal motivation.
  - Foster flexible and playful thinking.
  - Introduce children to creative people.

Language Development

Vocabulary and Grammar
- Thinking about words becomes less tied to actions and perceptual aspects and more analytical.
- Children's advances in logical reasoning and analytical skills helps them understand grammar.

Reading
- Controversy surrounds the issue as to the best way to teach children to read.
- The **whole-language approach** stresses that reading instruction should parallel children's natural language learning. Reading materials should be whole and meaningful.
- The **basic-skills-and-phonetics approach** emphasizes that reading instruction should teach phonetics and its basic rules for translating written symbols into sounds. Early reading instruction should involve simplified materials.
- Experts support combining the approaches (balanced instruction).
  - There is strong evidence that the decoding skills involved in recognizing sounds and words is an important skills for learning to read.
  - There is good evidence that children benefit from the whole-language approach of being immersed in a natural world of print.

Bilingualism
- Ten million children in the U.S. come from homes in which English is not the primary language.
- **Bilingual education** is the preferred strategy of schools for the past two decades and aims to teach academic subjects to immigrant children in their native languages (most often Spanish) while slowly and simultaneously adding English instruction.
- Researchers have found that bilingualism does not interfere with performance in either language.
  - Bilingualism has positive effects on children's cognitive development (attention control, concept formation, analytical reassigning, cognitive flexibility, and cognitive complexity).
- Controversy surrounds issues regarding bilingualism.
  - Proponents argue that teaching immigrant children in their native language stresses value for the native culture, increases self-esteem, and makes academic success more likely.
  - Critics argue that it harms immigrant children by failing to instruct them in English.
- Adults make faster initial progress when learning a second language, but their eventual success with the second language is not as great or easy as children's.

Learning Objectives

1. Explain the physical changes that take place during middle and late childhood, including motor development.
2. Discuss the importance of exercise and the effects of sports.
3. Discuss the most prevalent health issues during this time period—accidents and injuries, obesity, and childhood cancer.
4. Discuss what a learning disability is and the types of learning disabilities children have.
5. Consider how the educational system helps children with disabilities.
6. Understand Piaget's theory of concrete operations, and examine how his theories are applied to teachingas well as criticisms of his theory.
7. Describe how information processing examines cognitive development, including changes in memory, critical thinking, and metacognition.
8. Discuss what intelligence is, how it is measured, and the difficulty in measuring it.
9. Explain Sternberg's and Gardner's alternative theories of intelligence.
10. Examine the controversies surrounding intelligence, including culturally-biased tests and the misuse of intelligence tests.
11. Discuss mental retardation and its two causes.
12. Explain what giftedness is and the characteristics of a gifted child.
13. Understand what creativity is and ways to foster it in children.
14. Describe the two approaches to reading and the effectiveness of each.
15. Discuss bilingual education and the positions of both the critics and supporters of it.

Key Terms

attention deficit hyperactivity
   disorder (ADHD)
basic-skills-and-phonetics
approach
   bilingual education
brainstorming
control processes
convergent thinking
creativity
critical thinking
cultural-familial retardation
culture-fair tests
divergent thinking
dyslexia
giftedness
inclusion
individual differences
individualized education plan (IEP)

Individuals with Disabilities
   Education Act (IDEA)
intelligence
intelligence quotient (IQ)
learning disability
least restrictive environment (LRE)
long-term memory
mainstreaming
mental age (MA)
mental retardation
metacognition
neo-Piagetians
organic retardation
Public Law 94-142
seriation
transitivity
triarchic theory of intelligence
whole-language approach

Key People

Teresa Amabile

Alfred Binet

Jacqueline and Martin Brooks

John Dewey

Howard Gardner

J.P. Guilford

Deanna Kuhn

Jean Piaget

Michael Pressley

Theophile Simon

Charles Spearman

William Stern

Robert J. Sternberg

Lewis Terman

L.L. Thurstone

David Weschler

Ellen Winner

Lecture Suggestions

Lecture Suggestion 1: The Long-Term Consequences of Childhood Obesity The purpose of this lecture is to extend the textbook's discussion of the long-term physical and psychological consequences of childhood obesity. Must et al. (1992) have documented morbidity and mortality rates related to obesity in adolescence. Obese adolescents are at greater risk for death and adult obesity. These relationships are stronger for females than males. As the textbook discusses, both males and females suffer psychological and social consequences of childhood obesity (pulmonary problems, hip problems, high blood pressure and elevated blood cholesterol, low self-esteem, depression, and exclusion from peer groups).

- Gortmaker et al. (1993) studied the long-term effects of childhood obesity by assessing young adults who were obese as adolescents. These individuals had less education, less income, and were less likely to be married than the individuals who were not obese as adolescents. These effects were apparent despite the statistical control of initial SES and aptitude scores.
- These results cannot be explained by chronic health problems that interfere with academic or career success. Gortmaker et al. ingeniously compared a group of individuals with chronic health problems (diabetes, cerebral palsy) to the individuals who had been obese as adolescents. The individuals with chronic health problems did not suffer from the same consequences.
- What could explain the developmental pattern of obese individuals?
  - The authors speculate that the negative effects of early obesity are more likely due to stigmatization and discrimination. Overweight individuals are negatively labeled which decreases their chances of successful career progression and mate selection.
- Obesity may be an important factor in determining class and success. This speculation calls into question the long-held assumption of the unidirectional relationship between SES and obesity.
- Sources: Gortmaker, S.L., Must, A., Perrin, J.M., Sobol, A.M., & Dietz, W.H. (1993). Social and economic consequences of overweight in adolescence and young adulthood. *The New England Journal of Medicine, 329*, 1008-1012. Must, A., Jacques, P.F., Dallal, G.E., Bajema, C.J., & Dietz, W.H. (1992). Long-term morbidity and mortality of overweight adolescents: A follow-up of the Harvard Growth Study of 1922 to 1935. *The New England Journal of Medicine, 327*, 1350-1355.

Lecture Suggestion 2: ADHD—An Intolerance for Childhood Playfulness The purpose of this lecture is to examine Panksepp's (1998) ideas that attention deficit hyperactivity disorder (ADHD) is overdiagnosed and reflects an intolerance for normal childhood behavior. ADHD is the most common childhood disorder with approximately 15 percent of American children diagnosed (8 million children). This is an increase from 1 percent of the population in 1902 when this disorder was first recognized. Given that there is no neurological explanation for this increase, Panksepp speculates that the increase in standardized educational experiences has lead to intolerance for normal playfulness.

Children with ADHD are often given psychostimulants which promote attention and markedly reduce children's urge to play, especially rough-and-tumble play (Panksepp et al., 1987). This bothers Panksepp, as we do not fully understand the impact that play has on the developing brain and the added concern that we do not understand the long-term neurological consequences of psychostimulant drugs. Could it be that adults want to reduce children's rambunctiousness due to inadequate space and opportunity for children to express the natural biological need to play? After all, the biological need to play intrudes into classroom activities when opportunity and space are limited. Thus, Panksepp proposes that ADHD needs to be reconceptualized as a symptom of contemporary society and our attempt to control normal playfulness in children and not as a symptom of neurological imbalance or a disorder.

- Is ADHD a normal variant of human diversity?

Given the research on the heritability of temperament and the concordance of symptoms of ADHD for siblings, Panksepp argues that symptoms of ADHD are natural variations of child playfulness. The simple criteria used to diagnosis ADHD contributes to the frequency of medicating children. These children may be normal, highly playful children who have difficulty adjusting to some institutional expectations. Some of the symptoms can be interpreted in evolutionary terms. Distractibility may be useful to monitor a changing environment. Difficulty following instructions may reflect independent thought and judgement. Acting without regard for consequences may reflect risk-taking. Panksepp argues that we should nurture these characteristics and adjust societal expectations rather than medicate these children.

- What are the neural differences in individuals with ADHD?

The major difference in the brains of individuals with ADHD is a 5 percent reduction in overall size of the frontal areas. The size difference is accompanied by the lack of right-left asymmetries (right is smaller) (Castellanoes et al., 1996). The frontal lobes are necessary for long-term planning and the elaboration of complex behavioral strategies. The increased activity level and rough-and-tumble play demonstrated by children with ADHD is related to damage in these areas. Barkley (1997) theorizes that ADHD is a result of deficient behavioral inhibition, a function that allows better behavioral flexibility, foresight, and regulation of behavior. Environmental factors such as play may improve frontal lobe functions permanently.

- Do psychostimulants promote any long-term benefits or problems?

Psychostimulants promote activity in areas of the brain that control attention and goal-directed behavior (Pliszka et al., 1996). While these drugs do improve attention and focus temporarily, long-term benefits have not been found (if medication is terminated, ADHD symptoms return). The long-term problems outweigh the short-term benefits. Side effects of these psychostimulants have been found as well (children don't like the way the drugs make them feel, small decrease in physical growth). Continued behavior problems in adulthood have been reported. There is inconsistent evidence regarding the increased likelihood of drug abuse as it is difficult to tease apart whether these consequences are due to constitutional differences or to the long-term use of psychostimulants.

- What else might we do to address such childhood problems?

While there have been some lasting effects of combined cognitive and behavioral interventions, an alternative proposed by Panksepp is a rough-and-tumble intervention. The innate desire to engage in rough-and-tumble play may facilitate the normal maturation of children's brains. Providing children with abundant opportunity to play may reduce impulsivity. The logic is as follows. We know that frontal areas mature with age and that the frequency of play decreases with age, and animals with frontal area damage tend to be more playful (Panksepp et al, 1995).

The question remains, "Does rough-and-tumble play facilitate frontal lobe maturation?" Panksepp is testing this hypothesis. Rats with smaller frontal lobes are hyperactive and playful. After considerable play opportunities, they exhibit greater than normal decline in their play behavior as they mature. Panksepp et al. (1997) argue that playful experiences may regulate the brain's "play circuits."

In conclusion, despite 50 years of research there is not sufficient evidence regarding extreme biological or psychological deviance in individuals with ADHD to warrant the degree of current medical intervention. Many children's behavior has been modified with these drugs and has resulted in control of classroom behavior, increased attention for academic pursuits, and less peer ostracism of children due to the controlled behavior. Despite these benefits, Panksepp argues that the reduction in play behaviors may harm children's brain development and long-term control of behavior.

- Sources: Barkley, R.A. (1997). *ADHD and the nature of self-control.* New York: Guilford Press. Castellanoes, F.X., Giedd, J.N., March, W.L., Hamburger, S.D., Vaituzis, A.C., Dickerstein, D.P., Sarfatti, S.E., Vauss, Y.C., Snell, J.W., Rajapakse, J.C., & Rapoport, J.L. (1996). Quantitative brain magnetic resonance imaging in attention-deficit hyperactivity disorder. *Archives of General Psychiatry, 53,* 607-616. Panksepp, J. (1998). Attention deficit hyperactivity disorders, psychostimulant, and Intolerance of childhood playfulness: A tragedy in the making? *Current Directions in Psychological Science, 7,* 91-97. Panksepp, J., Normalsell, L.A., Cox, J.F., Crepeau, L., & Sacks, D.S. (1987). Psychopharmacology of social play. In J. Mos (ed.), *Ethnopharmocology of social behavior* (pp. 132-144). Dordrecht, The Netherlands: Duphar. Panksepp, J., Normalsell, L.A., Cox, J.F., & Siviy, S. (1995). Effects of neonatal decortication on the social play of juvenile rats. *Physiology & Behavior, 56,* 429-443. Panksepp, J, Burgdorf, J., Turner, C., & Walter, M. (1997). A new animal model for ADHD: Unilateral frontal lobe damage in neonatal rats. *Society for Neuroscience Abstracts, 23,* 691. Pierce, R.C., & Kalvas, P. (1997). A circuitry model of the expression of behavioral sensitization to amphetamine-like stimulants. *Brain Research Reviews, 25,* 192-216. Pliszka, S.R., McCraken, J.T., & Mass, J.W. (1996). Catecholamines in attention-deficit hyperactivity disorder: Current perspectives. *Journal of the American Academy of Child and Adolescent Psychiatry, 35,* 264-272. Robinson, T., & Berridge, K. (1993). The neural basis of drug craving: An incentive-sensitization theory of addiction. *Brain Research Reviews, 18,* 247-291.

Lecture Suggestion 3: Observational Issues in Identifying Children with ADHD There are several issues concerning the need for systematic observation in order to accurately diagnose a child with ADHD and to correctly characterize the syndrome. A discussion of these issues provides additional lessons about the use of observation in both practical and scientific applications.

First, discuss the reasons that ADHD typically is not identified until children are in the first or second grade. A basic point is that the normal, everyday behavior of preschool children is so "hyperactive" in its own right that the behavior does not necessarily draw attention to children who have the disorder. Another way of stating this is that we do not have a sufficient observational basis for identifying ADHD early on. Most of the symptoms of ADHD typically become troublesome when children engage in structured activities. Prior to entering the school system, the impulsivity and attention deficits are not problematic given that most activities are unstructured. Furthermore, identification of this "abnormality" depends heavily on careful identification of normal behavioral patterns among children. Most parents do not have the experience to differentiate typical playfulness in young children from atypical behavior.

Second, consider the possibility that hyperactivity is less a problem of too many behaviors and more a problem of too much disorganized behavior. In the 1970s, researchers made systematic, comparative observations of normal children, hyperactive children, and hyperactive children being treated with Ritalin. They found that those receiving Ritalin did not "slow down," but rather became more organized in their play. This finding called into question the notion that Ritalin (a stimulant) has a truly paradoxical effect (tranquilizing), and gave more support to the idea that the drug acts on brain processes that monitor and organize behavior (see Lecture Suggestion 2: ADHD—An Intolerance for Childhood Playfulness).

Thus, casual observation of ADHD is inadequate to characterize the disorder. Careful descriptions are needed of both "normal" children and those who have the syndrome, as well as detailed, systematic observations of the behavior of the children in question.

- Assessments need to be multidimensional. Assessment should include parent, teacher, and possibly peer reports, plus observation in the naturalistic setting.
  - Parents can observe their child in a variety of settings and note fluctuations in behavior in response to varying demands in different situations.
  - Teachers can use various rating scales to facilitate their observations of the child's behavior on a daily basis. These scales also provide a normative comparison relative to other children's behavior in the same settings. This normative perspective is important for comparisons of children of the same age and setting expectations.

- Systematic observations in play and school settings help experts quantify time spent off-task and provide information on the child's functioning. These are important observations of current behavior given that parent and teacher observations may be biased or confounded by past behavior.
- Sociometric assessment can highlight peer popularity, rejection, social loneliness, and social anxiety which may influence children's behavior.

Lecture Suggestion 4: Environmental Influences on Literacy The purpose of this lecture is to examine research findings related to environmental influences on children's literacy. Santrock addresses the controversy between the phonics method and the whole-word method to teaching reading. While these methods obviously factor into children's learning to read, early experiences also influence this ability. Considerable research has examined adults' conversations with children and the influence of parent-child interactions on literacy and language development (Crain-Thoreson & Dale, 1992; Huttenlocher, 1997; Snow, 1993).

- Reading development is influenced by early literacy activities such as "reading" picture books and story telling. Parents that ask their child to retell a story are facilitating the young child's ability to read. Snow found that children's vocabulary is enhanced by exposure to adults who use relatively uncommon words in everyday conversations with the child. Family contexts, especially adult-child conversations, increase the likelihood of the child developing a larger vocabulary and ability to recognize the words in print thus providing a strong foundation for literacy.
- Crain-Thoreson and Dale found that parental instruction in letter naming, sounds, and frequency of story reading was predictive of reading precocity at age 4 (knowledge of print conventions, invented spelling, and awareness of phonology).
- Huttenlocher reports that mothers influence children's vocabulary and grammatical structure as well. Children of "chatty" mothers averaged 131 more words than children of less talkative mothers by 20 months (by 24 months the difference was 295 words). There are differences in complexity of sentence structure relative to children's environments as well. Children who are exposed to their mother's use of complex sentences (dependent clauses, such as "When…" or "because…") are much more likely to use complex sentences. These early experiences impact a child's ability to read.
- Sources: Crain-Thoreson & Dale, P.S. (1992). Do early talkers become early readers? Linguistic precocity, preschool language, and emergent literacy. *Developmental Psychology, 28*, 421-429. Huttenlocher, J. (1997). In How to build a baby's brain by S. Begley, *Newsweek*, 1997 (spring/summer), 28-32. Snow, C.E. (1993). Families as social contexts for literacy development. *New Directions in Child Development (61, pp. 11-25).* San Francisco: Jossey-Bass.

Classroom Activities

Classroom Activity 1: Weight Control for a Young Child The purpose of this activity is to have students assess the options regarding an overweight 7-year-old child. In small groups, students should pretend to be parents of a 7-year-old who is overweight and who never exercises. Should the parents intervene? Students should list the pros and cons of intervening in the child's life. What might they do to help their child become better physically conditioned? Have them design a plan that would help the child.
Logistics:
- Group size: Small group discussion and full class discussion.
- Approximate time: Small groups (15 minutes) and full class discussion (20 minutes).
- Source: King, M. B., & Clark, D. E. (1990). *Instructor's manual to accompany children.* Dubuque, IA: Wm. C. Brown Communications, Inc.

Classroom Activity 2: Time to Tell Time? This activity highlights the development of understanding how to tell time. Have students discuss what they remember when they learned to read a clock. How did they deal with the time segments in school? Did they always lose track of time? Do they remember how long car trips seemed to take, or how endless sermons were? How did anticipation about holidays affect time? Ask them if all children learn that time is an important variable. Have students generate methods to teach children how to tell time.

Use the following information to enliven discussion and introduce new points and questions:
- Middle-class children are introduced to an organized sense of time early in life—they tend to see parents go to work at a certain time and return at a certain time, meals are scheduled, bedtime is regular, and alarm clocks are used to get them up on time for school.
- Children reared in poverty do not see adults going to work at regular times, and they are less likely to have consistent meal or bed times. As a result, they can be overwhelmed by the school day being divided into segments. They have difficulty conforming to schedules before they understand time.
- During middle childhood, children gradually improve their ability to estimate time periods.
  - By second grade, most can name the days of the week; most third-graders can name the months of the year; by fifth grade they can start with any day (month) and figure out which day (month) is three from now; by tenth grade they can start at any day (month) and count backwards.

Logistics
- Group size: Full class discussion.
- Approximate time: Full class discussion (20 minutes).
- Source: Friedman, W. (1986). The development of children's knowledge of temporal structure. *Child Development, 57*, 1386-1400. Taylor, E. (1989, February 27). Time is not on their side. *Time*, 74.

Classroom Activity 3: Is Psychology Just Common Sense? The goal of this activity is to have students predict the findings of the research studies that you present. It is sometimes assumed that psychology is "just common sense" and that the research findings are "obvious." First, describe each of the following research studies, and have students try to predict the findings. Second, describe the results and discuss why students were able to accurately or inaccurately predict the findings.
- Third-graders were shown two identical glasses filled equally full of colored liquid and asked to predict what would happen if the contents of one glass were poured into a wider glass. (Get a prediction here.)
  - About 90 percent of children predict that the level would be lower in the wider container. However, a tube was secretly connected to the third container. As water was poured into the wide container, extra water was added. The wider container actually filled up to a higher level than the narrower container. How did the third-graders answer the question: "Is there the same amount of water in the two containers?" (Get predictions and reasons here.) Over half replied that the wider container had more water. Forty-two percent said that the amount of liquid was the same. Explanations included "a trick glass that makes things look big."
- In one experiment, 6-year-olds and 9-year-olds were shown a small bit of an animal picture—not enough for them to predict what the animal was. They were then asked to predict whether another person could identify the animal from the same amount of information. What did the children say? (Get predictions and reasons here.)
  - Forty-four percent of the 6-year-olds said the other person would be able to identify the animal. Almost all of the 9-year-olds correctly realized that the other person also would not be able to identify the animal.
- Researchers asked first- and fourth-graders to imagine that they were playing with a friend (some were told the friend had been at their house before, and some were told the friend had never been over before) in the kitchen and they were asking the friend to get a particular toy from their bedroom. How well did the children do in giving toy-finding instructions? (Get predictions and reasons here.)

258

- Interestingly, both first- and fourth-graders provided more information to the friend who had never visited the house. Overall, however, fourth-graders gave more precise information about locating the toy.
- Both this example and the one above show the gradual improvements in middle childhood in the ability to judge how much information other people have and how much they need.

Logistics
- Group size: Full class discussion.
- Approximate time: Full class discussion (20 minutes).
- Source: Olson, D. R., & Astington, J. W. (1987). Seeing and knowing: On the ascription of mental states to young children. *Canadian Journal of Psychology, 41*, 399-411.Sonnenshein, S. (1988). The development of referential communication: Speaking to different listeners. *Child Development, 59*, 694-70.

Classroom Activity 4: Training Children to Use Memory Strategies The goal of this activity is to have students plan a lesson to teach a group of preschool children and a group of third-grade children memory strategies that would aid in their assigned learning tasks. After reviewing the information on memory strategies presented in the text, either as a class or in small groups, have them discuss the information. They should begin by listing the various memory strategies. Next, they should list the cognitive abilities of preschool and third-grade children. Using the information they generated, the students should develop a strategy for teaching the two age groups strategies that will aid their learning.
- Spontaneous maintenance rehearsal appears at about 5 years. Children from 5 to 10 can be taught this form of rehearsal. The youngest ones can be taught to repeat the material to be remembered. Organization, which appears spontaneously around 10, can be taught to children. The youngest children could be taught to put the remembered material into piles. Elementary school children can use imagery in the form of the keyword method. Third-grade students could probably be coached in semantic elaboration because they show spontaneous inferencing.

Logistics
- Group size: Small group and/or full class discussion.
- Approximate time: Small group (25 minutes) and/or full class discussion (30 minutes).
- Source: King, M. B., & Clark, D. B. (1989). *Instructor's manual to accompany Santrock and Yussen's child development: An introduction*, 4th ed. Dubuque, IA: Wm. C. Brown Communications, Inc.

Classroom Activity 5: Use of IQ Scores for Special Education Placement Have the students in small groups write a letter to an imaginary sister or brother whose 5-year-old child was just given an IQ test and received a score of 65. The parents have been told that the child will be placed in a class for the mentally retarded. Have the students advise their sibling.
- Here are some advice suggestions. You should not accept such a decision based only on an IQ test. Some specific local problem, such as illness or the death of a friend or pet, might cause the deficiency. The child may not have paid much attention during the test. IQ scores at young ages do not have the predictive power of IQ scores over the years. Parents should insist on (or even obtain themselves) a more extensive evaluation. They should work with the child to encourage and promote the sorts of skills the test indicates are missing. Remember a correlation as high as .8 only accounts for 64 percent of the variability, so there is plenty of room for the score to change even in one year. It would be informative if you knew your state laws, because some states do not permit such an assignment on the basis of an IQ score alone.

Logistics:
- Group size: Small group and/or full class discussion.
- Approximate time: Small group (25 minutes) and/or full class discussion (30 minutes).
- Source: King, M. B., & Clark, D. E. (1989). *Instructors manual to accompany Santrock and Yussen's child development: An introduction*, 4th ed. Dubuque, IA: Wm. C. Brown Communications, Inc.

Classroom Activity 6: Child Prodigies This activity focuses on child prodigies and complements the textbook's discussion of giftedness. Have the class discuss whether or not child prodigies or geniuses are well-adjusted or maladjusted individuals. Do they have more mental problems? Are they odd? Do they fail to live up to their expectations? In what ways can schools and families help bright youngsters adjust to their circumstances? Contrast the findings of Terman's longitudinal study of William James Sidis provided here.

- William James Sidis, the son of Russian immigrants, was taught by his father to read by age 3, type by 4, and read Russian, French, and German at 5 and Hebrew, Greek, and Latin by 6. Before he was 7, he passed out of seventh grade and passed a medical school examination on the human body. By 10, he understood integral calculus. At 12, he entered Harvard. By adolescence, he lost his goals and dropped out of graduate school. He lost a teaching job, was arrested at a radical demonstration, refused to attend his father's funeral, and became a cynical and eccentric person holding clerical jobs. He was poor and unemployed when he died at 46 from a brain hemorrhage. Rumors existed that he committed suicide.

The Sidis example has been given many times as a reason that schools should not have acceleration and enrichment programs. However, more case examples suggest that "burnout" is rare and successes are much more likely. Have students propose alternative explanations for Sidis's decline. Have them suggest ways to help child geniuses.

Logistics:
- Group size: Full class discussion.
- Approximate time: 15 minutes for full class discussion.
- Source: Montour, K. (1977). William James Sidis, the broken twig. *American Psychologist, 32,* 265-279. Townsend, J. K., & Gensley, J. T. (1978). The experts read to stereotyping gifted children. *The Gifted Child Quarterly, 22,* 217-219.

Classroom Activity 7: Critical Thinking Multiple-Choice Questions and Suggested Answers Discuss the answers to the critical thinking multiple-choice questions (**Handout 1**). Question 1 differs from previous exercises in that it requires students to use information they learn in chapter 10 to evaluate a program for children. Or more broadly, this material could be used to have students evaluate the sports programs of their own elementary school years, be they school programs, city athletic leagues, or YMCA programs. The "trick" in this question is using the material in ways that are relevant to the aims and goals of the Chinese sports schools. For example, alternative "e" is certainly true, but it is irrelevant. The schools are designed to foster special talent, so handicapped individuals are deliberately excluded. The same idea is true for choice "a," because the school only admits children who are advanced in motor development compared to their peers. Discuss with students the notion that criticism can occur on different levels and have different purposes. In the case of the sports schools, Santrock seems to be more concerned with the fates of the children who attend them rather than with broader social or political issues.

Question 2 is similar to exercises students have done for the previous cognition chapters. Their task is to integrate information in the chapter and draw appropriate conclusions about the material. This is essentially a comprehension exercise, and students will probably do it well.

Question 3 is based on material from the second edition of Santrock's *Children*. The main point of this exercise is to get students to see how the contemporary debate about national differences in mathematics achievement has been framed entirely in terms of nurture differences between countries like Japan and the United States. Commentators have seemingly assumed that there are no differences between Japanese and United States children that could account for the observed performance differences, and they have been willing to accept causal interpretations about the influence of observed differences in educational practices. This is particularly interesting in comparison with the willingness of many to entertain seriously the idea that racial differences in intellectual level and achievement in the United States are based on genetic or motivational differences between classes and races of people. You may want to discuss this irony as preparation for this exercise. The answers are presented as **Handout 2**.

- Materials: Handout 2 (the critical thinking multiple-choice questions) and Handout 3 (answers).
- Group size: Small groups to discuss the questions, then a full class discussion.
- Approximate time: Small groups (15 minutes), full class discussion of any questions (15 minutes).

Classroom Activity 8: Critical Thinking Essay Questions and Suggestions for Helping Students Answer the Essays Discuss the students' answers to the critical thinking essay questions (**Handout 3**). The purpose of this activity is threefold. First, the answering of these questions facilitates students' understanding of concepts in chapter 10. Second, this type of essay question affords the students an opportunity to apply the concepts to their own lives, which will facilitate their retention of the material. Third, the essay format also will give students practice expressing themselves in written form. Ideas to help students answer the critical thinking essay questions are provided as **Handout 4**.
Logistics:
- Materials: Handout 3 (essay questions) and Handout 4 (helpful suggestions for the answers).
- Group size: Individual, then full class.
- Approximate time: Individual (60 minutes), full class discussion of any questions (30 minutes).

Personal Applications

Personal Application 1: That's My Kid! The purpose of this exercise is for students to reflect on their childhood activities. By middle childhood, children are very active, and often become involved in various extracurricular activities. There are many benefits to participation in such activities, physical activity and social experiences, but there can be detriments if parents approach their children's activities with an improper perspective.
- Instructions for Students: Recall the activities of your childhood. What did you participate in? Were these activities your parents' idea or yours? Did they simply suggest things and offer you a choice, or were you enrolled without being consulted? Did they positively support and encourage your interests and participation? Were they demanding and critical, exerting pressure on you to perform? How did your early experiences with these endeavors influence your subsequent behavior and attitudes about being involved in particular activities? Any remaining impact today?
- Use in the Classroom: Explore the ways in which parents approach directing their children's interest in various activities. What might determine how they respond to their children's performance, and what various results might manifest themselves in children's behavior and attitudes? Which do you think is better developmentally: children participating in a number of different activities, one at a time; children participating in a number of different activities simultaneously; children participating in a single activity, and developing their skills over an extended period of time? What are the possible benefits and disadvantages of each?

Personal Application 2: Remember the Time... The purpose of this exercise is to demonstrate to students the long-term memory capabilities of middle childhood, through recollection of their own childhood experiences. Memory development continues during middle and late childhood, enabling children to encode information in such a way as to significantly contribute to their long-term memory.
- Instructions for Students: Recall, in as much detail as you can, an event from your childhood—when you were somewhere between the ages of 6 and 10. What do you think enabled you to remember this experience for all of these years? Did you think at the time that it was something you'd never forget? Are you certain that what you remember is accurate or have you "filled in the blanks" with you imagination over the years? How much can you remember from this period in your life? Was recalling this event easy or difficult? Do you have many more recollections from your childhood? If so, is there something similar about them which may lead to your remembering them? If not, why might that be, and at what point in your life do you begin to have lots of memories?

- Use in the Classroom: This may be a fun and interesting format for a class discussion on children's memory encoding. If students are willing to share their various childhood stories, they may provide amusing examples of children's information processing, and serve as prompts for exploring the accuracy of recall. And you can share your own childhood memories too!

Personal Application 3: Smart Move The purpose of this exercise is to prompt students to assess their intellectual strengths from the various perspectives of multiple kinds of intelligence. Rather than assume our intellectual functioning can be summed up in a single number—the score on a traditional IQ test—some theorists believe that we have particular intellectual strengths and weaknesses. Robert Sternberg's triarchic theory of intelligence identifies three areas of intelligence: analytical, creative, and practical. Individuals can be strong in any or all of the three domains. Howard Gardner theorizes eight different types of intelligence, addressing everything from verbal functioning to music and interpersonal skills. Both approaches assume an individual's intelligence profile will manifest itself in their academic and life functioning.
- Instructions for Students: Identify your intellectual profile based on both Sternberg's and Gardner's categories. What areas are you strong in? In what areas do you demonstrate weaknesses? How have these strengths and weaknesses impacted your experiences in school? How have they played a role in your decision as to what to major in and what career path you'll take? Have they influenced you socially in any way? Discuss your opinion of assessing intelligence as such.
- Use in the Classroom: Discuss intelligence in general. Can it be measured accurately? Should it be assessed at all? How might this be problematic to individuals or society as a whole? Is the concept of the IQ as relevant and important as that of the existence of multiple intelligences? What practical use might be made of Sternberg's and Gardner's theories? How early on in life should intelligence—in any form—be assessed? Who should be privy to this information and why? Discuss students' views on breeding for intelligence—what effect might this have on society? Also, have students develop their own items for fairly (no cultural, ethnic, or gender bias) assessing intelligence. This will demonstrate the tremendous challenge of working in this field of human development.
- Sources: Gardner, H. (1993). *Multiple Intelligences.* New York: Basic Books. Sternberg, R.J. (1999). Intelligence. In M.A. Runco & S. Pritzker (Eds.), *Encyclopedia of creativity.* San Diego: Academic Press.

Personal Application 4: Exploring Your Creativity The purpose of this exercise is to encourage students to think about the creativity within themselves to gain a more complete perspective of it's role in life-span development. Some developmental psychologists debate whether or not creativity is an aspect of intelligence. Regardless of their perspective, psychologists do agree that creativity is an important aspect of thinking and functioning in life.
- Instructions for Students: Describe the ways in which you are creative. Don't limit yourself to thinking of creativity as only manifesting itself in artistic ability. There are numerous ways in which individuals can be creative—what are yours? Provide examples. If you do not believe you are in any way creative, describe the efforts you've made to be creative. What were the results? Why don't you think you've developed creative abilities? What might you do to expand your creative functioning?
- Use in the Classroom: Construct a brainstorming activity or present a unique problem to be solved. Place students who believe they are creative in small groups with those who say they aren't. Have groups work together to creatively solve a problem, or develop something new. Afterwards, have groups share their efforts, and have the self-proclaimed "non-creative students" discuss what they observed and learned from their creative peers. Try another exercise in which the less creative students can apply what they've learned. What changed in their approach to the situation? How did they think about it differently? Conclude by pointing out, through studies and their methodologies, that science, and certainly developmental psychology, is a very creative field!

Research Project Ideas

Research Project 1: Current Exercise Levels In this exercise, your students will interview three people about their current exercise levels. One subject should be 5 years old, one 10 years old, and one 18 to 20. (If the students are between 18 and 20 years old, they may use themselves as one of the subjects.) The project will have to be approved by the human subjects review board at your school and they will need to get a signed informed consent form from the children's parents. See the section on Ethics, Human Subjects, and Informed Consent at the front of this Instructor's Manual. They can use the interview questions on **Handout 5** to record each person's responses and to answer the questions that follow.

- In what kinds of activities does the 5-year-old engage? How much time a week does the 5-year-old spend exercising? How often does the 5-year-old exercise?
- In what kinds of activities does the 10-year-old engage? How much time a week does the 10-year-old spend exercising? How often does the 10-year-old exercise?
- In what kinds of activities does the 18-year-old engage? How much time a week does the 18-year-old spend exercising? How often does the 18-year-old exercise?
- What differences do you find in activity level between the three different ages? Are there differences in the kinds of exercise engaged in at the different ages? If so, what are these?
- Could variables other than age determine differences between your subjects' reported activity levels? What are these?
- Use in the Classroom: Have the students present their data from the research project. Examine the data for age and sex differences in patterns of exercise. What activities do males and females perform? How do these differ at different ages? Is amount of exercise a function of age or of sex? What other variables might account for differences between individuals besides age and sex?
  - One might expect males to be more active than females, and regular exercise for all individuals to increase with age. The latter trend might be from a conscious decision to exercise. However, it could be that children are more active than adolescents and therefore exercise more. Individual variation can include parental models and reinforcement for participating in sports.

Research Project 2: Assessment of a Preoperational and a Concrete Operational Thinker The purpose of this exercise is for students to see an example of a preoperational and a concrete operational reasoner. Students should pair up with another class member and test two children, a 4- to 5-year-old child and an 8- to 9-year-old child, using several of Piaget's tasks. They should administer two conservation and two classification tasks to each child, and then compare the children's responses with each other and attempt to interpret those responses in view of Piaget's theory. In order to test the two children, they will need to clear this through the human subjects review board at your school and get a signed informed consent form from the children's parents. See the section on Ethics, Human Subjects, and Informed Consent at the front of this Instructor's Manual.

A description of the tasks, the data sheet for recording the observations, and a list of questions to answer are presented as **Handout 6**.

- **Conservation Task 1:** Conservation of number task. Make two sets of ten identical items. Each set should be a different color (e.g., one set of ten blue poker chips and one set of ten white poker chips). Place one row of ten same-colored items in front of the child. Ask the child to make an identical row with the other set. Ask the child if the two rows have the same number of items or if one row has more. Do not go on until the rows are identical in number and arrangement and the child agrees that the two rows are the same. Now spread one row out and push the other row together so that the display looks as follows:

OOOOOOOOOO
o o o o o o o o o o

- Ask the child if the rows are the same or if one row has more. Ask the child why it is the same or why one has more, and which one, if either, has more. If the child says one row has more, ask the child where the more came from. Record all responses.

- **Conservation Task 2:** Conservation of liquid task. Pour an identical amount of juice into two identical glasses. Ask the child if the two glasses have the same amount, and adjust the volume in each glass until the child agrees that both have the same. Now pour the liquid from one glass into a taller, thinner glass. Ask the child if the amount of juice is the same in both glasses or if one has more. If the child thinks one has more, ask which one. Have the child justify the judgment of having the same or different amount. Record all responses.

- **Classification Task 1:** Classification of groups. Present the child with cutouts of big and small triangles, circles, and squares. Some of the shapes should be red, some blue, and some green. Ask the child to put together those things that go together. Record how the child sorts the objects. Now ask the child if there is another way to put the objects together. Record the second sort.

- **Classification Task 2:** Present the child with a set of wooden beads, with ten red and two blue. (You can substitute poker chips or M&Ms.) Ask the child if there are more red beads or more blue beads. If the child were to make a train with the red beads and another train with the blue beads, which train would be longer? Now ask the child if there are more red beads or more wooden beads. If the child were to make a train with the red beads and another train with the wooden beads, which train would be longer?

Questions:
- Which tasks did the 4- to 5-year-old child solve? How would you characterize the nature of the child's responses to the questions?
- Which tasks did the 8- to 9-year-old child solve? How would you characterize the nature of the child's responses to the questions?
- How would you characterize the differences between the performance of the younger and older child on these tasks?
- What do these observations tell you about Piaget's theory? How would the children be classified into Piaget's stages based on their responses to your problems?
- Use in the Classroom: Have students present data from the research project in class. Pool the data for the two age groups, and compare mean performance for each age group. What kinds of behaviors were seen in the 4- to 5-year-olds? What kinds of justifications did they give for their answers? What kinds of answers did they give? How did the 8- to 9-year-olds differ from them? How do the class data relate to Piaget's theory?
  - The expectation is that the 4- to 5-year-olds will not be able to do either the simple classification task or the class inclusion task. The 4- to 5-year-olds are also nonconservers for liquid and probably for numbers. The 8- to 9-year-olds will be able to do all the classification and conservation tasks.

Film and Video List

The following films and videos supplement the content of chapter 10. Contact information for film distributors can be found at the front of this Instructor's Manual under Film and Video Sources.

All about ADD, Part 1 (Insight Media, 108 minutes). This video outlines eight symptoms of ADD and their effects on home, school, and social life. In addition, it traces the prognosis and causes of ADD.

All about ADD, Part 2 (Insight Media, 85 minutes). This program uses clinical examples to illustrate diagnosis and treatment of ADD.

The Diagnosis and Treatment of Attention Deficit Disorder in Children (Films for the Humanities and Sciences, 29 minutes). This program demonstrates the diagnosis of Attention Deficit Disorder and the available treatments. It follows children at home and school with and without medication.

Dyslexia: A Different Kind of Mind (Films for the Humanities and Sciences, 29 minutes). This program focuses on children with dyslexia and how new teaching techniques help them succeed in school.

The Elementary Mind (Insight Media, 30 minutes). This video looks at concrete operations, conceptualization, memory strategies, mental effort, and controversies in measuring intelligence.

The Gifted Child (Films for the Humanities and Sciences, 24 minutes). This program identifies characteristics of a gifted child and addresses educational needs to facilitate in the understanding the gifted children. Having a gifted child can present challenges for teachers, parents and childcare providers.

Intelligence (Insight Media, 30 minutes). This video covers the definition of intelligence, origins and design of intelligence tests, and the controversy about whether the tests measure aptitude or achievement.

Intelligence, Creativity, and Thinking Styles (Films for the Humanities and Sciences, 30 minutes). This program discusses IQ and triarchic theories of intelligence. It discusses school reform issues and the roles of teachers and family in shaping intelligence.

Kids' Sports (Films for the Humanities and Sciences, 30 minutes). This program scrutinizes the current state of organized youth sports. It looks at how the old values of fun and fair play have been undermined.

Medication for ADD (Insight Media, , 80 minutes). This program covers the benefits, side effects, and duration of stimulants, tricyclics, Prozac, and other medications.

Middle Childhood: Cognitive Growth and Development (Magna Systems, 28 minutes). This program discusses Piaget's theory of concrete operational development and information-processing abilities during middle childhood. In addition, topics related to language are examined.

Middle Childhood: Physical Growth and Development (Magna Systems, 28 minutes). This video explores the physical changes that take place between the ages of 6 and 12 years and related topics.

Obesity: Pain and Prejudice (Films for the Humanities and Sciences, 40 minutes). This program was developed in reference to a mother convicted of child abuse after her seriously overweight daughter died as a result of obesity. The topics discussed include prejudice against the overweight population, failing medical systems, society's habit of equating beauty with being thin, what constitutes obesity, and obesity as it relates to health issues.

Out of Control: Hyperactive Children (Filmakers Library, 14 minutes). This video deals with children that are hyperactive by exploring their problems and treatment with both drugs and therapy.

Stress, Health, and Coping (Insight Media, 30 minutes). This program uses case studies to explore daily stressors, loss of love, and post traumatic stress disorder. Narration by Norman Cousins covers Selye's GAS, stress and illness, and methods of coping with stress.

Understanding Attention Deficit Hyperactivity Disorder (Films for the Humanities and Sciences, 20 minutes). This program offers diverse and candid opinions from both sides of the debate as to whether Attention Deficit Hyperactivity Disorder is physiological or psychological in origin. It also discusses treatment including medication and behavior modification.

Understanding Learning Disabilities (Films for the Humanities and Sciences, 16 minutes).This program offers expert insight into the nature of learning disabilities, why they may also be accompanied by Attention Deficit Hyperactivity Disorder or social disorders, and what can be done to help children learn to compensate and succeed.

Web Site Suggestions

The URLs for general sites, common to all chapters, can be found at the front of this Instructor's Manual under Useful Web Sites. At the time of publication, all sites were current and active, however, please be advised that you may occasionally encounter a dead link.

Attention Deficit Hyperactivity Disorder, Dyslexia, Learning Disabilities
http://www.cdipage.com/index.htm

Children with Learning Disabilities
http://www.aacap.org/web/aacap/publications/factsfam/ld.htm

Creativity Home Page
http://www.ozemail.com.au/~caveman/Creative/

Gifted Children
http://www.kidsource.com/Forums?14@@.ee6b4d3

Learning to Read and Whole-Language Ideology
http://www.heinemann.com/info/08894f3.html

Mental Retardation
http://www.healthanswers.com/database/ami/converted/001523.html

Twice Exceptional - Gifted and Learning Disabled
http://www.bow.k12.nh.us/rmann/gtld/gtldfull/index.html

Whole Language versus Phonics
http://www.teachers.net/chatboard/topic5021/11.10.97.18.34.50.html

Critical Thinking Multiple-Choice Questions

1. The following vignette (quoted from the 6th edition of Santrock's *Life-Span Development*) sketches life for children who attend sports schools in China to prepare for the Olympics.

    Standing on the balance beam at a sports school in Beijing, China, 6-year-old Zhang Liyin stretches her arms outward as she gets ready to perform a backflip. She wears the bright-red gymnastic suit of the elite—a suit given to only the best ten girls in her class of 6- to 8-year-olds. But her face wears a dreadful expression; she can't drum up enough confidence to do the flip. Maybe it is because she has had a rough week; a purple bruise decorates one leg, and a nasty gash disfigures the other. Her coach, a woman in her twenties, makes Zhang jump from the beam and escorts her to the high bar, where she is instructed to hang for 3 minutes. If Zhang falls, she must pick herself up and try again. But she does not fall, and she is escorted back to the beam, where her coach puts her through another tedious routine.

    Zhang attends the sports school in the afternoon. The sports schools are a privilege given to only 260,000 of China's 200 million students of elementary to college age. The Communist party has decided that sports is one avenue China can pursue to prove that China has arrived in the modern world. The sports schools designed to produce Olympic champions were the reason for China's success in the 1984, 1988, and 1992 Olympics. These schools are the only road to Olympic stardom in China. There are precious few neighborhood playgrounds. And for every 3.5 million people, there is only one gymnasium.

    Many of the students who attend the sports schools in the afternoon live and study at the schools as well. Only a few attend a normal school and then come to a sports school in the afternoon. Because of her young age, Zhang stays at home during the mornings and goes to the sports school from noon until 6pm. A part-timer like Zhang can stay enrolled until she no longer shows potential to move up to the next step. Any child who seems to lack potential is asked to leave.

    Zhang was playing in a kindergarten class when a coach from a sports school spotted her. She was selected because of her broad shoulders, narrow hips, straight legs, symmetrical limbs, open-minded attitude, vivaciousness, and outgoing personality. If Zhang continues to show progress, she could be asked to move to full-time next year. At age 7, she would then go to school there and live in a dorm 6 days a week. If she becomes extremely competent at gymnastics, Zhang could be moved to Shishahia, where the elite gymnasts train and compete (Reilly, 1988).

    Although Santrock does not explicitly criticize these sports schools, the tone of his treatment conveys his disapproval of them. Which of the following topics presented in chapter 10 provides a basis for the most severe criticism of sports schools in China? Circle the letter of the best answer and explain why it is the best answer and why each other answer is not as good.

    a. The training program in the sports schools does not conform to the developmental timetable for gross and fine motor skills.
    b. Children in the sports schools are required to be too active.
    c. The program is imposing competitive values from another culture on the children.
    d. The training programs are too stressful for children.
    e. There is no place for handicapped children in the training program.

2. In chapter 8, you learned about preoperational thinking. In chapter 10, you now are learning about concrete operational thinking. In chapter 13, you will learn about formal operational thinking. After you review the appropriate sections in these three chapters, indicate which of the following cases best illustrates concrete operations. Hint: There is more than one example of concrete operational thinking. Circle the letters of the best answers and explain why they are the best answers and why each other answer is not as good.

   a. Katie is asked, "Do you have a brother?" She says, "Yes." Then she is asked, "Does he have a sister?" She answers, "No."

   b. Ray says, "A fly is like both insects and birds. It's like birds because it flies, but it's like insects because it has six legs."

   c. Tim is working on analogies. He declares, "Biking is to pedaling as riding in a car is to stepping on the gas pedal because they both make the vehicle go!"

   d. Bobby states, "I understand how this nickel and these five pennies are the same as this dime."

   e. Her teacher asks Mary, "How can the scale be brought back into balance?" Mary replies, "The only way to do that is to remove the weight that made one pan sink lower than the other."

3. Read the following passage entitled "Achievement in Math Requires Time and Practice: Comparisons of Children in the United States and Japan."

   Harold Stevenson and his colleagues (1986) recently conducted a detailed investigation of math achievement in first- and fifth-grade children from the United States and Japan. The final sample included 240 first-graders and 240 fifth-graders from each country. Extensive time was spent developing the math test that was given to the children, who were observed in their classrooms, and additional information was obtained from mothers, teachers, and the children themselves. The findings of Stevenson et al. revealed that Japanese children clearly outscored the American children on the math test in both the first and fifth grades. Japanese first-grade boys outscored U.S. first-grade boys 20.7 to 16.6, and Japanese first-grade girls outscored U.S. first-grade girls 19.5 to 17.6. In the fifth-grade, the highest average score of any of the American classrooms fell below the worst-performing score of the Japanese classrooms, with Japanese fifth-grade boys outscoring their U.S. counterparts 53.0 to 45.0, and Japanese fifth-grade girls outscoring their U.S. counterparts 53.5 to 43.8.

   What are some reasons for these dramatic differences between American and Japanese children's math achievement? Curriculum did not seem to be a factor. Neither did the educational background of the children's parents. And neither did intelligence; the American children sample actually scored slightly higher than the Japanese children on such components of intelligence as vocabulary, general information, verbal ability, and perceptual speed. Possibly the Japanese teachers had more experience? Apparently, this was not the case, since in terms of educational degrees and years of teaching experiences, no differences were found. The amount of time spent in school and math classes probably was an important factor. The Japanese school year consists of 240 days of instruction and each school week is 6 days long. The American school year consists of 178 days of instruction and each school week is 5 days long. In the fifth grade, Japanese children were in school an average of 37.3 hours per week, American children only 30 hours. Observations in the children's classrooms revealed that Japanese teachers spent far more time teaching math than did American teachers; approximately one-fourth of total classroom time in the first grade was spent in math instruction in Japan, only approximately one-tenth in the United States. Observations also indicated that the Japanese children attended more efficiently to what the teacher was saying than American children did. And Japanese children spent far more time doing homework than American children—on weekends, 66 minutes versus 18 minutes, respectively.

And in another recent investigation, Chinese children were assigned more homework and spent more time on homework than Japanese children, who, in turn, were assigned more homework and spent more time on homework than American children (Chen & Stevenson, 1989). Chinese children had more positive attitudes about homework than Japanese children, who in turn had more positive attitudes about homework than American children. The conclusion: Learning requires time and practice. When either is reduced, learning is impaired.

- Source: Chen, C., & Stevenson, H. W. (1989). Homework: A cross-cultural examination. *Child Development, 60,* 551-561.

On the basis of this information, indicate which of the following statements constitutes an assumption rather than an inference or an observation. Circle the letter of the best answer and explain why it is the best answer and why each other answer is not as good. Hint: There is more than one assumption.

a. There are no genetic differences between Japanese and American children that could influence mathematics achievement.
b. The differences between Japanese and American children's scores are smallest for first-grade girls.
c. The difference in achievement is caused by the amount of time spent in school.
d. Differences in achievement are not associated with differences in teacher experience.
e. Japanese and American children are equally motivated to achieve in mathematics.

Suggested Answers for Critical Thinking Multiple-Choice Questions

1. The vignette (quoted from the 6th edition of Santrock's *Life-Span Development*) you read sketches life for children who attend sports schools in China to prepare for the Olympics. Although Santrock does not explicitly criticize these sports schools, the tone of his treatment conveys his disapproval of them. Which of the following topics presented in chapter 10 provides a basis for the most severe criticism of sports schools in China? Circle the letter of the best answer and explain why it is the best answer and why each other answer is not as good.

a. The training program in the sports schools does not conform to the developmental timetable for gross and fine motor skills is not the basis for the criticism. The programs do not require that children do what they are not able to do. Only children who are relatively advanced in their motor development are accepted in the program.

b. Children in the sports schools are required to be too active is not the basis for the criticism. Children in middle to late childhood need a great deal of physical activity. Although challenging, the sports schools probably provide a superb physical regimen for children in this age bracket.

c. The program is imposing competitive values from another culture on the children is not the basis for the criticism. In fact, there is no discussion of the expression of cultural values in sport in the chapter. The Chinese programs are as much an expression of Chinese culture as they are an expression of values held in other cultures about sports achievement.

d. The training programs are too stressful for children is the basis of the criticism. The physical training is hard and injury-producing. There are few opportunities for rest and relaxation, particularly after setbacks. Children suffer punishment and occasional humiliation. If we apply the findings from North American children, the Chinese children in these schools often experience stressful daily hassles. Moreover, they are likely to experience these in combination, which multiplies the stress children undergo.

e. There is no place for handicapped children in the training program is not the basis for the criticism. The main reason is that point is irrelevant. The schools are not intended to serve all children. They admit only children who have exceptional talent for gymnastics.

2. In chapter 8, you learned about preoperational thinking. In chapter 10, you now are learning about concrete operational thinking. In chapter 13, you will learn about formal operational thinking. After you review the appropriate sections in these three chapters, indicate which of the following cases best illustrates concrete operations. Hint: There is more than one example of concrete operational thinking. Circle the letters of the best answers and explain why they are the best answers and why each other answer is not as good.

a. Katie is asked, "Do you have a brother?" She says, "Yes." Then she is asked, "Does he have a sister?" She answers, "No." is not an example of concrete operational thinking. Katie fails to understand that sibling relationships are reciprocal, which is a sign of preoperational thinking (irreversibility).

b. Ray says, "A fly is like both insects and birds. It's like birds because it flies, but it's like insects because it has six legs." is an example of concrete operational thinking. In this example, Ray is able to understand that flies have attributes that place them in more than one category (creatures that fly and creatures with six legs). According to Piaget this is a concrete operational skill.

c. Tim is working on analogies. He declares, "Biking is to pedaling as riding in a car is to stepping on the gas pedal because they both make the vehicle go!" is not an example of concrete operational thinking. In this example, Tim declares that he understands the equivalence of two abstract relationships, which is an aspect of formal operations.

d. Bobby states, "I understand how this nickel and these five pennies are the same as this dime." is an example of concrete operational thinking. Bobby is working with two concrete representations of money and is able to add the values of the nickels and pennies to confirm their equivalence to the dime. The equivalence also implies reversibility. All of these points characterize concrete operational thinking.

e. Her teacher asks Mary, "How can the scale be brought back into balance?" Mary replies, "The only way to do that is to remove the weight that made one pan sink lower than the other." is an example of concrete operational thinking. In this example, Mary shows reversibility. However, she can only think of one solution to the problem and fails to realize that there are several ways to balance a scale, an aspect of concrete operations.

3. After reading the vignette entitled, " Achievement in Math Requires Time and Practice: Comparisons of Children in the United States and Japan," indicate which of the following statements constitutes an assumption rather than an inference or an observation. (Hint: There is more than one assumption.) Circle the letters of the best answers and explain why they are the best answers and why each other answer is not as good.

a. There are no genetic differences between Japanese and American children that could influence mathematics achievement is an assumption. There are no data on this point, yet it must be true if we want to say that the differences in performance are due to different educational practices. An interesting point is that this is not assumed in discussions of differences between intelligence scores of African American and White children.

b. The differences between Japanese and American children's scores are smallest for first-grade girls is an observation. It is a direct statement describing the children's scores.

c. The difference in achievement is caused by the amount of time spent in school is an inference. It is an interpretation of the finding that Japanese students both spend more time in school and have higher mathematics achievement scores. There is nothing in these facts that indicates a necessary connection between them.

d. Differences in achievement are not associated with differences in teacher experience is an observation. No association between these two variables was found.

e. Japanese and American children are equally motivated to achieve in mathematics is an assumption. Motivation is a relevant concern, but apparently no data were collected about it. Thus the researchers assumed that motivation was equal for both Japanese and American students.

Critical Thinking Essay Questions

Your answers to this kind of question demonstrate an ability to comprehend and apply ideas discussed in this chapter.

1. Describe physical growth and changes in gross and fine motor skills during middle and late childhood.

2. Imagine that you are a parent of children who want to compete in sports. Explain how you would evaluate the pros and cons of their participation in high-pressure sports.

3. Describe the consequences of childhood obesity and explain why middle and late childhood is an especially difficult time for a child to be obese.

4. Differentiate between inclusion and mainstreaming and discuss the challenges to teaching of including children with disabilities, such as learning disabilities and attention deficit hyperactivity disorder, in regular classrooms.

5. Explain and give examples of characteristics of concrete operational thought according to Piaget.

6. Discuss at least three findings that challenge Piaget's theory about cognitive development.

7. Explain why and how information-processing psychologists distinguish among control processes and learner characteristics.

8. Compare and contrast metacognitive knowledge and critical thinking. Also, explain how these ideas relate to education and everyday life.

9. Compare and contrast Binet's and Sternberg's views of intelligence.

10. Explain why developmentalists try to create culture-fair tests, and evaluate their success to date.

11. Explain why and how mental retardation, giftedness, and creativity reflect the extremes of intelligence.

12. Discuss how the development of concrete operations and other aspects of cognitive development may lead to improvement in reading during middle and late childhood.

13. What is bilingual education? What is known about bilingualism? How successful have bilingual education programs been?

Ideas to Help You Answer Critical Thinking Essay Questions

1. As you discuss the physical changes, relate them to specific examples of both gross and fine motor skills. Address how the particular skills result from the physical changes that have taken place, and compare later functioning based on physical development to earlier limitations in motor ability.

2. You might want to create a pros and cons list for a variety of different sports. Do some tend to be more demanding than others? Consider that you are doing this task to assist your child in choosing a particular sport or sports to participate in. What would be your recommendations and why?

3. Begin by painting a picture of the experiences of an obese child. Consider various activities children engage in at school and on the playground. Consider the importance of friendships at this stage in life. Consider the logistical aspects of an obese child—fitting into standard size desks, sitting on a school bus, being required to engage in physical fitness activities, and the physical consequences of doing so.

4. Answer this question not only from the teacher's perspective, but from the perspective of a parent of a learning disabled child. What experience would you want for your child and why? Briefly discuss the issue of how difficult it is to meet both the parents' and teachers' needs.

5. Begin your discussion of concrete operational thought with a description of preoperational cognitive functioning. This will highlight the accomplishments that occur with the onset of concrete thinking.

6. Prior to each finding that challenges Piaget, present Piagetian theory, reasoning, and experimentation.

7. Begin by presenting a brief introduction to the information-processing approach. What aspects of cognitive development does it address, and from what perspective? After this address the issues of control processes and learner characteristics, and the rationale behind these aspects of the theory.

8. Define metacognitive knowledge and critical thinking, providing specific examples of each. Proceed with your comparison in terms of their role and relationship to education and our daily functioning.

9. Make a list of the issues each theory addresses. Your comparison can begin at this point: do they deal with the same aspects of intellectual functioning? Continue to look at their particular theoretical perspectives, methods of assessment, and application to real life.

10. What is the purpose of having culture-fair tests? How are they used in a practical sense? Provide examples of such tests and items that have been considered culturally biased.

11. Define what is meant by intelligence. If we know an individual's level of intelligence, of what use is that information? What if there were no such assessments for intellectual functioning? How might that affect education and our dealings with individuals regarding their intellectual ability? Tie all of these issues into the concept of intellectual extremes.

12. Provide an overview of concrete cognitive functioning. What kinds of thought are present? How does it differ from earlier thought processes? Then present the concepts behind reading and learning to read. What is the cognitive nature of reading?

13. Present the definition of bilingualism, followed by an itemized list as to what is known about its nature. Discuss bilingual education programs based on these factors, and address their relative failure or success in these terms.

Current Exercise Levels

In this exercise, you will interview three people about their current exercise levels. One subject should be 5 years old, one 10 years old, and one 18 to 20. (If you are between 18 and 20 years old, you may use yourself as one of the subjects.) Use the interview questions to record each person's responses. Then, answer the questions that follow.

DATA SHEET

	Person 1 Sex___ Age ___	Person 2 Sex___ Age ___	Person 3 Sex ___ Age ___
How often do you exercise each week?			
What kinds of activities do you do?			
How much time do you spend exercising each week?			

Questions:
- In what kinds of activities does the 5-year-old engage? How much time a week does the 5-year-old spend exercising? How often does the 5-year-old exercise?

- In what kinds of activities does the 10-year-old engage? How much time a week does the 10-year-old spend exercising? How often does the 10-year-old exercise?

- In what kinds of activities does the 18-year-old engage? How much time a week does the 18-year-old spend exercising? How often does the 18-year-old exercise?

- What differences do you find in activity level between the three different ages? Are there differences in the kinds of exercise engaged in at the different ages? If so, what are these?

- Could variables other than age determine differences between your subjects' reported activity levels? What are these?

Assessment of a Preoperational and a Concrete Operational Thinker

The purpose of this exercise is for you to see an example of a preoperational and a concrete operational reasoner. Pair up with another class member and test two children, a 4- to 5-year-old child and an 8- to 9-year-old child, using several of Piaget's tasks. Administer two conservation and two classification tasks to each child, and then compare the children's responses with each other and attempt to interpret those responses in view of Piaget's theory. In order to test the two children, you will need to clear this through the human subjects review board at your school and get a signed informed consent form from the children's parents. A description of the tasks, the data sheet for recording the observations, and a list of questions to answer are presented below.

Conservation Tasks

Conservation Task 1: Conservation of number task. Make two sets of ten identical items. Each set should have a different color (e.g., one set of ten blue poker chips and one set of ten white poker chips). Place one row of ten same-colored items in front of the child. Ask the child to make an identical row with the other set. Ask the child if the two rows have the same amount of items or if one row has more. Do not go on until the rows are identical in number and arrangement and the child agrees that the two rows are the same. Now spread one row out and push the other row together so that the display looks as follows:

OOOOOOOOOO
O O O O O O O O O O

Ask the child if the rows are the same or if one row has more. Ask the child why it is the same or why one has more and which one, if either, has more. If the child says one row has more, ask the child where the more came from. Record all responses.

Conservation Task 2: Conservation of liquid task. Pour an identical amount of juice into two identical glasses. Ask the child if the two glasses have the same amount, and adjust the volume in each glass until the child agrees that both have the same. Now pour the liquid from one glass into a taller, thinner glass. Ask the child if the amount of juice is the same in both glasses or if one has more. If the child thinks one has more, ask which one. Have the child justify the judgment of having the same or different amount. Record all responses.

Classification Tasks

Classification Task 1: Classification of groups. Present the child with cutouts of big and small triangles, circles, and squares. Some of the shapes should be red, some blue, and some green. Ask the child to put together those things that go together. Record how the child sorts the objects. Now ask the child if there is another way to put the objects together. Record the second sort.

Classification Task 2: Present the child with a set of wooden beads, with ten red and two blue. (You can substitute poker chips or M&Ms.) Ask the child if there are more red beads or more blue beads. If the child were to make a train with the red beads and another train with the blue beads, which train would be longer? Now ask the child if there are more red beads or more wooden beads. If the child were to make a train with the red beads and another train with the wooden beads, which train would be longer?

	Child 1	Child 2
Task	Sex ____ Age ____	Sex ___ Age ____

Conservation Task 1:
    Creation of row
    Response
    Justification

Conservation Task 2:
    Response
    Justification

Classification Task 1:
    First ordering
    Second ordering

Classification Task 2:
    Response: red > blue?
    Response: red > wooden?

Questions:
- Which tasks did the 4- to 5-year-old child solve? How would you characterize the nature of the child's responses to the questions?

- Which tasks did the 8- to 9-year-old child solve? How would you characterize the nature of the child's responses to the questions?

- How would you characterize the differences between the performance of the younger and older child on these tasks?

- What do these observations tell you about Piaget's theory? How would the children be classified into Piaget's stages based on their responses to your problems?

Chapter 11: Socioemotional Development in Middle and Late Childhood

Total Teaching Package Outline

Lecture Outline	Resource References
Socioemotional Development in Middle and Late Childhood	PowerPoint Presentation: See www.mhhe.com Cognitive Maps: See Appendix A
Emotional and Personality Development • The Self	F/V: Middle Childhood: Social and Emotional Dev.
-The Development of Self-Understanding	LO1
-Self-Esteem and Self-Concept	LO2 OHT92 & IB: Four Ways to Improve Self-Esteem OHT99: Behavioral Indicators of Self-Esteem OHT155: Self-Esteem Is Affected Differently PA1: I Love Me! PA2: Role Model WS: Family.Com: Your Child's Self-Esteem
-Industry Versus Inferiority	LO3
• Emotional Development -Developmental Changes	LO4
-Emotional Intelligence	PA3: Your EQ F/V: Emotional Intelligence WS: Emotions and Emotional Intelligence
• Moral Development -Kohlberg's Theory of Moral Development	LO5 LO6 LO7 IB: Kohlberg's Stages of Moral Development RP1: Kohlberg's Moral Dilemmas WS: Kohlberg's Theory of Moral Development
-Prosocial Behavior and Altruism	IB: Strategies to Increase Prosocial Behavior F/V: Friendship, Gender, and Morality F/V: Helping and Prosocial Behavior F/V: Obedience
• Gender -Gender Stereotypes	LO8
-Gender Similarities and Differences	WS: Gender Equity for Mathematics and Science
-Gender-Role Classification	LO9 OHT89 & IB: Gender-Role Classification RP2: Gender Roles and Television
-Gender in Context	F/V: Gender Socialization

Families • Parent-Child Issues	LO10 CA1: Parent-Child Communication CA2: Common Parenting Situations CA3: Rights of Grandparents
• Societal Changes in Families	F/V: Not All Parents Are Straight
-Stepfamilies	LO11
-Latchkey Children	LO12 WS: Latchkey Children
Peers	F/V: Peer Culture
• Peer Statuses	LO13 LS1: The Effects of Peer Rejection
• Bullying	LO14 LS2: Aggression CA4: Intervention for Aggressive Children
• Social Cognition	LO15 LS3: Cognitive Interventions with Socially Dysfunctional Youth F/V: Prejudice: The Eye of the Storm
• Friends	LO16 OHT127 & IB: The Functions of Friendship PA4: Best Buddies

Schools
• The Transition to Elementary School
 	
• Socioeconomic Status and Ethnicity in
  Schools
     -The Education of Students from Low
       Socioeconomic Backgrounds
     -Ethnicity in Schools
 	
• Cross-Cultural Comparisons of Achievement
	LO17
	LS4: Should Parents Pay Their Children When
	         They Earn High Grades in School?
	
	LO18
	LS6: Academic Success and Cultural Influence

Review	CA5: Critical Thinking Multiple-Choice CA6: Critical Thinking Essays

Chapter Outline

EMOTIONAL AND PERSONALITY DEVELOPMENT

The Self

The Development of Self-Understanding

- In middle and late childhood, self-understanding shifts from defining oneself through external characteristics to defining oneself through internal characteristics (preferences, personality traits, social memberships, or social comparisons).

Self-Esteem and Self-Concept

What Are Self-Esteem and Self-Concept?

- **Self-esteem** (self-worth or self-image) refers to global evaluations of the self.
- **Self-concept** refers to domain-specific evaluations of the self.

Research on Self-Esteem

- Self-esteem remains relatively stable, though it can change in response to life transitions.
- Social comparisons can influence self-esteem.

Increasing Children's Self-Esteem

- Children's self-esteem can be improved through:
    - Identification of the causes of low self-esteem and the domains of competence important to the self.
    - Emotional support and social approval.
    - Achievement and self-efficacy
        - Self-efficacy refers to individuals' belief that they can master a situation and produce positive outcomes.
    - Coping with problems, rather than avoiding problems.

Industry Versus Inferiority

- Erikson's 4th stage, industry versus inferiority, occurs during the elementary school years.
- When children are encouraged in their efforts to make, build, and work, their sense of industry increases.
- Inferiority develops if their efforts are regarded as "mischief" or "making a mess."

Emotional Development

Developmental Changes

- The developmental changes that occur during middle and late childhood include:
    - An increased understanding of such complex emotions as pride and shame.
    - An increased understanding that more than one emotion can be experienced in a situation.
    - An increased tendency to take into account the events leading up to an emotional reaction.
    - Improved ability to suppress and conceal emotion.
    - The ability to use self-initiated strategies to redirect emotions.

Emotional Intelligence

- The concept of emotional intelligence initially was proposed in 1990 as a form of social intelligence that involves the ability to monitor one's own and others' feelings and emotions, to discriminate among them, and to use this information to guide one's thinking and action.
- In Goleman's view, emotional intelligence includes:
    - Developing emotional self-awareness.
    - Managing emotions.
    - Reading emotions.
    - Handling relationships.

Moral Development
- Kohlberg extended Piaget's theory of moral development by emphasizing the importance of opportunities to take the perspective of others.

Kohlberg's Theory of Moral Development
- Kohlberg's theory stresses that moral development unfolds in stages.
- Using moral dilemmas, Kohlberg investigated the nature of moral thought with a focus on individuals' reasoning behind their answers to the moral dilemmas.
  - **Internalization** is the developmental change from behavior that is externally controlled to behavior that is controlled by internal standards and principles.
  - As children and adolescents develop, their moral thoughts become more internalized.
- Kohlberg's theory includes three levels of moral development:
Kohlberg's Level 1: Preconventional Reasoning
  - **Preconventional reasoning** is the lowest level in Kohlberg's theory of moral development. At this level, the individual shows no internalization of moral values—moral reasoning is controlled by external rewards and punishments
    - Stage 1: In the **heteronomous morality** stage, moral thinking is often tied to punishment.
    - Stage 2: In the **individualism, instrumental purpose and exchange** stage, individuals pursue their own interests but also let others do the same.
Kohlberg's Level 2: Conventional Reasoning
  - **Conventional reasoning** is the second level in Kohlberg's theory of moral development. At this level, internalization is intermediate. Individuals abide by certain standards (internal) but they are the standards of others (external) such as parents or the laws of society.
    - Stage 3: In the **mutual interpersonal expectations, relationships, and interpersonal conformity** stage, individuals value trust, caring, and loyalty to others as a basis of moral judgements.
    - Stage 4: In the **social systems morality** stage, moral judgements are based on understanding the social order, law, justice, and duty.
Kohlberg's Level 3: Postconventional Reasoning
  - **Postconventional reasoning** is the highest level in Kohlberg's theory of moral development. At this level, morality is completely internalized and is not based on others' standards. The individual recognizes alternative moral courses, explores the options, and then decides on a personal moral code.
    - Stage 5: In the **social contract or utility and individual rights** stage, individuals reason that values, rights, and principles transcend the law.
    - Stage 6: In the **universal ethical principles** stage, the person has developed a moral standard based on universal human rights.
- Kohlberg assumed that theses stages occur in sequence and are age-related.
- The moral stages appeared somewhat later than Kohlberg proposed and stage 6 was elusive.
- The first four stages appear to be culturally universal, though cultural diversity characterizes stages 5 and 6.
Kohlberg's Critics
Moral Thought and Moral Behavior
  - His theory has been criticized for placing too much emphasis on moral thought and not enough emphasis on moral behavior.

Culture and Moral Development
- Kohlberg's theory has been criticized for being culturally biased. Research has found that moral reasoning is more culturally specific than he envisioned and that his scoring system does not recognize higher-level reasoning in certain cultural groups.

Family Processes and Moral Development
- Critics claim that Kohlberg underestimated the contribution of family relationships to moral development. Parents' moral values and inductive discipline can influence children's moral development.

Gender and the Care Perspective
- Gilligan states that Kohlberg's theory does not adequately reflect relationships and concern for others.
  - The **justice perspective** is a moral perspective that focuses on the rights of the individual; individuals stand alone and independently make moral decisions.
  - The **care perspective** is a moral perspective that views people in terms of their connectedness with others and emphasizes interpersonal communication, relationships with others, and concern for others.
  - Gilligan speculated that Kohlberg's theory was biased against females because she assumed that females use the care perspective, whereas Kohlberg emphasized the justice perspective.

Prosocial Behavior and Altruism
- Moral behavior can involve negative, antisocial acts (lying, cheating, or stealing) and it can involve positive acts (empathy or altruism).
  - **Altruism** is an unselfish interest in helping someone else.
- Damon described a developmental sequence of altruism (sharing):
  - Three-year-olds share for the fun of social play ritual or imitation.
  - By 4 years, a combination of empathic awareness and adult encouragement produce an obligation to share.
  - By school age, children express a more objective idea about fairness or equality.
  - Middle or late childhood emphasizes benevolence and merit.
- Adult influence appears to have little influence over the development of altruism.

Gender
Gender Stereotypes
- **Gender stereotypes** are broad categories that reflect our impressions and beliefs about females and males.
  - Stereotypes help people simplify the complexity of everyday experiences and are very difficult to abandon.
- As gender equality increases, male and female stereotypes diminish.

Gender Similarities and Differences
- When looking at differences between the sexes, it is important to keep in mind that the differences are averages (not all females versus all males).
- Even when differences are reported, there is considerable overlap between the sexes.
- The differences may be due primarily to biological factors, sociocultural factors, or both.
  Physical Similarities and Differences
  - Females have a longer life expectancy than males.
  - Females are less likely to develop physical or mental disorders.
  - Females have twice the body fat as males usually around the breasts and hips.
  - Metabolic activity in the brain is similar for males and females except for the areas of the brain involving emotional expression and physical expression (females' brains are more active).

Cognitive Similarities and Differences
- Most research finds that males are better at math and visuospatial skills.
- Recent research finds that boys did slightly better than girls in math and science, yet girls were far superior students overall.

Socioemotional Similarities and Differences
- Boys are more aggressive and active than girls especially when provoked.
  - Biological (heredity and hormones) and environmental (cultural expectations, adult and peer models, and social agents reward aggression in boys) factors explain the differences.
- Males show less self-regulation of emotions, which can lead to behavioral problems.

Gender Controversy
- The belief that gender differences are small or nonexistent is rooted in a feminist commitment to gender similarities and is seen as important for political equality.
  - Eagly argues that there are gender differences that need to be addressed.

Gender-Role Classification

What Is Gender-Role Classification?
- Gender-role classification focuses on how masculine, feminine, or androgynous an individual is.
  - Rather than describing masculinity and femininity as a continuum in which more of one means less of the other, it was proposed that individuals can have both masculine and feminine traits.
  - **Androgyny** is the presence of desirable masculine and feminine characteristics in the same person.
    - Bem argues that androgynous individuals are more flexible, competent, and mentally healthy compared to their masculine and feminine counterparts.
- Gender-role classification more appropriately depends on the context involved (intimate relationships, academic, or work settings).

Androgyny and Education
- It is easier to teach androgyny to girls than to boys and it is easier to teach it before the middle school grades.
- Some advocates argue that traditional sex-typing is harmful for all students, but especially for girls as it has prevented many from experiencing equal opportunities.
- Detractors argue that androgyny education is too value-laden and ignores the diversity of gender roles in our society.

Gender-Role Transcendence
- **Gender-role transcendence** is the view that when an individual's competence is at issue, it should be conceptualized on a personal basis, rather than on the basis of masculinity, femininity, or androgyny.
  - Parents should rear their children to be competent boys and girls, not masculine, feminine, or androgynous, as gender-role classification leads to too much stereotyping.

Gender in Context
- Considering gender in context allows us to conceptualize gender not as a traitlike category, but as a person-situation interaction.
- For example, one stereotype is that females are more likely to help others than males.
  - Yet it depends on the context, as females are more likely to help children with personal problems and to engage in caregiving, while males are more likely to help in situations in which they feel a sense of competence or if danger is involved.
- Although androgyny and multiple gender roles are often available for American children to choose from, in many countries around the world, traditional gender roles are still in place.

FAMILIES
- Parents spend considerably less time with their children in middle and late childhood, including less time in caregiving, instruction, reading, talking, and playing.

Parent-Child Issues
- Parents are still powerful and important socializing agents during this period.
- New parent-child issues emerge and discipline changes.
    - Discipline is often easier during this period given children's cognitive advances which allow for more reasoning.
    - Parents use less physical discipline, and use more deprivation of privileges, appeals to the child's self-esteem, guilt, and reminders of children's responsibility.
    - Some control is transferred from parent to child, although the process is gradual and involves coregulation.
- Coregulation involves monitoring, guiding, and supporting children at a distance, effective use of direct contact with children, and strengthening children's ability to monitor their own behavior, adopt appropriate conduct standards, and to sense when adult help is warranted.

Societal Changes in Families
Stepfamilies
- Because of their parents' successive marital transitions, about half of all children whose parents divorce will have a stepfather within four years of parental separation.
- As in divorced families, children in stepfamilies have more adjustment problems than children in nondivorced families.
    - These problems include academic problems, externalizing and internalizing problems, lower self-esteem, early sexual activity, delinquency, etc.
- Early adolescence appears to be an especially difficult time for these transitions.
    - Restabalization may take up to five years in stepfamilies.
- **Boundary ambiguity** is the uncertainty in stepfamilies about who is in or out of the family and who is performing or responsible for certain tasks in the family system.
    - The parenting of the stepfather and stepmother undergoes changes with time, and stepmothers have a more difficult time.
- Children in blended families have more problems than children in stepfamilies.
Latchkey Children
- Latchkey children are often without parental supervision for 2 to 4 hours a day during the school year and for the entire day during the summer months.
    - A slight majority of latchkey children have had a negative experience (grow up too fast, engage in problem behaviors).
- Diversity characterizes latchkey children, as authoritative parenting and parental monitoring help children cope, especially with resisting peer pressure.

PEERS
Peer Statuses
- **Popular children** are frequently nominated as a best friend and are rarely disliked by their peers.
    - Popular children give out reinforcements, listen carefully, maintain open communication with peers, are happy, show enthusiasm and concern for others, and are self-confident.
- **Neglected children** are infrequently nominated as a best friend but are not disliked by their peers.
- **Rejected children** are infrequently nominated as someone's best friend and are actively disliked by their peers.
- **Controversial children** are frequently nominated both as someone's best friend and as being disliked.

- Rejected children often have the most serious adjustment problems (delinquency, aggression, or dropping out of school) later in life than do neglected children.
  - Some rejected children are shy and withdrawn (10-20 percent of rejected children).
- Training that focuses on social skills, peer group entry, and communication skills are often successfully targeted toward rejected children.

Bullying
- Some children are victimized by bullies—one study found that 25 percent of children are frequently bullied and 10 percent are chronically bullied.
  - Victims of bullies are often parented in an intrusive manner, which may influence children's assertiveness and independence.
  - Parents of bullies are often rejecting, authoritarian, or permissive about their child's aggressiveness.
- The short-term consequences of being bullied include depression, loss of interest in school, and avoiding school.
- The long-term effects include depression and low self-esteem.
- Bullies are more likely to commit crimes in adulthood.

Social Cognition
- Social cognition involves thoughts about social matters.
- Dodge argues that children go through five steps in processing information about their social world.
  - They decode social cues, interpret social cues, search for a response, select an optimal response, and enact that response.
    - Aggressive boys are more likely to perceive another child's actions as hostile when the intention is actually ambiguous.
    - Aggressive boys also respond more quickly, less efficiently, and less reflectively which leads to more conflicts.
- From a social cognitive perspective, maladjusted children do not have adequate social cognitive skills to interact effectively with others.

Friends
- Children's friendships serve six functions:
  - Companionship: Friendship provides children with a familiar playmate who will spend time with them and engage in collaborative activities.
  - Stimulation: Friendship provides children with interesting information, excitement, and amusement.
  - Physical support: Friendship provides time, resources, and assistance.
  - Ego support: Friendship provides the expectation of support, encouragement, and feedback, which helps children perceive themselves as competent, attractive, and worthwhile.
  - Social comparison: Friendship provides information about where the child stands vis-a-vis others and whether the child is doing OK.
  - Intimacy and affection: Friendship provides children with a warm, close, trusting relationship with another individual in which self-disclosure takes place.
- Two of friendship's most common characteristics are intimacy and similarity.
  - **Intimacy in friendships** involves self-disclosure and the sharing of private thoughts.
    - Intimate relationships may not appear until early adolescence.
  - Friends are more similar than dissimilar in terms of age, sex, race, attitudes, activities, etc.

SCHOOLS
- Children spend more than 10,000 hours in the classroom as members of a small society in which there are tasks to be accomplished, people to be socialized and socialized by, and rules that define and limit behaviors, feelings, and attitudes.

The Transition to Elementary School
- Children take on a new role as a school-child, interact and develop relationships with new significant others, adopt new reference groups, and develop new standards by which to judge themselves.
  - A special concern is that early schooling emphasizes negative feedback to children.
    - Children's self-esteem is lower in later elementary school than in early elementary school.
  - Children's learning is integrated.
    - Children do not need to distinguish learning by subject area. Curriculum can be planned and selected by children.

Socioeconomic Status and Ethnicity in Schools
- Children from low-income, ethnic minority backgrounds have more difficulties in school than do their middle-SES status, White counterparts because schools have not done a good job of educating low-income minority students to overcome the barriers to their achievement.

The Education of Students from Low Socioeconomic Backgrounds
- Many children in poverty face problems at home and school that present barriers to learning.
  - Families may have low-educational standards, be illiterate, lack sufficient funds for educational materials and supplies, experience malnutrition, and live in high crime areas.
  - Children from impoverished areas attend schools that have fewer resources, more students with lower achievement test scores, lower graduation rates, fewer college-bound students, and less experienced teachers.
  - These schools often encourage rote learning, as opposed to critical thinking skills.
- Antipoverty programs are emphasizing two-generational intervention.
  - Services focus on children (education, day care) and parents (adult education, literacy and job skill training).
  - These programs have been more successful with parents than children.

Ethnicity in Schools
- School segregation is still prevalent in American schools.
- The school experiences of students from different ethnic groups vary considerable.
  - African American and Latino students are less likely to be enrolled in academic, college preparatory programs.
  - Asian Americans are more likely than other ethnic minority groups to take advanced math and science courses.
- The vast majority of teachers at large minority schools are not minorities themselves.
  - Critics of the American education system state that institutional racism permeates our schools. Many teachers fail to challenge children of color to achieve.
- Strategies for improving relations between ethnically diverse students are provided:
  - Turn the class into a jigsaw classroom.
  - Encourage students to have positive personal contact with diverse other students.
  - Encourage students to engage in perspective taking.
  - Help students think critically and be emotionally intelligent when cultural issues are involved.
  - Reduce bias.
  - View the school and community as a team to help support teaching efforts.
  - Be a competent cultural mediator.

Cross-Cultural Comparisons of Achievement
- American children are more achievement-oriented than children in many countries, but are less achievement-oriented than many children in Asian countries, such as China, Taiwan, and Japan.
  - American children's performance in math and science are considerably lower.
  - The gap between Asian and American students widens the longer the children are in school.
    - Asian students spend considerably more time in school than American children.
    - Asian parents had considerably higher education and achievement standards than American parents do.
- Critics of the cross-national and international comparisons argue that, in many comparisons, U.S. children are being compared with a "select" group of children from other countries.

Learning Objectives

1. Understand the shift in development of self-understanding during middle and late childhood.
2. Define self-esteem and self-concept, and discuss ways to increase children's self-esteem.
3. Explain Erik Erikson's fourth stage of psychosocial development
4. Examine the changes in emotional development that take place in this period and discuss emotional intelligence.
5. Describe Kohlberg's theory of moral development, as well as criticisms of it.
6. Discuss Carol Gilligan's alternate theory of moral development.
7. Define prosocial behavior and altruism, and understand ways to increase altruism in children.
8. Examine gender stereotypes and gender similarities and differences.
9. Discuss gender-role classification, including androgyny and gender-role transcendence, and the importance of considering gender in context.
10. Explain how parent-child interaction in the family changes during middle and late childhood.
11. Describe both the short-term and long-term effects of living in stepfamilies.
12. Define the term latchkey children and elaborate on ways to reduce the risk to these children.
13. Expound on the four peer statuses.
14. Identify the parent-child relationships that characterize bullies and victims, as well as the effects of bullying and strategies to reduce bullying.
15. Explain what social cognition is and why it is important.
16. Examine the importance of children's friendships.
17. Discuss the transition to elementary school, how socioeconomic status and ethnicity impact education, and ways to improve relations among ethnically diverse groups.
18. Examine the cross-cultural differences in levels of achievement.

Key Terms

altruism
androgyny
boundary ambiguity
care perspective
controversial children
conventional reasoning
gender-role transcendence
gender stereotypes
heteronomous morality
individualism, instrumental purpose and exchange
internalization
intimacy in friendships
justice perspective

mutual interpersonal expectations, relationships, and interpersonal conformity
neglected children
popular children
postconventional reasoning
preconventional reasoning
rejected children
self-concept
self-esteem
social contract or utility and individual rights
social systems morality
universal ethical principles

Key People

Elliot Aronson
Sandra Bem
William Damon
Kenneth Dodge
Alice Eagly
Nancy Eisenberg
Erik Erikson
Carol Gilligan
Daniel Goleman
Susan Harter

Willard Hartup
Janet Shibley Hyde
Carol Jacklin
Lawrence Kohlberg
Jonathan Kozol
Joan Lipsitz
Eleanor Maccoby
John Ogbu
Margaret Beale Spencer
Harold Stevensen

Lecture Suggestions

Lecture Suggestion 1: The Effects of Peer Rejection This lecture extends the textbook's discussion regarding the difficulties that children who are rejected by their peers often experience. What effect does friendship play in the effects of peer rejection? Bagwell et al. (1999) conducted a 12-year longitudinal study to examine the role of friendships and peer rejection on adult adjustment. Thirty young adults who had stable, reciprocal best friends in the fifth grade were compared to 30 young adults who had been friendless in the fifth grade.

- Mutual friendships and low levels of peer rejection were related to successful adult adjustment.
- Peer rejection in the fifth grade was linked to low levels of social interaction, and less favorable school performance, vocational competence, and aspiration levels.
- Thus, peer rejection is associated with adulthood adjustment problems.
- Children's experience with peer rejection has stronger long-term implications than does friendship for success and educational endeavors.
- Children with a close friend tended to have a higher sense of general self-worth.
- Bagwell et al. conclude that close friendships provide a context for validation of self-worth and development of personal strengths.
- Psychopathological symptoms in adulthood are associated with peer rejection and the absence of friends in childhood.
- The researchers conclude that a mutual friendship is equally important as being accepted by peers.
- Source: Bagwell, C.L., Newcomb, A.F., & Bukowski, W.M. (1999). Preadolescent friendship and peer rejection as predictors of adult adjustment. *Child Development, 70,* 140-153.

Lecture Suggestion 2: Aggression The purpose of this lecture is to extend students' understanding of aggression. Most people assume that males are more aggressive than females. This assumption is accurate to a certain extent, depending on how aggression is defined. Researchers now differentiate between different types of aggression.

- Overt aggression is the type of aggression that most of us recognize as it involves physical or verbal behaviors that directly harm or threaten others (pushing, hitting, kicking, name calling, or verbal insults).
  - Most research on aggression has focused on this type of aggression and researchers have found that males are more likely to engage in this form of aggression (Crick, 1997).
  - Overt aggression is linked with social-psychological adjustment. That is, engaging in overt aggression is associated with externalizing behaviors (defiant behavior, delinquency, and impulsivity).

- Relational aggression involves harming others through attempts to disrupt relationships (rumor spreading, threatening to withdraw friendships, or excluding a particular person).
  - Relational aggression is more common among females than males. Relational aggression is linked with internalizing behaviors (depression, anxiety, and somatic symptoms).
- Consistency with gender expectations impacts children's social-psychological adjustment.
  - Crick found that a child was more likely to suffer maladjustment if he or she engaged in gender nonnormative aggression. That is, if a male engaged in more relational aggression or if females engaged in more overt aggression, they are more likely to be rejected by peers and experience higher levels of psychological maladjustment.
- Research has found gender differences relative to the relationship between aggression and peer relations (Rys & Bear, 1997).
  - Peer rejection was more strongly associated with overt aggression than with relational aggression for boys. For girls, the opposite was found; relational aggression was more strongly associated with peer rejection.
    - Just because his/her peers reject an aggressive child, this does not preclude the development of one reciprocated friendship with another child (Lecture Suggestion 1: The Effects of Peer Rejection).
- Sources: Crick, N.R. (1997). Engagement in gender normative versus nonnormative forms of aggression: Links to social-psychological adjustment. *Developmental Psychology, 33*, 610-617. Rys, G.S., & Bear, G.G. (1997). Relational aggression and peer relations: Gender and developmental issues. *Merrill-Palmer Quarterly, 43*, 87-106.

Lecture Suggestion 3: Cognitive Interventions with Socially Dysfunctional Youth The purpose of this lecture is to extend Santrock's brief introduction to Dodge's social information-processing model. This material is useful as an illustration of the practical value of research on social cognition. It is also an opportunity to review the information-processing approach to cognitive development and to illustrate how this approach has branched into other research areas.

Proponents of theories of social cognition claim that immature or poorly functioning thought about social relationships and processes is a fundamental cause of antisocial or disordered social behavior. Dodge and colleagues have attempted to show that problems lie in the steps or processes of social cognition (Crick & Dodge, 1994; Dodge et al., 1986). Crick and Dodge (1994) have proposed a social information-processing model.

The child brings a data base or memories to all social situations. The data base includes memories, acquired rules, social schemas, and social knowledge that the child has gained from his/her experiences. The memories include past interactions with peers and adults. The rules for behavior are acquired from other children, adults, or created upon reflection of social interactions. Social schemas are memory structures that organize information and are created through reflection of events. Social knowledge is the collection of memories for specific events, rules, and schemas.

There is a dynamic bidirectional relationship between a child's data base and his/her processing of social information. Social knowledge influences how the child processes information in a specific situation and their inferences about a specific situation contribute to his/her social knowledge (thus, changing the data base for future interactions). There are bidirectional relationships between a child's data base and each step in the information-processing system.

- Step 1 involves encoding internal and external cues. Children need to assess the social situation and take in social cues effectively in order to behave appropriately.
  - Aggressive children pick up fewer social cues before drawing inferences about people and situations than do nonaggressive children (Slaby & Guerra, 1988).
  - Aggressive children selectively attend to aggressive cues in situations (Gouze, 1987) and base their inferences on the most recent cues and ignore other relevant cues (Dodge, 1986).
  - Aggressive children's encoding of social situations is less complete and more biased than that of nonaggressive children.

- Step 2 involves interpreting the social cues and making inferences based on the interpretation. Attributions about the causes of, or reasons for, behaviors are made. Was the action intentional, and if so was it intentionally negative or positive. Inferences are influenced by past interactions with others. Other interpretative processes include evaluation of goal attainment, evaluation of past performance, self-evaluations, and evaluations of others. There is a feedback loop between step 2 and step 1. Children may seek additional social cues if they are having difficulty interpreting situational cues.
  - Aggressive children often interpret ambiguous acts as hostile. They only interpret the act as hostile if the behavior affects them; they do not if the act is not directed toward them (Crick & Dodge, 1994).
  - Dodge (1980) states that this interpretation is based in reality as aggressive children are more often the target of hostile acts.
- Step 3 involves clarifying goals. If conflict arises, clarification between the social partners is necessary with the resolution of conflict as the optimal outcome (focus on relationship goals). Arousal regulation is part of clarifying goals.
  - Aggressive children are more likely to have self-focused goals (Rabiner & Gordon, 1992).
- Step 4 involves response access or construction. Children can use a response that they have used in the past by recalling strategies to use in the current situation. Or, if a novel situation occurs or past strategies have not been successful, children may need to construct a novel response.
  - Aggressive children are more likely to respond in a less socially competent manner (hostile) (Slaby & Guerra, 1988).
- Step 5 involves making a response decision. Ideally, this should include response evaluation, outcome expectations, self-efficacy evaluations, and response selection.
  - Aggressive children perceive hostile responses more positively (Crick & Dodge, 1994).
- Step 6 involves the enactment of the response that was chosen in the previous step. This step is not officially part of information processing as it is completed in step 5. However, given the cyclical nature of interactions, peer responses to the enactment create additional social cues, thus the process begins again.

This model serves as a foundation for interventions as researchers have found that aggressive children have potential to be deficient in each and every step along the way. See Classroom Activity 4: Intervention for Aggressive Children for a complementary exercise.

- Sources: Crick N.R., & Dodge, K.A. (1994). A review and reformulation of social information-processing mechanisms in children's social adjustment. *Psychological Bulletin, 115*, 74-101. Dodge, K.A. (1980). Social cognition and children's aggressive behavior. *Child Development, 51*, 162-170. Dodge, K.A. (1986). A social information processing model of social competence in children. In M. Perlmutter (Ed.), *Minnesota Symposia on Child Psychology* (Vol. 18, pp. 77-125.). Hillsdale, NJ: Erlbaum. Dodge, K. A., Pettit, G. S., McClaskey, C. L., & Brown, M. M. (1986). Social competence in children: With commentary by John M. Gottman. *Monographs of the Society for Research in Child Development, 51* (2, Serial No. 213). Gouze, K.R. (1987). Attention and social problem solving as correlates of aggression in preschool males. *Journal of Abnormal Child Psychology, 15*, 181-197. Rabiner, D.L., & Gordon, L.V. (1992). The coordination of conflicting social goals: Differences between rejected and nonrejected boys. *Child Development, 63*, 1344-1350. Slaby, R.G., & Guerra, N.G. (1988). Cognitive mediators of aggression in adolescent offenders: 1. Assessment. *Developmental Psychology, 24*, 580-588.

Lecture Suggestion 4: Should Parents Pay Their Children When They Earn High Grades in School? The purpose of this lecture is to examine the issue of whether extrinsic rewards undermine intrinsic academic motivation. We all probably recall knowing someone in school who got $5 for every A they earned in school. Does this motivate children to do well in school? Research has found that encouragement of autonomous functioning, individual challenge, and positive feedback stimulates an intrinsic motivation to achieve (Deci & Ryan, 1985). If the environment is highly controlling however, the internal forces for mastery-achievement may be undermined. Parents that use surveillance and frequent rewards socialize their children to be motivated by and desire extrinsic rewards.

Ginsburg and Bronstein (1993) studied the relationship between parents' behavior and children's extrinsic/intrinsic orientation and school performance. Two specific parenting behaviors were related to extrinsic motivation and lower school performance. They found that overcontrolling parents (extreme supervision of homework completion) had children who were more likely to rely on external sources for evaluation. Their grades and achievement scores were lower as well. Parents that relied on external rewards also had children with extrinsic motivation and lower school performance.

Ginsburg and Bronstein speculate that extrinsically rewarded children use external criteria to assess their performance, which alters the child's perception of himself. This may undermine his ability to self-regulate and choose appropriate work. The child does not learn how to judge his own performance.

Children's mastery behaviors and an intrinsic motivation were positively correlated with parental encouragement. The authors propose that parents should be involved in children's academic activities, yet remain sensitive to the child's concerns and feelings by allowing the child to be involved in decision-making. Encouragement of intrinsic motivation, which is bidirectional and reciprocal, will foster independent self-evaluation and academic success. The goal is for the child to develop the ability to self-regulate and take responsibility for academic success; thus, the parents are not solely responsible for their child's outcome. What are some ways that parents can foster the development of intrinsic motivation?

Are grades in school undermining intrinsic motivation? Covington (2000) concludes that students enjoy learning and will be more likely to value what they are learning if desired grade achievement is attained through learning primarily for task-oriented, not self-aggrandizing or failure-avoiding, reasons or if they are personally interested in what they are studying. Further, their appreciation for what they are learning is more based on interest in the subject matter than the earned grade.

- Sources: Covington, M.V. (2000). Intrinsic versus extrinsic motivation in schools: A reconciliation. *Current Directions in Psychological Science, 9,* 22-25. Deci, E.L., & Ryan, R.M. (1985). *Intrinsic motivation and self-determination in human behavior.* New York: Plenum. Ginsburg, G.S., & Bronstein, P. (1993). Family factors related to children's intrinsic/extrinsic motivational orientation and academic performance. *Child Development, 64,* 1461-1474.

Lecture Suggestion 6: Academic Success and Cultural Influences on Peer Groups Santrock stresses that adolescence is a time when peers have increasing influence over adolescent behavior. Nonetheless, parents continue to influence adolescents, especially in the area of academic achievement. Steinberg (1990) examined whether adolescents from different cultural groups are influenced by peers and parents differently (15,000 high school students from nine high schools in Wisconsin and California). Children raised by authoritative parents, regardless of cultural group (White, African American, Latino, and Asian American), showed fewer emotional problems, had higher self-esteem, and had fewer behavioral problems.

Interesting differences emerged for the cultural groups with respect to academic achievement. White children raised by authoritative parents were more academically successful. In contrast, peer groups had great influence on school attitudes and behavior for African American, Latino, and Asian American students. These attitudes influenced how much time students spent studying, their enjoyment of school, and their classroom behaviors.

Differences between these groups emerged as well. Asian American students were positively influenced by their peers' positive regard for academic achievement. Latino and African American adolescents did less well in school. Steinberg speculates that these adolescents had more difficulty finding a peer group that stressed academic success, thus they were in conflict between their parents' positive regard for academic achievement and the negative influence of their peers. Oftentimes, African American students do not do well in school for fear of being unpopular with their peers (Fordham & Ogbu, 1986). Yet, high-ability African American students who attended school with other high-achieving students did not feel anxious about losing peer support for being academically successful, and consequently were more successful.

High school peer groups are highly segregated along cultural lines. Steinberg thinks that cultural segregation limits minority individuals' choice of peer group. If minority students are not part of a peer group that values academic success, it will be more difficult for them to benefit from positive parenting and be influenced by parents' positive regard for academic success.

- Sources: Fordham, S., & Ogbu, J.U. (1986). Black students' school success: Pragmatic strategy of pyrrhic victory? *Harvard Educational Review, 58*, 54-84. Steinberg, L. (1990). Autonomy, conflict, and harmony in the family relationship. In S. Feldman and G. Eliot (Eds.). *At the threshold The developing adolescent.* Cambridge, MA: Harvard University.

Classroom Activities

Classroom Activity 1: Parent-Child Communication The purpose of this activity is to assess the effect of harsh communication patterns between parents and children and to generate alternative patterns of communication. Parent-child relationships may include sentences that "shoot the other person down," which often add fuel to bickering situations. Share these statements with students using **Handout 1**. In small groups, the students should discuss whether they have ever used or heard these kinds of statements. Then they should discuss the manifest and latent meanings of these statements and generate healthier statements.

- I don't understand why you do these things.
- How could you do such a thing?
- I've never heard of such a thing.
- How could someone with your brains and your background do such a thing?
- I'm stumped, you really have confused me.
- You are going too fast. Please go over it one more time so I'll understand.
- You should know how I'm suffering.
- I cannot believe you are going to do that now, when _____.
- I do not understand how one little_____ is going to hurt you.
- You never tell me what you're thinking.
- Do it for me.
- You've offended me.
- I demand an apology.

Logistics:
- Materials: Handout 1 ("Shoot the Other Person Down" Activity).
- Group size: Small group and full class discussion.
- Approximate time: Small group (30 minutes) and full class discussion (15 minutes).
- Sources: Dyer, W. (1978). *Pulling your own strings.* New York: Thomas Y. Crowell Co.

Classroom Activity 2: Common Parenting Situations Divide the class into groups of three to six students and have them wrestle with common parenting situations (**Handout 2**). Students should present their individual views and reasons for each problem situation, and then they should try to reach a consensus about how to handle the situation. The groups can present their finalized position to the larger class and discover whether each group used similar solutions. A variation is to have students resolve these problems using a particular parenting style, such as authoritarian, permissive-indulgent, authoritative.

- Your 9-year-old and your 11-year-old want to play Nintendo all the time.
- The fifth-grade math teacher sends a note home saying that your child rarely does his homework and is easily distracted in class.
- Your 10-year-old daughter wants to know why you won't let her wear makeup, nylons, and earrings. She says all her friends do.
- You find out that your sixth-grader has removed a couple of cans of beer from your refrigerator.
- Your third-grader and peers seem to delight in sprinkling their conversation with an assortment of swearwords.

- Your fourth-grader starts to insist that she will only wear certain expensive brands of jeans, shoes, and tops; and they are so expensive that your budget could not afford very much.
- Your second-grader insists he doesn't need a baby-sitter anymore.
- Your fifth-grader thinks she is old enough to date and is interested in a seventh-grade guy.

Logistics:
- Materials: Handout 2 (Parenting Situations Activity).
- Group size: Small group and full class discussion.
- Approximate time: Small group (30 minutes) and full class discussion (30 minutes).
- Sources: Simons, J. A. (1987). How Would You Handle It?: A Classroom Activity. Ankeny, IA: Des Moines Area Community College.

Classroom Activity 3: Rights of Grandparents This activity examines the rights of grandparents regarding visitation. As family structures have changed due to increases in divorce and single parenting, grandparents' roles have also changed. As a result, more decisions about grandparents' visitation rights are being made by courts and state legislatures. Since the mid-1970s, all fifty states have passed laws granting grandparents the right to petition the courts for legally-enforced visitation privileges. Before this time period, grandparents had no rights to their grandchildren except by consent of the children's parents.

- Early court decisions (e.g., *Odell v. Lutz*, 1947) emphasized parental autonomy and ruled that grandparent visitation rights would undermine parental authority. In fact, grandparent visitation rights could subject children to intergenerational conflict (e.g., *Noll v. Noll*, 1950). These rulings also went along with the long tradition that the legal system should only intervene in the family in extreme circumstances. Early granting of grandparent visitation rights (e.g., *Benner v. Benner*, 1952) came in cases in which the grandchildren had lived with the grandparents for extended periods, or in cases in which the parents were deemed "unfit" and the grandparents were given custody. Recent rulings are more likely to view grandparent visitation as a way of preserving the child's continued contact with a family line and as a way of providing an alternative source for family support. These decisions are most likely made when children have experienced the death of a parent, or long-term separation from one parent due to divorce. Even then, courts make the determination of grandparent visitation rights based on the children's "best interests." Thus, to some degree, courts are recognizing the importance of the extended family, the possible psychological support of the older generation to children, and, in general, the political clout of older Americans.
- Have students discuss the pros and cons of regulated and enforced grandparent visitation rights. Part of the discussion can involve the roles that grandparents play in grandchildren's lives (e.g., alternative caregivers, playmates, family historians and transmitters of family values and traditions, advice givers to parents). Part of the discussion should deal with how to resolve intergenerational conflict, how to determine the "children's best interests," the consequences of grandparent visitation rights on family functioning, and how to resolve the grandparent policy.

Logistics:
- Group size: Small group.
- Approximate time: Small group (20 minutes).
- Source: Thompson, R. A., Tinsley, B. R., Scalora, M. J., & Parke, R. D. (1989). Grandparents' visitation rights: Legalizing the ties that bind. *American Psychologist, 44*, 1217-1222.

Classroom Activity 4: Intervention for Aggressive Children The purpose of the activity is for students to design an intervention program for aggressive children using Crick and Dodge's (1994) steps for processing social situations. Santrock introduced Dodge's original theory in the textbook. He states that children go through five steps in processing information about their social world. Children decode social cues, interpret the social cues, search for a response, select an optimal response, and enact that response. Using information from Lecture Suggestion 3: Cognitive Interventions with Socially Dysfunctional Youth, presented as **Handout 3**, have students design an intervention to help aggressive children process social information better.

Logistics:
- Materials: Handout 3 (Intervention for Aggressive Children Activity).
- Group size: Small group.
- Approximate time: Small group (30 minutes).
- Source: Crick, N.R., & Dodge, K.A. (1994). A review and reformulation of social information-processing mechanisms in children's social adjustment. *Psychological Bulletin, 115*, 74-101.

Classroom Activity 5: Critical Thinking Multiple-Choice Questions and Suggested Answers Discuss the answers to the critical thinking multiple-choice exercises in **Handout 4**. Question 1 is a new type of exercise. You will probably find that students are not clear about the nature of the three approaches to cognition, and you may want to prepare them for this assignment by doing a systematic review of the three. Begin simply by asking whether students can name the three approaches. As they do so, list them in a row across the top of a blackboard or overhead. Next, list the issues pertinent to the nature of development down the left side, such as continuity versus discontinuity (include research strategies and measurements, as well). Then have students suggest the stance each approach takes on the issues, and identify the dominant research strategies and methods associated with each approach. This will provide a method for doing the exercise and serve as a good review of these approaches.

Question 2 will require a review of Bronfenbrenner's ecological theory. Again, begin by asking students what they remember about the theory. Prompt them to identify and define the five systems and have them give examples of each. Emend their understanding as suggested by their answers.

Question 3 was prompted by material in the second edition of Santrock's *Children*. Even though it has been adapted for *Life-Span Development*, you may want to review the earlier treatment because it discusses important methodological and conceptual, as well as developmental, issues in the study of gender-role acquisition by children. This would fit nicely with the lecture on measuring gender-role orientation and would help students to identify the two assumptions in the exercise. In any case, you may want to tell students that the pertinent assumption in this example is not stated directly in the text. The concern about recognizing inferences initiated during the last several chapters continues in this exercise, and you may want to continue discussing with students how to determine when an author is presenting conceptual possibilities as opposed to empirical statements. For example, "b" seems to be a self-evident factual statement, but as it appears in the text it is really a conclusion of a syllogism: male stereotypes are more favorable to men than female stereotypes are to women (observation); stereotypes influence the development of individuals (assumption); therefore, gender-role stereotypes harm women more than men (conclusion). You might want to examine claims made in the text in just this way as a means of preparing students to identify inferences in this question. **Handout 5** presents the answers to the multiple-choice critical thinking questions.

Logistics:
- Materials: Handout 4 (the critical thinking multiple-choice questions) and Handout 5 (answers).
- Group size: Small groups to discuss the questions, then a full class discussion.
- Approximate time: Small groups (15 to 20 minutes), full class discussion of any questions (15 minutes).

Classroom Activity 6: Critical Thinking Essay Questions and Suggestions for Helping Students Answer the Essays Discuss the students' answers to the critical thinking essay questions on **Handout 6**. Several objectives can be met with these questions. First, the answering of these questions facilitates students' understanding of concepts in chapter 11. Second, this type of essay question affords the students an opportunity to apply the concepts to their own lives, which will facilitate their retention of the material. Third, the essay format also will give students practice expressing themselves in written form. Ideas to help students answer the critical thinking essay questions are provided as **Handout 7**.

Logistics:

- Materials: Handout 6 (essay questions) and Handout 7 (helpful suggestions for the answers).
- Group size: Individual, then full class.
- Approximate time: Individual (60 minutes), full class discussion of any questions (30 minutes).

Personal Applications

Personal Application 1: I Love Me! The purpose of this exercise is to help students differentiate between the notions of self-concept and self-esteem. These two terms are often mistakenly used interchangeably, but they refer to different things. Self-concept refers to one's assessment of one's abilities and functioning in a certain area of life. For example, Joe acknowledges he's very good in math and it comes easy to him, yet he's not too coordinated on the basketball court. Self-esteem is one's emotional reaction to those judgements of self-concept. Therefore, even though Joe may not be good at basketball, he may still have high self-esteem if that is not particularly important to him and doing well in school is. However, if all of Joe's friends are athletes and pressure him to be like them, he may suffer from lower self-esteem, because he judges himself weak in that area.

- Instructions for Students: Describe your self-concept profile. Delineate all areas of life (physical, social, intellectual and academic, emotional, achievement, etc.) and present your matter-of-fact judgement of how you function in each. Then explain your self-esteem with regard to each area—how you *feel* about your competence in each area. It is possible to have varying levels of self-esteem based on the different domains of your life. Summarize by discussing your overall self-esteem, and what you might do to improve it in particular areas.
- Use in the Classroom: Have students do this exercise in class, sharing their acknowledged strong points and weak areas. Compare and contrast their resulting profiles of self-esteem based on their self-concepts to demonstrate how personal self-esteem is determined by what is important to us in life.

Personal Application 2: Role Model The purpose of this exercise is for students to explore the influence of social comparison in their judgements about self. During middle and late childhood, children begin turning to their peers as a point of comparison for their self-concept and self-esteem. As they no longer rely solely on themselves to determine whether they feel competent or inferior with regard to various aspects of their lives, others become a focal point with which to assess progress and ability. This often remains the case throughout our lives.

- Instructions for Students: Discuss the process you employ to assess yourself. What is it you use to determine your level of functioning in school? Your progress toward your goals? Your intellectual and creative ability? Your physical appearance and degree of being in shape? Your social prowess—ability to be a good friend, communicator, listener, lover, husband or wife, mother, daughter, sister (father, son, brother)? Are you stressed, relaxed, content, fortunate, well compensated at work? What do you use to determine the answers to all of these questions?
- Use in the Classroom: After having students share the degree to which they compare themselves to others in order to assess their own functioning, discuss this phenomenon. Are they comfortable with doing this? Do they feel they should be able to have their own internal standards and ignore the status of others around them? Do they think it's logical and acceptable to turn to others to assess one's self?

How important is it to judge other's behaviors and attitudes? If we didn't do so, wouldn't that remove the concept of acceptable and unacceptable behavior? Should everyone, regardless of their functioning, be considered equal? After addressing these issues, ask students how they choose whom to compare themselves with.

- Source: Goleman, D. (1995). *Emotional intelligence*. New York: Basic Books.

Personal Application 3: Your EQ The purpose of this exercise is to familiarize students with the concept of emotional intelligence through the exploration of their own emotional awareness. In 1990, Daniel Goleman published a book in which he introduced a new concept he called emotional intelligence. It involves four primary areas: 1) emotional self-awareness, 2) managing emotions, 3) reading emotions, and 4) handling relationships.

- Instructions for Students: Review Goleman's categories of emotional intelligence and discuss your level of functioning in each area. Be open and honest in your evaluation of yourself, and delineate your strengths and weaknesses in each category. How have your weaknesses in particular areas affected you? What might you do to improve your emotional functioning in these areas? How motivated are you to change?
- Use in the Classroom: Discuss the importance of acknowledging an emotional intelligence. What effects might an awareness of this bring about? Have students debate whether this would be a worthwhile focus in public schools, or whether it would be a waste of time and funds. Have them provide specific examples of the usefulness, or lack of, developing emotional intelligence. Is this an area that we can really link the term *intelligence*? Why or why not? What practical applications could result from work in this area? What kinds of careers might individuals who are strong in this area pursue? Is it a separate domain of intelligence, or is it related to intelligence in other domains?

Personal Application 4: Best Buddies The purpose of this exercise is to have students reflect on their childhood friendships with regard to the various elements identified as significant in peer relations. Friendship is a major area of study for life-span developmentalists. Children's social interactions serve a variety of functions, and friendships providing their own special contributions, both cognitively and emotionally.

- Instructions for Students: Write about your best friend from childhood. How did you meet and become friends? What did you do together? What did you like best about him or her? What did you fight about? What did you learn from your friend, and what did you teach your friend? Are you still friends? If so, how has your relationship grown and changed over the years? If not, when and why did the friendship end? Review the text coverage f friendships and the six functions they serve in early and middle childhood, to guide you in your thinking.
- Use in the Classroom: Compare childhood friendship to adult friendship. Regarding the six functions that have been delineated for childhood friendships, which ones apply to adult relationships? What is different between adult friends? The same? What about the gender of our friends and issues surrounding that? Compare and contrast friendships of the same and opposite sex then and now. Are the perspectives on these different for men and women? Have each gender dispel misunderstandings they have about each other regarding friendships, their functions, benefits, difficulties, etc.

Research Project Ideas

Research Project 1: Kohlberg's Moral Dilemmas This research project exposes students to Kohlberg's (1976) moral dilemmas. They should present the following four moral dilemmas to four children. Two of the children should be in early elementary school and the other two should be in late elementary school. Have the children respond to each dilemma and explain their responses. A description of the dilemmas, the data sheet for recording the responses, and a list of questions to answer are presented as **Handout 8**. In order to test the children, students will need to clear this through the human subjects review board at your school and get a signed informed consent form from the children's parents. See the section on Ethics, Human Subjects, and Informed Consent at the front of this Instructor's Manual.

After collecting the data, students should analyze their results according to Kohlberg's six stages. Do their reasons fit into his categories? Why or why not? How do their patterns of results support or not support his stage model? Are all their subjects' responses in one stage? What kind of mixture or patterning is evident? What age differences were apparent?

- Dilemma 1: In Europe, a woman is near death from cancer. There is one drug that the doctors think might save her. It is a form of radium that a druggist in the same town has recently discovered. The drug is expensive to make, but the druggist is charging ten times what the drug cost him to make. He paid $200 for the radium and is charging $2,000 for a small dose of the drug. The sick woman's husband, Heinz, goes to everyone he knows to borrow the money, but he can get together only about $1,000. He tells the druggist his wife is dying and asks him to sell the drug for $1,000 now and the rest later. The druggist says, "No, I discovered the drug and I'm going to make money from it." Heinz is desperate and considers breaking into the man's store to steal the drug for his wife. Should he? Why or why not?
- Dilemma 2: John and Mary are taking a class together and are strongly attracted to one another. They want to have sex together, but John is married, though the marriage is having difficulties. Should they sleep together? Why or why not?
- Dilemma 3: Dr. Johnson makes decisions about which patients have access to a kidney machine. Patients who do not get access will die. There are far more people who need the machine than can be accommodated by it, so there is a waiting list for those not yet on it. Dr. Johnson's young daughter is injured in a car accident and has kidney damage. She needs access to the machine to live. Should Dr. Johnson take another patient off the machine to put his daughter on? Why or why not?
- Dilemma 4: You are shopping with a friend when you notice that your friend is shoplifting. You look around and notice that the store manager is watching you. What should you do? Why?
- Sources: King, M. B., & Clark, D. E. (1989). *Instructor's manual to accompany Santrock and Yussen's child development: An introduction,* 4th ed. Dubuque, IA: Wm. C. Brown Communications, Inc. Kohlberg, L. (1976). Moral stages and moralization: The cognitive-developmental approach. In T. Lickona (Ed.), *Moral development and behavior.* New York: Holt, Rinehart, and Winston.

Research Project 2: Gender Roles and Television In this project, students will be required to evaluate three prime-time television shows for gender-role stereotyping. They should pick three shows between 7:00pm and 9:00pm that children tend to watch. After collecting their data, they should answer the provided questions in report form. For each show, they should record the following information using **Handout 9**:

- the number of male and female main characters
- the occupations of main male and female characters
- thematic connections between males and females (e.g., female in distress and male as rescuer)
- personality characteristics of one male and one female from the show (use the Bem androgyny scale to determine masculinity, femininity, or androgyny)

Questions:

- In the shows you watched, were more main roles taken by males or females? What kinds of occupations did the males have? What kinds of occupations did the females have? Were there status differences in the occupations of the males and females? What were they?
- What kinds of themes connected the males and females in the television programs you watched? Were the themes stereotyped for male-female relationships?
- What were the sex-typed categories of the males portrayed on television: masculine, cross-sexed, androgynous?
- What were the sex-typed categories of the females portrayed on television: feminine, cross-sexed, androgynous?
- What do you think these models are teaching children about what it means to be a male or a female in our society? Do you think these models are a fair representation of the way women and men act in the real world?

- Use in Classroom: Have students present their information from the research project in class. Examine the data overall, looking at: (1) the relative number of males and females in primary roles; (2) the relative status of the males' and females' occupations; (3) the thematic relationships presented between males and females, and the extent to which these tie into sex stereotyping; and (4) the relative presentation of androgynous, cross-sexed, and sex-stereotyped males and females on television. Ask the students to examine specific programs for differences. Are some shows more stereotyped than others? Which ones are less stereotyped? In the stereotyped programs, is one sex portrayed as more advantageous or as better than the other? Which one? How do the class data relate to the data on stereotypes presented in the text? If the programs generally support gender-role stereotypes, how does this affect the developing child? If males are presented as the more interesting and preferred sex, could this account for the tomboyish behavior of some girls in middle childhood? How?

  - It is expected that there are still more males than females represented, and that the males have higher-status occupations. Frequently women are still portrayed as the romantic interest or the damsel in distress who must be rescued by the male. The majority of males and females portrayed on television are sex-typed rather than androgynous, and the data would be expected to show this. These models present children with an idea of what it is to be a man or a woman in our culture. To the extent that the male role is more valued and interesting, it could provide a model of activities for both females and males, and may contribute to the tomboyish behavior of some girls in middle childhood.

Film and Video List

The following films and videos supplement the content of chapter 11. Contact information for film distributors can be found at the front of this Instructor's Manual under Film and Video Sources.

Emotional Intelligence: The Key to Social Skills (Films for the Humanities and Sciences, 29 minutes). Schools now hold the task of teaching social skills to children. This program looks at teaching techniques that help students develop emotional intelligence and social skills.

Friendship, Gender, and Morality (Insight Media, 30 minutes). This video explores the functions of friendship and gender in moral development.

Gender Socialization (Insight Media, 60 minutes). This video examines interactions between gender, race, and class and their effects on self-esteem, emotions, and world view.

Helping and Prosocial Behavior (Insight Media, 30 minutes). This program explores why people help each other and discusses modeling effects and diffusion of responsibility.

Not All Parents Are Straight (Cinema Guild, 58 minutes). This video examines the dynamics of the parent-child relationship within several different households where children are raised by gay and lesbian parents. It forces viewers to confront their own unexamined assumptions or biases on these matters.

Middle Childhood: Social and Emotional Development (Magna Systems, 28 minutes). This video explores the development of self, growth in social cognition, family relations, etc.

Obedience (MINN, 45 minutes). This black-and-white film of Milgram's classic research on obedience to authority can stimulate class discussion of moral development.

Peer Culture (Insight Media, 30 minutes). This video examines conflicts as children move into greater involvement with their peers and features *los abandonados* in an analysis of the peer group as a microsociety.

Prejudice: The Eye of the Storm (Insight Media, 25 minutes). This award winning film on video illustrates a third-grade teacher's lesson on prejudice (the blue-eye/brown-eye demonstration).

Web Site Suggestions

The URLs for general sites, common to all chapters, can be found at the front of this Instructor's Manual under Useful Web Sites. At the time of publication, all sites were current and active, however, please be advised that you may occasionally encounter a dead link.

Emotions and Emotional Intelligence
http://trochim.human.cornell.edu/gallery/young/emotion.htm

Family.Com: Parenting New England—Your Child's Self-Esteem
http://www.family.com/Features/family_1997_03/nhpt/nhpt199703_esteem/nhpt199703_esteem.htm

Gender Equity for Mathematics and Science
http://www.woodrow.org/teachers/math/gender/03f-greene.html
http://www.woodrow.org/teachers/math/gender/02fennema.html

Kohlberg's Theory of Moral Development
http://www.dushkin.com/connectext/psy/ch03/kohlberg.mhtml

Latchkey Children
http://www.ci.phoenix.az.us/FIRE/keykids.html

Handout 1 (CA 1)

"Shoot the Other Person Down" Activity

The purpose of this activity is to assess the effect of harsh communication patterns between parents and children and to generate alternative patterns of communication. Parent-child relationships may include sentences that "shoot the other person down," which often add fuel to bickering situations.

1. Discuss whether you have ever used or heard these kinds of statements.
   - I don't understand why you do these things.
   - How could you do such a thing?
   - I've never heard of such a thing.
   - How could someone with your brains and your background do such a thing?
   - I'm stumped, you really have confused me.
   - You are going too fast. Please go over it one more time so I'll understand.
   - You should know how I'm suffering.
   - I cannot believe you are going to do that now, when _____.
   - I do not understand how one little _____ is going to hurt you.
   - You never tell me what you're thinking.
   - Do it for me.
   - You've offended me.
   - I demand an apology.

2. Discuss the manifest and latent meanings of these statements.
   - I don't understand why you do these things.
   - How could you do such a thing?
   - I've never heard of such a thing.
   - How could someone with your brains and your background do such a thing?
   - I'm stumped, you really have confused me.
   - You are going too fast. Please go over it one more time so I'll understand.
   - You should know how I'm suffering.
   - I cannot believe you are going to do that now, when _____.
   - I do not understand how one little _____ is going to hurt you.
   - You never tell me what you're thinking.
   - Do it for me.
   - You've offended me.
   - I demand an apology.

3. For each statement, generate a healthier alternative statement.
   - I don't understand why you do these things.
   - How could you do such a thing?
   - I've never heard of such a thing.
   - How could someone with your brains and your background do such a thing?
   - I'm stumped, you really have confused me.
   - You are going too fast. Please go over it one more time so I'll understand.
   - You should know how I'm suffering.
   - I cannot believe you are going to do that now, when _____.
   - I do not understand how one little _____ is going to hurt you.
   - You never tell me what you're thinking.
   - Do it for me.
   - You've offended me.
   - I demand an apology.

Parenting Situations Activity

The purpose of this activity is to wrestle with common parenting situations. In a small group, each group member should present his/her own views about how to handle each situation and reasons why that approach would work. The goal is to try to reach a consensus about how to handle each situation.

1. Your 9-year-old and your 11-year-old want to play Nintendo all the time.

2. The fifth-grade math teacher sends a note home saying that your child rarely does his homework   and is easily distracted in class.

3. Your 10-year-old daughter wants to know why you won't let her wear makeup, nylons, and earrings. She says all her friends do.

4. You find out that your sixth-grader has removed a couple of cans of beer from our refrigerator.

5. Your third-grader and peers seem to delight in sprinkling their conversation with an assortment of swearwords.

6. Your fourth-grader starts to insist that she will only wear certain expensive brands of jeans, shoes, and tops; they are so expensive that your budget could not afford very much.

7. Your second-grader insists he doesn't need a baby-sitter anymore.

8. Your fifth-grader thinks she is old enough to date and is interested in a seventh-grade guy.

Intervention for Aggressive Children Activity

The purpose of the activity is for you to design an intervention program for aggressive children using Crick and Dodge's (1994) steps for processing social situations. Santrock introduced Dodge's original theory in the textbook. He states that children go through five steps in processing information about their social world. Children decode social cues, interpret the social cues, search for a response, select an optimal response, and enact that response.

- Source: Crick N.R., & Dodge, K.A. (1994). A review and reformulation of social information-processing mechanisms in children's social adjustment. *Psychological Bulletin, 115,* 74-101.

- Step 1 involves encoding internal and external cues.
- Step 2 involves interpreting the social cues and making inferences based on the interpretation.
- Step 3 involves clarifying goals. If conflict arises, clarification between the social partners is necessary with the resolution of conflict as the optimal outcome (focus on relationship goals). Arousal regulation is part of clarifying goals.
- Step 4 involves response access or construction. Children can use a response that they have used in the past by recalling strategies to use in the current situation. Or, if a novel situation occurs or past strategies have not been successful, children may need to construct a novel response.
- Step 5 involves making a response decision. Ideally, this should include response evaluation, outcome expectations, self-efficacy evaluations, and response selection.
- Step 6 involves the enactment of the response that was chosen in the previous step.
  - This step is not officially part of information processing as the information processing is completed in step 5. However, given the cyclical nature of interactions, peer responses to the enactment create additional social cues thus, the process repeats.

Critical Thinking Multiple-Choice Questions

1. The study of cognitive development and intelligence has provided a model for studying other aspects of psychological development. For example, researchers have applied the methods and theories originally devised to study children's minds to aspects of children's personality and social development. This exercise requires you to identify the approach to intelligence that seems to have been most influential in research on each topic below. Present reasons for each of your choices, and also indicate which approach appears to have been most widely used in the works on personality and social development presented by your author. Note that this exercise differs from previous ones in that you do not have to identify a best answer; to the contrary, you should develop arguments for each item!
   a. aptitude-treatment interaction
   b. social cognition
   c. peer statuses
   d. masculinity, femininity, and androgyny
   e. moral development

2. Review the brief description of Bronfenbrenner's ecological model of sociocultural influences in chapter 2. Then, determine which of the following findings reported in chapter 11 is correctly matched with one of the systems described in the model. Circle the letter of the best answer and explain why it is the best answer and why each other answer is not as good.
   a. Microsystem: Children spend less time with their parents because they are spending more time with their peers.
   b. Mesosystem: Children from middle-class families enjoy school more than children from lower-class families.
   c. Chronosystem: The gender roles that children are encouraged to adopt today are more diverse than those prevalent a decade ago.
   d. Macrosystem: Peers influence children's development by accepting, neglecting, or rejecting each other.
   e. Exosystem: Adolescents who have stepparents are more likely to experience problems in close relationships outside the family.

3. In this chapter, Santrock describes attempts to define and measure gender roles. Which of the following statements constitutes an assumption made by gender-role researchers, rather than an inference or an observation? Circle the letter of the best answer and explain why it is the best answer and why each other answer is not as good.
   a. Girls should grow up to be feminine and boys should grow up to be masculine.
   b. Gender-role stereotypes are more harmful to females than to males.
   c. Femininity and masculinity are separable aspects of personality that have their own unique characteristics.
   d. Androgynous individuals are more flexible and mentally healthier than masculine or feminine individuals.
   e. Females and males should transcend gender-role characteristics.

Suggested Answers for Critical Thinking Multiple-Choice Questions

1. The study of cognitive development and intelligence has provided a model for studying other aspects of psychological development. For example, researchers have applied the methods and theories originally devised to study children's minds to aspects of children's personality and social development. This exercise requires you to identify the approach to intelligence that seems to have been most influential in research on each topic below. Present reasons for each of your choices, and also indicate which approach appears to have been most widely used in the works on personality and social development presented by your author. Note that this exercise differs from previous ones in that you do not have to identify a best answer; to the contrary, you should develop arguments for each item!

    a. Aptitude-treatment interaction is an example of the individual differences approach. The key idea is that teaching practices are to be adapted to specific characteristics of students. Hence, the specific ways that student aptitudes and personalities differ have to be identified in order to match them with appropriate treatments.

    b. Social cognition is an example of the information-processing approach. The most obvious clue is Dodge's five-stage analysis of social cognition: decoding social cues, interpreting the cues, searching for a response, selecting an optimal response, and enacting the response. This is the way the information-processing approach breaks down cognitive tasks.

    c. Peer statuses are an example of the individual differences approach. The four peer statuses are based on children nominating other children as being liked or disliked. The stress is on likability as a quantifiable trait, which most closely resembles the individual differences approach to intelligence.

    d. Masculinity, femininity, and androgyny is an example of the individual differences approach. As in "c" the stress is on measuring the dimensions (traits) of masculinity and femininity, which are then used to classify sex-role orientation. These classifications are not developmental in the sense that Piagetian classifications are, and the emphasis in this work is on how individuals' sex-role orientations vary from one another.

    e. Moral development is an example of the cognitive developmental, or Piagetian, approach. Kohlberg's work is explicitly an extension of Piaget's and shows many of the classic Piagetian characteristics. For example, children's solutions to moral dilemmas are classified, not quantified; stages of moral development are supposedly universal. The emphasis of the approach is on characterizing the development and differentiation of the moral stages, not on how individuals who possess them differ or on how individuals process information related to moral decision making.

2. Review the brief description of Bronfenbrenner's ecological model of sociocultural influences in chapter 2. Then, determine which of the following findings reported in chapter 11 is correctly matched with one of the systems described in the model. Circle the letter of the best answer and explain why it is the best answer and why each other answer is not as good.

    a. Microsystem: Children spend less time with their parents because they are spending more time with their peers does not match. The situation described is a mesosystem; children's experience in one system (peer) is influencing their experience in another (family).

    b. Mesosystem: Children from middle-class families enjoy school more than children from lower-class families does match. Here, variations in family experience (one microsystem) influence adaptation to school (another microsystem).

c. <u>Chronosystem: The gender roles that children are encouraged to adopt today are more diverse than those prevalent a decade ago</u> does not match. The statement describes a pervasive cultural influence, which is called an aspect of the macrosystem in Bronfenbrenner's analysis. Chronosystems are the changes over the course of the lives of individuals that cause their lives to vary from those of other individuals who have lived through different historical changes. If the focus of the statement was something about how changing gender roles influence the gender-role development of different generations, then the statement would exemplify the chronosystem.

d. <u>Macrosystem: Peers influence children's development by accepting, neglecting, or rejecting each other</u> does not match. The statement describes variations of influence in peer relationships, which occur in microsystems. The variables of acceptance, rejection, or neglect do not define culture-level influences, but rather the quality of interactions in specific situations.

e. <u>Exosystem: Adolescents who have stepparents are more likely to experience problems in close relationships outside the family</u> does not match. This statement describes how experience in one microsystem (stepparent families) influences experience in another (close relationships). The individual in question, an adolescent, has influence in both situations, so this cannot be called an exosystem.

3. In this chapter, Santrock describes attempts to define and measure gender roles. Which of the following statements constitutes an assumption made by gender-role researchers, rather than an inference or an observation? Circle the letter of the best answer and explain why it is the best answer and why each other answer is not as good.

a. <u>Girls should grow up to be feminine and boys should grow up to be masculine</u> is an assumption, but it is not one that is made by gender researchers today. Santrock mentions this point as being an assumption held by previous generations of researchers.

b. <u>Gender-role stereotypes are more harmful to females than to males</u> is an inference. It is based on the observation that males enjoy more favorable gender stereotypes, which (logically) suggests that they will be less harmed by them than women. However, the actual claim is not supported in the chapter with direct evidence.

c. <u>Femininity and masculinity are separable aspects of personality that have their own unique characteristics</u> is the assumption. This belief led researchers to develop separate scales for masculinity and femininity. However, the belief itself has not been independently confirmed, and the text does not present either argument or evidence for its validity.

d. <u>Androgynous individuals are more flexible and mentally healthier than masculine or feminine individuals</u> is an observation. The statement is presented as a description of individuals who are classified as androgynous.

e. <u>Females and males should transcend gender-role characteristics</u> is an inference. It is the conclusion of Pleck's argument that gender-role classifications create false dichotomies or contrasts, and that individuals are actually unique and must resolve gender issues on their own terms.

Critical Thinking Essay Questions

Your answers to this kind of question demonstrate an ability to comprehend and apply ideas discussed in this chapter.

1. How do developmentalists measure self-esteem? Also, indicate and explain what factors influence the self-esteem of children.

2. Describe how emotional intelligence is different from intelligence as described in chapter 10.

3. Explain Kohlberg's theory of moral development, and indicate three criticisms of his approach.

4. Define *altruism*, and indicate how this concept relates to moral development.

5. Explain the concept of a gender-role stereotype.

6. Summarize the differences and similarities between the sexes.

7. Define *androgyny* and *gender-role transcendence*, and explain why some theorists prefer one concept over the other one.

8. Explain the kinds of problems that parents confront with their children regarding school and discipline, and how parents change their disciplinary practices as children grow older.

9. Discuss factors that contribute to or detract from children's adjustment to life in a stepfamily.

10. What are latchkey children? What kinds of problems do they face when parents are absent? How can parents diminish or heighten the difficulties faced by latchkey children?

11. Compare and contrast popular, rejected, controversial, and neglected children.

12. Identify and explain what factors influence who will be your friend.

13. Explain how entering school changes children's lives.

14. Explain what is meant by saying that schools are middle-class institutions that favor middle-class students.

Ideas to Help You Answer Critical Thinking Essay Questions

1. Begin by defining *self-esteem*. As you describe how developmentalists measure it, discuss how valid their approach seems to be. In other words, are their assessments really "getting at" self-esteem? Why or why not? The way in which they measure this phenomenon should also highlight what factors influence self-esteem. Include this in your discussion.

2. Approach this discussion from the fact that both concepts include the term *intelligence*. As you discuss the differences between them, draw the connection between the two based on their shared terminology.

3. Prior to presenting Kohlberg's theory, define *morality*. Can there be more than one definition? If so, what perspective does Kohlberg take? How does this color his theory and the stages within it? Do the criticisms address this issue or something else?

4. As you relate altruism to moral development, again consider how *morality* is defined. Does altruism's role change with varying conceptualizations of morality?

5. Prior to explaining the concept, present a gender-role stereotype for each gender. As you explain the concept, refer back to your descriptions.

6. This is a great prompt for a chart. Delineate the items/issues along which you will compare, then fill in the grid with the appropriate gender-related descriptions. Once you have visually mapped this out, write a summary describing what you found.

7. Describe an androgynous individual. What characteristics does he/she have? How might he/she behave in certain situations? Create a similar descriptive scenario with a gender-transcendent individual. Proceed to address the theoretical considerations of each of these.

8. Although you should review the textbook for coverage of important issues, approach this question from a personal perspective. When explaining these problems and the discipline issue, do so with examples from your own childhood. Not only will this make it more interesting and relevant, you will discover you understand the issues more clearly.

9. If you have had such an experience yourself, include personal examples in your discussion. What factors made your transition and adjustment easier? What things made it more difficult? If this is not something familiar to you, talk with a friend who went through this for some additional insight.

10. As you define latchkey children, present the various contributions to their situation. Being a latchkey child carries with it many implications regarding family situations and parental circumstances. Identify these as you discuss the experiences these children have, and it may lead to some original thought on your part as to parental contributions to their children's well-being or, in some cases, difficulties.

11. There are particular realms in which these children are initially identified. Present them, their significance, and how each type of child functions along these lines.

12. Begin with the factors presented in your text. Include comments about whether these factors played a role in your friendships. Why did they or didn't they? Does your text address any interactions between factors?

13. As you address this question, don't just focus on the children themselves, but the impact the start of school has on parents. Then discuss how the change in parents will also serve to influence the children's new life circumstances.

14. Begin this question by explaining your socioeconomic perspective. Were you middle class or not? Given your experiences, add a personal commentary on what the text covers in this regard.

Moral Dilemmas Activity

Present the following four moral dilemmas to four children. Two of the children should be in early elementary school and the other two should be in late elementary school. Have the children respond to each dilemma and explain their responses. In order to test the children, students will need to clear this through the human subjects review board at your school and get a signed informed consent form from the children's parents.

- Dilemma 1: In Europe, a woman is near death from cancer. There is one drug that the doctors think might save her. It is a form of radium that a druggist in the same town has recently discovered. The drug is expensive to make, but the druggist is charging ten times what the drug cost him to make. He paid $200 for the radium and is charging $2,000 for a small dose of the drug. The sick woman's husband, Heinz, goes to everyone he knows to borrow the money, but he can get together only about $1,000. He tells the druggist his wife is dying and asks him to sell the drug for $1,000 now and the rest later. The druggist says, "No, I discovered the drug and I'm going to make money from it." Heinz is desperate and considers breaking into the man's store to steal the drug for his wife. Should he? Why or why not?

- Dilemma 2: John and Mary are taking a class together and are strongly attracted to one another. They want to have sex together, but John is married, though the marriage is having difficulties. Should they sleep together? Why or why not?

- Dilemma 3: Dr. Johnson makes decisions about which patients have access to a kidney machine. Patients who do not get access will die. There are far more people who need the machine than can be accommodated by it, so there is a waiting list for those not yet on it. Dr. Johnson's young daughter is injured in a car accident and has kidney damage. She needs access to the machine to live. Should Dr. Johnson take another patient off the machine to put his daughter on? Why or why not?

- Dilemma 4: You are shopping with a friend when you notice that your friend is shoplifting. You look around and notice that the store manager is watching you. What should you do? Why?

Questions:
- Do your subjects' reasons fit into Kohlberg's categories? Why or why not?

- How do your patterns of results support or not support his stage model?

- Are all your subjects' responses in one stage? What kind of mixture or patterning is evident?

- What age differences were apparent?

Handout 9 (RP 2)

Gender Roles and Television

In this project, you will be required to evaluate three prime-time television shows for gender role stereotyping. Pick three shows between 7:00pm and 9:00pm that children tend to watch. After collecting your data, answer the questions that follow in a brief report. For each show, you should record the following information:

- number of male and female main characters
- occupations of main male and female characters
- thematic connections between males and females (e.g., female in distress and male as rescuer)
- personality characteristics of one male and one female from the show (use the Bem androgyny scale to determine masculinity, femininity, or androgyny)

1. Program _____
   Number:

   Occupations:

   Connections:

   Sex Type:

2. Program _____
   Number:

   Occupations:

   Connections:

   Sex Type:

3. Program _____
   Number:

   Occupations:

   Connections:

   Sex Type:

Handout 9 (RP 2) continued

Questions:

- In the shows you watched, were more main roles taken by males or females? What kinds of occupations did the males have? What kinds of occupations did the females have? Were there status differences in the occupations of the males and females? What were they?

- What kinds of themes connected the males and females in the television programs you watched? Were the themes stereotyped for male-female relationships?

- What were the sex-typed categories of the males portrayed on television: masculine, cross-sexed, androgynous?

- What were the sex-typed categories of the females portrayed on television: feminine, cross-sexed, androgynous?

- What do you think these models are teaching children about what it means to be a male or a female in our society? Do you think these models are a fair representation of the way women and men act in the real world?

Chapter 12: Physical and Cognitive Development in Adolescence

Total Teaching Package Outline

Lecture Outline	Resource References
Physical and Cognitive Development in Adolescence	PowerPoint Presentation: See www.mhhe.com Cognitive Maps: See Appendix A
The Nature of Adolescence	LO1 CA1: Defining Adolescence CA2: Societal Influence on the Stage of Adolescence F/V: Adolescence: Physical Growth and Dev. F/V: Adolescence: The Prolonged Transition
Puberty • Puberty's Boundaries and Determinants	LO2 OHT95, OHT122, OHT144, OHT146-148: Puberty LS1: Myths about Puberty F/V: Puberty WS: Puberty 101
• Hormonal Changes	OHT120: Hormone Levels by Sex & Pubertal Stage OHT121: Glands Involved in Pubertal Change OHT107: Usual Sequence of Physiological Changes
• Height, Weight, and Sexual Maturation -Height and Weight	OHT145: Height at Different Ages
-Sexual Maturation	PA1: That Awkward Stage
-Individual Variation in Puberty	RP1: Secular Trend
• Body Image	
• Early and Late Maturation	LO3 CA3: The Stars and the Nerds
Adolescent Sexuality	LO4
• Developing a Sexual Identity	LS2: The Development of Homosexuality
• The Progression of Adolescent Sexual Behaviors	OHT96: Adolescent Sexual Intercourse OHT133: Teenagers and Sexual Intercourse F/V: Truth, Sex, and Videotape
• Risk Factors for Sexual Problems	
• Contraceptive Use	OHT 134: Contraceptive Use by Adolescent Females
• Sexually Transmitted Diseases (STDs)	OHT97: Understanding AIDS F/V: Common Threads: Stories from the Quilt

• Adolescent Pregnancy
   -Consequences of Adolescent Pregnancy
   -Reducing Adolescent Pregnancy
	LO5
	OHT135: Trends in the Teenage Birth Rate
	OHT166: An Overview of Adolescent Pregnancy
	LS3: Teenage Pregnancy: Trends in Teenage Births
	F/V: Grounded for Life: Teenage Pregnancy
	WS: Teenage Pregnancy Prevention Initiative

Adolescent Problems and Health
 	
• Substance Use and Abuse
 	
   -Alcohol
 	
   -Cigarette Smoking
 	
   -The Roles of Development, Parents, and
    Peers
 	
• Eating Disorders
   -Anorexia Nervosa
   -Bulimia Nervosa
 	
• Adolescent Health
   -Adolescence: A Critical Juncture in Health
 	
   -Leading Causes of Death in Adolescence
	CA4: Parenting Regarding Adolescent Problem
	         Behavior
	LO6
	OHT110, 141 & IB, OHT169-172: Substance Use
	
	LO7
	
	PA2: Ah, Immortality!
	
	LO8
	
	LO9
	F/V: The Cult of the Beautiful Body
	F/V: Eating Disorders: The Inner Voice
	F/V: Eating Disorders: Approaches to Treatment
	F/V: Having your Cake: Goodbye to Bulimia
	F/V: The Silent Hunger: Anorexia and Bulimia
	F/V: Slim Hopes: Media's Obsession with Thinness
	WS: Eating Disorders
	
	LO10
	WS: National Center for Health Statistics
	
	WS: Teen Health Home Page

Adolescent Cognition
 	
• Piaget's Theory
 	
• Adolescent Egocentrism
 	
• Information Processing
   -Decision Making
   -Critical Thinking
	F/V: Adolescence: Cognitive and Moral Dev.
	
	LO11
	OHT93 & IB: Formal Operational Thought
	CA5: Training for Formal Operational Thought
	CA6: Piaget's Formal Operations
	PA3: Let Me Mull This Over…
	RP2: Piaget's Pendulum and Chemical Problems
	WS: Formal Operations Test
	
	LO12
	F/V: Teenage Mind and Body
	
	LO13
	OHT123: Algebra Problem
	OHT124: Approaches to Adolescent Learning
	LS4: Do Video Games Improve Spatial
	         Reasoning Skills?

Schools • The Transition to Middle or Junior High School	LO14 CA7: Free College Tuition? CA8: Uniforms for Adolescents?
• Effective Schools for Young Adolescents • High School Dropouts	LO15 LO16 OHT112: School Dropout Rates OHT113: Growth in High School Graduation

• Moral Education
  -The Hidden Curriculum
  -Character Education
  -Values Clarification
  -Cognitive Moral Development
  -Service Learning
	LO17
	CA9: Morality High

Review	CA10: Death of a Salesman CA11: Critical Thinking Multiple-Choice CA12: Critical Thinking Essays F/V: Adolescent Development F/V: Teenage Mind and Body F/V: Teens: What Makes Them Tick?

Chapter Outline

THE NATURE OF ADOLESCENCE
• Many stereotypes of adolescents are too negative.
  • Many adolescents today successfully negotiate the path from childhood to adulthood.
  • More adolescents, especially African Americans, graduate high school than in the past, and most have positive self-concepts and positive relationships with others.
  • Too many adolescents are not provided with adequate opportunities and support to become competent adults.
• It is important to view adolescents as a heterogeneous group because a different portrayal emerges, depending on the particular set of adolescents being described.

PUBERTY
Puberty's Boundaries and Determinants
• **Puberty** is a period of rapid physical maturation involving hormonal and bodily changes that occur primarily during early adolescence.
  • Puberty is the most important marker of the beginning of adolescence, however, for most individuals it is over before adolescence has ended.
  • The average age of **menarche**, a girl's first menstruation, has been declining an average of 4 months per decade for the past century due to improved nutrition, health, heredity, and body mass.
  • Puberty is not a single, sudden event.

Hormonal Changes
- **Hormones** are powerful chemical substances secreted by the endocrine glands and carried through the body by the bloodstream.
- The endocrine system's influence on puberty involves an interaction of the hypothalamus, the pituitary gland, and the gonads.
  - The **hypothalamus** is a structure in the higher portion of the brain that monitors eating, drinking, and sex.
  - The **pituitary gland** is an endocrine gland that controls growth and regulates other glands.
  - The **gonads** are the sex glands (testes in males, ovaries in females).
- **Testosterone** is a hormone associated in boys with the development of genitals, an increase in height, and a change in voice.
  - Males have an eighteenfold increase in testosterone during puberty.
- **Estradiol** is a hormone associated in girls with breasts, and uterine and skeletal development.
  - Females have an eighteenfold increase in estradiol during puberty.
- Males and females both have testosterone and estradiol, however, the proportion of the two hormones differs for males and females.
- Hormone levels in adolescents can influence behavior and behavior can also affect hormonal levels.
  - There is a complex bidirectional relationship between hormones and behavior.

Height, Weight, and Sexual Maturation
  Height and Weight
- The onset of pubertal growth occurs on the average at 9.5 years for girls and 11.5 for boys.
  - Girls grow an average of 3.5 inches per year during pubertal change, boys average 4 inches.
  Sexual Maturation
- Male pubertal characteristics develop in the following order:
  - Increase in penis and testicle size, appearance of straight pubic hair, minor voice change, first ejaculation, appearance of kinky pubic hair, onset of maximum growth, growth of armpit hair, detectable voice changes, and growth of facial hair.
- Female pubertal characteristics develop in the following order:
  - breasts enlarge or pubic hair appears, armpit hair, simultaneously growth in height and widening of the hips, then menarche.
  Individual Variation in Puberty
- The normal range is wide enough that, given two groups of the same age, some might have completed puberty before the other one begins the sequence.
  - Menarche is considered within a normal range if it appears between the ages of 9 and 15.

Body Image
- Adolescents are preoccupied with their bodies and develop individual images of what their bodies are like.
  - Compared to boys, girls are less happy with their bodies and have progressively more negative body images as puberty occurs.

Early and Late Maturation
- Early-maturing boys perceive themselves more positively and have more successful peer relations than late-maturing boys.
- In adulthood, late-maturing boys have a stronger sense of identity than early-maturing boys
- Early-maturing girls experience more vulnerability to problems (smoke, drink, be depressed, strive for more independence).
- Some researchers question whether puberty's effects are as strong as once believed.

ADOLESCENT SEXUALITY
- Adolescence is a time of sexual exploration and experimentation, of sexual fantasies and realities, or incorporating sexuality in to one's identity.

Developing a Sexual Identity
- The process of mastering emerging sexual feelings and forming a sense of sexual identity is multifaceted.
- Sexual identity involves an indication of sexual orientation, activities, interest, and styles of behavior that interfaces with other developing identities.
  - Homosexual identities, attractions, and behaviors increase with age.
  - Harmful stigmatization of homosexuality involves self-devaluation of the homosexual adolescent and may result in passing, the process of hiding one's real social identity.

The Progression of Adolescent Sexual Behaviors
- A predictable progression of sexual behaviors includes necking, petting, sexual intercourse, and oral sex.
  - National statistics reveal that 80 percent of girls and 70 percent of boys are virgins at age 15.
  - Ten percent of 19-year-olds have not had sexual intercourse.
  - Sexual intercourse occurs approximately 8 years before marriage.
  - Most adolescent females' first voluntary sexual partners are younger, the same age, or no more than two years older than they are.

Risk Factors for Sexual Problems
- Adolescents who engage in sex at early ages (before age 16) and experience a number of partners over time are the least effective users of contraception and are at risk for early, unintended pregnancy and for sexually transmitted diseases and other behaviors (drug use, delinquency).
- Adolescents in low-income neighborhoods are often more sexually active and have higher pregnancy rates.

Contraceptive Use
- Two risks associated with unprotected sex include unintended pregnancy and sexually transmitted diseases.
  - Adolescents are increasing their use of contraceptives, but large numbers still do not use contraceptives, or use them inconsistently.
  - Young adolescents and those from low-income backgrounds are less likely to use contraceptives than their older, middle-income counterparts.

Sexually Transmitted Diseases
- Sexually transmitted diseases (STDs) are contracted primarily through sexual contact, which is not limited to sexual intercourse.
  - Oral-genital and anal-genital contact also can be involved in STDs.
- Approximately 25 percent of sexually active adolescents have an STD (genital herpes, HIV, gonorrhea).

Adolescent Pregnancy
- More than 5,000 American adolescents become pregnant every year.
  - Though this number is lower than in the 1950s and 1960s, the difference is the steady rise in births to unmarried teenagers.
  - Most teen pregnancies are unintended (80%).
  - America's adolescent pregnancy rate is among the highest in the Western world.

- There was a decrease in adolescent pregnancies in the 1990s, especially for 15- to 17-year-old African Americans.
  - Fear of STDs (AIDS), school/community health centers, and great hope for the future are likely reasons for this decrease.

Consequences of Adolescent Pregnancy
- Adolescent pregnancy increases health risks for both the mother and the baby (low-birthweight, neurological problems, and childhood illnesses).
- It is important to note that it often is not pregnancy alone that places adolescents at risk.
  - Adolescent mothers often come from low-income circumstances and were not doing well in school prior to their pregnancy.

Reducing Adolescent Pregnancy
- Recommendations for reducing the high rate of adolescent pregnancy include: sex education and family planning, access to contraceptive methods, the life options approach, broad community involvement and support, and encouragement of abstinence for young adolescents.

ADOLESCENT PROBLEMS AND HEALTH

Substance Use and Abuse
- The 1960s and 1970s were times of marked increase in the use of illicit drugs.
- Drug use began to decline in the 1980s, increased in the mid 1990s, and then declined in the late 1990s.
- The U.S. has the highest adolescent drug use rate of any industrialized nation.
  - These statistics are likely to be an underestimation, as they do not include high school dropouts, who have a higher rate of drug use.

Alcohol
- Alcohol is a depressant and the most widely used drug by adolescents.
  - Alcoholism is the third leading cause of death in the U.S.
  - Many car accidents and acts of violence occur under the influence of alcohol.
- Alcohol use is prevalent for adolescents, however, heavy drinking has decreased. This trend has not been seen in college-age students.

Cigarette smoking
- Most individuals who smoke cigarettes begin this habit in childhood or adolescence.
- Adolescent smoking has recently decreased, though approximately one-third of high school seniors smoke cigarettes.
- Early smoking causes permanent genetic changes in the lungs and forever increases the risk of lung cancer.

The Roles of Development, Parents, and Peers
- Drug use in childhood or early adolescence has more detrimental long-term effects than when its onset occurs in late adolescence.
  - When adolescents use drugs to cope with stress, they enter adult roles of marriage and work prematurely, without adequate socioemotional growth, and experience greater failure in adult roles.
- Positive relationships with parents and others are important in reducing adolescents' drug use.
  - If parents and peers use drugs, adolescents are more likely to use drugs.

Eating Disorders
- There are two primary eating disorders in adolescence.

Anorexia Nervosa
- **Anorexia nervosa** is an eating disorder that involves the relentless pursuit of thinness through starvation.

- Three main characteristics of anorexia nervosa are:
  - Weighing less than 85 percent of what is considered normal for age and height.
  - Having an intense fear of gaining weight.
  - Having a distorted image of one's body shape.
- Anorexia often begins in early to middle teenage years, often following an episode of dieting and the occurrence of a life stress.
  - Anorexia is ten times more likely to characterize females than males.
  - Many of these individuals react to high expectations from well-educated wealthy families by trying to control their weight.

Bulimia Nervosa
- **Bulimia nervosa** is an eating disorder in which the individual consistently follows a binge-and-purge eating pattern.
  - Most binge-purgers are females in their late teens or early 20s and are of normal weight.
- As with anorexics, most bulimics are preoccupied with food, have a strong fear of becoming overweight, and are depressed or anxious.

Adolescent Health
  Adolescence: A Critical Juncture in Health
- Adolescence is an important time in the development of healthy or unhealthy behavioral patterns.
- U.S. adolescents exercise less and eat more junk food than other adolescents.
- Health goals for adolescents include reducing health-compromising behaviors and increasing health-enhancing behaviors.

Leading Causes of Death in Adolescence
- The three leading causes of death in adolescence are accidents (more than half of all deaths for 10- to 19-year-olds), suicide (suicide rate has tripled since 1950), and homicide (especially African American males).

ADOLESCENT COGNITION
Piaget's Theory
- Abstractness and idealism, as well as hypothetical-deductive reasoning, are highlighted in formal operational thought.
  - Formal operation thought involves the ability to reason about what is possible and hypothetical, as opposed to what is real, and the ability to reflect on one's own thoughts.
  - **Hypothetical-deductive reasoning** is the formal operational concept that adolescents have the cognitive ability to develop hypotheses, or best guesses, about ways to solve problems, such as an algebraic equation. Then they systematically deduce, or conclude, which is the best path to follow in solving the equation.
- Critics argue that there is more variation in individuals' formal operational abilities than Piaget envisioned.
  - Many young adolescents are not formal operational thinkers but rather are consolidating their concrete operational thought.
- Formal operational thought occurs in two phases:
  - Assimilation characterizes early adolescence (reality is overwhelming).
  - Accommodation characterizes middle adolescence (intellectual balance is restored through consolidation of formal operational thought).

Adolescent Egocentrism
- **Adolescent egocentrism** is the heightened self-consciousness of adolescents, which is reflected in their belief that others are as interested in them as they themselves are, and in their sense of personal uniqueness.

- Adolescent egocentrism can be divided into two types of social thinking:
  - **Imaginary audience** refers to the heightened self-consciousness of adolescents that is reflected in their belief that others are as interested in them as they themselves are. The imaginary audience involves attention-getting behavior—the attempt to be noticed, visible, and "on stage."
  - **Personal fable** is the part of adolescent egocentrism that involves an adolescent's sense of uniqueness and invulnerability.

Information Processing
- Two important aspects of changes in information processing in adolescence involve decision making and critical thinking.

Decision Making
- Adolescence is a time of increased decision making.
- Older adolescents are more competent than younger adolescents are.

Critical Thinking
- The following are cognitive changes that allow for the improved critical thinking in adolescence.
  - Increased speed, automaticity, and capacity of information processing, which free cognitive resources for other purposes.
  - More breadth of content knowledge in a variety of domains.
  - Increased ability to construct new combinations of knowledge.
  - A greater range and more spontaneous use of strategies or procedures for applying or obtaining knowledge, such as planning, considering alternatives, and cognitive monitoring.
  - In order to develop critical thinking skills in adolescence, basic literacy and math skills must be acquired in childhood.

SCHOOLS

The Transition to Middle or Junior High School
- The emergence of junior high schools in the 1920s and 1930s was justified on the basis of the physical, cognitive, and social changes that characterize early adolescence and the need for more schools in response to a growing student population.
- Middle schools have become popular in recent years and coincide with puberty's earlier arrival.
  - Critics worry that these schools are watered-down versions of high schools mimicking their curricular and extracurricular activities.
  - Critics also stress that many high schools foster passivity rather than autonomy and that schools should create a variety of pathways for students to achieve an identity.
- The transition to middle or junior high school coincides with many social (increased responsibility, achievement focus), familial (dependence on parents), and individual (puberty, body image, formal operation thought) changes in the adolescent's life.
  - **Top-dog phenomenon** describes the circumstance of moving from the top position (in elementary school, being the oldest, biggest, and most powerful students in the school) to the lowest position (in middle or junior high school, being the youngest, smallest, and least powerful students in the school).
    - This can lower students' satisfaction with school and commitment to school.

Effective Schools for Young Adolescents
- Successful schools for young adolescents take individual differences in development seriously, show a deep concern for what is known about early adolescence, and emphasize social and emotional development as much as intellectual development.

- In 1989, the Carnegie Corporation recommended a major redesign of middle schools.
  - Develop smaller "communities" to lessen the impersonal nature of large middle schools.
  - Lower student-to-counselor ratios to 10-to-1.
  - Involve parents and community leaders in schools.
  - Develop curricula that produce students who are literate, understand the sciences, and have a sense of health, ethics, and citizenship.
  - Have teachers team teach in more flexibly designed curriculum blocks that integrate several disciplines.
  - Boost students' health and fitness with more in-school programs and help students who need public health care to get it.

High School Dropouts
- The dropout rate overall declined considerably in the second half of the twentieth century.
  - The dropout rates for Latino and Native American youth are still very high.

Moral Education
  The Hidden Curriculum
  - Every school has a **hidden curriculum** that provides moral education.
    - The moral atmosphere that is part of every school conveys the hidden curriculum. School and classroom rules, teachers, school administrators, and educational materials create the moral atmosphere.
  Character Education
  - **Character education** is a direct approach that involves teaching students a basic moral literacy to prevent them from engaging in immoral behavior and doing harm to themselves or others.
    - Every school should have explicit moral code (lying, cheating, and stealing) that is clearly communicated to students and violations of the code should be met with sanctions.
  Values Clarification
  - **Values clarification** means helping people clarify what their lives are for and what is worth working for.
    - Students are encouraged to define their own values and understand the values of others.
  Cognitive Moral Education
  - **Cognitive moral education** is a concept based on the belief that students should learn to value such things as democracy and justice as their moral reasoning develops.
    - Kohlberg's theory of moral development has been the basis for a number of cognitive moral education programs.
  Service Learning
  - **Service learning** is a form of education that promotes social responsibility and service to the community.
  - Researchers have found that service learning benefits students in a number of ways:
    - Their grades improve, they become more motivated, and they set more goals.
    - Their self-esteem improves.
    - They become less alienated.
    - They increasingly reflect on society's political organization and moral order.
    - Required community service has increased in high schools.

Learning Objectives

1. Understand the nature of adolescence including how adolescents view themselves and how others view them.
2. Describe the physical, hormonal, and psychological changes that take place during puberty.
3. Discuss how the timing of pubertal changes impacts females and males.
4. Elaborate on adolescent sexuality, including development of a sexual identity, progression of sexual behaviors, contraceptive use, and STDs.
5. Examine adolescent pregnancy including statistics, consequences, and ways to reduce rates.
6. Discuss substance abuse among adolescents, being certain to identify which drugs are on the rise and which ones are declining in use.
7. Address the rates and effects of alcohol and nicotine use among teens.
8. Identify the role development, parents, and peers play in the decision to partake in alcohol, drug, and nicotine use.
9. Differentiate between anorexia nervosa and bulimia nervosa.
10. Describe adolescent health and the leading causes of death in adolescence.
11. Discuss Piaget's stage of formal operational thought.
12. Define adolescent egocentrism and distinguish between Elkind's two types of social thinking.
13. Elaborate on how decision making and critical thinking change during adolescence.
14. Examine the transition from elementary school to junior high school, including the criteria of an effective school.
15. Address the rate, causes, and effects of high school drop outs.
16. Discuss how schools in the United States differ from schools in other countries.
17. Discuss programs and services designed to teach moral education.

Key Terms

adolescent egocentrism
anorexia nervosa
bulimia nervosa
character education
cognitive moral education
estradiol
gonads
hidden curriculum
hormones
hypothalamus

hypothetical-deductive reasoning
imaginary audience
menarche
personal fable
pituitary gland
puberty
service learning
testosterone
top-dog phenomenon
values clarification

Key People

David Elkind
Lloyd Johnston, Patrick O'Malley, and Gerald Bachman

Lawrence Kohlberg
Joan Lipsitz
Jean Piaget

Lecture Suggestions

Lecture Suggestion 1: Myths about Puberty The purpose of this lecture is to introduce the general topic of puberty. Dacey and Kenny (1997) highlight three myths about puberty. Consider presenting these myths to your students as statements. Ask your class how many of them think that they are true. Then present the information that Dacey and Kenny use to counter these myths. Your students will likely get a kick out of the history of the term *puberty*. It comes from the Latin word *pubescere* which means to grow hairy.

- Puberty Starts at One Point in Time
  - As Santrock discusses in the textbook, the process of puberty takes several years. Hormonal changes that stimulate the biological changes actually start around age 8.5 for females and 9.5 for males. Yet, adolescents do not complete puberty until the mid to late teens.
    - Recall that the changes that occur during puberty include biological, psychological, and social factors. Thus, the term biopsychosocial captures the essence of puberty.
      - The hormonal changes interact with psychological adjustment that is necessary during puberty and these in turn interact with social relationships with peers and family.
- Puberty Strikes Without Warning
  - The mechanisms for pubertal changes are present prenatally for males and females. For example, females are born with a full complement of eggs and males experience penile erections in utero during sleep (Calderone, 1985). Hormones suppress the onset of puberty until early adolescence, though the reproductive system is fully present in infancy.
- Puberty is the Result of Raging Hormones
  - This myth is a half-truth as hormones do play an important role in puberty. However, it is important to think methodologically about this statement. Given the biopsychosocial nature of puberty it is difficult to tease apart the contributions of each of these factors. Hormones do not act alone as they are influenced and influencing social and psychological aspects of the individual. For example, the adolescent is cognitively interpreting the biological changes that are occurring. Thus, is the mood swing a result of the hormonal changes or the adolescent's interpretation (confusion) of the physical changes that are occurring?
- Sources: Calderone, M. (1985). Adolescent sexuality: Elements and genesis. *Journal of American Academy of Pediatrics* (Supplement). 699-703. Dacey, J. & Kenny, M. (1997). *Adolescent development* (2nd ed.). Madison, WI: Brown and Benchmark.

Lecture Suggestion 2: The Development of Homosexuality For some individuals, adolescence is a time for acknowledgement of homosexual feelings. Retrospective studies have provided us with a basic understanding of this development. Prospective longitudinal studies are essential for us to gain a better understanding of this complex development. Discuss with your students why it is important to use prospective studies (less societal distortion, "real-time" versus memories of issues, etc.)

Paroki (1987) has outlined the sequence of homosexual orientation development. He interviewed 120 gay and lesbian adolescents about their sexual identity development. The same sequence was described by most of the adolescents.

- Realization of one's desire to have same-sex relationships.
- Development of guilt, shame, fear of discovery, and a sense of abnormality.
- Attempt to change or be heterosexual through behavior or fantasy.
- Failure to become heterosexual and the development of low self-esteem due to this failure.
- Investigation of homosexual lifestyle through various methods (literature, sexual activity).
- Acceptance and development of a positive gay/lesbian identity.

Most adult homosexuals recall feeling "different" around the age of 13 (Isay, 1989). Rodriguez (1988) found that an awareness of same-sex attraction emerged around the age of 11, though acknowledgement of the feelings as homosexual didn't occur until age 16. By age 20, many have adopted the self-label as homosexual. D'Augelli et al. (1987) found that for lesbians same-sex feelings developed by age 16 and self-labeling occurred around age 21.

Paroki (1987) also inquired about where the adolescents he interviewed had learned about homosexuality. Most males learned about being gay through sexual experiences, whereas females learned about lesbianism through television and other media.

High self-esteem is more common for individuals who achieve early and positive acceptance of their homosexual identity. It is unclear in which direction this relationship functions. Does having high self-esteem facilitate coming to terms with one's sexual orientation or does coming to terms with one's sexual orientation enhance self-esteem (Savin-Williams & Rodriguez, 1993)? This relationship is more complicated for homosexual adolescents given the social stigmas and stereotypes that exist.

Many homosexual individuals agonize over the issue of revealing their sexual orientation. Lying about or concealing one's true sexual orientation can affect one's psychological well-being. Significant risks are taken when revealing a homosexual orientation. Possible consequences include loss of friendships, physical harm, loss of family support (emotional and financial), and barriers to career development. Social isolation and identity issues are linked to adolescent suicide. Gibson (1989) found that 30 percent of teenage suicides are related to homosexuality due to social prejudice and stressors. Schools have failed to acknowledge homosexual adolescents and thus have not provided social support systems for these adolescents.

- Sources: D'Augelli, D.A., Collins, C., & Hart, M.M. (1987). Social support patterns of lesbian women in a rural helping network. *Journal of Rural Community Psychology, 8*, 12-22. Gibson, P. (1989). Gay male and lesbian youth suicide. In *ADAMHA, Report of the secretary's task force on youth suicide* (Vol. 3, pp.110-142). DHHS Pub. No. Washington, DC: US Government Printing Office. Isay, R.A. (*1989). Being homosexual: Gay men and their development.* New York: Farrar-Straus-Giroux. Paroki, P. (1987). Health care delivery and the concerns of gay and lesbian adolescents. *Journal of Adolescent Health Care, 8*, 188-192. Rodriguez, R.A.,(1988). *Significant events in gay identity development: Gay men in Utah.* Paper presented at the 96th Annual Convention of the American Psychological Association, Atlanta. Savin-Williams, R.C., & Rodriguez, R.A. (1993). A developmental, clinical perspective on lesbian, gay male and bisexual youths. In T.P. Gullotta, G.R. Adams, & R. Montemayor (Eds.), *Adolescent sexuality, advances in adolescent development: An annual book series*, Vol. 5 (pp.77-101). Newbury Park, CA: Sage.

Lecture Suggestion 3: Teenage Pregnancy and Trends in Teenage Births The purpose of this lecture is to examine teenage pregnancy and the trends for teenage births in the United States (Ventura et al., 1998). The National Center for Health Statistics website is a gold mine of interesting statistics http://www.cdc.gov/nchs/.

- Approximately 500,000 American adolescents give birth every year. The vast majority of these adolescents are not married.
- Teenage birth rates are defined as the number of births per 1,000 adolescents.
  - The teenage birth rate decreased in all 50 states.
  - In 1996, there were 54.7 live births per 1,000 15- to 19-year-olds, down 4 percent from the year before.
  - There was an overall decline of 24 percent between 1991 and 1996. This follows the 24 percent increase in teenage birth rates between 1986 and 1991.
- The percentage of teenagers that remain unmarried has changed dramatically in past decades.
  - In 1950, 23 percent of teenagers that gave birth were not married, compared to 84 percent in 1996.
  - This change is due to the increase in birth rates among unmarried teenagers and the decline in marriage among teenagers. The majority of unmarried women giving birth are not teenagers.
- Comparisons between demographic groups can be made based on teenage birth rates.
  - African American teenagers had a significant drop in teen birth rates with a 21 percent decline between 1991 and 1996 (1996 rate was 91.7 per 1,000).

- Several factors have contributed to the decline in teenage birth rates in the 1990s. Teenagers are more likely to use contraceptives (condoms during first intercourse, and injectable or implant contraceptives for African American teens).

One major concern surrounding teenage pregnancy is the issue of prenatal care. Teenagers are significantly less likely to receive adequate prenatal care, they are more likely to smoke, and they are less likely to gain sufficient weight during the pregnancy. These behaviors influence the babies' health (increased risk for low birthweight, long-term disabilities, and infant mortality).

Another concern is the issue of cognitive readiness for parenting. Adolescents who were not cognitively ready for parenting were more likely to experience serious parenting stress and less likely to engage in responsive parenting (Sommer et al., 1993).

It is important that students understand that the negative consequences associated with teenage pregnancy are not necessarily the result of teen pregnancy, rather the negative consequences are associated with preexisting conditions or background characteristics of the teenager. Coley and Chase-Lansdale (1998) review research to support this conceptual idea. Individuals that live in poverty and that have lower educational aspirations are more likely to become pregnant as teenagers. Individuals in low-income environments with lower educational aspirations are more likely to live in poverty as an adult, have lower status jobs, and have children with lower cognitive capabilities. Thus, it is important to examine these preexisting characteristics when examining the consequences of teenage pregnancy.

- Sources: Coley, R.L., & Chase-Lansdale, P.L. (1998). Adolescent pregnancy and parenting: Recent evidence and future directions. *American Psychologist, 53,* 152-166. Sommer, K., Whitman, T.L., Borkowski, J.G., Schellenbach, C., Maxwell, S., & Keogh, D. (1993). Cognitive readiness and adolescent parenting. *Developmental Psychology, 29,* 389-398. Ventura, S.J., Curtin, S.C., Mathews, T.J. (1998). Teenage births in the Untied States: National and state trends, 1990-96. *National Vital Statistics System.* Hyattsville, MD: National Center for Health Statistics. http://www.cdc.gov/nchs/

Lecture Suggestion 4: Do Video Games Improve Spatial Reasoning Skills? This lecture will allow you to examine the relationship between video game playing and cognitive development in adolescence. Contrary to what many want to believe, there is no evidence to support the claim that video game playing causes any significant ill effects (Subrahmanyam & Greenfield, 1994). This is good news as more than 34 perccent of American households have a Nintendo game system.

Current research has examined the potential advantages of playing video games. Given the vast importance of computer competence in today's adult work world, video game playing may be beneficial. Video games may enhance adolescents' understanding and exposure to computers. Subrahmanyam and Greenfield speculate that they may also enhance eye-hand coordination, numerical concepts, decision making, and the ability to follow directions.

Greenfield (1994) found that action video games improve spatial relational skills. Despite males' advantage of having better spatial relation skills, there were no gender differences in the rate of improvement in spatial skills after playing a video game for 6 hours (none of the individuals had played any video games the previous year) (Okagaki & Greenfield, 1994). Given the influence of stimulation on the development of spatial skills, Subrahmanyam and Greenfield propose that video game playing may contribute to gender equality in spatial skills. In addition to the influence on spatial skills, researchers have found that video game playing may improve individuals' ability to divide their attention while attending to a task (Greenfield et al., 1994).

- Sources: Greenfield, P.M. (1994). Cognitive effects of video games: Guest editor's introduction. Video games as cultural artifacts. *Journal of Applied Developmental Psychology, 15,* 3-12. Greenfield, P.M., DeWinstanley, P., Kilpatrick, H., & Kaye, D. (1994). Action video games and informal education: Effects on strategies for dividing visual attention. *Journal of Applied Developmental Psychology, 15,* 105-123. Okagaki, L., & Greenfield, P.M. (1994). Effect of video game playing on measures of spatial performance: Gender effects in late adolescence. *Journal of Applied Developmental Psychology, 15,* 33-58. Subrahmanyam, K., & Greenfield, P.M. (1994). Effect of video game practice on spatial skills in girls and boys. *Journal of Applied Developmental Psychology, 15,* 13-32.

Classroom Activities

Classroom Activity 1: Defining Adolescence A good way to discuss the problem of defining adolescence as a stage or period in life is to ask students to identify the formal signs or markers that signify adolescence has begun or ended. You may want to have students prepare for the discussion by answering the following questions either as an out-of-class assignment or as an in-class writing exercise.

- How do you define adolescence? In your answer, indicate what you believe about (a) when adolescence begins and ends (give ages); (b) what, besides age, indicates that adolescence is beginning or ending, and what the "signs" are that mark the boundaries of this time of life; and (c) what, if anything, makes adolescence a special time of life.

Structure your discussion by writing "beginning" and "end" on a chalkboard or overhead. Ask students simply to call out what they think marks the beginning and end of adolescence, and write their suggestions on the board. Solicit many answers. The two lists you get should permit you to discuss and illustrate many of the problems developmentalists face when they try to define and understand adolescence. For example, you should have lists that contain many different kinds of markers as well as different ages. You can discuss whether each sign of the beginning or end of adolescence occurs at the same time as the others. Are the changes simultaneous? Is one more important or fundamental than the others? Does one capture the essence of adolescence? Do the signs that mark the end of adolescence parallel those that mark the beginning? The lists you get should help you to illustrate the senses in which adolescence is (or is not) both a biological fact and a social invention. You can also use them to consider the value of thinking of adolescence as a stage as opposed to a less well-defined period in life. This activity also provides an agenda of topics for the unit on adolescence.
Logistics:
- Group size: Individual and full class.
- Approximate time: Individual (15 minutes) and full class discussion (20 minutes).

Classroom Activity 2: Societal Influence on the Stage of Adolescence G. Stanley Hall coined the term *adolescence* at the beginning of the twentieth century, thus it is a relatively new developmental stage. Ask students to "brainstorm" the societal changes and influences that produced the need for an adolescence stage.

- How did the industrial revolution create a need for an adolescence stage? What effects did the need for more education have on the teenage years? Could modern society exist without an adolescence stage? How might society change if teenagers were allowed to compete as equals with adults in the workforce? What are the advantages and disadvantages of adolescence? Why does society hurry individuals through childhood and then suspend them in a prolonged period of adolescence?
Logistics:
- Group size: Individual and full class.
- Approximate time: Individual (15 minutes) and full class discussion (20 minutes).
- Source: Simons, J. A., Irwin, D. B., & Drinnin, B. A. (1987). *Instructor's manual to accompany psychology: The search for understanding.* St. Paul, MN: West Publishing.

Classroom Activity 3: The Stars and the Nerds A way to illustrate the classic findings about the relationship between early or late maturation and aspects of personality and social development among adolescent boys is to do what we call "The Stars and the Nerds" activity. This activity is fun and nearly always stimulates student discussion about the relationship between physical and psychological development at puberty, as well as their spontaneous application of the material to their own lives.

Begin by asking the class to think about the most popular boy in their seventh-, eighth-, or ninth-grade class. Have students try to form an image of the person that they can then describe to you. Give them a minute, then solicit their physical and psychological descriptions. Write their answers on a chalkboard or on an overhead under the "Star" heading. You may have occasion to ask for clarification or additional comments on the meaning of the characteristic or observation. You should find that students have fun thinking of these characteristics and describing the individuals they have in mind.

When you finish collecting descriptions of the "stars," announce that you now want a description of the class "nerd," or least popular boy. Arrange student responses under the "Nerd" heading as you collect them. This phrase will undoubtedly pass with a certain amount of hilarity, which generally should contribute to, rather than detract from, the exercise.

Finally, ask students to study the paired sets of characteristics and comment on any pattern among the respective lists of psychological and physical characteristics that they notice.

- You should find indications that (a) the popular boy was an early maturer and the unpopular boy was a late maturer, and (b) the popular boy enjoyed a considerable range of personal and social advantages compared to the unpopular boy. Comment on the extent to which this mirrors the classic and contemporary work on early versus late maturation. If you have time, you may want to repeat the activity for students' recollection of popular versus unpopular girls (or do it this way in the first place), and find out whether the results are similar. The literature suggests that they should not be.

Logistics:
- Group size: Full class.
- Approximate time: Full class discussion (10-20 minutes).
- Source: Simons, J. A., Irwin, D. B., & Drinnin, B. A. (1987). *Instructor's manual to accompany psychology: The search for understanding.* St. Paul, MN: West Publishing.

Classroom Activity 4: Parenting Regarding Adolescent Problem Behavior Divide the class into small groups, and give each group a different problem to discuss (e.g., a child with an alcohol abuse problem, an adolescent with anorexia nervosa, a pregnant teenager). How would they, as parents, respond to a child with that difficulty? Should the parent report their adolescent's criminal behavior to the police? Should they commit their adolescent to the hospital for anorexia nervosa? Have each group present their plan to the class.

Logistics:
- Group size: Small group and full class.
- Approximate time: Small group (15 minutes) and full class discussion (20 minutes).
- Source: King, M. B., & Clark, D. B. (1990). *Instructor's manual to accompany children.* Dubuque, IA: Wm. C. Brown Communications, Inc.

Classroom Activity 5: Training for Formal Operational Thought The purpose of this activity is for students to review adolescents' cognitive abilities and discuss potential strategies for enhancing cognitive abilities. Ask groups of four to six students to design a curriculum for promoting formal operational reasoning in concrete operational children. During the first part of the discussion, the students should specify what changes normally take place between those two stages. After the initial discussion, the students should identify what activities might promote those changes.

Logistics:
- Group size: Small group and full class.
- Approximate time: Small group (15 minutes) and full class discussion (20 minutes).
- Source: King, M. B., & Clark, D. B. (1990). *Instructor's manual to accompany children.* Dubuque, IA: Wm. C. Brown Communications, Inc.

Classroom Activity 6: Piaget's Formal Operations This activity focuses on Piaget's formal operational stage. In small groups, students should use **Handout 1** for the following two tasks. Group members will attempt to solve Piaget's pendulum task and Piaget's chemical task and then analyze their problem-solving process for aspects of formal operational reasoning.

- Pendulum Task
  - Demonstrate a pendulum with various lengths of string and a number of equal weights. Group members are to identify the variable(s) that determine(s) the speed of the pendulum swing. The possible variables to manipulate are length, weight, height of the drop, and force of the drop.
- Chemical Task
  - Display five numbered flasks with each containing one of the following colorless chemicals: water, hydrogen peroxide, potassium iodine, acid, and thiosulfate. Have the students determine which combination of chemicals produces a mixture with the color yellow.

Each task is a combination problem. They are solved by systematically manipulating each of the variables and all of the possible combinations of variables to identify the correct solution.

- For the pendulum problem, the problem solver must manipulate the length of the string, the number of weights, the force with which the weight is swung, and the height from which the weight is dropped.
- In the chemistry task, the solution to the problem is to try each chemical until the solution to the problem is found.

Logistics:
- Materials: Handout 1 (Formal Operations Activity).
- Group size: Small group.
- Approximate time: Small group (60 minutes).
- Source: King, M. B., & Clark, D. E. (1989). *Instructor's manual to accompany Santrock & Yussen's child development: An introduction*, 4th ed. Dubuque, IA.: Wm. C. Brown Communications, Inc.

Classroom Activity 7: Free College Tuition? In 1981, sixth-graders (mostly Hispanic) of P.S. 121 in East Harlem were addressed by 71-year-old Eugene Lang, a self-made millionaire. On impulse he told them, "If you can somehow manage to graduate from high school, I'll pay your college tuition." In 1990, 34 of 61 students were enrolled at least part-time in colleges, with about one-third of them completing their junior year. Another nine of the students had Lang help them find jobs after graduating from high school. When Lang decided to "adopt" this class, he met with them regularly, giving them support, encouragement, and advice.

Since then, other individuals have adopted classes, and the I Have A Dream Foundation in New York City helps successful businesspersons adopt a class for $300,000.

- What do you think of such programs? What are the advantages and disadvantages? How might you accomplish the same level of enthusiasm and success with a program that would do more than "hit and miss" certain sixth-grade classes?

Logistics:
- Group size: Full class.
- Approximate time: Full class discussion (10 minutes).

Classroom Activity 8: Uniforms for Adolescents? This activity addresses adolescents' rights and typically stimulates significant discussion and controversy. Should high schools be able to have and enforce dress codes? What restrictions in clothing are reasonable? Would public schools be better off requiring uniforms? What are your personal experiences with school dress codes? How does clothing affect behavioral and academic performance in the schools? Who should establish the dress code?

After students have discussed these questions in small groups, supplement the discussion with additional information. In the 1970s and 1980s, dozens of federal judges have had to make rulings on whether the constitutional guarantees of privacy and free speech apply to the length of skirts and boots, and to other aspects of clothing such as designer clothes. There is no consensus among these rulings. How would you rule?

Take the discussion in the direction of other rights or non-rights of high school students. Do high school students have rights to free speech? They used to. In 1943, the Supreme Court (*Barnette v. West*

Virginia) ruled that it was within a student's right to refuse to salute the flag. In 1969, the Supreme Court (*Tinker v. Des Moines Independent Community School District*) ruled that students have constitutional rights to freedom of speech and expression in their schools, when it agreed that students could not be suspended for wearing black armbands to protest the Vietnam War. But in 1990, in about 25 states, school athletes must submit to mandatory urine testing for cocaine, steroids, marijuana, and alcohol. In Arkansas, school administrators are allowed to use breathalyzer tests, blood tests, and polygraph tests on students, and drug-sniffing dogs are used in schools. According to a 1985 Supreme Court decision (*New Jersey v. TLO*), regardless of the Fourth Amendment, students' lockers, gym bags, and purses are subject to spot searches. In a January 1988 ruling (*Hazelwood v. Missouri*), the Supreme Court even ruled that administrators have the right to censor school newspapers. Justice Byron R. White wrote, "A school need not tolerate student speech that is inconsistent with its basic educational mission even though the government could not censor similar speech outside the school."

Do students need their freedoms limited in order to protect them from the dangers of current times? How do issues of confidentiality, privacy, consent, and autonomy relate to teenagers? Why is society growing less tolerant of minors' free speech and more willing to assault their privacy (e.g., 67 percent of adults support mandatory drug testing for all high school students)? If teenagers would benefit from limited freedom, is the same true for adults?

Logistics:
- Group size: Small group and full class.
- Approximate time: Small group (20 minutes) and full class discussion (30 minutes).
- Sources: Bentayou, F. (1990, April). Children, behave. *Omni*, 33. Leslie, C. (1989, Nov. 27). Hey, hairball! You're gone! *Newsweek*, 79.

Classroom Activity 9: Morality High The purpose of this exercise is to have students consider the role of schools in developing morality in students. Beginning with John Dewey's "hidden curriculum" and including Kohlberg's acknowledgement of the importance of the moral atmosphere of the school, developmentalists are recognizing school-taught morality as an important cognitive issue.

- In small groups, have students describe the moral atmosphere of their junior high and high school. Were there any overt attempts made to teach morality and encourage students to develop their values? If so, what were they? If not, do you think there should have been? Do you think it could have had a positive effect on the students you went to school with? Do you think this is even an area that schools should be involved in, or is it most appropriate to leave it to the parents?

This topic makes great discussion or debate material. Take a poll to see the distribution of students who think schools should offer "morality training" and those who don't believe it belongs in the schools. Set up teams for debate if possible. Another option is to have students break up into groups and design a "morality program" for a junior high or high school. Remind them to review the social and cognitive functioning of children at the particular age they are dealing with. Have groups present their programs to the class, and discuss. Create a list of reasons for having such programs and how they might impact society.

Logistics:
- Group size: Small group and full class.
- Approximate time: Small groups (30 minutes) and full class discussion (30 minutes).
- Sources: Dewey, J. (1993). *How we think*. Lexington, MA: D.C. Heath. Kohlberg, L. (1986). A current statement of some theoretical issues. In S. Modgil & C. Modgil (Eds.), *Lawrence Kohlberg*. Philedelphia Falmer.

Classroom Activity 10: Death of a Salesman The purpose of this activity is to have students apply concepts of adolescence to a movie. Biff, the adolescent son in Arthur Miller's *Death of a Salesman*, provides many examples from an adolescent's life. Consider showing this video in class and then lead a discussion regarding relevant concepts from the chapter.

Logistics:
- Materials: *Death of a Salesman* movie.
- Group size: Full class.
- Approximate time: Video and full class discussion (3 hours).

Classroom Activity 11: Critical Thinking Multiple-Choice Questions and Suggested Answers Discuss the answers to the critical thinking multiple-choice questions on **Handout 2**. Question 1 requires a careful review of the major theoretical perspectives as well as the chapter material. Have students review chapter 2, previous lectures, activities, and exercises, or discuss with them directly how the theoretical perspectives are used in chapter 12. The challenge is that none of the perspectives is mentioned by name (except Erikson's view of delinquency), and students have to recognize each theory from the content of the discussion. To help them decide which one is most extensively represented in the chapter, suggest that students make a table in which they list each theory across the top row and each problem or disturbance in the first column. They then can enter in the table how each theory is or is not used to understand each topic. The result should be that the first three alternatives are used explicitly, but only behavioral theories (social cognitive theory) are used in all.

For question 2, an important point to clarify for students is that the various characteristics or types of formal operational thinking are not mutually exclusive. They are separate but logically related aspects. The task in this question, then, is to identify which characteristic of adolescent thinking is most emphasized in Cleveland Wilkes's comments. In fact, a good answer would identify and highlight how each characteristic of thought is present in Wilkes's comments, but also identify which seems to be most ascendant or pronounced.

Question 3 tests students' understanding of Piaget's theory of cognitive development. They need to recall concepts from the four stages of Piaget's theory. This is an opportunity to review the entire theory and test students' general understanding. The answers are provided as **Handout 3**.

Logistics:
- Materials: Handout 2 (the critical thinking multiple-choice questions) and Handout 3 (answers).
- Group size: Small groups to discuss the questions, then a full class discussion.
- Approximate time: Small groups (15 to 20 minutes), full class discussion of any questions (15 minutes).

Classroom Activity 12: Critical Thinking Essay Questions and Suggestions for Helping Students Answer the Essays Discuss the students' answers to the critical thinking essay questions provided in **Handout 4**. Several objectives can be met with these questions. First, the answering of these questions facilitates students' understanding of concepts in chapter 12. Second, this type of essay question affords the students an opportunity to apply the concepts to their own lives, which will facilitate their retention of the material. Third, the essay format also will give students practice expressing themselves in written form. Ideas to help students answer the critical thinking essay questions are provided as **Handout 5**.

Logistics:
- Materials: Handout 3 (essay questions) and Handout 5 (helpful suggestions for the answers).
- Group size: Individual, then full class.
- Approximate time: Individual (60 minutes), full class discussion of any questions (30 minutes).

Personal Applications

Personal Application 1: That Awkward Stage The purpose of this exercise is for students to think about their experiences with puberty, and to remind them of the variation of individual rates of maturation. This is a particularly dramatic and often difficult stage of development, with physical changes influencing psychological and emotional changes, resulting in numerous behavioral changes. Not only are there individual differences with regard to maturation, but also in terms of how individuals adapt to all that they are developmentally going through.

- Instructions for Students: Recall your early adolescent years, and write about your particular experiences with puberty. Did you mature early or late? How did you feel about the changes taking place with you – physically and emotionally? What do you recall about your friends and classmates during this time? Were you able to recognize behavioral changes within both yourself and your friends? How did you change? How did they change? How did your parents and siblings respond to "the new you"? Overall, was this a difficult time or were you able to make it through pretty easily?
- Use in the Classroom: If they don't have enough to deal with in puberty already, today's preteens have many different experiences than those of years ago. Nothing seems to be sacred with regard to open sexuality and homosexuality, and kids are blatantly exposed to these things through a variety of mediums—newspapers, magazines, TV, movies, music, and the Internet. Have students discuss the impact of our very open and explicit society on developing teens. What cultural signals are they receiving? How are they responding to what appear to be norms and expectations in terms of dress, problem solving, and relationships? What impact might this have on society in the near future?

Personal Application 2: Ah, Immortality! The purpose of this exercise is for students to recall the daring nature of adolescents. Teenagers have a sense of immortality that impacts their decision making, in often dangerous situations. It is a time filled with experimenting and indulging in risky behavior.

- Instructions for Students: Think back to your teen years and write about the risky behaviors you engaged in. Did you only do such things once just to try it, or did you routinely engage in things that were pushing your luck? How much of a role did peer pressure play? Did you have any bad, frightening experiences that woke you up to the dangers you were engaged in, or did you function oblivious to the possibility that something bad could actually happen to you? Do you continue any bad habits that you started as an adolescent, such as smoking, using drugs, or heavy drinking? Were your parents aware of your behavior? How did you rationalize your behavior at the time?
- Use in the Classroom: If students are willing, have them share these stories. As students will most likely vary with regard to their risky pasts, try and determine what factors may have played a role in determining the adolescent paths chosen. Are students from a stable, close family those that did not engage in typical dangerous teen behavior? Is there any connection to how they were doing in school? Involvement in extracurricular activities? Why did they choose the friends they did? Did they keep their childhood friends during this transition, or did they drift to new social circles? What has changed since that time in their current state? Are there those who still function as if they're immortal, or have most taken on a more responsible lifestyle?

Personal Application 3: Let Me Mull This Over... Use this exercise to help students recognize the cognitive processes of an adolescent. Decision-making skills are enhanced with further cognitive development, and teens often find themselves in the position of having to make some big decisions.

- Instructions for Students: Recall a big decision that you made during adolescence: to go to college or not, which college to attend, who to take to the Prom, how far to take a romantic relationship, to get a job and where to work, how to spend the money you earned, etc. See if you can remember the thought processes that led you to make the choice you did. Did you feel prepared or unprepared to make such a decision? What factors were most important to consider when making your decision? Did anyone help you to reach the conclusion you did? Did you ask for their input or did they just give it? How did you feel after you made the decision? Was it the right one?

- Use in the Classroom: You can begin by having students share their stories if they're willing, but go beyond early adolescence and address the decisions they are faced with making now. Ask students what important decisions they've recently made, or will be faced with in the near future. How do they plan on going about making up their mind? Do they hope to have help from others? If so, who? Do they feel that there would be someone on campus who they could turn to for advice with a decision?

Research Project Ideas

Research Project 1: Secular Trend The purpose of this project is to examine the secular trend in the age, and other characteristics, of puberty in families. Students should ask their parents and grandparents the age at which each went through puberty (parents should give information on grandparents, if information is not available from grandparents directly). Older students may have mature children that can be included in this chart. They should record the age at which they went through puberty using **Handout 6** and then they should answer the following questions.

Questions:
- Does the age of onset of puberty differ for the three different generations represented in the data? If so, in what way?
- Does the age of onset of puberty differ for the two sexes? What is the direction of the difference?
- How do the findings on generational differences relate to the trends described in the text? Why might they be similar or different from the findings described in the text?
- How do the findings here on sex differences in age of puberty relate to data in the text?
- Use in the Classroom: Have the students present their research project data in class. Pool the data for the three generations, keeping the data separated by sex. What generational differences in age of puberty are seen for the group as a whole? What sex differences in age of puberty are seen for the group as a whole? How could these criteria affect the data? How do the results reported by the class support or refute the data presented in the text?

Research Project 2: Piaget's Pendulum and Chemical Problems Students should pair up with a classmate. One should present the other with Piaget's pendulum task. Then they should switch and the other one will present the other with Piaget's chemical task. Next, test an 11-year-old on the two tasks. Prior to the start of the research, the project must be approved by the human subjects review board at your school and the students must get a signed informed consent form from the child's parents. See the section at the front of this Instructor's Manual on Ethics, Human Subjects, and Informed Consent. Instructions for the tasks are provided below and on **Handout 7** for the students.

- For the pendulum task, provide a frame for a pendulum as well as various lengths of string and a number of weights of equal size. Instruct the subjects to assemble the pendulum and to identify the variable(s) that determine(s) the period of the pendulum swing. The possible variables to manipulate are length, weight, height of the drop, and force of the initial push. Record on the data sheet the variables that the subjects manipulate and the way in which subjects organize the manipulations.
- For the chemical task, provide water, hydrogen peroxide, potassium iodine, acid, and thiosulfate in five numbered flasks. All of the chemicals are initially clear liquids. The subjects must determine which combination of chemicals produces a mixture with the color yellow. Record on the data sheet the variables that the subjects manipulate and the way in which subjects organize the manipulations.
  - Both tasks present combination problems, which are solved by systematically manipulating each of the variables and all of the possible combinations of variables to identify the correct solution. These tasks test for aspects of formal operational reasoning. After making the observations, answer the questions that follow.

Questions:
- How did the student solve the tasks? How would you characterize the responses? Did the student systematically manipulate the variables?
- How did the 11-year-old solve the tasks? How would you characterize the 11-year-old's responses? Did he or she systematically manipulate the variables?
- What differences did you observe in performance of the younger and older adolescent? How would you characterize their performances according to Piaget's theory? Did you find evidence of formal operational reasoning in either, both, or neither of your subjects? How would you account for your findings? What is the nature of the difference between performances of the younger and older adolescent?

- Use in the Classroom: Have the students combine their data, identify trends in the results, and relate their results to Piaget's theory.
- This project relates to Classroom Activity 6: Piaget's Formal Operations.

Film and Video List

The following films and videos supplement the content of chapter 12. Contact information for film distributors can be found at the front of this Instructor's Manual under Film and Video Sources.

Adolescence: Cognitive and Moral Development (Magna Systems, 25 minutes). The focus of this video is the physical changes of puberty that are accompanied by changes in thinking and moral reasoning.

Adolescence: Physical Growth and Development (Magna Systems, 25 minutes). This program is concerned with physical changes during adolescence. In addition, the effects of early maturation and problem behaviors are discussed.

Adolescence: The Prolonged Transition (Insight Media, 30 minutes). This program uses historical and cross-cultural comparisons to question the view of adolescence as a social construction.

Adolescent Development (Insight Media, 30 minutes). This video covers diverse aspects of physical, social, and psychological development and discusses developmental tasks, puberty, self image, social cognition, formal operations, and Kohlberg's theory of moral development.

Common Threads: Stories from the Quilt (Direct Cinema Limited, 80 minutes). This documentary focuses on five people who died from AIDS and how their loved ones came to terms with the loss.

The Cult of the Beautiful Body (Films for the Humanities and Sciences, 30 minutes). This program discusses body consciousness and how Western society has reduced courtship to a one-dimensional experience based primarily on physical attraction. It discusses the pressure men feel to conform to an abstract physical ideal, the role of the media, and culture.

Eating Disorders: The Inner Voice (Films for the Humanities and Sciences, 30 minutes). Four women and men share their torment in dealing with the physical and emotional pain of eating disorders. Medical, psychological, and nutritional experts explain the types of eating disorders, their causes, and who is most at risk. Treatment options are also discussed.

Eating Disorders: New Approaches to Treatment (Films for the Humanities and Sciences, 28 minutes). This program examines the use of antidepressants and cognitive behavioral therapy to combat eating disorders. Prevention is also discussed.

Grounded for Life: Teenage Pregnancy (Films for the Humanities and Sciences, 30 minutes). This program examines the rising national trend of unplanned pregnancies in the teen population. It uses case studies and interviews with teenage mothers to illustrate the risk factors, motivations, and thought processes associated with this growing social problem.

Having your Cake: Goodbye to Bulimia (Films for the Humanities and Sciences, 24 minutes). Four women share the details of their battles with bulimia. The focus is on how the women let go of the self-destructive behavior and moved towards physical and emotional health.

Puberty (Films for the Humanities and Sciences, 18 minutes). This program describes the hormonally driven metamorphosis that takes place in females and males as they grow to physical, sexual, and emotional maturity. Microscopic, endoscopic, and thermal imaging show detailed aspects of the male and female reproductive systems.

The Silent Hunger: Anorexia and Bulimia (Films for the Humanities and Sciences, 46 minutes). This program discusses eating disorders and their causes. Seven females who have suffered from an eating disorder and various health professionals tell their stories.

Slim Hopes: Media's Obsession with Thinness (Media Education Foundation, 1995, 30 minutes). This video discusses media's fascination with thinness.

Teenage Mind and Body (Insight Media, 1992, 30 minutes). Elkind's ideas about the contrast between teenagers' abilities and interests and parents' hopes, formal operational thought, social cognition, and moral development are explored in this video.

Teens: What Makes Them Tick? (Films for the Humanities and Sciences, 43 minutes). In this *ABC News* special, John Stossel talks to teens and their parents and visits the Harvard Medical School's Brain Imaging Center to reveal some surprising physiological reasons for teen behavior.

Truth, Sex, and Videotape: What Teens Really Think and Do About Sex (Films for the Humanities and Sciences, 14 minutes). *ABC News* anchors Diane Sawyer and Sam Donaldson let five teenagers use video cameras to do their own investigative reporting on teenage sexuality.

Web Site Suggestions

The URLs for general sites, common to all chapters, can be found at the front of this Instructor's Manual under Useful Web Sites. At the time of publication, all sites were current and active, however, please be advised that you may occasionally encounter a dead link.

Eating Disorders
http://www.yahoo.com/Health/Mental_Health/Diseases_and_Conditions/Eating_Disorders/

Formal Operations Test
http://www.afunzone.com/fot.html

National Center for Health Statistics
http://www.cdc.gov/nchs/

Puberty 101
http://www.puberty101.com/

Teen Health Home Page
http://www.chebucto.ns.ca/Health/TeenHealth/

Teenage Pregnancy Prevention
http://www.teenpregnancy.org/

Formal Operations Activity

This activity focuses on Piaget's formal operational stage. First, attempt to solve Piaget's pendulum task and Piaget's chemical task. Second, analyze your problem-solving process for aspects of formal operational reasoning.

Pendulum Task: Demonstrate a pendulum with various lengths of string and a number of equal weights. Group members are to identify the variable(s) that determine(s) the speed of the pendulum swing. The possible variables to manipulate are length, weight, height of the drop, and force of the drop.

Chemical Task: Display five numbered flasks with each containing one of the following colorless chemicals: water, hydrogen peroxide, potassium iodine, acid, and thiosulfate. Determine which combination of chemicals produces a mixture with the color yellow.

Critical Thinking Multiple-Choice Questions

1. In addition to the problems and pitfalls associated with emerging sexuality, adolescents risk a variety of problems and disturbances. Much of the material in chapter 12 about these problems is descriptive, but some of it relates to the determinants of these disturbances. Which theoretical perspective (see chapter 2 for a review) appears to have provided the most insight into the greatest number of problems and disturbances? Circle the letter of the best answer and explain why it is the best answer and why each other answer is not as good.

    a. behavioral
    b. cognitive
    c. psychoanalytic
    d. ethological
    e. ecological

2. Read the following passage, "Image of an Adolescent," which appears in John Santrock's *Children* 3rd edition (1993):

    Cleveland Wilkes
        Cleveland Wilkes's family lives in Providence, Rhode Island. They never have much money. He and his parents know what unemployment can do to a family. Nonetheless, Cleveland, who is 17 years old, is known as "the dresser" to his friends because of his penchant for flamboyant clothes, especially shoes. What little money Cleveland manages to scrape together is all channeled into maintaining a wardrobe. In Cleveland's own words: "Whole world floats by around here. There ain't nothing you can't see on these streets. See more in a month here than a lifetime where the rich folks live, all protected from the bad world. I ain't saying it's so great here. Only thing we don't have is the thing we need most of: jobs. Ain't no jobs for us here. Not a one, man, and I know, too, 'cause I been looking for three years, and I ain't all that old. Country got no use for me, folks around here neither. Ain't nobody care too much what happens to us. Tell us, 'Ain't you boys got nothing better to do than stand around all day? What you find to talk about all these hours? And ain't you supposed to be in school? Ain't you supposed to be doing this or that?' If you want to know what the teenagers are doing on this side of town to pass the time of day, now you got it. We got so many folks out of work it's enough to blow your mind. I can hear my brain rotting it's been so long since I done anything. How they let this happen in a country like this having all these kids walking around the streets, got their hands jammed in their pockets, got their heads down? What do folks think these kids gonna do, when they go month after month, year after year without nothing that even smells like a job?" (Psychology Today, 1979). Cleveland Wilkes is a high school dropout. Unemployed, he is described by some as one of the forgotten half of America—those who are poor, lack a high school diploma, and do not have a job.
        Chapter 12 indicates that adolescent thought has several qualities hitherto missing in children's thinking. Which of the types of thinking listed below is best illustrated by Cleveland Wilkes's comments? Circle the letter of the best answer and explain why it is the best answer and why each other answer is not as good.

    a. abstract
    b. logical
    c. idealistic
    d. hypothetical deductive
    e. egocentric

3. Santrock discusses Piaget's formal operational thought stage, which is the last stage in Piaget's stage theory of cognitive development. This question requires that you recognize examples of thought from the four different Piagetian stages. Which of the types of thinking listed below best illustrates formal operational thought? Circle the letter of the best answer and explain why it is the best answer and why each other answer is not as good.

    a.   Steven doesn't think that his brother, Mike, has a brother.
    b.   Susan tries to trick her little brother into thinking he has less orange juice by pouring it into a short, wide glass.
    c.   Lily understands that the keys still exist even though her mom is hiding them behind her back.
    d.   Daniel understands that for the pendulum problem, the problem solver must manipulate the length of the string, the number of weights, the force with which the weight is swung, and the height from which the weight is dropped.
    e.   Adolescents have a larger short-term memory than younger children do.

Suggested Answers for Critical Thinking Multiple-Choice Questions

1. In addition to the problems and pitfalls associated with emerging sexuality, adolescents risk a variety of problems and disturbances. Much of the material in chapter 12 about these problems is descriptive, but some of it relates to the determinants of these disturbances. Which theoretical perspective (see chapter 2 for a review) appears to have provided the most insight into the greatest number of problems and disturbances? Circle the letter of the best answer and explain why it is the best answer and why each other answer is not as good.

    a. Behavioral is the best answer. In particular, analyses of problems and their causes most often include social learning accounts. For example, sexual scripts are learned by observation from others; problems associated with sex may be alleviated by media education campaigns and portrayals. Drug use seems to be most heavily influenced by peer or parent models. Modeling is proposed as a cause of eating disorders (imitation of societal standards), though the actual cause(s) of eating disorders is/are not known.

    b. Cognitive is not the best answer. Cognitive factors are cited mainly in the discussion of sexuality, the treatment of sexual scripts, and the influence of egocentrism on adolescents' response to warnings about the dangers of STDs and pregnancy. Distortions of body image are prevalent among eating-disordered individuals, but this is not cited as a causal factor. Cognitive or cognitive developmental influences are otherwise not directly invoked to explain other disturbances. Finally, the notion of scripts and egocentrism can be subsumed in the social cpognitive analysis (which is partly cognitive).

    c. Psychoanalytic is not the best answer. The psychoanalytic perspective is omitted completely from the discussion of sexual behavior and is present only by inference in the discussion of factors related to eating disorders (regression).

    d. Ethological is not the best answer. The ethological approach receives no attention in these treatments.

    e. Ecological is not the best answer. Bronfenbrenner's ecological theory is not directly invoked. It could be used to structure or organize the discussion of problems and disturbances because of the apparent influences of family, school, community, and culture. However, none of the various systems of the theory are invoked directly to explain problems and disturbances.

2. Having read the passage, "Image of an Adolescent," which appears in John Santrock's *Children* 3rd edition (1993), which of the types of thinking listed below is best illustrated by Cleveland Wilkes's comments? Circle the letter of the best answer and explain why it is the best answer and why each other answer is not as good.

    a. Abstract is not the best answer because there is no evidence of abstract thought in Cleveland's comments; rather, the reason lies in the implications of his comments. Cleveland is suggesting that things could be better in his life if he had a job. To think about this requires an ability to consider the possible rather than the real conditions of his life; this ability involves abstraction. In this case the focus of his comments is on a better, more ideal life, which suggests that "c" is a better answer.

    b. Logical is not the best answer. Again, the reason is not that there is no evidence of logical thinking in Cleveland's comments. For example, the argument that things would be better if people had jobs is a hypothetical-deductive statement. The reason that "c" is a better answer lies in the purpose of Cleveland's comments-to suggest the possibility of a better, more ideal life.

    c. Idealistic is the best answer. Cleveland is employing both abstract and logical thinking to create a vision of a better life. He is able to imagine other possibilities and a different life for himself and others, which sets apart and highlights the limited and limiting conditions of his own life.

    d. <u>Hypothetical deductive</u> is not the best answer. While Cleveland's comments are critical of his circumstances, they are not (as they stand) a full example of critical thinking. For example, they do not demonstrate thinking about both sides of an issue (assuming that there is a valid counterpoint to Cleveland's arguments) concerning the availability of jobs. Nor do they show Cleveland being open-minded about alternative lifestyles perhaps better suited to his economic circumstances.

    e. <u>Egocentric</u> is not the best answer. Missing is the preoccupation with what others think about Cleveland and his life or any sense of intense drama about the injustice of his circumstances. Cleveland's comments are too firmly rooted in believable economic conditions to have the fantasy-character of adolescent egocentrism.

3. Santrock discusses Piaget's formal operational thought stage, which is the last stage in Piaget's stage theory of cognitive development. This question requires that you recognize examples of thought from the four different Piagetian stages. Which of the types of thinking listed below best illustrates formal operational thought? Circle the letter of the best answer and explain why it is the best answer and why each other answer is not as good.

    a. The statement that <u>Steven doesn't think that his brother, Mike, has a brother</u> is an example of irreversibility or the lack of understanding of reciprocal relationships. This cognitive limitation characterizes Piaget's preoperational thought stage.

    b. The statement that <u>Susan tries to trick her little brother into thinking he has less orange juice by pouring it into a short, wide glass</u> is not an example of formal operational thought. Rather, it highlights Susan's understanding of conservation and her little brother's lack of understanding of conservation. Conservation is an ability achieved in Piaget's concrete operational stage.

    c. The statement that <u>Lily understands that the keys still exist even though her mom is hiding them behind her back</u> highlights Lily's understanding of object permanence, which is a characteristic of Piaget's sensorimotor stage.

    d. The statement that <u>Daniel understands that for the pendulum problem, the problem solver must manipulate the length of the string, the number of weights, the force with which the weight is swung, and the height from which the weight is dropped</u> provides an example of formal operational thought. It highlights systematic analysis and deductive reasoning.

    e. The statement that <u>adolescents have a larger short-term memory than younger children do</u> does not represent an issue related to Piaget's view of cognitive development. Rather, it is a statement regarding adolescents' cognitive abilities from an information-processing perspective.

Critical Thinking Essay Questions

Your answers to this kind of question demonstrate an ability to comprehend and apply ideas discussed in this chapter.

1. Identify major physical developmental changes of adolescence, and relate these to psychological changes.

2. Explain why physical development during puberty seems to cause so much more concern to individuals at this age than physical development does at any other ages.

3. Compare and contrast early- and late-maturers, and discuss positive and negative consequences for each type of individual.

4. How does the incidence of adolescent sexual activity and pregnancy in the United States and European countries compare and contrast?

5. Compare and contrast adolescents' use of alcohol and cigarettes.

6. Indicate causes of adolescent drug use, and discuss whether these operate independently or whether they interact.

7. Define and distinguish between anorexia nervosa and bulimia nervosa.

8. Discuss ways to reduce adolescents' health-compromising behaviors and increase adolescents' health-promoting behaviors.

9. Describe and give examples of the three major characteristics of formal operational thought.

10. Compare and contrast Piaget's views about concrete and formal operational thought.

11. Explain the concepts of adolescent egocentrism, imaginary audience, and personal fable. Include at least two original examples of each in your response.

12. Analyze your own middle school or junior high school. How did it rate in terms of the criteria for effective schools for adolescents discussed in this chapter?

13. Compare and contrast the various approaches to moral education in schools. Do you think any of these approaches is acceptable for a public school system? Explain.

Ideas to Help You Answer Critical Thinking Essay Questions

1. Create a graph of physical milestones and map out psychological changes. Now discuss specifically what is taking place in both realms and how they appear to be developmentally related.

2. As you address this question, use some examples of physical development from other ages. This will illustrate the tremendous difference and dramatic nature of puberty with regard to changes at other times in life.

3. Describe the process and outcome of maturation during adolescence. This will provide a good backdrop for discussing the effects of experiencing it early and experiencing it later on.

4. Relate the data you find to U.S. and European views and societal mores of sexuality.

5. Differentiate the issues surrounding use of each of these types of drugs. Having established exactly what using each involves and the potential consequences, make your comparison of teen use.

6. Delineate the kinds of drugs adolescents tend to use. Present information on what is most common and popular down to drugs that are used very rarely by teens. Are the causes of drug use different for different types of drugs? If so, how?

7. Do not simply present the definition of each—descriptively present an image of an individual suffering from each type of disorder.

8. Include in your discussion the challenges of doing this. Summarize aspects of adolescents' lives that lead to poor behavior in the first place, then consider ways that might make use of these same characteristics to promote healthier behavior.

9. This answer will be most effective if you begin with a description of concrete operational thought—the more limited thinking that exists prior to advancement to formal operational thought.

10. Identify the areas of importance with regard to cognitive functioning, according to Piaget. Provide some general background as to why he theoretically focuses on these, then make your comparison.

11. Include in your explanation the aspects of cognitive functioning that these concepts reflect. Rely on personal examples to make these concepts real.

12. Address each aspect of effective schools with regard to yours. Provide examples of why you think or don't think your middle school was effective. Did you see any evidence of an attempt to improve the school while you were there? Since you've been gone?

13. Based on the particular approach, how do you think the educators are defining *morality*? Does the notion of morality fluctuate based on the method of incorporating it into the school experience? Address this along with your assessment of appropriateness.

Secular Trend

The purpose of this project is to examine the secular trend in the age, and other characteristics, of puberty in families. Ask your parents and grandparents the age at which each went through puberty (parents should give information on grandparents, if information is not available from grandparents directly). Older students may have mature children that can be included in this chart. Record the age at which each person went through puberty and then answer the questions below. Write a brief report based on the provided questions.

DATA SHEET

Record age of puberty for:

Self ____
Mother ____
Father ____
Maternal:
    Grandmother ____
    Grandfather ____
Paternal:
    Grandmother ____
    Grandfather ____

Questions:

- Does the age of onset of puberty differ for the three different generations represented in the data? If so, in what way?

- Does the age of onset of puberty differ for the two sexes? What is the direction of the difference?

- How do the findings on generational differences relate to the trends described in the text? Why might they be similar or different from the findings described in the text?

- How do the findings here on sex differences concerning age of puberty relate to data in the text?

Handout 7 (RP 2)

Piaget's Pendulum Problem

Pair up with a classmate. One of you should present the other with Piaget's pendulum task. Then switch and the other one of you will present the other with Piaget's chemical task. Next, test an 11-year-old on the two tasks. Prior to the start of the research, the project must be approved by the human subjects review board at your school and the students must get a signed informed consent form from the child's parents. After making the observations, answer the questions that follow.

For the pendulum task, provide a frame for a pendulum as well as various lengths of string and a number of weights of equal size. Instruct the subjects to assemble the pendulum and to identify the variable(s) that determine(s) the period of the pendulum swing. The possible variables to manipulate are length, weight, height of the drop, and force of the initial push. Record on the data sheet the variables that the subjects manipulate and the way in which subjects organize the manipulations.

For the chemical task, provide water, hydrogen peroxide, potassium iodine, acid, and thiosulfate in five numbered flasks. All of the chemicals are initially clear liquids. The subjects must determine which combination of chemicals produces a mixture with the color yellow. Record on the data sheet the variables that the subjects manipulate and the way in which subjects organize the manipulations.

Task	Subject 1	Subject 2
	Sex ___ Age ___	Sex ___ Age ___
Pendulum Task:		

Chemical Task:

Questions:
• How did the student solve the tasks? How would you characterize the responses? Did the student systematically manipulate the variables?

• How did the 11-year-old solve the tasks? How would you characterize the 11-year-old's responses? Did he or she systematically manipulate the variables?

• What differences did you observe in performance of the younger and older adolescent? How would you characterize their performances according to Piaget's theory? Did you find evidence of formal operational reasoning in either, both, or neither of your subjects? How would you account for your findings? What is the nature of the difference between performances of the younger and older adolescent?

Chapter 13: Socioemotional Development in Adolescence

Total Teaching Package Outline

Lecture Outline	Resource References
Socioemotional Development in Adolescence	PowerPoint Presentation: See www.mhhe.com Cognitive Maps: See Appendix A
Identity	LO1 OHT98, 100 & IB, 101, 130-131, 162: Identity Dev.
• Some Contemporary Thoughts about Identity	PA1: That's Me! F/V: Adolescence: Crisis or Change? F/V: The Development of Self
• Identity Statuses and Development	LS1: Research on Identity: Erikson to Marcia CA1: Personal Development and Marcia's Statuses of Identity CA2: Examples of Marcia's Identity Statuses RP1: Teens and the Political Scene RP2: Marcia's Statuses of Identity
• Family Influences on Identity	LO2 PA2: Aw, Mom!
• Culture and Ethnicity, and Gender -Gender and Identity Development	PA3: Line Up, Boys and Girls
Families	LO3
• Autonomy and Attachment	WS: Parenting Today's Teen—Books on Teens F/V: Understanding Parenting Styles OHT104 & IB: Parent-Adolescent Relationships
• Parent-Adolescent Conflict	WS: Parent-Adolescent Conflict
Peers • Peer Groups	LO4 OHT94 & IB: Progression of Peer Group Relations OHT126: Peer Conformity OHT163: Susceptibility to Peer Pressure LS2: Academic Success and Cultural Influences PA4: One of the Gang F/V: Adolescence: Social and Emotional Dev. F/V: Teenage Relationships WS: Adolescent Peer Groups
-Cliques	LS3: Adolescent Subcultures
-Adolescent Groups Versus Children Groups	CA3: Friendships
• Friendships	

• Dating and Romantic Relationships	LO5 F/V: The Familiar Face of Love
-Types of Dating and Developmental Changes	WS: An Evaluation of Safe Dates
-Dating Scripts	
-Emotion and Romantic Relationships	
-Sociocultural Contexts and Dating	F/V: Still Killing Us Softly
Culture and Adolescent Development	F/V: American Adolescence
• Cross-Cultural Comparisons and Rites of Passage	LO6 CA4: Is Prom a Rite of Passage? F/V: Spark among the Ashes: A Bar Mitzvah
• Ethnicity -Ethnicity and Socioeconomic Status -Differences in Diversity	LO7
-Value Conflicts, Assimilation, and Pluralism	LO8
Adolescent Problems	
• Juvenile Delinquency	LO9
-Causes of Delinquency	IB: The Antecedents of Juvenile Delinquency
-Youth Violence	CA5: Field Trip to the Juvenile Detention Center
• Depression and Suicide -Depression	LO10 WS: Adolescent Depression
-Suicide	OHT142 & IB: Rate of Suicide Is Rising OHT174: Suicide OHT196: Suicide Rates in the US LS4: The Clustering and Contagion of Suicide CA6: What Is a Teacher to Do? F/V: Suicide: Dead is Forever F/V: Suicide: A Guide for Prevention F/V: Teen Suicide WS: Teen Suicide
• The Interrelation of Problems and Successful Prevention/Intervention Programs	LO11
Review	CA7: Contemporary Television and Adolescence CA8: Movies and Adolescent Concepts CA9: Critical Thinking Multiple-Choice CA10: Critical Thinking Essays

Chapter Outline

IDENTITY
- Identity versus identity confusion is the 5th stage in Erikson's psychosocial theory.
  - Exploration of roles and coping with differing roles results in a new sense of self (identity).
  - Identity confusion results from unsuccessful resolution of the identity crisis, which causes individuals to either withdraw or lose their identity in the crowd.
- Identity includes many components (career, political beliefs, relationships, sexual orientation, intelligence, cultural, etc.)
  Some Contemporary Thoughts about Identity
  - Current theorists view identity development as a complex, gradual ongoing process that extends beyond adolescence.

Identity Statuses and Development
- The extent to which an individual has experienced a crisis or commitment determines one's status.
  - **Crisis** (exploration) is a period of identity development during which the adolescent is choosing among meaningful alternatives.
  - **Commitment** is the part of identity development in which adolescents show a personal investment in what they are going to do.
- Marcia proposed that four identity statuses are possible relative to one's crisis and commitment.
  - **Identity diffusion** characterizes adolescents who have not yet experienced a crisis (that is, they have not yet explored meaningful alternatives) or made any commitments.
  - **Identity foreclosure** characterizes adolescents who have made a commitment but have not experienced a crisis.
  - **Identity moratorium** characterizes adolescents who are in the midst of a crisis, but their commitments are either absent of only vaguely defined.
  - **Identity achievement** characterizes adolescents who have undergone a crisis and have made a commitment.
  - Many adolescents are either in diffusion, foreclosure, or moratorium, with many college students progressing to achievement.
- Researchers believe that "MAMA" (moratorium-achiever-moratorium-achiever) is a common pattern of progression for identity.

Family Influences on Identity
- Both individuation and connectedness in parent-adolescent relationships are linked with progress in identity development.
  - **Individuality** consists of two dimensions: self-assertion, the ability to have and communicate a point of view, and separateness, the use of communication patterns to express how one is different from others.
  - **Connectedness** consists of two dimensions: mutuality—sensitivity to and respect for others' views—and permeability—openness to others' views.

Culture, Ethnicity, and Gender
- Given that adolescents can interpret ethnic and cultural information, and reflect upon past and future experiences, they confront their ethnicity for the first time.
- **Ethnic identity** is an enduring, basic aspect of the self that includes a sense of membership in an ethnic group and the attitudes and feelings related to that membership.
- Research has found that ethnic identity increases with age and higher levels of ethnic identity are linked with more positive attitudes towards one's own ethnic group as well as other groups.

Gender and Identity Development
- As societal roles have changed for females to include family and career, more similarities than differences have been found relative to identity development.
- Some researchers speculate that for males identity formation precedes intimacy, whereas the opposite is true for females.

FAMILIES
Autonomy and Attachment
- A hallmark of adolescence is a push for autonomy and responsibility.
- While some parents may have trouble with this transition, other parents facilitate the process by relinquishing control in areas where the adolescent can make reasonable decisions.
  - With adult guidance and support, adolescents can learn to make reasonable decisions.
- Security of attachment in early childhood facilitates peer relations and decreases the likelihood of problem behaviors in adolescence.

Parent-Adolescent Conflict
- The increase of conflict between parents and early adolescents isdue to a number of factors including biological changes of puberty, cognitive changes involving increased idealism and logical reasoning, social changes focused on independence and identity, maturational changes in parents, and expectations that are violated by parents and adolescents.
  - Parents who recognize that the transition to an adult takes time handle their youth more competently and calmly than those who expect immediate conformity to adult standards.
  - Much of the conflict that occurs centers around everyday events (cleaning up, clothes, curfews).
  - Serious conflict about major issues (drugs and delinquency) is rare.
- The conflict is usually moderate rather than severe and the increased conflict may serve the positive function of promoting autonomy and identity.
  - Approximately 20 percent of parent-adolescent relationships are characterized by prolonged, intense, repeated, unhealthy conflict and are associated with juvenile delinquency, school dropouts, pregnancy, moving out, etc.

PEERS
Peer Groups
- Conformity to peer pressure in adolescence can be positive and negative.
  - Positive aspects include a feeling of belonging, dressing alike and spending time with friends, and prosocial activities such as raising money for a good cause.
  - Negative aspects include the use of profanity, illegal and delinquent behavior, and teasing others.
  - Conformity peaks in 8th and 9th grades.
Cliques
- Allegiance to cliques can exert powerful control as an adolescent focuses on group identity rather than personal identity.
- There are usually three to six well-defined cliques in secondary schools.
- Jocks, populars, and independents tend to have higher self-esteem, whereas the nobodies tend to have the lowest.
Adolescent Groups Versus Children Groups
- Adolescent groups are more formal, more heterogeneous, and more mixed-gender than children groups.

Friendships
- Harry Stack Sullivan theorized that psychological importance and intimacy of close friendships increase in early adolescence.
- Research has found that
  - Adolescents disclose intimate and personal information more than younger children do.
  - Adolescents spend more time with their peers.
  - Adolescents rely on friends for companionship needs and intimacy.
  - Friendship in early adolescence was a significant predictor of self-worth in early adulthood.

Dating and Romantic Relationships
  Types of Dating and Developmental Changes
  - Dating in adolescence has several functions (explore one's attractiveness, figure out how to interact romantically, relevance to peer groups, attachment needs, and sexual needs).
  - Younger adolescents often begin to hang out together in heterosexual groups.
  - A special concern is that early dating is linked to developmental problems.
  - Cyberdating, dating over the Internet, is particularly popular among middle school students.
  Dating Scripts
  - **Dating scripts** are the cognitive models that guide individuals' dating interactions.
  - First dates are highly scripted along gender lines; males have more power initially.
  - Males and females often bring different motivations to the dating experience.
    - Females focus on interpersonal qualities and males focus on physical attractiveness.
  - Young adolescents focus on the affiliative qualities of companionship, intimacy, and support.
  Emotion and Romantic Relationships
  - Strong emotions are involved with adolescent dating. They can have a disruptive effect or they can give the adolescent a sense of mastery and competence if the emotions are managed.
  Sociocultural Contexts and Dating
  - Cultural values and religious beliefs often dictate the age at which dating begins, how much freedom is allowed, whether dates must be chaperoned, and the gender roles during dating.

CULTURE AND ADOLESCENT DEVELOPMENT
  Cross-Cultural Comparisons and Rites of Passage
  - Cultural values and beliefs influence adolescent development.
  - **Cross-cultural studies** involve the comparison of a culture with one or more other cultures, which provides information about the degree to which development is similar, or universal across cultures, or the degree to which it is culture-specific.
  - A **rite of passage** is a ceremony or ritual that marks an individual's transition from one status to another. Most rites of passage focus on the transition to adult status.
    - In primitive cultures, rites of passage are often well defined.
    - In contemporary America, rites of passage are ill defined. Some religious and social groups have initiation ceremonies that indicate an advance in maturity (bar mitzvah, confirmation).

Ethnicity
  Ethnicity and Socioeconomic Status
  - Much of the research on ethnic minority adolescents has not teased apart the influences of ethnicity and socioeconomic status (SES).
    - The interaction between SES and ethnicity can exaggerate the influence of ethnicity as ethnic minority individuals are over-represented in low SES.
    - While not all ethnic minority families are poor, poverty contributes to the stress of many ethnic minority adolescents.

Differences and Diversity
- There are many legitimate differences between many ethnic groups, as well as between ethnic groups and the White majority.
- Too often, differences between ethnic groups and the White majority have been interpreted as deficits on the part of the ethnic minority group.
- Another important dimension of ethnic minority groups is their diversity. Ethnic minority groups are not homogeneous; they have different social, historical, and economic backgrounds.
  - Failure to recognize diversity and individual variations results in the stereotyping of an ethnic minority group.

Value Conflicts, Assimilation, and Pluralism
- Value conflicts are often involved with individual responses to ethnic issues. One prominent value conflict involves assimilation versus pluralism.
  - **Assimilation** is the absorption of ethnic minority groups into the dominant group, which often means the loss of some of the values of the ethnic minority group.
  - **Pluralism** is the coexistence of distinct ethnic and cultural groups in the same society. Individuals who adopt a pluralistic stance usually advocate that cultural differences be maintained and appreciated.

ADOLESCENT PROBLEMS
Juvenile Delinquency
- **Juvenile delinquent** is a label applied to an adolescent who breaks the law or engages in behavior that is considered illegal.
  - The FBI estimate that at least 2 percent of all youth are involved in juvenile court cases.
  - Males are arrested more often than females are; though the gap is decreasing.
  - Delinquency rates for individuals from minority groups and low SES are especially high in proportion to the overall population of these groups.
  - Research suggests that prosecuting juveniles as adults may actually increase the long-term criminal offenses.

Causes of Delinquency
- Heredity, identity problems, community influences, and family experiences have been proposed as causes of juvenile delinquency.
  - An adolescent with a negative identity (fail to identify with acceptable social roles) may find support for his/her delinquent image among peers, which strengthens the negative identity.
  - The norms of many lower SES peer groups are antisocial and adolescents can gain attention and status by being delinquent.
  - Parental monitoring and parents' ability to discourage antisocial behavior are important.
  - Having delinquent peers also influences adolescents' antisocial behavior.

Youth Violence
- Violent youth are overwhelmingly male and driven by feelings of powerlessness.
- Youth violence is most prevalent in poverty-infested urban areas.
- Efforts at prevention should include developmentally appropriate schools, supportive families, conflict management classes, and youth and community organizations.

Depression and Suicide
   Depression
   - Adolescents have a higher rate of depression than children do.
   - Female adolescents are more likely to have mood and depressive disorders than male adolescents for several reasons.
      - Females tend to ruminate in their depressed mood and amplify it.
      - Females' self-images are more negative than males'.
      - Females face more discrimination than males.
   - Other factors that place adolescents at risk for depression include having a depressed parent, emotionally unavailable parents, parents who have high marital conflict and/or divorce, parents with financial difficulties, and poor peer relations.
   Suicide
   - Suicide in the U.S. has tripled since 1950 and is the 3rd leading cause of death for 15- to 24-year-olds.
   - Compared to females, males are about 3 times as likely to commit suicide.
   - Suicide attempts are 6 to 7 times more likely for homosexual adolescents than heterosexual adolescents.
   - Both proximal and distal factors influence an adolescent's decision to attempt suicide.

The Interrelation of Problems and Successful Prevention/Intervention Programs
- Researchers have found that problem behaviors are interrelated, as many as 10 percent of all adolescents in the U.S. have multiple-problem behaviors.
- Dryoos found a number of common components in programs designed to prevent or reduce adolescent problems.
   - They provide individual attention to high-risk adolescents, they develop community-wide intervention, and they include early identification.

Learning Objectives

1. Discuss the development of identity proposed by Erikson and Marcia.
2. Examine how family, culture and ethnicity, and gender influence adolescent development.
3. Describe how families change as adolescents seek autonomy, being sure to include factors related to parent-adolescent conflict.
4. Elaborate on the changes that take place with peer groups and the importance of friendships.
5. Discuss adolescent dating, including the functions of dating and dating scripts.
6. Define "rite of passage" and examine its importance in this culture and other cultures around the world.
7. Determine what role ethnicity and socioeconomic status play in adolescent development in this country.
8. Differentiate between assimilation and pluralism, indicating how these concepts impact the development of an ethnic identity.
9. Discuss the causes and antecedents of juvenile delinquency and the recent research conducted on youth violence.
10. Examine the nature of depression and causes of suicide in adolescents.
11. Discuss prevention and intervention programs that have been successful with at-risk youths.

Key Terms

assimilation
commitment
connectedness
crisis
cross-cultural studies
dating scripts
ethnic identity
identity achievement

identity diffusion
identity foreclosure
identity moratorium
individuality
juvenile delinquent
pluralism
rite of passage

Key People

Joy Dryfoos
Erik Erikson
G. Stanley Hall
Reed Larson and Marsye Richards

James Marcia
Harry Stack Sullivan
Stanley Sue
Alan Waterman

Lecture Suggestions

Lecture Suggestion 1: Research on Identity: Erikson to Marcia Erik Erikson's ideas about identity development during adolescence are the standard concepts used to organize and integrate diverse aspects of adolescent social development. They form a complex conceptual network that Erikson himself admits is not transparent. However, textbook treatments are necessarily brief and often distort or misrepresent the concepts. Although Santrock's treatment is accurate, it is brief, and a more detailed presentation may help clarify and deepen students' understanding of the theory. Give a lecture that is directly based on Erikson's writings collected in *Identity: Youth and Crisis* (1986). You will find that the first two or three essays give a full treatment of Erikson's ideas about identity. Quote them liberally as you characterize the richness, complexity, and ambiguity of Erikson's ideas. Notice how Erikson actually refuses to define the concept in a compact way, and explore his reasons for doing so. He offers several pithy characterizations of identity. Other interesting observations include his original idea that the identity crisis was entirely an unconscious process, but that modern fascination with the idea has almost mandated that it be excruciatingly conscious. As rich as Erikson's ideas are, the problem with them is that they are not operationalized in ways that appeal to researchers. With publication of his doctoral thesis in 1966, James Marcia changed things. Marcia proposed and demonstrated that a valid and reliable interview could yield a four-way classification of identity status derived from Erikson's theory. Supplement Santrock's summary of Marcia's work with a sampling of quotes from Marcia's research report. You may also wish to informally explore your students' identity statuses as part of the in-class activity suggested below (see Classroom Activity 1: Personal Development and Marcia's Statuses of Identity and Classroom Activity 2: Examples of Marcia's Identity Statuses). Marcia's work has been criticized. If you have time, explore some of the modifications by Grotevant (1992). Grotevant stresses that some aspects of identity, such as occupation ,are chosen, while other aspects, such as ethnicity and gender, are not chosen.

- Sources: Erikson, E. (1986). *Identity: Youth and crisis.* New York: W. W. Norton. Grotevant, H. D. (1992). Assigned and chosen identity components: A process perspective on their integration. In G. R. Adams, T.P. Gullotta, & R. Montemayor (Eds.), *Adolescent identity formation: Advances in adolescent development.* Newbury Park, CA: Sage. Marcia, J. E. (1966). Development and validation of ego identity status. *Journal of Personality and Social Psychology, 3,* 551-558.

Lecture Suggestion 2: Academic Success and Cultural Influences on Peer Groups Interesting differences emerge for cultural groups in the U.S. with respect to academic achievement. See Lecture Suggestion 6 from chapter 11 for a complete lecture idea. In a nutshell, White children raised by authoritative parents were more academically successful. In contrast, peer groups had great influence on school attitudes and behavior for African American, Latino, and Asian American students. These attitudes influenced how much time students spent studying, their enjoyment of school, and their classroom behaviors.

Lecture Suggestion 3: Adolescent Subcultures The purpose of the lecture is to examine elements of the adolescent subculture as described by Dacey and Kenny (1997).

- Propinquity or geographic closeness. Members of a subculture typically live near one another (or did know each other prior to joining the group).
- Unique values and norms. Atkinson (1989) states that all group members attempt to overcome limitations they perceive they would experience if they did not belong to the group. Members discern that there is some advantage to being a member of the group, regardless of the underlying reason (race, age, politics, and ethnic background). Adolescents often form a group with their agemates in response to adult dominance. Armsden and Greenberg (1987) found that adolescents who were devoted members of a group "reported greater satisfaction with themselves, a higher likelihood of seeking social support, and less symptomatic responses to stressful life events" (p. 427).
- Gender differences. LeCroy (1988) found that girls focus on emotional needs in their friendships (loyalty, trustworthiness, and emotional support) and seek just a few intimate friendships, whereas male relationships emphasize independence and resistance to adult control in their friendships.
- Peer group identity. Deep, sustained involvement with the peer group characterizes adolescence today. Given that more adolescents are continuing their education today, they spend a longer period with and being influenced by peers and less time with adults. Adolescents often use each other as models.
  - Newman and Newman (1976) proposed that early adolescence (13–17 years) was better characterized by the psychosocial stage of group identity versus alienation to highlight the importance of peer identity on personality development. Later adolescence would be better characterized by the individual identity versus role diffusion psychosocial substage.
    - Dacey and Kenny suggest that the ages noted for the group identity substage are more accurately represented by age 11 and 12 for females and males, respectively, in early adolescence. Middle adolescence begins around age 14 and late adolescence occurs between 17 and 19 years of age for adolescents in the Western Hemisphere.
- Sources: Armsden, G.C., & Greenberg, M.T. (1987). The inventory of parent and peer attachment: Individual differences and their relationship to psychological well-being in adolescence. *Journal of Youth and Adolescence, 16*, 427-454. Atkinson, R. (1989). Respectful, dutiful teenagers. *Psychology Today, 22*, 22-26. Dacey, J. & Kenny, M. (1997). *Adolescent development* (2nd ed.). Madison, WI: Brown and Benchmark. LeCroy, C. (1988). Parent-adolescent intimacy: Impact on adolescent functioning. *Adolescence, 23*, 137-147. Newman, P.R., & Newman, B.M. (1976). Early adolescence and its conflict: Group identity versus alienation. *Adolescence, 11*, 261-273.

Lecture Suggestion 4: The Clustering and Contagion of Suicide The purpose of this lecture is to examine two general types of suicide clusters. This lecture extends Santrock's brief discussion of adolescent suicide. Joiner (1999) distinguishes between the terms *suicide clusters* and *suicide contagion*.

- *Cluster* refers to the occurrence of two or more completed or attempted suicides that are not randomly "bunched" in space or time (suicides following the suicide of a celebrity or a series of suicides—(attempts or completed)—in the same high school). The term *cluster* does not indicate or imply why the cluster occurred, only that it did happen.
- *Contagion* implies a possible, albeit vague, explanation of why a cluster occurred.

Given that research has found that suicides occur at roughly the same rate across geographical regions in the U.S. and they are not influenced by the day of the week or the month, it is statistically unlikely that suicides would cluster by chance alone. Two general types of suicide clusters have been described, mass clusters and point clusters.

- Point clusters are suicides that are related in the local sense (related in space and time), usually by an institution. Brent et al. (1989) documented an example of a point cluster. In a relatively large high school (1,500 students), 2 students committed suicide within a 4-day time frame. In the following 14 days, 2 more students committed suicide, 7 other students attempted suicide, and 23 students reported suicidal ideation. The authors noted that 75 percent of the members of the cluster had at least one major psychiatric disorder, implying that they were vulnerable for suicide prior to the actual suicides. Friends of the victims were more influenced by the suicides than students who were less familiar with the victims (social contiguity is important).
  - Given that suicide runs in families and that the suicide of a family member would be devastating, it is interesting that within-family point clusters are very rare.
- Mass clusters are media-related phenomena as they are grouped by time, rather than space. They are in response to a publicized suicide. There is inconsistent support for this phenomenon. Phillips and Carstensen (1986) found that the increase in suicides does not always occur after a publicized suicide, though it does appear to influence adolescent suicides. In contrast Kessler et al. (1988) did not find a correlation between adolescent suicides and publicized suicides.

It is unclear whether contagion (the social or interpersonal transmission of suicide) is involved in suicide clusters. Not all incidences of cluster suicides involve contagion. For example, a third variable may better explain the mass suicides. Mass delusion (Heaven's Gate), a combination of delusion and coercion (Jonestown), or simultaneous exposure to trauma (Chernobyl) may explain the suicides.

Joiner states that contagion may not explain point-clustered suicides. He proposes an alternative view based on the following four factors.

- Severe negative life events are risk factors for suicide.
- Good social support buffers individuals against developing suicidal symptoms.
- Personal-based risk factors for suicide may influence behavior (personality disorders).
- People form relationships assortatively (people who have similar problems or characteristics).

Thus, people who are vulnerable to suicide may cluster prior to the appearance of suicidal symptoms. Point-cluster suicides may be prearranged or simultaneously exposed to severe negative life events that unduly affect the group of vulnerable individuals.

Joiner speculates that two issues are important to understand when addressing the relatively low frequency of point-cluster suicides.

- The factors (suicide, severe negative life events, low social support, and high person-based risk) that Joiner states must co-occur are themselves relatively rare. Each of the factors independently is rare, despite that contingency that they must co-occur to explain the phenomenon.
- The second issue revolves around the fact that attempted or completed suicides represent an extreme and severe psychopathology, which involves a high threshold. This high threshold in conjunction with the confluence of the other rare factors explains the low frequency of point-cluster suicides. Increased social support following a family member's suicide may explain the lack of point-cluster suicides within families.

Joiner concludes that the evidence for mass clusters is lacking, however, there is support of point-cluster suicides. Contagion may not be the best explanation for the occurrence of point-cluster suicides.

- Sources: Brent, D.A., Kerr, M.M., Goldstein, C., & Bozigar, J. (1989). An outbreak of suicide and suicidal behavior in a high school. *Journal of the American Academy of Child & Adolescent Psychiatry, 28,* 918-924. Joiner, T.E. (1999). The clustering and contagion of suicide. *Current Directions in Psychological Science, 8,* 89-92. Kessler, R.C., Downey, G., Milavsky, J.R., & Stipp, H. (1988). Clustering of teenage suicides after television news stories about suicides: A reconsideration. *American Journal of Psychiatry, 145,* 1379-1383. Phillips, D.P., & Carstensen, L.L. (1986). Clustering of teenage suicides after television news stories about suicides. *New England Journal of Medicine, 315,* 685-689.

Classroom Activities

Classroom Activity 1: Personal Development and Marcia's Statuses of Identity This activity relates students' goals and values to Marcia's statuses of identity. Have students write a description of their vocational goals, personal goals, political goals, and moral values. For example, with regard to vocational goals, they could indicate what their current vocational goals are, when and how they decided upon them, what their last vocational goal was, and why it changed (change of major in college is one possibility of a concrete event they could cite). They could also write what their parents would like them to do.

In small groups, the students should classify each group member according to Marcia's identity statuses: identity-achieved, identity moratorium, identity foreclosure, and identity-diffused. Have students discuss the possible role of the college experience in generating an identity crisis, especially in terms of changing majors and exposure to alternative political, moral, or religious views.

Logistics:
- Group size: Small group.
- Approximate time: Small group (25 minutes).
- Sources: King, M. B., & Clark, D. E. (1990). *Instructor's manual to accompany children*. Dubuque, IA: Wm. C. Brown Communications, Inc.

Classroom Activity 2: Examples of Marcia's Identity Statuses Marcia expanded on Erikson's description of the conflicts encountered at the identity versus identity confusion stage. Four types of resolution are described: identity diffusion, identity foreclosure, identity moratorium, and identity achievement. The resolutions vary on two dimensions—the presence or absence of a crisis and the presence or absence of a sense of commitment to an identity. After describing each type of resolution, students should be able to give examples of people experiencing the different resolutions. To test their ability to do so, you may want to give them some examples (**Handout 1**) and ask them to identify the status of the adolescent in each scenario.
- Marsha is a 14-year-old who, when asked what she wants to do when she graduates from high school, replies, "Maybe I will get married and have some children, or maybe I will be a neurosurgeon, or a fashion designer." (identity moratorium)
- Seventeen-year-old Suzanne is questioning the tenets of the religion in which she was brought up. She is, for the first time, examining her beliefs and considering other belief systems. At the end of the period, she chooses to follow the same religion as her parents. (identity achievement)
- Lorraine is 16 years old and, when asked what she wants to do when she graduates from high school, replies, "I never really thought about it. I guess I will decide when the time comes." (identity diffusion)
- After Bill graduates from high school, he plans to go into his father's business. He has been talking this over with his parents since he was a preschooler and is eager to fulfill his parents' expectations. (identity foreclosure)
- Michael was asked to debate issues concerning premarital sex in his health class. His parents always taught him that premarital sex was wrong and that they would be very disappointed if they discovered that he had participated. After thoroughly investigating the consequences of premarital sex, Michael came out against it. (identity achievement)

Logistics:
- Materials: Handout 1 (Identity Status Activity)
- Group size: Small group.
- Approximate time: Small group (10 minutes).

Classroom Activity 3: Friendships This activity focuses on friendships. Ask students to describe the first friendship they can remember and a more recent friendship. What did they do with their first friend? What did they know about that friend? What about their recent friend? How does the intimacy in the two friendships differ? How does this difference confirm or deny the developmental data presented in the text? Are there general characteristics for earlier or later friendships?

- Early friendships are generally based on proximity and similarity. Friendships later in life involve more intimacy than friendships early in life. Younger friendships might be expected to focus on play activities; friendships of older individuals might focus more on conversation and sharing ideas and feelings. Students are likely to remember more details about their friends in junior high school and high school relative to their memories of specific activities. Because of the more intimate nature of friendships in the later years of school, they probably learned more about these people at the time. There is also a time confound to explain the difference.

Logistics:
- Group size: Small group and full class discussion.
- Approximate time: Small group (15 minutes) and full class discussion (15 minutes).
- Sources: King, M. B., & Clark, D. E. (1989). *Instructors' manual to accompany Santrock and Yussen's child development: An introduction,* 4th ed. Dubuque, IA: Wm. C. Brown Communications, Inc.

Classroom Activity 4: Is Prom a Rite of Passage? One of the rites of passage in American society is the senior prom, and nowadays high school proms are expensive. Some retailers estimate that males must spend at least $300 for a prom (tux rental, prom tickets, corsage, dinner, and limousine), with costs often going toward $800. Females can easily spend $400 to $600. Some schools charge as much as $200 per couple for the prom. Some prom couples also go away for the weekend after the prom. The average 16- to 19-year-old gets $1,250 in allowance each year. Seventy-five percent of teens have two working parents and fewer siblings, so there is more expendable income. Fifty-six percent of all teenagers have jobs. Teens who work 35 hours or more each week have weekly median earnings of $204; those with part-time jobs average $75 a paycheck.

- Have your students discuss the following questions: How can proms be so expensive? How do prom-goers afford this rite of passage? Do you think it is fair that proms are so expensive? What can schools do to reduce the price of prom night?

Logistics:
- Group size: Full class.
- Approximate time: Full class discussion (15 minutes).
- Sources: Hodgin, D. (1990, May 14). Reaching deep to put on the prom. *Insight*, 40-41.

Classroom Activity 5: Field Trip to the Local Juvenile Detention Center There are many ways to describe the behavior of juvenile delinquents. Statistics and data about their characteristics, though important, may not always be learned as efficiently as we would like. One way to help the statistics come to life is to take a field trip to the local juvenile detention center. Most facilities will allow tours if the groups are not too big. If possible, the tour should include a look at the holding tanks, solitary confinement, day rooms, and offices. Staff are usually willing to give a short presentation about the services they provide and the clientele they serve. Before going, prepare students with a lecture on forms of detention and encourage them to form a list of questions to ask the juvenile court staff. If your class is too large, recruit a subset of students to go to the detention center. Have them report back to the full class.

If a trip to a juvenile detention center is not possible, you may want to focus the classroom activity on how statistics about delinquency are gathered. Break students into groups and have them design a study to determine the frequency of drug use in high school. Be sure you point out some of the problems associated with asking the students directly about their drug usage behavior. Also point out the problems with questionnaires, gaining permission from parents, and the ethical issues involved.

Logistics:
- Materials: Tour of juvenile detention center.
- Group size: Full class or a small group from your class.
- Approximate time: Full class discussion regarding the field trip (30 minutes).

Classroom Activity 6: What Is a Teacher to Do? Interventions for a Suicidal Adolescents Have students discuss what they would do if they were a high school teacher and suspected that a student of theirs was potentially suicidal. What obligations would they have to the student? What kinds of things could they do to help that individual? Should people have the right to take their own lives?

Logistics:
- Group size: Small group and full class discussion.
- Approximate time: Small group (15 minutes) and full class discussion (15 minutes).
- Sources: King, M. B., & Clark, D. B. (1990). *Instructor's manual to accompany children*. Dubuque, IA: Wm. C. Brown Communications, Inc.

Classroom Activity 7: Contemporary Television and Adolescence The purpose of this activity is to have students apply concepts from the chapter to characters in contemporary television shows (*Buffy, Dawson's Creek, Malcom in the Middle, The Simpsons*, etc). This activity can be carried out several ways. One option is to videotape a contemporary sitcom and have the students watch the show together in class. Another option is to have students watch a sitcom on their own and return to class to discuss their results.

Regardless of which option is employed the goal is for students to apply concepts (peer influences, autonomy vs. attachment, parent-conflict, identity development, etc.) from the chapter. This exercise reinforces the concepts that they are learning and helps students make connections between everyday life (if we can call TV shows everyday life!) and psychological concepts. Students typically enjoy this activity and learn from it.
- Use in the Classroom: Were students able to apply the concepts? Have them provide examples to the class. Did the shows demonstrate evidence to support these concepts or refute them?

Logistics:
- Materials: If you use the first option, you will need to videotape a contemporary TV sitcom.
- Group size: Individual and/or full class.
- Approximate time: Individual (45-75 minutes) and full class discussion (30 minutes) or full class viewing of videotape and discussion (75 minutes).

Classroom Activity 8: Movies and Adolescent Concepts The purpose of this activity is to have students apply concepts from the chapter to characters in commercial movies (*The Breakfast Club, Boyz in the Hood, Stand by Me, The Ten Things I Hate About You*). Have students watch a movie on their own and return to class to discuss the results. The goal is for students to apply concepts (peer relations, cognitive development, peer influences, autonomy vs. attachment, parent-conflict, identity development, etc.) from the chapter. This exercise reinforces the concepts that they are learning and helps students make connections between everyday life and psychological concepts. Students typically enjoy this activity and learn from it.
- Use in the Classroom: Were students able to apply the concepts? Have them provide examples to the class. Did the movies accurately depict adolescence?

Logistics:
- Group size: Individual and full class.
- Approximate time: Individual (3 hours) and full class discussion (30 minutes).

Classroom Activity 9: Critical Thinking Multiple-Choice Questions and Suggested Answers Discuss the answers to the critical thinking multiple-choice questions on **Handout 2**. Question 1 is a type of problem that should by now be familiar to students. Nevertheless, remind them of the issues involved in the Nature of Development box in chapter 1, and determine whether they want a guided review of the issues pertinent to this exercise.

Question 2 is different from the other critical thinking questions. This one requires an overview of the chapter, followed by a judgment about the nature of the material contained in the chapter. You may want to discuss with your class the nature of knowledge in developmental psychology and how to determine whether information is empirical or theoretical in nature. This exercise is an opportunity to apply the work students have been doing on learning the differences between inferences, observations, and assumptions in a broader way. Another basis for discussion is to have students practice using these statements to characterize a previous chapter or chapters in the adolescence unit or in a previous unit.

Question 3 involves separating assumptions, inferences, and observations. If you have not already done so, you may want to discuss with students the variety of statements they have come to identify as assumptions in the series of problems they have done. Discuss with them how well they think they are able to identify assumptions and whether they feel confident that they can do so on their own. **Handout 3** provides the answers to the critical thinking multiple-choice questions

Logistics:
- Materials: Handout 2 (the critical thinking multiple-choice questions) and Handout 3 (answers).
- Group size: Small groups to discuss the questions, then a full class discussion.
- Approximate time: Small groups (15 to 20 minutes), full class discussion of any questions (15 minutes).

Classroom Activity 10: Critical Thinking Essay Questions and Suggestions for Helping Students Answer the Essays Discuss students' answers to the critical thinking essay questions provided as **Handout 4**. Several objectives can be met with these questions. First, the answering of these questions facilitates students' understanding of concepts in chapter 13. Second, this type of essay question affords the students an opportunity to apply the concepts to their own lives, which will facilitate their retention of the material. Third, the essay format also will give students practice expressing themselves in written form. Ideas to help students answer the critical thinking essay questions are provided as **Handout 5**.

Logistics:
- Materials: Handout 4 (essay questions) and Handout 5 (helpful suggestions for the answers).
- Group size: Individual, then full class.
- Approximate time: Individual (60 minutes), full class discussion of any questions (30 minutes).

Personal Applications

Personal Application 1: That's Me! The purpose of this exercise is for students to begin thinking about the importance of identity by getting in touch with their own. Erikson highlights the significance of developing a positive identity in his psychosocial stage of identity versus identity confusion. He theorizes that how individuals explore their beliefs, values, and roles in life will determine whether they will form an identity or proceed through life experiencing confusion as to who they really are.
- Instructions for Students: In the introduction to the section on identity, your text lists all of the aspects of an individual's identity (such as career, political views, and culture). Describe yourself with regard to each aspect of identity, then summarize to what extent you feel you've established a strong sense of self.
- Use in the Classroom: Discuss the development of personal identity. Have students reflect on their sense of self as children, and what has changed as to their self-perceptions now. Talk about the process of re-evaluating and rethinking values and ideals from childhood in order to establish their new adult identity. Has everyone finished this stage or are some still working on it? If they are still in the process of developing their identity, see if they will share what they are going through while doing so. Is anyone concerned about experiencing identity confusion? Explore this fascinating process, and share your own stories as well.

Personal Application 2: Aw, Mom! You can use this exercise to demonstrate the connection between parenting styles and the process of identity formation. The way in which parents include and/or respond to their adolescents during this critical time in life has been found to result in particular identity experiences as related to Marcia's identity statuses.

- Instructions for Students: Discuss your family experiences as an adolescent. What was your role in the family? How were your ideas responded to? How much influence and input did your parents have in what you did? After establishing your parents parenting style, discuss how you feel it has influenced your identity status.
- Use in the Classroom: Take a poll in class, categorizing students as to the parenting styles they experienced. Now compare and contrast their perceptions as to how they were affected by their experiences at home. Are students of the same background reacting similarly to their experiences or are you finding diversity within groups? If so, what might explain these differences? Have students consider different theoretical perspectives to explain findings within the class.
- Source: Marcia, J.E. (1980). Ego identity development. In J. Adelson (Ed.), *Handbook of adolescent psychology*. New York: Wiley.

Personal Application 3: Line Up, Boys and Girls The purpose of this exercise is to have students explore their identity formation in the context of their gender. It is a known fact that boys and girls are socialized differently and the results emerge time and time again in developmental research. Identity issues are no exception, as the factors that come to play in determining personal roles, goals, values, etc. are often gender based.

- Instructions for Students: Discuss your identity and the process you've gone through (or are going through) for identity formation with regard to your gender. What issues have come into play that specifically relate to your being male or female? What particular considerations have you been faced with concerning your gender? Which sex do you think has an easier time of identity formation and why?
- Use in the Classroom: This makes an excellent topic for class discussion. Pose all of the above questions and get specific examples along with answers. Do responses fall along gender lines, or is there variation among men and women in how they perceive the influences of gender on identity formation?

Personal Application 4: One of the Gang This exercise allows students to reflect on their experiences with peer pressure and think about its role in adolescent development. Teens do many things simply because their friends do it, and in order to fit in and be accepted. These behaviors are often negative in nature, and regardless of whether they even like engaging in certain things or not, teens will still do them due to the pressure to be one of the gang.

- Instructions for Students: Write about the role peer pressure played (or still plays) in your life. What things did you do, just to fit in? Who were the people you were trying to impress and why were they so important? Were you aware of what you were doing, or did you actually convince yourself that things were *your* decision? What were the results of your conformity?
- Use in the Classroom: Discuss peer pressure and its role in identity formation in adolescence and beyond. Have students speculate about what might occur during identity formation that might lead an individual to continue to succumb to peer pressure later in life. Ask students to provide, or provide yourself, examples of adults conforming to the wishes of others. Why do they still do so? Does it happen at all stages of adulthood or does it taper off with the later stages? What might have contributed to individuals who are incredibly independent thinkers and nonconformists?

Research Project Ideas

Research Project 1: Teens and the Political Scene Adolescent interest in politics varies from generation to generation. In the 1960s, teenagers were more active in political rallies and demonstrations than previous or later generations. In the 1970s, however, adolescents could look forward to voting at age 18 where previous generations had to wait until 21.

- First, have students interview early, middle, and late adolescents on their political attitudes and behaviors (See **Handout 6**). Possible interview questions include:
  - How important is it to vote? Why? What issues do you think politicians should put most of their efforts in (e.g., education, poverty, health, defense, economy, crime, family)? Would you ever want to be a politician (e.g., member of a school board, city council member, state legislator, congressional representative)? Have you ever participated in a political convention? What did you do? Do you hold political discussions with your friends? Family? Do you watch television news or read the newspaper regularly? What are the three most important global issues? National issues? State and local issues? Which label fits you best: political optimist-idealist, political cynic, apolitical? If you are old enough to vote, are you registered? If not, do you plan to register when you are 18? With which political party do you most identify? Why? Do your political views agree more with your parents' or with your friends' views? How informed do you believe you are on political and governmental issues?
- Second, they should note whether the imaginary audience, personal fable, and idealism have more significance in the younger rather than the older adolescents. Do adolescents think that politics can alleviate human problems? Do they tend to be conservative or liberal? Do they know information about the political system?
  - Early adolescents should be the most idealistic about finding solutions to political dilemmas, and they are the most likely to believe that their parents have not done all they could have done to solve problems such as homelessness, famine, and conflict.
- Source: Simons, J. A. (1985). Teens and the political scene: A classroom activity. Ankeny, IA: Des Moines Area Community College.

Research Project 2: Marcia's Statuses of Identity This project examines Marcia's statuses of identity in college students (18 to 20 years old). Using **Handout 7**, students should interview ten college students (if the student is 18 to 20, he/she may be a subject) and then identify their current identity status. In a brief report, the students should answer the questions that follow.

From the following statements, choose the one that best reflects you currently:

a. "I believe that I have made commitments to my future career and life. A while back, however, I had a rough time deciding what I wanted to do with my life."

b. "I really don't know what I want to do with my life, but I am trying to make up my mind about my options. I guess I'm having an identity crisis."

c. "I know what commitments I am going to make in my life. Seems like I always have known where I'm heading. I can't remember it being very difficult to decide."

d. "I really don't know what I want to do with my life, but I'm not losing any sleep over it. Sometime I'll decide what I want to do, but not right now."

Questions:

- How did your ten subjects break down by identity achievement (a), identity moratorium (b), identity foreclosure (c), and identity diffusion (d)?
- Do female and male subjects tend to give the same responses?
- Do you think you would get similar answers if you used 18- to 20-year-old subjects who were not enrolled in college? Married young adults? Parents?
- Use in the Classroom: Have students pool their data. What is the most typical identity status? Least typical? Are there any sex differences? What identity statuses do your class members remember going through? How did different identity statuses affect emotions? Self-confidence? Self-esteem?

Film and Video List

The following films and videos supplement the content of chapter 13. Contact information for film distributors can be found at the front of this Instructor's Manual under Film and Video Sources.

Adolescence: Crisis or Change? (Insight Media, 60 minutes). This video explores development of autonomy, peer group relations, and personal identity. The featured theories include Erickson, Sullivan, and Ginzberg.

Adolescence: Social and Emotional Development (Magna Systems, 38 minutes). The search for identity in adolescence and the influence of parents and peers on this search are the focus of this video.

American Adolescence (Films for the Humanities and Sciences, 30 minutes). This program investigates the hurdles faced by today's teens and discusses how their hopes, fears, and expectations will shape American society.

The Development of Self (Insight Media, 60 minutes). This video discusses self-concept, self-esteem, and self-worth, with a focus on Harter's work. In addition, it relates development in these areas to puberty and clinical disorders.

The Familiar Face of Love (Filmakers Library, 47 minutes). This video involves a study of love and looks at how and why we choose our mates.

Spark among the Ashes: A Bar Mitzvah in Poland (Filmakers Library, 56 minutes). This video illustrates the rites of passage into adulthood through religious ceremonies and provides cross-cultural examples.

Still Killing Us Softly: Advertising's Image of Women (Cambridge Documentary Films, 30 minutes). This program uses magazine, newspaper, album, and billboard ads to illustrate effects on sexual roles, expression, and violence.

Suicide: Dead is Forever (Films for the Humanities and Sciences, 28 minutes). This program looks at the lives of those who commit suicide and the survivors left behind. Experts explain risk factors, statistics, and warning signs while discussing the impact of teen suicide on both society and the victims' friends and family.

Suicide: A Guide for Prevention (Films for the Humanities and Sciences, 26 minutes). In this video, suicide myths are replaced with factors related to suicide such as who is at risk, warning signs, triggers and interventions. Discussion includes how careful assessment and compassionate dialogue between parasuicides and medical staff is vital.

Teen Suicide (Films for the Humanities and Sciences, 35 minutes). This program examines the reason why teens consider, attempt, or commit suicide and stresses specific measures to help prevent suicide. Viewers learn how to recognize warning signs, how to help, and where to go for assistance.

Teenage Relationships (Insight Media, 30 minutes). Social development during early and late adolescence is examined in this video.

Understanding Parenting Styles: Authoritarian-Democratic-Permissive (Films for the Humanities and Sciences, 27 minutes). This program shows teen interactions with their parents and three parenting styles.

Web Site Suggestions

The URLs for general sites, common to all chapters, can be found at the front of this Instructor's Manual under Useful Web Sites. At the time of publication, all sites were current and active, however, please be advised that you may occasionally encounter a dead link.

Adolescent Depression
http://health.yahoo.com/health/Diseases_and_Conditions/Disease_Feed_Data/Adolescent_depression/

Adolescent Peer Groups
http://www.personal.psu.edu/faculty/n/x/nxd10/peers2.htm

American Academy of Child and Adolescent Psychiatry: Teen Suicide
http://www.aacap.org/web/aacap/publications/factsfam/suicide.htm

An Evaluation of Safe Dates, an Adolescent Dating Violence Prevention Program
http://www.apha.org/news/publications/journal/foshee.htm

Parenting Today's Teen—Books for Those Who Live with and Work with Teens
http://www.parentingteens.com/

Identity Status Activity

To test your understanding of Marcia's four identity statuses, identify the status of the adolescent in each of the five scenarios. Be sure to explain your reasoning behind your choices.

1. Marsha is a 14-year-old who, when asked what she wants to do when she graduates from high school, replies, "Maybe I will get married and have some children, or maybe I will be a neurosurgeon, or a fashion designer."

2. Seventeen-year-old Suzanne is questioning the tenets of the religion in which she was brought up. She is, for the first time, examining her beliefs and considering other belief systems. At the end of the period, she chooses to follow the same religion as her parents.

3. Lorraine is 16 years old and, when asked what she wants to do when she graduates from high school, replies, "I never really thought about it. I guess I will decide when the time comes."

4. After Bill graduates from high school, he plans to go into his father's business. He has been talking this over with his parents since he was a preschooler and is eager to fulfill his parents' expectations.

5. Michael was asked to debate issues concerning premarital sex in his health class. His parents always taught him that premarital sex was wrong and that they would be very disappointed if they discovered that he had participated. After thoroughly investigating the consequences of premarital sex, Michael came out against it.

Critical Thinking Multiple-Choice Questions

1. Listed below are several aspects of development, each paired with a topic in adolescent social development. Only one of these statements aptly illustrates the aspect paired with it. Which one is it? Circle the letter of the best answer and explain why it is the best answer and why each other answer is not as good.

   a. Maturation: Parent-adolescent conflict
   b. Stability: Parent-adolescent attachment
   c. Quantitative change: Identity development
   d. Cognitive processes: Formation of adolescent groups
   e. Critical period: Rites of passage

2. Which statement best characterizes what we know about the social development of adolescents? Circle the letter of the best answer and explain why it is the best answer and why each other answer is not as good.

   a. Our knowledge is mainly descriptive.
   b. We understand the causes and determinants of adolescent personality and social development.
   c. There are few data available about adolescent personality and social development, so we rely mainly on theory and speculation.
   d. Research on each aspect of adolescent social development has been stimulated by a theory associated with it.
   e. Theory has made relatively little contribution to our understanding of adolescent personality and social development.

3. Contrary to what was previously believed, needs for autonomy and attachment appear to be complementary influences on adolescent social development. Needs for autonomy push adolescents to discover their strengths and limitations, whereas needs for attachment keep them connected to adults who nurture and support their explorations. It is therefore appropriate to allow adolescents to have control over some aspects of their lives. Which of the following is an assumption, rather than an inference or an observation, that underlies advice based on these conclusions? Circle the letter of the best answer and explain why it is the best answer and why each other answer is not as good.

   a. The key limitation on adolescents' ability to make good decisions is lack of knowledge.
   b. Attachment to parents contributes to social adjustment.
   c. Adolescents who are securely attached to their parents experience little depression.
   d. Attachment to parents promotes positive relationships with peers.
   e. Parents who recognize the attachment-autonomy connection will not experience conflict with their teenage children.

Suggested Answers for Critical Thinking Multiple-Choice Questions

1. Listed below are several aspects of development, each paired with a topic in adolescent social development. Only one of these statements aptly illustrates the aspect paired with it. Which one is it? Circle the letter of the best answer and explain why it is the best answer and why each other answer is not as good.

   a. <u>Maturation: Parent-adolescent conflict</u> is not the best answer. Parent-adolescent conflict is only partly, and not necessarily directly, based on maturation, which is but one factor cited as a possible cause of conflict. In any case, the idea of maturation is that there is an "orderly sequence of changes dictated by a genetic blueprint." There is nothing in chapter 13 that suggests that this is a cause of parent-adolescent conflict or that parent-adolescent conflict represents this sort of developmental process.

   b. <u>Stability: Parent-adolescent attachment</u> is the best answer. The idea is that secure attachment seems to be a stable characteristic across both time and situations. Early and concurrent attachment to parents is related to secure attachment to friends, lovers, and spouses.

   c. <u>Quantitative change: Identity development</u> is not the best answer. Identity development involves qualitative changes in individuals' ideas about who they are. Marcia's system classifies identity into different types, which represent differently organized concepts about the self and adaptations to life's demands. This is a classic example of qualitative development.

   d. <u>Cognitive processes: Formation of adolescent groups</u> is not the best answer. The treatment of the topic focuses on social processes. Nothing is said about cognitive factors that may influence individuals' participation in groups.

   e. <u>Critical period: Rites of passage</u> is not the best answer. A rite of passage is a social event that is not keyed to any particular developmental phase. Nor is there evidence that the timing of a rite of passage is crucial for any aspect of development.

2. Which statement best characterizes what we know about the social development of adolescents? Circle the letter of the best answer and explain why it is the best answer and why each other answer is not as good.

   a. <u>Our knowledge is mainly descriptive</u> best characterizes what we know. The core of chapter 13 is made of observational and correlational studies of different aspects of adolescent social development. For example, the discussion of families focuses on accurately characterizing the nature of parent-adolescent conflict, as well as establishing a more valid statement of the relationship between attachment and autonomy. Likewise, material on peer relations describes the characteristics of adolescents' groups and group information.

   b. <u>We understand the causes and determinants of adolescent personality and social development</u> does not best characterize what we know. The reason is that the reported research is correlational. Although it suggests hypotheses about causal mechanisms, it does not confirm them.

   c. <u>There are few data available about adolescent personality and social development, so we rely mainly on theory and speculation</u> does not best characterize what we know. In fact, there are many studies of personality and social development in chapter 13. These describe diverse aspects of family structure and function; peer group formation, structure, and function; culturally variable aspects of development; and the nature and course of identity development.

   d. <u>Research on each aspect of adolescent social development has been stimulated by a theory associated with it</u> does not best characterize what we know. As presented in chapter 13, only one area of research was clearly motivated by theory: identity development. Research on the other subjects seems to have been driven mainly by empirical or pragmatic concerns. For example, as suggested in "a," much of the work describes aspects of social development.

Handout 3 (CA 9) continued

e. <u>Theory has made relatively little contribution to our understanding of adolescent personality and social development</u> does not best characterize what we know. It is contradicted by the value of Erikson's theory as a means of integrating what we know about family, peer, and cultural correlates of identity development. This theory has played an important role in organizing diverse facts and suggesting new research directions.

3. Contrary to what was previously believed, needs for autonomy and attachment appear to be complementary influences on adolescent social development. Needs for autonomy push adolescents to discover their strengths and limitations, whereas needs for attachment keep them connected to adults who nurture and support their explorations. It is therefore appropriate to allow adolescents to have control over some aspects of their lives. Which of the following is an assumption, rather than an inference or an observation, that underlies advice based on these conclusions? Circle the letter of the best answer and explain why it is the best answer and why each other answer is not as good.

a. <u>The key limitation of adolescents' ability to make good decisions is lack of knowledge</u> is the assumption. The specific advice is to allow teenagers to make decisions when they have enough knowledge about the choices they have—that is, to relinquish control over these decisions. This appears to assume that knowledge is the main factor determining the quality of decisions because it does not mention that other factors could influence decision making. However, chapter 12 describes several other factors (e.g., logical thinking, specific limitations on adolescents' decision-making capacities associated with age) that probably have a strong influence on adolescent decision making and probably should be included in decisions about granting autonomy.

b. <u>Attachment to parents contributes to social adjustment</u> is an inference. It is one interpretation of the correlational data, which have established a connection between quality of attachment and quality of social adjustment

c. <u>Adolescents who are securely attached to their parents experience little depression</u> is an observation. Research has documented this association.

d. <u>Attachment to parents promotes positive relationships with peers</u> is an inference, for the same reason that "b" is. The supporting evidence is correlational.

e. <u>Parents who recognize the attachment-autonomy connection will not experience conflict with their teenage children</u> is an inference. It is an extension of information presented in the text about optimal ways to parent adolescents, a hypothesis about the effects of recommended parenting practices. It is also an incorrect extension of the information, because work done to date appears to suggest that some degree of conflict is probably both necessary and desirable. For example, some kinds of conflict appear to promote identity development.

Handout 4 (CA 10)
Critical Thinking Essay Questions

Your answers to this kind of question demonstrate an ability to comprehend and apply ideas discussed in this chapter.

1. Show how the vignette at the beginning of chapter 13 illustrates themes of the chapter.

2. Explain Marcia's four identity statuses, and indicate specific life events that would channel personality toward each of the four identity statuses.

3. Explain the relationship between attachment and autonomy, and evaluate the claim that secure attachment promotes personal adjustment.

4. Compare and contrast the old and new models of parent-adolescent relationships. Which appears to be more accurate? Support your conclusion with recent findings.

5. How does the maturation of parents influence parent-adolescent relationships?

6. Explain the roles that peers play in the lives of adolescents; highlight both positive and negative peer influences.

7. Compare and contrast children and adolescent groups.

8. Describe developmental trends in dating for boys and girls, and discuss how both cognitive and cultural factors may explain those trends.

9. What is a rite of passage? Explain at least two examples of rites of passage in your own life.

10. Explain what it means to say that social class confounds ethnic explanations for adolescent development.

11. Discuss the harm done by researchers and laymen alike when each fails to respect differences between ethnic groups and differences within ethnic groups.

12. Explain the concepts of assimilation and pluralism. Relate these concepts to value conflicts.

13. Imagine that you are in a situation with a potentially suicidal individual. Explain what you should and should not do.

Ideas to Help You Answer Critical Thinking Essay Questions

1. Begin by making a list of all the themes presented in the chapter. Introduce each theme, with a brief description of its characteristics, then present the aspect of the vignette as an example of the theme.

2. Review the sections of the text that present all of the various influences on identity formation. Create specific examples reflecting each of the influences as you discuss Marcia's statuses.

3. Addressing this question requires specifically defining all the critical terms involved. It is important to know exactly what is meant by 1) attachment, 2) autonomy, 3) secure attachment, and 4) personal adjustment. Be sure to explain each of these concepts from a developmental perspective, so as to clarify exactly what you are describing when you discuss the relationship between attachment and autonomy and its implications for personal adjustment.

4. Identify the issues of importance with regard to the parent-adolescent relationship. Create a grid with similarities and differences between the two views, relating to each issue. As you discuss the recent findings and their implications for accuracy, feel free to address any additional issues you think are relevant, and use your own experiences to evaluate the accuracy of the views.

5. To assist you in answering this question, think back to your teen years. Recall your parents and the parents of your friends. How did they differ maturationally? How did your relationship with your parents differ from those of your friends and their parents? Can you now explain those differences?

6. For each role, write your own vignette illustrating it. Feel free to pull examples from your childhood, and create quotes from peer interactions and experiences.

7. Go beyond the text for this question. Recall, in detail, your childhood groups and those that you were a part of in adolescence. What differences exist in your own perceptions of the two?

8. You might be able to enhance your response to this question by reflecting on the progression of your own dating experiences. When did you have your first boyfriend or girlfriend? What were your expectations for the relationship? What did you do as a couple? What characterized your next romantic relationship? How was it different from the first? Continue on to illustrate development.

9. Recall a traditional, commonly recognized rite of passage, or one that may be more personal in nature (within your own family or community). Don't limit yourself to typical notions and "ceremonies."

10. Recall that the term *confound* indicates a connection and possible interaction between factors.

11. Begin by illustrating a difference *between* ethnic groups, and a difference *within* ethnic groups. Having painted those pictures, address the question.

12. Include specific examples in your explanation of the concepts and you may find an obvious introduction to addressing the issue of value conflicts from this perspective.

13. Things are often explained best when informing other people. Thus, incorporate into your scenario that your situation is that of an individual working for a suicide hotline. You have a caller on the phone, and you are training people to take calls. This call is a demonstration, so you must clearly explain what should and should not be done.

Handout 6 (RP 1)

Teens and the Political Scene

Adolescent interest in politics varies from generation to generation. In the 1960s, teenagers were more active in political rallies and demonstrations than previous or later generations. In the 1970s, however, adolescents could look forward to voting at age 18 where previous generations had to wait until 21. The purpose of this research project is to examine the relationship between age and political attitudes.

You will need to interview early, middle, and late adolescents on their political attitudes and behaviors. It is important to use the same questions for all of the adolescents that you interview. Spend some time generating the standardized list of interview questions.
- Possible interview questions include:
    - How important is it to vote? Why?
    - What issues do you think politicians should put most of their efforts in (e.g., education, poverty, health, defense, economy, crime, family)?
    - Would you ever want to be a politician (e.g., member of a school board, city council member, state legislator, congressional representative)?
    - Have you ever participated in a political convention? What did you do?
    - Do you hold political discussions with your friends? Family?
    - Do your political views agree more with your parents' or with your friends' views?
    - Do you watch television news or read the newspaper regularly?
    - What are the three most important global issues? National issues? State and local issues?
    - Which label fits you best: political optimist-idealist, political cynic, apolitical?
    - If you are old enough to vote, are you registered? If not, do you plan to register when you are 18?
    - With which political party do you most identify? Why?
    - How informed do you believe you are on political and governmental issues?

After you have completed the three interviews examine the answers.
- Did you notice any age differences?
- Did cognitive characteristics such as imaginary audience, personal fable, and idealism influence the younger adolescents more than the other adolescents?
- Do adolescents think that politics can alleviate human problems?
- Do they tend to be conservative or liberal?
- Do they know information about the political system?

- Source: Simons, J. A. (1985). Teens and the political scene: A classroom activity. Ankeny, IA: Des Moines Area Community College.

Marcia's Statuses of Identity

This project examines Marcia's statuses of identity in college students (18 to 20 years old). Interview ten college students (if you are 18 to 20, you may be a subject) and then identify their current identity status. In a brief report, answer the questions that follow.

Instructions to subjects:

From the following statements, choose the one that best reflects you currently:

a. "I believe that I have made commitments to my future career and life. A while back, however, I had a rough time deciding what I wanted to do with my life."
b. "I really don't know what I want to do with my life, but I am trying to make up my mind about my options. I guess I'm having an identity crisis."
c. "I know what commitments I am going to make in my life. Seems like I always have known where I'm heading. I can't remember it being very difficult to decide."
d. "I really don't know what I want to do with my life, but I'm not losing any sleep over it. Sometime I'll decide what I want to do, but not right now."

DATA SHEET

Subject:	Sex:	Age:	Statement Choice:
1	F/M	18/19/20	a/b/c/d
2	F/M	18/19/20	a/b/c/d
3	F/M	18/19/20	a/b/c/d
4	F/M	18/19/20	a/b/c/d
5	F/M	18/19/20	a/b/c/d
6	F/M	18/19/20	a/b/c/d
7	F/M	18/19/20	a/b/c/d
8	F/M	18/19/20	a/b/c/d
9	F/M	18/19/20	a/b/c/d
10	F/M	18/19/20	a/b/c/d

Questions:

• How did your ten subjects break down by identity achievement (a), identity moratorium (b), identity foreclosure (c), and identity diffusion (d)?

• Do female and male subjects tend to give the same responses?

• Do you think you would get similar answers if you used 18- to 20-year-old subjects who were not enrolled in college? Married young adults? Parents?

Chapter 14: Physical and Cognitive Development in Early Adulthood

Total Teaching Package Outline

Lecture Outline	Resource References
Physical and Cognitive Development in Early Adulthood	PowerPoint Presentation: See www.mhhe.com Cognitive Maps: See Appendix A
The Transition from Adolescence to Adulthood	LS1: Allport's Dimensions of Maturity
• The Criteria for Becoming an Adult	LO1 OHT150: Consequences of Attaining Adult Status F/V: Adulthood
• The Transition from High School to College	LO2 PA1: Free At Last!
Physical Development	CA1: Healthy Living? F/V: Woman and Man
• The Peak and Slowdown in Physical Performance	LO3
• Eating and Weight -Obesity	LO4 WS: Weight Control and Statistics LS2: Obesity
-Dieting	
• Regular Exercise	CA2: Body Perception PA2: Stretch, 2, 3, 4...
• Substance Abuse	LO5
-Alcohol -Cigarette Smoking -Addiction	RP1: College Students and the Use of Alcohol LO6 WS: The Science Behind Drug Addiction WS: Alcohol and Drug Addiction
Sexuality	LS3: Guest Lecture Ideas on Sexuality F/V: Sociology and Sexuality

• Sexual Orientation
    -Heterosexual Attitudes and Behavior
    -Homosexual Attitudes and Behavior
	
	 LO7
	 LO8

• Sexually Transmitted Diseases
    -Gonorrhea
    -Syphilis
    -Chlamydia
    -Genital Herpes
    -HPV
    -AIDS
    -Protecting Against STDs
	LO9
	
	 RP2: AIDS in Your Community
	 WS: The AIDS Knowledge Base

• Forcible Sexual Behavior and Harassment
   -Rape
 	
   -Sexual Harassment
	LO10
	WS: Rape and Sexual Assault

Cognitive Development
• Cognitive Stages
   -Piaget's View
 	
   -Realistic and Pragmatic Thinking
   -Reflective and Relativistic Thinking
   -Is There a Fifth, Post-Formal Stage?
 	
• Creativity
   -Adult Developmental Changes
   -Csikszentmihalyi's Ideas
	LO11
	OHT175 & IB: Cognitive Stages of Adulthood
	
	LS4: Self, Knowledge, and Morality
	
	CA3: Reflecting on Your Life
	
	LO12
	PA3: Get Those Juices Flowing!

Careers and Work • Developmental Changes • Personality Types • Values and Careers • Monitoring the Occupational Outlook Handbook • The Skills Employers Want • Finding the Right Career • Work	LO13 PA4: Dream Job LO14 CA4: Need For Achievement and Career Dev. WS: Advanced Education and Career Dev. LO15 F/V: One Nation Under Stress F/V: Stress F/V: Stress: Keeping Your Cool OHT176 & IB: Life Contour of Work CA5: Gender and Multiple Roles
Review	LS5: A Note on Qualitative Research CA6: Qualitative Research CA7: Critical Thinking Multiple-Choice CA8: Critical Thinking Essays

Chapter Outline

THE TRANSITION FROM ADOLESCENCE TO ADULTHOOD
The Criteria for Becoming an Adult
- The age period from 18-25 has been labeled "emerging adulthood" as individuals have often left the dependency of childhood but have not yet assumed adult responsibilities.
- Two criteria for adult status are economic independence and independent decision making.

The Transition from High School to College
- There is both continuity and change in the transition from high school to college.
- The transition can involve positive and negative features.
  - Positive features include feeling more grownup, increased freedom, exploration of new ideas.
  - Negative features include increased stress and more depression.
- More individuals are becoming college educated in the U.S. than in the past.
  - An increasing number of students are returning to college.

PHYSICAL DEVELOPMENT
- Physical status both reaches its peak and begins to decline in early adulthood.
The Peak and Slowdown in Physical Performance
- Peak physical status is often reached between 18 and 30 years of age.
- Individuals are often at their healthiest in early adulthood.
  - College students understand how to prevent illness and promote health, yet they have unrealistic, overly optimistic expectations about their future health risks.
- Bad health habits are often formed.
- Decline in physical performance occurs in early adulthood.
  - Muscle tone and strength decline around age 30.

Eating and Weight
Obesity
Pervasiveness and Costs
- Approximately one-third of the American population is overweight enough to be at increased health risk.
- The prevalence of obesity has risen 8 percent in the 1990s.
- Health care costs linked to obesity are estimated to be $46 billion per year.
- Obesity is associated with increased risk of hypertension, diabetes, and heart disease.
Heredity
- Some individuals do inherit a tendency to be overweight.
- Identical twins have similar weights even when reared apart.
Set Point and Metabolism
- The amount of stored fat in your body is an important factor in your set point.
  - **Set point** is the weight maintained when no effort is made to gain or lose weight.
- Another factor in weight is **basal metabolism rate (BMR)**, the minimal amount of energy an individual uses in a resting state.
  - BMR declines with age and females have lower BMR than males.
Environmental Factors
- Strong evidence of the environment's influence on weight is the doubling of the rate of obesity in the U.S. since 1900.
  - Obesity is six times more prevalent among women with low incomes than among women with high incomes.
  - Americans are also more obese than Europeans.

371

Dieting

Dieting

The Diet Scene

- Many divergent interests are involved in the topic of dieting (public, health professionals, policy makers, media, and diet and food industries).

Restrained Eating

- **Restrained eaters** are individuals who chronically restrict their food intake to control their weight.
- When restrained eaters stop dieting, they tend to binge eat.

Do Diets Work?

- Few people are successful in keeping weight off long-term, though some are successful.

Exercise

- Exercise not only burns calories, but also continues to elevate the person's metabolic rate for several hours after the exercise.
- Exercise lowers a person's set point for weight, which makes it easier to maintain a lower weight.

Dieting: Harm or Benefit?

- Dieting can be harmful, especially when a person is in a recurring cycle of dieting and weight gain.
- When overweight people diet and maintain their weight loss, it can have positive effects such as less depression and reduction in their risk for a number of health impairing disorders.

Regular Exercise

- **Aerobic exercise** is sustained exercise—jogging, swimming, or cycling, for example—that stimulates heart and lung activity.
- Experts recommend that adults engage in 30 minutes or more of moderate-intensity physical activity 5-7 days a week.
  - Only 20 percent of adults in the U.S. are active at these levels.
- Both moderate and intense exercise produce important physical and psychological gains, such as lowered risk of heart disease and lowered anxiety.

Substance Abuse

Alcohol

- Almost half of all U.S. college students say they drink heavily.
  - Most acknowledge that their heavy drinking affects them.
- Although some reduction in alcohol use has occurred among college freshmen, binge drinking is still a major concern.
- By the mid-twenties, a reduction in drug use often takes place.
  - College students drink more than youths who end their education after high school.
  - Those who don't go to college smoke more.
  - Singles use marijuana more than married individuals.
  - Drinking is heaviest among singles and divorced individuals. Becoming engaged, married, or even remarried quickly brings down alcohol use.

Cigarette Smoking

- Research evidence underscores the dangers of smoking or being around those who smoke.
- The prevalence of smoking in men has dropped from 50 percent in 1965 to about 25 percent today.
- A number of strategies, such as nicotine substitutes, have shown some success in getting smokers to quit, but quitting is difficult because of the addictive properties of nicotine.

Addiction
- **Addiction** is a pattern of behavior characterized by an overwhelming involvement with using a drug and securing its supply.
  - Addiction can occur despite adverse consequences of the drug use.
  - Addiction can refer to physical and/or psychological dependence.
  - Controversy continues concerning whether addictions are diseases.
  - Two models of addiction have been proposed.
    - The **disease model of addiction** describes addictions as biologically based, lifelong diseases that involve a loss of control over behavior and require medical and/or spiritual treatment for recovery.
    - The **life-process model of addiction** states that addiction is not a disease but rather a habitual response and a source of gratification or security that can be understood only in the context of social relationships and experiences.

SEXUALITY
  Sexual Orientation
  Heterosexual Attitudes and Behavior
- The 1994 Sex in America survey was a major improvement over earlier sex surveys.
- The major findings include:
  - Americans tend to fall into three categories:
    - One-third have sex twice a week or more.
    - One-third have sex a few times a month.
    - One-third have sex a few times a year or not at all.
  - Married couples have the most sex.
  - Most Americans do not engage in kinky sexual acts.
  - Adultery is clearly the exception rather than the rule.
  - Men think about sex far more than women do.
  Homosexual Attitudes and Behavior
- It is generally accepted to view sexual orientation along a continuum from exclusively heterosexual to exclusively homosexual.
  - Some individuals are bisexual as they are sexually attracted to people of both sexes.
- Homosexuals and heterosexuals have similar physiological responses during sexual arousal and seem to be aroused by the same types of tactile stimulation.
- Research has found no differences between homosexuals and heterosexuals in a wide range of attitudes, behaviors, and adjustments.
- An individual's sexual preference likely is the result of a combination of genetic, hormonal, cognitive, and environmental factors.

  Sexually Transmitted Diseases
- **Sexually transmitted diseases (STDs)** are diseases that are contracted primarily through sexual contact. This contact is not limited to vaginal intercourse but includes oral-genital and anal-genital contact as well.
  - STDs are an increasing health problem.
  Gonorrhea
- **Gonorrhea** is a sexually transmitted disease that is commonly called the "drip" or the "clap."
- It is reported to be one of the most common STDs in the United States and is caused by a bacterium from the gonococcus family, which thrives in the moist mucous membranes lining the mouth, throat, vagina, cervix, urethra, and anal tract.
- Gonorrhea can be successfully treated in its early stages with antibiotics.

Syphilis
- **Syphilis** is a sexually transmitted disease caused by the bacterium *Treponema pallidum*, a member of the spirochete family.
- Syphilis can be effectively treated in its early stages, however it can cause paralysis or even death in its advanced stages.

Chlamydia
- **Chlamydia**, the most common of all sexually transmitted diseases, is named for *Chlamydia trachomitis*, an organism that spreads by sexual contact and infects the genital organs.
- About 10 percent of all college students have chlamydia.
- Females are asymptomatic and chlamydia is the number one preventable cause of female infertility.

Genital Herpes
- **Genital herpes** is a sexually transmitted disease caused by a large family of viruses with many different strains. These strains produce other, nonsexually transmitted diseases such as chicken pox and mononucleosis.
- There is no cure for genital herpes, though the painful symptoms can be treated.

HPV
- **HPV** is a virus (human papillomavirus) that causes warts on people. A few types of the virus cause warts on the genitals.
- Physicians can treat HPV, though it is thought that HPV does not go away.

AIDS
- **AIDS** is a sexually transmitted disease that is caused by the human immunodeficiency virus (HIV), which destroys the body's immune system.
  - Deaths due to AIDS have begun to decline in the U.S. due to education and more effective drug treatments.
  - AIDS is increasing in Africa; 4 million people in Africa had AIDS in 2000.
- Experts say that AIDS can be transmitted only by sexual contact, sharing hypodermic needles, blood transfusion, or other direct contact of cuts or mucous membranes with blood and sexual fluids.

Protecting Against STDs
- Some good strategies for protection against AIDS and other STDs include:
  - Know your and your partner's risk status.
  - Obtain medical examinations.
  - Have protected sex.
  - Don't have sex with multiple partners.

Forcible Sexual Behavior and Harassment
Rape
- **Rape** is forcible sexual intercourse with a person who does not give consent.
- Of increasing concern is **date or acquaintance rape**, which is coercive sexual activity directed at someone with whom the individual is at least casually acquainted.
  - Two-thirds of college males admit to fondling females against their will and one-half admit to forced sexual activity.
  - Why is rape so pervasive in the U.S.?
    - Males are socialized to be sexually aggressive, to regard women as inferior beings, and to view their own pleasure as the most important objective.
- Rape is a traumatic experience for the victim and those close to her. Common consequences include depression, fear, anxiety, and sexual dysfunction.

Sexual Harassment
- Sexual harassment can include sexist remarks, covert sexual contact, and sexual assault.
- This occurs when one person uses his/her power over another individual in a sexual manner.

COGNITIVE DEVELOPMENT

Cognitive Stages

Piaget's View

- Piaget thought that young adults were quantitatively advanced in their thinking (they have more knowledge), however, they are qualitatively similar.

Realistic and Pragmatic Thinking

- Some experts argue that the idealism of Piaget's formal operational stage declines in young adulthood, replaced by more realistic, pragmatic thinking.
- Schaie argues that adults use information differently than adolescents.

Reflective and Relativistic Thinking

- Perry said that adolescents often engage in dualistic, absolute thinking, whereas young adults are more likely to engage in reflective, relativistic thinking.

Is There a Fifth, Post-Formal Stage?

- **Post-formal thought** is qualitatively different than Piaget's formal operational thought.
- Post-formal thought involves understanding that the correct answer to a problem requires reflective thinking, may vary from one situation to another, and that the search for truth is often an ongoing, never-ending process.
- Also part of the fifth stage is the belief that solutions to problems need to be realistic and that emotion and subjective factors can influence thinking.
- Some critics argue that the research evidence does not fully support a qualitatively more advanced stage of thinking beyond formal operations.

Creativity

Adult Developmental Changes

- Creativity peaks in adulthood, often in the forties, and then declines.
  - The magnitude of decline is often slight.
  - The creativity-age link varies by domain.
  - There is extensive individual variation in lifetime creative output.

Csikszentmihalyi's Ideas

- Csikszentmihalyi interviewed 90 leading figures in art, business, government, education, and science to learn how creativity works.
- He found that creative people regularly experience a state he called flow, a heightened state of pleasure when engaging in mental and physical challenges that absorb us.
- The following are ways to cultivate your curiosity and interest:
  - Try to be surprised by something every day.
  - Try to surprise at least one person every day.
  - Write down each day what surprised you and how you surprised others.
  - When something sparks your interest, follow it.
  - Wake up in the morning with a specific goal to look forward to.
  - Take charge of your schedule.
  - Spend time in settings that stimulate your creativity.

CAREERS AND WORK

Developmental Changes

- Many young children have idealistic fantasies about a career.
- In the late teens, early twenties, their career thinking has usually turned more serious.
- By their early to mid twenties, many individuals have completed their education or training and started in a career.
- In the remainder of early adulthood, they seek to establish their emerging career and start moving up the career ladder.

Personality Types
- **Personality type theory** is John Holland's view that it is important for individuals to select a career that matches up well with their personality type.
- Holland proposed six basic career-related personality types:
  - Realistic
  - Investigative
  - Artistic
  - Social
  - Enterprising
  - Conventional
- Most individuals are a combination of two or three types.
- The basic idea of matching the abilities and attitudes of individuals to particular careers is important.

Values and Careers
- It is important to match up a career to your values. There are many different values, ranging from the importance of money to working in a preferred geographical location.

Monitoring the Occupational Outlook Handbook
- Service-producing industries will account for the most jobs in America in the next decade.
- Employment in the computer industry is projected to grow rapidly.
- Jobs that require a college education will be the fastest-growing and highest paying.
- Labor force participation of women will increase and so will that of Latinos and African Americans.

The Skills Employers Want
- In most careers today, communication skills and career skills are at the top of the lists of what employers want in prospective employees.
- Employers look for evidence in the candidate's accomplishments and experiences of leadership positions, involvement in campus organizations and extracurricular activities, relevant experiences in internships, part-time work or co-ops, and good grades.

Finding the Right Career
- Personality types and values are important in finding the right career.
- It is a good idea to have several careers in mind rather than just one.
- Seeing a career counselor, engaging in personal networking, and exploring Internet networks and resources are good strategies.

Work
- Work defines people in fundamental ways and is a key aspect of their identity.
  - Most individuals spend about one-third of their adult life at work.
- People often become stressed if they are unable to work.
- Work also can produce stress, as when there is a heavy work load and time pressure.
- The increasing number of women who work in careers outside the home has led to new work-related issues.
  - A special concern of many women is how to effectively juggle a career with family responsibilities.

Learning Objectives

1. Discuss the criteria for becoming an adult.
2. Elaborate on the transition from high school to college.
3. Explain the changes in physical development that occur during early adulthood.
4. Explain the causes of and concerns about obesity, and then discuss the issues surrounding dieting and exercise.
5. Explore the issue of substance abuse in the college population.
6. Define addiction and explain the two models of addiction.
7. Examine heterosexual attitudes and behaviors during early adulthood.
8. Examine homosexual attitudes and behaviors during early adulthood.
9. Describe the sexually transmitted diseases prevalent among young adults, and discuss ways to protect against them.
10. Elaborate on the factors associated with rape and sexual harassment.
11. Address the ways in which cognition changes during early adulthood.
12. Explain the changes that take place in creativity in early adulthood and ways to encourage it.
13. Indicate the development changes that take place in career choices, and describe Holland's career-related personality types.
14. Explain the process of choosing a career and what employers look for.
15. Discuss the importance of work and how it shapes the identity of the young adult.

Key Terms

addiction
aerobic exercise
AIDS
basal metabolism rate (BMR)
chlamydia
date or acquaintance rape
disease model of addiction
genital herpes
gonorrhea

HPV
life-process model of addiction
personality type theory
post-formal thought
rape
restrained eaters
set point
sexually transmitted diseases (STDs)
syphilis

Key People

Jeffrey Arnett
Jerald Bachman
Laura Brown
Faye Crosby
Mihaly Csikszentmihalyi

John Holland
Simon LeVay
Robert Micheal
William Perry
Jean Piaget
K. Warner Schaie

Lecture Suggestions

Lecture Suggestion 1: Allport's Dimensions of Maturity The purpose of this lecture is to examine Allport's dimensions of maturity. There are many tasks that need to be accomplished in early adulthood, including the establishment of an intimate relationship, the beginnings of family, and the decision about careers. One of the tasks that deserves attention is maturity. Most of the traditional-aged students in your classes (i.e., late adolescence and early adulthood) will be currently working on these dimensions in their own lives. Some areas will demand their undivided attention, others can be worked on in concert. You may want to engage the students in conversation about which dimensions are the most difficult to establish. Also, ask the students whether the dimensions of maturity apply to their lives. Are they dealing with the issues Allport identified, or was he off the mark? This lecture is a unique way to introduce the section on early adulthood.

Allport's dimensions of maturity are described below:

- Extension of self: doing something for its own sake, not because others want you to, or because it is expected of you.
- Relating warmly to others: developing intimate relations and displaying compassion.
- Emotional security, which includes:
  - self acceptance: including acceptance of one's faults.
  - emotional acceptance: accepting emotional responses without letting them take control.
  - frustration tolerance: an ability to handle high levels of stress.
  - confidence in self-expression: control over emotional expression.
- Realistic perception: perceiving situations accurately.
- Possession of skills and competencies: being aware of skills and displaying pride in personal abilities.
- Knowledge of the self, which includes:
  - what one can do.
  - what one cannot do.
  - what one ought to do.
- Establishing unifying philosophy of life: finding a guiding purpose, establishing ideals, identifying needs, developing goals, and adopting values.
- Source: Allport, B. (1950). *The nature of personality: Selected papers.* Cambridge, MA: Addison-Wesley.

Lecture Suggestion 2: Obesity The purpose of this lecture is to elaborate on Santrock's discussion of obesity in the U.S. adult population. The prevalence of obesity has increased since the 1980s. This is a major issue as obesity is strongly correlated with cardiovascular disease and diabetes. Cardiovascular disease is the number one killer in the U.S. In addition, economically speaking, obesity-related morbidity may account for almost 7 percent of U.S. health care costs.

Mokdad et al. (1999) monitored obesity trends by state and geographical region since 1991 using a large population-based survey. Six states were not included due to missing data. Body Mass Index (BMI) was calculated by dividing self-reported weight in kilograms by the square of height in meters. Obesity was indicated as a BMI of 30 or higher. Leisure-time physical activity was assessed and classified as inactive; irregular active; regular, not intense; and regular intense.

- Prevalence of obesity increased from 12 percent in 1991 to 17.9 percent in 1998.
- Obesity increased in women and men and across all sociodemographic groups.
  - The highest increase occurred among the youngest ages and higher education levels.
  - For Hispanic men, the prevalence increased from 10 percent to 18.3 percent and for Hispanic women from 13.2 percent to 23.4 percent.

- Prevalence and increase in prevalence since 1991 of obesity differed by state and region.
  - Thirty-seven states had obesity levels higher than 15 percent (with a range of 31.9-67.2 in the mid-Atlantic and South Atlantic regions of the US).
  - Delaware had the lowest magnitude of change from 1991 to 1998 with 11 percent and Georgia had the greatest change (101.8 percent).
- In 1998, the level of leisure-time physical activity was 28.6 percent inactive, 28.2 percent irregularly active, 29.6 percent regular not intense, and 13.6 percent regular intense.
  - These numbers indicate that physical activity has not changed substantially since 1991.

"Rarely do chronic conditions such as obesity spread with the speed and dispersion characteristic of a communicable disease epidemic." (Mokdad, p. 1520). A frightening aspect of this research is that these numbers are considered to be conservative estimates for two main reasons. First, these statistics are based on self-report. The concern arises from the fact that most people underestimate their weight; thus, the prevalence statistics presented here are conservative. Second, this survey was conducted by telephone thus it likely underrepresented individuals in lower SES, which is a factor related to obesity.

Why is obesity such a problem in the U.S.? What are some societal changes that potentially account for this epidemic-like change? Have students discuss potential intervention strategies for reducing the number of obese people in the U.S.

- Source: Mokdad, A.H., Serdula, M.K., Dietz, W.H., Bowman, B.A., Marks, J.S., & Koplan, J.P. (1999). The spread of the obesity epidemic in the United States, 1991-1998. *JAMA, 282*, 1519-1522.

Lecture Suggestion 3: Guest Lecture Ideas on Sexuality Chapter 14 spends a considerable amount of time focusing on issues of sexuality. Students may find it interesting to further investigate this topic in class. Invite to your class several individuals from your community, such as relationship counselors, gay rights activists, and fellow colleagues who conduct research on sexuality in early adulthood. Have a panel discussion on such topics as the causes of homosexuality, similarities and differences between homosexual and heterosexual relationships, and biases about sexual orientation in our culture as well as in research. You may also want to invite both heterosexual and homosexual individuals who are HIV positive. This lecture suggestion complements Research Project 2: AIDS in Your Community.

Lecture Suggestion 4: Self, Knowledge, and Morality - What Does Personal Epistemology Mean? This lecture is a good opportunity to integrate cognitive development and morality. This lecture suggestion is based on the book *Women's Ways of Knowing* by Belenky (1986). The opening paragraph sets the stage for understanding the orientation of the authors as they look at cognitive and moral development among women. The first paragraph notes that most of us are not preoccupied with questions of epistemology. That is, we do not often explicitly ask ourselves "What is truth?" or "What is authority?" Nor do we ask about the nature of evidence or how we know what we know. However, the author argue that to ask and to attempt to answer these questions has a profound effect on our understanding of ourselves, our notion of morality, teaching, learning, and our understanding of our impact on the events of the world. Further, the implication of this argument is that even if we do not explicitly ask ourselves these questions, we implicitly ask them in the way we respond to teaching and learning, in making moral decisions, and in creating our public and private personae.

These ways of knowing ourselves as moral agents can be understood in terms of Richard Rorty's concept of a "final vocabulary." Rorty (1989) argues in *Contingency, Irony, and Solidarity* that all of us have in the back of our heads, and often use, a set of words to justify our actions, beliefs, and lives. We use these words to formulate praise of our friends and contempt of our enemies. Our long-term projects, our deepest self-doubts, and our highest hopes are expressed in these words. We tell the story of our lives, sometimes reflecting on the past, sometimes projecting into the future, using these words. Rorty calls these words a person's "final vocabulary" because we cannot justify them beyond using them.

The idea of "final vocabulary" helps us understand how Belenky and her colleagues pieced together the pictures of the development of self, voice, and mind (even though they did not specifically build on or use the work of Richard Rorty). They did it by listening to the interviewees' "final vocabulary." The deepest self-doubts of the people they interviewed, and their definitions of friends and enemies makes Belenky's book about both cognition and morality. By contrast, the assumptions made by Belenky and her colleagues are quite different from the basic assumptions of Kohlberg. For example, Lawrence Kohlberg (1981) looks primarily at reasoning and its relationship to morality. Belenky and her colleagues believe that understanding the self as a knower shapes moral decisions, not reasoning ability per se. In other words, Kohlberg would argue that people cannot think at conventional levels of morality unless they are capable of taking the perspective of someone else. They need to have that cognitive ability to think at moral reasoning level. Belenky would argue, on the other hand, that if I see knowledge handed down from authority (What is the nature of truth?), I will think of myself differently and act differently than if I see knowledge as gained from personal experience, or from following a set of procedures.

While Belenky and her colleagues and Kohlberg all listen and pay attention to the specific words of their subjects, Belenky is likely to look closer at the words that relate to a life story, to long-term projects, and to deepest hopes and fears, whereas Kohlberg is likely to look at particular words that relate to the specific dilemmas that he presents to his subjects.

- Sources: Belenky, M. (1986). *Women's ways of knowing: The development of self, voice, and mind.* New York: Basic Books. Kohlberg, L. (1981). *The philosophy of moral development.* New York: Harper and Row. Rorty, R. (1989). *Contingency, irony, and solidarity.* Cambridge, MA: Cambridge University Press.

Lecture Suggestion 5: A Note on Qualitative Research Many studies of adult development rely on qualitative research methods; indeed, much of the material in chapter 14 is based on these. Now is a good time to clarify the differences between qualitative and quantitative research studies. Given space constraints, this lecture suggestion focuses on a few points: purpose, method, and reporting style.

- Purpose
  - Qualitative studies are intended to describe a given phenomenon in all its complexity. Quantitative studies, specifically experimental studies, are designed to show a cause and effect relationship between a limited number of variables. An elegant experimental design would control all but one or two key variables, and demonstrate a clear cause and effect relationship. An elegant qualitative study would present a multidimensional description of a complex activity or process.
- Method
  - Qualitative methods include in-depth interviews, participant observation, and unobtrusive measures. Researchers are very much a part of the study, and their task is to develop their skills as a human instrument of data collection and analysis. Because the data collected is primarily people's words and actions, the data are extensive and the number of subjects studied is usually small. Experimental studies are the archetypal quantitative study. An experimental study contains one group of subjects who receive a treatment (experimental group), while a like group of subjects receives no treatment (control group). The data collected is specific and can often be translated into numbers. The power of a quantitative study is often dependent on a large number of subjects.
- Reporting
  - Qualitative research projects have thorough descriptions as their central tenet. Quantitative studies are reported in a technical and highly consistent manner, with statistical levels of significance as an essential part of the study.

There is a debate as to the compatibility of qualitative and quantitative studies. Each addresses topics in different ways. One way to understand whether a topic for research might be studied by qualitative or quantitative methods is to make two statements: "I would like to understand more about..." versus "I would like to prove that..." If you want to understand more about something, a qualitative study might be the approach to take. If you want to prove something, look to a quantitative study. This lecture suggestion complements Classroom Activity 6: Qualitative Research.

- Source: Fetterman, D. (1988). *Qualitative approaches to evaluation in education: The silent scientific revolution.* New York: Praeger.

Classroom Activities

Classroom Activity 1: Healthy Living? The purpose of this activity is to get students to think about the quality of their life. This is a useful exercise at any age, but you can relate this to what we know about well-being in early adulthood. Early adulthood brings new responsibilities and stress. How people cope with this added pressure affects them physically and sets the stage for future development. Have your students answer yes or no to each of the following questions. At the end, have them total the number of yes answers. A score of 10 to 12 is considered a healthy lifestyle; 4 to 9 suggests the need for some lifestyle changes; and 0 to 3 suggests a need to reassess one's lifestyle. The questions are presented as **Handout 1**.

- I love my job most of the time.
- I use my seat belt.
- I am within 5 pounds of what my ideal weight should he.
- I know three methods of reducing stress excluding drugs or alcohol.
- I feel that I have a good support system.
- I do not smoke.
- I sleep 6 to 8 hours a night.
- I engage in regular physical activities at least three times a week such as walking briskly, running, swimming, or biking.
- I have seven or fewer alcoholic drinks a week.
- I know my blood pressure.
- I follow sensible eating habits such as eating breakfast every day, and limiting salt, sugar, and fat intake.
- I have a positive mental attitude.

Discuss as a class how each of these could potentially affect their current psychological and physical health and how each could potentially affect their future psychological and physical health. Which ones are within their control to change? How difficult would it be to change them? How could they go about making changes to improve their current lifestyle?

Logistics:
- Materials: Handout 1 (Lifestyle Questionnaire)
- Group size: Individual and full class.
- Approximate time: Individual (5 minutes) and full class (15 minutes).
- Source: Croc, P. (1990, May 21). Testing your health habits. *Newsweek*, special advertising section, 4.

Classroom Activity 2: Body Perception This exercise focuses on body perception and can be done first at the students' present ages, and then repeated with the students imagining what their physical aspects will be like in late adulthood. If you select this option, collect their papers for use with chapter 18. The exercise can be done individually or in small groups. The questions are presented as **Handout 2**.
Logistics:
- Materials: Handout 2 (Body Perception Questionnaire Activity).
- Group size: Individual or small groups.
- Approximate time: Individual (15 minutes), small group (25 minutes).

Classroom Activity 3: Reflecting on Your Life In chapter 14, Schaie's theory of adult cognitive development is presented. He believes that in early adulthood we typically switch from acquiring knowledge to applying knowledge. The purpose of this exercise is to determine how students are beginning to apply their knowledge to their own lives. Have students examine their life goals by doing the following exercise. Spend approximately 3 minutes on each part of this exercise. Each student needs four sheets of paper.

- At the top of the first paper write: What are my goals for my life?
- At the top of the second paper write: What do I want to do for the next 3 years?
- At the top of the third paper write: If I had only 6 months to live, how would I choose to live my life?
  - Look over your three sets of answers.
- At the top of the fourth paper write: My three most important goals. Next, write about your most important goals.
- When the students have completed the task, ask the following questions:
  - What kinds of goals (i.e., personal, career, family, community, social, spiritual) did you choose?
  - Were the same goals present on all your lists?
  - How would your lists be different if you had done this exercise 5 years ago?

Logistics:
- Materials: Each student will need four sheets of paper.
- Group size: Individual and full class.
- Approximate time: Individual (15 minutes) and full class (10 minutes).
- Source: Simons, J. A., Irwin, D. B., and Drinnin, B. A. (1987). *Instructor's manual to accompany psychology, the search for understanding*. St. Paul: West Publishing.

Classroom Activity 4: Need for Achievement and Career Development The end of chapter 14 focuses on careers and work. It presents theories of career selection. One characteristic that influences any career decision is the need for achievement. The three main styles of expressing achievement (and each of these has three substyles) are the direct style, the instrumental style, and the relational style.
- With direct achievemente, individuals confront tasks directly and want to achieve tasks through their own efforts.
- With instrumental achievement, individuals achieve by promoting themselves or others.
- With relational achievement, individuals achieve by contributing to others accomplishments.

Your preferences for different achievement styles develop throughout childhood and adolescence, though they can be modified during the adult years. Gender roles are one significant influence on achievement style preferences. For example, more males are socialized to have a direct achievement style and more females are socialized to have a relational achievement style. Family members, friends, and cultural messages further shape and differentiate your achievement choices.

This activity is presented as **Handout 3**. Have students rank each of the substyles for how typical they are of their own achievement patterns. The instructions for students are as follows: For each of the following scales record a 0 if the style is very atypical of you, a 1 if you occasionally use the style, a 2 if you believe you are average in this pattern, and a 3 if you think that you often use the particular style. After rating the substyles, go back and rank the three major styles (direct style, instrumental style, and relational style) from 1 (most typical for you) to 3 (least typical for you).

When students are finished with their rankings, you may want to divide them into small groups to discuss the questions below. These discussion questions are presented as **Handout 4**.
- How do you feel about your individual pattern?
- Are you able to work on achievement in ways that are satisfying to you?
- How would you change school, work, and family situations to better fit your needs?
- Have you chosen career goals that will enable you to achieve in ways that fit your pattern?
- What kinds of changes would you like to make in your achievement style?
- What kinds of changes in your achievement style have occurred over your life so far?
- Regardless of your current achievement style, which substyle do you wish was your most prominent style?
- Can you identify achievement styles of your family members? Among your friends?
- Do you have similar or dissimilar styles to family and friends?
- How do you think cultural and worldwide influences affect the prominence of different types of achievement styles from generation to generation?

Logistics:
- Materials: Handout 3 (Achievement Styles Questionnaire) and Handout 4 (Discussion).
- Group size: Individual and small group.
- Approximate time: Individual (15 minutes) and small group (30 minutes).
- Source:. Lipman-Blumen, J., Handley-Isakin, A., and Leavitt, H. J. (1983). Achieving styles in men and women: A model, an instrument, and some findings. In J. T. Spence (Ed.), *Achievement and achievement motives: Psychological and sociological approaches*. San Francisco: W. H. Freeman.

Classroom Activity 5: Gender and Multiple Roles Most Americans have multiple roles - work, family, schooling, and so on. How do males and females cope with having a variety of goals? Have class members provide examples. Introduce the ideas of Eccles (1987), who claims that women worry about reconciling their career and personal goals while men tend to compartmentalize their goals. What about their socialization leads to this gender difference? How is it exhibited, for example, by behaviors within the family (e.g., men don't say "I'm not sure if I want to have children because it will interfere with my career.")?
Logistics:
- Group size: Full class.
- Approximate time: Full class (25 minutes).
- Source: Eccles, J. S. (1987). Gender roles and women's achievement-related decisions. *Psychology of Women's Quarterly, 11*, 135-172.

Classroom Activity 6: Qualitative Research This exercise complements Lecture Suggestion 5: A Note on Qualitative Research. Many studies of adult development rely on qualitative research methods; indeed, much of the material in chapter 14 is based on these. The goal of this activity is to identify as many research examples of qualitative research from the chapter as you can. Recall that the main differences focus on the purpose, method, and reporting style of the research.
Logistics:
- Group size: Small group.
- Approximate time: Small group (60 minutes).
- Source: Fetterman, D. (1988). *Qualitative approaches to evaluation in education: The silent scientific revolution*. New York: Praeger.

Classroom Activity 7: Critical Thinking Multiple-Choice Questions and Suggested Answers Discuss the answers to the critical thinking multiple-choice questions presented as **Handout 5**. Question 1 will demand a review of the nature of evidence, particularly in light of the types of evidence each of the five generalizations demands. The basic point is that many of these claims are about causal relationships, yet only one is based on experimental research.

Question 2 is again concerned with identifying a fundamental assertion or basic belief that shapes a debate. The other statements are either given as claims of fact in support of an argument, or the conclusions of points that the author has made in an argument.

Question 3 challenges students to examine the uncertain and tenuous nature of early adulthood in terms of the various theories of cognitive development discussed in the chapter. The main idea is that only one of the theories' stages (as presented in chapter 14) addresses uncertainty created by cognitive development. The others seem to stress cognitive competence and realism. The answers are presented as **Handout 6**.
Logistics:
- Materials: Handout 5 (the critical thinking multiple-choice questions) and Handout 6 (answers).
- Group size: Small groups to discuss the questions, then a full class discussion.
- Approximate time: Small groups (15 to 20 minutes), full class discussion of any questions (15 minutes).

Classroom Activity 8: Critical Thinking Essay Questions and Suggestions for Helping Students Answer the Essays Discuss students' answers to the critical thinking essay questions presented in **Handout 7**. The purpose of this exercise is threefold. First, answering the essay questions further facilitates students' understanding of concepts in chapter 14. Second, this type of essay question affords the students an opportunity to apply the concepts to their own lives, which will facilitate their retention of the material. Third, the essay format also gives students practice expressing themselves in written form. Ideas to help students answer the critical thinking essay questions are provided as **Handout 8**.

Logistics:
- Materials: Handout 7 (essay questions) and Handout 8 (helpful suggestions for the answers).
- Group size: Individual, then full class.
- Approximate time: Individual (60 minutes), full class discussion of any questions (30 minutes).

Personal Applications

Personal Application 1: Free At Last! The purpose of this exercise is for students to recognize the significance of the period of transition from high school to college. There are positive experiences related to this time in life, along with negative ones. It is often a time of newfound independence, setting adolescents on the path toward true adulthood, yet today's college freshman report being more stressed and depressed than those from the 1980s (Santrock & Halonen, 1999).

- Instructions for Students: Talk about your transition from high school to college. How did your life circumstances change? How prepared did you feel going into this new phase of your life? How prepared did you discover you actually were? In what ways did you meet your expectations for success, and in what ways did you discover that you needed guidance? How are you faring now? What has been the most significant change, and what is the most significant thing you've learned in this time period?
- Use in the Classroom: Create a list from students' input about the major life changes that take place in the transition from high school to college. Have them share what things were most unexpected, what they've had the most difficulty adjusting to, and how they perceive themselves now that they are established college students. Tie this into the criteria for adulthood.
- Source: Santrock, J.W., & Halonen, J.A. (1999). *Mastering the college experience*. Belmont, CA: Wadsworth.

Personal Application 2: Stretch, 2, 3, 4... Use this exercise to get students thinking about the state of their personal health. Early adulthood is the healthiest time of life. We are the strongest physically, are the least prone to disease and infections, and studies show that young adults are highly aware of what it takes to be healthy (Turk, Rudy, & Salovey, 1984).

- Instructions for Students: Present your lifestyle profile. Include descriptions of your eating habits, exercise, substance use (and/or abuse), and health risks. Assess your functioning in all areas. Where are you succeeding in living well? What areas do you need to work on? What is your worst health-threatening habit? How might you improve these things to live a better and more healthy life?
- Use in the Classroom: Talk to students about their health and lifestyle concerns. Weinstein (1984) found that although college students know what it takes to prevent illness and promote health, they report they would never have a heart attack or drinking problem, but that other students would. Assess your students' realistic awareness of how their current habits truly affect their well-being. Are they aware of the potential consequences of getting very little or no sleep on a regular basis? Do they know about the diminished capacity of their functioning when they don't eat healthy, well-balanced meals? If they report not regularly doing things that promote healthy living, find out what is preventing them from doing so. Have the class brainstorm ideas for ways to overcome the obstacles faced by college students for living a healthy life.
- Sources: Turk, D.C., Rudy, T.E., & Salovey, P. (1984). Health protection: Attitudes and behaviors of LPN's teachers, and college students. *Health Psychology, 3*, 189-210. Weinstein, N.D. (1984). Reducing unrealistic optimism about illness susceptibility. *Health Psychology*, 3, 431-457.

Personal Application 3: Get Those Juices Flowing! The purpose of this exercise is to encourage students to think about their own creativity. Csikszentmihalyi coined the term "flow" to identify a heightened state of pleasure we experience when we are engaged in mental and physical challenges that absorb us. It is also his belief that everyone is capable of experiencing flow.

- Instructions for Students: Ponder your creativity. Read the section in your text on flow and expand your concept of what constitutes creativity. In what ways are you creative? Give some examples of your own creativity. If you don't consider yourself creative, address each aspect of flow and your experiences with it. Can you determine that you have experienced at least some of what it takes to be creative? What might you do to try to expand your creative potential? Remember, it's in all of us!
- Use in the Classroom: Discuss the concept of creativity and explore flow. Have students present examples of things they find to be most indicative of creativity. Have them share personal experiences with the elements of flow. Have Csikszentmihalyi's ideas changed anyone's concept of creativity? Has anyone in the class witnessed their own growth in the area of creativity? Have you? Come prepared for this discussion with your own examples of personal creativity, and your favorite illustrations of creativity from others.
- Source: Csikszentmihalyi, M. (1997). *Finding Flow*. New York: Basic Books.

Personal Application 4: Dream Job This exercise offers an opportunity to get students thinking about their future careers. It is no surprise that when individuals find a job they feel personally well-suited to, they enjoy it more and are more successful at it. It is important to explore what personal characteristics match well with particular occupations in order to successfully pursue a satisfying career path.

- Instructions for Students: Read the section in your text covering John Holland's career-related personality types. Which ones describe you? Give examples as to how you match particular ones. Do these match the career you're pursuing? Do they match a career you've considered, but for whatever reason are not currently exploring? Where do your personal values fit in? Does your career path reflect what's most important to you in life? Why or why not?
- Use in the Classroom: Have students choose the personality type that fits them the best. Group students accordingly and have them compare notes on personal values, majors, and career aspirations. Do they share similarities or has someone discovered they may be travelling down the wrong path? Have the class come together as a group and discuss the notion of personality matching careers. Share your own story about what aspects of your personality suit your profession. Provide insight as to how important finding the right match is.

Research Project Ideas

Research Project 1: College Students and the Use of Alcohol The purpose of this project is to collect information about alcohol use in early adulthood (**Handout 9**). Students will interview five friends who are in early adulthood about their history of alcohol use. If they are in early adulthood themselves, they can also respond to the questions, as one of the five individuals. Have students use the interview questions on the data sheet (**Handout 10**), record each person's responses, and then write a report describing what they found and how that relates to the information in the text about alcohol use in early adulthood. Instruct the students to be sure to answer the questions that follow.
Questions:

- What is the average frequency of drinking in your subjects? What is the range among individuals? Are there large individual differences in frequency of drinking? Are there age or sex differences?
- What is the average age at which your subjects first drank? What is the range among individuals? Are there large individual differences in the age at which they started drinking? Are there age or sex differences?

- On the average, how much do these subjects consume when they drink? What is the range among individuals? Are there large individual differences in the amount they drink? Are there age or sex differences?
- How often, overall, does this group get drunk? What is the range among individuals? Are there large individual differences in frequency of drunkenness? Are there age or sex differences?
- How do your data compare with data on alcohol use in early adulthood presented in the text? Does your data support or refute the text?
- Use in the Classroom: Have students present and pool their data in class. Identify trends in the data, and discuss the findings.

Research Project 2: AIDS in Your Community This project allows students to investigate the prevalence of AIDS in your community (**Handout 11**). After reading chapter 14, they should seek out the statistics on AIDS in your city by contacting someone at the Health Department. Next, students should research what services are available for AIDS education, testing, and treatment. They will need to contact the public school system to find out what information students are exposed to during the public school years. They may want to contact any hospitals or clinics in your area to find out about education and treatment as well. Your local Hospice may be a good source of information about what resources are available for people infected with HIV. Have students write a brief report detailing the efforts made by your community concerning the prevention of AIDS, education about the causes of AIDS, and treatment for individuals infected with the disease.

- Use in the Classroom: Have students present and pool their information in class. Evaluate how well you think your community is doing in terms of education, prevention, and treatment of AIDS. Discuss ways in which your community could improve in these areas. You may also want to broaden the discussion from your immediate area to your state as a whole.

Film and Video List

The following films and videos supplement the content of chapter 14. Contact information for film distributors can be found at the front of this Instructor's Manual under Film and Video Sources.

Adulthood (Insight Media, 3 volumes, 60 minutes each). This video examines the biological, social, and psychological forces in adulthood.

One Nation Under Stress (Films for the Humanities and Sciences, 52 minutes). This program helps viewers understand the causes and consequences of stress and how to cope with it.

Sociology and Sexuality (Insight Media, 10 lectures, 45 minutes each). Paul Root Wolpe explores sexuality, love, gender roles, and sexual orientation in a series of ten lectures.

Stress (Films for the Humanities and Sciences, 26 minutes). This film demonstrates methods of coping with stress such as biofeedback.

Stress:Keeping Your Cool (Films for the Humanities and Sciences, 36 minutes). This program demonstrates the impact that stress has on society and describes both positive and negative stress.

Woman and Man (Indiana University, 52 minutes). This video examines possible physiological differences between the sexes.

Web Site Suggestions

The URLs for general sites, common to all chapters, can be found at the front of this Instructor's Manual under Useful Web Sites. At the time of publication, all sites were current and active, however, please be advised that you may occasionally encounter a dead link.

Advanced Education and Career Development
http://www.aecd.gov.ab.ca/

The AIDS Knowledge Base
http://hivinsite.ucsf.edu/akb/1994/5-25/ref3.html

Alcohol and Drug Addiction Prevention and Treatment
http://www.caritasdata.co.uk/charity4/ch008454.htm

Rape and Sexual Assault: Information, Crisis Intervention, Therapy and Support Groups
http://www.icfs.org/bluebook/si000008.htm

The Science Behind Drug Addiction
http://www.the-scientist.library.upenn.edu/yr1995/august/drugs1_950821.html

Weight Control and Statistics
http://www.niddk.nih.gov/health/nutrit/nutrit.htm

Lifestyle Questionnaire

Indicate whether each of the statements is true for you by writing yes or no after each one. Total the number of yes answers.

1. I love my job most of the time.

2. I use my seat belt.

3. I am within 5 pounds of what my ideal weight should he.

4. I know three methods of reducing stress excluding drugs or alcohol.

5. I feel that I have a good support system.

6. I do not smoke.

7. I sleep 6 to 8 hours a night.

8. I engage in regular physical activities at least three times a week such as walking briskly, running, swimming, or biking.

9. I have seven or fewer alcoholic drinks a week.

10. I know my blood pressure.

11. I follow sensible eating habits such as eating breakfast every day, and limiting salt, sugar, and fat intake.

12. I have a positive mental attitude.

TOTAL SCORE _____

Handout 2 (CA 2)

Body Perception Questionnaire Activity

Answer each of the following questions regarding your perceptions of your **current body**.

1. What is the strongest part of your body?

2. What is the weakest part?

3. What is the oldest part?

4. What is the youngest part?

5. What do you consider the most attractive part of your body?

6. What is the least attractive?

7. Where does your body have the most warmth?

8. Where is your body coldest?

9. What is the most vulnerable part of your body—the place most quickly or easily hurt?

10. What is the smoothest part of your body?

11. What is the roughest part?

12. What is the hardest part?

13. Where do you carry tensions in your body?

14. What part of your body do you most want to change?

15. What do you least want to change?

16. What part of your body are you ashamed of?

17. What part of your body do you feel most proud of?

Body Perception Questionnaire Activity

Answer each of the following questions regarding your perceptions of your **body as you imagine them to be in late adulthood**.

1. What is the strongest part of your body?

2. What is the weakest part?

3. What is the oldest part?

4. What is the youngest part?

5. What do you consider the most attractive part of your body?

6. What is the least attractive?

7. Where does your body have the most warmth?

8. Where is your body coldest?

9. What is the most vulnerable part of your body—the place most quickly or easily hurt?

10. What is the smoothest part of your body?

11. What is the roughest part?

12. What is the hardest part?

13. Where do you carry tensions in your body?

14. What part of your body do you most want to change?

15. What do you least want to change?

16. What part of your body are you ashamed of?

17. What part of your body do you feel most proud of?

Handout 3 (CA 4)

Achievement Styles Questionnaire Activity

For each of the following scales, record a 0 if the style is very atypical of you, a 1 if you occasionally use the style, a 2 if you believe you are average in this pattern, and a 3 if you think that you often use the particular style. After rating the substyles, go back and rank the three major styles (direct, instrumental, and relational) from 1 (most typical for you) to 3 (least typical for you).

_____ **Direct style**: I am an individual who likes to achieve and accomplish tasks by my own efforts. I confront tasks directly.

    _____ Intrinsic substyle: I tend to compare myself to some standard of performance excellence. For example, I am satisfied with A's and B's and would like to make the dean's list. I like to see "well written" on a paper I have done. I try to do work that meets the high standards set by my boss.

    _____ Competitive substyle: I tend to express achievement by trying to do better than others do. For example, I like to get grades that are higher than other students in the class. It is as important to win an athletic competition as it is to do well. I like to hear that my ideas are better than others.

    _____ Power substyle: I like to be in charge of and have control over others in order to accomplish achievement goals. For example, I would like to organize and lead a study group in order to improve my grades. I would like to be chairperson of a student organization. I would like a career in management or other area in which I am in charge of other personnel.

_____ **Instrumental style**: I tend to use myself and others as a way to meet my achievement goals.

    _____ Personal substyle: I often achieve by making use of my status, influence, reputation, and personal characteristics. For example, I try to dress for success in order to make a good impression on the people with whom I work. I would like to earn a doctorate degree because I think I would be better able to meet my goals if I could sign Ph.D. after my name. I would like to be on the dean's list or an officer in state organizations because this would help me achieve more.

    _____ Social substyle: I tend to use networking to achieve my goals. For example, I plan to join a fraternity or sorority because other members can provide lifelong social and career connections. I think it is important to belong to lots of organizations because you meet people who are able to help you get things accomplished. I try to associate socially with people I admire and with whom I hope to work.

    _____ Reliant substyle: I tend to achieve by depending on others for direction. For example, before studying or writing papers I usually ask instructors and classmates what I should do and how I should do it. I think it's important to get lots of input and feedback from others in order to know how to work on a task correctly. I often get advice on what to do from others rather than deciding goals by myself.

_____ **Relational style**: I tend to achieve by contributing to the accomplishments of other persons.

   _____ Collaborative substyle: I tend to achieve through group effort that includes the sharing of both responsibility and credit. For example, I prefer classes in which projects are done in small groups with shared responsibilities and a common grade. I would rather co-author a paper than write alone. I like working on issues with a group of peers.

   _____ Contributory substyle: I tend to play a secondary role of helping others to achieve. For example, I would be willing to work and financially support a spouse while he or she went to college. I like to offer suggestions in committees, but I would not enjoy being the chairperson of the committee. I would enjoy playing supportive roles in arenas such as politics and charitable organizations.

   _____ Vicarious substyle: I tend to satisfy my own achievement needs by identifying with the success of other persons who are important to me. For example, I get a lot of school pride when our athletic teams win. I would just as soon help my offspring to accomplish something important than to achieve that accomplishment myself. It is very satisfying to see a co-worker have a great success. I feel like I can identify with the co-worker's achievements.

Handout 4 (CA 4)

Achievement Style Discussion Activity

When you are finished with your rankings, divide into small groups to discuss the questions below.

1. How do you feel about your individual pattern?

2. Are you able to work on achievement in ways that are satisfying to you?

3. How would you change school, work, and family situations to better fit your needs?

4. Have you chosen career goals that will enable you to achieve in ways that fit your pattern?

5. What kinds of changes would you like to make in your achievement style?

6. What kinds of changes in your achievement style have occurred over your life so far?

7. Regardless of your current achievement style, which substyle do you wish was your most prominent style?

8. Can you identify achievement styles of your family members?

9. Can you identify achievement styles of your friends?

10. Do you have similar or dissimilar styles to family and friends?

11. How do you think cultural and worldwide influences affect the prominence of different types of achievement styles from generation to generation?

Critical Thinking Multiple-Choice Questions

1. There is a great deal of practical information in chapter 14 about the value of exercise in early adulthood. While this information is useful, an uncritical thinker might be tempted to draw conclusions from it that are not warranted by the type of research that generated the data. Review the inferences you might draw from the information about physical exercise in early adulthood listed below, and identify which is the best supported conclusion. Circle the letter of the best answer and explain why it is the best answer and why each other answer is not as good.

   a. Peak human performances are determined by the human genetic code.
   b. Unrealistic optimism about their health leads college students to behave in unhealthy ways.
   c. The key to effective weight control is to control eating habits.
   d. Intensive exercise programs (e.g., running 10 miles each week) will cause more harm than good.
   e. Moderate or intense exercise benefits our physical and mental health.

2. Attitudes toward homosexuality improved and then worsened during the past 15 years. At the same time, efforts to understand homosexuality increased, but, to date, the determinants of sexual orientation are not well understood. Which of the following represents an assumption, rather than an inference or an observation, that influences current scientific attempts to understand homosexuality? Circle the letter of the best answer and explain why it is the best answer and why each other answer is not as good.

   a. Homosexual and heterosexual individuals respond to the same types of tactile stimulation.
   b. Homosexuality is not a psychological disorder.
   c. No one factor alone causes homosexual behavior.
   d. There is a critical period during infancy for the formation of a homosexual orientation.
   e. Children raised by homosexual parents are no more likely to become homosexual than children raised by heterosexual parents.

3. Early in chapter 14, Santrock suggests that there is an uncertain, temporary, or unsettled character to early adulthood. Santrock then discusses various ways youths experiment with life before they settle into the decision-making clarity of adulthood. Later in the chapter, Santrock describes several theories of adult cognitive development that might be applied to understanding young adults' uncertainties from another point of view. Of the following stages or characteristics taken from the various theories, which best explains youths' delay in making decisions? Circle the letter of the best answer and explain why it is the best answer and why each other answer is not as good.

   a. formal operations (Piaget)
   b. pragmatic constraints view (Labouvie-Vief)
   c. relativistic thinking (Perry)
   d. post-formal operations (Piaget)
   e. investigative (Holland)

Suggested Answers for Critical Thinking Multiple-Choice Questions

1. There is a great deal of practical information in chapter 14 about the value of exercise in early adulthood. While this information is useful, an uncritical thinker might be tempted to draw conclusions from it that are not warranted by the type of research that generated the data. Review the inferences you might draw from the information about physical exercise in early adulthood listed below, and identify which is the best supported conclusion. Circle the letter of the best answer and explain why it is the best answer and why each other answer is not as good.

    a. <u>Peak human performances are determined by the human genetic code</u> is not the best answer. The chief problem is that the basically descriptive and correlational research Santrock reports can only suggest this hypothesis; they do not test it. Needed are twin studies or other formal studies of heredity/environment interactions.

    b. <u>Unrealistic optimism about their health leads college students to behave in unhealthy ways</u> is not the best answer. Although college students can be described as being optimistic about their health, Santrock does not report either correlational or experimental work that shows that this belief relates to or causes specific health habits.

    c. <u>The key to effective weight control is to control eating habits</u> is not the best answer. The bottom line is that the vast majority of dieters (90 percent) regain most of the weight they lose, even among participants in the best diet programs (e.g., Weight Watchers).

    d. <u>Intensive exercise programs (e.g., running 10 miles each week) will cause more harm than good</u> is not the best answer. No evidence is presented or discussed that would support this conclusion.

    e. <u>Moderate or intense exercise benefits our physical and mental health</u> is the best answer. This conclusion is based on elaborate studies of 17,000 male alumni of Harvard University that contrasted high-intensity, moderate, and no exercise programs, and found physical and psychological changes only among participants in the moderate exercise program.

2. Attitudes toward homosexuality improved and then worsened during the past 15 years. At the same time efforts to understand homosexuality increased, but, to date, the determinants of sexual orientation are not well understood. Which of the following represents an assumption, rather than an inference or an observation, that influences current scientific attempts to understand homosexuality? Circle the letter of the best answer and explain why it is the best answer and why each other answer is not as good.

    a. <u>Homosexual and heterosexual individuals respond to the same types of tactile stimulation</u> is an observation. The statement represents a finding from studies that compare what sexually arouses homosexual and heterosexual individuals.

    b. <u>Homosexuality is not a psychological disorder</u> is an inference. Both heterosexual and homosexual people are equally (well or ill) adjusted. In other words, the point seems to be that sexual orientation does not stem from some sort of psychological malfunction, because no such malfunction can be found in other aspects of homosexual individuals' lives.

    c. <u>No one factor alone causes homosexual behavior</u> is the assumption. In the treatment of causes or determinants of homosexuality, Santrock indicates that most experts believe this to be true. Reasons for the point of view are not given; rather, this belief is stated as a rule or guide for finding out what the determinants of homosexuality (and therefore also heterosexuality) are.

    d. <u>There is a critical period during infancy for the formation of a homosexual orientation</u> is an inference. It is presented as the "prenatal development" hypothesis and is offered as one explanation of homosexuality (and heterosexuality).

e. <u>Children raised by homosexual parents are no more likely to become homosexual than children raised by heterosexual parents</u> is an observation. It is a statement derived from longitudinal research in which this pattern was recorded.

3. Early in chapter 14, Santrock suggests that there is an uncertain, temporary, or unsettled character to early adulthood. Santrock then discusses various ways youths experiment with life before they settle into the decision-making clarity of adulthood. Later in the chapter, Santrock describes several theories of adult cognitive development that might be applied to understanding young adults' uncertainties from another point of view. Of the following stages or characteristics taken from the various theories, which best explains youths' delay in making decisions? Circle the letter of the best answer and explain why it is the best answer and why each other answer is not as good.

a. <u>Formal operations (Piaget)</u> is not the best answer. Assuming that young adults have come into full possession of formal operations, their thinking should exhibit the full flower of abstract logical thought. These capacities should promote clarity of thought rather than indecision.

b. <u>Pragmatic constraints view (Labouvie-Vief)</u> is not the best answer. Labouvie-Vief's view stresses a direct, seemingly resigned but mature adaptation to life's realities and constraints that is based on commitment, specialization, and dedication to finding a social niche.

c. <u>Relativistic thinking (Perry)</u> is the best answer. Perry indicates that relativistic thinking challenges the black or white certainties based on authority of the previous dualistic stage; after what may be a period of decisiveness, another period of uncertainty develops when the relativistic thinkers' opinions are challenged by others.

d. <u>Post-formal operations (Piaget)</u> is not the best answer. Post-formal thinking involves understanding that the correct answer to a problem requires reflective thought and that answers vary depending of the situation. These realizations should promote clarity of thought rather than indecision.

e. <u>Investigative (Holland)</u> is not the best answer. Investigative refers to one of Holland's career-related personality types.

Critical Thinking Essay Questions

Your answers to these kinds of questions demonstrate an ability to comprehend and apply ideas discussed in this chapter.

1. Compare and contrast the transition to college with the transition to middle school.

2. Is young adulthood better characterized as a period of health-improving lifestyles or health-impairing lifestyles?

3. What advice would you offer to someone who is considering a weight-loss program? Use information presented in chapter 14 to support your recommendations.

4. Indicate the sort of exercise program that current research on exercise best supports.

5. Compare and contrast the two major perceptions on addiction? Which do you agree with?

6. Does research support the following two statements, "Single Americans are obsessed with sex" and "Sexual orientation is biologically determined"?

7. Give at least three examples of coerced sexual activity, and discuss whether the consequences for the victim are similar or different in each case.

8. Compare and contrast two approaches to adult cognitive development

9. Describe ways in which you cultivate your own curiosity and interest. How do they compare to Csikszentmihalyi's ideas?

10. Compare and contrast the two theories of career development.

11. Develop and describe your own personal career plan.

12. What factors would encourage and discourage you from entering into a dual-career marriage?

Ideas to Help You Answer Critical Thinking Essay Questions

1. Describe your own recent experiences, along with your memories from entering middle school to set the foundation for your comparison. After you've "told your stories," point out the critical issues that identify these time periods as developmentally significant (e.g., top-dog phenomenon). Explain their similarities and differences.

2. Is this a black-and-white question? Can you present evidence for both possibilities?

3. Imagine you are a nutritionist who is talking with a client. In addition to the individual's physical needs for a weight-loss program, consider the societal influences that might have brought him/her to this point. Also, will your advice be the same for everyone? How might it differ for varying client profiles?

4. Present this information to a new patron at your health club. Remember, they're paying a lot of money, so they'll want to know what's best for them and why.

5. Present scenarios of addicts from each perspective, then expand to compare the two.

6. Expand on what each of these statements is really saying; what is the full scope of each issue? After you've presented what is being purported by each, present the research that either supports or refutes them.

7. To help you develop clear, specific descriptions, image that you are an expert testifying in a court case where the details and distinction between the three examples are critical.

8. Begin by describing the criteria that developmentalists use to identify an individual as an "adult," and explain the important issues related to cognition at this stage.

9. Begin by writing very "free form" about your curiosity and interest exploration. Go with the flow of your thoughts and don't censor yourself. After this experience, present Csikszentmihalyi's ideas and discuss how your profile matches up.

10. Identify the basic issues of importance related to this issue. Who are these theories geared toward?

11. Begin by brainstorming all the possibilities that appeal to you. Don't hold back—include your dreams along with your more practical ideas. Then address each one (even…especially… your dream) and how you might reach each of them.

12. Be realistic about this one—answer it from the head and the heart. If you haven't already, you may actually face this in the not-so-distant future.

Handout 9 (RP 1)

College Students and the Use of Alcohol

The purpose of this project is to collect information about alcohol use in early adulthood. Interview five friends who are in early adulthood about their history of alcohol use. If you are in early adulthood, you can respond to the questions yourself, as one of the five individuals.

Use the interview questions on the data sheet (Handout 10), record each person's responses, and then write a report describing what you found and how that relates to the information in the text about alcohol use in early adulthood. Be sure to answer the questions that follow.

Questions:

- What is the average frequency of drinking in your subjects? What is the range among individuals? Are there large individual differences in frequency of drinking? Are there age or sex differences?

- What is the average age at which your subjects first drank? What is the range among individuals? Are there large individual differences in the age at which they started drinking? Are there age or sex differences?

- On the average, how much do these subjects consume when they drink? What is the range among individuals? Are there large individual differences in the amount they drink? Are there age or sex differences?

- How often, overall, does this group get drunk? What is the range among individuals? Are there large individual differences in frequency of drunkenness? Are there age or sex differences?

- How do your data compare with data on alcohol use in early adulthood presented in the text? Does your data support or refute the text?

College Students and the Use of Alcohol Data Sheet

You will want to have five copies of this data sheet (one for each subject).

Person _____
Gender _____
Age _____

Interview Questions:

1. How often do you have a drink?

2. At what age did you first drink?

3. When you take a drink, how much do you drink?

4. Do you ever get drunk?

5. If you answered "yes" to question 4, how frequently?

6. Do you drink alone?

7. Do you drink in the morning?

8. Do you ever drink and drive?

9. Is anyone in your family an alcoholic?

AIDS in Your Community

The purpose of the project is to investigate the prevalence of AIDS in your community. After reading chapter 14, seek out the statistics on AIDS in your city by contacting someone at the Health Department. Next, you should research what services are available for AIDS education, testing, and treatment. You will need to contact the public school system to find out what information students are exposed to during the public school years. You may want to contact any hospitals or clinics in your area to find out about education and treatment as well. Your local Hospice may be a good source of information about what resources are available for people infected with HIV. Write a brief report detailing the efforts made by your community concerning the prevention of AIDS, education about the causes of AIDS, and treatment for individuals infected with the disease. Indicate what further steps your community could take to improve prevention, education, and treatment of/for AIDS.

Chapter 15: Socioemotional Development in Early Adulthood

Total Teaching Package Outline

Lecture Outline	Resource References
Socioemotional Development in Early Adulthood	PowerPoint Presentation: See www.mhhe.com Cognitive Maps: See Appendix A
Continuity and Discontinuity from Childhood to Adulthood	LO1 PA1: The More Things Change, the More They Stay the Same
• Temperament • Attachment	LO2
Attraction, Love, and Close Relationships	F/V: Gender and Relationships F/V: Love, Love Me Do F/V: Men and Women: Talking Together
• Attraction -Familiarity and Similarity	LO3 CA1: Mate Selection
-Physical Attraction	PA2: Ten Things I Like about You
• The Faces of Love	F/V: The Familiar Face of Love
-Intimacy	LO4, LO5, LO6 OHT164: Age Differences in Intimacy
-Romantic Love	LO7 LS1: Who Is the Lucky One? LS2: Ideal Standards in Close Relationships CA2: Ideal Standards for Romantic Partners F/V: Love
-Affectionate Love	LO8 OHT177 & IB: Sternberg's Triangle of Love
-Friendship	
• Loneliness	LO9

Marriage and the Family
• The Family Life Cycle
  -Leaving Home and Becoming a Single Adult
  -Joining of Families through Marriage: New Couple
  -Becoming Parents and a Family with Children
  -The Family with Adolescents
  -The Family at Midlife
  -The Family in Later Life
	LO10

Marriage	CA3: Sign On the Dotted Line? Prenuptial Contracts
-Marital Trends	LO11 IB: Increase in Age at First Marriage in the U.S. OHT165: First Marriages
-Marital Expectations and Myths	LO12 RP1: The Marriage Quiz
-What Makes Marriage Work	LS3: Love and Marriage F/V: Bobby and Rosie: Anatomy of a Marriage F/V: Love, Lust, and Marriage F/V: The Marriage Partnership
-The Benefits of a Good Marriage	
• Gender and Emotion in Marriages	LO13
• Parental Roles	LO14 WS: The In-Site to Parenting
The Diversity of Adult Lifestyles	LO15
• Single Adults	IB: Increase in Single Adults (1970-1998) CA4: Pressure to Pair Up
• Cohabiting Adults	IB: Increase in Cohabitation in the U.S.
• Divorced Adults	IB: Divorce Rate in Relation to Years Married LS4: Paternity Laws Lag Behind Science WS: Divorce Source WS: Resource for Divorce and Remarriage
• Remarried Adults	
• Gay and Lesbian Adults	F/V: Gay Couples: The Nature of Relationships
Gender, Relationships, and Self-Development	LS5: Gender Differences and Language CA5: Connectedness CA6: Gender Face-Off PA3: Understanding Me F/V: In My Country F/V: Woman and Man F/V: Gender and Communication
• Women's Development	LO16 F/V: Dear Lisa: A Letter to my Sister
• Men's Development	LO17 F/V: Dedicated, Not Deadbeat F/V: Juggling Family and Work F/V: Man, Oh Man WS: Fatherhood

Review	CA7: Critical Thinking Multiple-Choice
	CA8: Critical Thinking Essays
	RP2: Gender and Age Roles in Magazine
	Advertisements

Chapter Outline

CONTINUITY AND DISCONTINUITY FROM CHILDHOOD TO ADULTHOOD
- The first 20 years are important in predicting an adult's personality, but so, too, are continuing experiences in the adult years.
- The smaller the time intervals over which researchers measure personality characteristics, the more similar an individual will look from one measurement to the next.

Temperament
- Temperament is an individual's behavioral style and characteristic way of emotional responding.
  - High activity level in young children is linked with being outgoing young adults.
    - Young adults show fewer mood swings, are more responsible, and engage in less risk-taking than adolescents.
  - Temperament in childhood is linked with adjustment in early adulthood.
    - Easy children are well-adjusted young adults; difficult children are not.
    - Individuals with an inhibited temperament in childhood are less likely to be assertive, experience social support, and to delay in entering a stable job track.
    - Children with high emotional control continued to handle their emotions well as adults.

Attachment
- Attachment classifications can be used to describe adults.
- Researchers have found that the quality of attachment relationships in childhood is linked with the quality of adult romantic relationships.
- Attachment styles in young adulthood are linked with their attachment history, although attachment styles can change in adulthood as adults experience relationships.

ATTRACTION, LOVE, AND CLOSE RELATIONSHIPS
Attraction
Familiarity and Similarity
- Familiarity precedes a close relationship.
- Individuals associate with people who are similar to them with respect to attitudes, behavior, intelligence, personality, other friends, values, lifestyle, and physical attractiveness, etc.
  - **Consensus validation** provides an explanation of why people are attracted to others who are similar to them.
  - Our own attitudes and behavior are supported and validated when someone else's attitudes and behavior are similar to ours.

Physical Attraction
- Physical attraction is usually more important in the early part of a relationship.
  - Criteria of physical attractiveness vary across cultures and historical time.
- Research supports the **matching hypothesis** that states while we may prefer a more attractive person in the abstract, in the real world we end up choosing someone who is close to our own level of attractiveness.

The Faces of Love
Intimacy
Erikson's Stage: Intimacy vs. Isolation
- For Erikson, intimacy versus isolation is the key developmental issue in early adulthood.
  - Erikson thought that intimacy should follow the development of a stable identity.
- Intimacy involves finding oneself, yet losing oneself in another person.
- Isolation occurs if an individual is not able to form healthy friendships and an intimate relationship with another person.

The Role of Intimacy in Relationship Maturity
- White proposed a three level model of relationship maturity.
  - **Self-focused level** is the first level of relationship maturity, when one's perspective on another person or a relationship is concerned only with how it affects oneself.
  - **Role-focused level** is the second or intermediate level of relationship maturity, when one begins to perceive others as individuals in their own right. However, at this level, the perspective is stereotypical and emphasizes social acceptability.
  - **Individuated-connected level** is the highest level of relationship maturity, when one begins to understand oneself, as well as to have consideration for others' motivations and to anticipate their needs. Concern and caring involve emotional support and individualized expressions of interest.

Intimacy and Independence
- There is a delicate balance between intimacy and commitment, on the one hand, and independence and freedom on the other.

Romantic Love
- **Romantic love** is also called passionate love, Eros or "in love."; it has strong components of sexuality and infatuation, and it often predominates in the early part of a love relationship.
- Romantic love includes passion, sexuality, and a mixture of emotions, not all of which are positive (fear, anger, jealousy).

Affectionate Love
- **Affectionate love** or companionate love is the type of love that occurs when individuals desire to have the other person near and have a deep, caring affection for the person.
- As a relationship progresses, sexual attraction wanes, attachment anxieties either lessen or produce conflict and withdrawal, novelty is replaced with familiarity, and lovers either find themselves securely attached in a caring relationship or distressed and seeking a new relationship.
- Sternberg proposed the **triangular theory of love** that includes three components of love.
  - Passion is the physical and sexual attraction to another.
  - Intimacy is the emotional feelings of warmth, closeness, and sharing in a relationship.
  - Commitment is the cognitive appraisal of the relationship and intent to maintain the relationship.
- Different patterns of love that result, depending on the combination of passion, intimacy, and commitment experienced.

Friendship
What Is Friendship?
- **Friendship** is a form of close relationship that involves enjoyment (we like to spend time with our friends), acceptance (we accept our friends without trying to change them), trust (we assume our friends will act in our best interest), respect (we think our friends make good judgments), mutual assistance (we help and support our friends and they us), confiding (we share experiences and confidential matters with a friend), understanding (we feel that a friend knows us well and understands what we like), and spontaneity (we feel free to be ourselves around a friend).

- Friendships serve many functions such as companionship, intimacy/affection, emotional support, a buffer against stress, and a source of self-esteem.

Female, Male, and Female-Male Friendship
- Sex differences occur in adult friendships.
  - Self-disclosure and emotional support are more common in female friendships.
  - Adult male friendships are more competitive and involve sharing useful information, while keeping one's distance.
- There are more same-sex friendships than cross-sex friendships in adulthood.
  - Cross-sex friendships provide opportunities to learn more about the opposite sex and acquire information that has historically been reserved more for one sex.
  - Problems can arise as well, due to differing expectations about the function of friendships and ambiguity regarding sexual boundaries.

Loneliness
- Married individuals are less lonely than never married, divorced, or widowed individuals.
- Loneliness often emerges when people make life transitions, so it is not surprising than loneliness is common among college freshmen.
  - Lonely men are more likely to blame themselves for their loneliness because men are socialized to initiate relationships.
  - Lonely women are more likely to blame external factors because they are traditionally socialized to wait and respond to other's initiation of social interaction.
- A number of strategies can be used to help lonely individuals become more socially connected.
  - Participate in activities that you can do with others.
  - Be aware of the early warning signs of loneliness.
  - Draw a diagram of your social network.
  - Engage in positive behaviors when you meet new people.
  - See a counselor or read a book on loneliness.

MARRIAGE AND THE FAMILY
The Family Life Cycle
- There are six stages in the family life cycle.

Leaving Home and Becoming a Single Adult
- **Leaving home and becoming a single adult** is the fist stage in the family life cycle and involves launching.
  - **Launching** is the process in which youths move into adulthood and exit their family of origin.

The Joining of Families Through Marriage: The New Couple
- The **new couple** is the second stage in the family life cycle, in which two individuals from separate families of origin unite to form a new family system.

Becoming Parents and a Family with Children
- **Becoming parents and a family with children** is the third stage in the family life cycle. Entering this stage requires that adults now move up a generation and become caregivers to the younger generation.

The Family with Adolescents
- The **family with adolescents** represents the fourth stage of the family life cycle. Adolescence is a period of development in which individuals push for autonomy and seek to develop their own identity.

The Family at Midlife
- The **family at midlife** is the fifth stage in the family cycle. It is a time of launching children, playing an important role in linking generations, and adapting to midlife changes in development.

The Family in Later Life
- The **family in later life** is the sixth stage in the family life cycle. Retirement alters a couple's lifestyle, requiring adaptation. Grandparenting also characterizes many families in this stage.

Marriage
Marital Trends
- Even though adults are remaining single longer and the divorce rate is high, we still show a strong predilection for marriage.
  - The average duration of marriage in the U.S. is just over 9 years.
  - In 1998, the average age for first marriages was 25 years for women and 27 years for men.
- The age at which individuals marry, expectations about what the marriage will be like, and the developmental course of marriage may vary not only across historical time within a culture, but also across cultures.
Marital Expectations and Myths
- Unrealistic expectations about marriage contribute to marital dissatisfaction and divorce.
  - College students have unrealistic expectations about marriage as indicated by their failing of the "marriage quiz." Females and students with a less romantic perception of marriage missed fewer items.
- Some myths about marriage include:
  - Avoiding conflict will ruin your marriage.
    - Couples have different styles of conflict. Trouble arises if the individuals in the couple have different styles of handling conflict (avoid, fight, discuss).
  - Affairs are the main cause of divorce.
    - The opposite pattern is more common. Extramarital affairs are usually the result of marital dissatisfaction.
    - In one study, only 20 percent of divorced men and women said that an extramarital affair was even partially to blame.
  - Men are not biologically made for marriage.
    - This myth is based on the assumption that men are philanderers and ill-suited for monogamy. Interestingly, as more women are employed outside of the home, the rate of extramarital affairs by women has exceeded the rate for males.
  - Women and men are from different plants.
    - Gender differences may contribute to marital problems, however, they usually don't cause the problems.
What Makes Marriages Work
- Gottman has conducted the most extensive research on what makes marriages work by interviewing couples, observing their interactions, and assessing their physiological functioning during interactions.
- Gottman has found seven main principles that determine whether a marriage will work or not:
  - Establishing love maps.
    - Individuals in successful marriages have personal insights and detailed maps of each other's life and world which they use to express their understanding of each other.
  - Nurturing fondness and admiration.
    - Partners sing each others' praises.
  - Turning toward each other instead of away.
    - Spouses respect each other and appreciate each other's point of view even if they don't agree with it.
  - Letting your partner influence you.
    - A willingness to share power and to respect the other person's view is a prerequisite to compromising.

- Solving solvable conflicts.
  - Two types of problems occur in marriages.
    - An example of a perpetual problem is when one partner wants a baby and the other one does not. Perpetual problems are problems that will not go away and represent two-thirds of marital problems.
      - Couples do not need to solve their perpetual problems for the marriage to work. Conflict resolution is not about making one person change, it is about negotiating and accommodating each other.
    - Solvable problems include not helping each other reduce daily stresses and not being verbally affectionate.
  - Overcoming gridlock.
    - The key to ending gridlock is not to solve the problem, but to move from gridlock to dialogue and be patient.
  - Creating shared meaning.
    - Shared meaning comes from talking candidly and respectfully with each other and sharing goals and working towards those goals.

The Benefits of a Good Marriage
- An unhappy marriage increases an individual's risk of getting sick and shortens one's life span.
- Benefits include better physical (less heart disease) and mental (less anxiety, depression, and substance abuse) health, as well as a longer life by about 4 years on the average.

Gender and Emotion in Marriages
- Overall, women are more expressive and affectionate in marriage, and this difference bothers many women.

Parental Roles
- For some, the parental role is well planned and coordinated. For others, there is surprise and sometimes chaos.
  - Parenting consists of a number of interpersonal skills and emotional demands, yet there is little in the way of formal education for this task.
  - Many learn parenting practices from their parents, which can perpetuate both desirable and undesirable practices.
  - There are many myths about parenting, among them the myth that the birth of a child will save a failing marriage.
- Families are becoming smaller, and many women are delaying childbirth until they have become well established in a career.
- Advantages of having children earlier in adulthood include:
  - parents are likely to have more physical energy,
  - fewer medical problems with pregnancy and childbirth, and
  - parents are less likely to build up expectations for their children.
- Advantages for having children late include:
  - parents will have had more time to consider their goals in life,
  - parents are more mature and will be able to benefit from their life experience to engage in more competent parenting, and
  - parents will be better established in their careers and will have more income for child-rearing expenses.

THE DIVERSITY OF ADULT LIFESTYLES

Single Adults

- Being single has become an increasingly prominent lifestyle.
    - In 1998, more than 46 million adult Americans (24 percent of total adult population) who never married lived alone.
        - This number is three times greater than in 1970.
- Myths and stereotypes about singles abound, ranging from "swinging single" to "desperately lonely, suicidal single."
- Advantages of living alone include time to make decisions about one's life, time to develop personal resources to meet goals, freedom to make autonomous decisions and own schedule and interests, opportunity to explore own ideas, and privacy.
- Disadvantages include lack of intimacy with others, loneliness, and finding a niche in a marriage-oriented society.

Cohabiting Adults

- Cohabitation refers to living together in a sexual relationship without being married.
- Cohabitation is an increasing lifestyle for many adults.
    - Almost 7 percent of all couples are cohabiting, with most being temporary.
- Advantages of cohabiting include less pressure to live up to expectations attached with being a "wife" or a "husband," relationships tend to be more equal, and dissolution of cohabitation carries less stigma than divorce.
- Disadvantages include potential disapproval by parents, difficulty with owing property jointly, and legal rights on the dissolution of the relationship are less certain.
    - Cohabitation does not lead to greater marital satisfaction, but rather to no differences or differences suggesting that cohabitation is not good for a marriage.

Divorced Adults

- Divorce has increased dramatically, although its rate of increase has begun to slow.
- Divorce rates are higher in disadvantaged groups.
    - Youthful marriages, low educational level, premarital pregnancy, and low income are associated with increases in divorce.
- Divorce usually occurs early in the marriage, peaking in the 5th to 10th years of marriage.
- Both divorced men and women complain about loneliness, diminished self-esteem, anxiety about the unknown, and difficulty in forming new intimate relationships.
    - Separated and divorced women and men have higher rates of psychiatric disorders, clinical depression, alcoholism, and psychosomatic disorders.
- In the first year following divorce, a disequilibrium in the divorced adult's behavior occurs, but by several years after the divorce, more stability has been achieved.
    - The displaced homemaker may encounter excessive stress due to a decline in income.
    - Men do not go through divorce unscathed either.

Remarried Adults

- On average, divorced adults remarry within 4 years after their divorce with men doing this sooner than women.
- Stepfamilies are complex, as the new couple must define and strengthen their marriage while at the same time renegotiate the biological-child relationships and establish stepparent-stepchild and stepsibling relationships.
    - Only one-third of stepfamily couples stay remarried.
- Adjustment within a stepfamily is difficult due to stress related to child rearing.
- Strategies that help remarried couples cope with the stress of living in a stepfamily include having realistic expectations and developing new positive relationships within the family.

Gay and Lesbian Adults
- One consistent research finding about gay and lesbian couples is how similar they are to heterosexual couples.
- There are a number of misconceptions about homosexual couples including:
  - the myth that one partner is masculine and the other one feminine,
  - the myth that homosexual couples engage in high levels of sexual activity, and
  - the myth that homosexuals do not get involved in long-term relationships.
- Researchers have found that the children of gay and lesbian parents are as well-adjusted as those of heterosexual couples.
  - The overwhelming majority of children raised by homosexual parents have a heterosexual orientation.

GENDER, RELATIONSHIPS, AND SELF-DEVELOPMENT
Women's Development
- Many experts believe it is important for females to retain their competencies and interest in relationships, but also to direct more effort into self-development.
- Tannen distinguishes between rapport talk and report talk.
  - Rapport talk is the language of conversation and a way of establishing connections and negotiating relationships.
  - Report talk is public speaking, which men feel more comfortable doing.
    - For men, talk is for information, while for women talk is for interaction.

Men's Development
- Men have been successful at achieving but the male role involves considerable strain.
- According to Pleck's role-strain view, male roles are contradictory and inconsistent.
  - Men are often stressed when they violate men's roles and they are also harmed when they do act in accord with men's roles.
- The following areas can cause males considerable strain.
  - Health: Men live 8 to 10 years less than women do and experience more stress-related disorders (alcoholism, accidents, suicide) and homicide.
  - Male-female relationships: Too often men disparage women, act violently towards women, and are unwilling to have equal relationships with women.
  - Male-male relationships: The male role has left men with inadequate positive, emotional connections with other males.
- Levant recommends that every man should reexamine his beliefs about manhood, separate out the valuable aspects of the male role, and get rid of those parts of the masculine role that are destructive.

Learning Objectives

1. Discuss continuity and discontinuity from childhood to adulthood.
2. Address how temperament and attachment influence adulthood.
3. Elaborate on the factors that motivate attraction.
4. Discuss Erik Erikson's sixth stage of cognitive development.
5. Define the three levels of relationship maturity.
6. Indicate ways in which adults balance intimacy and independence.
7. Differentiate between romantic love and affectionate love, then explain Sternberg's triangular theory of love.
8. Discuss friendship and related gender differences.
9. Define loneliness and ways to decrease it.

10. Describe the stages of the family life cycle.
11. Explain recent marital trends and how the view of marriage differs throughout the world.
12. Elaborate on marital myths, what makes marriages work, and the benefits of a good marriage.
13. Discuss gender differences in expectations for marital relationships.
14. Explain the expectations of parenting and common parenting myths.
15. Elaborate on the diversity of adult lifestyles.
16. Address how women develop during early adulthood.
17. Address how men develop during early adulthood.

Key Terms

affectionate love
becoming parents and a family
   with children
consensual validation
family at midlife
family in later life
family with adolescents
friendship
individuated-connected level

launching
leaving home and becoming a
   single adult
matching hypothesis
new couple
role-focused level
romantic love
self-focused level
triangular theory of love

Key People

Ellen Berscheid
Erik Erikson
John Gottman
Cindy Hazan and Phillip Shaver
Harriet Lerner
Jean Baker Miller

Joseph Pleck
Zick Rubin
Robert J. Sternberg
Deborah Tanner
Theodore Wachs
Kathleen White

Lecture Suggestions

Lecture Suggestion 1: Who Is the Lucky One? The purpose of this lecture is to extend Santrock's brief discussion of mate selection. Students are usually fascinated by Udry's filter theory of mate selection. Given that most young adults in the U.S. do not participate in arranged marriages, most of your students will engage in the process of trying to find a partner to enter into a marriage or a marriage-like relationship. Udry's (1971) theory is based on the notion that potential partners must pass through a series of "filters" in the process of mate selection. These filters screen out unacceptable partners at various stages of the intimate relationship. The filters are presented below:

- Propinquity: All possible dating partners are first screened by geographical location.
- Attractiveness: This "accessible" individual attribute can be observed early in the process and is used to screen out undesirable individuals.
  - Cross-culturally, males value physical attractiveness more than females, whereas females value economic earning power more.
- Social Background: Similarity is the key in this filter. People tend to marry individuals who are similar in religion, political affiliation, education, occupation, and social class.
  - Education and occupation have become more important, while religion has become less important in mate selection.
- Consensus: This filter involves similarity in specific attitudes and values, thus it is goes a step further than the broad social background filter.

411

- Complementarity: Does this individual complement me or complete me? Individuals seek partners that fit well with them.
- Readiness for Marriage: Are both partners ready to get married or commit to a marriage-like relationship? Discrepancies in this filter can terminate a relationship despite the success of the previous filters.
- This lecture suggestion complements Classroom Activity 1: Mate Selection.
- Source: Udry, J.R. (1971). *The social context of marriage* (2nd ed.). New York: Lippincott.

Lecture Suggestion 2: Ideal Standards in Close Relationships This lecture provides an opportunity to examine Simpson, Fletcher, and Campbell's Ideal Standards Model (ISM). Students are typically very interested in the development of intimate relationships, as many of them are currently dealing with these issues in their lives. How do you know if you are in a good or bad relationship? How do you know if you should proceed and become more involved with a particular person? The researchers propose that the answers to these questions are determined by the consistency between ideal standards and perceptions of the current partner or relationship.

Ideals guide and regulate interpersonal interactions. The ISM assumes that partner and relationship ideals predate and influence decision making in relationships. Ideals are comprised of three interlocking components: perceptions of the self, the partner, and the relationship. The ideals will guide who to date and what to expect in a relationship. Simpson et al. state that partner and relationship ideals are based around three evaluative dimensions.
- Warmth, commitment, and intimacy.
- Health, passion, and attractiveness.
- Status and resources.

There are several reasons why people do not strive to "have it all" by seeking incredibly attractive, rich, and warm partners. First, few people actually fit that description; thus, the pool is relatively small. Second, few people could attract such a person. Third, most people, even if they could attract such a person, would have difficulty keeping such a person. In other words, most people make trade-offs regarding these attributes when deciding whom to date and marry.

Simpson et al. states that ideals serve three functions. Discrepancies between one's ideals and reality are used to evaluate, explain, and regulate. Individuals need to evaluate the quality of their current partners and relationships. They need to explain or understand the current status and interactions within the relationship (explain conflict or satisfaction). Individuals also need to regulate and modify their relationships (predict and control the relationship).

People often positively enhance or idealize one's romantic partner and current relationship. This is beneficial given it facilitates and motivates one to maintain the relationship despite the odds that the relationship will end. ISM assumes that partner and relationship idealization may conflict with the desire to be accurate. Trying to understand and attribute motives and beliefs to others is adaptive in situations where you are trying to decide whether to maintain a relationship. Enhancement of one's partner and relationship and the desire to be accurate in one's perceptions and predictions are at odds. Simpson et al. propose that these patterns of behaviors operate in different situations. In highly threatening interactions or in relationships that are stable and comfortable, the enhancement pattern may increase, whereas in situations that require unbiased accurate judgements (to get married or have a child), the accuracy pattern should be dominant.

The researchers are currently testing the Ideal Standards Model. Men and women rated student generated lists of traits that characterize an ideal romantic partner and relationship.
- Three ideal-partner factors were found. Intimacy, warmth, trust, and loyalty were noted for partner characteristics. Personality and appearance characteristics included attractiveness, energy, and health of partner. The third factor included partner's social status and resources.
- Two ideal-relationship factors were revealed: intimacy, loyalty, and stability of the relationship, and the importance of passion and excitement in the relationship.

Another group of men and women rated their current partners relative to their ideal standards and rated their relationship satisfaction. Individuals that reported smaller discrepancies between their ideal standards and their perceptions reported greater relationship satisfaction.

In order to examine possible causal relationships between ideals, perceptions, and satisfaction, they conducted a longitudinal study of newly formed dating couples. Greater consistency between ideals and perception of the current partner or relationship predicted increases in relationship satisfaction over time. However, high initial levels of relationship satisfaction did not predict changes in levels of consistency between ideals and perceptions. The researchers conclude that cognitive comparisons between ideals and perceptions of current partner and relationship influence the initial stages of dating relationships.

These researchers have several interesting questions that they would like to pursue regarding their model. How do individuals establish and adjust their ideal standards over time? How do ideals function and change within an intimate relationship? How do similarities in partner and relationship ideals facilitate relationship functioning and quality?

- Classroom Activity 2: Ideal Standards for Romantic Partners and Relationships complements this lecture suggestion.
- Sources: Fletcher, G.J.O., & Simpson, J.A. (2000). Ideal standards in close relationships: Their structure and function. *Current Directions in Psychological Science, 9,* 102-105. Simpson, J.A., Fletcher, G.J.O., & Campbell, L.J. (2000). The structure and functions of ideal standards in close relationships. In G.J.O. Fletcher & M.S. Clark (Eds.), *Blackwell handbook of social psychology: Interpersonal processes.* London: Blackwell.

Lecture Suggestion 3: Love and Marriage You may want to discuss the types of love involved in relationships that occur in early adulthood, such as the love that forms the foundation for a successful marriage. However, many of your students, even those already married, may not be familiar with the many tasks associated with establishing a marriage. Ciano-Boyce and Turner list twenty such tasks.

- establishing the routines of daily living
- learning how to make important decisions together
- building new friendships as a couple
- developing a relationship with in-laws
- establishing a budget
- developing a "double person" mentality for shopping and spending
- establishing religious habits
- deciding on a contraceptive method
- learning how to negotiate conflicts
- learning how to give and take while living together
- allocating responsibility
- developing effective communication patterns
- establishing a shared core-value system
- identifying family rules
- creating common goals
- deciding on leisure-time activities and community involvement
- establishing financial credit
- developing a satisfying sex life
- finding a balance between togetherness and a respect for individuality
- establishing traditions as a family

Each of these can be elaborated on as appropriate. Newly married students may have some insight into how difficult some of these tasks are. Soon-to-be-married students may want to begin to work some of them out. Those who have been married for some time may have some suggestions to ease the transition.

Once the marriage relationship is established, many individuals choose to start a family. There are several tasks associated with the addition of children to the marriage unit.

- physical maintenance: food, shelter, clothing, and health care
- allocation of resources: possessions, space, time, and affection
- division of labor: income, chores, and child care
- socialization of family members: basic behaviors (aggression, sleeping habits, elimination, and sexual drives) and complex behaviors (attitudes, social orientation, biases, and involvement)
- reproduction, recruitment, and release of family members:
- maintenance of order: establishing clear lines of leadership and communication
- placement of members in the larger society: community interactions (e.g., schools, parks, stores), culture (e.g., plays, museums), and world events (e.g., reading newspapers)
- maintenance of motivation and morals: passing on family rituals and providing support

These tasks can seem overwhelming to a newly established family, but by identifying them and indicating that some of them will take longer than others, individuals in the early adulthood period may have a better understanding of the stress and conflict they are possibly feeling during the period.

- Source: Ciano-Boyce, C., & Turner, B. (1988). Sex stereotypes and clinical judgments of mental health among marital and family therapists. *Journal of Independent Social Work, 3,* 57-70.

Lecture Suggestion 4: Current Paternity Laws Lag Behind Science The purpose of this lecture is to examine men's rights regarding paternity. A recent *New York Times* (2001) article described an interesting, yet disturbing case involving nonpaternity and child support. Morgan Wise sought genetic testing following one of "his son's" diagnoses with cystic fibrosis. The doctor told him that he was not a carrier of cystic fibrosis. This statement in and of itself was a wake-up call because in order for a child to have this disorder both biological parents must be carriers of the recessive allele. Mr. Wise's doctor told him that he was not the biological father of three of the four children born during his marriage to Wanda Fryar. Mr. Wise had already divorced his wife before the paternity determination was discovered. Interestingly, the court that heard his divorce would not consider the genetic evidence and refused to allow him to stop paying child support for the three boys. Yet, the court did cut off visitation rights, even with his biological daughter.

Traditionally, children born within a marriage were assumed to be fathered by the husband because paternity was impossible to determine. However, paternity tests are routine in the US today. According to the American Association of Blood Banks, 280,000 paternity tests were conducted in 1999. The man being tested was not the biological father in 28 percent of the tests. The National Conference of Commissioners on Uniform State Laws found that 5–10 percent of marital children are not the biological children the husband. Most states have not updated their laws and men are being forced to continue supporting children they did not father. It is particularly disconcerting that family courts will not acknowledge the scientific evidence when criminal courts are using DNA evidence to prove innocence regardless of time frame. Some states will consider genetic evidence within 2 years of the child's birth, others allow 5 years. In Ohio, a new law was passed last year stating that if genetic testing determined nonpaternity, the man was relieved of child support.

There are differing views regarding men's rights.

- Some argue that men should not try to get out of paying child support, regardless of paternity.
- Others argue that a man should not have to support a child that he was duped into thinking was his, when the child was not his biologically.
- Others argue that it would be acceptable to relieve the non-biological father of financial responsibilities, only if the biological father assumes the responsibility.

Have your students consider each of these stated positions and the following questions. What makes a parental relationship? If biology is held supreme, what are the implications for same-sex parental relationships? What are the consequences for adoptive parents? Does the refusal to acknowledge biological evidence reward women for deception?

- Source: Lewin, T. (2001, March 11). In genetic testing for paternity, law often lags behind science. *The New York Times* (1 and 19).

414

Lecture Suggestion 5: Gender Differences and Evaluative Language One of the difficulties in exploring difference is that "different" often carries an unintended implication of better or worse. This is especially true in the exploration of gender differences. Even when the researchers themselves are careful to avoid implying that difference is equal to better or worse, others can easily read that into research. Two examples will help to clarify the point.

First, individuation is defined as "to develop a healthy adult personality of one's own." Thus individuation is a good thing to develop. Yet, women have more difficulty with individuation than do men. However, men and women appear to be equally functional. It could be argued that women and men have different problems with individuation; perhaps men err on the side of distantiation and isolation, and women on the side of connectedness. Gilligan (1982) refers to women as being connected and men as being separate. The concepts imply good and less good, although that is not intended by Gilligan. In fact she goes out of her way to state that these concepts are not better or worse.

Second, these issues are related to larger issues in psychology and society. The discipline of psychology has not yet come to grips with how to explain or give meaning to facts. There is currently a tension in psychology between positivistic explanations and hermeneutic explanations. The social issue has to do with how individuals are to be treated and thought of within a pluralistic society. Both these larger issues need to be addressed if psychology is to maintain its place as an important discipline of human inquiry and if individuals are to be validated within society.

- Source; Gilligan, C. (1982). *In a different voice: Psychological theory and women's development*. Cambridge, MA: Harvard University Press.

Classroom Activities

Classroom Activity 1: Mate Selection One of the primary tasks facing young adults is to form intimate relationships. You can begin this activity by discussing filter theories of mate selection (Udry, 1971). Filter theories suggest that we use a series of filters to select an appropriate mate. The number of filters varies depending on the theorist. Describe some of these filters (Lecture Suggestion 1: Who is the Lucky One?) and then ask students to get into groups and discuss the filters. Have your students discuss the validity of this theory. Are there other filters that could be added (family and friend acceptance filter, sexual compatibility filter, etc.)? Is the order appropriate? Ask them if they believe these filters are actually used by people in selecting marriage partners. How do they think the filters have changed in the last 10, 20, or 30 years?
Logistics:
- Group size: Small group.
- Approximate time: Small group discussion (15 minutes).
- Sources: Udry, J. (1971). Marital alternatives and marital disruption. *Journal of Marriage and the Family, 43,* 889-897.

Classroom Activity 2: Ideal Standards for Romantic Partners and Relationships The purpose of this activity is to examine potential gender differences in ideal standards for romantic partners and relationships. This exercise complements Lecture Suggestion 2: Ideal Standards in Close Relationships. Have students generate a list of characteristics and traits for their ideal romantic partner. Then, have students generate a list of characteristics and traits for their ideal romantic relationship. Fletcher et al. (1999) found the following factors related to ideal partners and ideal relationships.
- Three ideal-partner factors were found. Intimacy, warmth, trust, and loyalty were noted for partner characteristics. Personality and appearance characteristics included attractiveness, energy, and health of partner. The third factor included partner's social status and resources.
- Two ideal-relationship factors were revealed: intimacy, loyalty, and stability of the relationship, and the importance of passion and excitement in the relationship.

- Use in the Classroom: Separate the males and females. Have the males and females compile their characteristics and traits for both their ideal partner and ideal relationship. Then, have the males and females independently rank their top five characteristics for an ideal partner and an ideal relationship. As a full class, list on the board the top five rankings for both the ideal partner and ideal relationship. Are they similar or different? Why? How do they compare to the Fletcher et al. findings?

Logistics:
- Group size: Individual. Two groups based on gender. Full class discussion.
- Approximate time: Individual (10 minutes). Gender groups (25 minutes). Full class (20 minutes).
- Sources: Fletcher, G.J.O., Simpson, J.A., Thomas, G., & Giles, L. (1999). Ideals in intimate relationships. *Journal of Personality and Social Psychology, 76*, 72-89.

Classroom Activity 3: Sign on the Dotted Line? Prenuptial Contracts The purpose of this exercise is to afford students an opportunity to examine the issue of premarital contracts. Premarital contracts explicitly state how property and finances are to be divided up in the case of marital dissolution. Have your students discuss relevant psychosocial issues in early adulthood. What is the nature and/or function of premarital contracts? Students should generate a list of pros and cons for premarital contracts.
- Use in the Classroom: As a full class, compile the list of pros and cons. Is there group consensus? Are there gender differences regarding the utility of premarital contracts? Is there consensus between single, married, and divorced students?

Logistics:
- Group size: Small group and full class.
- Approximate time: Small group discussion (20 minutes) and full class discussion (20 minutes).

Classroom Activity 4: Pressure to Pair Up Many of the students in your class will be in the early adulthood period. A good number of them will be struggling with decisions about marriage and careers and starting families. One way to help them identify the choices they are making on a daily basis is to get them to focus on being single (**Handout 1**). Ask students to write down the age at which they hope to marry or move into a long-term, exclusive relationship with a significant other. Ask those students who are married or already in long-term intimate relationships to indicate the age at which that relationship started. Then ask students to identify, on a 7-point scale, how much pressure they feel or felt to become involved in a marriage or a marriage-like relationship from the following sources:
- family
- peers
- society
- desire to have children
- desire to alleviate loneliness
- type of activities they enjoy
- desire to finish their education (key this one backwards)

Total the responses to arrive at a pressure-to-get-married score. Next, have the students subtract the age they are from the age they think they should be when they establish their intimate relationship. Have the married students respond as they would have before they got married, and have them subtract the age that they first thought about getting married from the age they were when they actually got married. Collect the data and run a quick correlation on it to see if there is a significant relationship. If there are enough married students, do two analyses.

Discuss the results and have students offer explanations for the findings the class obtained. During the discussion, you may want to highlight some of the advantages and disadvantages of being single that were mentioned in the text.

Logistics:
- Materials: Handout 1 (Pressure to Pair Up).
- Group size: Full class.
- Approximate time: Full class discussion (30 minutes).

Classroom Activity 5: Connectedness A number of theorists have suggested that intimacy is the goal of young adulthood. Some feminist psychologists have talked about this in terms of connections and webs of relationships. Carol Gilligan views this process of finding oneself and valuing oneself within the context of connectedness as a growing edge of women. A growing edge is a personal frontier of knowledge. With this theoretical perspective in mind, and with the individuation index and the interview schedule from *Women's Ways of Knowing* as guides, you can have a class discussion about connectedness. Below you see the connectedness index. This is also presented as **Handout 2** for the students.

Connectedness Index

- List several relationships that have been important to you over the past several years.
- How have these relationships helped to shape who you are?
- How have you helped to shape these persons who helped to shape you?
- List two situations in which you solved a problem that took your own needs into consideration along with the needs of the other people involved in the problem.

Logistics:

- Materials: Handout 2 (Connectedness).
- Group size: Full class.
- Approximate time: Full class discussion (30 minutes).
- Sources: Belenky, M. (1986). *Women's ways of knowing: The development of self, voice, and mind.* New York: Basic Books. Gilligan, C. (1982). *In a different voice: Psychological theory and women's development.* Cambridge, MA: Harvard University Press. Morehouse, R. E., & Vestal, L. B. (1994). *Instructor's manual with test item file to accompany human development*, (2nd ed.) by John Dacey and John Travers. Dubuque, IA: Wm. C. Brown Communications, Inc.

Classroom Activity 6: Gender Face-Off Have students e-mail you 3 to 5 questions they have for or about the opposite sex related to friendship, intimacy, romantic love, and affectionate love, during the week prior to class. Assure them that after you have recorded their participation upon receiving their questions, their names will not be connected to what they ask. As you gather the questions, create a list to pose the men and to the women. The next class period, have the men sit on one side of the room and the women sit on the other side of the room. As the moderator, you will simply pose the questions to each gender group and let them answer. Encourage all students to participate and contribute their opinions, perceptions, and beliefs. Have the group that's listening pay close attention to what the other gender has to say, and point out that in some cases (as you'll see during this activity) not all men and not all women think alike when it comes to relationships. Students will really enjoy this activity and probably want to continue long after class is over!

Logistics:

- Group size: Individual and full class.
- Approximate time: Individual (10 minutes) and full class discussion (30 minutes).

Classroom Activity 7: Critical Thinking Multiple-Choice Questions and Suggested Answers Discuss the critical thinking multiple-choice questions in **Handout 3**. The answers to these questions are presented as **Handout 4**. By this time in the semester, we hope that question 1 is not very taxing for your students, and we advise that you simply remind them to review the relevant material in chapter 2 if they cannot think of good reasons for accepting/rejecting alternatives. If a class review is desirable, have students review material before class and report back.

Question 2 requires students to correlate concepts they learn at separate points in chapter 15. They will find the task easier if you have them identify the defining features of each style and level of relationship separately discussed in the chapter. The match for "a" is not perfect, but glaring contradictions are found among all the others.

Question 3 tests students understanding of the myths regarding marriage in the textbook. Be sure that students understand that they are not selecting one correct answer, rather they are to explain why the statement is either a myth or a true statement.

Logistics:
- Materials: Handout 3 (the critical thinking multiple-choice questions) and Handout 4 (answers).
- Group size: Small groups to discuss the questions, then a full class discussion.
- Approximate time: Small groups (15 to 20 minutes), full class discussion of any questions (15 minutes).

Classroom Activity 8: Critical Thinking Essay Questions and Suggestions for Helping Students Answer the Essays Discuss students' answers to the critical thinking essay questions presented in **Handout 5**. The purpose of this exercise is threefold. First, answering the essay questions further facilitates students' understanding of concepts in chapter 15. Second, this type of essay question affords the students an opportunity to apply the concepts to their own lives, which will facilitate their retention of the material. Third, the essay format also gives students practice expressing themselves in written form. Ideas to help students answer the critical thinking essay questions are provided as **Handout 6**.
Logistics:
- Materials: Handout 5 (essay questions) and Handout 6 (helpful suggestions for the answers).
- Group size: Individual, then full class.
- Approximate time: Individual (60 minutes), full class discussion of any questions (30 minutes).

Personal Applications

Personal Application 1: The More Things Change, the More They Stay the Same The purpose of this exercise is to get students to think about the particular continuities of their development across their life so far. Certainly, we no longer believe that an individual's personality is fully in place by age 6 as Freud claimed, yet the research indicates that both temperament and attachment are two strong influences on adult behavior.
- Instructions for Students: Reflect on your life thus far and discuss how aspects from both your childhood temperament and the attachment relationship you had with your parents are manifested in your current behavior patterns. Also talk about areas in which there are discontinuities. Overall, do you see yourself more as a product of your growing up years, or are you forging new trails as an adult? To successfully do this exercise, you need to take a hard, honest look at yourself at all times in your life.
- Use in the Classroom: Ask students to share examples of how they can—or cannot—map their current behavioral patterns onto aspects of their childhood. Discuss what changes have taken place over their lives and how this has either contributed to changes in their behaviors or how their behavior patterns have withstood the varying influences and circumstances they've encountered over the years. You may begin the discussion by offering your own examples to help get students to share. Also, explore the varying strengths of temperament and attachment in influencing adult behavior. Which seems to be more profound and long-lasting? Which do students find it easier to attribute current behavior to? Is there a more valid argument for the strength of one of these influences over another?

Personal Application 2: Ten Things I Like about You This exercise will get students thinking about the aspects of interpersonal attraction. Many factors influence what draws us to another person, and it is an important area explored by psychologists.
- Instructions for Students: Before you read, or re-read this section in your text, make a list of all of the qualities and characteristics that attract you to someone. Be honest and don't censor yourself. After you've made your list, read what psychologists have discovered about what attracts people to one another. How are these things reflected in your list? Did you learn something about why it is you view others the way you do? Can you illustrate these factors with personal experiences with attraction? Is there any aspect of attraction that you didn't realize influenced you?

- Use in the Classroom: Collect everyone's list (they can make a copy for you without their name, if they wish to remain anonymous) and create a chart on the board with all the characteristics and the frequency with which students mentioned them on their lists. What do they find? Have students discuss and comment on what they and their classmates listed as important aspects for attraction. For those items listed by only one or two people, see if they'll talk about why those things are important to them—and have the rest of the class comment on why they didn't list them. For the popular items, is there consensus among students as to how they perceive them, or do different students view the same characteristics differently with regard to their role in attraction?

Personal Application 3: Understanding Me The purpose of this activity is to help students connect with the ideas discussed with regard to findings in the areas of men and women's development. Psychologists have found that it is important to explore what goes on in the lives and minds of adults as they continue to develop, and that there are different issues faced by men and women. Better understanding these issues relevant to both sexes is an important goal, and can help adults lead fuller, more satisfying lives.
- Instructions for Students: Read the section in your text related to the development of your particular gender. Write about what you learned and how you find it relevant to you at this time in your life. What issues are you dealing with at this time with regard to your personal growth and understanding? What issue is the most challenging to you? In what areas to you feel good about how you function and perceive yourself? What areas do you need to work on the most? Do you have a better idea now about how you might approach them?
- Use in the Classroom: This subject provides another great opportunity for the genders to learn from each other. After everyone has explored themselves with regard to these issues, discuss these important aspects of self-development, and have the men and women enlighten each other on what is important to their development and functioning.

Research Project Ideas

Research Project 1: The Marriage Quiz In chapter 15, Santrock discusses marital expectations and myths. He presents Jeffrey Larson's (1988) research, which uses a "Marriage Quiz" to measure people's ideas about marriage. Larson demonstrates that college students have relatively unrealistic views of marriage. Provide a copy of the quiz (**Handout 7**) and instruct the students to have as many college men and women that they know respond to it. If they can, they should try to get equal numbers of men and women, and representatives of first through fourth year college students.

Score respondents' answers and then determine the mean score. If they know how, they should also compute a standard deviation for the scores. If the students were able to obtain responses from men and women in some or all college ranks (e.g., first through fourth year), compute means (and standard deviations) for each group. Next, students should prepare a table that displays these means. With the table as a base, instruct the students to write a brief report in which they indicate whether Larson's claims apply to their college or university. Advise students to answer the questions that follow the quiz in their report:

Answer the following items as true or false.
1. A husband's marital satisfaction is usually lower if his wife is employed full-time than if she is a full-time homemaker.
2. Today most young, single, never-married people will eventually get married.
3. In most marriages, having a child improves marital satisfaction for both spouses.
4. The best single predictor of overall marital satisfaction is the quality of a couple's sex life.
5. The divorce rate in America increased from 1960 to 1980.
6. A greater percentage of wives are in the workforce today than in 1970.
7. Marital satisfaction for a wife is usually lower if she is employed full-time than if she is a full-time homemaker.

8. If my spouse loves me, he/she should instinctively know what I want and need to be happy.
9. In a marriage in which the wife is employed full-time, the husband usually assumes an equal share of the housekeeping.
10. For most couples marital satisfaction gradually increases from the first years of marriage throughout the childbearing years, the teen years, the empty-nest period, and retirement.
11. No matter how I behave, my spouse should love me simply because he/she is my spouse.
12. One of the most frequent marital problems is poor communication.
13. Husbands usually make more lifestyle adjustments in marriage than wives do.
14. Couples who cohabited before marriage usually report greater marital satisfaction than couples who did not.
15. I can change my spouse by pointing out his/her inadequacies, errors, etc.

- Answers: 1. F 2. T 3. F 4. F 5. T 6. T 7. F 8. F 9. F 10. F 11. F 12. T 13. F 14. F 15. F
- Questions:
    - On average, how many items did your respondents pass?
    - How did women compare to men?
    - How did younger respondents compare to older respondents?
    - Can you think of other comparisons to make, or other questions to ask, that would yield interesting ideas concerning young adults' expectations about and knowledge of marriage?
    - Do your results support Larson's claim that most college students have unrealistic expectations about marriage?
    - Do your peers have similarly unrealistic expectations of marriage or is there wide variety in their expectations?
    - Why do you think people develop unrealistic expectations for marriage?
- Use in the Classroom: Have students form groups of four to six people, preferably balanced between men and women. Instruct individuals in groups to present their findings to each other, with the goal of identifying both common expectations and unique ones. Make sure someone in each group keeps track of these for reporting to the class at large. Also, have the groups pool their data in one large table. Aside from what you find out, this will provide a lesson about the effects of sampling variations on research results.
- Source: Larson, J. (1988). The marriage quiz: College students' beliefs in selected myths about marriage. *Family Relations, 37*, 3-11.

Research Project 2: Gender and Age Roles in Magazine Advertisements This project is a good opportunity to make a connection between the stage of the life span just covered (adolescence), the current stage of emphasis (early adulthood), and the two stages to be discussed next (middle and late adulthood). In this project, students investigate gender and age stereotypes in magazines. Using **Handout 8** instruct students to look at one widely circulated magazine and evaluate how ads depict males and females of various ages (adolescence, early, middle, and late adulthood). They should evaluate physical appearance, personality, and behaviors as they are depicted in the magazine ads. They can use the chart presented as **Handout 9** to help them organize their impressions. Tally up the number of persons in each age group that appeared in ads and determine what percentage of ads depicted each age group. You might want to assign specific magazines to students so that you can explore the effects of type of magazine on gender images (e.g., *Sports Illustrated* vs. *Ladies Home Journal*) or age images (e.g., *Seventeen* vs. *Modern Maturity*). Another variation is to have students evaluate two issues of the same magazine, a current issue and one more than 20 years old, to explore changes in images over the years. Following data collection, have students write a brief report addressing the following questions.
Questions:
- Are all age groups represented in advertisements?
- Who is underrepresented and overrepresented? Why do you think that is so?
- Compare the various groups in terms of the characteristics you observed portrayed for each in the advertisements. What generalizations about age and gender do these portrayals convey?

420

- Compare your findings to those obtained by someone who looked at a different magazine. Are your findings similar or different?
- What do you conclude if they are similar? Different?
- If they are different, do the differences sensibly relate to differences in the apparent purpose or style of the magazines?

• Use in the Classroom: Class discussion will be enhanced if you include some examples of actual ads and have students evaluate them. Class members will want to discuss their favorite examples of stereotyping from the magazines they check out.

Film and Video List

The following films and videos supplement the content of chapter 15. Contact information for film distributors can be found at the front of this Instructor's Manual under Film and Video Sources.

Bobby and Rosie: Anatomy of a Marriage (The Glendon Association, 47 minutes). In this video a clinical psychologist unravels the dynamics operating in a relationship and discloses the basic reasons why couples have trouble maintaining satisfactory sexual relations.

Dedicated, Not Deadbeat (Films for the Humanities and Sciences, 56 minutes). This program introduces dedicated young fathers who want to break the chain of "deadbeat dads." Issues include welfare reform and the need for counseling.

Dear Lisa: A Letter to My Sister (Insight Media, 45 minutes). This video presents interviews of thirteen women of different ages, races, education levels, and SES. In addition, it investigates sex-typed toys and play, women in the workplace, body image and self-esteem, motherhood, relationships, and sexual assault.

Gay Couples: The Nature of Relationships (Films for the Humanities and Sciences, 50 minutes). This program features sociologist Dr. Schwartz, as she documents the lives of two couples, one gay and one lesbian.

Gender and Communication: She Talks, He Talks (Insight Media, 22 minutes). This video describes sex differences in communication and examines their causes.

Gender and Relationships (Insight Media, 30 minutes). This video explores uncertainties in our understanding of love, affection, and sexual attraction.

In My Country: An International Perspective on Gender (Insight Media, 91 minutes). This video is a resource for studying cultural attitudes and gender. The coverage includes household labor, discipline of children, marriage decisions, control of money, rape, care of the elderly, and attitudes toward homosexuals. The presentation includes interviews of people from several countries.

Juggling Family and Work (Films for the Humanities and Sciences, 56 minutes). This program follows three men who, when forced to choose between family and career, chose their family. They discuss the implications of that choice and its impact on their career and conceptions of themselves as fathers and the new opportunities that have developed.

Love (Films for the Humanities and Sciences, 53 minutes). This program seeks to understand love's social rituals and its interrelated physiological imperatives. Topics such as pair bonding, platonic, courtly and romantic models of love, homosexuality, inhibitions vs. promiscuity, and flirting are discussed.

Love, Love Me Do: How Sex Differences Affect Relationships (Films for the Humanities and Sciences, 51 minutes). This program discusses the influence of sex-related brain differences on love, marriage, reproduction, and parenthood. It uses images from art, television, and hidden-camera footage.

Love, Lust, and Marriage: Why We Stay and Why We Stray (Films for the Humanities and Sciences, 46 minutes). *ABC News* correspondent John Stossel discusses the modern-day notion of love, with all of its attendant expectations. This program presents research that suggests that married couples are actually healthier-and claim to be happier as well.

Man, Oh Man: Growing Up Male in America (Insight Media, 18 minutes). This video looks at societal pressures on men through the eyes of a young woman.

The Marriage Partnership (Films for the Humanities and Sciences, 19 minutes). This program explores the steps that cultivate strong marriages in relation to the high divorce rate. Experts and married couples offer ways in which newlyweds can become equal partners-for life.

Men and Women: Talking Together (Insight Media, 58 minutes). Deborah Tannen and Robert Bly talk about communication between the sexes before a live audience.

The Familiar Face of Love (Filmmaker's Library, 47 minutes). This video presents a study of love and loving that looks at how we choose our mates and why. John Money narrates and explores the concept of a *love map*.

Woman and Man (Films for the Humanities and Sciences, 52 minutes). This program looks at some of the differences between men and women and how these role differences are beginning to fade.

Web Site Suggestions

The URLs for general sites, common to all chapters, can be found at the front of this Instructor's Manual under Useful Web Sites. At the time of publication, all sites were current and active, however, please be advised that you may occasionally encounter a dead link.

Divorce Source: Family Law, Custody, Alimony, Support, and Visitation
http://www.divorcesource.com/

Fatherhood: Improving Data and Research on Male Fertility, Family Formation, and Fatherhood
http://fatherhood.hhs.gov/CFSForum/front.htm

The In-Site to Parenting
http://www.babybag.com/

Resource for Divorce and Remarriage
http://www.maritalstatus.com/

Handout 1 (CA 4)

Pressure to Pair Up

Many students are struggling with decisions about marriage and careers and starting families. One way to help you identify the choices you are making on a daily basis is to focus on being single.

- Write down the age at which you hope to marry or move into a long-term, exclusive relationship with a significant other.

- If you are already married or in a long-term committed relationship, indicate at what age the relationship started.

- Then identify, on a 7-point scale, how much pressure you feel or felt to become involved in a marriage or a marriage-like relationship from the following sources:
  _____ family
  _____ peers
  _____ society
  _____ desire to have children
  _____ desire to alleviate loneliness
  _____ type of activities you enjoy
  _____ desire to finish your education (key this one backwards)

- Total the responses to arrive at a pressure-to-get-married score.

- Next, subtract the age you are from the age you think you should be when you establish your intimate relationship.

- Married students respond as you would have before you got married, and subtract the age that you first thought about getting married from the age you were when you actually got married.

Handout 2 (CA 5)

Connectedness Index Activity

Answer the following.

1. List several relationships that have been important to you over the past several years.

2. How have these relationships helped to shape who you are?

3. How have you helped to shape these persons who helped to shape you?

4. List two situations in which you solved a problem that took your own needs into consideration along with the needs of the other people involved in the problem.

Critical Thinking Multiple-Choice Questions

1. The major focus of chapter 15 is relationships with others, whether it be friendship or love, companionship or intimacy. Which theoretical perspective indicates that this is an appropriate focus for the study of socioemotional development in early adulthood? Circle the letter of the best answer and explain why it is the best answer and why each other answer is not as good.

    a. psychoanalytic
    b. behavioral
    c. cognitive
    d. ecological
    e. eclectic

2. Early in chapter 15, Santrock outlines different ways to classify forms of love. Later in the chapter, he sketches several intimacy styles and levels of relationship maturity. Which of the following pairs of love form, intimacy style, or relationship maturity is most logical according to Santrock's summary of each aspect of relationships? Circle the letter of the best answer and explain why it is the best answer and why each other answer is not as good.

    a. consummate, individuated-connected
    b. fatuous love, individuated-connected
    c. companionate love, role-focused level
    d. isolated love, self-focused level
    e. infatuated love, role-focused level

3. Santrock discusses marital expectations and myths in chapter 15. Which of the following illustrate myths regarding marriage and which of the following are true regarding marriage? Note that there will be more than one of each. Be sure to explain why the statement is either a myth or a true statement.

    a. Avoiding conflict will ruin your marriage.
    b. Affairs are the main cause of divorce.
    c. Unhappily married couples express unrealistic expectations about marriage.
    d. Men are not biologically made for marriage.
    e. College students have unrealistic expectations about marriage.

Suggested Answers for Critical Thinking Multiple-Choice Questions

1. The major focus of chapter 15 is relationships with others, whether it be friendship or love, companionship or intimacy. Which theoretical perspective indicates that this is an appropriate focus for the study of socioemotional development in early adulthood? Circle the letter of the best answer and explain why it is the best answer and why each other answer is not as good.

    a. Psychoanalytic is the best answer. Specifically, Erikson's theory specifies that early adulthood is a stage of intimacy versus isolation, which seems to be the theme of chapter 15.
    b. Behavioral is not the best answer. The behavioral approach would probably focus on the nature of reciprocal responses in social settings that shape adult social behavior; or focus on social and cultural models as guides for adult social behavior.
    c. Cognitive is not the best answer. The cognitive theories would stress social cognition, whether of a Piagetian or an information-processing type, as the basis of social development in early adulthood.
    d. Ecological is not the best answer. Ecological theory would require a more broadly conceived analysis of the situational, cross-situational, cultural, and temporal factors in early adult social behavior and social development.
    e. Eclectic is not the best answer. An eclectic approach would combine the theories mentioned in "a" through "d" in an analysis of early adult social behavior.

2. Early in chapter 15, Santrock outlines different ways to classify forms of love. Later in the chapter, he sketches levels of relationship maturity. Which of the following pairs of love styles and relationship maturity levels, is most logical according to Santrock's summary of each aspect of relationships? Circle the letter of the best answer and explain why it is the best answer and why each other answer is not as good.

    a. Consummate, individuated-connected is the best answer. Both of these represent the highest level of love and relationship maturity. They involve understanding of self and partner.
    b. Fatuous love, individuated-connected is not the best answer. Fatuous love includes passion and commitment without intimacy—love at a distance. Individuated-connected maturity represents understanding self and partner in an intimate relationship.
    c. Companionate love, role-focused level is not the best answer. The chief fault is that the role-focused level of intimacy is weak on commitment, but companionate love is very strong on it.
    d. Isolated love, self-focused level is not the best answer. Isolated love is not one of the types of love discussed. People at a self-focused level in relationships are, by definition, in relationships.
    e. Infatuated love, role-focused level is not the best answer. The infatuated love is focused chiefly on sexual activity, whereas the role-focused level is concerned mainly with defining, if not enacting, communication and mutual understanding.

3. Santrock discusses marital expectations and myths in chapter 15. Which of the following illustrate myths regarding marriage and which of the following are true statements regarding marriage? Note that there will be more than one of each. Be sure to explain why the statement is either a myth or a true statement.

   a. The statement <u>avoiding conflict will ruin your marriage</u> represents a myth. Couples have different styles to deal with conflict. The most important factor is whether the marital partners agree with how to deal with conflict (avoid, fight, or discuss the problem).
   b. The statement <u>affairs are the main cause of divorce</u> represents a myth. In most cases, infidelity is the result of marital dissatisfaction. Only 20 percent of divorced men and women reported that an extramarital affair was even partially to blame for the divorce.
   c. This statement is true. Epstein and Eidelson found that <u>unhappily married couples express unrealistic expectations about marriage.</u>
   d. The statement <u>men are not biologically made for marriage</u> represents a myth. This statement is based on the assumption that men are philanderers and ill-suited for monogamy. Interestingly, as more women pursue careers outside of the home, the number of extramarital affairs for women slightly exceeds those of men.
   e. This statement is true. Larson found that <u>college students have unrealistic expectations about marriage.</u> College students responded incorrectly to almost half of the questions on his marriage quiz. Female students and students with a less romantic perception of marriage missed fewer items.

Critical Thinking Essay Questions

Your answers to this kind of question demonstrate an ability to comprehend and apply ideas discussed in this chapter.

1. Describe the continuities and discontinuities from childhood to adulthood.

2. Explain what factors initially attract one individual to another.

3. Define and distinguish between romantic love, affectionate love, and friendship.

4. How would you explain Sternberg's triangular theory of love to a friend?

5. Explain what college students can do to reduce their feelings of loneliness.

6. List and briefly explain the successive stages in the family life cycle.

7. Compare and contrast the experience and implications of marriage for women and men.

8. Describe the lives of single adults, and evaluate the stereotype that single adults are abnormal.

9. Characterize the experiences of an individual who goes through a divorce.

10. Compare and contrast the relationship between gender issues women and men's development.

Handout 6 (CA 8)

Ideas to Help You Answer Critical Thinking Essay Questions

1. As you describe the continuities and discontinuities, use examples from your own development to illustrate the concepts, and to help you understand why this is an important issue considered by developmentalists.

2. Do not just rotely describe these factors based on the information presented in your text. Think about the people you've been attracted to and how these factors have come into play. Take the time to really consider the impact that they have, and expand on your basic explanations with a little personal insight.

3. Define and distinguish between these three types of relationships by painting a picture of what they are like. What do the individuals do together? How do they communicate? What do they communicate about? What challenges do they face? How do individuals perceive their participation in each relationship? What purpose does each serve in our lives? How do we feel when we aren't engaged in one or more of these relationship?

4. Imagine you are having a conversation about love, and your friend concludes that there is no way to really define or explain love ("It's one of those things you just can't put your finger on," he or she says.) This is when you kindly correct your friend and present Sternberg's theory.

5. In this case, you are a student advocate for your school—someone who works with new students to help them adjust to (and enjoy) college life. As freshman often have bouts of loneliness, part of your job is to give a presentation to incoming students on how to reduce their feelings of loneliness. Think about whether you have ever experienced these feelings. They can be pretty powerful, particularly at a time when there are so many other challenges you're facing. Make your presentation as effective as possible.

6. Look back through your own family history for the first part of this exercise, and try and project into the future as you address the family life cycle. Expand on each component with your own examples.

7. Begin by describing the experience and implications of marriage for your own gender. Consider whether this is how you've perceived it or not. Does this information surprise you? In what ways? What were your actual expectations? Now address these same things from your future spouse's perspective and consider those same questions. Do you think being aware of these differences will help you create a successful marriage? Why or why not?

8. If you are a single adult, enhance your description with experiences from your own life. Do you match the stereotype? Why or why not?

9. If your parents went through a divorce, use your position as observer to enhance your description. If your parents are still together, imagine being married—and having children—as you consider these experiences. Knowing what you know about this process, what do you make of the incredibly high incidence of divorce in our society? What are the implications of so many individuals experiencing this? What might it mean for the future of our society and for the children of the next several generations?

10. Delineate the issues related to gender development, then map out the experiences of males and females. Feel free to include illustrations based on your own experiences and those of your opposite sex siblings and friends.

The Marriage Quiz

In chapter 15, Santrock discusses marital expectations and myths. Santrock presented Jeffrey Larson's (1988) research, which uses a "Marriage Quiz" to measure people's ideas about marriage. Larson demonstrates that college students have relatively unrealistic views of marriage. Have as many college men and women that you can respond to Larson's quiz. Try to get equal numbers of men and women, and representatives of first through fourth year college students.

Score respondents' answers and then determine the mean score. If you know how, compute a standard deviation for the scores. If you were able to obtain responses from men and women in some or all college ranks (e.g., first through fourth year), compute means (and standard deviations) for each group. Next, prepare a table that displays these means. With the table as a base, write a brief report addressing whether Larson's claims apply to your college or university. In addition, answer the questions that follow the quiz in your report.

Answer the following items as true or false.
1. A husband's marital satisfaction is usually lower if his wife is employed full-time than if she is a full-time homemaker.

2. Today most young, single, never-married people will eventually get married.

3. In most marriages, having a child improves marital satisfaction for both spouses.

4. The best single predictor of overall marital satisfaction is the quality of a couple's sex life.

5. The divorce rate in America increased from 1960 to 1980.

6. A greater percentage of wives are in the workforce today than in 1970.

7. Marital satisfaction for a wife is usually lower if she is employed full-time than if she is a full-time homemaker.

8. If my spouse loves me, he/she should instinctively know what I want and need to be happy.

9. In a marriage in which the wife is employed full-time, the husband usually assumes an equal share of the housekeeping.

10. For most couples marital satisfaction gradually increases from the first years of marriage throughout the childbearing years, the teen years, the empty-nest period, and retirement.

11. No matter how I behave, my spouse should love me simply because he/she is my spouse.

12. One of the most frequent marital problems is poor communication.

13. Husbands usually make more lifestyle adjustments in marriage than wives do.

14. Couples who cohabited before marriage usually report greater marital satisfaction than couples who did not.

15. I can change my spouse by pointing out his/her inadequacies, errors, etc.

Handout 7 (RP 1) continued

Questions:

- On average, how many items did your respondents pass?

- How did women compare to men?

- How did younger respondents compare to older respondents?

- Can you think of other comparisons to make, or other questions to ask, that would yield interesting ideas concerning young adults' expectations about and knowledge of marriage?

- Do your results support Larson's claim that most college students have unrealistic expectations about marriage?

- Do your peers have similarly unrealistic expectations of marriage or is there wide variety in their expectations?

- Why do you think people develop unrealistic expectations for marriage?

Handout 8 (RP 2)

Gender and Age Roles in Magazine Advertisements

In this project, you will investigate gender and age stereotypes in magazines. Look at one widely circulated magazine and evaluate how ads depict males and females of various ages (adolescence, early, middle, and late adulthood). You should evaluate physical appearance, personality, and behaviors as they are depicted in the magazine ads. You can use the data sheet presented as **Handout 9** to help organize your impressions. After completing the data collection, write a brief report that answers the questions below.

Questions:

- Are all age groups represented in advertisements?

- Who is underrepresented and overrepresented? Why do you think that is so?

- Compare the various groups in terms of the characteristics you observed portrayed for each in the advertisements. What generalizations about age and gender do these portrayals convey?

- Compare your findings to those obtained by someone who looked at a different magazine. Are your findings similar or different?

- What do you conclude if they are similar? Different?

- If they are different, do the differences sensibly relate to differences in the apparent purpose or style of the magazines?

Data Sheet for Gender and Age Roles in Magazine Advertisements

Magazine Title _____   Issue date _____   Number of Ads _____

ADOLESCENTS:	BOYS	GIRLS
physical appearance:		
body message:		
clothes:		
facial expressions:		
personality:		
intelligence:		
activities:		
verbal comments:		
sexuality:		
other:		

YOUNG ADULTS:	MEN	WOMEN
physical appearance:		
body message:		
clothes:		
facial expressions:		
personality:		
intelligence:		
activities:		
verbal comments:		
sexuality:		
other:		

Handout 9 (RP 2) continued

MIDDLE ADULTS:	MEN	WOMEN
physical appearance:		
body message:		
clothes:		
facial expressions:		
personality:		
intelligence:		
activities:		
verbal comments:		
sexuality:		
other:		

ELDERLY ADULTS:	MEN	WOMEN
physical appearance:		
body message:		
clothes:		
facial expressions:		
personality:		
intelligence:		
activities:		
verbal comments:		
sexuality:		

Chapter 16: Physical and Cognitive Development in Middle Adulthood

Total Teaching Package Outline

Lecture Outline	Resource References
Physical and Cognitive Development in Middle Adulthood	PowerPoint Presentation: See www.mhhe.com Cognitive Maps: See Appendix A
Changing Middle Age	LO1 PA1: Young Whippersnappers

Physical Development
• Physical Changes
    -Noticeable Visible Signs
    -Height and Weight
    -Strength, Joints, and Bones
    -Vision
    -Hearing
    -Cardiovascular System
    -Sleep	

• Health and Disease
    -Health
 	
    -Chronic Disorders
	LO2
	WS: Health Statistics Sources
	
	IB: Leading Chronic Disorders in Middle Age
	F/V: Controlling Cholesterol
	F/V: Reducing Cardiovascular Disease

• Culture, Personality, Relationships, and Health
 	
    -Culture and Cardiovascular Disease
 	
    -Type A/Type B Behavior Patterns
 	
    -Hardiness
 	
    -Health and Social Relationships
	LO3
	LS1: Gender and Ethnic Differences in Health
	RP1: Song Lyric Values
	WS: Men's Health
	WS: Stress and Health Psychology
	WS: Women's Health
	
	LS2: The Concept of Stress
	CA1: Type A Behavior Pattern
	
	F/V: For Richer, For Poorer

• Mortality Rates	LO4 IB: Leading Causes of Death in Middle Adulthood

• Sexuality
    -Menopause
    -Hormone Replacement Therapy
    -Hormonal Changes in Middle-Aged Men
    -Sexual Attitudes and Behavior
	LO5
	CA2: Menopause
	RP2: Archival Research

Cognitive Development
•   Intelligence
     -Fluid and Crystallized Intelligence
 	
     -Seattle Longitudinal Study
 	
•   Information Processing
     -Speed of Information Processing
     -Memory
     -Expertise
     -Practical Problem Solving
	LO6
	IB: Fluid and Crystallized Intellectual Dev.
	
	IB: Intellectual Change in Middle Adulthood
	WS: The General Intelligence Factor
	
	LO7

Careers, Work, and Leisure • Job Satisfaction • Career Challenges and Changes • Leisure	LO8 LS3: Work, Leisure, and Intellectual Growth LS4: Social Structures Regarding Work, Leisure, and Education in Adulthood WS: Midlife Career Change

Religion and Meaning in Life
•   Religion and Adult Lives
 	
•   Religion and Health
     -Religion and Physical Health
     -Coping
     -Happiness
 	
•   Meaning in Life
	LO9
	
	CA3: Prayer and Stress

Review	LS5: Guest Lecture Idea CA4: The Song of Developmental Psychology CA5: Wise Consumers of Information CA6: Critical Thinking Multiple-Choice CA7: Critical Thinking Essays PA2: Friends in High Places

Chapter Outline

CHANGING MIDDLE AGE
- Developmentalists are beginning to study middle age more probably because of the dramatic increase in the number of individuals entering this period of life.
- As more people live into old age, what we think of as middle age seems to be occurring later.
  - Today, the average life expectancy is 77, 12 percent of the U.S. population is older than 65.
  - The age boundaries of middle age are not set in stone.
    - **Middle adulthood** is the developmental period that begins at approximately 40 years of age and extends to about 60 years of age.
- Middle age involves extensive individual variation.

PHYSICAL DEVELOPMENT
Physical Changes
- Midlife changes are often gradual.
- Genetic makeup and lifestyle factors play important roles in whether chronic diseases will appear and when.

Noticeable Visible Signs
- Physical appearance is one of the most noticeable signs of physical changes in middle adulthood and is usually apparent by the forties and fifties.
  - Outwardly, noticeable changes in physical appearance include wrinkles, age spots, and thinning and gray hair.
  - Many individuals engage in age-concealing behaviors (coloring hair, cosmetic surgery).
  - Signs of aging are interpreted differently for men and women.
    - Facial wrinkles and gray hair symbolize strength and maturity in men, but may be perceived as unattractive in women.

Height and Weight
- Individuals lose height in middle age and many gain weight.
  - Adults lose about one-half inch of height per decade beginning in their forties.
  - Body fat accounts for 20 percent or more in middle age.
- Obesity is associated with health problems and a shorter life span.

Strength, Joints, and Bones
- Muscle strength decreases noticeably in the mid forties, with 10 to 15 percent loss between 35 and 60 years.
- Tendons and ligaments become less efficient in middle adult years.
- Maximum bone density occurs by the late thirties, with progressive loss of bone after that.
  - Women experience twice the rate of bone loss as men.

Vision
- Accommodation of the eye (the ability to focus and maintain an image on the retina) experiences its sharpest decline between 40 and 59 years of age.

Hearing
- Hearing may also start to decline by the age of 40.
- Sensitivity to high pitches usually declines first and men experience it sooner than women do.

Cardiovascular System
- The heart and coronary arteries change in midlife and cholesterol level increases with age.
- Blood pressure increases in the forties and fifties.

Sleep
- The total number of hours slept usually remains the same as in early adulthood, but beginning in the forties, wakeful periods are more frequent and there is less of the deepest type of sleep.

Health and Disease
Health
- In middle age, the frequency of accidents declines and individuals are less susceptible to colds and allergies.

Chronic Disorders
- A slow onset and long duration characterize **chronic disorders**.
- Chronic disorders rarely appear in early adulthood, increase in middle adulthood, and become more common in late adulthood.
- Arthritis is the leading chronic disorder in middle age, followed by hypertension.
  - Men have more fatal chronic disorders (coronary heart disease, cancers and stroke), women have more non-fatal ones (arthritis, varicose veins, and bursitis) in middle age.

Culture, Personality, Relationships, and Health
- Emotional stability and personality are related to health in middle adulthood.
- Healthy individuals aged 35 to 50 were also the most calm, self-controlled, and most responsible.
  Culture and Cardiovascular Disease
  - Culture plays an important role in coronary disease.
    - Research has found that Japanese men in San Francisco had more coronary heart disease than Japanese men in Honolulu and Japan.
      - As the Japanese men migrated farther away from Japan, their health practices, such as diet, changed.
  Type A/Type B Behavioral Patterns
  - **Type A behavior pattern**, a cluster of characteristics, involves being excessively competitive, hard-driven, impatient, and hostile. It is thought to be related to the incidence of heart disease.
  - **Type B behavior pattern** involves a relaxed and easygoing nature.
    - The Type A behavior pattern has been proposed as having a link with heart disease, but it is primarily the hostility dimension of the pattern that is associated with heart disease.
      - People can develop the ability to control their anger and develop more trust in others, which may reduce their risk for heart disease.
  Hardiness
  - **Hardiness** is a personality style characterized by a sense of commitment (rather than alienation), control (rather than powerlessness), and a perception of problems as challenges (rather than threats).
    - Hardiness is a buffer of stress and is related to reduced illness.
  - Hardiness, exercise, and social support can alleviate stress and maintain health.
  Health and Social Relationships
  - Health in middle age is linked to the current quality of social relationships and to developmental pathways of relationships.
  - Individuals, who were on a positive relationship pathway from childhood to middle age, had significantly fewer biological problems (cardiovascular disease, physical decline).

Mortality Rates
- In middle age, the leading causes of death, in order, are Heart disease, cancer, cerebrovascular disease, accidents, and pulmonary disease.
  - Men experience higher mortality rates than women for all of the leading causes of death.

Sexuality
- **Climacteric** is a term that is used to describe the midlife transition in which fertility declines.
  Menopause
  - **Menopause** is the time in middle age, usually in the late forties or early fifties, when a woman's menstrual periods cease completely.
    - The average age at which women have their last period is 52.
  - The vast majority of women do not have serious physical or psychological problems related to menopause.
    - It is difficult to determine the extent to which cross-cultural variations in the menopause experience are due to genetic, dietary, reproductive, or cultural factors.
  Hormone Replacement Therapy
  - The two main types of hormone replacement therapy are estrogen alone (ERT) and estrogen combined with a progestin (combined therapy or HRT).
    - HRT reduces bone loss if the HRT is maintained.
    - It is unclear whether HRT is linked with breast cancer or cardiovascular disease.
  - The American Geriatric Association recommends HRT in post-menopausal women.

Hormonal Changes in Middle-Aged Men
- Men do not loss their ability to father children, although their testosterone levels drop off.
- A male menopause, like the dramatic decline in estrogen, does not occur.
  - Men's sexual desires can lessen and some men experience erectile dysfunction.
    - Viagra has been proven effective for treating erectile dysfunction.

Sexual Attitudes and Behavior
- Although the ability of men and women to function sexually shows little biological decline in middle age, sexual activity usually occurs on a less frequent basis than in early adulthood.
  - Career interests, family matters, energy level, and routine may contribute to this decline. The majority of middle-aged adults show a moderate or strong interest in sex.
  - Having a live-in partner was a significant determining factor for women's sexual activity.

COGNITIVE DEVELOPMENT
Intelligence
Fluid and Crystallized Intelligence
- Horn argues that **crystallized intelligence**, an individual's accumulated information and verbal skills, continues to increase in the middle adulthood years.
- **Fluid intelligence**, one's ability to reason abstractly, begins to decline in middle age.
  - Horn utilized a cross-sectional design; thus, these differences might be due to cohort effects related to educational differences rather than to age.

The Seattle Longitudinal Study
- Schaie focused on individual change and stability in intelligence longitudinally.
- He examined vocabulary, verbal memory, numerical ability, spatial orientation, inductive reasoning, and perceptual speed.
  - For both women and men, peak performance on vocabulary, verbal memory, inductive reasoning, and spatial orientation occurred in middle adulthood.
  - Decline occurred in numerical ability and perceptual speed.
- Schaie found that when assessed longitudinally intellectual abilities are less likely to decline and are more likely even to improve than when assessed cross-sectionally in middle age.

Information Processing
Speed of Information Processing
- Speed of information processing, often assessed through reaction time, declines in midlife.
Memory
- While Schaie found that verbal memory increased in middle age, some researchers have found that memory declines in middle age.
  - Memory is more likely to decline in middle age when individuals don't use effective memory strategies, such as organization and imagery.
Expertise
- **Expertise** involves having an extensive, highly organized knowledge and understanding of a particular domain.
- Expertise often increases in the middle adulthood years.
- Among the strategies that distinguish experts from novice are:
  - Experts are more likely to rely on their accumulated experience to solve problems.
  - Experts often automatically process information and analyze it more efficiently when solving a problem in their domain than a novice does.
  - Experts have better strategies for solving problems in their domain than novices do.
  - Experts are more creative and flexible in solving problems in their domain than novices.
- Practical Problem Solving
  - Practical problem solving often increases through the forties and fifties as individuals accumulate practical experience.

CAREERS, WORK, AND LEISURE
Job Satisfaction
- Work satisfaction increases steadily throughout the work life (from age 20 to at least 60) for both college-educated and non-college-educated men and women.
  - Satisfaction probably increases due to pay increases, higher positions, and more job security.
- Researchers have found that the greatest physical and psychological well-being characterizes people who are doing as much paid work as they would like to.

Career Challenges and Changes
- The current middle-aged worker faces challenges such as the globalization of work, rapid developments in information technologies, downsizing of organizations, and early retirement.
- Some midlife career changes are self-motivated; others imposed by others.

Leisure
- **Leisure** refers to the pleasant times after work when individuals are free to pursue activities and interests of their own choosing—hobbies, sports, or reading, for example.
- Midlife may be an especially important time for leisure because of the physical changes that occur and because of preparations for an active retirement.
  - Men who took vacations (compared to whose who did not) were 21 percent less likely to die over the 9-year period tested, and 32 percent less likely to die from coronary heart disease.
    - The qualities that lead men to pass on a vacation tend to promote heart disease (not trusting anyone to fill your position when gone).

RELIGION AND MEANING IN LIFE
Religion and Adult Lives
- Religion is an important dimension of many peoples' lives worldwide.
  - Females show a stronger interest in religion than males do.
  - Americans are becoming less committed to particular religious denominations.
    - They are more tolerant of other faiths and more focused on their own spiritual journeys.
- It is important to consider individual differences in religious interest.

Religion and Health
Religion and Physical Health
- In some cases, religion can be negatively linked to physical health, as when cults or religious sects restrict individuals from obtaining medical care.
- In mainstream religion, religion usually shows either a positive association or no association with physical health.
  - Religion may promote physical health for several reasons including lifestyle issues, social networks, and coping with stress.
Coping
- Psychologists disagree as to the effectiveness of religious commitment as a coping strategy.
Happiness
- Happy people tend to have a meaningful religious faith, but it is important to remember that the link is correctional, not causal.

Meaning in Life
- Frankl believes that examining the finiteness of our existence leads to exploration of meaning in life.
- Faced with death of older relatives and less time to live themselves, many middle-aged individuals increasingly examine life's meaning.

440

Learning Objectives

1. Discuss changing middle age and the physical changes that take place during middle adulthood.
2. Elaborate on prominent health issues and chronic disorders that individuals face in middle adulthood.
3. Explain how culture, personality, and relationships are related to health.
4. Indicate the way in which mortality rates changed during the twentieth century.
5. Discuss the changes that characterize the sexuality of men and women as they go through middle adulthood.
6. Describe the cognitive changes in intelligence that take place during this middle adulthood.
7. Discuss how speed of processing, memory, expertise, and problem solving are impacted by the aging process.
8. Examine how career, work, and leisure change from early adulthood.
9. Discuss the role that religion, spirituality, and meaning play during this stage of life.

Key Terms

chronic disorders
climacteric
crystallized intelligence
expertise
fluid intelligence

hardiness
leisure
menopause
middle adulthood
Type A behavior pattern
Type B behavior pattern

Key People

Gilbert Brim
John Clausen
Nancy Denney
Victor Frankl

Meyer Friedman and Ray Rosenman
John Horn
K. Warner Schaie
Lois Verbrugge

Lecture Suggestions

Lecture Suggestion 1: Gender and Ethnic Differences in Health The purpose of this lecture is to examine research on gender differences and ethnic differences in health. Information for this lecture suggestion was obtained from Lemme's (1995) *Development in Adulthood* textbook. Unfortunately, women and minorities have been ignored in the vast majority of medical research until relatively recently. The National Institutes of Health has recently funded a large longitudinal study to examine the effects of diet, smoking, and other risk factors on the development of disease, stroke, osteoporosis, and breast and colon cancer among older women and minorities.

- Research has found that despite the fact that men and women experience the same kinds of health problems, rates of various diseases and conditions vary.
  - Men are more likely to develop and die from the most serious fatal diseases (i.e., coronary heart disease).
  - Women are more likely to develop less acute serious conditions (i.e., arthritis and osteoporosis).
  - Heart disease occurs earlier for men than women.
    - Women are twice as likely as men to have a second heart attack and to die from the heart attack.
    - Given that there is a misconception that heart disease is a man's disease, many women are most diagnosed appropriately.

- Biological and genetic factors influence the gender differences regarding health.
- Women are at greater risk for functional impairment than older men are.
  - Interestingly, when socioeconomic status is controlled, the gender difference in functional impairment is eliminated (Maddox, 1991).
- Whites have fewer health problems than minorities in the U.S.
  - For minorities, health problems tend to develop earlier in life, are more severe, and more often fatal.
    - Asians are the exception; Asian Americans have a longer life expectancy than Whites.
- It is essential to examine the influence of SES, as it is one of the strongest predictors of health and illness (Adler et al., 1994).
  - Individuals in higher SES tend to have better health.
  - Rates of illness and mortality for almost all diseases and conditions follow this trend.
  - Poverty often results in poor nutrition, substandard housing, inadequate prenatal care, and limited health care (Otten et al., 1990).
    - Almost one-third of the excess mortality of African Americans (age 35-54) can be attributed to six risk factors (high blood pressure, high cholesterol, overweight, diabetes, smoking, and alcohol) (Otten et al., 1990).
      - The first four risk factors can be partly attributed to heredity, though lifestyle also plays a role in these factors as well.
  - Research has attempted to disentangle the SES-health relationship. How does SES influence the biological functions that determine health status?
    - It is important to examine health-related behaviors (Adler et al., 1994).
      - Smoking is inversely correlated with SES.
      - Physical activity and SES are positively correlated.
      - Some psychological variables (depression, hostility, and stress) are also inversely related to SES.
- Sources: Adler, N.E., Boyce, T., Chesney, M.A., Cohen, S., Folkman, S., Kahn, R.L., & Syme, S.L. (1994). Socioeconomic status and health: The challenge of the gradient. *American Psychologist, 49*, 15-24. Lemme, B.H. (1995). *Development in adulthood*. Boston: Allyn and Bacon. Maddox, G.L. (1991). Aging with a difference. Generations, 15, 7-10. Otten, M.W., Teutsch, S.M., Williamson, D.F., & Marks, J.S. (1990). The effect of known risk factors on the excess mortality of black adults in the United States. *Journal of the American Medical Association, 263*, 845-850.

Lecture Suggestion 2: The Concept of Stress This lecture can be used to examine the effects of stress on health. Knowing how the body responds to stress may help students see the connection between tension and disease. According to Hans Selye (1976), the physiological response to stress follows a predictable course as it goes through a series of stages. In the first stage, the alarm stage, the autonomic nervous system is activated, adrenaline begins to flow, cardiac output increases, blood pressure rises, the respiratory rate increases, and the pupils dilate. The body is ready to fight, flight, or fright (between fight and flight). This stage may last for just a few minutes or may go on for 24 hours or more.

In the next stage, the resistance stage, the body adapts to the stressor. Hormones are released to help cope with the physiological changes that are occurring and efforts are made to limit the stress response as much as possible. The resistance stage may last for a brief time or for years, depending on the nature of the stressor. A near car accident produces a residual response for about 20 minutes. A terminal illness may put the body in a resistance mode until death.

In the third stage of the stress response, the adaptation qualities of the body are depleted. The stage is called exhaustion and it is characterized by the development of a severe illness. The body can no longer fight off the stressor. The immune system is weakened. If the stress is not relieved, the body will eventually die. If the stressor is removed, the exhaustion stage serves as the beginning stage on the road to recovery. Repeated exposures to stressors that cause the exhaustion stage diminish the body's reserves and eventually lead to death.

Though almost everybody responds to stress in the same way, not everybody perceives the same activities or events to be stressful. One woman may experience severe stress at the loss of her husband in an automobile accident. Another woman may actually recover more quickly from stress due to the loss of her husband after a long illness. Thus, it is the perception of the event, not the event itself, that leads to the physiological response to stress.

Lazarus and Folkman (1984) argue one's cognitive interpretation of the situation determines whether that situation will produce stress for an individual. The person first engages in primary appraisal which is the assessment of an event to determine whether its implications are positive, negative, or neutral. Then, the individual engages in secondary appraisal which is the assessment of whether one coping abilities and resources are adequate to overcome the harm, threat, or challenge posed by the potential stressor.

Though individuals will appraise situations differently, research has found some factors that increase the likelihood that a situation will be perceived as stressful.
- Situations that produce negative emotions are more likely to produce stress.
- Situations that are uncontrollable or unpredictable are more likely to produce stress.
- Ambiguous situations are more likely to produce stress.
- When an individual is required to accomplish simultaneous tasks, stress is more likely to occur.
- Sources: Lazarus, R. & Folkman, S. (1984). *Stress, appraisal, and coping*. New York: Springer. Selye, H. (1976). *The stress of life*. New York: McGraw-Hill.

Lecture Suggestion 3: Work, Leisure, and Intellectual Growth The purpose of this lecture is to expand on Santrock's discussion of work and leisure. Kohn (1980) found that there is a reciprocal relationship between the degree of thought and independent judgment that work requires (substantive complexity) and a person's flexibility in coping with intellectual demands. People with more complex work requirements tend to be more cognitively flexible and they are more likely to continue to engage in complex work. There are several reasons why work complexity is tied to cognitive functioning. Mastery and success of complex work may increase individuals' confidence and cognitive abilities. Complex work may also broaden their horizons by opening them up to new experiences and encourage them to be more self-directed. Individuals who engage in complex work also are more likely to pursue intellectually demanding leisure activities. Several hypotheses have been proposed to explain the choice of work and leisure activities (Papalia et al., 1996).
- Spillover hypothesis: Learning is carried over from work to leisure or because personality factors influence the selection of leisure activities and work.
- Compensation hypothesis: Individuals pursue leisure activities to make up for what is missing at work.
- Resource provision-depletion hypothesis: "Work promotes or constrains certain kinds of leisure activities by providing or depleting resources of time, energy, and money" (Papalia et al., 1996, p. 304).
- Segmentation hypothesis: Work choices and leisure activities are independent.
- Sources: Kohn, M.L. (1980). Job complexity and adult personality. In N.J. Smelser & E.H. Erikson (Eds.), *Themes of work and love in adulthood*. Cambridge, MA: Harvard University Press. Papalia, D.E., Camp, C.J., & Feldman, R.D. (1996). *Adult development and aging*. New York: McGraw-Hill.

Lecture Suggestion 4: Social Structures Regarding Work, Leisure, and Education in Adulthood
This lecture summarizes Papalia and her colleagues' interpretation of Riley's (1994) work on social structures in adulthood. Riley proposed that there are two contrasting social structures regarding work, leisure, and education. Traditionally, age has determined one's role in industrialized societies. Traditional age-differentiated structures exemplify this emphasis on age. The primary role for young people is that of student with a focus on education. The primary role for young and middle-aged adults is that of worker. Then in late adulthood, adults focus on retirement and leisure activities.

Riley stresses that this structure is outdated. Society has changed and life expectancy has increased. It does not make sense to her that many adults will work like crazy in middle age and then spend one-third of their adult lifetime in retirement. This results in a structural lag, as many older adults can continue to contribute to society, yet opportunities are limited. The singular emphasis on either education, work, or leisure at each of these life stages is disadvantageous. People are not able to enjoy each period of life as much as they might if they were more diversified. In addition, they may be ill-prepared for the next phase if they focus on only one of these roles.

Riley encourages an age-integrated society. All roles (work, education, and leisure) should be open to all ages. People of all ages should be able to enjoy periods of education, work, and leisure throughout their adulthood. Striving for lifelong learning is exciting. People may experience less stress in their work lives if they take time for leisure activities throughout the life span.

- Sources: Papalia, D.E., Camp, C.J., & Feldman, R.D. (1996). *Adult development and aging.* New York: McGraw-Hill. Riley, M.W. (1994). Aging and society: Past, present, and future. *The Gerontologist, 34,* 436-444.

Lecture Suggestion 5: Guest Lecture Idea Have two middle-aged men and two middle-aged women come to class to talk about their experiences during this time of life. In order to highlight the diversity of experiences during middle age, you may want to invite one single man, one married man, one woman who stays home during the day, and one woman in the workforce. Be sure to ask them to talk about both the pros and cons of this stage of life. They can talk about physical and cognitive changes they are currently experiencing. Before the day of the guest lecture, have students review Erikson's theory of psychosocial development and prepare questions for the guest speakers about generativity.

Classroom Activities

Classroom Activity 1: Type A Behavior Pattern This activity is a good way to highlight the theme of continuity versus discontinuity by addressing the roots of the Type A behavior pattern. Discuss the following points before having students divide into groups to discuss the questions below. Type A behaviors consist of time urgency, impatience, competitive achievement striving, and aggressiveness-hostility. Although usually discussed as an adult health concern because pessimistic Type A persons have higher coronary heart disease risks, researchers now know that many children exhibit Type A behaviors and usually carry these behaviors into adulthood (Matthews, 1982). For example, some 3-year-olds seem to display Type A behaviors. They act aggressively, show signs of impatience and restlessness such as squirming and sighing, set high standards for themselves, and are extremely competitive.

Discuss what factors lead to Type A behaviors in children. At this time, little is known about the role of genetic factors or temperament on Type A levels, but some research suggests that parent-child interactions influence the amount of Type A behaviors in children. In one study, Type A boys received fewer positive evaluations of their performances from their mothers than did other boys. Therefore, Type A boys had to work harder, more competitively, and more anxiously to receive their mothers' approval (Matthews, 1977). Divide students into groups and have them discuss the questions below.

- What are the advantages and disadvantages of Type A behavior in children?
- How do you think Type A behavior develops in young children?
- How could adults intervene with Type A children to minimize the negative consequences of this behavior?
- What similarities and differences would you expect in the expression of Type A behavior pattern across the life span?

Logistics:
- Group size: Small group.
- Approximate time: Small group (20 minutes).
- Sources: Matthews, K. A. (1977). Caregiver-child interactions and the Type A coronary-prone behavior pattern. *Child Development, 48,* 1752-1756. Matthews, K. A. (1982). Psychological perspectives on the Type A behavior pattern. *Psychological Bulletin, 91,* 293-323.

Classroom Activity 2: Menopause The purpose of this exercise is highlight individual variability regarding menopause. Encourage your students to interview middle-age women about their experiences and attitudes about menopause. Encourage them to ask about expectations and attitudes about menopause for women who have not yet experienced menopause. Are they excited about it? Will they be relieved when it is over? If the women are postmenopausal, have your students ask about whether the women's expectations were realized by the actual process of menopause. Did they experience any physical or psychological symptoms? Have your students get into small groups to discuss the results of their interviews.

Logistics:
- Group size: Small group.
- Approximate time: Small group (20 minutes).
- Sources: Matthews, K. A. (1992). Myths and realities of the menopause. *Psychosomatic Medicine, 54*, 1-9

Classroom Activity 3: Prayer and Stress Most psychology classes avoid the topics of religion and spirituality, but students generally like to discuss them. We recommend you use passages from popular writers such as Scott Peck (1978) or Harold Kushner (1989) as a starting point for class discussion about religion and spirituality in terms of how they relate to the experience of stress and stress management.

Research on the use of transcendental meditation indicated that meditation with a mantra induces a relaxation response (i.e., lower metabolic rate, slower heart rate, lower blood pressure, slower breathing). The researchers looked at the effects of short prayers from the Christian and Jewish traditions as well (e.g., "Hail Mary, full of grace," "Shalom," "The Lord is my Shepherd"). These phrases also brought about the relaxation responses. Using traditional Western prayers worked better than meditation using the word "one" because subjects stuck with the meditation longer using prayers. When using longer prayers, the researchers found subjects reporting a "praying high." People high in spirituality (i.e., the feeling that there is a higher being) score higher on psychological health and have fewer stress-related symptoms.

Divide students into groups and have them discuss religion's effect on their own experience of stress. Do they agree with the researchers discussed? If they believe meditation reduces stress, they should discuss why this might be so. What other techniques do they find help to relieve stress?
Logistics:
- Group size: Small group.
- Approximate time: Small group (20 minutes).
- Sources: Kiesling, S., & Harris, T. G. (1989, Oct). The prayer war. *Psychology Today*, 65-66. Kushner, H. (1989). *Who needs God*. New York: Summit Books. Peck, M. S. (1978). *The road less traveled: A new psychology of love, traditional values and spiritual growth*. NY: Touchstone/Simon & Schuster.

Classroom Activity 4: The Song of Developmental Psychology Pick a currently popular song that addresses a theme relevant for people in midlife and analyze it in a fashion similar to the Images of Life-Span Development box that introduces chapter 16. Use the analysis suggested for Research Project 1 as a model. (This would be good preliminary instruction for that project.)
Logistics:
- Group size: Full class.
- Approximate time: Full class (25 minutes).

Classroom Activity 5: Wise Consumers of Information Find an article about middle age in the lifestyles section of your local newspaper, or in the similar section of a national magazine such as *Time* or *Newsweek*. Have your class read the article, then, in a subsequent class, take them through a review of it using the following guidelines for being a wise consumer of information about life-span development (Santrock, 1997). This could be a good way to prepare students for the second critical thinking multiple-choice question.

Guidelines for Being a Wise Consumer of Information:

- Not all information about life-span development in the media comes from professions with excellent credentials.
- Journalists are not trained as scientists, therefore the material they are reporting on may be difficult for them to interpret correctly.
- The media often wants to present sensationalized versions of the truth to boost ratings. For example, they may read a research article about theories for successful aging and then present a news report entitled "How to live to be 130."
- It may be difficult to accurately summarize a complicated research report in the brief amount of time or space news stories get, so important information may be left out.
- Know how to distinguish between nomothetic research and ideographic needs.
- Recognize how easy it is to overgeneralize from a small or clinical sample.
- Be aware that a single study is usually not the defining word about any aspect of development.
- Remember that causal conclusions cannot be made from correlational studies.
- Always consider the source of the information and evaluate its credibility.

Logistics:
- Group size: Full class.
- Approximate time: Full class (25 minutes).
- Source: Santrock, J. (1997). *Life-span development,* (6th ed.). Madison, WI: Brown & Benchmark.

Classroom Activity 6: Critical Thinking Multiple-Choice Questions and Suggested Answers Discuss the critical thinking multiple-choice questions presented as **Handout 1**. The answers to these questions are presented as **Handout 2**. You may find it necessary to review the material from chapter 1 on developmental issues to help students orient themselves to the first question. Unless you have made a point of keeping them aware of these issues, their ability to recognize them will be "rusty."

Question 2 is something completely new among the critical thinking multiple-choice questions that we have written for previous chapters. Again, unless you have been systematically reminding your students about the guidelines for being a consumer of information about life-span development, you will find them at something of a loss when confronted with this assignment. You may want to precede it with the classroom activity suggested above (Classroom Activity 5: Wise Consumers of Information), which involves analyzing a newspaper or magazine article. Another option is to simply lecture on the guidelines for being a wise consumer of information.

Question 3 presents some of the difficulties the parallel exercise for chapter 15 did. Prepare students again to determine how Santrock is using statements in his presentation in order to determine what are observations, inferences, and assumptions.

Logistics:
- Materials: Handout 1 (the critical thinking multiple-choice questions) and Handout 2 (answers).
- Group size: Small groups to discuss the questions, then a full class discussion.
- Approximate time: Small groups (15 minutes), full class discussion of any questions (15 minutes).

Classroom Activity 7: Critical Thinking Essay Questions and Suggestions for Helping Students Answer the Essays Discuss students' answers to the critical thinking essay questions presented in **Handout 3**. The purpose of this exercise is threefold. First, answering the essay questions further facilitates students' understanding of concepts in chapter 16. Second, this type of essay question affords the students an opportunity to apply the concepts to their own lives, which will facilitate their retention of the material. Third, the essay format also gives students practice expressing themselves in written form. Ideas to help students answer the critical thinking essay questions are provided as **Handout 4**.

Logistics:
- Materials: Handout 3 (essay questions) and Handout 4 (helpful suggestions for the answers).
- Group size: Individual, then full class.
- Approximate time: Individual (60 minutes), full class discussion of any questions (30 minutes).

Personal Applications

Personal Application 1: Young Whippersnappers The purpose of this exercise is to get students thinking about middle age. The perception of "middle age" has changed dramatically over the years as the average life span has increased, and older adults are remaining healthy and ambitious long after they were just a generation or two ago.

- Instructions for Students: Before you read this chapter, write about your perceptions of middle age. Don't try to anticipate what your book will teach you, simply discuss how you view the time of life commonly referred to as "middle age." When does it begin? How long does it last? What do you expect to be doing? What do you expect you will have accomplished by this time? What do you hope to accomplish by that time? What do you hope to accomplish during that time? What do you expect your psychological mind set about life will be? Are you looking forward to middle age or dreading it? Why?

- Use in the Classroom: Prior to beginning this chapter, create a chart on the board for all the relevant issues regarding middle age. Ask students their opinions, thoughts, and feelings about each factor. Map out their perceptions of middle age, and see how they vary (or not) among students. When do they think middle age is? How long does it last? What should people be able to do physically and cognitively at this time of life. What are their limitations due to being "middle aged"? What do they think people in this stage of life experience emotionally, socially, and sexually? What are their biggest concerns about reaching this stage of life? What do they most look forward to about reaching this stage? Discuss the reasoning behind their views.

Personal Application 2: Friends in High Places This exercise affords students an opportunity to think about individuals in the stage of life known as "middle age." There are many new conceptions about individuals at this stage of life with regard to positive functioning, yet many aspects of life begin to change and even decline.

- Instructions to students: Think about the people you know who are in middle adulthood. This may be your parents, your friends' parents, aunts and uncles, instructors, and co-workers. What do you know of their lives? How do they exhibit the characteristics discussed in your textbook related to middle age? Do you find a lot of consistency among them, or do they represent a wide range of individual differences? If you observe differences among them, what do you think accounts for the differences? Be sure to consider both current and past influences on behavior and mental functioning. Has thinking about these individuals with regard to the information from your text changed your perceptions of middle adulthood? Why or why not, and in what ways?

- Use in the Classroom: Have your students share their stories of those they know in middle adulthood. You may even have a student or two currently experiencing this stage of life, or you yourself may be in middle adulthood. Share your stories, mapping reality onto the information discussed in the text. What about this stage of life surprises your students the most?

Research Project Ideas

Research Project 1: Song Lyric Values Students should work on this project in pairs. Instruct them to locate the lyrics of five currently popular songs and five songs that were popular at least 10 years ago (they should stick to one type of music, e.g., rock, country, or folk, for both time periods). Have them work with their partner to evaluate each set of lyrics for: sexism, ageism, attitudes toward love, work, and life, and general values (**Handout 5**).

Students should rate each song as very positive (5), positive (4), neutral (3), negative (2), very negative (1), and absent (0) in each of the areas listed on the data sheet (**Handout 6**). Then for each group (songs popular now versus songs popular 10 years ago), add the five ratings together (0-25 total). Instruct students to keep brief notes about specific lyrics for discussion purposes. Have students write a brief report of their findings. They should answer the following questions in their report, using the information they gathered to support their answers.

Questions:
- What attitudes/values have remained consistently positive/negative over the years? Which have changed considerably?
- What external, world/national events occurred during each time period that might have influenced popular song lyrics?
- What values seem to appeal to today's middle-aged people? Why?
- How do you think song lyrics will change in the next 10 years? Why?
- Use in the Classroom: Students can provide many examples of song lyrics when discussing this project. Discuss related topics such as censorship of song lyrics for suggestivity or obscene language as well. Ask the students for examples of their all-time favorite lyrics, and their reasons for these preferences.

Research Project 2: Archival Research Throughout the text, there are several references to the importance of understanding cohort effects on the results of research studies. To learn about the power of the socioeconomic, religious, and political climate on attitudes, have students go to the library to do some archival research (**Handout 7**).

First, they should find out what popular magazines (e.g., *Reader's Digest*, *Woman's Day*, etc.) have been around since at least 1955, even earlier if possible. Next, they should choose five of these magazines and count the number of articles about sex that appeared in each magazine during the years 1955, 1965, 1975, 1985, 1995, and today. Also students should keep a list of the titles of the articles they find.

Handout 8 can be used to record the relevant information and to assist the students with their analyses. Instruct the students to compute averages for the rows and columns of numbers and enter these at the far right side of their table and at the bottom of their table. Next, they should use the number of articles for each magazine in each year to come to a conclusion about how attitudes toward sex and dissemination of information about sex have changed over the years. They will want to create a graph using the data they collected. They should summarize their results in a brief paper in which they answer at least the following questions.

Questions:
- How did the number of articles change over the years?
- How did the number of articles vary from one magazine to the next?
- Were the changes over the years the same or different for each magazine?
- What did you learn from the titles of the articles?
- Interpret your findings in terms of what you have learned in your text about changing attitudes toward sex and sexuality, and in terms of what your know about the intended audiences of each magazine.
- What is your evaluation of this method of finding out about sex attitudes and dissemination of information about sex?
- Use in Classroom: Have students report their findings. Perhaps an effective format would be to have groups of students work together on the project and then report their findings during something like a poster session at a research conference. To help motivate the students, you may want to invite a few colleagues to attend the "poster session" and judge the quality of the work. You may even want to offer an award for the best poster.

Film and Video List

The following films and videos supplement the content of chapter 16. Contact information for film distributors can be found at the front of this Instructor's Manual under Film and Video Sources.

Controlling Cholesterol (Films for the Humanities and Sciences, 28 minutes). This video discusses ways of preventing cardiovascular disease through diet and lower cholesterol levels.

For Richer, For Poorer (National Film Board of Canada, 30 minutes). This documentary tells the story of the realities of a woman's life after a marriage breakdown.

Reducing the Risks of Cardiovascular Disease (Films for the Humanities and Sciences, 29 minutes). This program provides an overview of how the heart functions and why a healthy heart is important. Heart problems are presented and emphasis is placed on prevention.

Web Site Suggestions

The URLs for general sites, common to all chapters, can be found at the front of this Instructor's Manual under Useful Web Sites. At the time of publication, all sites were current and active, however, please be advised that you may occasionally encounter a dead link.

The General Intelligence Factor
http://www.sciam.com/specialissues/1198intelligence/1198gottfred.html

Health Statistics Sources: Morbidity and Mortality Statistics
http://www.nlm.nih.gov/nichsr/stats/morbmort.html

Men's Health
http://dir.yahoo.com/Health/Men_s_Health/

Midlife Career Change
http://www.bestyears.com/careerchange.htm

Stress and Health Psychology
http://www.abacon.com/lefton/stress.html

Women's Health
http://dir.yahoo.com/Health/Women_s_Health/

Critical Thinking Multiple-Choice Questions

1. Chapter 16 includes a discussion of how lifestyle, health, and personality relate to each other. Which developmental issue (see chapter 1) seems to be emphasized the most in this discussion? Circle the letter of the best answer and explain why it is the best answer and why each other answer is not as good.

   a. continuity versus discontinuity
   b. early versus later experience
   c. stability versus change
   d. the influence of biological, social, and cognitive processes
   e. nature versus nurture

2. An important topic in chapter 16 is menopause. Apply Santrock's guidelines for being a wise consumer of information about life-span development that were explained in class. People generally have many misconceptions about this life transition in middle adulthood, based on flaws in their sources of information. For this question, indicate whether and how Santrock applies each of the guidelines listed below in his discussion of menopause.

   a. Know how to distinguish between nomothetic research and idiographic needs.
   b. Recognize how easy it is to overgeneralize from a small or clinical sample.
   c. Be aware that a single study is usually not the defining word about any aspect of life-span development.
   d. Remember that causal conclusions cannot be made from correlational studies.
   e. Always consider the source of the information and evaluate its credibility.

3. Santrock discusses the importance of leisure activities in middle adulthood. Which of the following statements best represents an inference, rather than an assumption or an observation? Circle the letter of the best answer and explain why it is the best answer and why each other answer is not as good.

   a. There is no one ideal leisure activity for all individuals in middle adulthood.
   b. Many adults view leisure as boring and unnecessary due to a strong work ethic.
   c. Men who went on an annual vacation were less likely to die over the study period.
   d. Not taking vacations causes early death.
   e. Leisure activities can ease the transition into retirement.

Suggested Answers to Critical Thinking Multiple-Choice Questions

1. Chapter 16 includes a discussion of how lifestyle, health, and personality relate to each other. Which developmental issue (see chapter 1) seems to be emphasized the most in this discussion? Circle the letter of the best answer and explain why it is the best answer and why each other answer is not as good.

    a. Continuity versus discontinuity is not the best answer. This issue involves determining the extent to which development proceeds in stages, or, more directly, the extent to which it is true that there are qualitatively distinct periods of development in the life span. Stages do not figure in the discussion of lifestyle, health, and personality.

    b. Early versus later experience is not the best answer. Although there is discussion of how personality characteristics and behavior patterns are related to long-term health status, the issue appears to be the consistency of personality or behavior pattern. For example, in some cases, changed patterns reduce risk, something that should not happen if the emphasis were on early versus later experience.

    c. Stability versus change is the best answer. The clue is that the greatest part of the discussion centers on personality types that are prone to health risks. If these are stable, so is the risk; if these change, the risk changes.

    d. The influence of biological, social, and cognitive processes is not the best answer. Although there is discussion of biological (temperamental and genetic influence), social (cultural factors), and cognitive processes as factors in the relationship between personality, health, and lifestyle, these factors are not found as broadly across the various topics discussed in this section as the focus on personality type or behavior pattern.

    e. Nature versus nurture is not the best answer. Again, nature/nurture issues are discussed with respect to some of the topics, but not as pervasively as the issues of personality type and behavior pattern.

2. An important topic in chapter 16 is menopause. Apply Santrock's guidelines for being a wise consumer of information about life-span development that were explained in class. People generally have many misconceptions about this life transition in middle adulthood, based on flaws in their sources of information. For this question, indicate whether and how Santrock applies each of the guidelines listed below in his discussion of menopause.

    a. Santrock does not seem to apply the know how to distinguish between nomothetic research and idiographic needs guideline explicitly, but it seems to be applied implicitly when he begins his discussion of menopause with comments and illustrative cases about the diversity of menopause's effects. The reader is given permission, so to speak, to realize that generalizations from research may not apply to herself.

    b. Santrock applies the recognize how easy it is to overgeneralize from a small or clinical sample guideline in his discussion of Sheehy's work, but makes no mention of sample size for the estrogen replacement therapy research.

    c. Santrock is silent on the be aware that a single study is usually not the defining word about any aspect of life-span development guideline. He relies on one large-scale study, thus indirectly addressing "b" to make generalizations about menopause's effects, and mentions that a few studies provide the basis of concern about estrogen replacement therapy. However, he does not fully and directly address the issue of need for multiple studies on menopause's effects.

d. Santrock does not address the issue of <u>remember that causal conclusions cannot be made from correlational studies</u> directly, even though it appears that most of the data forming the background for this section are correlational. This is an important issue when discussing the questions of whether biological changes produce psychological changes, especially when something like menopause has such pervasive social meaning (which itself could cause the psychological and behavioral changes associated with menopause).

e. Santrock comes close on the <u>always consider the source of the information and evaluate its credibility</u> guideline. He nearly suggests that Sheehy's work is not credible, but stops short of suggesting the author herself is not credible. Otherwise, nothing is said about the credibility of his sources.

3. Santrock discusses the importance of leisure activities in middle adulthood. Which of the following statements best represents an inference, rather than an assumption or an observation? Circle the letter of the best answer and explain why it is the best answer and why each other answer is not as good.

a. The statement <u>there is no one ideal leisure activity for all individuals in middle adulthood</u> is an assumption that Santrock alludes to. Santrock indicates that individuals choose different leisure activities. The assumption that there is one ideal activity has not been tested. Given the individual variability in middle adulthood, one would assume that there would not be one activity that would suffice for all midlife adults (or individuals at any age).

b. This statement <u>many adults view leisure as boring and unnecessary due to a strong work ethic</u> is an assumption. Santrock attempts to explain the observation that many American adults find leisure activities boring and unnecessary by mentioning the traditional work ethic of many Americans to work hard to achieve.

c. The statement that <u>men who went on an annual vacation were less likely to die over the study period</u> is an observation. Gump and Matthews found that vacationless men were also more likely to die from coronary heart diseases.

d. The statement that <u>not taking vacations causes early death</u> is the best answer as it is an inference. Gump and Matthews did not state that not taking vacations causes men to die earlier, however they did find that behaviors that sometimes have been described as part of the Type A behavioral pattern were found in men who did not take vacations.

e. The statement that <u>leisure activities can ease the transition into retirement</u> is an assumption. While this idea sounds good, it has not been tested empirically, thus it is an assumption.

Handout 3 (CA 7)

Critical Thinking Essay Questions

Your answers to these kinds of questions demonstrate an ability to comprehend and apply ideas discussed in this chapter.

1. Define middle age, and explain its changing nature.

2. Compare the physical changes that occur in middle adulthood to the physical changes that occur in early adulthood.

3. Define and distinguish between Type A behavior, Type B behavior, and hardiness, and explain the relationship between these personality factors and health.

4. Describe the biological changes in sexuality that occur during middle age, and evaluate stereotypes about midlife sexuality based on this information.

5. Characterize the nature and extent of heterosexual activity during middle age.

6. Compare and contrast the research findings on cognitive changes in adulthood relative to the research design used to collect the data. Describe how the research design influenced the findings.

7. Describe your own personal work pathway to date, and then project it into the future. Incorporate a discussion of your projected (or past) job satisfaction and midlife career change into your answer.

8. Discuss your present leisure interests. Also indicate and explain which of these interests you expect to change and which you expect to remain stable as you age.

9. Describe middle-aged adults' involvement in religion and discuss the benefits they receive from their involvement.

Ideas to Help You Answer Critical Thinking Essay Questions

1. Imagine you are a motivational speaker who talks to adults on the verge of "midlife." Your goal is to inform them about the new developmental journey they are about to embark on, and explain, fully and honestly, its changing nature.

2. Begin by identifying the areas/aspects of the body that change during each of these stages. Acknowledge whether they are exactly the same, or if one stage has more areas affected by physical change.

3. Distinguish between these factors through the use of descriptions of individuals with these personality types. What similarities and differences exist between them? After you compare your people, go further and make more specific comments about the relationship between these personalities and health.

4. Approach this assignment by addressing the changes characteristic of men and women. What areas overlap? Which gender has more stereotypes related to them and why?

5. Do this assignment by describing what a middle-aged couple might do on a date. Consider both a married and unmarried couple and compare.

6. Begin by delineating the aspects of cognitive change, then present each research design used to explore them. Conclude your discussion by addressing the possible confounds inherent in each design, resulting in its particular finding.

7. Make sure you include your college "career" as part of your work pathway. Present courses you've taken and plan to take, as well as your major and any internships or coops you've participated in or plan to pursue.

8. As you discuss your leisure interests, talk about when they began and what inspired your interest in them. Also talk about the changes that have already taken place in your various interests over your lifetime. What caused the changes? Do you think these same factors will influence changes in the future, or will new influences be present to alter your leisure interests?

9. After you've addressed this issue, consider the opposite scenario. What might the impact/effects be on the issues accompanying middle age for those who do not embrace and practice religion?

Song Lyric Values

Work on this project with one of your classmates. Locate the lyrics of five currently popular songs and five songs that were popular at least 10 years ago (stick to one type of music, e.g., rock, country, or folk, for both time periods). Work with your partner as a team to evaluate each set of lyrics for: sexism, ageism, attitudes toward love, work, and life, and general values.

Rate each song as very positive (5), positive (4), neutral (3), negative (2), very negative (1), and absent (0) in each of the areas listed on the data sheet (Handout 6). Then for each group (songs popular now versus songs popular 10 years ago), add the five ratings together (0-25 total). Keep brief notes about specific lyrics for discussion purposes. Write a brief report of your findings. Be sure to answer the following questions in your report, using the information you gathered to support your answers.

Questions:

- What attitudes/values have remained consistently positive/negative over the years? Which have changed considerably (either higher or lower)?

- What external, world/national events occurred during each time period that might have influenced popular song lyrics?

- What values seem to appeal to today's middle-aged people? Why?

- How do you think song lyrics will change in the next 10 years? Why?

Data Sheet for the Song Lyric Values Project

Observational area:	Current songs	Older songs (year)
Attitudes toward females:		
Attitudes toward males:		
Attitudes toward children:		
Attitudes toward teenagers:		
Attitudes toward adults:		
Attitudes toward older adults:		
Attitudes toward love:		
Attitudes toward family:		
Attitudes toward work:		
Attitudes toward country:		
Values:		
Wealth:		
Achievement:		

Handout 6 (RP 1) continued

Observational area:	Current songs	Older songs (year)
Education:		
Government:		
Serving others:		
Change:		
Drugs:		
Sex:		
Conflict:		
Beauty:		
Happiness:		
Self-sacrifice:		
Marriage:		

Comments:

Archival Research

Throughout the text, there are several references to the importance of understanding cohort effects on the results of research studies. To learn about the power of the socioeconomic, religious, and political climate on attitudes, go to the library and do some archival research.

First, find out what popular magazines (e.g., *Reader's Digest*, *Woman's Day*, etc.) have been around since at least 1955, even earlier if possible. Choose five of these magazines and count the number of articles about sex that appeared in each in 1955, 1965, 1975, 1985, 1995, and today. Also, keep a list of the titles of the articles you find. Use the table presented as Handout 8 to record the information. Enter the number of articles you found for each magazine for each year. Compute averages for the rows and columns of numbers and enter these at the far right side of your table and at the bottom of your table.

Use the number of articles for each magazine in each year to come to a conclusion about how attitudes toward sex and dissemination of information about sex have changed over the years. You should first generalize about these using the data for all magazines (column averages). Then, compare averages for each magazine (row averages). Finally, plot the individual article counts for each magazine over the years on a graph (use years as the horizontal or x-axis).

Summarize your results in a brief paper in which you answer at least the following questions.

Questions:

- How did the number of articles change over the years?

- How did the number of articles vary from one magazine to the next?

- Were the changes over the years the same or different for each magazine?

- What did you learn from the titles of the articles?

- Interpret your findings in terms of what you have learned in your text about changing attitudes toward sex and sexuality, and in terms of what you know about the intended audience of each magazine.

- What is your evaluation of this method of finding out about attitudes toward sex and dissemination of information about sex?

Data Table for the Archival Research Project

List the names of the magazines in the far left column. Then enter the number of articles you found about sex for each magazine for each year.

	1955	1965	1975	1985	1995	Today
magazine title #1						
magazine title #2						
magazine title #3						
magazine title #4						
magazine title #5						
Average:						

Chapter 17: Socioemotional Development in Middle Adulthood

Total Teaching Package Outline

Lecture Outline	Resource References
Socioemotional Development in Middle Adulthood	PowerPoint Presentation: See www.mhhe.com Cognitive Maps: See Appendix A
Personality Theories and Development in Middle Adulthood	CA1: Interviews about Middle Adulthood PA1: A Picture's Worth a Thousand Words F/V: Ageless America WS: Research on Successful Midlife Development
• Adult Stage Theories -Erikson's Stage of Generativity versus Stagnation	LO1 OHT181 & IB: Paths to Developing Generativity LS1: Trait Versus Stage Theories RP1: Adult Stage Theories in Biographies
-Levinson's Seasons of a Man's Life	LO2 OHT182 & IB: Adult Development Stages
-How Pervasive Are Midlife Crises?	LO3 LS2: Men's Psychological Health PA2: My Hero F/V: Doctor, Lawyer, Indian Chief F/V: The Midlife Passage WS: Midlife Crisis: Recent Research
-Individual Variations	
• Life-Events Approach	LO4
• Contexts of Midlife Development -Historical Contexts (Cohort Effects)	LO5
-Gender Contexts	CA2: Women in the Workforce
-Cultural Contexts	CA3: Middle Adulthood in the Movies
Stability and Change • Longitudinal Studies	LO6 LS3: Compare, Contrast, and Apply Longitudinal Studies
-Neugarten's Kansas City Study	
-Costa and McCrae's Baltimore Study	IB: The Big Five Factors of Personality
-Berkeley Longitudinal Studies	
-Helson's Mills College Study	WS: Ravenna Helson's Research
• Conclusions	

Close Relationships	

• Love and Marriage at Midlife
    -Affectionate Love
    -Marriage and Divorce
	LO7
	
	LO8
	LS4: Divorce at Midlife

• The Empty Nest and Its Refilling	LO9
• Parenting Conceptions	LS5: Parent Care in the Context of Women's Multiple Roles
• Sibling Relationships and Friendships	LO10LS6: Siblings
• Intergenerational Relationships	LO11 PA3: Generation Gap F/V: Parenting Our Parents WS: Sandwich Generation
Review	CA4: Critical Thinking Multiple-Choice CA5: Critical Thinking Essays RP2: Your Life Review

Chapter Outline

PERSONALITY THEORIES AND DEVELOPMENT IN MIDDLE AGE
    Adult Stage Theories
        Erikson's Stage of Generativity versus Stagnation
- Erikson's seventh stage, generativity vs. stagnation, occurs in middle adulthood.
  - Generativity encompasses adults' desire to leave a legacy of themselves to the next generation.
  - Stagnation develops when individuals sense that they have done nothing for the next generation.
- Four types of generativity have been identified:
  - Biological generativity: adults conceive and give birth to an infant.
  - Parental generativity: adults provide nurturance and guidance to children.
  - Work generativity: adults develop skills that are passed down to others.
  - Cultural generativity: adults create, renovate, or conserve some aspect of culture.
- Research has supported that generativity is an important dimension of middle age.

        Levinson's Seasons of a Man's Life
- Levinson developed his stage/transition theory based on interviews with 40 middle-aged men.
- He emphasized that developmental tasks must be mastered at each of these stages.
  - Changes in middle age focus on four conflicts:
    - being young vs. being old,
    - being destructive vs. being constructive,
    - being masculine vs. being feminine,
    - being attached vs. being separated from others.

How Pervasive Are Midlife Crises?
- Levinson views midlife as a crisis, believing that the middle-aged adult is suspended between the past and the future. Further, trying to cope with this gap threatens life's continuity.
  - He proposed that a majority of Americans, especially men, experience a midlife crisis.
- However, researchers have found that the incidence of midlife crises has been exaggerated.
  - The stage theories place too much emphasis on crises, especially midlife crises.
- There often is considerable individual variation in the way people experience midlife.

Individual Variations
- In the individual variation view, middle-aged adults interpret and give meaning to their lives.
  - The ability to set aside unproductive worries and preoccupations is an important factor in functioning under stress.

Life-Events Approach
- In the early version of the life-events approach, life events (marriage, divorce, and loss of a spouse) were viewed as taxing circumstances for individuals, forcing them to change their personality.
- The **contemporary life-events approach** emphasizes that how life events influence the individual's development depends not only on the life event, but also on mediating factors (physical health, family supports), the individual's adaptation to the life event (appraisal of the threat, coping strategies), the life-stage context, and the sociohistorical context.
  - Critics claim that this approach places too much emphasis on change and not enough on stability.
  - Other critics claim that daily stresses are ignored.

Contexts of Midlife Development
Historical Contexts (Cohort Effects)
- Neugarten states that the social environment of a particular cohort can alter its social clock.
  - **Social clock** is the timetable according to which individuals are expected to accomplish life's tasks (getting married, having children, and establishing a career).
    - Social clocks guide our lives and can cause stress if one's life is not synchronized with them.
    - There is little agreement with respect to order and particular ages for achievements.

Gender Contexts
- Critics say that the stage theories of adult development have a male bias.
  - They place too much emphasis on achievement and careers.
  - Stage theories do not adequately address women's concerns about relationships, interdependence, child rearing, and caring.
- As the roles of women have become more complex and varied, defining a normative sequence of development for them has become more difficult.
- Midlife is a heterogeneous period for women, as it is for men.
  - Some women experience late-life divorces and pressure to look younger.
  - Others capitalize on the vast opportunities now available to women in midlife and consider midlife the prime of their lives.

Cultural Contexts
- In many nonindustrialized societies, a woman's status often improves in middle age as she is freed from cumbersome restrictions, child-care and domestic chores are reduced, and her authority over the next generation increases.
- In many cultures, the concept of middle age is not clear though most cultures distinguish between young adults and old adults.

STABILITY AND CHANGE
Longitudinal Studies
Neugarten's Kansas City Study
- Neugarten's Kansas City Study involved the investigation of individuals 40- to 80-years-of-age over a 10-year period.
- Both stability and change in personality occurred.
  - Styles of coping, life satisfaction, and being goal-directed were the most stable.
  - Change was characterized by being passive and threatened by the environment.

Costa and McCrae's Baltimore Study
- Costa and McCrae focused on the **big five factors of personality**—emotional stability (neuroticism), extraversion, openness to experience, agreeableness, and conscientiousness.
- They studied a thousand college-educated men and women aged 20 to 96 longitudinally.
  - They concluded that considerable stability occurs in the five personality factors.

Berkeley Longitudinal Studies
- This study has examined 500 children and their parents from the 1920s longitudinally.
- The extremes in the stability-change argument were not supported.
  - The most stable characteristics were the degree to which individuals were intellectually oriented, self-confident, and open to new experiences.
  - The characteristics that changed the most included the extent to which individuals were nurturing or hostile and whether they had good self-control or not.

Helson's Mills College Study
- Helson et al. studied 132 women through their adulthood from the 1950s to 1980s.
- Three main groups of women were distinguished: family-oriented, career-oriented, and women who did not follow either path.
- Women from all of these paths experienced similar psychological changes over their adult years.
  - The women in the third group changed the least.
- Overall, there was a shift toward less traditional feminine characteristics between age 27 and the forties.
  - These changes may be a reflection of societal changes.
- In their early forties, women experienced many of the concerns that Levinson described for men.
  - Helson et al. concluded that rather than being in a midlife crisis, what was being experienced was a midlife consciousness.

Conclusions
- The longitudinal studies portray adults as becoming different but still remaining the same.
- Amid change, there is still some underlying coherence and stability.
- Some people change more than others.

CLOSE RELATIONSHIPS
Love and Marriage at Midlife
Affectionate Love
- Affectionate or companionate love increases in midlife, especially in marriages that have endured many years.
- Happily married couples emphasize different aspects in their relationships at different ages.
  - Passion and sexual intimacy were more important in early adulthood.
  - Feelings of affection and loyalty were more important in later life.
  - Young lovers rated communication more characteristic of their love than older adults did.
  - At all ages, the order of the following characteristics was the same—emotional security, communication, help and play behaviors, sexual intimacy, and loyalty.

Marriage and Divorce
- Partners who engage in mutual activities usually view their marriage more positively.
- Most married individuals in midlife consider their marriages satisfying.
  - Couples that divorce in middle age are usually alienated and avoidant.
  - Divorce between younger adults usually involves heated emotions and disappointment.
- In one study, divorce in middle age had more positive emotional effects for women than men.
- Marriage had more positive emotional effects for men than women.

The Empty Nest and Its Refilling
- In the **empty nest syndrome**, marital satisfaction decreases because parents derive considerable satisfaction from their children and the children's departure leaves parents with empty feelings.
- Research has found that the empty nest actually increases satisfaction.
- An increasing number of young adults are returning home to live with their parents.
  - Adult children appreciate the financial and emotional support their parents provide, and parents feel good that they can provide this support.
  - Some middle-aged parents experience serious conflict with their resident adult children.
    - When adult children return home, a disequilibrium in family life is created, which requires considerable adaptation on the part of parents and their adult children.

Parenting Conceptions
- In middle age, many individuals say they wish they had spent more time with their children, and fathers wish they had been better parents.
- The identity of middle-aged women is frequently cast against the background of their mothers.
- During middle age, many individuals restructure their perceptions of parents and parenting.

Sibling Relationships and Friendships
- Sibling relationships persist over the entire life span for most adults.
- The majority of sibling relationships in adulthood are close, especially if they were close in childhood.
- Friendships continue to be important in middle adulthood.

Intergenerational Relationships
- Continuing contact across generations in families usually occurs.
- Parent-child similarity is most noticeable in religion and politics, least noticeable in gender roles, lifestyle, and work orientation.
- Mothers and daughters have the closest relationship.
- The middle-age generation has been called the "sandwich" generation because it is caught between obligations to children and obligations to parents.
- The middle-aged generation plays an important role in linking generations.

Learning Objectives

1. Discuss Erik Erikson's seventh stage of development.
2. Elaborate on Levinson's research on life-span transitions.
3. Describe the research conducted on the midlife crisis.
4. Examine the contemporary life-events approach to development.
5. Explain how historical context, gender, and culture impact development.
6. Discuss the longitudinal studies conducted to examine the issue of stability versus change in middle adulthood.
7. Examine how love and marriage change as people grow older.

8. Discuss the causes for and results of divorce in middle age.
9. Explain the empty nest syndrome and the reasons adult children return home.
10. Examine how sibling relationships and friendships change during middle adulthood.
11. Describe the nature of intergenerational relationships during middle adulthood, including the role that gender and culture play.

Key Terms

big five factors of personality
contemporary life-events approach

empty nest syndrome
social clock

Key People

John Clausen
Paul Costa and Robert McCrae
Erik Erikson
Ravenna Helson

William James
Daniel Levinson
Bernice Neugarten
Carol Ryff
George Vaillant

Lecture Suggestions

Lecture Suggestion 1: Trait versus Stage Theories—Is There a Way to Sort Things Out? There may be no way to combine ideas from these different research traditions into one coherent theory, but an examination of underlying assumptions and philosophical underpinnings might help clarify the nature of the differences. Trait theories are biological at their base. They are closely related to theories of temperament in children. A trait by definition is a more or less permanent characteristic. Trait theorists, if pushed, would support the idea that a leader is born and not made. The least a trait theorist will allow is the idea that early influence shapes, more or less permanently, a person's personality. The level of analysis used by trait theorists is the trait. This is key to understanding their position because a trait is a cluster of behaviors and attitudes, not a single behavior or attitude. Thus, it is possible for some shift to occur in the behaviors and attitudes of a person without changing the trait.

Stage theorists tend to be interactionist and constructionist. The person and the environment mutually shape behaviors, learning, and action. These shapes form a construct within the person. The person is an active participant, but the environment, including other people, is a significant player. The level of analysis for many stage theorists is structure or stage.

The only way to find agreement between the theories is to find common questions, research methods, and, most importantly, units of analysis. Unless researchers agree on units of analysis, the debate will continue, with no resolution in sight.

Lecture Suggestion 2: Men's Psychological Health This lecture examines men's psychological well-being relative to work and family. It has been long thought that marriage can enhance a man's work, whereas marriage and family will interfere with a woman's work. For example, early in the twentieth century, if an educated woman wanted to teach at Wellesley College (a prestigious women's college), she had to give up the idea of getting married and having a family. Wellesley felt it was inappropriate to have married women on its faculty. They thought it was incompatible for women to have family and a career. In contrast, men's professional life was enhanced by marriage.

Barnett et al. (1992) surveyed men in dual-career families. They were interested in their work, marital, and parental roles. Each man received a "quality" score for role. The "quality" role was computed by subtracting the "concerns from that role" from the "rewards from that role" score.

465

The main finding from this study was that men's family roles (marital and parental) are just as important as men's work role. In addition, for men the various roles were interrelated. Good marital and parental relationships can make up for poor work experience. Psychological distress was most likely if the man was experiencing poor family relationships and negative work experiences.

Men and women seem to incorporate the parental role into their self-concept differently. For working women, motherhood is central to their sense of self and being a parent can often offset job concerns. In contrast, for working men, fatherhood is less central to their sense of self. However, the degree of satisfaction or reward from the parental role is important to the man's psychological well-being.

- Source: Barnett, R.C., Marshall, N.L., & Pleck, J.H. (1992). Men's multiple roles and their relationship to men's psychological distress. *Journal of Marriage and the Family, 54*, 358-367.

Lecture Suggestion 3: Compare, Contrast, and Apply Longitudinal Studies Obtain copies of some of the research reports generated by the four major longitudinal studies of personality change across the adult developmental period described in the text (Clausen, 1993; Costa & McCrae, 1980, 1989; Helson, Mitchell, & Moane, 1984; Helson & Wink, 1992; Neugarten, Havighurst, & Tobin, 1968).

For each of the studies:

- Identify the variables that were studied.
- Indicate how many subjects were recruited and how they were recruited.
- Describe the methods that were used to collect the data.
- Briefly, describe the results that were obtained.

It might be worthwhile to assign students the task of gathering the information, and then you can summarize it for the class. The basic components of the theories of adult personality are well presented in the text. A lecture could center on the strengths and weaknesses of each theory. After you've discussed the theories, you could have the students compare and contrast each one. Next, you could describe a scenario in which an adult engages in a particular behavior. Each theory could then be used to describe why the adult behaves in that way. One example would be a 40- to 50-year-old woman who is a habitual liar. What do the theories say about why she is a liar; how do they explain her behavior; and what do they predict will happen to the behavior as the middle-aged woman enters late adulthood? Other behaviors could also be examined, for example, altruism, aggressiveness, preoccupation with the body, or reclusiveness.

- Sources: Clausen, J.A. (1993). *American lives*. New York: Free Press. Costa, P.T., & McCrae, R.R. (1980). Still stable after all these years: Personality as a key to some issues in aging. In P. Baltes & O. Brim (Eds.), *Life-span development and behavior*. New York: Academic Press. Costa, P.T., & McCrae, R.R. (1989). Personality continuity and the changes of adult life. In M. Storandt & G. VandenBos (Eds.), *The adult years: Continuity and change*. Washington, DC: American Psychological Association. Helson, R., Mitchell, V., & Moane, G. (1984). Personality change in women from college to midlife. *Journal of Personality and Social Psychology, 53*, 176-186. Helson, R., & Wink, P. (1992). Personality change in women from the early 40s to early 50s. *Psychology and Aging, 7*, 46-55. Neugarten, B., Havighurst, R., & Tobin, S. (1968). Personality and patterns of aging. In B. Neugarten (Ed.), *Middle age and aging*. Chicago: University of Chicago Press.

Lecture Suggestion 4: Divorce at Midlife This chapter includes a discussion of love and marriage at midlife. You can expand on this theme by discussing the causes and consequences for both men and women of divorce during this stage of the life cycle. One strategy for covering this material could involve inviting a marriage counselor to come and discuss the causes and consequences of midlife divorce. You might want to ask them to discuss whether the problems that lead to divorce during middle age are the same as the problems presented by younger and older couples. Students will find this a very interesting topic, as many of them likely have divorced parents or are divorced themselves.

Lecture Suggestion 5: Parent Care in the Context of Women's Multiple Roles The purpose of this lecture is to examine the effect that women's multiple roles have on women's well-being. Women have taken the brunt of the rapid societal change. Based on a nationally representative sample of caregivers to older adults, 37.4 percent of all caregivers were adult children of the individual in need of care (Stone et al., 1987). Daughters were three times more likely than sons to care for an aging parent. Women are often caught between the demands of caregiver, wife, mother, and employee.

Stephens and Franks (1999) describe two opposing perspectives on this issue and conclude that neither perspective adequately captures the nature of this complex relationship The *competing-demands hypothesis* states that negative consequences will result from the multiple role demands that are placed on individuals. This idea is based on the notion of scarcity, which assumes that individuals have limited resources, and that role partners and social organizations require all of these limited resources (Goode, as cited Stephens & Franks, 1999). Role conflict is the norm as role obligations exceed the limited resources. The *expansion hypothesis* states that energy gains, not energy expenditures, characterize individuals with multiple roles (Marks, 1977). Thus, positive consequences result due to the enhancement of personal attributes and resources (self-esteem, identity, social and monetary gains).

Stephens and Franks (1995) claim that these perspectives are limited as they solely focus on the quantity of roles and they do not focus on the quality of the role experiences. Perspectives on quality of role experiences claim that two similar roles could involve different cost/benefit ratios within and across these roles (Barnett & Baruch as cited in Stephens & Franks, 1999). Thus, problems and rewards must be taken into account when examining the effect of multiple roles on well-being. Stephens and colleagues have addressed these perspectives in the context of adult daughters who assist their chronically ill and disabled parents, and offered the following conclusions.

Role Quality
- They found that these women report both rewarding and stressful experiences in their caregiving roles. Stress was most often a result of interpersonal conflict (criticisms, unresponsiveness, demanding), while the rewarding experiences involved the satisfaction that the parent is being well taken care of, fulfillment of family obligations, and time spent together. These women also assumed the role of wife and mother. "The stress of these roles detracted from their well-being beyond the negative effects of experiences in the parent-care role" (p.150). Yet, the positive or rewarding experiences of the additional roles were emphasized more than the stressful aspects. The positive aspects of the three roles influenced the women's psychological well-being after the stress had been accounted for.

Role Combinations
- Accumulation of roles was examined. Stephens and Franks examined how competing demands would influence well-being and whether role combinations would enhance well-being. High levels of stress in only one role (parent-care) led to better well-being than did a combination of high stress in the parent-care role and one other role, or all three roles. Another pattern emerged as well. High levels of rewards in only the parent-care role led to poorer well-being, than having additional rewarding roles. In summary, both the competing-demands and the expansion perspectives were supported.

Role Spillover
- The concept of spillover assumes that rewarding and stressful experiences in one role can "spillover" and influence experiences in other roles in a bidirectional fashion. From the competing-demands perspective, one would assume negative spillover or psychological interference between roles, whereas the expansion perspective would assume positive spillover between roles. The most frequent negative spillover was the lack of time available for time with the husband due to caregiving. Few women reported that their marriage interfered with the parent-care responsibilities, rather many reported that it enhanced the care that they provided. Positive self-esteem was the most frequent positive spillover from the parent-care role. Women with more negative spillover reported poorer well-being and women with more positive spillover

reported greater well-being. Again, both the competing-demands perspective and the expansion perspective were supported.

In conclusion, these perspectives should be viewed as complementary not opposing.

- Sources: Marks, S.R. (1977). Multiple roles and role strain: Some notes on human energy, time, and commitment. *American Sociological Review, 42,* 921-936. Stephens, M.A.P., & Franks, M.M. (1999). Parent care in the context's of women's multiple roles. *Current Directions in Psychological Science, 8,* 149-152. Stephens M.A.P. & Franks, M.M. (1995). Spillover between daughters' roles as caregiver and wife: Interference or enhancement? *Journal of Gerontology: Psychological Sciences, 508,* 9-17. Stephens, M.A.P., Franks, M.M., & Townsend A.L. (1994). Stress and rewards in women's multiple roles: The case of women in the middle. *Psychology and Aging, 9,* 45-52. Stone, R., Cafferata, G.L., & Sangl, J. (1987). Caregivers of the frail elderly: A national profile. *The Gerontologist, 27,* 616-626.

Lecture Suggestion 6: Siblings The purpose of this lecture is to extend Santrock's discussion of sibling relationships. Lemme (1995) highlights four unique aspects of sibling relationships.

- Shared genes: Siblings share between 33 and 66 percent of their genes (Scarr & Gracek, 1982), which emphasizes the involuntary nature of the relationship.
- Long-term: Sibling relationships are potentially the longest-lived of any family relationship.
- Shared history: Siblings have a shared history of family experiences, which can facilitate common interests and values.
- Equality: Siblings are likely to have an egalitarian relationship (relatively equal power).

Bedford (1989) described the normal course of sibling relationships over time as an "hourglass effect." In childhood, the level of involvement with siblings is extensive and the level of involvement decreases during adulthood and then increases again in later life. Gold (1987) studied sibling relationships for individuals over the age of 65. He found that 53 percent reported increased contact and emotional closeness in late adulthood and 80 percent enjoyed and sought increased contact with siblings. These changes occurred for several reasons, including increased free time, desire to resolve old conflicts, concern for sibling's health, desire to reminisce about their shared history, and greater need for social support. Gold also found that the siblings he studied indicated that the majority of older adults stated that siblings played a secondary role during young and middle adulthood, which supported the "hourglass effect."

- Sources: Bedford, V.H. (1989). A comparison of thematic apperception of sibling affiliation, conflict, and separation at two periods of adulthood. *International Journal of Aging and Human Development, 28,* 53-66. Gold, D.T. (1987). Siblings in old age: Something special. *Canadian Journal on Aging, 6,* 199-215. Lemme, B.H. (1995) *Development in adulthood.* Boston: Allyn and Bacon. Scarr, S. & Gracek, S. (1982). Similarities and differences among siblings. In M.E. Lamb & B. Sutton-Smith (Eds.), *Sibling relationships: Their nature and significance across the lifespan* (pp. 357-381). Hillsdale, NJ: Erlbaum.

Classroom Activities

Classroom Activity 1: Interviews about Middle Adulthood Most of your students will not be in the middle adulthood period of development yet. One way to get them to think about what kinds of issues they will deal with in their forties and fifties is to get them to ask their parents and grandparents about the experiences they are having, or did have, during their midlife transition.

There is considerable debate about whether there is such a thing as a midlife crisis. Some investigators argue that socioeconomic, cultural, and historical events may combine to determine whether the midlife period is one of transition or one of crisis. Students will develop a better understanding of the influence of cohort factors on the experiences associated with middle adulthood by collecting intergenerational data.

With the students' help, generate a list of biological, cognitive, emotional, and social changes that commonly occur during middle adulthood. Once the list is generated, set up a 7-point Likert type scale for each item. Use "had an impact" and "did not have an impact," or some other comparative terms, as poles.

You may also want to put a couple of open-ended questions on the form, such as, "What did you like best about being 40?" and "What did you like least about being 40?"

Ask the students to administer the questionnaire to their parents and their grandparents or take it themselves if appropriate. If a sufficient sample size cannot be obtained this way, ask the students to find at least one 40-year-old and one 60-year-old who would be willing to complete the questionnaire, anonymously of course.

Compile the data and discuss the results. Students should be able to draw some conclusions about the possibility of cohort effects. They, by now, should also be able to point out flaws in the design and suggest ways to make it a better study. At the conclusion of the discussion, ask the students what, if anything, the data contribute to the debate about the existence of a midlife crisis.

Logistics:
- Group size: Full class, individual, and full class.
- Approximate time: Full class (20 minutes), individual (1 hour), and full class (30 minutes).

Classroom Activity 2: Women in the Workforce This activity examines issues related to women in the workplace. Two areas can be explored: The glass ceiling (women can see the top of the corporate world but do not have access to it), and differing experiences of women depending on when they entered the workforce (in the '60s, '70s, '80s, or '90s). Additionally, students can study differences between women in nontraditional jobs (building trades, factory work, or other male-dominated professions) compared to women in traditional women's work (teaching, social work, hair styling, and related areas). How are the opportunities and barriers similar and different?

Logistics:
- Group size: Full class.
- Approximate time: Full class (20 minutes).

Classroom Activity 3: Middle Adulthood in the Movies Have students watch two movies that have middle-aged people as the main characters (e.g., *The First Wives Club*, *As Good as it Gets*, or *Thelma and Louise*). In your class discussion, ask students to describe the portrayal of the characters. Do the moviemakers do a good job of characterizing what people in midlife are typically like? Compare and contrast the movie portrayals with information presented in chapters 16 and 17. If the students were to make a movie to accurately reflect what people in midlife are like, what characters would they have?

Logistics:
- Group size: Individual and full class.
- Approximate time: Individual (3 hours) and full class (20 minutes).

Classroom Activity 4: Critical Thinking Multiple-Choice Questions and Suggested Answers Discuss the critical thinking multiple-choice questions presented in **Handout 1**. Question 1 should be fairly easy by now, but you may want to orient students (or find out if they are oriented) to the appropriate segment of the reading alluded to in the question.

Question 2 is by now a familiar sort of question that requires students to apply material in the chapter to the Images of Life-Span Development box that opens the chapter. Students may benefit from an in-class analysis of the sketch of Sarah's and Wanda's lives that highlights the relevant features of their own lives in terms of the various theories discussed in the chapter.

Question 3 concerns an unstated assumption, and by this time in your course may not represent a new challenge. We suggest that you urge students to work on this one alone with minimal input from you. The answers to these questions are presented as **Handout 2**.

Logistics:
- Materials: Handout 1 (the critical thinking multiple-choice questions) and Handout 2 (answers).
- Group size: Small groups to discuss the questions, then a full class discussion.
- Approximate time: Small groups (15 to 20 minutes), full class discussion of any questions (15 minutes).

Classroom Activity 5: Critical Thinking Essay Questions and Suggestions for Helping Students Answer the Essays Discuss students' answers to the critical thinking essay questions presented in **Handout 3**. The purpose of this exercise is threefold. First, answering the essay questions further facilitates students' understanding of concepts in chapter 17. Second, this type of essay question affords the students an opportunity to apply the concepts to their own lives, which will facilitate their retention of the material. Third, the essay format also gives students practice expressing themselves in written form. Ideas to help students answer the critical thinking essay questions are provided as **Handout 4**.

Logistics:
- Materials: Handout 3 (essay questions) and Handout 4 (helpful suggestions for the answers).
- Group size: Individual, then full class.
- Approximate time: Individual (60 minutes), full class discussion of any questions (30 minutes).

Personal Applications

Personal Application 1: A Picture's Worth a Thousand Words This exercise will get students to tune in to the portrayal of middle-aged individuals in the media. The media is a huge influence in societal thinking and perceptions—about anything and everything! Through movies, television shows and advertising, and magazines, it can positively or negatively mold our thinking about individuals of different age groups, including those in middle adulthood.

- Instructions for Students: Begin paying attention to the media portrayals of individuals in middle age and note what you see. How are they portrayed in movie roles? Do these roles reflect what you've learned about adults in this stage of life, or are they unrealistic? If so, in what ways? How about appearances on talk shows and news programs—what issues are they concerned with? There are numerous commercials featuring adults in middle adulthood—how are they presented and for what products or services? What magazine articles address issues of middle adulthood, and what do they generally have to say? Does the media present an overall positive or negative view of this stage of life? How accurate is it? Does it make you feel good when you think about growing older and reaching this time of your life? Why?

- Use in the Classroom: Have students present their media findings with examples in class. Discuss what they found and their reaction to it. How might they suggest doing a better job of dealing with this stage of life with regard to all aspects of media portrayal? Is this even necessary? You may want to find your own examples as well. Address the various adult stage theories and issues of love and marriage, coping, midlife crises, menopause, religion, job satisfaction, and intergenerational relationships.

Personal Application 2: My Hero The purpose of this exercise is to have students think about the generativity aspect of Erikson's midlife stage, generativity vs. stagnation. Erikson believes that generativity encompasses adults' desire to leave a legacy of themselves to the next generation. They can develop generativity in numerous ways with the result being that the adult achieves a kind of immortality.

- Instructions for Students: Write about several of your middle-aged "heroes." Identify adults who have or are doing something particularly inspiring *during this stage of their life*. Talk about what they've done that represents their generativity. Can you see how this reflects their perspective of experiencing this stage of life? In what ways? What have you learned from these individuals? Do they motivate you to do more with your life, particularly as you get older? (Hint: you can choose someone you don't know personally, such as an athlete, politician, activist, or well-known individual.)

- Use in the Classroom: Make a list of students' choices for inspiring models of generativity. Come prepared with your own list of individuals and discuss the characteristics of Erikson's stage with regard to these individuals.

Personal Application 3: Generation Gap The purpose of this exercise is to have students think about the intergenerational relationships they have been a part of. With each new generation, personality characteristics, attitudes, and values are replicated or changed. The relationship between parents and their adult children have been found to be related to the nature of their earlier relationship.

- Instructions for Students: Reflect on the aspects of your relationships with individuals in middle adulthood. What characterizes them? What is the nature of your interactions? On what things do you see eye-to-eye? Where do you disagree? How effective is your communication with one another? What things do you wish they could or would try to understand? What would make your relationships better and closer? For each area you discuss, provide reasons as to why you believe your relationship works that way. Use the information in your text to guide you.

- Use in the Classroom: Explore these intergenerational relationships with the class as a whole. Have students address the topics listed in the book (such as religion, politics, gender roles, lifestyle, work orientation, and child rearing) with regard to their views and those of the middle-aged others in their life. Have them present where they agree and where the discrepancies lie. Keep track of everyone's responses and not whether there is a consistency among these relationships or if there appears to be variation. If students are willing, also have them share their history in the relationships they discuss, and how their past interactions may be contributing to what they're experiencing now.

Research Project Ideas

Research Project 1: Adult Stage Theories in Biographies Chapter 17 presents three major adult stage theories (Erikson's, Levinson's, and Vaillant's), each of which attempts to capture the focal points of adult life-span development. An intriguing aspect of these theories is that they essentially are based on biographies. Some biographies were of famous people or of people the theorists knew as clients or participants in life-span developmental research. For example, Erikson based his theory on his clients, and both Erikson and Levinson applied their theories to the lives of famous people.

For this research project, have students find out how well one of the theories applies to a specific biography (**Handout 5**). In other words, they will (a) locate and read the biography of any person who interests them (Bill Clinton, Colin Powell, Martin Sheen, Joe Montana); and (b) determine whether or not the events of that person's life illustrate the adult stages specified in either Erikson's, Levinson's, or Vaillant's theory (they will not do all three theories—encourage them to choose the one that appeals most to them).

Instruct students to present their findings in a table like the one on **Handout 6**. In addition, they need to write a brief report in which they summarize how well the theory they are applying captures the life of the person they read about. If they believe the theory applies, tell them to be sure to describe the facts of the person's life that they think support the theory. If they believe the theory does not apply, they should explain how they reached that conclusion. For example, show why the events of the person's life do not fit the stages of the theory.

Research Project 2: Your Life Review The following discussion appeared in Santrock's 7th edition of *Life-Span Development* (p. 475).

Frank just turned 45 years old yesterday. As he realizes that he has become "middle aged," he recognizes that his life is, almost certainly, at least half over. As he reflects back on his time, he begins to consider his goals from when he was younger. In doing so, he realizes that some of his aspirations have been met with success, other with disappointment. Looking back allows Frank the chance to assess where he has been, where he is now, and where he is headed. Given that he still has, at the most, half of his life to go, he can make some adjustments to reach many of the goals he has not yet achieved.

As you read chapter 17, people frequently engage in a process of reviewing their lives when they enter their middle years and beyond. This process, often referred to as "life reviews," can be highly beneficial. Although dwelling on the past will rarely result in greater productivity or progress, taking a look at how things are going and how they got there can help us work toward the future. Of course, it is not necessary for a person to be in the middle years to do something like a life review.

One way you can assess your life situation is to consider each aspect of your life and its history, one segment at a time. For example, think about Frank, discussed above. As he wonders about his life situation, he is likely to take many aspects into account. He may ponder his career, family life, education, relationships, and many other things. However, if his thinking is unorganized, he will probably miss some of the connections among aspects of his life and may not see how he could see a new path. Thus, rather than just thinking about one's life, it is possible to examine its developmental course. One way to do this is to list out several life areas and note how they have gone along throughout life. For example, consider your family. Questions that you can pose to yourself include these: "What was most important about my childhood?" "What major events have changed my family?" "What aspects of my family life am I most and least satisfied with right now?" "How would I like to see my family life in the future, and what can I do to bring it there?" Regarding your career path, consider questions such as these: "How did I get into the work I am currently in?" "How far along have I progressed with respect to my personal goals?" "What can I do to progress along as I have wished?" "Do I need to adjust my goals for the future?"

A life review also benefits when you identify several areas of your life and then write down your perspectives about the past, present, and future prospects of each. Consider the areas listed (family, friends, education, career, travel, financial security, and religious/spiritual), as well as any others that may hold more personal meaning to you. The end result of this process can be a broader view of life that is put together in a meaningful, whole picture.

An alternative means of life review involves taking a more chronological approach. For example, a person may construct what is called a "life line." Rather than examine specific aspects of your life one at time, you can evaluate your life one period or phase at a time. Construct a time line, starting as far back as your like—with your birth, say, or even with where your family came from before your birth. Then, looking at your infancy, childhood, adolescence, and adulthood, list out all of the major events of your life and where they brought you.

Other strategies you can follow include discussing your life with older family members, constructing a family tree, and keeping an extensive diary. Regardless of the exact method you use, engaging in a personal life review can give you a clearer picture of yourself and place your life into perspective.

Even though your students may not be in middle age yet, they will learn more about the concept of a life review (and something about themselves) if they attempt to do one (**Handout 7**). Have them use the Life Review Chart presented as **Handout 8**. Based on what they learn from this process, they should write a brief report in which they indicate whether doing this life review gave them a broader view of middle adulthood.

An interesting addition to their project would be to have a middle-aged person also carry out a life review by filling out a life review chart. Students should summarize what they learn about the person's ideas about his or her past, present, and future life, and compare that review to their own. Also, have them indicate whether the findings are in line with information about life-span developmental changes reported in the text.

Film and Video List

The following films and videos supplement the content of chapter 17. Contact information for film distributors can be found at the front of this Instructor's Manual under Film and Video Sources.

Ageless America (Films for the Humanities and Sciences, 52 minutes). Caring for the elderly, women's longer lifespan, aging in middle-aged individuals, sandwich generation, and the process and problems of aging are discussed.

Doctor, Lawyer, Indian Chief (National Film Board of Canada, 29 minutes). This forward-looking documentary chronicles the lives of five Native American women who become successful in their respective careers.

The Midlife Passage (Films for the Humanities and Sciences, 24 minutes). In this video, individuals discuss issues of dissatisfaction with successes, awareness of fleeting time, and consciousness of having tried to live up to others' expectations. In addition, they discuss their efforts to reassess their lives, satisfaction in making peace with the past and determination to steer their remaining years mindfully.

Parenting Our Parents (Films for the Humanities and Sciences, 26 minutes). This film deals with the sandwich generation and discusses alternative care arrangements for aging parents.

Web Site Suggestions

The URLs for general sites, common to all chapters, can be found at the front of this Instructor's Manual under Useful Web Sites. At the time of publication, all sites were current and active, however, please be advised that you may occasionally encounter a dead link.

Midlife Crisis: Recent Research
http://www.hope.edu/academic/psychology/335/webrep2/crisis.html

Ravenna Helson's Research
http://psychology.berkeley.edu/helson-sp.htm

Research Network on Successful Midlife Development
http://midmac.med.harvard.edu/

Sandwich Generation
http://marriage.about.com/people/marriage/cs/sandwich/

Critical Thinking Multiple-Choice Questions

1. Which pair of developmental concepts is highlighted in Santrock's treatment of intergenerational relationships? Circle the letter of the best answer and explain why it is the best answer and why each other answer is not as good.

    a. nature versus nurture
    b. continuity versus discontinuity
    c. early versus late experience
    d. stability versus change
    e. social versus cognitive processes

2. Chapter 17 presents a number of theories and perspectives on socioemotional development in middle adulthood. Which of these best captures the contrasting lives of Sarah and Wanda sketched in the Images of Life-Span Development box, "Middle Age Variations," that opens the chapter? Circle the letter of the best answer and explain why it is the best answer and why each other answer is not as good.

    a. Erikson's generativity versus stagnation
    b. Gould's midlife crisis
    c. Levinson's transition to middle adulthood
    d. Contemporary life-events theory
    e. individual variation (e.g., Farrel and Rosenberg's study)

3. Levinson studied the life paths of men, whereas Helson studied the life paths of women. Although these researchers found similar patterns in both sexes, their interpretation of their findings about the influence of midlife concerns was different. Which of the following represents an assumption of one of these researchers, rather than an inference or an observation, that produced these different interpretations? Circle the letter of the best answer and explain why it is the best answer and why each other answer is not as good.

    a. The transition at midlife forces people to choose between opposite possibilities (polarities).
    b. Adult development requires mastery of developmental tasks experienced in successive stages.
    c. Most of the men in Levinson's study found the midlife transition painful.
    d. Helson found a shift toward less traditionally feminine attitudes between the ages of 27 and the early forties among women.
    e. Women who did not commit themselves in early adulthood to a lifestyle pattern faced fewer challenges.

Suggested Answers for Critical Thinking Multiple-Choice Questions

1. Which pair of developmental concepts is highlighted in Santrock's treatment of intergenerational relationships even though he is talking about cross-generational patterns? Circle the letter of the best answer and explain why it is the best answer and why each other answer is not as good.

   a. Nature versus nurture is not the best answer. The main reason is that little is said about the mechanisms that produce the degree of stability/change in personality characteristics, attitudes, or values that occurs across generations.

   b. Continuity versus discontinuity is not the best answer. Santrock does not explore possible ways that succeeding generations differ qualitatively from each other.

   c. Early versus late experience is not the best answer. Again, early determinants versus later plasticity are not a focus on the material. For example, a possible discussion could have been how parental influence exerted early in a child's life may enhance or detract from cross-generational similarity (e.g., following Freud); but there is no such discussion.

   d. Stability versus change is the best answer. Specifically, Santrock says, "With each new generation, personality characteristics, attitudes, and values are either replicated or changed." This highlights the stability/change issue.

   e. Social versus cognitive processes is not the best answer. This is a possible alternative answer, even though it is not so directly underscored. Santrock does discuss how social interactions and contexts are involved in intergenerational relationships; however, he does not discuss what role cognitive processes play.

2. Chapter 17 presents a number of theories and perspectives on socioemotional development in middle adulthood. Which of these best captures the contrasting lives of Sarah and Wanda sketched in the Images of Life-Span Development box, "Middle Age Variations," that opens the chapter? Circle the letter of the best answer and explain why it is the best answer and why each other answer is not as good.

   a. Erikson's generativity versus stagnation is not the best answer. The chief contrast between Sarah and Wanda is their relative satisfaction between whom they have become and what they have yet to be, rather than on their satisfaction with what they have handed to posterity.

   b. Gould's midlife crisis is not the best answer. Neither woman seems to be possessed of the sense of urgency that seems to be Gould's criterion for a midlife crisis.

   c. Levinson's transition to middle adulthood is not the best answer. None of Levinson's four conflicts is the center Sarah or Wanda's woes or joys. The issue for Levinson is resolving life's polarities, whereas Sarah and Wanda seem to exemplify despair versus zestful contentment with their lives.

   d. The contemporary life-events theory is the best answer. It emphasizes that how life events influence the individual's development depends not only on the life event, but also on mediating factors (physical health, family supports), the individual's adaptation to the life event (appraisal of the threat, coping strategies), the life-stage context, and the sociohistorical context. It is apparent that Wanda and Sarah for example have different levels of social support and coping strategies.

   e. Individual variation (e.g., Farrel and Rosenberg's study) is not the best answer. The main reason for arguing this is that you can find appropriate contrasts that appear to illustrate Vaillant's idea. Of course, Sarah and Wanda could represent individual variations in adjustment to middle age; but Santrock seems to have a more definite purpose in sketching their contrasting situations.

3.   Levinson studied the life paths of men, whereas Helson studied the life paths of women. Although these researchers found similar patterns in both sexes, their interpretation of their findings about the influence of midlife concerns was different. Which of the following represents an assumption of one of these researchers, rather than an inference or an observation, that produced these different interpretations?

Circle the letter of the best answer and explain why it is the best answer and why each other answer is not as good.

a.   The transition at midlife forces people to choose between opposite possibilities is not the best answer. It is an inference Levinson drew from his observations of things that were troubling to men at midlife.

b.   Adult development requires mastery of developmental tasks experienced in successive stages is the best answer. This is an assumption Levinson makes that Helson does not, which seems to lead Levinson to life's events and decisions as a series of crises and integrations that occur over the life-span. In contrast, Helson seems to believe that women embark on a limited set of alternative "life journeys," during which they may pause and reflect (in more or less normative ways) on the distance they have come.

c.   Most of the men in Levinson's study found the midlife transition painful is not the best answer. This is an observation Levinson reports about men's emotional reactions to their midlife situations.

d.   Helson found a shift toward less traditionally feminine attitudes between the ages of 27 and the early forties among women is not the best answer. This is also an observation, reported by Helson, about women's gender-role attitudes.

e.   Women who did not commit themselves in early adulthood to a lifestyle pattern faced fewer challenges is not the best answer. Helson also reported this as a fact, presumably a state of affairs observable in review of the life events of the less-challenged women.

Critical Thinking Essay Questions

Your answers to these kinds of questions demonstrate an ability to comprehend and apply ideas discussed in this chapter.

1. Compare and contrast two of the theories of personality development in middle age. Are these theories mutually contradictory, or do they add to and enrich each other?

2. Evaluate whether midlife entails a crisis in development according to each of the adult stage theories.

3. Explain how the concepts of cohort and social clock affect the view that midlife is a period of crisis.

4. Defend or refute the view that adult stage theories express a male bias.

5. Explain whether middle age is a universal or culturally-specific concept.

6. Explain and give examples of the life-events approach in your own words.

7. What does it mean to say that there is individual variation in adult personality development?

8. Summarize the results of longitudinal studies of adult personality development, and relate the findings of these studies to the theories of adult personality development.

9. Describe the nature of love and marriage during middle adulthood.

10. Define the empty nest syndrome, and explain its relationship to marital satisfaction.

11. Imagine a situation in which adult children move back into their parent's home. Describe the concerns from both the young adult's and the parent's perspectives, and summarize important issues for discussion by both parties.

12. Define and provide at least two examples of intergenerational relationships.

Ideas to Help You Answer Critical Thinking Essay Questions

1. Present each theory in full with related examples, relevant research, etc. After these have been explicitly mapped out, make your comparisons and draw your conclusions.

2. Define what is meant by "crisis" with regard to each theory. Does it vary?

3. Prior to addressing this issue, clearly define *cohort* and *social clock effect* to substantiate your explanation.

4. First, simply present how each theory addresses males and male issues. Then explain your perspective, pulling examples from your discussion of each theory.

5. Begin by presenting a general overview of the developmental stage of middle age, then address the notion of its universality.

6. Read the section describing the life-events approach in your text. Stop and think about it. Do you really understand it? Are you aware of all the relevant issues? Can you provide examples of research and findings? As you write your answer, imagine that you are an instructor and you are describing it to a student who missed class on that day of lecture. Keep in mind you must be thorough and communicate the information clearly—in your own words.

7. As you answer this, draw examples from your own experiences with, interactions involving, and knowledge of people in middle adulthood.

8. Research studies are ideally based on theories. Delineate the issues addressed in the studies (such as age, behaviors, cognition) and match them with the issues addressed in the theories. Are there any gaps in either the research or the theories?

9. To enhance your discussion, present your description in relation to what you learned about love and marriage in early adulthood.

10. Have your parents experienced this yet? If so, what have you observed with regard to issues of marital satisfaction?

11. Consider various situations in which adult children move back into their parent's home and how they might *differentially* affect the issues presented in the question.

12. Include in your discussion and provide examples of conflict and concern, areas of agreement, factors contributing to closeness, reasons for the significance of the relationships, and the important role they play in individuals' lives.

Adult Stage Theories in Biographies

Chapter 17 presents three major adult stage theories (Erikson's, Levinson's, and Vaillant's), each of which attempts to capture the focal points of adult life-span development. An intriguing aspect of these theories is that they essentially are based on biographies. Some biographies were of famous people or of people the theorists knew as clients or participants in life-span developmental research. For example, Erikson based his theory on his clients, and both Erikson and Levinson applied their theories to the lives of famous people.

Your task for this research project is to find out how well one of the theories applies to a specific biography. In other words, you will (a) locate and read the biography of any person who interests you (Bill Clinton, Colin Powell, Martin Sheen, Joe Montana); and (b) determine whether or not the events of that person's life illustrate the adult stages specified in either Erikson's, Levinson's, or Vaillant's theory (do not do all three theories—choose the one that appeals most to you).

Present your findings in a table (Handout 6). In addition, write a brief report in which you summarize how well the theory you are applying captures the life of the person you read about. If you believe the theory applies, be sure to describe the facts of the person's life that you think agree with the theory. If you believe the theory does not apply, be sure to explain how you reached that conclusion. For example, show why the events of the person's life do not fit the stages of the theory.

Data Sheet for the Adult Stage Theories in Biographies Project

On the left side of your table, indicate the stages of adult life for the theory you are applying. On the right side of your table indicate whether or not you found evidence that the person you are studying passed through the stage or experienced the specified crisis. If the person did pass through the stage or experience the crisis, enter a brief note about the events of his or her life that support your claim.

Theory you are applying: _____
Age of person you are studying: _____
Gender of person you are studying: _____

<u>Stage of Adult Life</u>   <u>Evidence of this Stage</u>

1.

2.

3.

4.

5.

6.

Your Life Review

Even though you may not be in middle age yet, you will learn more about the concept of a life review (and something about yourself) if you attempt to do one. Use the Life Review Chart presented as Handout 8. Based on what you learn from this process, write a brief report in which you indicate whether doing this life review gave you a broader view on middle adulthood.

An interesting addition to your project would be to have a middle-aged person also carry out a life review by filling out a life review chart. Summarize what you learn about the person's ideas about his or her past, present, and future life, and compare that review to yours. Also, indicate whether the findings are in line with information about life-span developmental changes reported in the text.

Handout 8 (RP 2)

Your Life Review Chart

	Past	Present	Future
Family:			
Friends:			
Education:			
Career:			
Travel:			
Financial Security:			
Religious/Spiritual:			

Chapter 18: Physical Development in Late Adulthood

Total Teaching Package Outline

Lecture Outline	Resource References
Physical Development in Late Adulthood	PowerPoint Presentation: See www.mhhe.com Cognitive Maps: See Appendix A
Longevity	LS1: Gerontology Careers and You CA1: Facts on Aging Quiz PA1: Family Tree
• Life Expectancy and Life Span	LO1 OHT2 & IB, OHT3 & IB, OHT4 & IB 4, OHT184-185 & IB, OHT190: Life Expectancy CA2: Life Expectancy Quiz RP1: Variations in Life Expectancy
-Centenarians	LO2 F/V: Living Past A Hundred F/V: 100-something WS: Living to 100
-Sex Differences in Longevity	LO3 LS2: Longevity as a Function of Age, Sex, and Race
• The Young Old, the Old Old, and the Oldest Old	LO4
• Biological Theories of Aging -Cellular Clock Theory -Free-Radical Theory -Hormonal Stress Theory	LO5 LS3: Primary versus Secondary Aging
The Course of Physical Development in Late Adulthood	LO6 CA3: Compensation for Physical Changes PA2: "Chronologically Challenged!" F/V: The Death Knell of Old Age F/V: You Won't Need Running Shoes, Darling
• The Aging Brain -The Aging Brain's Plasticity and Adaptiveness	LS4: Changes in the Brain
• Physical Appearance	F/V: Aging and Sagging
• Sensory Development -Vision -Hearing -Smell and Taste -Touch -Pain	LO7 IB: Vision and Hearing Decline

• The Circulatory System • The Respiratory System • Sexuality	 LO8 LS5: Sexuality and Aging F/V: Sexuality and Aging

Health
 	
• Health Problems
 	
    -Causes of Death in Older Adults
 	
    -Arthritis
 	
    -Osteoporosis
 	
    -Accidents
 	
• The Robust Oldest Old
 	
• Exercise, Nutrition, and Weight
 	
    -Exercise
 	
    -Nutrition and Weight
 	
    -The Growing Vitamin and Aging
     Controversy
 	
• Health Treatment
    -Care Options
 	
    -Giving Options for Control and Teaching
     Coping Skills
 	
    -The Older Adult and Health-Care
     Providers
	PA3: It's Never Too Early…
	F/V: Aging and Health
	
	LO9
	IB: Most Prevalent Chronic Conditions
	
	OHT186 & IB: Leading Causes of Death
	
	LO10
	
	F/V: Osteoarthritis and Rheumatoid Arthritis
	F/V: Osteoporosis: Progress and Prevention
	WS: Osteoporosis and Other Bone Diseases
	
	LO11
	
	LO12
	
	RP2: Physical Fitness for the Elderly in Your
	     Community
	F/V: A Case Study of Successful Aging
	WS: Physical Aging and Exercise
	
	LS6: Caloric Restriction
	
	LO13
	CA4: Health Care Debate
	F/V: Caring for the Elderly
	WS: Medicare Information
	
	LO14

Review	CA5: Critical Thinking Multiple-Choice
	CA6: Critical Thinking Essays
	WS: Administration on Aging
	WS: APA-Adult Development and Aging
	WS: APA Division 20 Newsletters
	WS: Gerontology Society of America
	WS: Resources on Aging Online Directory
	WS: National Association of Area Agencies on Aging
	WS: National Institute of Aging
	WS: Society for Research in Adult Development

Chapter Outline

LONGEVITY

Life Expectancy and Life Span

- Although a greater percentage of persons live to an older age, the life span has remained virtually unchanged since the beginning of recorded history.
  - **Life span** is the upper boundary of life, the maximum number of years an individual can live.
    - The maximum life span of human beings is approximately 120 years of age.
    - Improvements in medicine, nutrition, exercise, and lifestyle have increased our life expectancy an average of 30 additional years since 1900.
  - **Life expectancy** is the number of years that will probably be lived by the average person born in a particular year.
    - Life expectancy of individuals born today in the U.S. is 77 years (80 for women, 74 for men).
    - Differences in life expectancies across countries are due to such factors as health conditions and medical care throughout the life span.

Centenarians

- An increasing number of people are living to be 100 years or older.
  - Many of these people are healthy for most of their older years and seem to cope with stress effectively.
- The most important factors in longevity are heredity, family history, health (weight, diet, smoking, and exercise), education, personality, and lifestyle.
  - The rapid growth in the 85+ and 100+ age categories suggests that potential changes lie ahead.
    - Retiring at age 65 may be too young.
    - Increasing health and longer productivity of the elderly may offset some of the economic burden of the graying of America.
    - A more positive view of individuals in late adulthood may need to be created.

Sex Difference in Longevity

- Females live about 6 years longer on average than males do.
- Females outnumber males at the age of 25, and the gap widens from there.
  - The sex difference is likely due to biological (infection resistance) and social (health attitudes, habits, lifestyles, and occupation) factors.

The Young Old, the Old Old, and the Oldest Old
- The young old are 65-74 years of age, the old old are 75 years and older, and the oldest old are 85 years and older.
  - Many experts on aging prefer to talk about the functioning of individuals in late adulthood, rather than age.
    - Some 85-year-olds function far better than some 65-year-olds.
  - The needs, capacities, and resources of the oldest old are often different than their younger counterparts.
    - Today's oldest old are much more likely to be living in institutions, less likely to be married, and more likely to have low educational attainment.
  - Every period or subperiod of development is heterogeneous.
    - Significant numbers of the oldest old function effectively and are in good health.

Biological Theories of Aging
  Cellular Clock Theory
  - The **cellular clock theory** is Hayflick's view that cells can divide a maximum of about 75 to 80 times and that as we age, our cells become increasingly less capable of dividing.
    - In the last decade, scientists have found that telomeres are involved in explaining why cells lose their dividing capabilities.
      - Telomeres are DNA sequences that cap chromosomes.
  Free-Radical Theory
  - The **free-radical theory** states that people age because inside their cells normal metabolism produces unstable oxygen molecules known as free radicals. These molecules ricochet around the cells, damaging DNA and other cellular structures.
  Hormonal Stress Theory
  - The **hormonal stress theory** states that aging in the body's hormonal system may lower resilience to stress and increase the likelihood of disease.
  - With aging, the hormones stimulated by stress remain elevated longer than when the individuals were young, which is associated with increased risk for many diseases.

THE COURSE OF PHYSICAL DEVELOPMENT IN LATE ADULTHOOD
- Acknowledgement of variability in rates of decline in functioning has generated increased attention for factors involved in the maintenance of functional abilities with age.
  The Aging Brain
    The Aging Brain's Plasticity and Adaptiveness
    - Adults continue to grow new brain cells throughout their lives.
      - The brain occupies less of the cranial cavity after 50 years of age.
    - We lose some neurons as we age, but how many is debated.
    - The aging brain retains considerable plasticity and adaptiveness.
    - Lack of dendritic growth in the elderly could be due to a lack of environmental stimulation.
    - The brain has the capacity to virtually rewire itself to compensate for loss in older adults.

Physical Appearance
- The most obvious signs of aging are wrinkled skin and age spots on the skin.
  - Men lose about $1\frac{1}{4}$ inches by the age of 70. Women lose about 2 inches by the age of 75.
  - Weight often decreases after age 60 because of the loss of muscle.

Sensory Development
Vision
- The visual system declines but the vast majority of older adults can have their vision corrected so they can continue to work and function in the world.
- Some of the changes that occur include: Night vision decreases, dark adaptation is slower, cataracts (cloudy opaque areas in the lens that prevent light from passing through), glaucoma (disease involves hardening of the eyeball because of fluid buildup), and macular degeneration (disease involving deterioration of the retina).

Hearing
- Hearing declines often begin in middle age but usually do not become much of an impediment until late adulthood.
  - It is estimated that 15 percent of the population over age 65 is legally deaf, usually due to degeneration of the cochlea.
- Hearing aids can diminish hearing problems for many older adults.

Smell and Taste
- Smell and taste may decline although the decline is minimal in healthy older adults.

Touch
- Changes in touch sensitivity are associated with aging although this does not present a problem for most older adults.
  - Touch sensitivity decreases more in the lower extremities than in the upper extremities.

Pain
- Older adults are less sensitive to pain and suffer from it less than younger adults.

The Circulatory System
- When heart disease is absent, the amount of blood pumped is the same regardless of an adult's age.
  - High blood pressure is no longer just accepted but rather is treated with medication, exercise, and/or a healthy diet.
- Blood pressure may rise with age because of illness, obesity, anxiety, stiffening of blood vessels, or lack of exercise.

The Respiratory System
- Lung capacity drops 40 percent between the ages of 20 and 80, even without disease.
  - Older adults can improve lung functioning with diaphragm-strengthening exercises.

Sexuality
- Aging in late adulthood does include some changes in sexual performance, more so for males than females (orgasm is less frequent for males, more direct stimulation is needed).
- There are no known age limits to sexual activity.

HEALTH
Health Problems
- As we age, the probability of disease or illness increases.
  - Chronic disorders are rare in early adulthood, increase in middle adulthood, and become common in late adulthood.
    - The most common chronic problems are arthritis and hypertension.
  - Low income is strongly related to health problems in late adulthood.
    - Three times as many poor as nonpoor older adults report that their activities are limited by chronic disorders.

Causes of Death in Older Adults
- Nearly three-fourths of older adults die of heart disease, cancer, or cerebrovascular disease.
  - If all cardiovascular and kidney diseases were eradicated, the average live expectancy would increase by approximately 10 years.

Arthritis
- **Arthritis** is an inflammation of the joints accompanied by pain, stiffness, and movement problems. Arthritis is especially common in older adults.
  - There is no known cure for arthritis, though symptoms can be reduced with drugs, range-of-motion exercises, and weight reduction.

Osteoporosis
- **Osteoporosis** is an aging disorder involving an extensive loss of bone tissue. Osteoporosis is the main reason many older adults walk with a marked stoop. Women are especially vulnerable to osteoporosis, the leading cause of broken bones in women.
  - Almost two-thirds of all women over the age of 60 are affected by osteoporosis, especially White, thin, and small-framed women.
  - This aging disorder is related to deficiencies in calcium, vitamin D, estrogen depletion, and lack of exercise.
    - Prevention of osteoporosis is important in early and middle adulthood.
    - Prevention focuses on calcium-rich foods, exercise, and avoiding smoking.

Accidents
- Accidents are the seventh leading cause of death in late adulthood.
- Accidents are usually more debilitating to older adults than to younger adults.

The Robust Oldest Old
- Early portrayals of the oldest old were too negative; there is cause for optimism in the development of new regimens and interventions.
  - A sizable portion of individuals over age 80 are free of disability, able to cope with their disabilities free of assistance, or able to recover their functioning over time.

Exercise, Nutrition, and Weight
Exercise
- The physical benefits of exercise have been clearly demonstrated in older adults.
  - In one study, sedentary participants were more than twice as likely to die during the 8-year time span than those who were moderately fit.
  - Beginning moderately vigorous physical activity from the forties through the eighties was associated with a 23 percent lower risk of death, quitting smoking with a 41 percent lower death risk.
- Aerobic exercise and weight lifting are recommended if the adults are physically capable.

Nutrition and Weight
- Scientists have accumulated considerable evidence that food restriction in laboratory animals can increase the animal's life span.
- Experts recommend a well-balanced, low-fat diet that includes the nutritional factors needed to maintain good health.
  - Leaner men do live longer, healthier lives.

The Growing Vitamin and Aging Controversy
- The controversy focuses on whether vitamin supplements, especially the antioxidants vitamin C, vitamin E, and beta-carotene, can slow the aging process and improve older adults' health.
  - There is no evidence that antioxidants can increase the human life span, but some experts believe that they can reduce a person's risk of becoming frail and sick in later adult years.
  - Critics stress that the studies that have been conducted are correlational and not experimental.

Health Treatment

Care Options

- Although only 5 percent of adults over 65 reside in nursing homes, 23 percent of adults over age 85 do.
    - The quality of nursing homes varies enormously.
    - Alternatives to nursing homes include home health care, day-care centers, and preventive medicine clinics.

Giving Options for Control and Teaching Coping Skills

- An important factor related to health, and even survival, in a nursing home is the patient's feelings of control and self-determination.
    - Simply giving nursing home residents options for control and teaching coping skills can change their behavior and improve their health.
    - When older adults thought of themselves as younger, they had improved posture, gait, a more positive outlook, better memory, and improved eyesight.
        - Loss of control may even be worse than lack of control.

The Older Adult and Health-Care Providers

- The attitudes of both the health-care provider and the older adult patient are important aspects of the older adult's health care.
    - Too often health-care personnel share society's negative view of older adults.
        - Health-care personnel tend to be less responsive to older patients.
- Older adults should be encouraged to take a more active role in their own health care.

Learning Objectives

1. Distinguish between life expectancy and life span, including mention of cross-cultural differences.
2. Elaborate on the characteristics associated with being a centenarian.
3. Describe the sex differences in longevity and what may account for them.
4. Be able to determine differences between the young old, the old old, and the oldest old.
5. Discuss the biological theories of aging.
6. Elaborate on the course of physical development in late adulthood and the changes that take place in the brain as we age.
7. Indicate the physical and sensory changes that occur in the older adult.
8. Discuss how sexual performance is impacted by aging.
9. Describe common health problems in late adulthood, and expound on the causes of death in older adults.
10. Discuss arthritis and osteoporosis, including the symptoms, causes, and possible treatments for each.
11. Describe the robust oldest old.
12. Discuss the role of exercise, nutrition, and weight in late adulthood, as well as the vitamin controversy.
13. Explain care options for the elderly and ways to improve their care in the nursing home.
14. Describe the relationship between health-care providers and the older adult.

Key Terms

arthritis

cellular clock theory

free-radical theory

hormonal stress theory

life expectancy

life span

osteoporosis

Key People

Ellen Langer
Stanley Rapaport

Judith Rodin
Richard Schultz

Lecture Suggestions

Lecture Suggestion 1: Gerontology Careers and You As you begin this section of the course, which focuses on aging, you might want to start with a lecture on gerontology careers. The growing population of older people is creating new jobs for young people such as doctors, occupational therapists, nurses, physiotherapists, architects, engineers, professors, family counselors, clergy, and directors/workers in senior centers. In the next decade, there is going to be growing demand for workers in these areas as the number of aging Americans increases. In a study done by the Association for Gerontology in Higher Education (AGHE) and the University of Southern California in 1992, the researchers concluded that 1,639 colleges (55 percent) in the United States offered courses in aging. This was an increase of 11 percent since 1985. This might be a good opportunity for a discussion of how your students might get involved in careers in gerontology. For a thorough discussion of how each of these fields will grow as a result of the aging population, see Novak's (1997) book.

The following is a quote from Lobenstine (1994). "Do you find enjoyment in being with older persons? Do you empathize with the needs of the elderly and feel a desire to be an advocate for them? Are you intrigued with wanting to understand the process of why we age? Do you have a basic concern for people and their special needs? Consider preparing for a career in the field of aging!"

- Sources: Lobenstine, J.C. (1994). Consider a career in the field of aging. A brochure for the Association for Gerontology in Higher Education. Novak, M. (1997). *Issues in aging: An introduction to gerontology*. New York: Longman.

Lecture Suggestion 2: Longevity as a Function of Age, Sex, and Race In keeping with the cultural and gender themes carried throughout the text, focus one lecture on the interactive effects of age, race, and sex on longevity. Obtain a copy of the latest longevity data. *Vital Statistics* publishes new data every year on the life expectancy of Americans as well as other cultures. Collect data from a few time periods (e.g., 1950, 1975, and 2000), and break the life expectancy tables down by sex, race, and age. You can include culture also, but it gets a little confusing to try to do it all at once, particularly if there is a four-way interaction. Several trends can be monitored including the following:

- The gap in genders: Females are still living longer, but is the gap between males and females widening or shrinking? Why might the trend be changing or why might it be staying the same? Does the increase in women in the workforce appear to be affecting the gap?
- The increase in life expectancy: Are 20-year-olds in 2000 expected to live longer than 20-year-olds in 1950? Have the gains in life expectancy tapered off?
- The effect of race: African American women who survived until the age of 60 had a higher life expectancy than White women who survived until the age of 60. This result was true even though life expectancies at birth for African Americans is lower than for Whites. Have the students attempt to explain such findings if they appear in your data.
- The interactive effects of age, sex, and race: Do the trends for different ages, different sexes, and different races have to be qualified? Is your life expectancy dependent on more than just how old you currently are?

Have students postulate as to why the results you described exist. Help them focus their discussion around economic and educational opportunities and health practices.

Lecture Suggestion 3: Primary versus Secondary Aging This lecture clarifies the nature of aging by making a distinction between primary and secondary aging. Primary aging refers to the normal and intrinsic processes of biological aging that are genetically programmed and that take place despite good health and the absence of disease. Despite the universal nature of primary aging, environmental factors can modify the effects. Lemme (1995) highlighted the following characteristics of primary aging:

- Complex process of age-related structural and functional change over time
- Cumulative
- Changes that reduce functioning
- Progressive, gradual changes
- Intrinsic, not caused by external factors
- Inevitable
- Universal
- Irreversible
- Changes that begin after physical and reproductive maturity has been reached
- Results in death

Secondary aging refers to age-related declines that are pathological and result from extrinsic factors (disease, environment, and behavior). Examples of secondary aging include the effects of smoking on wrinkles, respiratory disease and heart disease, the effects of sun exposure on cancer, cataract formation, wrinkles, and the effects of noise pollution on hearing loss. Approximately one-third to one-half of the health problems among the elderly are linked to inadequate nutrition (Hendricks & Hendricks, 1986). Secondary aging is identifiable because these effects occur among only part of the population. They are preventable and potentially reversible.

- Sources: Hendricks, J., & Hendricks, C.D. (1986). *Aging in mass socieity: Myth and realities.* Boston: Little, Brown. Lemme, B.H. (1995) *Development in adulthood.* Boston: Allyn and Bacon.

Lecture Suggestion 5: Changes in the Brain The purpose of this lecture is to extend Santrock's brief discussion of brain changes with age. The cerebral cortex, where higher-order mental activities occur, progressively loses brain tissue. By age 70, 5 percent of the total brain mass is lost, by age 80, 10 percent, and by age 90, 20 percent (Minckler & Boyd, as cited in Lemme, 1995). The frontal lobe (working memory) and the hippocampus (memory) also experience progressive loss, which may account for the memory and executive deficits seen in older adults (Mittenberg et al., 1989).

Gur et al. (as cited in Lemme, 1995) found that brain atrophy (reduced brain volume and increased cerebrospinal fluid) is greater for men (especially in the left hemisphere). In addition, the changes that females experienced were more symmetrical, which accounts for the finding that females experience fewer changes in mental functions controlled by the left hemisphere (verbal abilities). Gur et al. speculate that female sex hormones (estrogen) may protect the brain from these age-related changes and buffer them from some of the age-related changes in cognitive functioning.

- Sources: Lemme, B.H. (1995) *Development in adulthood.* Boston: Allyn and Bacon. Mittenberg W., Seidenberg, M., O'Leary, D.S., & DiGiulio, D.V. (1989). Changes in cerebral functioning associated with normal aging. *Journal of Clinical and Experimental Neuropsychology, 11,* 918-932.

Lecture Suggestion 6: Sexuality and Aging This lecture affords an opportunity to highlight six facts on human sexuality and aging. Dr. Cross (1993), an internal medicine specialist, states that the care of elderly could be significantly improved if health-care personnel understood the following facts.

Fact 1: All older people are sexual.

- Granted not all older people are sexually active, however, they all have sexual beliefs, values, memories, and feelings. The same could be said for younger adults. It is incorrect to assume that older adults have lost their sexual competence, desire, and sexual interest. It is unfortunate that many younger adults believe this assumption, however, it is tragic that many older adults also buy into this myth. Many sexual older adults experience guilt and anxiety for experiencing normal sexual feelings.

Fact 2: Many older people have a need for a good sexual relationship.

- With age, individuals need to adapt to physical and mental changes. They are experiencing physical changes and limitations, social changes, and potentially cognitive changes. Thus, intimacy, warmth, and security from a good sexual relationship can facilitate individuals' adaptation to these changes.

Fact 3: Sexual physiology changes with age.

- It is important for aging individuals and health-care providers to understand the gradual physiological changes that occur with age. Older men have less frequent erections, it takes longer for erections to occur, the penis is less firm, and erections are more easily lost. Ejaculation takes longer, is less forceful, and produces less semen. The refractory period is longer as well. If a man is consumed by sexual prowess and doesn't understand these normative changes, he may experience performance anxiety, impotence, and panic. Conversely, if a man understands these changes, he can compensate for them. Women also experience some physiological changes as the result of menopause. Vaginal dryness can make sexual intercourse painful, though saliva, commercial lubricants, or hormone replacement therapy can alleviate this problem.

Fact 4: Social attitudes are often frustrating.

- Unfortunately, society holds many negative attitudes regarding older people's sexuality and tends to deny the sexuality of the aged. Self-satisfaction could be encouraged for the many single older women. Unfortunately, many nursing homes discourage sexual relationships.

Fact 5: Use it or lose it.

- Sexual functioning is a physiologic function that tends to deteriorate if it is not used. Thus, in order to remain sexually competent, it is important to engage in sexual activity.

Fact 6: Older folks do it better.

- If we go beyond a focus on the firmness of the penis and the moistness of the vagina, and focus on satisfaction, the elderly can enjoy several advantages. They tend to have considerable sexual experience, more free time, and are more secure in their identities.

- Source: Cross, R.J. (1993). What doctors and others need to know: Six facts on human sexuality and aging. *Sex Information and Education Council of the U.S.*

Lecture Suggestion 6: Caloric Restriction The purpose of this lecture is to expand Santrock's brief mention of the effects of caloric restriction on longevity. Seventy years ago, researchers at Cornell University made an extraordinary discovery. By placing a rat on a very low-calorie diet, McCay et al. (as cited in Weindruch, 1996) extended the outer limit of the animals' life span by 33 percent (from 3 years to 4). They subsequently found that rats on low-calorie diets stayed youthful longer and suffered fewer late-life diseases than did their normally fed counterparts.

Since the 1930s caloric restriction has been the only intervention shown convincingly to slow aging in rodents and in creatures ranging from single-celled protozoa to roundworms, fruit flies, and fish. Can this work be extended to humans? Even if this does turn out to be a fountain of youth for humans, it might not catch on. Historically, humans' adherence to strict diets has not been impressive. Several laboratories around the country (University of Wisconsin, for example) are working to understand the cellular and molecular basis of how caloric restriction retards aging in animals. If the nutritional needs of the dieters are carefully guarded, research has found an astonishing range of benefits in animals. In most studies, the test animals (mice and rats) consume 30-50 percent fewer calories than are ingested by control animals. Thus, they weigh 30-50 percent less as well. It is important to note that these animals are not malnourished, as they receive enough protein, fat, vitamins, and minerals to maintain efficient operation of their tissues. The results consistently increase not only the average life span of a population, but also the maximum life span (the lifetime of the longest-surviving members of the group). In addition, low-calorie diets in rodents have postponed most major diseases that are common late in life, including cancers of the breast, prostate, immune system, and gastrointestinal tract. An important caveat is that the restriction of fat, protein, or carbohydrates without caloric reduction does not increase the maximum life span of rodents.

As a step toward understanding caloric reduction's effects on humans, the results need to be confirmed with monkeys, as they are more similar to humans. These studies are very time-consuming because monkeys live much longer than mice or rats. Preliminary analyses have focused on the effects of caloric restriction on biomarkers of aging. These attributes generally change with age and may help predict future health over the life span. Roth and colleagues (as cited in Weindruch, 1996) began one of the monkey studies in 1987 by examining rhesus monkeys (average life span of 30-40 years) and squirrel monkeys (life span of 20 years). The preliminary results show that the dieting animals seem healthy and happy (and eager for their meals). Blood pressure and glucose levels are lower, insulin sensitivity is greater, and the levels of insulin in the blood are lower than in the control animals.

One explanation for the effects focuses on limiting injury of mitochondria by free radicals. Mitochondria are the tiny intracellular structures that serve as the power plants of the cells. Free radicals are highly reactive molecules (usually derived from oxygen) that carry unpaired electrons at their surface. Molecules in this state are prone to destructively oxidizing or snatching electrons from any compound they encounter. Free radicals have been suspected of contributing to aging since the 1950s. Mitochondria are thought to create most of the free radicals in cells. Once formed, free radicals can damage protein, fats, and DNA anywhere in the cell. As the cells become less efficient, the body is less able to cope with challenges to its stability.

- Source: Weindruch, R. (1996). Caloric restriction and aging. *Scientific American*, 46-52.

Classroom Activities

Classroom Activity 1: Facts on Aging Quiz A good way to start a unit on aging is to give students a "quiz" on aging (**Handout 1**). It is interesting to see how much they know about aging prior to reading the chapters on late adulthood. Administer the quiz and then determine who in the class knows the most about getting old. Surprisingly, or maybe not so surprisingly, there is no correlation between knowledge about aging and a person's current age. After scoring the quiz, open up the floor for discussion. Students are encouraged to ask why they got a particular statement wrong. If no discussion is forthcoming, jump in with some facts about a few of your favorite items. The questions and notes regarding the answers are presented below.

1. Most women experience severe physical symptoms during menopause.
   - FALSE: Menopause is defined as 12 consecutive months without menstruation (median age 50-52 years). Age of menarche and menopause are not related. Smokers experience menopause 1-2 years earlier. Historically menopause has been viewed as negative ("partial death," "estrogen deficient," or "ovarian failure"). Hot flashes and night sweats are primary symptoms. Secondary symptoms include weight gain, vaginal dryness, depression, and irritability. Approximately 20 percent experience no symptoms, whereas 19 percent have very bothersome symptoms.
2. Most adult children can't wait to ship their aging parents off to a "home."
   - FALSE: 25 percent of females over 60 have a parent living with them in their home.
3. Most people over 65 are in nursing homes or other institutions.
   - FALSE: Only 5.4 percent of people over 65 are in institutions because of incapacitating physical or mental illness (22 percent over 85 years).
4. Most people over 65 are financially insecure.
   - FALSE: in 1990, 12.2 percent of older persons lived below the official poverty level; 22.7 percent of total population is below 1.5 times the poverty level compared to 26.3 percent of older persons (10 percent White, 32 percent African American, and 22 percent Latino live in poverty).

5. Comparing younger and older people at one point in time will tell us what the younger people will be like when they are old.
   - FALSE: Cohort and time of measurement issues.
6. Nuclear families in today's society have little contact with kin.
   - FALSE: Most people are fairly close to aging parents, technology helps (email, telephone). Forty percent see at least one child two or more times a week, 22 percent see one or more of their children daily. Contact increases as the parents' age increases. Working class individuals have more contact (larger families, geographically close).
7. Aged drivers have fewer accidents per driver than those under age 65.
   - TRUE: The main reason is that they limit when they drive and they drive less aggressively.
8. Most people have the same career for a lifetime.
   - FALSE: Most people have 4 to 7 jobs per lifetime. Women's career paths tend to be discontinuous.
9. The shock of retirement often results in deteriorating physical and mental health.
   - FALSE: Satisfaction increases if individuals prepare for it. Satisfaction is predicted by health, money, and education.
10. Personality is relatively stable during the adult years.
    - TRUE: Most aspects of personality are stable over adulthood. Oftentimes people attribute characteristics to an individual because of the age of the person, when actually the person has always been that way.
11. Over three-fourths of the aged are healthy enough to carry out their normal activities.
    - TRUE: Most do not experience debilitating illnesses.
12. Those who are most able in their youth decline the fastest in old age.
    - FALSE: Activity level and education level influence ability.
13. Women live longer than men do because they don't work as hard.
    - FALSE: Women live 6-7 years longer than men worldwide due to biology, estrogen, and behavior (smoke and drink less).
14. In general, old people tend to be pretty much alike.
    - FALSE: There is more variance or difference in older individuals than younger people due to accumulated experiences.
15. Unmarried people are more susceptible to mental disorders than married people.
    - DEPENDS: Married women have a much higher incidence of mental disorders than married men, but single, divorced, or widowed men have higher rates than women. Can't be biological due to marital status differences. Some blame "housewife" status.

Logistics:
- Materials: Handout 1 (Aging quiz).
- Group size: Small group and full class.
- Approximate time: Small group (20 minutes), full class (20 minutes).

Classroom Activity 2: Life Expectancy Quiz Santrock has included a copy of a longevity quiz in his text. Have students complete the scale, share their life expectancy, and discuss which items add years to your life and which items take away years. In addition, discuss what areas are not mentioned on the quiz but should be, such as diet, risk taking behavior, and the health of the person filling out the quiz. This will require students to integrate what they are learning about the influences on longevity with their own life experiences.

After discussing longevity, it may be a good idea to reassure students that to some extent they control their own destiny. The idea for this lecture comes from a *Newsweek* article entitled "How to Live to 100." It seems that the fastest growing segment of the United States population is the over 100 group. It is estimated that more than 200,000 Americans will be over 100 by the year 2020. The three recommendations about how to live to 100 made in the article are: (1) exercise; (2) healthy eating; and (3) staying connected to others. In your lecture, discuss or expand on each of these points.

Logistics:
- Materials: Life expectancy quiz from the textbook.
- Group size: Individual and full class.
- Approximate time: Individual (10 minutes), full class (20 minutes).
- Source: Cowley, G. (1997, June 30). How to live to 100. *Newsweek*.

Classroom Activity 3: Compensation for Physical Changes The purpose of this exercise is to have students think about some ways to compensate for the changes that occur in late adulthood. As a class, have them list as many "tools" or resources that are available to compensate for these changes. Write them on the board. The list may include the following: large print books, books on tape, hearing aids, motorized shopping carts, and elevator chairs along the staircase. Have your students generate additional resources. Encourage them to be creative.
Logistics:
- Group size: Full class.
- Approximate time: Full class (20 minutes).

Classroom Activity 4: Heath Care Debate In chapter 18, Santrock discusses the health care of the elderly. A good way to engage students in this topic is to set up a debate about how society should meet the health-care needs of the elderly. You may want to read two opposing views on this issue by Sager (1990) and Lamm (1990). Divide the class into two groups. Assign one group to argue the position that states that the elderly should be granted full access to health care. Assign the other group to argue that the elderly can't be granted full access to health care. Structure the class as a debate. You may want to ask a colleague to join you in judging the debate. Remind students that they must provide quality arguments to support their position. Students will most likely need to do some library research to support their position. Most students will find this activity stimulating and will become quite passionate about their position.
Logistics:
- Group size: Small group and full class.
- Approximate time: Small group (30 minutes), full class (30 minutes).
- Source: Sources: Lamm, R. (1990). The elderly cannot be guaranteed full access to health care. In D. Bender & B. Leone (Series Eds.) *The elderly: Opposing viewpoints*. San Diego, CA: Greenhaven Press. Sager, A. (1990). The elderly should be guaranteed full access to health care. In D. Bender & B. Leone (Series Eds.) *The elderly: Opposing viewpoints*. San Diego, CA: Greenhaven Press.

Classroom Activity 5: Critical Thinking Multiple-Choice Questions and Suggested Answers Discuss the critical thinking multiple-choice questions presented as **Handout 2**. Question 1 emphasizes a theme of life-span developmental psychology which states that development results from the interaction of many factors. An important feature of this question, though, is that it requires students to draw on most of the material of the chapter in order to form an appropriate conclusion. Because this is fairly unusual for the critical thinking multiple-choice questions, you may want to take time with your students to discuss which material is relevant to the question. This could produce a valuable discussion about the sometimes vague concepts of biological process, environmental influence, and experience.

Question 2 revisits the issue of whether potential applications of text material are justified by the evidence that exists for these claims. The main point is that each claim addresses a cause-effect relationship, and therefore requires experimental research as justification. All but one of the claims is based on findings from experiments.

Question 3 requires that students apply what they are learning to the chapter opening vignette. The answers to the critical thinking multiple-choice questions are presented as **Handout 3.**
Logistics:
- Materials: Handout 2 (the critical thinking multiple-choice questions) and Handout 3 (answers).
- Group size: Small groups to discuss the questions, then a full class discussion.
- Approximate time: Small groups (15 minutes), full class discussion of any questions (15 minutes).

Classroom Activity 6: Critical Thinking Essay Questions and Suggestions for Helping Students Answer the Essays Discuss students' answers to the critical thinking essay questions presented in **Handout 4**. The purpose of this exercise is threefold. First, answering the critical thinking essay questions further facilitates students' understanding of concepts in chapter 18. Second, this type of essay question affords the students an opportunity to apply the concepts to their own lives, which will facilitate their retention of the material. Third, the essay format also gives students practice expressing themselves in written form. Ideas to help students answer the critical thinking essay questions are provided as **Handout 5**.

Logistics:

- Materials: Handout 4 (essay questions) and Handout 5 (helpful suggestions for the answers).
- Group size: Individual, then full class.
- Approximate time: Individual (60 minutes), full class discussion of any questions (30 minutes).

Personal Applications

Personal Application 1: Family Tree The purpose of this exercise is to get students thinking about longevity with regard to their own family members. With changes in technology, medical and otherwise, lifestyles are changing in such a way that the human life span is ever increasing in length. More people are living longer and perceiving their later years more positively than ever before. Many individuals are beginning new endeavors at a significantly later age than was previously considered possible, and they are remaining active, physically and mentally, long into their later years.

- Instructions for Students: You may need some assistance from your parents for this exercise in order to get all the information you need. Write about the lives of the older generations of your family. How long did each person live? What were their living conditions and lifestyles? What caused their death? What factors other than the direct cause of death might have contributed to their death or the decline in their health? Discuss any factors you think might be related to their being male or female.
- Use in the Classroom: Create a grid on the board with age of death on one axis and cause of death on the other. Gather data points from students as they share what they know of their elder generations' life spans and causes of death. Once you've plotted your points, look for any trends or similarities based on generations. If there appears to be no connection between the age at which people died and the cause of their death, collect stories as to their living conditions and lifestyles. Can you now make the connection between positive, healthy lifestyles (physical and mental) and longevity?

Personal Application 2: I'm Not Old, I'm "Chronologically Challenged!" This exercise can help connect students with the physical characteristics of late adulthood through real-life experience. Despite an increase in longevity, the human body still undergoes a great deal of decline in its physical functioning and appearance late in life.

- Instructions for Students: Think about any individuals you currently know and occasionally see who are in late adulthood, or reflect on time you spent with your grandparents when they were alive. What do/did you notice about them physically? What aspects of their physical functioning are affected by their age? What physical abilities appear to still be intact? What disabilities do you think are most difficult to adapt to and live with? Can you recall when you noticed the beginning of the decline in aspects of their functioning? If you can't, ask them to share with you when *they* did. What is most difficult for them about their physical functioning at this time in life? Use the issues presented in your text to guide you.
- Use in the Classroom: Proceed through the issues presented in the text and have students share their observations and experiences with elderly people and their physical characteristics. As you notice that not all people in this stage of life suffer from apparent limiting decline in each area, what aspects of their lifestyles might contribute to this?

Personal Application 3: It's Never Too Early... The purpose of this exercise is to have students consider what aspects of their current lifestyle may ultimately effect their experiences when they reach late adulthood. As researchers learn more about how the human body ages and what it experiences during the later years of life, the more we can prepare for what is to come, by living healthy, positive lifestyles now.

- Instructions for Students: Describe your current lifestyle—both physically (your eating habits, exercise routine, bad habits, scheduled doctor and dentist visits, etc.) and mentally (your tendency to become stressed, how important leisure activities are to you, how you perceive yourself, your current life circumstances, how you view the future, etc.). How do you believe each of the factors of your current lifestyle will effect what you will experience when you reach late adulthood? What aspects of your life might you change to improve the possibility that you will live a healthier, more positive and productive life in late adulthood? How critical do you think it is that you begin these changes now, rather than wait until you reach middle adulthood?

- Use in the Classroom: Expand this discussion in the classroom. How able are students to see the connection between what they do now and the end result with regard to their existence late in life and, ultimately, their longevity? What aspects of personal functioning now do they see as related to those later years, and which ones do they feel will not influence what will determine their elderly physical characteristics? Make sure they are able to back up their responses with reasoning and evidence.

Research Project Ideas

Research Project 1: Variations in Life Expectancy You may want to assign this research project (**Handout 6**) after completing Classroom Activity 2: Life Expectancy Quiz. Have students administer the life expectancy questionnaire, found in chapter 18, to at least five male and five female acquaintances (or alternatively, to any two or more groups of college students they would like to compare). After they have collected the data, they should add (or subtract) the total points indicated to each individual's basic life expectancy (71 for males, 78 for females; add 10 to these basic figures for each respondent over 50 years of age). Once they have collected their data, they should prepare a table in which they tally the number of individuals in each of their groups who indicated that a question applied to them. Next, they should calculate the average life expectancy for each group. Finally, students should write a brief report that summarizes their findings by answering at least the following questions:
Questions:

- Is the pattern of answers for the groups similar or different?
- Which categories of answers tend to be added to or subtracted from each group's life expectancy?
- Does one group have a greater overall life expectancy than the other?
- What conclusions can you draw about the basic life expectancies of each group?
- If the answers to question 14 of the life expectancy quiz indicate interesting group differences, why do you think these differences exist?
- Use in the Classroom: This activity would lend itself well to full class discussion, small group interactions, or single student presentations. Ask students to indicate what benefit there may be from doing such an exercise. Also, discuss how life expectancy quizzes such as this one will change in the future.

Research Project 2: Physical Fitness for the Elderly in Your Community There is a tremendous amount of research available today that points to the importance of exercise for successful aging. This project will allow students to see if the message is getting out (**Handout 7**). For this project, students will investigate the physical fitness programs available for elderly people in your community. They should call any senior centers in your area to find out what programs are available. They can also visit the local gyms to see if there are any special programs available for elderly people. The students should visit the gym on three occasions (preferably at different times of day and different days of the week) and make a note of what percentage of the people exercising are elderly (i.e., over 65). They may also want to note what kinds of activities the elderly clients are engaged in. Students should interview four people, one in each of the following age groups: twenties, forties, sixties, and over-seventies They should ask them the questions that follow.

Questions:

- How often do you exercise?
- What types of exercise do you regularly engage in?
- Do you typically exercise alone or with other people?
- How long have you been regularly exercising?
- How long do you plan to regularly exercise in the future?
- Why do you exercise?

After completing the interviews, students should compare and contrast the answers given by people in the different age groups. They should write a brief report summarizing their findings and indicating how well the message about the benefits of exercise for successful aging has been received in their community. Instruct the students to make a proposal for their city government about improvements in programs/facilities for the elderly to promote physical fitness.

- Use in the Classroom: Have students get into groups to discuss their proposals and create a more comprehensive program based on the ideas of each of the group members. Have the groups report to the class and compare group proposals.

Film and Video List

The following films and videos supplement the content of chapter 18. Contact information for film distributors can be found at the front of this Instructor's Manual under Film and Video Sources.

Aging and Sagging (Films for the Humanities and Sciences, 24 minutes). This program discusses the need to help the aging population redefine themselves as role models and to reincorporate them into society as a valuable resource.

The Aging Process (Films for the Humanities and Sciences, 19 minutes). This program looks at the effects of aging on the human mind and body, different theories about why the body wears out, lifestyle habits that affect longevity, and quality of life. It also discusses how it is never too late to live more healthfully.

Caring for the Elderly (Films for the Humanities and Sciences, 19 minutes). This video provides an overview of care available for elderly adults such as day care, group homes, respite care, and nursing homes.

A Case Study of Successful Aging (Morton Publishing, 46 minutes). This video shows case studies of three people, two elderly and one young, and how physical activity can make life better during old age.

The Death Knell of Old Age (Films for the Humanities and Sciences, 24 minutes). This program uses 3-D imaging to track the end of life in an 87-year-old man. It shows the intricate workings of the body in its final stages.

Living Past A Hundred (Films for the Humanities and Sciences, 57 minutes). This program presents commentary from leading scientists and case studies of centenarians to illustrate elements that influence life expectancy. This program also discusses the impact of the lengthening life span.

100-something (Films for the Humanities and Sciences, 47 minutes). In this video, doctors search for a connection between life expectancy and the genetic, physical, psychological, and cognitive dimensions of aging. In addition, centenarians share their experiences.

Osteoarthritis and Rheumatoid Arthritis (Films for the Humanities and Sciences, 19 minutes). This program distinguishes between the two types of arthritis and describes the nature of the diseases and treatments.

Osteoporosis: Progress and Prevention (Films for the Humanities and Sciences, 24 minutes). This program explains current innovative treatments, assessment techniques, and preventive measures that women can take in the battle against osteoporosis. The connection between osteoporosis, menopause, and estrogen is examined and new drug therapies that can halt bone density loss are discussed.

Sexuality and Aging (Insight Media, 60 minutes). This video explores attitudes, myths, facts, and research about sexuality in old age.

You Won't Need Running Shoes, Darling (Terra Nova Films, 53 minutes). This is a personal and honest film that tells the story of Mildred and Bob Todd, retired octogenarians. They savor life but have some health problems. Their daughter films their life over a 2-year period.

Web Site Suggestions

The URLs for general sites, common to all chapters, can be found at the front of this Instructor's Manual under Useful Web Sites. At the time of publication, all sites were current and active, however, please be advised that you may occasionally encounter a dead link.

Administration on Aging
http://www.aoa.dhhs.gov/siteindex.html
http://www.aoa.dhhs.gov/aoa/wn.html

APA's Site on Adult Development and Aging Division 20
http://www.iog.wayne.edu/apadiv20/apadiv20.htm

APA Division 20 Newsletters
http://www.iog.wayne.edu/APADIV20/student.htm

Gerontology Society of America
http://www.geron.org/
http://www.aoa.dhhs.gov/aoa/webres/a-quick.htm

Resources on Aging Online Directory
http://www.aoa.dhhs.gov/aoa/pages/jpostlst.html

Living to 100
http://www.livingto100.com/

Medicare Information
http://www.medicareinfo.com/

National Association of Area Agencies on Aging
http://www.n4a.org/

National Institute of Aging
http://www.nih.gov/nia/

Osteoporosis and Other Bone Diseases
http://www.osteo.org/

Physical Aging and Exercise
http://www.hope.edu/academic/psychology/335/webrep/exercise.html

Society for Research in Adult Development
http://www.tiac.net/users/commons/srad/index.html

Handout 1 (CA 1)

Aging Quiz

Indicate whether each of the following statements is true or false.

1. Most women experience severe physical symptoms during menopause.

2. Most adult children can't wait to ship their aging parents off to a "home."

3. Most people over 65 are in nursing homes or other institutions.

4. Most people over 65 are financially insecure.

5. Comparing younger and older people at one point in time will tell us what the younger people will be like when they are old.

6. Nuclear families in today's society have little contact with kin.

7. Aged drivers have fewer accidents per driver than those under age 65.

8. Most people have the same career for a lifetime.

9. The shock of retirement often results in deteriorating physical and mental health.

10. Personality is relatively stable during the adult years.

11. Over three-fourths of the aged are healthy enough to carry out their normal activities.

12. Those who are most able in their youth decline the fastest in old age.

13. Women live longer than men because they don't work as hard.

14. In general, old people tend to be pretty much alike.

15. Unmarried people are more susceptible to mental disorders than married people.

Handout 2 (CA 5)

Critical Thinking Multiple-Choice Questions

1. A significant portion of chapter 18 concerns the causes and effects of aging and death. Which of the following statements most accurately summarizes what we know about these causes? Circle the letter of the best answer and explain why it is the best answer and why each other answer is not as good.

    a. Genetic factors cause aging and death.
    b. Biological processes cause aging and death.
    c. A combination of environmental, biological, and experiential factors produce aging and death.
    d. The main cause of aging and death is wear and tear on the body due to stress.
    e. We do not really know what causes aging and death.

2. Santrock describes a number of ways to improve the lives of the elderly and makes several suggestions about how to do so in chapter 18. Which two of the following of his recommendations (direct or implied) are least well supported by the evidence he presents? Circle the letters of the best answers and explain why each is a good answer and why each other answer is not as good.

    a. Give elderly nursing home patients control over their environment.
    b. Involve elderly people in aerobic exercise programs.
    c. Get elderly men to lose weight.
    d. Take vitamin E to prevent heart disease.
    e. Teach elderly nursing home residents to assert themselves.

3. The vignette about Sadie Halperin in the Images of Life-Span Development box illustrates several concepts and research findings that are discussed in the section of late adulthood (chapters 18-20). Which of the following statements does Sadie's case least well illustrate? Circle the letter of the best answer and explain why it is the best answer and why each other answer is not as good.

    a. There are numerous physical changes in late adulthood.
    b. There are several benefits from exercise.
    c. Social support is an important part of aging.
    d. Weight lifting can help prevent osteoporosis.
    e. The oldest old group is heterogeneous and diversified.

Suggested Answers for Critical Thinking Multiple-Choice Questions

1. A significant portion of chapter 18 concerns the causes and effects of aging and death. Which of the following statements most accurately summarizes what we know about these causes? Circle the letter of the best answer and explain why it is the best answer and why each other answer is not as good.

   a. Genetic factors cause aging and death is not the best answer. The chapter discusses several environmental and lifestyle factors that contribute to the course of aging and the time of eventual death.

   b. Biological processes cause aging and death is not the best answer. The main reason is that there appears to be a genetic limit on the life span of human cells; so biological processes per se are not the only factor, and, as in "a," environmental factors contribute to the process as well.

   c. A combination of environmental, biological, and experiential factors produce aging and death is the best answer. The text, for example, refers to genetic limits, biological processes (hormones), environmental, and lifestyle (exercise) factors that are related to life expectancy.

   d. The main cause of aging and death is wear and tear on the body due to stress is not the best answer. See "c."

   e. We do not really know what causes aging and death is not the best answer. While in some sense this is true, we have enough evidence to know what factors are involved; the mechanism, however, does not seem to be known.

2. Santrock describes a number of ways to improve the lives of the elderly and makes several suggestions about how to do so in chapter 18. Which two of the following of his recommendations (direct or implied) is least well supported by the evidence he presents? Circle the letter of the best answer and explain why it is the best answer and why each other answer is not as good.

   a. Give elderly nursing home patients control over their environment is not the best answer. This claim is supported by experimental evidence (e.g., Rodin & Langer's work).

   b. Involve elderly people in aerobic exercise programs is not the best answer. Blumethal and others' experimental work supports this claim.

   c. Get elderly men to lose weight is one of the best answers. Although there is experimental work with animals that supports the claim, the research with humans is correlational and subject to alternative interpretations.

   d. Take vitamin E to prevent heart disease is one of the best answers. One reason is that the description of Rimm's work on this issue does not make it clear whether the work is experimental or correlational. A more important reason is that a large-scale correlational study in Finland suggested no influence of vitamin E supplements on heart disease risk.

   e. Teach elderly nursing home residents to assert themselves is not the best answer. Rodin's experimental work supports this claim.

3. The vignette about Sadie Halperin in the Images of Life-Span Development box illustrates several concepts and research findings that are discussed in the section of late adulthood (chapters 18-20). Which of the following statements does Sadie's case least well illustrate? Circle the letter of the best answer and explain why it is the best answer and why each other answer is not as good.

    a. The statement that there are numerous physical changes in late adulthood is not the best answer. The vignette regarding Sadie Halperin eludes to the many physical changes that occur in late adulthood. For example, the chapter discusses respiratory changes and skeletal changes that are mentioned in the vignette.

    b. The statement that there are several benefits from exercise is not the best answer. Sadie provides a good example of several of the benefits of exercise that are described in the chapter. For example, the benefits of exercise on cardiovascular fitness and stability while walking are both mentioned.

    c. The statement that social support is an important part of aging is the best answer. The vignette does not address any aspect of social interactions or social support.

    d. The statement that weight lifting can help prevent osteoporosis is not the best answer. The chapter discusses the benefits of weight lifting for osteoporosis. Women between 50 and 70 who lifted weights lowered their risk of osteoporosis and resulting broken bones, while their balance and muscular strength improved.

    e. The statement that the oldest old group is heterogeneous and diversified is not the best answer. Sadie illustrates that not all individuals in the oldest old subgroup are inactive and plagued by illness. Sadie demonstrates activity by pursuing weight lifting and remaining active through shopping, cooking, and walking.

Handout 4 (CA 6)

Critical Thinking Essay Questions

Your answers to these kinds of questions demonstrate an ability to comprehend and apply ideas discussed in this chapter.

1. Define and distinguish between life expectancy and life span. Also identify factors that influence life expectancy.

2. Explain whether old age is a relatively differentiated or undifferentiated period in life-span development.

3. Compare and contrast the biological theories of aging.

4. Summarize the physical changes that occur in late adulthood with respect to the brain, sensory capacities, circulatory and respiratory systems, and sexuality.

5. Indicate and explain at least three chronic disorders that affect the health of older adults.

6. What do the robust oldest old reveal about stereotyped views of late adulthood?

7. Discuss the role of exercise, nutrition, and weight in the health of elderly adults.

8. Explain and evaluate the controversy regarding vitamins and aging.

9. Explain the rationale for providing options and teaching coping skills to residents of nursing homes.

10. Evaluate whether health-care providers treat older adults better or worse than other developmental age groups such as middle-aged or young adults.

Ideas to Help You Answer Critical Thinking Essay Questions

1. Identifying factors that influence life expectancy should be *part of* your definition and discussion of the distinction between life expectancy and life span.

2. As you explain your answer, present examples and compare and contrast old age with other periods of development.

3. Begin by identifying issues that each theory considers, then discuss how they perceive them. Where is there overlap? Where do they diverge?

4. As you discuss the changes, consider the interrelatedness of change in all of these areas. How do changes in one area influence, and become influenced by, changes in the other areas?

5. Before consulting the text, try to come up with the disorders on your own from what you've observed, or what you associate with being elderly.

6. Begin your discussion by presenting some of the stereotyped views of this stage of life, then present the profile of the robust oldest old for comparison.

7. Answer this question as if you are a counselor or physician addressing a group of senior citizens who will be directly affected, rather than just reporting the basic information.

8. Again, imagine you are someone working closely with elderly individuals and are guiding them with regard to important decisions about their health and well-being.

9. For this question, imagine that you are the director of a nursing home addressing your staff—those who need this information and perspective for responding most effectively to their patients.

10. Begin by identifying the issues that you will consider, then present the information with regard to each issue for each age group.

Variations in Life Expectancy

Administer the life expectancy questionnaire, found in chapter 18, to at least five male and five female acquaintances (or alternatively, to any two or more groups of college students you would like to compare). After you have collected the data, you should add (or subtract) the total points indicated to each individual's basic life expectancy (74 for males, 780 for females; add 10 to these basic figures for each respondent over 50 years of age). Once you have collected your data, you should prepare a table in which you tally the number of individuals in each of your groups who indicated that a question applied to them. Next, calculate the average life expectancy for each group. Finally, write a brief report that summarizes your findings by answering at least the following questions:

Questions:

- Is the pattern of answers for the groups similar or different?

- Which categories of answers tend to be added to or subtracted from each group's life expectancy?

- Does one group have a greater overall life expectancy than the other?

- What conclusions can you draw about the basic life expectancies of each group?

- If the answers to question 14 of the life expectancy quiz indicate interesting group differences, why do you think these differences exist?

Physical Fitness for the Elderly in Your Community

There is a tremendous amount of research available today that points to the importance of exercise for successful aging. This project will allow you to see if this message is getting out to the public. For this project, investigate the physical fitness programs available for elderly people in your community. Call any senior centers in your area to find out what programs are available. You can also visit the local gyms to see if there are any special programs available for elderly people. Visit the gym on three occasions (preferably at different times of day and different days of the week) and make a note of what percentage of the people exercising are elderly (i.e., over 65). You may also want to note what kinds of activities the elderly clients are involved in. Interview four people, one in each of the following age groups: : twenties, forties, sixties, and over-seventies They should ask them the questions that follow.

Questions:

- How often do you exercise?

- What types of exercise do you regularly engage in?

- Do you typically exercise alone or with other people?

- How long have you been regularly exercising?

- How long do you plan to regularly exercise in the future?

- Why do you exercise?

After completing the interviews, compare and contrast the answers given by people in the different age groups. Write a brief report summarizing your findings and indicating how well the message about the benefits of exercise for successful aging has been received in your community. Finally, make a proposal for your city government about improvements in programs/facilities for the elderly to promote physical fitness.

Chapter 19: Cognitive Development in Late Adulthood

Total Teaching Package Outline

Lecture Outline	Reference Resources
Cognitive Development in Late Adulthood	PowerPoint Presentation: See www.mhhe.com Cognitive Maps: See Appendix A
Cognitive Functioning in Older Adults	F/V: The Mind: Aging
• The Multidimensional, Multidirectional Nature of Cognition	LO1 OHT188 & IB: Comparisons of Reasoning Ability
-Cognitive Mechanics and Cognitive Pragmatics	IB: Theorized Age Changes in Cognitive Mechanics and Pragmatics
-Sensory/Motor and Speed-of-Processing Dimensions	
-Memory	LO2 PA1: Remembering When… RP1: Free Recall among College Students and Older Adults WS: Memory and Aging
-Wisdom	PA2: In Age There Is Wisdom F/V: Wind Grass Song F/V: The Wit and Wisdom of Aging

• Education, Work, and Health: Links to Cognitive Functioning
    -Education
    -Work
    -Health
	LO3
	
	CA1: Nontraditional College Students

• Use It or Lose It	CA2: Body Perception in Later Adulthood
• Training Cognitive Skills	LO4
Work and Retirement • Work	LO5 LS1: Work for Seniors
• Retirement in the United States and Other Countries	LO6 CA3: Panel Discussion Regarding Retirement WS: A Guide to Retirement Planning WS: AARP
• Adjustment to Retirement	LS2: Retirement and the Busy Ethic CA4: Elderhostel PA3: Ah, The Easy Life! WS: Elderhostel

The Mental Health of Older Adults	
• The Nature of Mental Health in Older Adults	LO7
• Depression	F/V: A Desperate Act: Suicide and the Elderly
• Dementia and Alzheimer's Disease	LO8
-Dementia	WS: Aging and Dementia
-Alzheimer's Disease	LS3: Diagnosing Alzheimer's Disease LS4: Current Research on Alzheimer's Disease CA5: Panel Discussion Regarding Alzheimer's Disease F/V: Alzheimer's Disease: How Families Cope F/V: The Alzheimer's Mystery F/V: Alzheimer's: The Tangled Mind F/V: When the Mind Fail WS: Alzheimer's Disease WS: The Nun Study
-Multi-Infarct Dementia -Parkinson's Disease	F/V: Nerves WS: Parkinson's Disease
• Fear of Victimization, Crime, and Elder Maltreatment	LO9 LS5: Elder Abuse F/V: Elder Abuse: America's Growing Crime WS: Elder Abuse Law
• Meeting the Mental Health Needs of Older Adults	LO10 RP2: Physical and Mental Health Care of the Elderly
Religion in Late Adulthood	LO11
Review	CA6: Critical Thinking Multiple-Choice CA7: Critical Thinking Essays F/V: Older Voices WS: Aging Quiz

Chapter Outline

COGNITIVE FUNCTIONING IN OLDER ADULTS
   The Multidimensional, Multidirectional Nature of Cognition
- Cognition in adulthood is multidimensional.
- Cognitive change in adulthood is multidirectional.
   Cognitive Mechanics and Cognitive Pragmatics
- Baltes distinguishes between cognitive mechanics and cognitive pragmatics.
  - **Cognitive mechanics** are the hardware of the mind and reflect the neurophysiology architecture of the brain developed through evolution.
    - Cognitive mechanics involve the speed and accuracy of the processes involving sensory input, visual and motor memory, discrimination, comparison, and categorization.

- **Cognitive pragmatics** are the culture-based software programs of the mind.
    - Cognitive pragmatics include reading and writing skills, language comprehension, educational qualifications, professional skills, and also the type of knowledge about the self and life skill that help us to master or cope with life.
- Cognitive mechanics are more likely to decline in older adults than are cognitive pragmatics.

Sensory/Motor and Speed-of-Processing Dimensions
- Sensory functioning is a strong late-life predictor of individual differences in intelligence.
    - Speed of processing information declines in late adulthood.
    - There is individual variation in this decline.
    - It is unclear how much this decline affects daily living.

Memory
- Memory does change during aging, but not all memory changes with age in the same way.

Episodic Memory
- **Episodic memory** is the retention of information about the where and when of life's happenings.
    - Younger adults have better episodic memory than older adults.
- Older adults think that they can remember older events better than more recent events, though research has not supported these claims.

Semantic Memory
- **Semantic memory** is a person's knowledge about the world. It includes a person's fields of expertise (such as knowledge of chess, for a skilled chess player); general academic knowledge of the sort learned in school (such as knowledge of geometry), and "everyday knowledge" about meanings of words, famous individuals, important places, and common things (such as who Nelson Mandela and Mahatma Gandhi are).
    - Semantic memory appears to be independent of an individual's personal identity with the past.
    - Older adults often take longer to retrieve semantic information, but they usually can retrieve it.
- Episodic memory declines more in older adults than semantic memory.

Cognitive Resources: Working Memory and Perceptual Speed
- One view of memory suggests that a limited number of cognitive resources can be devoted to any one cognitive task.
- Two important cognitive resource mechanisms are working memory and perceptual speed.
    - **Working memory** is the concept currently used to describe short-term memory as a place for mental work. Working memory is like a mental "workbench" that allows individuals to manipulate and assemble information when making decisions, solving problems, and comprehending written and spoken language.
    - Perceptual speed is the ability to perform simple perceptual-motor tasks such as deciding whether pairs of two-digit or two-letter strings are the same or different.
- Researchers have found declines in working memory and perceptual speed in older adults.

Explicit and Implicit Memory
- **Explicit memory** (declarative memory) refers to memory of facts and experiences that individuals consciously know and can state.
- **Implicit memory** (procedural memory) refers to memory without conscious recollection; it involves skills and routine procedures that are automatically performed.
- Implicit memory is less likely to be adversely affected by aging than explicit memory.

Memory Beliefs
- An increasing number of studies are finding that people's beliefs about memory play an important role in their memory performance.

Noncognitive Factors
- Noncognitive factors (health, education, and SES) are linked to memory in older adults.
  - Good health does not eliminate memory decline.
- Critics claim that most memory research occurs in laboratories and lacks external validity.

Conclusions about Memory and Aging
- Some aspects of memory decline in older adults.
  - Decline occurs in episodic and working memory, but not in semantic memory.
  - Decline in perceptual speed is associated with memory decline.
- Successful aging does not eliminate memory decline, but reduces it and facilitates adaptation to the decline.

Wisdom
- **Wisdom** is expert knowledge about the practical aspect of life that permits excellent judgement about important matters.
- Although theorists propose that older adults have wisdom, researchers usually find that younger adults show as much wisdom as older adults.

Education, Work, and Health: Links to Cognitive Functioning
- Education, work, and health are three important influences on the cognitive functioning of older adults.
- It is also important to examine cohort effects when studying cognitive functioning in older adults.

Education
- Successive generations of Americans have been better educated.
  - Education is positively correlated with scores on intelligence tests.
  - Older adults may return to education for a number of reasons (to understand their own aging, to learn about societal and technological changes, to remain competitive in the workforce, to enhance their self-discovery and leisure activities, may facilitate the transition to retirement).

Work
- Successive generations have had work experiences that include a stronger emphasis on cognitively oriented labor.
  - The increased emphasis on information processing in jobs likely enhances an individual's intellectual abilities.

Health
- Successive generations have been healthier in late adulthood due to medical advances.
  - Poor health is related to decreased performance on intelligence tests in older adults.
  - Exercise is linked to higher cognitive functioning in older adults.
- The **terminal drop hypothesis** states that death is preceded by a decrease in cognitive functioning over approximately a 5-year period prior to death.
  - The chronic diseases that older adults are more likely to have may decrease their motivation, alertness, and energy to perform competently on tests.
  - The terminal drop hypothesis was supported for tests of vocabulary, not for numerical facility and perceptual speed.

Use It or Lose It
- Researchers are finding that older adults, who engage in cognitive activities, especially challenging ones, have higher cognitive functioning than those who don't use their cognitive skills.

Training Cognitive Skills
- Two main conclusions can be derived from research on training cognitive skills in older adults.
    - There is plasticity, and training can improve the cognitive skills of many older adults.
    - There is some loss in plasticity in late adulthood.
        - Using individualized training, researchers improved the spatial orientation and reasoning skills of two-thirds of the adults.
        - **Mnemonics** are techniques designed to make memory more efficient and can be used to improve older adults' cognitive skills.
    - Greater time spent in communication and leisure activities is linked with positive training effects.

WORK AND RETIREMENT
Work
- Today, the percentage of men over 65 who continue to work full-time is less than at the beginning of the twentieth century.
- An important change involved in adults' work patterns is the increase in part-time work.
    - Some individuals continue a life of strong work productivity throughout late adulthood.
        - Good health, a strong psychological commitment to work, and distaste for retirement are the most important characteristics related to continued employment into old age.
        - Cognitive ability is one of the best predictors of job performance in the elderly.
        - Older workers have lower rates of absenteeism, fewer accidents, and increased job satisfaction compared to younger workers.

Retirement in the United States and Other Countries
- Retirement is a late twentieth century phenomenon in the United States.
    - On average, today's workers will spend 10-15 percent of their lives in retirement.
    - Eighty percent of baby boomers expect to work during retirement for a variety of reasons (enjoyment, income, new career interest).
    - The U.S. has extended the mandatory retirement age upward to 70 years old.
    - Congress voted to ban mandatory retirement for all but a few occupations (police officers, fire fighters, and pilots) where safety is an issue.
        - Efforts have been made to reduce age discrimination in work-related circumstances.
        - Many European countries have lowered the age for mandatory retirement.

Adjustment to Retirement
- Individuals who are healthy, have adequate income, are active, are better educated, have an extended social network of friends and family, and are satisfied with their lives before they retire adjust better to retirement.
- Flexibility is also a key factor to retirement adjustment.
    - It is important to plan psychologically as well as financially for retirement.
    - Individuals who retire involuntarily are more unhealthy, depressed, and poorly adjusted than those who retire voluntarily.

THE MENTAL HEALTH OF OLDER ADULTS
The Nature of Mental Health in Older Adults
- The cost of mental health disorders in older adults is estimated at more than $40 billion per year in the U.S.
    - More important is the loss of human potential and the suffering.
- There is not a higher incidence of mental disorders in older adults than in younger adults.

Depression
- **Major depression** is a mood disorder in which the individual is deeply unhappy, demoralized, self-derogatory, and bored. The individual with major depression does not feel well, loses stamina easily, has a poor appetite, and is listless and unmotivated.
  - Depression has been called the "common cold" of mental disorders.
- The most common predictors of depression in older adults are earlier depressive symptoms, poor health, loss events such as death of a spouse, and low social support.
  - As many as 80 percent of older adults with depressive symptoms receive no treatment at all.
- Combinations of medications and psychotherapy produce significant improvements in almost 4 out of 5 elderly adults with depression.
  - Nearly 25 percent of individuals who commit suicide in the U.S. are 65 years of age or older.

Dementia and Alzheimer's Disease
Dementia
- **Dementia** is a global term for any neurological disorder in which the primary symptoms involve a deterioration of mental functioning.
  - It is estimated that 20 percent of individuals over the age of 80 have dementia.
  - The most common form of dementia is **Alzheimer's disease**, a progressive, irreversible disorder that is characterized by gradual deterioration of memory, reasoning, language, and eventually physical functioning.
Alzheimer's Disease
- Approximately 2.5 million people over the age of 65 in the U.S. have Alzheimer's disease.
  - It is predicted to triple in the next 50 years, as increasing numbers of people live to old age.
- Alzheimer's disease can be either early-onset (initially occurring in individuals younger than 65 years) or late-onset (initial onset after 65 years of age).
  - Early onset is rare (about 10 percent of all cases).
Causes and Treatments
- Special efforts are being made to discover the causes of Alzheimer's disease and effective treatments of it.
  - Alzheimer's disease involves a deficiency in the important brain messenger chemical acetylcholine, which plays an important role in memory.
- Efforts to identify the cause of Alzheimer's have not been successful.
  - Among the main characteristics of Alzheimer's disease are the increasing number of tangles (tied bundles of protein that impact the functioning of the neurons) and plaques (deposits that accumulate in the brain's blood vessels).
    - An abnormal gene may be responsible for as many as one-third of all cases of Alzheimer's disease.
Early Detection of Alzheimer's Disease
- Special brain scans, analysis of spinal fluids, and a sophisticated urine test are being used to detect Alzheimer's disease before its symptoms appear.
Stages
- Alzheimer's disease involves a predictable, progressive decline in physical, cognitive, and social functioning.
- Most individuals with Alzheimer's disease live 8 years after symptoms first appear.
Caring for Individuals with Alzheimer's Disease
- A special concern is the care of Alzheimer's patients and the burden it places on caregivers.
  - Depression has been reported in 50 percent of family caregivers.
  - Respite care can periodically relieve the caregiver from the burden of chronic caregiving.

Multi-Infarct Dementia
- **Multi-infarct dementia** involves a sporadic and progressive loss of intellectual functioning caused by repeated temporary obstruction of blood flow in cerebral arteries.
  - It is estimated that 15-25 percent of dementia involves multi-infarct dementia.
    - Multi-infarct dementia is more common among men with high blood pressure.
    - Individuals can recover from multi-infarct dementia.

Parkinson's Disease
- Another dementia is **Parkinson's disease**, a chronic, progressive disease characterized by muscle tremors, slowing of movement, and partial facial paralysis.
  - It is triggered by degeneration of dopamine-producing neurons in the brain.

Fear of Victimization, Crime, and Elder Maltreatment
- Some of the physical decline and limitations that characterize development in late adulthood contribute to a sense of vulnerability and fear among older adults.
  - Almost one-fourth of older adults say they have a basic fear of being the victim of a crime.
  - Older women are more likely to be victimized or abused than older men.

Meeting the Mental Health Needs of Older Adults
- Older adults receive disproportionately fewer mental health services.
  - A number of barriers to mental health treatment in older adults exist (expense, biases of health-care providers, failed diagnoses).
- There are many different types of mental health treatment available.
- Some mechanisms of change that improve mental health of older adults are:
  - Fostering a sense of control, self-efficacy, and hope.
  - Establishing a relationship with a helper.
  - Providing or elucidating a sense of meaning.
  - Promoting education activities and the development of skills.

RELIGION IN LATE ADULTHOOD
- Many elderly are spiritual leaders in their church and community.
- Religious interest increases in old age (put faith into practice, and attend services).
  - For some, religious practice is associated with sense of well-being.
    - Religion and religious organizations can meet important psychological needs in older adults, offering social support and an opportunity to assume leadership roles.

Learning Objectives

1. Explain the multidimensional, multidirectional nature of change in cognitive functioning
2. Discuss the different types of memory, memory changes, and wisdom.
3. Explain the relationship to cognitive functioning of education, work, and health.
4. Elaborate on the training of cognitive skills.
5. Explain the work trends among older adults.
6. Discuss retirement in the United States and in other countries, including factors that aid adjustment to retirement.
7. Describe the nature of mental disorders in older adults, being sure to mention the predictors of and treatment for depression.
8. Discuss the different types of dementia, including their causes, symptoms, and treatments.
9. Identify the effects of fear of victimization, crime, and elder maltreatment on older adults.
10. Expound on ways in which society can meet the mental health needs of older adults.
11. Discuss the role of religion in late adulthood.

Key Terms

Alzheimer's disease
cognitive mechanics
cognitive pragmatics
dementia
episodic memory
explicit memory
implicit memory
major depression

mnemonics
multi-infarct dementia
Parkinson's disease
semantic memory
terminal drop hypothesis
wisdom
working memory

Key People

Marilyn Albert
Paul Baltes
Fredda Blanchard-Fields

K. Warner Schaie
Sherry Willis

Lecture Suggestion

Lecture Suggestion 1: Work for Seniors Though difficult to get data on, it might be interesting to examine the hiring practices of fast-food restaurants like McDonalds or Wendys. In the past few years, more and more retired adults have found a second career in fast-food restaurants. Money, the prime motivator for some younger workers, may not be the prime motivator for most of the older workers. Most of the older employees enjoy the social interactions, like the work, and want to get out of the house for a portion of each week. The company benefits by hiring dependable employees, with low absenteeism rates, who have few accidents, and who possess mature attitudes about work and dealing with customers. The society benefits from this arrangement because there are fewer and fewer young people to fill low-level service industry and fast-food vacancies.

A discussion of this trend in hiring can be touched upon in a lecture about what older adults do for work after they retire. Most of them work, maybe not right away after retirement, but a fairly large percentage of retired adults go back to work in a part-time position sometime during their retirement. Others postpone retirement, still others find new full-time positions after their first retirement.

Those who do not work in paying jobs often find volunteer jobs. Retired Seniors Volunteer Program places volunteers in all types of positions. SCORE, a volunteer organization that relies on the expertise of retired business executives, is gaining in popularity. Foster grandparents bridge the generation gap by helping teenagers raise their babies. Scores of hospitals, schools, and long-term care facilities depend on their senior volunteers to provide much-needed services in their institutions.

The barriers that traditionally kept people in work are being removed with individual retirement plans offering incentives for early retirement. The barriers that forced people into retirement because of their age have been removed for most occupations so employees can work until they no longer want to, or until their health prevents them from performing their duties. However, difficulties arise concerning how to assess the ability of workers to maintain their positions. Who decides when a worker is no longer safe and should be removed from his or her post? And what if the employer decides that an employee must go, but the employee does not agree? If the employee is fired, is it age discrimination? If the employee is not fired, is it reverse age discrimination? No easy answers to these difficult questions are being found.

Changes in the job market and the educational requirements for entry level positions are keeping some older workers out of some jobs. Other elderly people are taking continuing education courses at local community colleges and universities. Clearly, the options available for older adults are better than ever. Certainly ageism exists and must be fought on every front, but employment and educational opportunities exist, and are being pursued by a growing older population.

Lecture Suggestion 2: Retirement and the Busy Ethic—So, What Do You Do to Keep Yourself Busy? The purpose of this lecture is to summarize Ekerdt's (1986) interesting article on the moral continuity between work and retirement. He distinguishes between a work ethic and a busy ethic. An ethic is a set of beliefs and values that identifies what is good and affirms ideals of conduct. The busy ethic stresses leisure that is earnest, occupied, and filled with activity. The busy ethic is partly based on the work ethic that has predominated in the twentieth century. The work ethic encompasses habits such as diligence, initiative, temperance, self-reliance, and the capacity for deferred gratification. Hanlon (1983) found that persons approaching retirement maintain a commitment to work and subscribe to values about work. Ekerdt asks the question, "what do people do with a work ethic when they no longer work?"

The busy ethic facilitates the transition from work to retirement. Transitions are easier if beliefs are continuous between the two phases. Thus, the transition is facilitated when action in retirement is built upon or integrated with the existing values of the persons. According to Ekerdt, the suggestion that retirees need to unlearn the work ethic is misguided. Rather two devices transform the work ethic. The busy ethic and an ideology of pensions capture moral continuity between work and retirement. The ideology of pensions is based on the idea that the "inoccupation of retirees is considered to have been earned by virtue of having formerly been productive. This veteranship status (Nelson, 1982) justifies the receipt of income without work, preserves the self-respect of retirees, and keeps retirement consistent with the dominant societal prestige system, which rewards members primarily to the extent that they are economically productive" (Ekerdt, 1986, p. 240). Ekerdt proposes that activity that is analogous to work validates retirement.

The busy ethic serves several purposes:

- It legitimates leisure activities.
- It defends retirees against negative judgements (senescence, obsolescence).
- It provides a definition for retirement.
- It "domesticates" retirement by adapting retired life to societal norms.

The retirees themselves, family, friends, and institutions (marketers of products and services, the gerontology profession, and the popular media) support the busy ethic. The busy ethic is most appropriately applied to the young-old and to individuals who are not incapacitated by chronic illness. Not all retirees subscribe to the busy ethic, though the majority do. Ekerdt states that "one cannot talk to retirees for very long without hearing the rhetoric of busyness" (p.244).

- Source: Ekerdt, D.J. (1986). The busy ethic: Moral continuity between work and retirement. The Gerontologist, June, 239-244. Hanlon, M.D. (1983). *Age and the commitment to work.* Flushing, NY: Queens College, City University of New York, Department of Urban Studies (ERIC Document Reproduction Service, #ED 243 003). Nelson, D.W. (1982). Alternative images of old age as the bases for policy. In B.L. Neugarten (Ed.), *Age or need? Public policies for older people.* Beverly Hills, CA: Sage.

Lecture Suggestion 3: Diagnosing Alzheimer's Disease One of the most difficult diagnoses made by geriatricians is that of Alzheimer's disease. Electromagnetic scanning devices are improving the prospects of diagnosis, however, an autopsy is still the most reliable source for a correct diagnosis. A discussion of why the disease is hard to diagnose catches the interest of future physicians in the class. Listing the symptoms of Alzheimer's next to the symptoms of depression and asking students to differentiate between the two often catches the interest of the future clinical psychologists in the class. Future nurses are surprised at the similarities between the disease and low-grade infections in the kidney or liver. Future cognitive psychologists are interested in the changes in memory that closely mirror those accompanying some forms of neurology trauma. In short, the disease is difficult to diagnose, hard to treat, has no known causes, and wreaks havoc on the sufferers and their families.

The latest attempts at discovering a cause may be successful in improving diagnosis and may eventually lead to preventative measures, treatment, and maybe even a cure. The research suggests a genetic cause, and investigators are close to isolating a chromosome (See Lecture Suggestion 4: Current Research on Alzheimer's Disease). Doctors and neuropsychologists continue to struggle with the diagnosis, patients continue to deteriorate, and families suffer seemingly endless years of worry and concern. Your lecture may spark a budding scientist to work on discovering the cause, improving the reliability of the diagnosis, improving the treatment, or counseling the patient or the family who suffers along with them.

The following information was quoted from press releases on Alzheimer's disease research findings from the National Institute on Aging (NIA) http://www.alzheimers.org/nianews/nianews.html. The NIA operates the Alzheimer's Disease Education and Referral Center (ADEAR), which provides information to health professionals and the public on AD and memory impairment. For more information about Alzheimer's disease, contact ADEAR at 1-800-438-4380, or at www.alzheimers.org.

Structural Magnetic Resonance Imaging (MRI) could become an important tool for characterizing and diagnosing Alzheimer's disease (AD) in its very early stages, well before clinical signs appear, according to a new study by researchers in Boston. The study, which measured the volume of specific regions of the brain affected early in the disease process, is a significant step toward ultimately predicting who may be at risk for AD and who might benefit from drug treatments that could prevent the disease or slow its progression. The research, conducted by Marilyn Albert, Ph.D., and her colleagues at Massachusetts General Hospital (MGH) and Harvard Medical School, with collaborators at Brandeis and Boston Universities and Brigham & Women's Hospital, is reported in the April 2000 issue of the Annals of Neurology.

"The study was designed to see whether people in the 'preclinical' phase of AD—people with mild memory impairments who would develop AD at the end of the study—could be identified accurately, in advance of showing outward signs of the disease. At the outset of the study, the 119 participants were divided into two groups—normal and those with mild memory difficulties—and each received a baseline MRI scan. Over 3 years, the participants were followed to determine who developed AD, which was diagnosed by a standard medical evaluation. Researchers then went back to the MRIs that had been taken 3 years earlier to see if the scans could prove useful in predicting who would develop AD. The average age of study participants was the early 70s."

Previous research had indicated that measurements of hippocampal volume could identify some cases of AD before a patient met clinical criteria for dementia. But the Boston researchers were seeking to improve accuracy by honing in on select areas of the brain involved at an earlier stage in the disease process. Albert and colleagues looked at differences in volume in a number of areas, focusing on the entorhinal cortex and the banks of the superior temporal sulcus, both involved in memory, and the anterior cingulate, which affects "executive" functions such as organizing, planning, and switching back and forth among tasks and ideas. Recent studies have shown several of these areas to be affected by a significant loss of neurons early in the AD process.

The researchers found that they could identify people who would develop AD over time based on measurements of these brain regions. The MRIs were 100 percent accurate in discriminating between the participants who were normal and those from a third group looked at by Albert's team who already had mild AD. They were 93 percent accurate in discriminating between participants who were normal and those who initially had memory impairments and ultimately developed AD; the entorhinal cortex in the case of the people "converting" to AD had about 37 percent less volume than the entorhinal cortex of those who remained normal, probably reflecting a loss of brain cells. Other comparisons showed a relatively high accuracy rate as well, although it was more difficult to distinguish the people who continued to have memory problems but did not progress to AD from those who eventually converted to AD.

Albert emphasizes the importance of developing such diagnostic techniques at this time, in concert with the development and testing of dozens of new drugs it is hoped will prevent or slow the progression of AD. "Effective treatments for Alzheimer's disease are likely to be ready over the next decade or so," she notes. "In the not too distant future, we may be able to use MRI, in combination with other measures, to identify people at highest risk who can be effectively treated as these new therapies come along." Albert says that these types of measurements might be useful in monitoring response to treatments as well.

The researchers caution, however, that their MRI technique will need to be further refined and validated before it can be used in everyday practice by neurologists and MRI technicians. Albert points to the study's value in getting scientists on the "right track" about what to measure. But, she says, more research in several areas will need to be done, including follow-up of patients over a longer period of time to more precisely gauge the predictive value of the MRIs. Also, the researchers would like to look at functional MRIs and other imaging techniques to see if accuracy can be improved.

There has been enormous progress in improving clinical diagnosis of dementia and Alzheimer's disease. But research from the Honolulu-Asia Aging Study by G. Webster Ross, M.D., of the Veterans Administration and colleagues from the NIA and other institutions shows that a majority of families may fail to recognize or address symptoms. In the study group of 191 Japanese-American men with dementia, for example, 52 percent of families said they did not see the symptoms at all in patients who were in the early stages of the disease. For patients whose families did recognize a memory problem, 53 percent did not receive a medical workup for memory impairment. As treatments become available, especially for the early stages of Alzheimer's disease, early detection and assessment of dementia will become more important, the researchers say. Cognitive screening and public education programs may need to be developed to help increase awareness.

- Source: http://www.alzheimers.org/nianews/nianews.html

Lecture Suggestion 4: Current Research on Alzheimer's Disease Research on Alzheimer's disease is entering a new, highly productive phase and the pace of promising developments is accelerating. The following information was quoted from press releases announcing Alzheimer's disease research findings from the National Institute on Aging (NIA) (http://www.alzheimers.org/nianews/nianews.html.) The NIA operates the Alzheimer's Disease Education and Referral Center (ADEAR), which provides information to health professionals and the public on AD and memory impairment. For more information about Alzheimer's disease, contact ADEAR at 1-800-438-4380, or through its web site www.alzheimers.org.

Vaccines

In the last few years, research has intensified into ways to prevent or lower the formation of plaques and tangles in the brain that are the major hallmarks of AD. These characteristics, along with inflammation and other pathological changes in the brain, cause damage that eventually can lead to dementia. Amyloid plaques occur when individual peptide fragments clipped from a larger protein, called the amyloid precursor protein, or APP, clump together in the brain. Scientists in both the public and the private sectors are trying to interfere with production of the protein fragment, beta amyloid, or inhibit its clumping into plaques. In a vaccine, some part of the beta amyloid peptide would be administered, at an age and in doses and routes yet to be determined, triggering an immune response against the offending peptide and possibly protecting against disease development. While the exact mechanisms behind the beta amyloid vaccine are not fully understood, researchers believe that the vaccine generates antibodies that bind to beta amyloid in the mouse brain and enhance its removal from the nervous system. The long-term effects of this vaccine on normal brain function need further study.

Nasal administration of synthetic beta amyloid peptide reduces potentially damaging Alzheimer's disease-like plaques in the brains of test mice and may one day be tested in clinical trials for its ability to vaccinate against plaque formation in people with Alzheimer's disease (AD), according to a new study by researchers at Harvard Medical School. The findings are a significant step forward for the concept that an immunological approach, using vaccines, might one day be effective against Alzheimer's disease in humans. The research is a collaboration of the laboratories of Howard L. Weiner, M.D., and Dennis J. Selkoe, M.D., at Harvard and Brigham and Women's Hospital. Cynthia Lemere, Ph.D., in the Selkoe group, and Ruth Maron, Ph.D., in the Weiner group, led the experiments. The findings are reported in the October 2000 issue of the

Annals of Neurology. The National Institute on Aging (NIA) and the National Institute of Allergy and Infectious Disease (NIAID), both part of the Federal government's National Institutes of Health, supported the study.

The Harvard study delivered the beta-amyloid peptide nasally, using a method somewhat like the inhalers used to deliver allergy and asthma medicines. Scientists are interested in testing the delivery of the peptide nasally because it may be better tolerated in humans than repetitive injections over the long-term. In this study, the strength of antibodies resulting from nasal administration of the vaccine was not as great as that from the injection approach, although still significantly effective against plaque formation. The study also identified cellular immune responses in the brains of mice treated nasally with amyloid that may contribute to reducing plaque levels. Apart from the way the vaccine was administered and differences in the strength of the response, the latest study, in most other respects, is consistent with the Elan work, demonstrating that an immunological intervention—such as a vaccine—can lower plaque formation associated with AD.

Investigation of a Number of Influential Genetic and Environmental Factors
apoE-E4 allele

The apoE-E4 allele, while an important genetic risk factor, may account for a fairly small fraction of the disease in the general population. Denis A. Evans, M.D., Rush Alzheimer's Disease Center and Rush Institute on Aging, Rush-Presbyterian-St. Luke's Medical Center in Chicago, and colleagues from other institutions, found an approximately two-fold increased risk of developing Alzheimer's disease associated with apoE-E4 in an East Boston, Massachusetts, population. In this population, an estimated 13.7 percent of all Alzheimer's disease was attributable to this allele. This finding suggests that studies to identify other environmental and genetic risk factors should continue.

Chromosome 10

Three new, separate research studies suggest that a gene or genes on chromosome 10 may be risk factors for late-onset Alzheimer's disease (AD). The findings, reported in the December 22, 2000, issue of *Science*, are important new evidence that more than one gene may play a role in development of AD later in life. AD is a progressive, degenerative disorder, characterized by amyloid plaques and neurofibrillary tangles in the brain, resulting in loss of memory and, finally, in loss of mental and physical function. Scientists involved in the trio of studies reported today by teams at a number of different laboratories think that this newly discovered genetic influence on late-onset AD may possibly involve the processing of the amyloid ß protein (Aß), a peptide important in the formation of AD's hallmark amyloid plaques.

For the past several years, a particular form of the apolipoprotein E (APOE) gene on chromosome 19 has been the only widely recognized genetic risk factor in late onset Alzheimer's disease. Scientists have long suspected that more than one gene may be involved in increasing an individual's risk of developing late-onset AD. Some reports have shown evidence of a risk factor gene on a region of chromosome 12, and investigators worldwide have searched intensively for other genes, on other chromosomes, that might also play a role.

Even with such progress, considerably more testing to pinpoint the identity of the suspect genes needs to be done, researchers say. Scientists will have to sort through each of the hundred or so genes in these chromosome regions to find the gene or genes that might be at work in AD. There are two types of AD—early-onset and late-onset. In early-onset AD, symptoms first appear before age 60. Some early-onset disease runs in families and involves autosomal dominant, or inherited, mutations that are believed to be the actual cause of the disease. So far, three early-onset genes with AD-causing mutations have been identified. Early-onset AD is rare, about 5-10 percent of cases.

The findings reported on December 22 concern late-onset AD, the most common form of the disease, which develops in people 60 and older and is thought to be less likely to occur in families. Late-onset AD may run in some families, but a gene may not be the absolute determinant of whether an individual will develop AD. Rather, the role of genes involved in late onset may be to modify the risk of developing AD by affecting factors involved in the formation of plaques and tangles or other AD-related pathologies in the brain. Scientists hope that by identifying and understanding the function of risk factor genes, as well as possible non-genetic factors like severe head injury, estrogen use, or education that may influence the development of AD, treatments can be developed and the progression of the disease can be slowed or stopped. It is estimated that up to 4 million Americans currently suffer from AD.

Presenilin 1 gene

Another study by F. Lopera, M.D., of Antioquia University, Medellin, Colombia, and researchers at various U.S. institutions, whose work on this project has been supported by the NIA, characterized the pathological and symptomatic variations in a large, early-onset family in Antioquia, Colombia. All affected members of the family share the same mutation in the presenilin 1 gene and show similar disease symptoms and progression. Age of onset, however, varied widely, ranging from 34 to 62 years. This, too, suggests that other genetic and environmental factors may be at work. The researchers and NIA scientists believe that further study of this particular family will yield important information about influences on the age of onset.

Genetics of Alzheimer's Disease and Genetic Testing

The notion that Alzheimer's disease can be caused by a number of different genetic factors is echoed in a review article on the genetics of Alzheimer's disease by Corinne Lendon, Ph.D., Frank Ashall, D. Phil., and Alison Goate, D.Phil., at Washington University. A great deal of progress has been made leading to the identification of three genes whose mutations can cause familial forms of early-onset disease, they note. But it is likely that additional genetic and environmental factors need to be identified, especially in late-onset disease. Much needs to be learned, for example, about how the disease develops, especially the role of beta-amyloid in neurofibrillary tangles, chronic inflammation, and neuronal cell loss.

Stephen Post, Ph.D., of Case Western Reserve University, reports on the findings of the National Study Group of leading genetics researchers, ethicists, and public policy experts, supported by the NHGRI. The panel was set up to review emerging information on genetic testing, taking into consideration the views of people in focus groups convened by the Alzheimer's Association. It concludes that apoE testing is not recommended for people without dementia. For those few people in whom early-onset disease occurs, an estimated 1-2 percent of all cases, genetic predictive testing may be possible, but must be applied with extensive counseling and with adequate safeguards for confidentiality. The panel also expressed concern about the public's incorrect impression that a predictive genetic test exists for the vast majority of people whose disease is late-onset. The potential for discrimination in life and health insurance, especially long-term care insurance, and other possible adverse consequences of testing also are pointed out.

- Source: http://www.alzheimers.org/nianews/nianews.html

Lecture Suggestion 5: Elder Abuse The purpose of this lecture is to expand upon Santrock's discussion of elder abuse. This lecture is based on an article by Rosalie Wolf (1996). Elder abuse is multifaceted as it includes mistreatment as either an act of commission (abuse) or omission (neglect). It can be either intentional or unintentional. Some elder abuse involves a conscious attempt to inflict harm. Other cases of abuse may be unintentional due to infirmity, lack of knowledge, or laziness on the part of the caregiver. The frequency, intensity, severity, duration, and consequences of elder abuse influence the outcome. There are four main types of elder mistreatment.

- Physical abuse: infliction of physical pain or injury (restraining, hitting, and molesting).
- Psychological abuse: infliction of mental anguish (threatening, humiliating).
- Financial abuse: illegal or improper exploitation of funds.
- Neglect: failure to fulfill a caretaking obligation (denial of food or health services).

The issue is complicated by the varying definitions (state-by-state) of abuse. Inconsistent definitions have made it difficult to monitor and assess the prevalence of elder abuse.

Prevalence

- It is estimated that between 4 and 10 percent of all individuals over 65 years of age are abused. One study in Boston found that 3.2 percent had experienced physical abuse, verbal aggression, and/or neglect since they turned 65 years old. Abuse by adult children was less common (24 percent) compared to spouse abuse (58 percent). Cases that come to the attention of adult protective services are thought to be a small portion of the estimated one and one-half million to two million cases of elder abuse and neglect in the United States.

Risk Factors and Characteristics

- Interestingly, stress factors (poverty, job status, loss of family support, etc.) do not seem to be an important risk factor for elder abuse. The cycle of violence hypothesis (victims will become perpetrators) has not been supported by research.
- Other forms of domestic violence and alcohol are associated with elder abuse. Research has also found support for codependence (the unhealthy dependency of the perpetrator on the victim and vice versa) and the disturbed psychological state of the perpetrator, impairment of the victim, and social isolation of the family.

Three profiles emerged from an analysis of 328 cases of mistreatment (physical and psychological abuse, neglect, and financial abuse).

Physical and psychological abuse:

- Perpetrators often had a history of psychopathology and were financially dependent on the victim.
- The victims tend to be relatively independent in their daily activities, though they were emotionally unhealthy.
- Family members are most likely to be the perpetrators (spouses, adult children).
- The violence may be the result of poor interpersonal relationships that were intensified due to illness or financial concerns.

Neglect:

- Neglect victims are more likely to be widowed, very old, cognitively and physically impaired, with few social contacts. Neither psychological nor financial dependency was an issue for the caregivers.

Financial abuse:

- The victims tend to be unmarried with few social contacts. The physical and mental state of the victims are relatively unimportant in financial abuse cases. The risk factors are the perpetrator's financial need or greed and loneliness.

Comparisons have been made between spousal abuse and parent abuse cases. Spouse abuse was most likely to involve physical abuse, poor emotional health, and dependence on the spouse for companionship. Abusing spouses often have medical concerns and physical deterioration. For some individuals, the accumulation of stress from an unhappy marriage and physical illness results in spouse abuse. Adult children were more likely to neglect or psychologically abuse their elderly parent. The adult children often have financial concerns, and a history of mental illness and alcoholism.

- Source: Wolf, R.S. (1996). Understanding elder abuse and neglect. *Aging, 367,* 4-13.

Classroom Activities

Classroom Activity 1: Nontraditional College Students Santrock reports in chapter 19 that more older adults than ever before are going to college. He indicates that college performance among these individuals is related to intelligence and information-processing skills, but he is only able to speculate on the variety of reasons older people go to college. Ask students to speculate on the reasons people of traditional age attend college and why older people do. If people in your class know older students, have them ask these students why they are attending college. Relate what they report to material presented in the text.

Logistics:
- Group size: Full class.
- Approximate time: Full class (20 minutes).

Classroom Activity 2: Body Perception in Later Adulthood This exercise was introduced in chapter 14 and it focuses on body perception. If your students completed this activity during chapter 14, return their handouts to them. If this exercise is new to them, have them complete **Handout 1** prior to reading the chapter. Encourage them to imagine what their physical aspects will be like in late adulthood. Once the Handout questions are completed, reconvene as a full class. How accurate were they regarding their physical abilities? How accurate were they regarding their physical appearance? Were there any obvious gender differences regarding students' perceptions? If so, why?

Logistics:
- Materials: Handout 1 (Body Perception Questionnaire Activity).
- Group size: Individual and full class.
- Approximate time: Individual (15 minutes), full class (25 minutes).

Classroom Activity 3: Panel Discussion Regarding Retirement Invite several older adults into your classroom to discuss their retirement. How did they prepare for it financially? How did they prepare for it psychologically? Does the busy ethic from Lecture Suggestion 2: Retirement and the Busy Ethic—So, What Do You Do to Keep Yourself Busy? relate to these individuals? Are there gender differences?

Logistics:
- Group size: Full class.
- Approximate time: Full class (60 minutes).

Classroom Activity 4: Elderhostel The purpose of this exercise is to expose students to the Elderhostel program. Encourage students to visit the following web site: http://www.elderhostel.org. Have them explore all of the fascinating programs available to elderly adults. Encourage them to pick the one program that they are most interested in. They should print the relevant program and bring it to class. Have them get into small groups to discuss the advantages of participating in that particular program. Many of the advantages will be similar for the various programs, though there may be some differences. Can they think of any disadvantages or negatives associated with the programs offered by the Elderhostel organization?

Logistics:
- Group size: Small group.
- Approximate time: Small group (25 minutes).
- Source: http://www.elderhostel.org

Classroom Activity 5: Panel Discussion Regarding Alzheimer's Disease Many communities have support groups for spouses and families of Alzheimer's patients. Consider inviting a panel of spouses, family members, and group coordinators to class. Students should be instructed to prepare a list of questions for the guests to answer. Questions should be based on their understanding of the disease, their knowledge of other support groups, and should focus on the unique stresses of Alzheimer's disease for those who have the disease and those who care for Alzheimer's victims.

Logistics:
- Group size: Full class.
- Approximate time: Full class (60 minutes).

Classroom Activity 6: Critical Thinking Multiple-Choice Questions and Suggested Answers Discuss the critical thinking multiple-choice questions presented in **Handout 2**. The answers to these questions are presented as **Handout 3**. For question 1, you may want to precede the assignment with a review of the key features of each approach to cognitive development. We recommend this, because this is your "last shot" at these topics and some students will still not be clear on the distinctions among the approaches.

Question 2 requires integration of information from other chapters on late adulthood. The phrase "use it or lose it" applies for various aspects of development.

Question 3 asks the student to once again identify assumptions, inferences, and observations.

Logistics:
- Materials: Handout 2 (the critical thinking multiple-choice questions) and Handout 3 (answers).
- Group size: Small groups to discuss the questions, then a full class discussion.
- Approximate time: Small groups (15 to 20 minutes), full class discussion of any questions (15 minutes).

Classroom Activity 7: Critical Thinking Essay Questions and Suggestions for Helping Students Answer the Essays Discuss students' answers to the critical thinking essay questions presented in **Handout 4**. The purpose of this exercise is threefold. First, answering the essay questions further facilitates students' understanding of concepts in chapter 19. Second, this type of essay question affords the students an opportunity to apply the concepts to their own lives which will facilitate their retention of the material. Third, the essay format also gives students practice expressing themselves in written form. Ideas to help students answer the critical thinking essay questions are provided as **Handout 5**.

Logistics:
- Materials: Handout 4 (essay questions) and Handout 5 (helpful suggestions for the answers).
- Group size: Individual, then full class.
- Approximate time: Individual (60 minutes), full class discussion of any questions (30 minutes).

Personal Applications

Personal Application 1: Remembering When.... The purpose of this exercise is to have students think about memory in late adulthood. Although decline exists in various aspects of memory in late adulthood, many elderly people comfortably enjoy sharing memories from long ago. They seem to recall events from years past in incredible detail.
- Instructions for Students: Recall your favorite story from an elderly person in your life. Although you may not remember all the details, tell as much of it as you can. Does he or she have more than one favorite memory to share (often repeatedly!)? What is the nature of the memories (are they from their childhood and personal experiences? Are they from a dramatic historical occurrence such as the war or Great Depression? Do they involve their children and married life? A family vacation?)? Do you notice any gaps in the story? Does the story change as you hear it time and time again? In what way? Do you sense (or do they acknowledge) that their memory occasionally fails them, or are they "filling in the gaps" with their imagination?

- Use in the Classroom: Discuss aspects of memory in late adulthood. Discuss the strengths and weaknesses apparent from everyone's stories (feel free to share those you've heard from those in older generations). Are their similar themes in the memories classmates have heard? Are there similarities in the extent of detail provided? What do these similarities (and any differences you find) indicate? What memories do your students currently have that they believe will remain throughout their lifetime?

Personal Application 2: In Age There Is Wisdom This exercise is a good way to get students thinking about one of the major benefits of late adulthood—that of having wisdom. Wisdom is defined as expert knowledge about the practical aspects of life that permits excellent judgement about important matters. The only way to obtain wisdom is to acquire and accumulate it over many years, although recent research has found no age differences in the amount of wisdom in young adults and older adults.

- Instructions for Students: Share some of the wisdom you have learned from an older adult. This can be someone you know personally, or someone well-known in the media. Why is this wisdom valuable to you? Do you view it as something strongly connected with the person who espoused it, or do you believe many people share this particular insight? What do you think the individual experienced to lead them to acquire this wisdom? Given research has indicated young adults can be considered to have much wisdom as well, what significant wisdom do you feel you have acquired at this point? What experiences led you to this knowledge and understanding of the world?

- Use in the Classroom: Have everyone come to class prepared to share their favorite words of wisdom. You may even want to write them all down and make copies for each student to keep. Where did they obtain this wisdom? Who do they feel has had the greatest impact on their accumulation of wisdom? (Most likely you will find that the majority is older adults!) Conclude class with students sharing their own personal words of wisdom—and the experiences behind the lessons they've learned.

Personal Application 3: Ah, the Easy Life! The purpose of this exercise is to have students think about the phenomenon of retirement. The perception that one is simply free of working is lacking in many significant areas. After working for typically 40 years, individuals suddenly find themselves with a very unstructured environment, a lack of regular social interaction with co-workers, and a greatly reduced income. There are many aspects to a healthy adaptation and functioning in retirement during this stage of life.

- Instructions for Students: What is your perception of retirement? What issues are of concern to those on the verge of ending their regular days of employment? What impressions of retirement do you get from the media and those around you? How have these helped to form your notion of retirement? Although this may seem like an eternity from now, what do you envision your retirement to be like? What will you do with your time? How will you fare financially? How will you function socially? Is this a time you look forward to eventually or is this something that scares you and you'd rather not consider at this time? How important is it to you to prepare yourself, particularly financially, for the time when you will no longer be working?

- Use in the Classroom: Have students present their "retirement plans." Where will they live? What will they do? Where will their money come from? What do they most look forward to about this time in their life? What do they feel most apprehensive about? Have them tell you why it can be beneficial to start addressing these issues now—even though many have not even begun their careers yet!

Research Project Ideas

Research Project 1: Free Recall Among College Students and Older Adults Chapter 19 reports on various aspects of memory function among older adults compared to younger people, but indicates little specific information about how well older adults can recall information they have just studied compared to younger people. Students can discover something about this by carrying out this research project (**Handout 6**). Prior to the start of the research, the project must be approved by the human subjects review board at your school and the students must get a signed informed consent form from the participants. See the section entitled Ethics, Human Subjects, and Informed Consent at the front of this Instructor's Manual.

They should each locate at least four elderly people and four college age peers to participate in their project. They will make appointments to work individually with each person, allowing at least a half an hour to do their "experiment." Before the appointment, they need to get paper and pencils for their respondents to use. **Handout 7** lists the words they can give their respondents to try to memorize.

At the start of the interview, students should explain their project to the respondents. During this time they should note carefully on their data sheet (**Handout 8**) how the person receives the instructions. For example, are they relaxed? Comfortable? Do they make spontaneous remarks about their memory, or their anticipated performance? Tell students to write down their observations as soon as they can.

Next, they should do the memory "test." Students should give the sheet listing the words (Handout 7) to each person and let them study the words for exactly one minute. When the minute is past, they should retrieve the sheet and ask the person to recite numbers backwards from 99 by threes for 30 seconds. This is a standard control for remembering from short-term rather than long-term memory. Immediately after 30 seconds have passed, students should give their respondent a sheet of paper and a pencil and ask them to write as many of the words as they can.

Tell the students to give respondents as much time as they want; note how much time they take. Observe them carefully, again noting their comfort levels, possibly jotting down their spontaneous remarks. When they say they are finished, the student should retrieve the sheet they have given them, give them another, and ask them to try again. Give them as much time to remember as they want.

When they have finished the second memory trial, students will briefly interview their respondents about their experience. Were they comfortable? Did they enjoy the task? Did they feel confident? Do they feel they performed well? Throughout this interview, the students should be as supportive and as interested as they can, and assure people that they appreciate their willingness to participate in their project. If the student has time, they might try to answer any questions the respondents have about human memory.

Students should summarize their data in a table that lists the number of words each person in each age group was able to recall, and how much time they spent trying to recall, for each trial. They should compute averages (means) and list these in their table. They also need to indicate how well and fast the subjects remembered on the first and second trials. Next, they will need to summarize their observations about the reactions to the task of people in each group. Note how many people in each group were comfortable, anxious, confident; note whether there were comments typically expressed by each group. Finally, students should study the order in which respondents remembered the words. Did they appear to have used any of the words' characteristics to help themselves remember?

Students should then write a brief paper in which they report their data. Instruct them to be sure to describe the people who participated, including their sex, age, race/ethnicity, and current "life situation." In addition, students should discuss their results in terms of information reported in their text. They should try to determine whether such things as emotional reaction, confidence, time spent remembering, and use of word characteristics were related to number of words recalled. What do they conclude about the relative recall performance levels of college students versus elderly adults?

- Use in the Classroom: Have students divide into small groups and compile their data. After each group has compiled their data and drawn some conclusions about the relative recall ability of college students versus elderly adults, discuss these conclusions as a class. Ask the students to discuss any problems they had with their "experiments" and how they would correct these problems in future studies.

Research Project 2: Physical and Mental Health Care of the Elderly What is your community's response to the physical and mental health needs of its aging people? Have students find out by doing a survey of agencies and businesses that provide services for these needs (**Handout 9**). They could begin by searching the Yellow Pages of the phone book under "Social Services Agencies," but they should be aware that not all services are listed there. Another place to search is "First Call for Help," a locally run national network of information of referral and crisis intervention phone services. Have students gather at least the following information on the agencies and businesses they identify:
- name of the agency
- services it provides
- cost of services
- whether it employs paid employees or volunteers
- who are its clients
- how many clients it serves

They should also try to determine to what extent the needs of local elderly people are being met by these services. For example, does each agency have a waiting list of people they cannot serve yet? Students should summarize their findings in a report in which they answer the following questions.

Questions:
- What is the range of services available?
- What is the average cost of services? Who pays these costs?
- Do people who provide basic services appear to be paid adequately?
- Do elderly people in general have access to physical and mental health care in your community? Do some groups (e.g., social classes) have better access? Worse?
- If you were to provide a new service, what would it be?
- Use in the Classroom: Discuss the findings of students' projects. Create a list of the social service agencies available for the elderly in your community. Have students present their ideas for new services that should be provided.

Film and Video List

The following films and videos supplement the content of chapter 19. Contact information for film distributors can be found at the front of this Instructor's Manual under Film and Video Sources.

Alzheimer's Disease: How Families Cope (Films for the Humanities and Sciences, 28 minutes). Practical information on how to manage Alzheimer's is discussed for the patient and caregiver.

The Alzheimer's Mystery (Films for the Humanities and Sciences, 48 minutes). This program traces the initiative to understand the disease and shows families and patients describing how they cope with the illness. Medical professionals address the disease's pathology, research, and the importance of compassionate health care.

Alzheimer's: The Tangled Mind (Films for the Humanities and Sciences, 75 minutes). This program looks into one couple's experience with Alzheimer's disease. It chronicles the life of a prominent husband, father, professor, and pianist.

A Desperate Act: Suicide and the Elderly (Films for the Humanities and Sciences, 23 minutes). This program addresses the chronic depression that leads many senior citizens to take their own lives. Promoting prevention, intervention, and follow-up, medical experts use three case studies as a basis for discussing the warning signs of depression and treatment through counseling, education, medication, and other therapies.

Elder Abuse: America's Growing Crime (Films for the Humanities and Sciences, 16 minutes). *ABC News* correspondents Diane Sawyer and Marti Emerald probe what is quickly becoming the fastest-growing family crime in the U.S. Several cases of elder abuse are investigated and the efforts of crusaders against such treatment are discussed.

The Mind: Aging (PBS, 60 minutes). This video examines what happens to the brain and mind during the aging process. It includes a discussion of the role of genetics and the environment in degenerative diseases such as Alzheimer's disease.

Nerves (Insight Media, 24 minutes). This BBC animated video discusses propagation, synapses, and transmitters, and explores disorders such as Alzheimer's disease and Parkinson's disease.

Older Voices: Interviewing Older Adults (Insight Media, 46 minutes). This video is designed to train interviewers to use flexible techniques for interviewing elderly people.

When the Mind Fails: A Guide to Alzheimer's Disease (Films for the Humanities and Sciences, 58 minutes). This program provides steps for care giving and patients. Case studies and medical insights provide the means to display such steps.

Wind Grass Song: The Voice of Our Grandmothers (Women Make Movies, 20 minutes). This video is based on interviews with Oklahoma women aged 85 to 101. It presents a unique vision of life on the land through invaluable oral histories.

The Wit and Wisdom of Aging (Films for the Humanities and Sciences, 26 minutes). This video tells the story of Norman Cousins and his fight with a fatal disease. It shows the effects of emotions on health and the immune system.

Web Site Suggestions

The URLs for general sites, common to all chapters, can be found at the front of this Instructor's Manual under Useful Web Sites. At the time of publication, all sites were current and active, however, please be advised that you may occasionally encounter a dead link.

AARP: American Association of Retired Persons
http://www.aarp.org/whatnew/whatnw.html

Aging and Dementia
http://www.med.nyu.edu/clnres95/agedemen.htm

Aging Quiz
http://crab.rutgers.edu/~deppen/agingIQ.htm

Alzheimer's Disease
http://www.alzheimers.org/
http://www.alzheimers.org/nianews/nianews.html

Elder Abuse Law
http://www.elderabuselaw.com/library/cases/cahf-dhs-smy.html

Elderhostel
http://www.elderhostel.org

A Guide to Retirement Planning
http://www.schwab.com/retire/employer-retirement.html

Memory and Aging
http://www.nymemory.org/

The Nun Study
http://www.coa.uky.edu/nunnet/

Parkinson's Disease
http://health.yahoo.com/health/Diseases_and_Conditions/Disease_Feed_Data/Parkinson_s_disease/

Body Perception Questionnaire Activity

Answer each of the following questions regarding your perceptions of your body *as you imagine them to be in late adulthood.*

1. What is the strongest part of your body?

2. What is the weakest part?

3. What is the oldest part?

4. What is the youngest part?

5. What do you consider the most attractive part of your body?

6. What is the least attractive?

7. Where does your body have the most warmth?

8. Where is your body coldest?

9. What is the most vulnerable part of your body—the place most quickly or easily hurt?

10. What is the smoothest part of your body?

11. What is the roughest part?

12. What is the hardest part?

13. Where do you carry tensions in your body?

14. What part of your body do you most want to change?

15. What do you least want to change?

16. What part of your body are you ashamed of?

17. What part of your body do you feel most proud of?

Critical Thinking Multiple-Choice Questions

1. Throughout the text, you have learned about different approaches to cognitive development. For example, in chapter 2 you learned about the Piagetian and information-processing approaches; in chapters 6 and 8 you learned about the individual differences approach; and in chapter 14 you learned about the stage theories of LaBouvie-Vief and Schaie. Which of these approaches has generated what we know about cognitive changes in old age? Circle the letters of as many answers as apply and explain why they are the best answers and why each other answer is not as good.

   a. Piagetian approach
   b. Information-processing approach
   c. Individual differences approach
   d. LaBouvie-Vief's approach
   e. Schaie's approach

2. Santrock emphasizes the adage, "Use it or Lose it," throughout the section on late adulthood. Identify the statements below regarding physical and cognitive aspects of aging that reflect this philosophy. Circle the letters of as many answers as apply and explain why they are the best answers and why each other answer is not as good.

   a. Crossword puzzles can facilitate the maintenance of cognitive abilities.
   b. Attendance at concerts and lectures can help buffer against cognitive decline.
   c. Weight lifting can facilitate the maintenance of physical abilities.
   d. Sexual activity can decrease one's sexual interest and competence.
   e. Aerobic exercise can enhance one's physical functioning.

3. Toward the end of chapter 19, Santrock discusses the problem of meeting the mental health needs of older adults. Which of the following statements is an assumption, rather than an inference or an observation, that underlies Santrock's claim that we are not meeting the mental health care needs of the elderly? Circle the letter of the best answer and explain why it is the best answer and why each other answer is not as good.

   a. Older adults receive proportionately fewer mental health services than do younger people.
   b. Psychologists fail to treat older adults because they perceive that older adults have a poor prognosis for therapy success.
   c. Psychotherapists like to work with young, attractive, verbal, intelligent, and successful clients.
   d. Medicare currently pays lower percentages for mental health care than for physical health care.
   e. As the population of older adults increases, so will the number of those who need mental health services.

Suggested Answers for Critical Thinking Multiple-Choice Questions

1. Throughout the text, you have learned about different approaches to cognitive development. For example, in chapter 2 you learned about the Piagetian and information-processing approaches; in chapters 6 and 8 you learned about the individual differences approach; and in chapter 14 you learned about the stage theories of LaBouvie-Vief and Schaie. Which of these approaches has generated what we know about cognitive changes in old age? Circle the letter of the best answer and explain why it is the best answer and why each other answer is not as good.

   a. Piagetian approach is not the best answer. There is no discussion of formal reasoning skills per se in this chapter and there is no implicit or explicit treatment of stages of cognitive development in old age.

   b. Information-processing approach is the best answer. The focus on speed of processing, memory, problem solving, training cognitive skills, and cognitive mechanics versus cognitive pragmatics is very much the information-processing focus.

   c. Individual differences approach is not the best answer. If research regarding crystallized and fluid intelligence had been discussed, then the individual differences approach would have been a good answer.

   d. LaBouvie-Vief's approach is not the best answer. There seems to be little discussion of the nature of "realities constraints" to which older adults adapt in the material of chapter 19.

   e. Schaie's approach is not the best answer. Nothing is included in the chapter concerning Schaie's reintegrative stage, though appropriate places for this to be included in the chapter could be the sections titled "Education," "Work," and "Wisdom." The main problem is that the issues raised in these sections do not seem to resemble the concerns cited as characteristic of Schaie's reintegrative stage.

2. Santrock emphasizes the adage, "Use it or Lose it," throughout the section on late adulthood. Identify the statements below regarding physical and cognitive aspects of aging that reflect this philosophy. Circle the letters of as many answers as apply and explain why they are the best answers and why each other answer is not as good.

   a. The statement crossword puzzles can facilitate the maintenance of cognitive abilities reflects a true statement. Cognitive aging expert Albert mentioned doing crossword puzzles as one activity that can benefit the maintenance of cognitive skills in older adults.

   b. The statement attendance at concerts and lectures can help buffer against cognitive decline is also accurate. Hultsch et al. found that intellectually engaging activities served as a buffer against cognitive decline for older adults.

   c. The statement weight lifting can facilitate the maintenance of physical abilities is accurate. As discussed in chapter 18, weight lifting can help prevent osteoporosis and facilitate one's ability to balance and prevent broken bones.

   d. The statement sexual activity can decrease one's sexual interest and competence is not accurate. While Santrock does not explicitly state that consistent sexual activity facilitates sexual functioning, research has found this to be the case.

   e. The statement aerobic exercise can enhance one's physical functioning is accurate. As discussed in chapter 18, aerobic exercise can enhance one's respiratory and circulatory functioning.

3. Toward the end of chapter 19, Santrock discusses the problem of meeting the mental health needs of older adults. Which of the following statements is an assumption, rather than in inference or an observation, that underlies Santrock's claim that we are not meeting the mental health care needs of the elderly? Circle the letter of the best answer and explain why it is the best answer and why each other answer is not as good.

   a. <u>Older adults receive proportionately fewer mental health services than do younger people</u> is not the best answer. It is an observation based on the relative proportions of older and younger people in the population and the number of services each group receives.

   b. <u>Psychologists fail to treat older adults because they perceive that older adults have a poor prognosis for therapy success</u> is not the best answer. It is an inference that is proposed as an explanation for the fact that psychologists often do not see elderly patients. No confirming evidence appears in the relevant passages.

   c. <u>Psychotherapists like to work with young, attractive, verbal, intelligent, and successful clients</u> is the best answer. This is the assumption. Santrock does not provide any data to support this statement.

   d. <u>Medicare currently pays lower percentages for mental health care than for physical health care</u> is not the best answer. It is an observation that Santrock cites as relevant to the problem of meeting the mental health needs of older adults.

   e. <u>As the population of older adults increases, so will the number of those who need mental health services</u> is not the best answer. It is an inference, a projection of future mental health needs, based partly on the fact that there will be more individuals in late adulthood in the next century.

Critical Thinking Essay Questions

Your answers to these kinds of questions demonstrate an ability to comprehend and apply ideas discussed in this chapter.

1. Define and distinguish between cognitive mechanics and cognitive pragmatics, and use what information is given in chapter 19 to draw conclusions about changes in each during late adulthood.

2. Identify and explain changes in memory in late adulthood.

3. Explain how education, work, and health affect cognitive performance for older adults.

4. Define wisdom, and explain whether it changes over the course of adult development.

5. Explain the nature and meaning of terminal drop to an elderly friend.

6. Explain the benefits of cognitive training research for both elderly adults and those who study the cognitive abilities of elderly adults.

7. Compare work and retirement in the United States with work and retirement in other countries.

8. Describe some factors that influence one's adjustment to retirement and satisfaction with retirement.

9. Indicate and explain the major mental health problems and concerns of older adults.

10. Describe the similarities and differences between dementia associated with Alzheimer's disease, multi-infarct dementia, and Parkinson's disease.

11. Evaluate the prospects of mental health care of the elderly.

12. Describe the nature of elderly people's involvement in and benefits received from religion.

Ideas to Help You Answer Critical Thinking Essay Questions

1. Distinguish means to address them with regard to each other—how they're related, how they are different, etc. Are their changes related? Do they impact one another?

2. Provide examples to illustrate the differences between memory functioning at earlier stages and old age.

3. Address each (education, work, health) with regard to each cognitive issue (memory, information processing, etc.)

4. Provide examples of "wisdom" from individuals of various ages (including children)—and even yourself!

5. Consider who your audience is, and adapt the tone of your writing accordingly.

6. First, present the notion of cognitive training including information such as how it works, expected outcomes, etc.

7. What are the issues involved in this aspect of life-span development? Are they the same for most countries? Different? If so, how? Follow your explanation up with a personal commentary.

8. Outline the basics of retirement—what changes have occurred from the previous working lifestyle? What issues do people have to face?

9. Clearly identify health related concerns from those which are not. How much overlap is there?

10. Define each condition first. Proceed by highlighting the overlap and shared characteristics, the defining characteristics, etc.

11. Begin by describing what's available. How easily accessible is each? Affordable? Beneficial? Then make an evaluative assessment.

12. Be sure and relate these two issues—involvement and benefits. Could their benefits change as their involvement changes? Do the elderly alter their involvement to "up" their benefits?

Free Recall among College Students and Older Adults

Prior to the start of the research, the project must be approved by the human subjects review board at your school and the students must get a signed informed consent form from the participants. See the section entitled Ethics, Human Subjects, and Informed Consent at the front of this Instructor's Manual. Locate at least four elderly people and four of your college age peers to participate in your project. Make appointments to work individually with each person, allowing at least a half an hour to do your "experiment." Before the appointment, get paper and pencils for your respondents to use to write down the words they remember from the list. **Handout 7** lists the words that you can give your respondents to test their memory.

At the start of the interview, explain your project to your respondents. During this time, note carefully on your data sheet (**Handout 8**) how they receive the instructions. For example, are they relaxed? Comfortable? Do they make spontaneous remarks about their memory, or their anticipated performance? Be sure to note your observations as soon as you can.

Next, do the memory "test." Give the sheet listing the words to each person and let them study the words for exactly one minute. When the minute is past, retrieve the sheet and ask the person to recite numbers backwards from 99 by threes for 30 seconds. This is a standard control for remembering from short-term rather than long-term memory. Immediately after 30 seconds have passed, give your respondent a sheet of paper and a pencil and ask them to write as many of the words from the list as they can.

Give respondents as much time as they want; note how much time they take. Observe them carefully, again noting their comfort levels, possibly jotting down their spontaneous remarks. When they say they are finished, retrieve the sheet you have given them, give them another, and ask them to try again. Give them as much time to remember as they want.

When they have finished the second memory trial, briefly interview your respondents about their experience. Were they comfortable? Did they enjoy the task? Did they feel confident? Do they feel they performed well? Throughout this interview, be as supportive and as interested as you can, and assure them that you appreciate their willingness to participate in your project. If you have time, you might try to answer any questions they have about human memory.

Summarize your data in a table that lists the number of words each person in each age group was able to recall, and how much time they spent trying to recall, for each trial. Compute averages (means) and list these in your table. Indicate how well and fast they remembered on the first and second trials. Next, summarize your observations about the reactions of people in each group to the task. Note how many people in each group were comfortable, anxious, confident; record whether there were comments typically expressed by each group. Finally, study the order in which respondents remembered the words. Did they appear to have used any of the words' characteristics to help themselves remember?

Write a brief paper in which you report your data. Be sure to describe the people who participated, including their sex, age, race/ethnicity, and current "life situation." Discuss your results in terms of information reported in your text. Try to determine whether such things as emotional reaction, confidence, time spent remembering, and use of word characteristics were related to number of words recalled. What do you conclude about the relative recall performance levels of college students versus elderly adults?

Handout 7 (RP 1)

Words to be Remembered for Free Recall among College Students and Older Adults Project

Study the words below for one minute. You will be asked to recall as many words as possible after a brief delay.

street

trail

Abe

chair

beer

rain

ape

drape

pear

ham

hail

tail

Claire

lamb

pony

sleet

lane

cone

phone

brain

grape

Tony

Sam

lamp

Handout 8 (RP 1)

Data Sheet for Free Recall among College Students and Older Adults Project

For each respondent record the following information.

Before the Memory Task

1	2	3	4	5
Very Uncomfortable				Very Comfortable

1	2	3	4	5
Very Anxious				Not at all Anxious

1	2	3	4	5
Not at all Confident				Very Confident

Comments Made:

During the Memory Task

1	2	3	4	5
Very Uncomfortable				Very Comfortable

1	2	3	4	5
Very Anxious				Not at all Anxious

1	2	3	4	5
Not at all Confident				Very Confident

Comments Made:

Handout 8 (RP 1) continued

<u>After the Memory Task</u>

1	2	3	4	5
Very Uncomfortable				Very Comfortable

1	2	3	4	5
Very Anxious				Not at all Anxious

1	2	3	4	5
Not at all Confident				Very Confident

Comments Made:

Physical and Mental Health Care of the Elderly

What is your community's response to the physical and mental health needs of its aging people? Find out by doing a survey of agencies and businesses that provide services for these needs. You could begin by searching the Yellow Pages of the phone book under "Social Services Agencies," but be aware that not all services are listed there. Another place to search is "First Call for Help," a locally run national network of information of referral and crisis intervention phone services.

Gather at least the following information on the agencies and businesses you identify:
- name of the agency
- services it provides
- cost of services
- whether it employs paid employees or volunteers
- who are its clients
- how many clients it serves

Try also to determine to what extent the needs of local elderly people are being met by these services. For example, does each agency have a waiting list of people they cannot serve yet? Summarize your findings in a report in which you answer the following questions.

Questions:

- What is the range of services available?

- What is the average cost of services? Who pays these costs?

- Do people who provide basic services appear to be paid adequately?

- Do elderly people in general have access to physical and mental health care in your community? Do some groups (e.g., social classes) have better access? Worse?

- If you were to provide a new service, what would it be?

Chapter 20: Socioemotional Development in Late Adulthood

Total Teaching Package Outline

Lecture Outline	Resource References
Socioemotional Development in Late Adulthood	PowerPoint Presentation: See www.mhhe.com Cognitive Maps: See Appendix A
Theories of Socioemotional Development	PA1: Aging by the Numbers RP1: Collecting a Life Story F/V: Older Voices: Interviewing Older Adults WS: The New England Centenarian Study
• Erikson's Theory	LO1 F/V: On Old Age F/V: On Old Age II
-Robert Peck's Reworking of Erikson's Final Stage -Life Review	LO2 LS1: Life Review
• Disengagement Theory	LO3 OHT189 & IB: Social Breakdown
• Activity Theory	
• Socioemotional Selectivity Theory	LS2: Socioemotional Selectivity Theory
• Selective Optimization with Compensation Theory	
Older Adults in Society	
• Stereotyping Older Adults	LO4 CA1: Media and Late Adulthood PA2: What a Geezer! WS: Ageism
• Policy Issues in an Aging Society	LO5 LS3: Intergenerational Politics CA2: Social Security PA3: It Will Be You Some Day
• Income	LO6 OHT194: Sources of Income for Older Americans CA3: Debate: Are Elderly Americans Poor? WS: Economics of Aging Publications
• Living Arrangements	LO7 OHT195: Living Arrangements LS4: Choosing a Nursing Home LS5: Alternative Living Arrangements WS: Directory of Nursing Homes

Families and Social Relationships • The Aging Couple	LO8 RP2: The Aging Couple F/V: Love, Intimacy, and Sexuality F/V: Sexuality and Aging
• Grandparenting -Satisfaction with Grandparenting -Grandparent Roles and Styles -The Changing Profile of Grandparents	LO9 WS: Articles on Grandparenting CA4: Grandparenting Styles
• Friendship	LO10
• Social Support and Social Integration	LO11

Ethnicity, Gender, and Culture
• Ethnicity and Gender
    -Ethnicity
 	
    -Gender
 	
    -Racism and Sexism
 	
• Culture
	LO12
	
	WS: Women and Successful Aging
	
	LO13
	F/V: To Be Old, Black, and Poor

Successful Aging	LO14 LS6: Successful Aging F/V: Aging Successfully
Review	CA5: Critical Thinking Multiple-Choice CA6: Critical Thinking Essays

Chapter Outline

THEORIES OF SOCIOEMOTIONAL DEVELOPMENT
    Erikson's Theory
- **Integrity versus despair** is Erikson's eighth and final stage of development, which individuals experience during late adulthood.
  - This involves reflecting on the past and either piecing together a positive review or concluding that one's life has not been well spent.

    Robert Peck's Reworking of Erikson's Final Stage
- Peck reworked Erikson's final stage by describing three tasks that older adults face.
  - **Differentiation versus role preoccupation** is Peck's developmental task in which older adults must redefine their worth in terms of something other than work roles.
  - **Body transcendence versus body preoccupation** is Peck's developmental task in which older adults must cope with declining physical well-being.
  - **Ego transcendence versus ego preoccupation** is Peck's developmental task in which older adults must recognize that, while death is inevitable and probably not too far away, they feel at ease with themselves by realizing that they have contributed to the future through the competent rearing of their children or through their vocation and ideas.

Life Review
- Life review involves looking back at one's life experiences, evaluating them, interpreting them, and often reinterpreting them.

Disengagement Theory
- **Disengagement theory** states that to cope effectively older adults should gradually withdraw from society.
  - According to this theory, older adults develop increasing self-preoccupation, decreasing emotional ties with others, and decreasing interest in society's affairs which leads to enhanced life satisfaction.
- This theory is no longer viable.

Activity Theory
- **Activity theory** states that the more active and involved older adults are, the more likely they will be satisfied with their lives.
- Researchers have found strong support for this theory.

Socioemotional Selectivity Theory
- **Socioemotional selectivity theory** states that older adults become more selective about their social networks. Because they place a high value on emotional satisfaction, older adults often spend more time with familiar individuals with whom they have had rewarding relationships.
  - Carstensen argues that older adults deliberately withdraw from social contact with individuals peripheral to their lives, while they maintain or increase contact with close friends and some family members.
  - Socioemotional selectivity theory focuses on the types of goals that individuals are motivated to achieve.
    - Motivation for knowledge-based goals starts high in early years, peaks in adolescence and early adulthood, then declines in middle and late adulthood.
    - Motivation for emotional goals is high in infancy and early childhood, declines from middle childhood through early adulthood, and increases in middle and late adulthood.

Selective Optimization with Compensation Theory
- **Selective optimization with compensation theory** states that successful aging is linked with three main factors: selection, optimization, and compensation.
  - Selection is based on the concept that older adults have a reduced capacity and loss of functioning, which require a reduction in performance in most life domains.
  - Optimization suggests that it is possible to maintain performance in some areas through continued practice and technology.
  - Compensation involves altering and modifying how one carries out previous tasks in order to increase the level of functioning.
- The process of selective optimization with compensation is likely to be effective whenever loss is prominent in a person's life.

OLDER ADULTS IN SOCIETY
Stereotyping Older Adults
- **Ageism** is prejudice against others because of their age, especially prejudice against older adults.
  - Many negative stereotypes for the elderly exist today.
    - Young, middle-aged, and older adults hold many of the same stereotypes about individuals in late adulthood.

Policy Issues in an Aging Society
- These include the status of the economy and the viability of the Social Security system, the provision of health care, supports for caregiving families, and generational inequity.
  - It is incorrect to describe older adults as consumers and younger adults as producers.
  - About one-third of the total health bill of the U.S. is for the care of older adults, who comprise only 12 percent of the population.
    - Health-care personnel need to be trained and be available to provide home services and to share authority with the patient.
- **Eldercare** is the physical and emotional caretaking of older members of the family, whether that care is day-to-day physical assistance or responsibility for arranging and overseeing such care.
- **Generational inequity** states that an aging society is being unfair to its younger members because older adults pile up advantages by receiving an inequitably large allocation of resources.

Income
- The elderly poor are a special concern.
  - Approximately 10 to 12 percent of the elderly live in poverty.
  - More than 25 percent of older women who live alone live in poverty.
  - Poverty rates among ethnic minorities are 2-3 times higher than the rate for Whites.
  - The oldest old is the age group most likely to be living in poverty.
- Many middle-aged individuals do not adequately plan for retirement.

Living Arrangements
- Most older adults (95 percent) live in the community, not in institutions.
  - Almost two-thirds of older adults live with family members.
- Twenty-three percent of adults 85 years and over live in institutions.

FAMILIES AND SOCIAL RELATIONSHIPS
The Aging Couple
- Retirement alters a couple's lifestyle and requires adaptation.
- Married older adults are often happier than single older adults.
- Regarding sexuality, many older couples emphasize intimacy over sexual prowess.

Grandparenting
Satisfaction with Grandparenting
- Most grandparents are satisfied with their role.
- Middle-aged grandparents are more involved in caregiving and discipline than older grandparents.
- Frequency of contact predicted satisfaction with grandparenting.
Grandparent Roles and Styles
- Three prominent meanings have been attached to being a grandparent (biological reward and continuity, emotional fulfillment and companionship, or a remote role).
- Three styles have been identified (formal, fun-seeking, and distinct figure).
The Changing Profile of Grandparents
- The profile of grandparents is changing, due to such factors as divorce and remarriage.
- A single grandmother raises almost half of grandchildren who move in with grandparents.
- Grandparents who take in grandchildren are in better health, are better educated, and more likely to be working outside of the home.
- Grandparents are being granted visitation privileges to see their grandchildren in the case of divorce.

Friendship
- People choose close friends over new friends, as they grow older.
- There is more continuity than change in friendships for older adults.
- There is more change in male than female friendships.
- Friends play an important role in the support systems of older adults.

Social Support and Social Integration
- Social support is linked with improved physical and mental health in older adults.
- Social integration plays an important role.
  - Being lonely and socially isolated is a significant health risk factor in older adults.
  - Older adults who participate in more organizations live longer than their counterparts who have low participation rates.
  - Older adults often have fewer peripheral social ties but a strong motivation for spending time in relationships with close friends and family members that are rewarding.

ETHNICITY, GENDER, AND CULTURE
Ethnicity and Gender
Ethnicity
- Of special concern are the ethnic minority elderly, especially African Americans and Latinos, who are overrepresented in the elderly poor.
  - Aging minorities have to cope with the double burden of ageism and racism (double jeopardy).
    - Both the wealth and the health of ethnic minority elderly decrease more rapidly than for elderly Whites.
    - Extension of family networks helps elderly minority group members cope with the essentials of living and gives them a sense of being loved.
  - There is considerable variation in aging minorities.
Gender
- There is stronger evidence that men become more feminine (nurturing, sensitive) as older adults than there is that women become more masculine (assertive).
Racism and Sexism
- Many women face a double jeopardy of ageism and sexism.
  - The poverty rate for elderly females is almost double that of elderly males.
- Female, ethnic minority individuals may face triple jeopardy (ageism, sexism, and racism).

Culture
- The following factors are most likely to predict high status for the elderly in a culture.
  - Older persons have valuable knowledge.
  - Older persons control key family/community resources.
  - Older persons are permitted to engage in useful and valued functions as long as possible.
  - There is role continuity throughout the life span.
  - Age-related role changes involve greater responsibility, authority, and advisory capacity.
  - The extended family is a common family arrangement in the culture, and the older person is integrated into the extended family.
- Historically, respect for older adults in China and Japan was high, but today their status is more variable.

SUCCESSFUL AGING
- Increasingly, the positive aspects of older adults are being studied.
- Factors linked to successful aging include an active lifestyle, positive coping skills, good social relationships and support, and self-efficacy.

Learning Objectives

1. Discuss Erikson's eighth stage of psychosocial development and Robert Peck's reworking of this final stage.
2. Explain the life review process.
3. Elaborate on the four theories of socioemotional development.
4. Discuss the stereotyping of older adults.
5. Indicate the policy issues we face in an aging society.
6. Discuss how income changes for the elderly.
7. Discuss the living arrangements of the elderly.
8. Describe the aging couple, including marriage, dating, and sexuality.
9. Explore aspects of grandparenting such as their satisfaction, their roles and styles, and changing characteristics.
10. Describe how friendship changes as we grow old.
11. Elaborate on the importance of social support and social integration for older adults.
12. Explain the roles of ethnicity, gender, and culture in aging.
13. Describe the factors associated with holding a high position in a culture.
14. Expound on the factors related to successful aging.

Key Terms

activity theory
ageism
body transcendence versus body
   preoccupation
differentiation versus role
   preoccupation
disengagement theory

ego transcendence versus
   ego preoccupation
eldercare
generational inequity
integrity versus despair
selective optimization with
   compensation theory
socioemotional selectivity theory

Key People

Paul Baltes
Robert Butler
Laura Carstensen

Erik Erikson
Bernice Neugarten
Robert Peck

Lecture Suggestions

Lecture Suggestion 1: Successful Aging This lecture extends Santrock's discussion of Peck's early attempt to identify factors related to successful aging. Peck (1955) expanded upon Erikson's psychosocial development in middle and late adulthood. Peck identified seven psychological developments that he considered crucial for a healthy adaptation to aging.

Given that aging is a gradual process, psychological developments in middle adulthood affect whether one experiences successful aging. The first four adjustments focus on middle adulthood.

Valuing wisdom versus valuing physical powers.
- Wisdom compensates for diminished physical abilities and loss of youthful appearance.

Socializing versus sexualizing in human relationships.
- Middle-aged adults recognize men and women as companions or friends rather than primarily as sex objects. Individuals are valued for their attributes and unique characteristics.

Emotional flexibility versus emotional impoverishment.

- Emotional flexibility involves the shifting of emotional investment between people and between activities. This is an important ability as people age and change roles (child to adult, parents die, or one's spouse dies).

Mental flexibility versus mental rigidity.

- It is important to remain mentally flexible and open to new ideas.

The following three life adjustments occur during late adulthood.

Broader, self-definition versus preoccupation with work roles.

- This adjustment focuses on the transition from defining oneself as a worker to defining oneself as a nonworking person. The retiree needs to broaden his/her interests and restructure his/her life around the new interests and the nonemployed self.

Transcendence of the body versus preoccupation with the body.

- This adjustment involves compensation for physical decline that accompanies aging. Adjustment to late adulthood is facilitated by focusing on relationships and activities that do not demand perfect health. Activities that stress social and mental abilities should be emphasized.

Transcendence of the ego versus preoccupation with the ego.

- Peck considers the acceptance of death a crucial part of successful aging. Part of this acceptance involves reflecting back upon one's achievements and accomplishments. Concern shifts from one's own needs and accomplishments to the contribution that these have on the well-being of others.

- Source: Peck, R.C. (1955). Psychological developments in the second half of life. In J.E. Anderson (Ed.), *Psychological aspects of aging*. Washington, DC: American Psychological Association.

Lecture Suggestion 2: Life Review The purpose of this lecture is to expand Santrock's discussion of life reviews. Information for this lecture suggestion was obtained from Papalia et al.'s (1996) *Adult Development and Aging* textbook. Sherman (1991) has identified three types of reminiscences.

- Reminiscences for pleasure are the most common type. They enhance mood and self-image.
- Reminiscences for self-understanding occur in approximately 25 percent of older adults. This type can help resolve past problems and find meaning in life. This type facilitates ego integrity and positive mental health. In order to have ego integrity, individuals must review positive and negative memories.
- Reminiscences to solve present problems and cope with losses occurs in approximately 10 percent of older adults. This type revolves around current issues.

Wong and Watt (1991) have further examined types of reminiscences.

- Integrative reminiscences help people resolve old conflicts and reconcile disappointments and disparity between idealized memories and reality. This helps people accept their lives.
- Instrumental reminiscences facilitate coping with current problems by using coping strategies that have been successful in the past.
- Escapist reminiscences "glorify" past memories. The occurring theme is that the past was significantly better than the present.
- Obsessive reminiscences emphasize the negative and result in guilt, bitterness, and despair.

Wong and Watt found that individuals who are aging successfully engage in more integrative or instrumental styles and fewer escapist or obsessive styles of reminiscences.

- Sources: Papalia, D.E., Camp, C.J., & Feldman, R.D. (1996). *Adult development and aging*. New York: McGraw-Hill. Sherman, E. (1991). *Reminiscences and the self in old age*. New York: Springer. Wong, P.T.P., & Watt, L.M. (1991). What types of reminiscences are associated with successful aging? *Psychology and Aging, 6*, 272-279.

Lecture Suggestion 3: Socioemotional Selectivity Theory This lecture allows you to expand Santrock's discussion of Carstensen's socioemotional selectivity theory. This theory states that older adults structure their social environments by retaining meaningful social relationships and eliminating relationships that are not emotionally rewarding. Social contact is guided by two primary goals (emotion regulation and acquisition of knowledge). The same set of social goals exists throughout the life span, however, the salience of specific goals depends on one's stage in the life span. The theory proposes that the regulation of emotion becomes increasingly salient in adulthood, while the acquisition of information and the desire to meet unfamiliar people decreases. Preferences for social partners change as a result of the shift of goals. During infancy and old age, emotion regulation is the primary goal, which results in a preference for familiar social partners. Novel, unfamiliar social partners are preferred when information seeking is the goal. This goal peaks during adolescence and young adulthood. It is important to note that emotion regulation and information seeking goals are present throughout the life span, however, the relative salience changes. Carstensen (1996) has described her systematic program of research regarding her theory of socioemotional selectivity. There is empirical support that individuals actively mold their social environments by retaining meaningful social relationships and eliminating relationships that are not emotionally rewarding.

Several research findings are presented.

- Reduction in social contacts is a gradual process; it does not begin suddenly in old age.
  - The reduction of social contacts over the life span results in an increasing tendency to reserve social contacts for those people who have the most positive emotional potential. Using longitudinal and cross-sectional data, Carstensen et al found that social selectivity is not confined to older adulthood. The reduction of social contact is most pronounced in nonemotional relationships. The rates of interactions and emotional closeness remained stable or increased for intimate relationships throughout adulthood. Social networks are smaller for older adults due to the reduction in acquaintances, not fewer confidants. There is an active selection of social contacts.
15. Emotional concerns will become more important in old age or whenever the future is limited.
    16. Carstensen found that the magnitude of autonomic arousal during an emotional experience was slightly diminished for older adults, however, the intensity of reported subjective experience was no different for older individuals compared to younger individuals.
  - Three dimensions have been highlighted relative to social goals.
    - Anticipated affect involves the positive-negative valence of the prospective interaction.
    - Future possibilities involve the potential for continued contact.
    - Information seeking involves the amount of information that can be provided by the prospective social partners.
      - Older participants focused on the affective dimension more than the younger ones.
      - Younger participants focused on the future possibilities and information seeking more than the older participants. In addition, younger participants were eager to engage with a novel social partner compared to older participants.
  - With age, the emotional aspects of social relationships become increasingly important. As a side note, the researchers did not observe any memory decrements when the older adults were recalling emotionally significant events.
  - Researchers experimentally manipulated future expectations (limited future and extended future).
    - Regardless of age, if one's future is perceived to be limited, then the individual prefers to interact with a familiar social partner.
    - Regardless of age, if one's future is perceived to be extended, then the individual prefers to engage with a novel social partner.
    - In conclusion, they found that future expectations influence one's choice of social partners.
- Source: Carstensen, L.L. (1996). Socioemotional selectivity: A life span developmental account of social behavior. In M.R. Merrens & G.G. Brannigan (Eds.), *The developmental psychologists: Research adventures across the life span*. New York: McGraw-Hill.

Lecture Suggestion 4: Intergenerational Politics Rosenbaum and Button (1993) have written a very interesting article for *The Gerontologist* concerning the potential for future political confrontations between the growing number of older Americans and the rest of the country. They state that for the last 20 years people have been predicting political confrontations between the old and the young in this country. However, now people are beginning to report that this confrontation is unlikely to happen. Rosenbaum and Button believe that this revision may be premature. The reason for this inappropriate revision, they believe, is because researchers have been looking for evidence in the wrong place and at the wrong time. In a study of attitudes in Florida (a state where 1 in 5 residents is retired), Rosenbaum and Button found that there is reason to believe political conflict is likely to occur in the future. Consider starting your lecture by asking students opinions about several political issues such as increasing taxes, limiting Medicare, welfare reform, and political fundraising reform. Ask them to also speculate on how elderly Americans would see these issues.

Rosenbaum and Button found evidence in their survey of adults in Florida regarding a variety of political and economic issues. They were concerned with the extent of agreement within age categories and the extent of disagreement between age categories. The goal was to assess general similarities and differences. A substantial portion of the younger respondents (approximately one-third to over one-half) considered older adults in their community to be an economic burden, an economically selfish voting bloc, a generationally divisive influence, or an unconstructive community element. Both older and younger respondents had a latent disaffection for the aging's community impact and civic behavior. The researchers found complimentary and beneficial images of older adults as well. For example, older and young respondents thought that older adults had "about the right amount of political power." There was a statistically significant correlation between critical appraisals of the elderly and the number of older adults in the respondents' home counties. Especially for younger respondents, the greater the number of older adults in their community the more negative the view of the aging population.

Several of the findings did not support some widely held beliefs about the aging population. Older respondents were no more likely than younger respondents to be opposed to new school taxes. The younger respondents were also divided about whether to support new school taxes. Older adults were no more likely to be involved in community activities than were the younger respondents.

Rosenbaum and Button think that there are several reasons why they found evidence of generational tension, whereas previous studies failed to reveal differences. They asked whether the respondents thought the older adults actually needed and/or deserved the entitlements they received. They focused on local and community concerns, where many of the tensions may precipitate. Concerns at the national level (e.g., Social Security) may evolve from persistent thoughts on the legitimacy of the entitlements and the negative stereotypes of the aging.

Rosenbaum and Button think that their survey findings point to the likelihood of intergenerational conflict. The reality is that the older population will increase and younger individuals will be in contact with more older adults regarding community and civic issues. These factors may exacerbate generational tensions and extend intergenerational concern to the national level. In support, Torres-Gil (1992, pp. 76, 87) thinks that if younger individuals transform their image of older adults as poor and in need of entitlement to an image of "selfish and concerned only with personal pension and income benefits," intergenerational tension is likely.

- Source: Rosenbaum, W., & Button, J. (1993). The unquiet future of intergenerational politics. *The Gerontologist*, August, 481-490. Torres-Gil, G. (1992). *The new aging*. New York: Auburn House.

Lecture Suggestion 5: Choosing a Nursing Home This lecture outlines guidelines for choosing a nursing home for a loved one. The guidelines were provided by Jackie Fitzpatrick in the St. Raphael's Better Health publication and reprinted in *Annual Editions Aging 1998/1999*.

Read the state inspection report (state survey) on the facility.

- This report should be posted at the facility. These reports contain any deficiencies and violations of federal law regarding health, safety, and quality of life. They also should give a picture as to how the facility treats its residents. It would be prudent to be skeptical if a nursing home director fails to provide the requested report.

Inspect the facility yourself.

- Be sure to visit the nursing home prior to placing an elderly individual in the home. It is a good idea to repeatedly visit the facility unannounced at various times of day. During your visits talk with the residents and the staff.

Make sure the facility and the residents are clean.

- During your visits, observe the cleanliness of the nursing home (odors?) and the elderly individuals (well groomed and dressed).

Focus on the quality of the care provided.

- While it is nice to have attractive decor, the care that the residents receive is more important. Does the staff respect the residents? What activities are provided (social, cognitive, spiritual)? Are restraints used? (It is illegal to use restraints unless medically justified or ordered by a physician.)

Look for safety hazards.

- During your inspection, keep in mind that the elderly person may have an unsteady gait or poor eyesight.

Observe the attitude of the staff.

- Are there sufficient numbers of staff members to care for the number of residents? Are they warm, interactive, and engaged with the residents? Do they like their jobs and the residents?

If possible, visit at mealtime.

- Check to see if the food is nutritionally sound. Does it taste good too? Do the residents eat in the dining room so that they can socialize? If a resident needs help, is a staff member available and willing to help feed the resident?

Investigate the care plans.

- Do the residents have appropriate care plans? Have they been properly implemented? The care plan should address nutritional requirements, physical and speech needs, and range-of-motion exercises, etc.

Once you choose a good nursing home, it is important to monitor the care that your loved one is receiving. Let the nursing home personnel know when they are doing a good job and if a problem happens to arise.

- Source: Fitzpatrick J. (1996) St. Raphael's Better Health publication and reprinted in *Annual Editions Aging 1998/1999*. McGraw-Hill.

Lecture Suggestion 6: Alternative Living Arrangements for the Elderly The purpose of this lecture is to introduce two relatively new alternative living arrangements for elderly individuals. One fairly new alternative for retired couples is living in an age-segregated community. These communities take several forms. The more established type of age-segregated community is the so-called "sunshine community." These communities, usually in the southwestern United States, offer older couples a carefree way to stay active. They provide activities such as golf, tennis, bridge, and bingo, as well as community dances and socials. They are seen as allowing older people to make their own choices about how they remain active. To visit, children and grandchildren must be invited, and their stay must be short. Ideally, this takes some pressure off the elderly. The flip side of this arrangement is that it may isolate some people and restrict their freedom to have people visit as long as they like.

A newer alternative is local, medical-center run, independent living quarters. These centers are often set up like condominiums with complete independent living quarters, but with access to common areas for meals, activities, and socialization. One of the special features of these centers is their easy access to 24 hour-a-day medical services. This allows individuals with chronic problems (such as diabetes) to live independently and relatively anxiety free. These communities offer an alternative to living in a nursing home or with a relative. A person or couple can choose to live in the same community, stay independent, and not be a burden on family.

Classroom Activities

Classroom Activity 1: Media and Late Adulthood This exercise allows students to examine how older adults are portrayed in the media. Two interesting films related to late adulthood are *Grumpy Old Men* and *Cocoon*. Consider showing one of these films in class. Encourage students to apply concepts from the late adulthood chapters to the films. They can use concepts from chapters 18-21. Have them think about how accurate the portrayals are of older adults. What impact do these images have on society? Do they impact older adults differently than they impact younger adults?

Logistics:
- Materials: *Grumpy Old Men* or *Cocoon* videos.
- Group size: Full class.
- Approximate time: Full class (2 and a half hours).

Classroom Activity 2: Social Security The Social Security system is a mystery to most people. One way to unravel the mystery is to invite a Social Security employee to come speak to your class about how the system works, what ensures its survival, who gets benefits, and how one finds out about eligibility.

Students should be given enough of an overview of the system to be able to form appropriate questions to ask the speaker. The speaker should be told in advance what the topic of his or her talk should be and what kind of questions can be expected. With a little preparation, this class activity could be one of the most informative and helpful sessions of all.

Ask your students to call the Social Security office and ask for a form to request a summary of their benefits. The form takes a few days to arrive and the summary about 6 weeks, which means you will have to plan well in advance for this activity. It would be most beneficial to have as many students order their summaries before the speaker arrives as possible.

Logistics:
- Materials: Students need to request a summary of their Social Security benefits.
- Group size: Individual and guest lecture to full class.
- Approximate time: Individual (30 minutes), guest lecture to full class (45 minutes).

Classroom Activity 3: Classroom Debate: Are Elderly Americans Poor? In chapter 20, Santrock discusses the number of elderly people living below the poverty level. A good way to engage students in this topic is to set up a debate about whether it is accurate to think of the elderly as poor. Two opposing views on this issue by England (1990) and by the Families USA Foundation (1990) can provide a basis for the debate. Divide the class into two groups. Assign one group to argue the position that states that the elderly are poor. Assign the other group to argue that the elderly are not poor. Structure the class as a debate. You may want to ask a colleague to join you in judging the debate. Remind students that they must provide quality arguments to support their position. Students will most likely need to do some library research to support their argument. Most students will find this activity stimulating and will become quite passionate about their position.

Logistics:
- Group size: Small group, individual, small group, and full class.
- Approximate time: Small group (15 minutes), individual (1 hour), small group (30 minutes), and full class (45 minutes).
- Sources: England, R. (1990). The elderly are not poor. In *The elderly: Opposing viewpoints*. San Diego, CA: Greenhaven Press. Families USA Foundation. (1990). The elderly are poor. In *The elderly: Opposing viewpoints*. San Diego, CA: Greenhaven Press.

Classroom Activity 4: Grandparenting Styles Ask each student to write down eight to ten characteristics that describe each of their grandparents. After they have produced the descriptions, have them trade characteristic lists with another member of the class. On the basis of the descriptions provided, students should try to identify the grandparenting style used by each grandparent. The lists should be returned to their creator. Give feedback about the appropriateness of the classifications made. It might also be interesting to have the students record the ages of their grandparents. The last part of the class period could be spent trying to determine whether grandparents of different ages use different grandparenting styles.

Logistics:
- Group size: Individual, dyads, and full class.
- Approximate time: Individual (10 minutes), dyads (5 minutes), and full class (20 minutes).

Classroom Activity 5: Successful Aging Brochures This exercise affords students an opportunity to be creative. Have students create a pamphlet or brochure on successful aging for older adults. Students should use the information from the textbook regarding successful aging, the benefits of exercise, and the benefits of good nutrition, etc. to inform older adults about successful aging. It will be important for students to be respectful, yet informative, in their approach. They should keep in mind the cognitive abilities and sensory abilities of older adults and target their pamphlet accordingly. Encourage them to be creative. One option is to turn this exercise into a friendly contest. They can work in groups to design their brochure and then anonymously present each brochure prior to having a vote as to the "best" brochure.

Logistics:
- Group size: Small group (out of class) and full class.
- Approximate time: Small group (45 minutes) and full class (15 minutes).

Classroom Activity 6: Critical Thinking Multiple-Choice Questions and Suggested Answers Discuss the critical thinking multiple-choice questions (**Handout 1**). Question 1 provides a good basis for one last treatment of the developmental issues that define the core themes of life-span developmental psychology. Your discussion might entail an attempt to delineate how concern about these developmental issues varies, depending on the age span of the individuals studied and the extent to which these issues can be addressed given the state of the field in the new century.

Question 2 continues the task of applying concepts from the chapter to the opening vignette. As you may have done in earlier chapters, you may want to analyze the relevant components of Bob's case prior to requiring students to do the exercise.

The key to question 3 is to have students identify which statement is most in character with Neugarten's concerns; the other statements constitute observations or inferences that individuals on both sides of the debate can accept. The answers to these questions are presented as **Handout 2**.

Logistics:
- Materials: Handout 1 (the critical thinking multiple-choice questions) and Handout 2 (answers).
- Group size: Small groups to discuss the questions, then a full class discussion.
- Approximate time: Small groups (15 to 20 minutes), full class discussion of any questions (15 minutes).

Classroom Activity 7: Critical Thinking Essay Questions and Suggestions for Helping Students Answer the Essays Discuss students' answers to the critical thinking essay questions presented in **Handout 3**. The purpose of this exercise is threefold. First, answering the essay questions further facilitates students' understanding of concepts in chapter 20. Second, this type of essay question affords the students an opportunity to apply the concepts to their own lives, which will facilitate their retention of the material. Third, the essay format also gives students practice expressing themselves in written form. Ideas to help students answer the critical thinking essay questions are provided as **Handout 4**.

Logistics:
- Materials: Handout 3 (essay questions) and Handout 4 (helpful suggestions for the answers).
- Group size: Individual, then full class.
- Approximate time: Individual (60 minutes), full class discussion of any questions (30 minutes).

Personal Applications

Personal Application 1: Aging by the Numbers The purpose of this exercise is to help familiarize students with each of the theories about aging with regard to real life examples. Many theoretical perspectives have been put forth to try to explain what occurs from a socioemotional standpoint during late adulthood. Each one focuses on its own set of particular issues, offers its own behavioral profiles, and draws its own conclusions. As we consider each of these, we have to keep in mind that theories are neither true nor false, simply useful or not useful for understanding human behavior.

- Instructions for Students: Familiarize yourself with the tenets of each of the theoretical approaches to socioemotional development in late adulthood. Try to find examples of aspects of each (or contradictions to each) in your own experience with individuals in late adulthood. If your grandparents or great aunts and uncles are no longer living, or you don't have contact with them, see if you can get your parents to share information about their lives, their outlook, their social functioning and mental well-being. With the information that you gather, discuss the elements of each theory with regard to your own personal examples. From what you've observed, experienced, and learned, which theory do you think does the best job of addressing socioemotional development in late adulthood? Which one do you think is farthest off the mark—and why? How have these theories influenced your perspective on this stage of life (both positively and negatively)?
- Use in the Classroom: Expand on this topic in an in-class discussion. Present each theory and have students provide their own personal knowledge and examples of individuals who reflect what the theory purports (or the opposite of its claims). This is a wonderful review of this portion of the chapter, and it may lead to discussion and debate as to the most effective and applicable theory for this stage of development. You may encourage students to pool their personal "data" and begin developing their own theory to help understand and explain this facet of the life span.

Personal Application 2: What a Geezer! This exercise is a great way to expose students to the ugly reality of ageism. Ageism is proof that no stage of life is immune to the harshness of stereotyping, even old age. In fact, the elderly are prominent targets for negative attributes—regarding their driving, understanding the latest technology, and even just thinking and communicating. Imagine living a full and substantial life only to be reduced to a negative generalization by people less experienced and less wise than yourself!

- Instructions for Students: Be honest. Write about your ageist thoughts. In what ways do you view elderly people *in general*? How often do you find yourself frustrated when behind them in line at the grocery store, or predicting someone who is driving poorly is old? Do you think that ageism is a legitimate issue that needs to be addressed in society, or is it just a "politically correct" concern? How might such stereotyping effect those in late adulthood? How might your own responses to such generalizations have affected an older individual?
- Use in the Classroom: Have students present stereotypes of elderly people, and list them on the board. Use the list to generate a discussion about the problematic results from such views. Are there any *positive* generalizations about older people that are embraced in our society? You may want to prepare ahead of time by researching the cross-cultural attitudes towards society's elders, particularly in Asian cultures. Have students comment on the differences, including why they think they exist and what our society might do to begin the shift toward a more positive view of individuals in this stage of life.

Personal Application 3: It Will Be You Some Day The purpose of this exercise is to get students thinking about social policies related to late adulthood. As students are now of voting age, they too will have a say on such issues, even though they won't directly affect them. In most cases, voter apathy works to prevent people from being aware of, and understanding, issues that are not relevant to them. This, of course, can then backfire when they face these issues themselves one day.

- Instructions for Students: Read through the policy issues related to late adulthood described in your textbook. Take a moment to really think about one day facing such aspects in your own life. What issues really move you now? What policies do you feel very strongly about for those who are currently in late adulthood? What social problems make you angry? Which ones make you fearful of facing when you reach this stage of life? What issues are of the least concern? What could you do personally now, as a young person, to make an impact on the lives of elderly people? Remember, it will be you some day.
- Use in the Classroom: Carry this discussion into the classroom, with some pre-class research on current legislation in your area (city, county, state, nation) relating to social policy for the elderly. How apathetic are students about these issues? Have they changed their interest and involvement since studying this stage of life? Who do they know that it affects? Would they be willing to write a letter to their congressman to let their voice be heard? What issues might be present when they are in this stage that are not an issue now? What do they hope to see younger generations do for *them*?

Research Project Ideas

Research Project 1: Collecting a Life Story One way to understand aging is to study someone's life story **(Handout 5)**. This will not tell the students how people generally change over a lifetime, but it will give them ideas about the complexity of change, and the highs and lows of a person's life. It is also an opportunity for them to apply material about socioemotional development in late adulthood found in chapter 20.

After receiving IRB approval, students will need to do at least three interviews with the same individual to collect a life story. See the section at the front of this Instructor's Manual on Ethics, Human Subjects, and Informed Consent. Before having students complete this project, you might want to show and subsequently discuss the film *Older Voices: Interviewing Older Adults* to prepare them for their interviews. They should use the first interview to obtain their respondent's informed consent and to help the person become comfortable with them **(Handout 6)**. Students should be sure to explain that they will tape record the interviews, but that they will not use the person's name in any reports or discussions they have about them. In the second interview (and possible third or fourth), students will have the person tell their story. If necessary, the student should suggest a series of topics (e.g., childhood, marriage, work) during these interviews. Have them prepare questions that they can ask to help the person along. The last interview will be a summary and reflection on the previous interview. Each interview should take somewhere between 1 and 2 hours.

The next step ideally would be to transcribe the taped interviews, but this is probably too much work for your course (unless this is the major course project). If transcribing is not reasonable or possible, have the students listen carefully to the tapes and make notes about key ideas or themes from the interview; their respondent may have suggested these in the last interview. Students need to listen to the tapes to identify statements, stories, or reflections that illustrate the themes. After they have done this first review, they should listen to the tapes again for additional themes and illustrative material. Finally, from their notes they should prepare a table that lists the themes and the material that illustrated them.

Students will write a report in which they at least describe their respondent and characterize their experience of interviewing him or her. Next, they will summarize the individual's life story, including the table they prepared to identify its major themes. Then they will discuss in as much detail as they can how this person's story relates to the material in the text.

- Use in the Classroom: Have students get into small groups and discuss the themes they saw in the answers of their subjects. What kinds of similarities were there between the older people? What differences existed? You might want to point out the variability of experience in these people's responses. Sometimes students mistakenly believe that "all old people are just alike."

Research Project 2: The Aging Couple An important topic in chapter 20 is the aging couple. The time after retirement can bring many changes to a couple's relationship. Have students read this section of the text prior to completing this project.

In this research project (**Handout 7**), students will need to interview both members of an elderly couple. Before having students complete this project, you might want to show and subsequently discuss the film *Older Voices: Interviewing Older Adults* to prepare them for their interviews. They will want to first interview each person separately and then together as a couple. **Handout 8** provides some sample questions that students can ask the couple. They should, however, create their own questions to add to the interview.

After they have completed the interview, students should write a report describing the interview questions and summarizing the responses of the couple. In addition, they should address the following questions in their paper.

Questions:
- How old were the members of the couple?
- How long have they known each other?
- If they are married, how long have they been married?
- When interviewed separately, were there any questions that they responded to differently?
- Do you believe they are happy with each other? Why or why not?
- If they are happy, to what would you attribute their relationship success?
- How do you think their responses would differ from a couple in their twenties, thirties, or forties?
- What did you learn about relationships in late adulthood?

Sample Questions:
- How did you meet your partner?
- How long have you known each other?
- Tell me about your relationship.
- Are you married?
- How long have you been married?
- What do you like best about your partner?
- What do you like best about your relationship?
- What do you like least about your relationship?
- How has your relationship changed over the years?
- How do you anticipate your relationship changing in the future?

- Use in the Classroom: Have students present their findings and discuss how they think younger couples would have responded to their questions. Ask students to indicate what they learned about relationships in late adulthood. Connect what they report with the information presented in the.

Film and Video List

The following films and videos supplement the content of chapter 20. Contact information for film distributors can be found at the front of this Instructor's Manual under Film and Video Sources.

Aging Successfully: Psychological Aspects of Growing Old (Davidson Films, 30 minutes). Paul and Margaret Baltes present their model of "Selection, Optimization, and Compensation" as an example of successful aging. They discuss the personality characteristics that generally lead to positive aging experiences.

Love, Intimacy, and Sexuality (Annenberg/CPB Collection, 60 minutes). In this program, older couples speak frankly about their enjoyment of sex. Experts examine physical and emotional issues of sexuality.

Older Voices: Interviewing Older Adults (Insight Media, 46 minutes). This video is designed to train interviewers to use flexible techniques for interviewing elderly people.

On Old Age: A Conversation with Joan Erikson at 90 (Davidson Films, 38 minutes). Joan Erikson and her husband Erik formulated their eight stage life cycle theory during their middle-aged years, and in this video she talks about how they romanticized the eighth stage (she is currently in this stage).

On Old Age II: A Conversation with Joan Erikson at 92 (Davidson Films, 38 minutes). Joan Erikson discusses her search for a better living situation for her frail husband and then his subsequent death. In this video, she proposes a ninth stage of psychosocial development.

Sexuality and Aging (Fanlight Productions, 59 minutes). This video explores the attitudes, myths, and facts concerning the experience of romance and sexuality for older adults.

To Be Old, Black, and Poor (Films for the Humanities and Sciences, 52 minutes). This program shows the painful life of a black, poor, and elderly individual in the U.S. It records a couple's struggle to survive.

Web Site Suggestions

The URLs for general sites, common to all chapters, can be found at the front of this Instructor's Manual under Useful Web Sites. At the time of publication, all sites were current and active, however, please be advised that you may occasionally encounter a dead link.

Ageism
http://www.owen-withee.k12.wi.us/TEACHER/tolerance/page3.htm

Articles on Grandparenting
http://seniors-site.com/grandpar/g_articl.html

Directory of Nursing Homes
http://www.d-net.com/min/min10129.htm

Economics of Aging Publications
http://www.nber.org/programs/a/aging_pubs.html

The New England Centenarian Study
http://www.med.harvard.edu/programs/necs/

Program for Women and Successful Aging
http://www.unomaha.edu/~wwwpa/gero/acpwsa.html

Critical Thinking Multiple-Choice Questions

1. Which life-span developmental issue does Santrock appear to emphasize in his treatment of socioemotional development in late adulthood? Circle the letter of the best answer and explain why it is the best answer and why each other answer is not as good.

    a. social over biological processes
    b. discontinuity over continuity
    c. nurture over nature
    d. later experience over earlier experience
    e. change over stability

2. The vignette about Bob Cousy in the Images of Life-Span Development box illustrates several aspects of personality development, life satisfaction, and successful aging. Which of the following concepts does Bob's case illustrate least well? Circle the letter of the best answer and explain why it is the best answer and why each other answer is not as good.

    a. body transcendence
    b. feeling in control
    c. despair
    d. life satisfaction
    e. selective optimization with compensation

3. Bernice Neugarten's proposed solution to the problem of generational inequity questions one of the basic assumptions motivating criticisms of the advantages enjoyed by the elderly. Which of the following represents Neugarten's alternative assumption, rather than an inference or an observation? Circle the letter of the best answer and explain why it is the best answer and why each other answer is not as good.

    a. The problem is not one of generational inequity.
    b. The percentage of children living in poverty has been increasing.
    c. Baby boomers will receive lower Social Security payments than are presently being paid.
    d. We would do better to think about what a positive spirit about aging would mean to America.
    e. Generational inequity produces intergenerational conflict and divisiveness in the society at large.

Suggested Answers for Critical Thinking Multiple-Choice Questions

1. Which life-span developmental issue does Santrock appear to emphasize in his treatment of socioemotional development in late adulthood? Circle the letter of the best answer and explain why it is the best answer and why each other answer is not as good.

   a. <u>Social over biological processes</u> is the best answer. The focus on social worlds of older adults, ethnicity, gender, and culture all seem to give priority to social over biological processes in this chapter. This stands in some contrast to the treatment of biological processes relevant to cognitive change discussed in the previous chapter.

   b. <u>Discontinuity over continuity</u> is not the best answer, even though there is discussion of Erikson's final stage of psychosocial development, and the focus on grandparenting stresses its difference from parenting.

   c. <u>Nurture over nature</u> is not the best answer. There simply is no treatment of these issues in this chapter.

   d. <u>Later experience over earlier experience</u> is not the best answer. Nothing is discussed concerning how earlier life experiences in childhood influence socioemotional development in old age.

   e. <u>Change over stability</u> is not the best answer. The issue of the extent to which personality remains constant versus the extent to which it changes is not addressed. However, the chapter does discuss the nature of personality changes as older people adapt to the constraints of aging and nearing death.

2. The vignette about Bob Cousy in the Images of Life-Span Development box illustrates several aspects of personality development, life satisfaction, and successful aging. Which of the following concepts does Bob's case least well illustrate? Circle the letter of the best answer and explain why it is the best answer and why each other answer is not as good.

   a. <u>Body transcendence</u> is not the best answer. Bob's remarks suggest that he has been able to cope with his changing physical abilities and is experiencing body transcendence.

   b. <u>Feeling in control</u> is not the best answer. Bob comments that he feels in control of his destiny given that he remains actively involved in basketball through his role as a broadcaster.

   c. <u>Despair</u> is the best answer. Bob does not discuss being unhappy, depressed, or dissatisfied with his life, in fact his statements reflect that he has achieved integrity. d.   <u>Life satisfaction</u> is not the best answer. While Bob does not directly address whether he is satisfied with his life, he eludes to it with his comments about being active and enjoying time with his wife, family , and close friends.

   e. <u>Selective optimization with compensation</u> is not the best answer. Bob speaks directly of this issue with the shift in his physical activities. He still enjoys competition, yet he now competes in golf and tennis rather than in basketball. This suggests that Bob is selectively optimizing and compensating.

3. Bernice Neugarten's proposed solution to the problem of generational inequity questions one of the basic assumptions that motivates criticisms of the advantages enjoyed by the elderly. Which of the following represents Neugarten's alternative assumption, rather than an inference or an observation? Circle the letter of the best answer and explain why it is the best answer and why each other answer is not as good.

   a. <u>The problem is not one of generational inequity</u> is the best answer. Neugarten questions the assumption that we have to trade off childcare and eldercare. She proposes that the basic problem is the nation's willingness to care for any of its "dependent and neglected" populations.

   b. <u>The percentage of children living in poverty has been increasing</u> is not the best answer. It is an observation cited in contrast to the fact that elderly people are receiving more services.

   c. <u>Baby boomers will receive lower Social Security payments than are presently being paid</u> is not the best answer. It is an inference in that it is a projection based on current population distributions and their effect on the Social Security system.

   d. <u>We would do better to think about what a positive spirit about aging would mean to America</u> is not the best answer. It is an inference, Neugarten's conclusion to her argument that we have to question the generational inequity issue.

   e. <u>Generational inequity produces intergenerational conflict and divisiveness in the society at large</u> is not the best answer. It is an inference, a deduction about how beliefs about generational inequity impair social unity and consequently the quality of life for old and young alike.

Critical Thinking Essay Questions

Your answers to these kinds of questions demonstrate an ability to comprehend and apply ideas discussed in this chapter.

1. Describe the tasks and themes of personality development during late adulthood.

2. Compare and contrast three socioemotional theories of aging.

3. Define *ageism*, and provide two original examples of ageism.

4. Imagine that you are an elderly adult. Indicate and explain the policy issues of concern to you.

5. Indicate where elderly adults live.

6. Explain what an elderly, ethnic female can expect to experience during late adulthood.

7. If you were an elderly adult, what could you expect to happen to aspects of your social relations such as lifestyle, dating, and friendship?

8. Discuss the diversity of grandparenting functions and roles.

9. Evaluate your own culture's regard for the elderly in terms of the seven factors most likely to predict high status for the elderly.

10. Explain how the selective optimization with compensation model could help you age successfully.

Ideas to Help You Answer Critical Thinking Essay Questions

1. Imagine that you are sharing this information with elderly individuals. What will they want to know? What questions might they have? How might you best present the material to both inform them and keep them positive about this stage of life?

2. Begin by fully presenting each theory—their characteristics, perceptions, issues. Make a grid to highlight similarities and differences.

3. Address the notion of how broad or specific the term *ageism* really is. The term *sexual harassment*, for example, can include a wide range of behaviors and circumstances. Is ageism pretty easily defined and identified, or does a gray area exist as to what might be included in the concept? Provide examples to back your argument.

4. Provide your background: education, SES level, family status, career, and any other relevant information (you may want to anticipate your future somewhat). Now address the policy issues.

5. Present this information as if you are addressing adult children of elderly parents. What are their options? What might their concerns be? What will you recommend? Anticipate a variety of circumstances.

6. Begin your discussion by explaining why this individual profile is significant to address. Be sure to address the issue of triple jeopardy.

7. End your discussion by addressing how this knowledge can be applied to benefit older individuals (or those not quite at this stage).

8. Use lots of examples of such things as interactions, activities, goals, etc.

9. Itemize the seven factors, then evaluate them. How does this make you feel about growing older?

10. Present what the model has to offer, then apply it to practical use.

Collecting a Life Story

One way to understand aging is to study someone's life story. This will not tell you how people generally change over a lifetime, but it will give you ideas about the complexity of change and highs and lows of a person's life. It is also an opportunity to apply material about socioemotional development in late adulthood found in chapter 20.

You will need to do at least three interviews with the same individual to collect a life story. You can use **Handout 6** to help you get started writing your interview questions. Use the first interview to obtain your respondent's informed consent and to help the person become comfortable with you. Be sure to explain that you will tape record the interviews, but that you will not use the person's name in any reports or discussions you have about them. In the second interview (and possible third or fourth), have the person tell their story (don't forget to turn on your tape recorder!). If necessary, suggest a series of topics (e.g., childhood, marriage, work) during these interviews. Be sure to prepare questions that you can ask to help the person along. The last interview will be a summary and reflection on the previous interview. Each interview should take somewhere between 1 and t2 hours.

The next step ideally would be to transcribe the taped interviews, but this is probably too much work for your course (unless this is the major course project). If transcribing is not reasonable or possible, listen carefully to the tapes and make notes about key ideas or themes from the interview; your respondent may have suggested these in the last interview. Listen to the tapes to identify statements, stories, or reflections that illustrate the themes. After you have done this first review, listen to the tapes again for additional themes and illustrative material. Finally, from your notes prepare a table that lists the themes and the material that illustrated them.

Write a report in which you at least describe your respondent and characterize your experience of interviewing him or her. Summarize the individual's life story, including the table you prepared to identify its major themes. Then discuss in as much detail as you can how this person's story relates to the material in the text.

Abbreviated Interview Schedule for Collecting a Life Story

First Interview

Introduce yourself and obtain informed consent for the interview. Explain how you will use the material. Listen to the tape of your first interview before doing the second. Determine what you want to know more about. Write out possible questions.

Sample question:
- What stands out for you as you look back over your life?

Probes (if necessary):
- Can you give an example of that?
- Explain what you mean by that.
- Tell me more about that point.
- That's interesting. Can you be more detailed?

Second Interview

Ask questions about:
- relationships
- careers
- family
- significant events

Listen to the tape of your second interview before doing the third. Determine what you want to know more about. Write out possible questions.

Third Interview

You might begin by saying, "Let's reflect on what we have been talking about in these conversations."
- Tell me about high points and low points in your life.
- What conflicts stand out for you?
- What did you learn from these conflicts?
- Is there anything else you would like to add?

The Aging Couple

An important topic in chapter 20 is the aging couple. The time after retirement can bring many changes to a couple's relationship. Before beginning this project, read the section of your text on the aging couple.

In this research project, you will need to interview both members of an elderly couple. You will want to first interview each person separately and then together as a couple. **Handout 8** provides some sample questions that you can ask the couple. You should, however, create your own questions to add to the interview.

After you have completed the interview, write a report describing your interview questions and summarizing the responses of the couple. In addition, you should address the following questions in your paper.

Questions:

• How old were the members of the couple?

• How long have they known each other?

• If they are married, how long have they been married?

• When interviewed separately, were there any questions that they responded to differently?

• Do you believe they are happy with each other? Why or why not?

• If they are happy, to what would you attribute there relationship success?

• How do you think their responses would differ from a couple in their twenties, thirties, or forties?

• What did you learn about relationships in late adulthood?

Handout 8 (RP 2)

Potential Interview Questions for the Aging Couple

These questions are meant to help you get started writing your own interview questions. You may want to look through chapter 20 of your textbook to help you come up with some other relevant questions. Remember to interview them separately first and then together as a couple.

Sample interview questions:

- How did you meet your partner?

- How long have you known each other?

- Tell me about your relationship.

- Are you married?

- How long have you been married?

- What do you like best about your partner?

- What do you like best about your relationship?

- What do you like least about your relationship?

- How has your relationship changed over the years?

- How do you anticipate your relationship changing in the future?

Chapter 21: Death and Grieving

Total Teaching Package Outline

Lecture Outline	Resource References
Death and Grieving	PowerPoint Presentation: See www.mhhe.com Cognitive Maps: See Appendix A
Defining Death and Life/Death Issues	LO1 WS: Int'l Conference on Death and Bereavement WS: Assoc. for Death Education and Counseling
• Issues in Determining Death	LS1: Defining Brain Death PA1: But I'm Not Dead Yet... WS: Definition of Brain Death
• Decisions Regarding Life, Death, and Health Care	LO2 WS: Growth House
-Natural Death Act and Advanced Directive	CA1: Advanced Directives F/V: Before I Die F/V: A Death of One's Own F/V: Difficult Decisions F/V: A Time to Change WS: Advanced Directives
-Euthanasia	LO3 CA2: The Right to Choose Debate WS: Euthanasia WS: Hemlock Organization WS: Last Rights
-Needed: Better Care for Dying Individuals	LO4 LS2: Hospice CA3: Field Trip to a Local Hospice RP1: Hospices in Your Community F/V: Toward a Better Death F/V: Letting Go: A Hospice Journey WS: Hospice Information
Death and Sociohistorical, Cultural Contexts • Changing Historical Circumstances • Death in Different Cultures	 LO5 LO6
A Developmental Perspective on Death • Causes of Death and Expectations about Death	 LO7
• Attitudes toward Death at Different Points in the Life Span -Childhood -Adolescence -Adulthood	LO8 F/V: Coping with Loss WS: Attitudes toward Death

Facing One's Own Death	LO9 CA4: Write Your Own Obituary
• Kubler-Ross' Stages of Dying	OHT197 & IB: Kubler-Ross's Stages of Dying F/V: Living with Dying
• Perceived Control and Denial	LO10
• The Contexts in Which People Die	LO11
Coping with the Death of Someone Else	PA2: The Loss of a Loved One RP1: Experiencing Others' Deaths F/V: Common Threads: Stories From the Quilt
• Communicating with a Dying Person	LO12 IB: Strategies for Communicating with a Dying Person

• Grieving
     -Dimensions of Grieving
     -Cultural Diversity in Healthy Grieving
	LO13
	 LS3: Grief
	 F/V: The Forgotten Mourner
	 F/V: Grief and Healing
	 F/V: The Pitch of Grief
	 F/V: When Children Grieve

• Making Sense of the World	WS: Crisis, Grief, and Healing
• Losing a Life Partner	LO14 WS: WidowNet
• Forms of Mourning and the Funeral	LO15 LS4: Reactions to Loss CA5: Field Trip to a Local Mortuary CA6: Funerals F/V: The Forgotten Mourner
Review	CA7: Critical Thinking Multiple-Choice CA8: Critical Thinking Essays

Chapter Outline

DEFINING DEATH AND LIFE/DEATH ISSUES

Issues in Determining Death

- Twenty-five years ago, determining if someone was dead was simpler than it is today.
- **Brain death** is a neurological definition of death, which states that a person is brain dead when all electrical activity of the brain has ceased for a specified period. A flat EEG (electroencephalogram) recording for a specified period of time is one criterion of brain death.
  - Medical experts debate whether this should mean the higher and lower brain functions or just the higher cortical functions.
  - Currently, most states have a statute endorsing the cessation of brain function (both higher and lower) as a standard for determining death.

Decisions Regarding Life, Death, and Health Care
- In cases of catastrophic illness or emergency circumstances, patients might not be able to respond adequately to participate in decisions about their medical care.
  Natural Death Act and Advanced Directive
  - A living will is a document designed to be filled in while the individual can still think clearly that expresses the person's desire that extraordinary medical procedures not be used to sustain life when the medical situation becomes hopeless.
  - The Natural Death Act permits individuals who have been diagnosed by two physicians as terminally ill to sign an advanced directive, which states that life-sustaining procedures may not be used to prolong their lives when death is imminent.
  Euthanasia
  - **Euthanasia** (easy death or "mercy killing") is the act of painlessly ending the lives of individuals who are suffering from an incurable disease or severe disability.
  - Distinctions are made between two types of euthanasia: passive and active.
    - **Passive euthanasia** occurs when a person is allowed to die by withholding available treatment, such as withdrawing a life-sustaining device.
    - **Active euthanasia** occurs when death is deliberately induced, as when a lethal dose of a drug is injected.
  Needed: Better Care for Dying Individuals
  - Death in the U.S. is often lonely, prolonged, and painful.
  - The following suggestions can help individuals avoid pain at the end of life.
    - Make a living will.
    - Have a power of attorney.
    - Give your doctor specific instructions.
    - If you want to die at home, let your family and doctor know.
    - Check to see whether your insurance covers home care and hospice care.
  - **Hospice** is a humanized program committed to making the end of life as free from pain, anxiety, and depression as possible. The hospice's goals contrast with those of a hospital, which are to cure illness and prolong life.
    - Hospice care has grown rapidly in the U.S.

DEATH AND SOCIOHISTORICAL, CULTURAL CONTEXTS
  Changing Historical Circumstances
  - The "when, where, and why people die" have changed historically.
    - Today, death occurs most often among the elderly.
    - More than 80 percent of all deaths in the U.S. now occur in a hospital or an institution.
  - Our exposure to death in the family has been minimized.

  Death in Different Cultures
  - Most societies throughout history have had philosophical or religious beliefs about death, and most societies have rituals that deal with death.
  - Most cultures do not view death as the end of existence; spiritual life is thought to continue.
  - The U.S. has been described as a death-denying and death-avoiding culture.
  - Death denial can take many forms.
    - The tendency of the funeral industry to gloss over death with lifelike qualities for the dead individual.
    - The adoption of euphemistic language for death.
    - The persistent search for a fountain of youth.
    - The rejection and isolation of the aged.
    - The adoption of the concept of a pleasant and rewarding afterlife.
    - The medical community's emphasis on the prolongation of biological life.

A DEVELOPMENTAL PERSPECTIVE ON DEATH

Causes of Death and Expectations about Death

- Although death is more likely to occur in late adulthood, death can come at any point in development.
  - In childhood, death occurs most often because of accidents (car, drowning, poisoning, fire, or falling) or illness (heart disease, cancer, or birth defects).
  - Death in adolescence is more likely to occur because of car accidents or homicide.
  - Older adults are more likely to die from chronic diseases (heart disease and cancer), whereas younger adults are more likely to die from accidents.
- The deaths of some persons, especially children and younger adults, are often perceived to be more tragic than those of others, such as very old adults, who have had an opportunity to live a long life.

Attitudes toward Death at Different Points in the Life Span

- Research has found that as children grow they develop a more mature approach to death.
  Childhood
  - Infants do not have a concept of death.
  - Preschool children also have little concept of death; often showing little or no upset at the sight of a dead animal or person.
    - Preschoolers sometimes blame themselves for a person's death.
  - In the elementary school years, children develop a more realistic orientation towards death.
    - By age 9, children recognize death's finality and universality.
  - Most psychologists believe honesty is the best strategy for helping children cope with death.
    - Young children need reassurance that they are loved and will not be abandoned.
  Adolescence
  - The prospect of death is so remote that it does not have much relevance for adolescents so it is often glossed over or kidded about.
  - Adolescents develop more abstract conceptions of death than children do.
  Adulthood
  - There is no evidence that a special orientation towards death emerges in early adulthood.
  - Middle adulthood is a time when adults show a heightened consciousness about death and death anxiety.
  - Older adults often show less death anxiety than middle-aged adults, but older adults experience and converse about death more.
  - Attitudes about death may vary considerably among adults of any age.

FACING ONE'S OWN DEATH

Kübler-Ross' Stages of Dying

- Kübler-Ross divided the behavior and thinking of dying persons into five stages.
  - **Denial and isolation**: the person denies that death is really going to take place.
  - **Anger**: the dying person recognizes that denial can no longer be maintained. Denial often gives way to anger, resentment, rage, and envy.
  - **Bargaining**: the person develops the hope that death can somehow be postponed or delayed.
  - **Depression**: the dying person comes to accept the certainty of death. At this point, a period of depression or preparatory grief may appear.
  - **Acceptance**: the person develops a sense of peace, an acceptance of one's fate, and, in many cases, a desire to be left alone.

- Critics argue that the existence of the five-stage sequence has not been demonstrated empirically and the stage interpretation neglects the patients' total life situations (support, illness details, family obligations, and institutional climate).
  - Not all individuals go through the same sequence.
  - Some individuals may struggle to the end.
- Supporters give Kübler-Ross credit for calling attention to people attempting to cope with life-threatening illnesses and her attention to the quality of life for dying persons and their families.

Perceived Control and Denial
- Perceived control and denial may work together as an adaptive orientation for the dying individual.
- When individuals are led to believe they can influence and control events (prolong life), they may become more alert and cheerful.
  - Denial may ward off learned helplessness and protect us from the tortuous feeling that we are going to die.
  - Denial can be adaptive and maladaptive depending on the circumstances.

The Contexts in Which People Die
- Most deaths in the US occur in hospitals.
  - Hospitals offer several advantages, such as a professional staff and medical technology.
- Most individuals say they would rather die at home. However, they worry that they will be a burden and they are concerned about the lack of medical care.

COPING WITH THE DEATH OF SOMEONE ELSE
- In the ratings of life's stresses that require the most adjustment, death of a spouse is the highest.

Communicating with a Dying Person
- Most psychologists believe that it is best for dying individuals and their significant others to know that they are dying so they can interact and communicate with each other on the basis of this mutual knowledge.
- Advantages of open awareness of dying include:
  - Dying individuals can close their lives in accord with their own ideas about death.
  - Dying individuals may be able to complete some plans and projects, make arrangements for survivors, and participate in death ritual decisions.
  - Dying individuals have the opportunity to reminisce and converse with loved ones.
  - Dying individuals will understand what is happening with their bodies and the interventions.
- Open communication should not dwell on pathology or preparation for death, but should emphasize the dying person's strengths.

Grieving

Dimensions of Grieving
- **Grief** is the emotional numbness, disbelief, separation anxiety, despair, sadness, and loneliness that accompany the loss of someone we love.
- Grief is multidimensional and in some cases may last for years.
- Researchers have found that the grieving process is more like a roller-coaster ride than an orderly progression of stages with clear-cut time frames.
  - Many grieving spouses still report that even though time has brought some healing, they have never gotten over the loss.
- Long-term grief is sometimes masked and can predispose individuals to become depressed and even suicidal.
  - Good family communication may help to reduce the incidence of depression and suicidal thoughts.

Cultural Diversity in Healthy Grieving
- Beliefs about continuing bonds with the deceased vary extensively across cultures.
- Diverse grieving patterns are culturally embedded practices.

Making Sense of the World
- The grieving process may stimulate individuals to strive to make sense out of their world.
- If the death is caused by an accident or a disaster, efforts to understand it are pursued more vigorously.

Losing a Life Partner
- The death of an intimate partner causes profound grief and often financial loss, loneliness, increased physical illness, and psychological disorders, including depression.
- Widows outnumber widowers by a ratio of 5 to 1 and they represent the poorest group in the U.S.
  - The poorer and less educated they are, the lonelier they tend to be.
- Optimal adjustment after a death depends on several factors.
  - Women do better than men because they tend to have stronger social support networks.
  - Older women do better than younger women because death is more expected.
  - Widowers usually have more money and are more likely to remarry.
- Social support benefits widows and widowers.

Forms of Mourning and the Funeral
- Mourning varies from culture to culture.
- The most important aspect of mourning in most cultures is the funeral.
- Research found that bereaved individuals who were personally religious derived more psychological benefit from a funeral, participated more actively in the rituals, and adjusted more positively to the loss.
- In recent years, the funeral industry has been the focus of controversy as critics claim that funeral directors are just trying to make money and that embalming is grotesque.
  - One way to avoid exploitation is to purchase funeral arrangements in advance, though few people opt for this strategy.

Learning Objectives

1. Discuss the definition of death and how it has changed.
2. Explain the living will and the advanced directive.
3. Distinguish between the different types of euthanasia.
4. Discuss current available care for the dying, and why better care is needed.
5. Elaborate on the changing historical circumstances regarding death.
6. Discuss how death is viewed in other cultures compared to the United States.
7. Describe the common causes of and expectations about death at different points in the life span.
8. Discuss the attitudes toward death that children, adolescents, and adults have.
9. Describe Kübler-Ross' five-stage theory of dying, and its criticisms.
10. Explain how perceived control and denial play a role for those who face death.
11. Discuss the contexts in which people die.
12. Describe ways to communicate with a dying person.
13. Explain the dimensions of grieving, elaborating on how different cultures grieve and how grieving can be used to make sense of the world.
14. Discuss how losing a partner impacts the individual.
15. Elaborate on forms of mourning and the meaning of the funeral.
16. Identify the mourning traditions of the Amish and the traditional Jews.

Key Terms

acceptance

active euthanasia

anger

bargaining

brain death

denial and isolation

depression

euthanasia

grief

hospice

passive euthanasia

Key People

Robert Kastenbaum

Elisabeth Kübler-Ross

Lecture Suggestions

Lecture Suggestion 1: Defining Brain Death The text offers a definition of brain death that includes the cessation of neurological activity. This definition is one of the criteria from the Harvard Criteria for determining whether an individual is dead. To expand the material in the text, present the Harvard Criteria. Start by discussing the reasons that we need a definition of death. Those reasons include: (1) medical—when to tell the family, when to turn off the life support; (2) legal—insurance, distribution of estate; (3) ethical—how to ensure dignity and sanctity of life; and (4) practical—organ donation.

The following discussion regarding a medical definition of death was quoted from the following web site: http://www.geocities.com/HotSprings/Oasis/2919/death.html.

Looking back throughout the history of medicine, there was a time when people believed that death occurred when the heart stopped and breathing ceased (Burnell 67). Cessation of respiration was often determined by placing a feather beneath the nose of the patient where it would move with the slightest breath. Cardiac activity was checked by simply placing one's ear on the patient's chest and listening for a heartbeat. Because little was known about states of limited or nonexistent consciousness in which a heartbeat was undetectable to the human ear, some people were buried alive, and it became clear that new methods were needed to verify death (Larue 11). But along with the development of technology designed for the purpose of more accurately determining death came technology that could keep a body alive almost indefinitely (Burnell 67). For example, some people who have experienced severe hypothermia and who exhibit all of the classic symptoms of death have been successfully resuscitated, and others under the influence of certain substances, such as anesthetizing or paralyzing drugs, may appear dead although they are still alive (Larue 11-12). The definition of death is further clouded by resuscitative measures that are only partially successful, resulting in an individual whose heart and lungs continue to function but whose brain is irreversibly damaged ("A Definition of Irreversible Coma" 337). Modern medical technology has enabled physicians to keep patients such as these biologically alive, although they are capable of existing only at a vegetative level (Wennberg 109).

Fewer than fifty years ago, a person who had stopped breathing and had no heartbeat was considered dead. Now, however, brain function is also considered in the definition of death (Burnell 16). In 1991, the Multi-Society Task Force on PVS (persistent vegetative state), a conglomerate of physicians, ethicists, and lawyers sponsored by the American Academy of Neurology, defined brain death as the "permanent absence of all brain functions, including those of the brain stem. Brain dead patients are irreversibly comatose and apneic and have lost all brain stem reflexes and cranial-nerve functions"(Part 1 1502). But due to the introduction of the electroencephalogram (EEG), which makes it possible to monitor the functioning of the brain, and the advent of organ transplantation, which makes the monitoring of brain activity necessary, the shift of attention towards the brain as the organ that ultimately signals death took place many years earlier (Hoefler and Kamoie 55).

The actual concept of brain death was introduced in a 1959 article by two French neurophysiologists, Mallaret and Goulon, who studied patients on artificial life support who showed no electrical brain activity. They concluded that these comatose patients were "beyond coma"(Burnell 68). No definitive standards of brain death emerged until a group of physicians, theologians, lawyers, and philosophers on the Harvard University faculty formed the Ad Hoc Committee of the Harvard Medical School to Examine the Definition of Brain Death early in 1968 (Barnard 31-32). According to the report of the Ad Hoc Committee in the Journal of the American Medical Association, a permanently nonfunctioning brain must exhibit four criteria: unreceptivity and unresponsitivity, in which there is a "total unawareness of externally applied stimuli;" no movements or breathing during a period of at least one hour in which the patient is continuously observed by physicians; no reflexes, such as blinking, eye movement, and stretch-of-tendon reflexes; and a flat electroencephalogram, assuming that the electrodes have been properly placed, the equipment is functioning normally, and the personnel operating it are competent (337-338). The Harvard Criteria, as these standards came to be known, have proven to be reliable indicators of brain death, and physicians have generally reached a consensus about continuing to apply them.

More recently, a commission created by former United States president Ronald Reagan in 1981, for the purpose of, among other things, establishing a definition of death, concluded that the diagnosis of death would require that physicians establish the presence or absence of brain activity, given that no bodily functions can occur spontaneously without the help of the brain (Burnell 68-69). From this new definition, it can be argued that death occurs at the moment that the brain activity necessary to control autonomous biological functions ceases. In fact, patients who are determined to be brain dead, based on the Harvard Criteria, are medically and legally dead, and no further medical treatment is required (McCuen and Boucher 25).

- Sources: http://www.geocities.com/HotSprings/Oasis/2919/death.html Barnard, C. (1980). *Good life, good death: A doctor's case for euthanasia and suicide.* Englewood Cliffs: Prentice-Hall, Inc. Burnell, G.M. (1993). *Final choices: To live or to die in an age of medical technology.* New York: Plenum Press. Hoefler, J.M., & Kamoie, B.E. (1994). *Deathright: Culture, medicine, politics, and the right to die.* Boulder: Westview Press. Larue, G.A. (1996). *Playing God: 50 religions' views on your right to die.* Wakefield: Moyer Bell. McCuen, G.E., & Boucher T. (1985). *Terminating life: Conflicting values in health care.* Hudson: Gary E. McCuen Publications, Inc. The Multi-Society Task Force on PVS. (1994). Medical aspects of the persistent vegetative state (first of two parts). *New England Journal of Medicine, 330* 1499-1508. The Multi-Society Task Force on PVS. (1994). Medical aspects of the persistent vegetative state (second of two parts). *New England Journal of Medicine, 330,* 1572-1578. Report of the Ad Hoc Committee of the Harvard Medical School to Examine the Definition of Brain Death. (1968) A definition of irreversible coma. *Journal of the American Medical Association, 205,* 337-340. Wennberg, R.N. (1989). Terminal choices: Euthanasia, suicide, and the right to die. Grand Rapids: William B. Eerdmans Publishing Company.

Lecture Suggestion 2: Hospice This lecture suggestion examines hospice care based on information from Gentile and Fello's article (1990). It is important to set admission criteria for a hospice. The authors have established a fairly rigid set of three criteria for admission:
- Completion of all active, curative treatment.
- Patient's awareness of diagnosis and prognosis.
- Patient and family's clear understanding of the goals of hospice care.

Hospice care emphasizes a multifaceted and comprehensive approach to a patient's medical, psychosocial, and spiritual problems. "Role blurring" which involves the overlapping of duties of various professional disciplines is encouraged to a certain extent. For example, a nurse may also engage in some counseling regarding how to approach a child about an impending death rather than waiting for a counselor to discuss the issues. Obviously, each team member has a specific area of expertise, which focuses his or her primary responsibilities. In other words, hospice team members need to be aware of and comfortable with role blurring and with their primary responsibilities, for which they are liable. A typical composition of hospice team members is noted below. The composition will vary depending on the specific model and whether the program is Medicare certified.

- Hospice nurse (coordinate care, principal support for patients and their families).
- Hospice aide (provide personal care and light housekeeping duties in the home).
- Counselor (support for families, seek out community resources, help with financial, legal, and insurance issues).
- Therapists (Physical, occupational, and speech therapists).
- Nutritionist (counsels family members on the special nutritional needs of the patient).
- Medical director (symptom management for patient, educate patient and staff regarding the illness).
- Chaplain (attend to the spiritual needs of the patients and their families).
- Volunteers (friend and companion for patients, home care, office help, fundraising).

Gentile and Fello mention that staff burnout is a common concern within the hospice setting given that the staff experiences successive losses. It is important to develop support systems, both formal and informal, for the team members to prevent burnout. They stress that it is necessary for each team member to continually evaluate job satisfaction, self-esteem, personal goals, and career goals.

- Source: Gentile, M. & Fello, M. (1990). Hospice care for the 1990s: A concept coming of age. *The Journal of Home Health Care Practice, 3,* 1-15.

Lecture Suggestion 3: Grief This lecture introduces anticipatory grief and discusses three phases of grief. Information for this lecture was obtained from Papalia et al.'s *Adult Development and Aging* text.

Anticipatory grief involves experiencing symptoms of grief while the person is still alive. Anticipatory grief is often experienced by the friends and family of a person who has been ill for a long time. Brown and Stoudemire found that anticipatory grief can facilitate coping with the actual death. There is inconsistent evidence as to whether preparation for widowhood actually facilitates adjustment. For some, it helps to prepare psychologically and practically to become a widow.

Brown and Stoudemire (1983) developed the most common and widely studied phases of grief. These phases may vary depending on the individual experiencing grief.

Shock and disbelief

- The time frame for this phase varies. It may last several weeks especially if the death was unexpected and sudden. Initially, the survivor is lost and confused. The shock and disbelief may buffer them against other intense reactions. Physical symptoms often accompany this phase (shortness of breath, tightening of the chest and throat, a feeling of emptiness in the abdomen). The initial numbness gradually shifts to overwhelming feelings of sadness.

Preoccupation with the memory of the dead person

- The time frame for this phase is approximately 6 months or longer. Physical symptoms continue with frequent crying, insomnia, loss of appetite, and fatigue. Much research has examined how widows cope with the loss of a spouse. She may relive her husband's death or their entire relationship. While a widow used to be considered emotionally disturbed if she talked to her dead husband, it is now considered common and potentially helpful to the widow (Lund, 1993). The widow may feel his presence, hear his voice, or see his face. These vivid perceptions tend to diminish over time, though they may persist for years.

Resolution

- This phase involves renewed interest in everyday activities. The realization that life must go on sparks an increase in social activity. Memories of the dead person persist, though the reaction to these memories changes. Rather than the sharp pain and longing, the memories provoke fond, positive feelings mingled with sadness.

- Sources: Brown, J.T., & Stoudemire, A. (1983). Normal and pathological grief. *Journal of the American Medical Association, 250,* 378-382. Lund, D.A. (1993). Widowhood: The coping response. In R. Kastenbaum (Ed.), *Encyclopedia of adult development* (pp. 537-541). Phoenix: Oryx. Papalia, D.E., Camp, C.J., & Feldman, R.D. (1996). *Adult development and aging.* New York: McGraw-Hill.

Lecture Suggestion 4: Reactions to Loss The purpose of this lecture is to examine the diversity of loss reactions. Information for this lecture suggestion was obtained from Papalia et al.'s (1996) *Adult Development and Aging* textbook. Lund (1993) found that many people do not experience grief in a linear fashion from shock to resolution. For many, grief occurs in a roller-coaster fashion with emotional ups and downs of varying lengths. The intensity of these emotional ups and downs may lessen with time, though they may never subside completely. Wortman and Silver (1989) reviewed studies of reactions to major loss. This discussion will focus on the loss of a loved one.

- Depression is far from universal. Only 15-35 percent of widows and widowers demonstrated signs of depression from 3 weeks to 2 years after the loss.
- The lack of initial distress does not inevitably lead to problems. Researchers found that the individuals that were most upset and troubled initially showed more problems up to 2 years later.
- Not everyone has to work through the loss. Individuals vary as to how they will cope.
- Not everyone rebounds quickly. The time frame of grief varies tremendously for individuals. Up to 40 percent of surviving spouses showed moderate to severe anxiety up to 4 years after the loss of their spouse (especially if it was a sudden death).
- Some people never accept the loss. Some individuals never resolve their grief. This is more common when the individual dies in an accident.

Wortman and Silver concluded that there are three main patterns of grieving.

- The mourner can proceed from high distress to low distress.
- The mourner does not experience intense distress (initially or later).
- The mourner remains distressed for a long period of time.

It is important to note that there is no one "right way" to mourn. Individuals experience the loss of a loved one differently and should be allowed to mourn differently.

- Sources: Lund, D.A. (1993). Widowhood: The coping response. In R. Kastenbaum (Ed.), *Encyclopedia of adult development* (pp. 537-541). Phoenix: Oryx. Papalia, D.E., Camp, C.J., & Feldman, R.D. (1996). *Adult development and aging*. New York: McGraw-Hill. Wortman, C.B., & Silver, R.C. (1989). The myths of coping with loss. *Journal of Consulting and Clinical Psychology, 57*, 349-357.

Classroom Activities

Classroom Activity 1: Advanced Directives The purpose of this activity is to expose students to advanced directives. For this exercise, invite an attorney to your class to describe the advantages and disadvantages of having a living will and a durable power of attorney for health care. If you are unable to get an attorney to come to your class, obtain a copy of a living will and the power of attorney form. You can download a living will from the following web site http://www.euthanasia.org/lwvh.html. You could have your students get into small groups to discuss their thoughts about these documents. Do any students have a living will? Do their parents? What are the advantages of having a living will? What are the potential disadvantages?
Logistics:
- Materials: A copy of a living will and a power of attorney form.
- Group size: Full class, or small group.
- Approximate time: Full class (60 minutes) or small group (20 minutes).

Classroom Activity 2: The Right to Choose Debate One of the most controversial topics of modern day is a person's right to choose to die. Chapter 21 mentions Dr. Jack Kevorkian who has assisted with numerous suicides of terminally ill people. Set up a class debate around three distinctly different perspectives, all of which have a position on this issue: the medical community, the legal community, and the individuals who want to die. People tend to have very strong opinions regarding euthanasia. Randomly divide the class into three groups and assign one of the three positions to each group. Given the random nature of the group selection, the groups will most likely consist of some individuals that support the assigned position and some individuals that oppose the assigned position. It will be important for them to rise above their personal beliefs and explore the assigned position. Encourage them to seek out support for their position. We have provided several articles to facilitate the debate.

The American Medical Association is clear on physician-assisted suicide. They believe that the purpose of physicians is to heal, therefore, suicide does not fulfill that mission. However, many doctors are opposing this stance and it may very well change in the near future. For a discussion of medicine's position on this topic, see a paper by Cotton (1995). An article by Kassirer (1997) in *The New England Journal of Medicine* discusses some of the legal issues surrounding physician-assisted suicide. Quill (1993) writes an article from the perspective of the patient. The idea for this debate came from readings in the *Annual Editions: Dying, Death, and Bereavement* (1998/1999).

Logistics:
- Group size: Small group, individual, small group, and full class.
- Approximate time: Small group (15 minutes), individual (1 hour), small group (30 minutes), and full class (45 minutes).
- Sources: *Annual editions: Dying, death, and bereavement* (1998/1999). Guilford, CT: Dushkin/McGraw-Hill. Cotton, P. (1995). Medicine's position is both pivotal and precarious in assisted-suicide debate. *Journal of American Medical Association, 273*, 363-364. Kassirer, J. (1997). The Supreme Court and physician-assisted suicide: The ultimate right. *The New England Journal of Medicine*, 50-53. Quill, T. (1993). Doctor, I want to die. Will you help me? *Journal of the American Medical Association, 270*, 870-875.

Classroom Activity 3: Field Trip to a Local Hospice Organize a trip to a local hospice. Many communities are fortunate to have a stand-alone hospice and many hospice directors are happy to provide tours. Many are also willing to come talk to classes about their philosophy of death and the services they provide. Before going to the hospice, prepare students by discussing what services are provided and what they can expect to see there. During the class period following the field trip, it may be a good idea to have students get into small groups and discuss what they learned and how they felt about the experience. You can go around to each group and make sure that everyone understands what a hospice does and that they have no unanswered questions. You may also want students to write a brief report about their impressions of the visit and what they learned.

Logistics:
- Group size: Full class, small group or individual.
- Approximate time: Full class (60 minutes), small group or individual (20 minutes).

Classroom Activity 4: Write Your Own Obituary One of the most challenging and productive activities for this chapter involves confronting our own deaths. This is not as frightening as it may sound, if approached carefully. You may want to begin by pointing out that none of us will get out of life alive. We will all die, some sooner than others. In the newspaper each day we read of people who died; the death notices and obituaries try to capture the essence of their lives for us, a sort of summary of their existence. Most students who have read obituaries know how unsatisfying they are, but few have thought to do anything about them. You might point out to students, if you hear such dissatisfaction, that most newspapers charge for the printing of the obituary, and small ones can easily cost $35 to $50 per day. Nonetheless, students should enjoy certain benefits without paying extra, and today they will. They will have a chance to write their own obituaries. Each student should write two: one as though he or she died today, at their present age; the other worded in such a way as though the student has lived through adulthood and has died at an old age, for example, at age 90.

The first obituary is realistic; it forces the confrontation with the possibility of death but is not typically very frightening. After all, we feel good, so why worry. The pain begins when the student starts listing the survivors or specifies the place of service or burial. Then it is real. However, this obituary has real value by showing how the student has already had significant impact on those they have known and cared about and how they will be missed.

The second obituary is idealistic in a sense, in that it permits the student to anticipate many years of life. On the other hand, obituaries are rather brief. It is difficult to capture 90 years in 3 column inches.

Students will have to select carefully the accomplishments they include, and this is the value of the exercise. It focuses their attention on the fact that life is finite; we simply do not know the borders. If the class is small enough, have students read their obituaries (either one) aloud. A point to stress is that we should try to live our lives to the fullest.

Logistics:
- Group size: Individual and full class.
- Approximate time: Individual (30 minutes) and full class (20 minutes).

Classroom Activity 5: Field Trip to a Local Mortuary People in the mortuary industry are in the service business and are almost always willing to offer tours, provide materials, or give talks about their industry and describe the services they provide. Despite their initial fears and complaints, students always convey positive feedback about their trip to the mortuary. During the class period following the field trip, it may be a good idea to have students get into small groups and discuss what they learned and how they felt about the experience. You can go around to each group and make sure that everyone understands what a mortuary does and that they have no unanswered questions. You may also want students to write a brief report about their impressions of the visit and what they learned.

Logistics:
- Group size: Full class, small group or individual.
- Approximate time: Full class (60 minutes) small group or individual (20 minutes).

Classroom Activity 6: Funerals The purpose of this exercise is for students to research the costs of funerals. The Federal Trade Commission mandates a general price list for services to protect the consumer. Have your students look up the cost of various components of a funeral to determine the potential cost. Itemized lists should be provided for funeral director, embalming, transferring the remains, limousine, visitations, funeral services, casket, flowers, burial clothing, register book, organist, clergy, etc. Have them bring the information to class for a discussion. Were they surprised at the total cost? What components of the service would they want at a funeral? Would the cost of the services alter their desires for various services?

Logistics:
- Group size: Individual and full class.
- Approximate time: Individual (45 minutes) and full class (20 minutes).

Classroom Activity 7: Critical Thinking Multiple-Choice Questions and Suggested Answers Discuss the critical thinking multiple-choice questions (**Handout 1**). Question 1 requires the students to recall the major theories of development outlined earlier in the textbook. You may want to spend a few minutes with the students discussing the major tenets of each theory.

Question 2 requires students to apply the material in chapter 21. You may want to discuss this question as a class after students have completed it because it can be difficult to answer.

Question 3 is the standard question asked in most chapters. For this question, students must determine which of the statements are assumptions rather than an inference or an observation. The answers to these questions are presented in **Handout 2**.

Logistics:
- Materials: Handout 1 (the critical thinking multiple-choice questions) and Handout 2 (answers).
- Group size: Small groups to discuss the questions, then a full class discussion.
- Approximate time: Small groups (15 to 20 minutes), full class discussion of any questions (15 minutes).

Classroom Activity 8: Critical Thinking Essay Questions and Suggestions for Helping Students Answer the Essays Discuss students' answers to the critical thinking essay questions presented in **Handout 3**. The purpose of this exercise is threefold. First, answering the essay questions further facilitates students' understanding of concepts in chapter 21. Second, this type of essay question affords the students an opportunity to apply the concepts to their own lives, which will facilitate their retention of the material. Third, the essay format also gives students practice expressing themselves in written form. Ideas to help students answer the critical thinking essay questions are provided as **Handout 4**.

Logistics:
- Materials: Handout 3 (essay questions) and Handout 4 (helpful suggestions for the answers).
- Group size: Individual, then full class.
- Approximate time: Individual (60 minutes), full class discussion of any questions (30 minutes).

Personal Applications

Personal Application 1: But I'm Not Dead Yet... This exercise will allow you to demonstrate to students the complexity of defining "death." As our body and our mind both contribute to our experiencing life, there is debate as to when we are actually officially "dead" if some of our body still functions, while most of our brain does not. It is a significant issue to consider, as it can influence decisions that are made in times of such horrific circumstances.

- Instructions for Students: At what point do you consider an individual "dead"? Think carefully about what you believe constitutes "life" to help you answer this more completely. What is your conclusion based on? Has this view changed over your lifetime? Why? If you were declared "brain dead" by a competent group of physicians, what would you want to be done? Would you consider a living will? What is your perspective on Dr. Kevorkian and his assistance to individuals who make the choice that their "lives" are a mere physical existence, too painful to enable them a true mental "life"?
- Use in the Classroom: This is a very powerful discussion topic, and it can lead to very strong views presented on all aspects of the topic. Bring into your class discussion the notion of modern technology and the advances made in medicine's ability to prolong life under many circumstances. Also consider what lies ahead in terms of assisting people to overcome what were once life-ending circumstances (technology such as cloning, stem cell implants, etc.). You are certain to elicit a great deal of critical thinking and emotional reactions.

Personal Application 2: The Loss of a Loved One The purpose of this exercise is to help students recognize the differing view and understanding of death at various stages in the life span. Very young children view death quite differently than older children, who vary still, from adolescents, young adults, and older adults. At each stage of life, death is understood and approached from a very different perspective.

- Instructions for Students: Share the experiences you have had with death thus far in your life. There is no need to go into difficult detail, just focus on the stages in your life during which someone you knew passed away, and try to recall your perception of it. What were your thoughts when you found out? Did you fully comprehend what was going on? Did you understand how it would affect your life? What was your emotional reaction? How did others around you act? Did their actions affect you? Do you think about the experience differently now that you are older? How do you think your experiences have affected the way you view your own death? Are you more apprehensive or more comfortable with the idea? Why?
- Use in the Classroom: Have students who are willing to share, do so. Try and collect stories from each stage of life and discuss the differences in perspectives on death. Have students comment on the notion of whether or not there is a singular view of death in our society. Do we all tend to fear it? Are people becoming more daring in their behavior due to a lessening of fear of dying? What factors might contribute to the attitudes of individuals who are highly risky in their behavior—those who appear to tempt fate often. What factors contribute to a fear of death? Are there any consistencies in responses, or do these issues seem to have a great deal of individual variation? How might developmentalists' knowledge of people's views of death at various stages help to develop a more "positive" or healthy view of death and dying?

Research Project Ideas

Research Project 1: Hospices in Your Community Santrock indicates that most people die in hospitals, but that increasingly people are turning to hospices as a context in which to die. Is this happening in your community? Have students find out by determining whether there are hospices in your community (**Handout 5**). These may be located within hospitals or adjacent to them; or they may be found in nursing homes or nursing care centers.

Once they have selected a hospice, students should learn as much as they can about it. One line of inquiry concerns social policy that affects the hospice. For example, hospitals cannot be reimbursed for providing long-term care for dying patients. Thus, important questions to ask concern the impact of Medicare, Medicaid, and private insurance payments. Some questions to ask are listed below.
Questions:
- What is the nature of the group that runs the hospice?
- How does the hospice serve the needs of the dying person and the person's family?
- Does the hospice do anything to teach about the meaning of death to the person who is dying and people close to that person?
- What services does the hospice provide for the survivors?
- How does this relate to who can afford hospice care?
- Who uses the service?
- What type of hospice care would local groups provide if the governmental policy and financial constraints did not limit them?

Students should summarize their findings in a brief paper in which they answer at least the questions listed above. Also, they will want to comment on how well what they learned coincides with what the text reports about attitudes toward death in the United States. If they can, they should determine how well the hospice or hospices they located implement what we know about how well people cope with their own or other individuals' deaths.
- Use in the Classroom: Have the students present their results and make recommendations for how these hospices can improve the care they give to dying people. This will be a good time to discuss how developmental psychology research can have a direct impact on people's lives.

Research Project 2: Experiencing Others' Deaths Commentators have observed that Americans have remarkably little direct experience of death compared to people of other nations. You also may have concluded this from information in the text (for example, most Americans die in hospitals). But is this true? This project will give students information about the nature and extent of their own and their peers' knowledge of, and experience with, death. By now you should be familiar with the section in the front of this Instructor's Manual on Ethics, Human Subjects, and Informed Consent.

Students will need to have at least five of their peers answer the questions below (**Handout 6**). They may have them respond in writing or in an interview. In either case, they will want to allow up to an hour for each person to respond. Of course, they will need institutional approval and their respondents' informed consent to carry out the project.

Students should summarize their findings by constructing an appropriate table or tables showing how people responded to the questions they asked. Then they will write a brief report in which they at least indicate the purpose of their project, describe the people who participated, summarize their results, and draw appropriate conclusions about their peers' knowledge of and experience with death. Instruct students to indicate whether what they learned illustrates points made in their textbook.
Questions about experiencing others' deaths:
- Has anyone you have known died? How many people?
- Who was the person in relation to you (e.g., brother, aunt, friend)?
- How and where did the person die?
- Were you present at the time of death? What was your reaction?

- If you were not present at the time of death, how did you react when you learned of the death?
- Did you view the body of the dead person at some time after death (e.g., at a funeral home)? What was your reaction to seeing the body?
- How involved were you in taking care of practical matters concerning the deceased?
- How involved were you in mourning the deceased?
- How involved were you in caring for other people who were mourning the deceased?
- For how long did the individual's death have a daily impact on you (e.g., thinking about the person every day)?
- Have you worked through any concerns the person's death created for you?
- Has it been difficult for you to answer these questions?

- Use in the Classroom: Have students present their results to the class. It might be easiest for them to display their tables on an overhead projector or hand out copies of their tables to the class. Based on these presentations, the class can attempt to draw some general conclusions about their knowledge of death, as well as their peers' experiences.

Film and Video List

The following films and videos supplement the content of chapter 21. Contact information for film distributors can be found at the front of this Instructor's Manual under Film and Video Sources.

Before I Die: Medical Care and Personal Choices (Films for the Humanities and Sciences, 60 minutes). This program brings experts together to debate medical and cultural issues related to prolonging the dying process.

Beyond Life and Death (Films for the Humanities and Sciences, 30 minutes). This program explores how beliefs about an afterlife affect the way people live their lives and approach death. Concepts of heaven and reincarnation are presented.

Common Threads: Stories from the Quilt (Direct Cinema Limited, 80 minutes). This documentary focuses on five people who died from AIDS and how their loved ones came to terms with the loss.

Coping with Loss (Films for the Humanities and Sciences, 19 minutes). This video deals with how children cope with death.

A Death of One's Own (Films for the Humanities and Sciences, 90 minutes). This program highlights the complexities of end-of-life choices, including the bitter debate over physician-assisted suicide. Three patients, their families, and their doctors discuss some of the hardest decisions, including how to pay for care, humane treatment, and how to balance dying and dignity.

Difficult Decisions: When a Loved One Approaches Death (Films for the Humanities and Sciences, 30 minutes). This program follows two families that must deal with life-and-death decisions in an ICU. Medical professionals help the families understand the process of making such difficult decisions.

The Forgotten Mourner (Films for the Humanities and Sciences, 28 minutes). This video looks at the effects of loss on those who are often overlooked in the mourning process: siblings, grandparents, people who have lost their lovers to AIDS, and parents who experience a miscarriage.

Grief and Healing (Films for the Humanities and Sciences, 30 minutes). In this program, seven people reflect on their experiences with loss, grief, and healing.

Letting Go: A Hospice Journey (Films for the Humanities and Sciences, 90 minutes). This program looks at three patients with terminal illnesses and how hospices care for them and help them learn to cope. It also shows the decision-making process of various medical professionals.

Living with Dying (Films for the Humanities and Sciences, 90 minutes). In this program, Bill Moyers describes the search for new ways of thinking and talking about dying. Patients and medical professionals alike come forward to examine the end of life with honesty, courage, and even humor, demonstrating that dying can be an incredibly rich experience both for the terminally ill and their loved ones.

The Pitch of Grief (Fanlight Productions, 30 minutes). This video provides a look at the emotional process of grieving through intimate interviews with four men and women who have lost loved ones.

A Time to Change (Films for the Humanities and Sciences, 90 minutes). This program discusses care at the end of life, and life-improvement techniques at the end-of-life.

When Children Grieve (Syracuse University, 20 minutes). This video shows interviews with children before and after the death of a parent.

Toward a Better Death (Films and Humanities and Sciences, 27 minutes) This program explores the choices open to terminally ill patients and their families. It presents available options for comfortable end-of-life care that attend to physical, emotional, and spiritual needs. Medical experts and caregivers discuss the difficult choices that arise, including the moral and legal controversies, and medical options available when a cure is no longer viable.

Web Site Suggestions

The URLs for general sites, common to all chapters, can be found at the front of this Instructor's Manual under Useful Web Sites. At the time of publication, all sites were current and active, however, please be advised that you may occasionally encounter a dead link.

Advanced Directives
http://www.aarp.org/programs/advdir/home.html

Association for Death Education and Counseling
http://www.adec.org/

Attitudes Toward Death
http://www.wwdc.com/death/attitudes.html

Crisis, Grief, and Healing
http://www.webhealing.com/

Definition of Brain Death
http://www.geocities.com/HotSprings/Oasis/2919/death.html

Euthanasia
http://www.euthanasia.org/lwvh.html

Growth House: An international gateway to resources for life-threatening illnesses and end-of-life issues
http://www.growthhouse.org/

Hemlock Organization
http://www.hemlock.org/

Hospice Information
http://www.americanhospice.org/

International Conference on Death and Bereavement
http://www.wwdc.com/death/kings/conference.html

Last Rights: The Right to Die Society in Canada
http://www.rights.org/deathnet/last_rights.html

WidowNet: For information and self-help resources for widows and widowers
http://www.fortnet.org/~goshorn/

Critical Thinking Multiple-Choice Questions

1. Recall that chapter 2 of your text presented several types of theories that psychologists use to understand life-span development. Which of the following theories is most applicable to the material in chapter 21? Circle the letter of the best answer and explain why it is the best answer and why each other answer is not as good.

   a. Psychoanalytic
   b. Cognitive
   c. Behavioral and social cognitive
   d. Ethological
   e. Ecological

2. At least one reason for including a chapter about death and dying in a text on life-span development is that knowledge about death and dying can help us accept the end of life. In that regard, which of the following statements represents the best application of information presented in chapter 21? Circle the letter of the best answer and explain why it is the best answer and why each other answer is not as good.

   a. The material prepares the reader to accept death and dying with dignity and equanimity.
   b. Chapter 21 provides clear ethical guidelines for difficult decisions about death and dying.
   c. An individual who reads chapter 21 more clearly understands what death is and how people react to it.
   d. Knowing the material in chapter 21 will enable a person to help a dying person accept death and die peacefully.
   e. Chapter 21 indicates how best to postpone death and optimize the quality of life.

3. The legal definition of death appears to be on the verge of changing. Which of the following statements represent assumptions, rather than inferences or observations, that are prompting this change? Circle the letters of the best answers and explain why they are the best answers and why each other answer is not as good.

   a. The higher portions of the brain often die sooner than the lower portions.
   b. Personality and intelligence are located in the higher cortical part of the brain.
   c. Most physicians define brain death as the death of both higher cortical functions and the lower brain stem functions.
   d. When higher cortical function is lost, a person is no longer a human being.
   e. The cessation of electrical activity in part of the brain indicates that that part of the brain can no longer function.

Suggested Answers for Critical Thinking Multiple-Choice Questions

1. Recall that chapter 2 of your text presented several types of theories that psychologists use to understand life span development. Which of the following theories is most applicable to the material in chapter 21? Circle the letter of the best answer and explain why it is the best answer and why each other answer is not as good.

   a. Psychoanalytic is not the best answer. Nothing is mentioned of the usual psychoanalytic themes. Were Erikson included in this chapter, a case could be made for this answer, but Erikson's views on the last stage of life were presented in chapter 20.

   b. Cognitive is the best answer. By far the largest amount of material in this chapter is about how individuals react to and understand their own and others' deaths. Even the treatment of cultural and historical contexts focuses on the understanding of death.

   c. Behavioral and social cognitive is not the best answer. The main reason for not choosing this answer is the predominant focus on how people understand death. A lesser role is given to information about the importance of being exposed to death and the influence of social rituals concerning death. But this material is not couched in social cognitive terms; nor is the material about understanding death explicitly and deliberately related to behavior.

   d. Ethological is not the best answer. Death is not placed in its genetic and evolutionary perspective, nor are ideas about how death is adapted for species survival explored.

   e. Ecological is not the best answer. Although this is touched on in the discussion of sociohistorical and cultural contexts, these influences do not form a part of the later discussions of understanding, facing, or coping with death.

2. At least one reason for including a chapter about death and dying in a text on life-span development is that knowledge about death and dying can help us accept the end of life. In that regard, which of the following statements represents the best application of information presented in chapter 21? Circle the letter of the best answer and explain why it is the best answer and why each other answer is not as good.

   a. The material prepares the reader to accept death and dying with dignity and equanimity is not the best answer. No information in the chapter is presented to suggest that specific knowledge about the nature and meaning of death influences the manner by which people face death.

   b. Chapter 21 provides clear ethical guidelines for difficult decisions about death and dying is not the best answer. Information about death and dying presented in this chapter can be used only inferentially to construct ethical guidelines for decisions about death and dying.

   c. An individual who reads chapter 21 more clearly understands what death is and how people react to it is the best answer. Chapter 21 is mainly descriptive, and is based primarily on descriptive research. There appears to be no systematic or experimental work that would provide a basis for believing that knowing the material in the chapter will produce the outcomes suggested in "a" and "d."

   d. Knowing the material in chapter 21 will enable a person to help a dying person accept death and die peacefully is not the best answer. As indicated in "a" and "c" above, relevant correlational or experimental (or even descriptive) information is lacking.

   e. Chapter 21 indicates how best to postpone death and optimize the quality of life is not the best answer. The chapter does not discuss how to prolong life, nor how to get the best of it. The chapter focuses on death itself.

3. The legal definition of death appears to be on the verge of changing. Which of the following statements represent assumptions, rather than inferences or observations, that are prompting this change? Circle the letters of the best answers and explain why they are the best answers and why each other answer is not as good.

   a. The higher portions of the brain often die sooner than the lower portions is not the best answer. Although the source of this fact is not given, it is stated as something objectively true and verified, that is, an observation pertinent to the issue of defining death.

   b. Personality and intelligence are located in the higher cortical part of the brain is one of the best answers. Santrock points out that it is a belief of people who support a brain death definition of death.

   c. Most physicians define brain death as the death of both higher cortical functions and the lower brain stem functions is not the best answer. It is clearly an observation pertinent to the claim that brain death is an increasingly accepted definition of death.

   d. When higher cortical function is lost, a person is no longer a human being is not the best answer. It is an inference from the claim in assumption stated in "a" and from an assumption that intelligence and personality are, in fact, the defining features of human beings.

   e. The cessation of electrical activity in part of the brain indicates that that part of the brain can no longer function is one of the best answers. If this claim is not true, counting a person who has undergone brain death as defined by EEG readings would wrongfully be considered dead in the event that brain function could have (however predictably or reliably) been revived.

Critical Thinking Essay Questions

Your answers to these kinds of questions demonstrate an ability to comprehend and apply ideas discussed in this chapter.

1. Indicate and explain the alternative definitions of death.

2. Distinguish between active and passive euthanasia, and indicate which type of euthanasia best characterizes the activities of Dr. Jack Kevorkian.

3. Provide at least two examples of practices that indicate death acceptance and death avoidance.

4. Explain how death might be defined and perceived by individuals at different stages of life-span development such as preschoolers, elementary school children, adolescents, and young, middle-aged, and older adults.

5. Describe the stages in Kübler-Ross' analysis of dying. Has research supported her stages?

6. Indicate and briefly explain different ways that people mourn the death of others.

7. Compare and contrast the alternative conceptions of grief.

8. What are some of the consequences associated with losing a life partner?

9. Defend or refute the contention that individuals who persistently hold on to the deceased should enter therapy.

Handout 4 (CA 8)

Ideas to Help You Answer Critical Thinking Essay Questions

1. Begin your discussion with an introduction as to why this is even necessary to address.

2. What issues (physiological, ethical, emotional, financial, etc.) do you see as related to this subject matter? Should everyone consider these? Why or why not?

3. Define what death acceptance and death avoidance are referring to as you provide your examples.

4. Make a time line illustrating how death is viewed as one ages. Identify what is changing at each stage.

5. Be certain you provide examples for evidence of your answer concerning the research.

6. Provide a definition and description of mourning. Is there a single definition, or does your answer lead you to conclude otherwise?

7. Is grief a relative term, or are there enough similarities among all people's experience that it has a universal definition?

8. Are the consequences always negative? Explain.

9. Present a personal profile of an individual "holding on to the deceased"? What does that phrase mean? After you've established this understanding and image, address the role of therapy.

Hospices in Your Community

Santrock indicates that most people die in hospitals, but that increasingly people are turning to hospices as a context in which to die. Is this happening in your community? Find out by determining whether there are hospices in your community. These may be located within hospitals or adjacent to them; or they may be found in nursing homes or nursing care centers.

Once you have selected a hospice, learn as much as you can about it. One line of inquiry concerns social policy that affects the hospice. For example, hospitals cannot be reimbursed for providing long-term care for dying patients. Thus, important questions to ask concern the impact of Medicare, Medicaid, and private insurance payments. Some questions to ask are listed below. Summarize your findings in a brief paper in which you answer at least the questions listed below. Also, comment on how well what you learned coincides with what your text reports about attitudes toward death in the United States. Determine how well the hospice or hospices you located implement what we know about how well people cope with their own or other individuals' deaths.

Questions:

- What is the nature of the group that runs the hospice?

- How does the hospice serve the needs of the dying person and the person's family?

- Does the hospice do anything to teach about the meaning of death to the person who is dying and people close to that person?

- What services does the hospice provide for the survivors?

- How does this relate to who can afford hospice care?

- Who uses the service?

- What type of hospice care would local groups provide if the governmental policy and financial constraints did not limit them?

Handout 6 (RP 2)

Experiencing Others' Deaths

Commentators have observed that Americans have remarkably little direct experience of death compared to people of other nations. You also may have concluded this from information in your text (for example, most Americans die in hospitals). But is this true? This project will give you information about the nature and extent of your own and your peers' knowledge of, and experience with, death.

Have at least five of your peers answer the questions below. You may have them respond in writing or in an interview (if the latter, be sure you are prepared to record their answers). In either case, be sure to allow up to an hour for each person to respond. Of course, you will need institutional approval and your respondents' informed consent to carry out your project.

Summarize your findings by constructing an appropriate table or tables showing how people responded to the questions you asked. Then, write a brief report in which you at least indicate the purpose of your project, describe the people who participated, summarize your results, and draw appropriate conclusions about your peers' experience of death, as well as your own. Try also to indicate whether what you learned illustrates points made in your textbook.

Questions about experiencing others' deaths:

- Has anyone you have known died? How many people?

- Who was the person in relation to you (e.g., brother, aunt, friend)?

- How and where did the person die?

- Were you present at the time of death? What was your reaction?

- If you were not present at the time of death, how did you react when you learned of the death?

- Did you view the body of the dead person at some time after death (e.g., at a funeral home)? What was your reaction to seeing the body?

- How involved were you in taking care of practical matters concerning the deceased?

- How involved were you in mourning the deceased?

- How involved were you in caring for other people who were mourning the deceased?

- For how long did the individual's death have a daily impact on you (e.g., thinking about the person every day)?

- Have you worked through any concerns the person's death created for you?

- Has it been difficult for you to answer these questions?

589

Appendix A: Cognitive Maps

Chapter 1

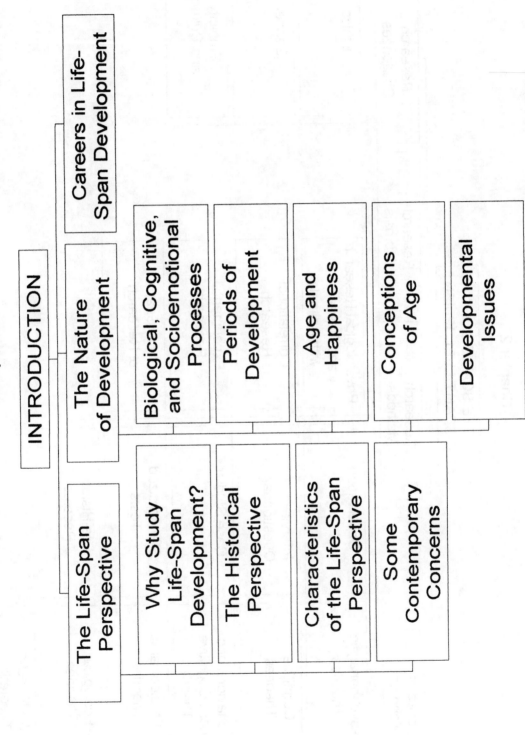

INTRODUCTION

The Life-Span Perspective

The Nature of Development

Careers in Life-Span Development

Why Study Life-Span Development?

The Historical Perspective

Characteristics of the Life-Span Perspective

Some Contemporary Concerns

Biological, Cognitive, and Socioemotional Processes

Periods of Development

Age and Happiness

Conceptions of Age

Developmental Issues

Chapter 2

THE SCIENCE OF
LIFE-SPAN DEVELOPMENT

Theories of
Development

Research
Methods

Research
Journals

Research
Challenges

Psychoanalytic
Theories

Cognitive
Theories

Behavioral and
Social Cognitive
Theories

Ethological
Theories

Ecological
Theories

An Eclectic
Theoretical
Orientation

Observation

Interviews and
Questionnaires

Case Studies

Standardized
Tests

Life-History
Records

Physiological Research
and Research
with Animals

Correlational
Research

Experimental
Research

Time Span
of Research

Ethics

Gender

Ethnicity
and Culture

Chapter 3

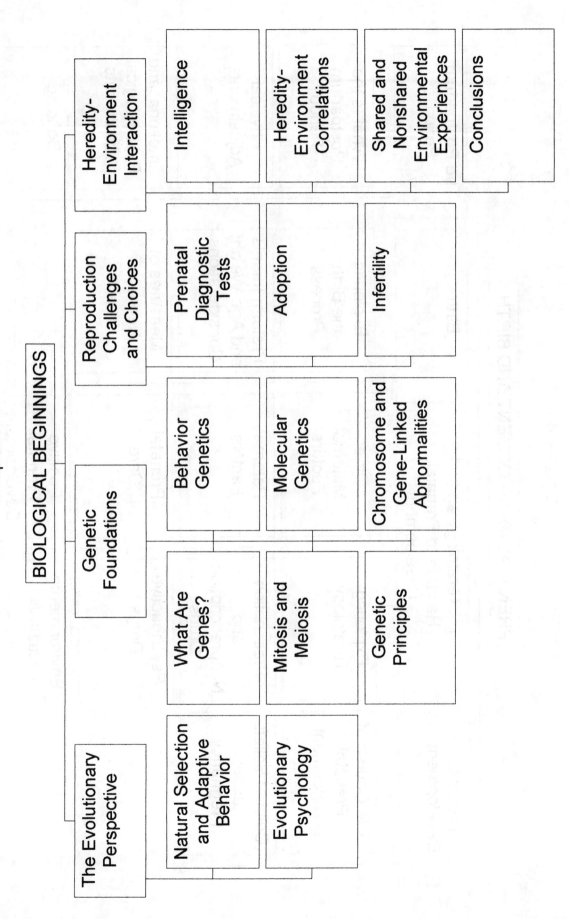

BIOLOGICAL BEGINNINGS

The Evolutionary Perspective

Natural Selection and Adaptive Behavior

Evolutionary Psychology

Genetic Foundations

What Are Genes?

Mitosis and Meiosis

Genetic Principles

Behavior Genetics

Molecular Genetics

Chromosome and Gene-Linked Abnormalities

Reproduction Challenges and Choices

Prenatal Diagnostic Tests

Adoption

Infertility

Heredity-Environment Interaction

Intelligence

Heredity-Environment Correlations

Shared and Nonshared Environmental Experiences

Conclusions

Chapter 4

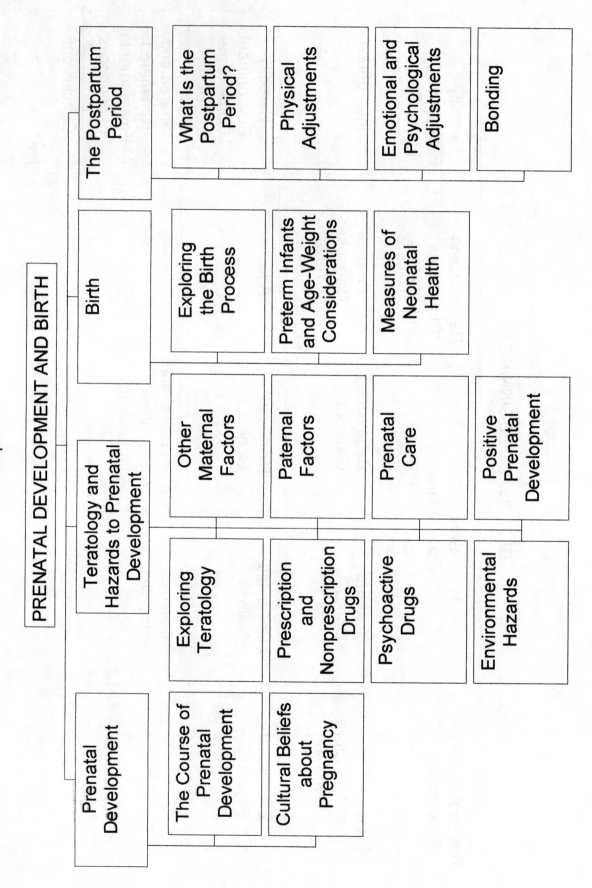

PRENATAL DEVELOPMENT AND BIRTH

Prenatal Development
- The Course of Prenatal Development
- Cultural Beliefs about Pregnancy

Teratology and Hazards to Prenatal Development
- Exploring Teratology
- Prescription and Nonprescription Drugs
- Psychoactive Drugs
- Environmental Hazards
- Other Maternal Factors
- Paternal Factors
- Prenatal Care
- Positive Prenatal Development

Birth
- Exploring the Birth Process
- Preterm Infants and Age-Weight Considerations
- Measures of Neonatal Health

The Postpartum Period
- What Is the Postpartum Period?
- Physical Adjustments
- Emotional and Psychological Adjustments
- Bonding

Chapter 5

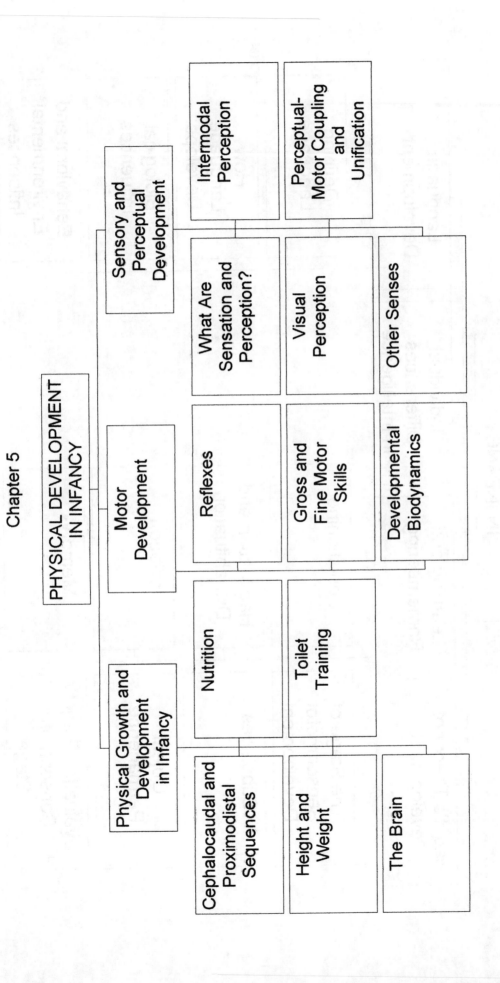

PHYSICAL DEVELOPMENT IN INFANCY

Physical Growth and Development in Infancy
- Cephalocaudal and Proximodistal Sequences
- Height and Weight
- The Brain
- Nutrition
- Toilet Training

Motor Development
- Reflexes
- Gross and Fine Motor Skills
- Developmental Biodynamics

Sensory and Perceptual Development
- What Are Sensation and Perception?
- Visual Perception
- Other Senses
- Intermodal Perception
- Perceptual-Motor Coupling and Unification

Chapter 6

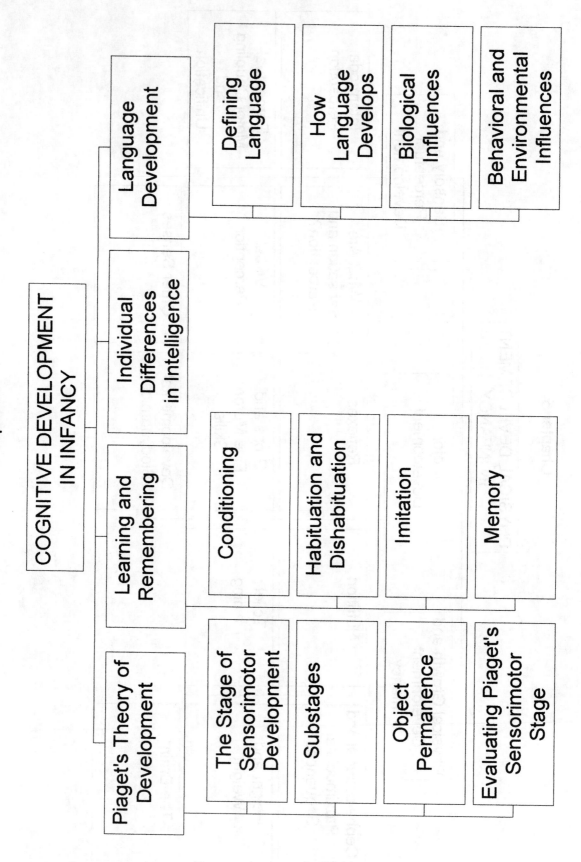

COGNITIVE DEVELOPMENT IN INFANCY

Piaget's Theory of Development

- The Stage of Sensorimotor Development
- Substages
- Object Permanence
- Evaluating Piaget's Sensorimotor Stage

Learning and Remembering

- Conditioning
- Habituation and Dishabituation
- Imitation
- Memory

Individual Differences in Intelligence

Language Development

- Defining Language
- How Language Develops
- Biological Influences
- Behavioral and Environmental Influences

Chapter 7

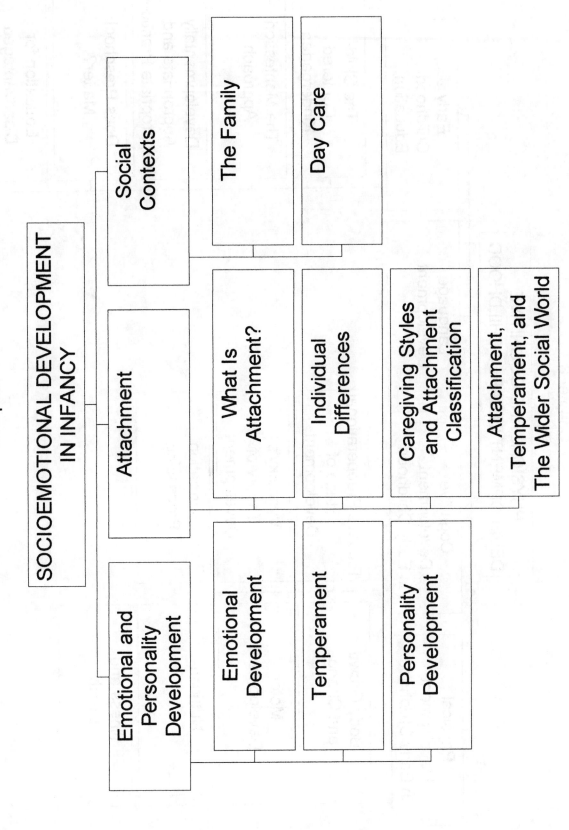

SOCIOEMOTIONAL DEVELOPMENT IN INFANCY

Emotional and Personality Development

- Emotional Development
- Temperament
- Personality Development

Attachment

- What Is Attachment?
- Individual Differences
- Caregiving Styles and Attachment Classification
- Attachment, Temperament, and The Wider Social World

Social Contexts

- The Family
- Day Care

Chapter 8

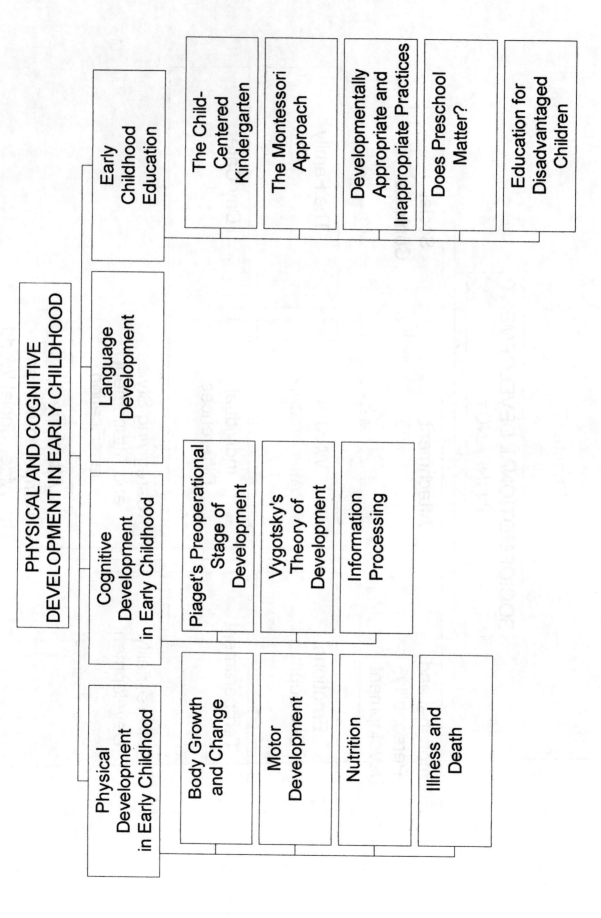

PHYSICAL AND COGNITIVE DEVELOPMENT IN EARLY CHILDHOOD

Physical Development in Early Childhood
- Body Growth and Change
- Motor Development
- Nutrition
- Illness and Death

Cognitive Development in Early Childhood
- Piaget's Preoperational Stage of Development
- Vygotsky's Theory of Development
- Information Processing

Language Development

Early Childhood Education
- The Child-Centered Kindergarten
- The Montessori Approach
- Developmentally Appropriate and Inappropriate Practices
- Does Preschool Matter?
- Education for Disadvantaged Children

Chapter 9

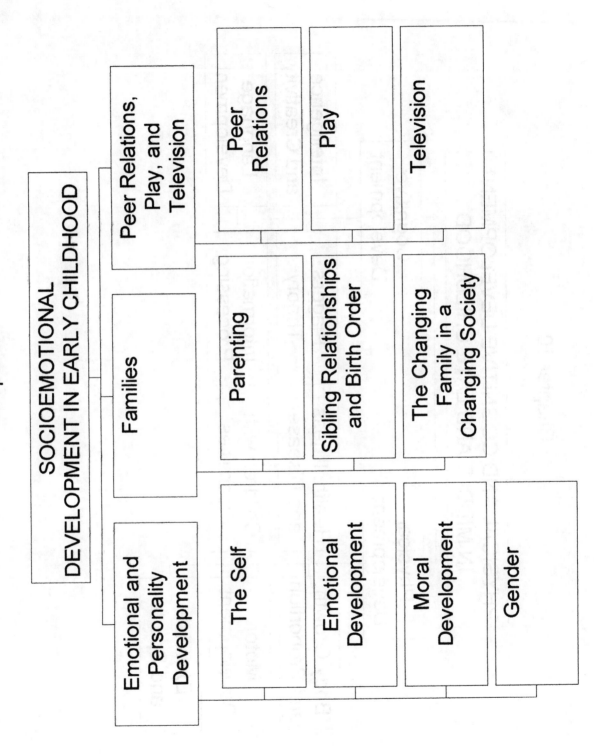

SOCIOEMOTIONAL DEVELOPMENT IN EARLY CHILDHOOD

Emotional and Personality Development
- The Self
- Emotional Development
- Moral Development
- Gender

Families
- Parenting
- Sibling Relationships and Birth Order
- The Changing Family in a Changing Society

Peer Relations, Play, and Television
- Peer Relations
- Play
- Television

Chapter 10

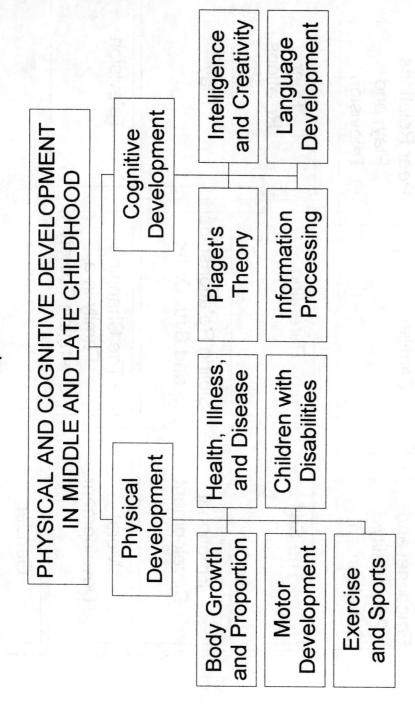

PHYSICAL AND COGNITIVE DEVELOPMENT
IN MIDDLE AND LATE CHILDHOOD

Physical Development

Cognitive Development

Body Growth and Proportion

Motor Development

Exercise and Sports

Health, Illness, and Disease

Children with Disabilities

Piaget's Theory

Information Processing

Intelligence and Creativity

Language Development

Chapter 11

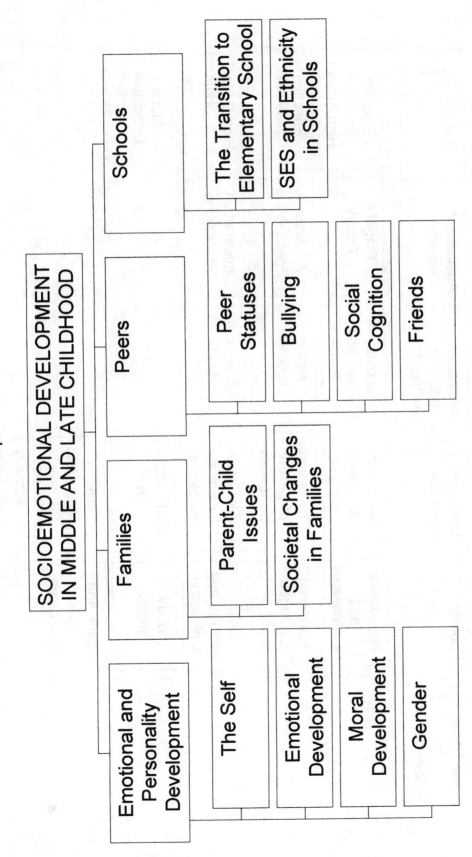

SOCIOEMOTIONAL DEVELOPMENT IN MIDDLE AND LATE CHILDHOOD

Emotional and Personality Development
- The Self
- Emotional Development
- Moral Development
- Gender

Families
- Parent-Child Issues
- Societal Changes in Families

Peers
- Peer Statuses
- Bullying
- Social Cognition
- Friends

Schools
- The Transition to Elementary School
- SES and Ethnicity in Schools

Chapter 12

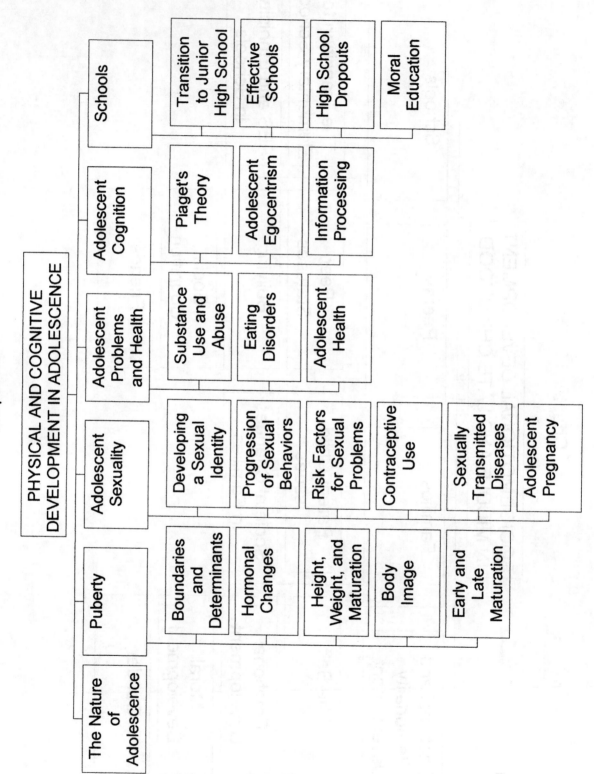

PHYSICAL AND COGNITIVE DEVELOPMENT IN ADOLESCENCE

The Nature of Adolescence

Puberty
- Boundaries and Determinants
- Hormonal Changes
- Height, Weight, and Maturation
- Body Image
- Early and Late Maturation

Adolescent Sexuality
- Developing a Sexual Identity
- Progression of Sexual Behaviors
- Risk Factors for Sexual Problems
- Contraceptive Use
- Sexually Transmitted Diseases
- Adolescent Pregnancy

Adolescent Problems and Health
- Substance Use and Abuse
- Eating Disorders
- Adolescent Health

Adolescent Cognition
- Piaget's Theory
- Adolescent Egocentrism
- Information Processing

Schools
- Transition to Junior High School
- Effective Schools
- High School Dropouts
- Moral Education

Chapter 13

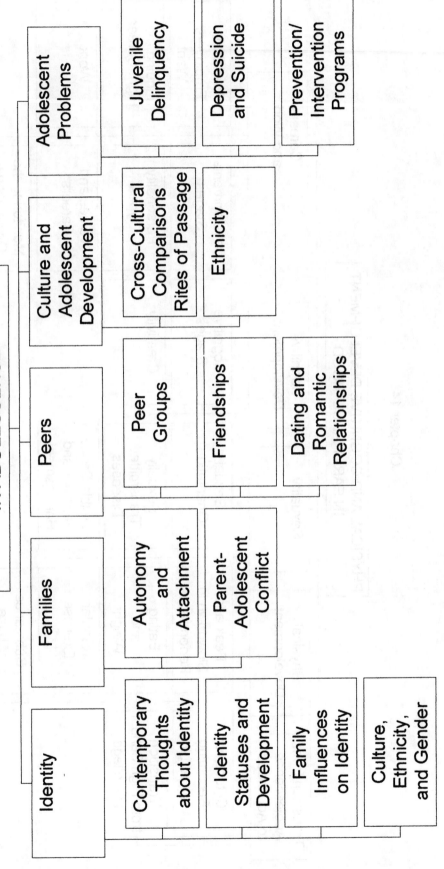

SOCIOEMOTIONAL DEVELOPMENT
IN ADOLESCENCE

Identity

- Contemporary Thoughts about Identity
- Identity Statuses and Development
- Family Influences on Identity
- Culture, Ethnicity, and Gender

Families

- Autonomy and Attachment
- Parent-Adolescent Conflict

Peers

- Peer Groups
- Friendships
- Dating and Romantic Relationships

Culture and Adolescent Development

- Cross-Cultural Comparisons Rites of Passage
- Ethnicity

Adolescent Problems

- Juvenile Delinquency
- Depression and Suicide
- Prevention/Intervention Programs

Chapter 14

PHYSICAL AND COGNITIVE DEVELOPMENT
IN EARLY ADULTHOOD

Transition from Adolescence to Adulthood
- Criteria for Becoming an Adult
- Transition from High School to College

Physical Development
- Peak and Slowdown in Performance
- Eating and Weight
- Regular Exercise
- Substance Abuse

Sexuality
- Sexual Orientation
- Sexually Transmitted Diseases
- Forcible Sexual Behavior and Harrassment

Cognitive Development
- Cognitive Stages
- Creativity

Careers and Work
- The Skills Employers Want
- Finding the Right Career
- Work
- Developmental Stages
- Personality Types
- Values and Careers
- Monitoring the Occupational Handbook

Chapter 15

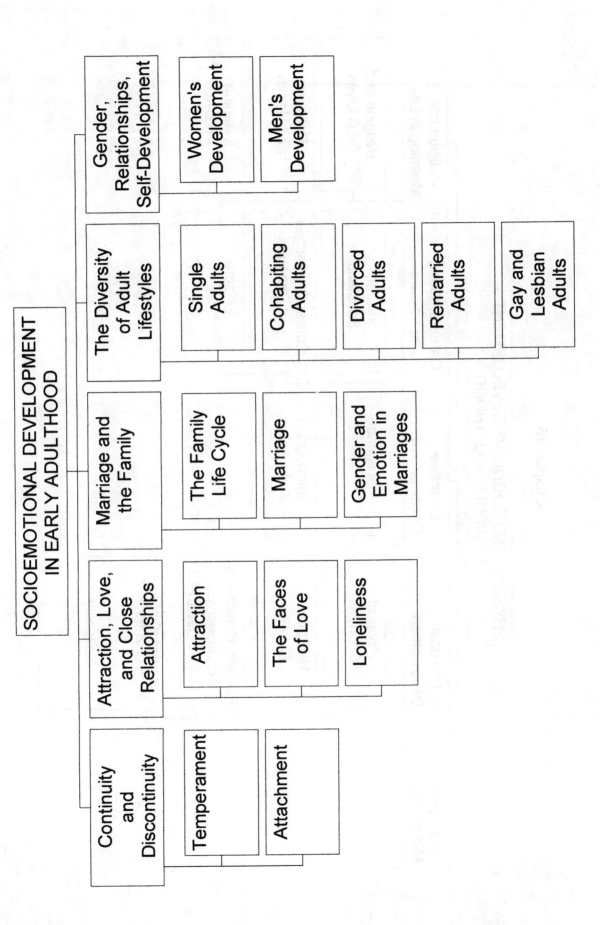

SOCIOEMOTIONAL DEVELOPMENT IN EARLY ADULTHOOD

Continuity and Discontinuity
- Temperament
- Attachment

Attraction, Love, and Close Relationships
- Attraction
- The Faces of Love
- Loneliness

Marriage and the Family
- The Family Life Cycle
- Marriage
- Gender and Emotion in Marriages

The Diversity of Adult Lifestyles
- Single Adults
- Cohabiting Adults
- Divorced Adults
- Remarried Adults
- Gay and Lesbian Adults

Gender, Relationships, Self-Development
- Women's Development
- Men's Development

Chapter 16

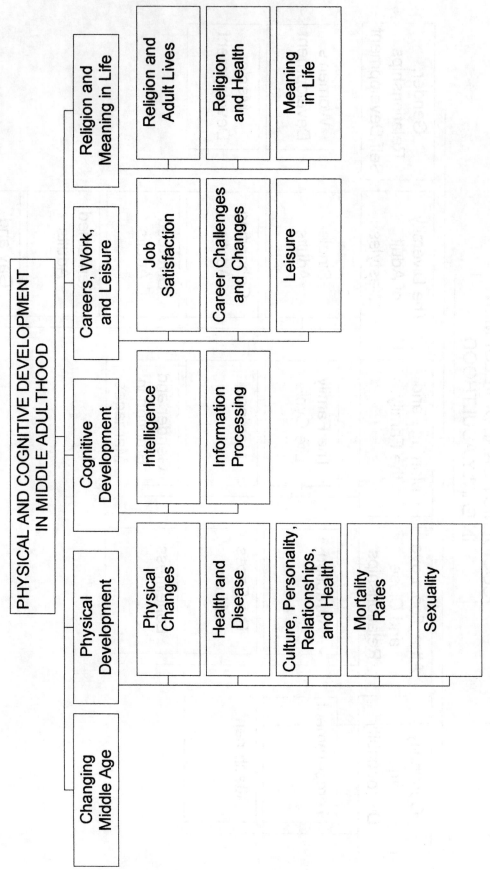

PHYSICAL AND COGNITIVE DEVELOPMENT
IN MIDDLE ADULTHOOD

Changing Middle Age

Physical Development
- Physical Changes
- Health and Disease
- Culture, Personality, Relationships, and Health
- Mortality Rates
- Sexuality

Cognitive Development
- Intelligence
- Information Processing

Careers, Work, and Leisure
- Job Satisfaction
- Career Challenges and Changes
- Leisure

Religion and Meaning in Life
- Religion and Adult Lives
- Religion and Health
- Meaning in Life

Chapter 17

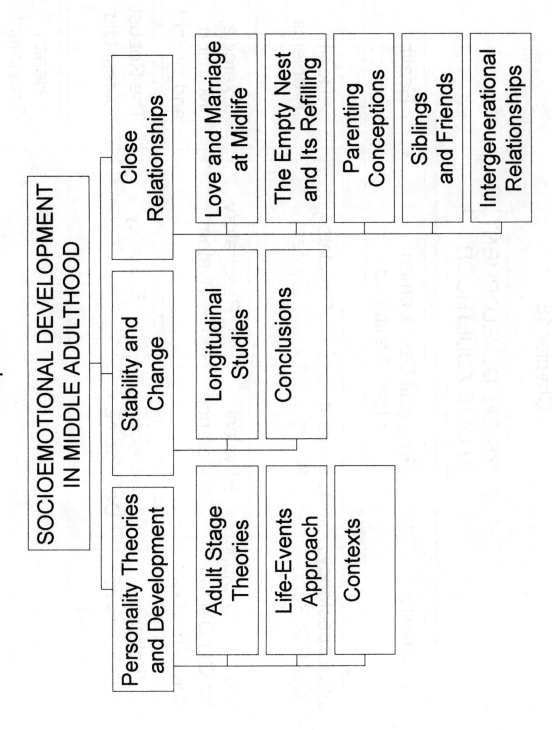

SOCIOEMOTIONAL DEVELOPMENT
IN MIDDLE ADULTHOOD

Personality Theories and Development

Adult Stage Theories

Life-Events Approach

Contexts

Stability and Change

Longitudinal Studies

Conclusions

Close Relationships

Love and Marriage at Midlife

The Empty Nest and Its Refilling

Parenting Conceptions

Siblings and Friends

Intergenerational Relationships

Chapter 18

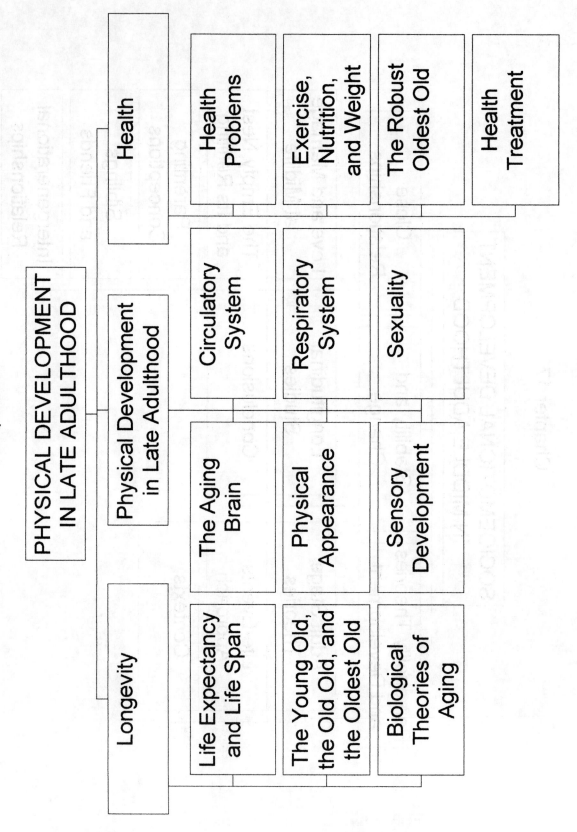

PHYSICAL DEVELOPMENT
IN LATE ADULTHOOD

Longevity

Physical Development
in Late Adulthood

Health

Life Expectancy
and Life Span

The Young Old,
the Old Old, and
the Oldest Old

Biological
Theories of
Aging

The Aging
Brain

Physical
Appearance

Sensory
Development

Circulatory
System

Respiratory
System

Sexuality

Health
Problems

Exercise,
Nutrition,
and Weight

The Robust
Oldest Old

Health
Treatment

Chapter 19

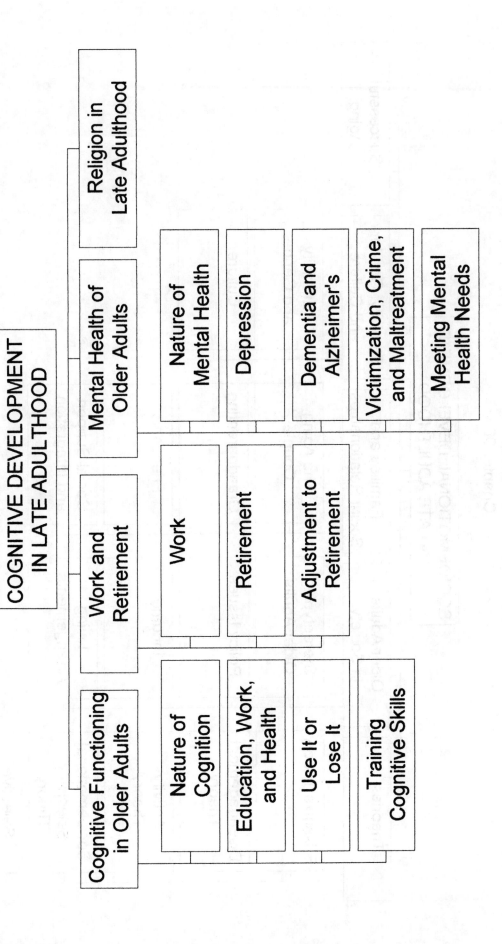

COGNITIVE DEVELOPMENT IN LATE ADULTHOOD

Cognitive Functioning in Older Adults
- Nature of Cognition
- Education, Work, and Health
- Use It or Lose It
- Training Cognitive Skills

Work and Retirement
- Work
- Retirement
- Adjustment to Retirement

Mental Health of Older Adults
- Nature of Mental Health
- Depression
- Dementia and Alzheimer's
- Victimization, Crime, and Maltreatment
- Meeting Mental Health Needs

Religion in Late Adulthood

Chapter 20

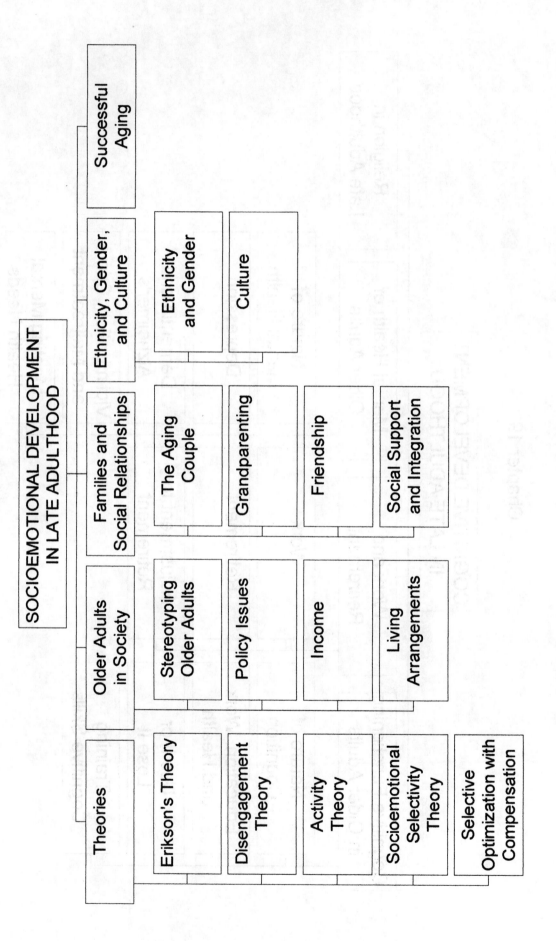

SOCIOEMOTIONAL DEVELOPMENT
IN LATE ADULTHOOD

Theories

- Erikson's Theory
- Disengagement Theory
- Activity Theory
- Socioemotional Selectivity Theory
- Selective Optimization with Compensation

Older Adults in Society

- Stereotyping Older Adults
- Policy Issues
- Income
- Living Arrangements

Families and Social Relationships

- The Aging Couple
- Grandparenting
- Friendship
- Social Support and Integration

Ethnicity, Gender, and Culture

- Ethnicity and Gender
- Culture

Successful Aging

Chapter 21

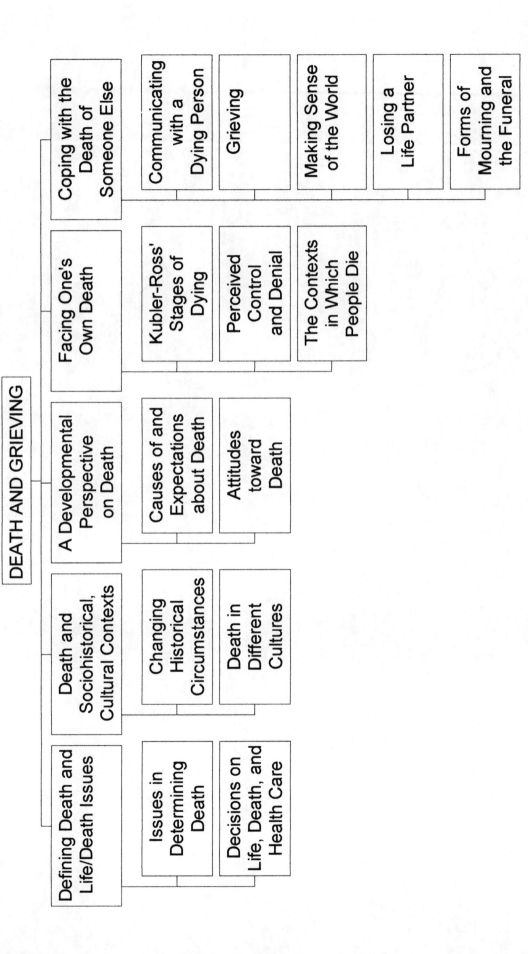

DEATH AND GRIEVING

Defining Death and Life/Death Issues
- Issues in Determining Death
- Decisions on Life, Death, and Health Care

Death and Sociohistorical, Cultural Contexts
- Changing Historical Circumstances
- Death in Different Cultures

A Developmental Perspective on Death
- Causes of and Expectations about Death
- Attitudes toward Death

Facing One's Own Death
- Kubler-Ross' Stages of Dying
- Perceived Control and Denial
- The Contexts in Which People Die

Coping with the Death of Someone Else
- Communicating with a Dying Person
- Grieving
- Making Sense of the World
- Losing a Life Partner
- Forms of Mourning and the Funeral